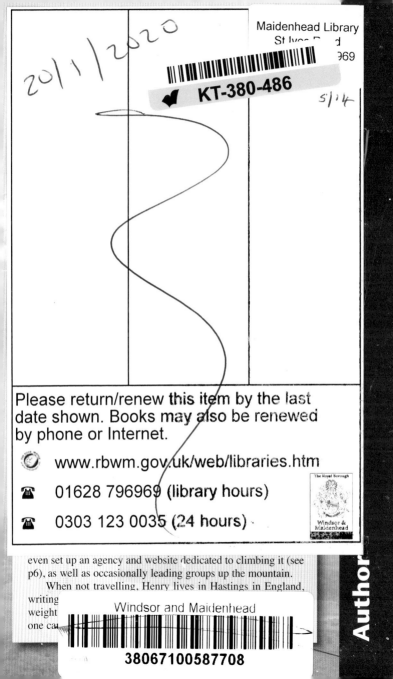

even set up an agency and website dedicated to climbing it (see
p6), as well as occasionally leading groups up the mountain.

When not travelling, Henry lives in Hastings in England,
writing
weight
one ca

Kilimanjaro – the trekking guide to Africa's highest mountain
First edition 2003; **this fourth edition 2014**

Publisher Trailblazer Publications ⌨ www.trailblazer-guides.com
The Old Manse, Tower Rd, Hindhead, Surrey, GU26 6SU, UK

British Library Cataloguing in Publication Data
A catalogue record for this book is available from the British Library

ISBN 978-1-905864-54-6

Editor: Anna Jacomb-Hood
Cartography: Nick Hill **Layout**: Anna Jacomb-Hood & Bryn Thomas
Proof-reading: Nicky Slade **Index**: Anna Jacomb-Hood & Jane Thomas

A request
The author and publisher have tried to ensure that this guide is as accurate and up to date
as possible. However, things change quickly in this part of the world. Agencies come and
go, trails are re-routed, prices rise and ... well, rise some more, governments are toppled
and glaciers shrink. If you notice any changes or corrections for the next edition of this
guide, please email Henry Stedman at ⌨ henry@climbmountkilimanjaro.com.
You can also contact Trailblazer via ⌨ www.trailblazer-guides.com. Those persons
making a significant contribution will be rewarded with a free copy of the next edition,
an acknowledgement in that edition and Henry's undying gratitude.

Acknowledgements
See p368 for a list of those who contributed to this edition.

Warning: mountain walking can be dangerous
Please read the notes on when to go (pp14-16), health and fitness (pp68-72) and on safe
trekking (pp222-32). Every effort has been made by the author and publisher to ensure
that the information contained herein is as accurate and up to date as possible. However,
they are unable to accept responsibility for any inconvenience, loss or injury sustained by
anyone as a result of the advice and information given in this guide.

Updated information will, as always, be available on:
⌨ **www.climbmountkilimanjaro.com**

Photos – Front cover: Kilimanjaro from the north © Torleif Svensson/Corbis.
Opposite: Kibo summit as seen from the east from the lower slopes of Mawenzi.
Overleaf: Looking towards Kilimanjaro from the crater of Mount Meru.

Printed on chlorine-free paper by D'Print (☎ +65-6581 3832), Singapore

Kilimanjaro

THE TREKKING GUIDE TO
AFRICA'S HIGHEST MOUNTAIN

also includes MOUNT MERU & guides to
Arusha, Moshi, Marangu, Nairobi & Dar es Salaam

HENRY STEDMAN

TRAILBLAZER PUBLICATIONS

Contents

PART 7: MOUNT MERU

PART 8: TRAIL GUIDE AND MAPS

PART 9: THE SUMMIT

APPENDICES

Contents

IN THIS EDITION

For this fourth edition, in terms of style and structure we have kept the book pretty much the same as the last one. We have, of course, given everything a thorough update, including our guides to the cities and towns and our review of the trekking agencies.

We have also walked routes again, both on Kilimanjaro and Meru, to satisfy ourselves that our descriptions are still accurate. Furthermore, we have finally got around to climbing one of the least popular routes on the mountain – the Shira Plateau Route – which we had previously done only in parts. To be honest, few people use the path anymore since much of it is now an emergency track for vehicles – but a couple of the more popular agencies in Tanzania not only promote it but also say it's a superior route. It was thus our duty to follow this path and see for ourselves what the fuss is all about; you can read our conclusions on p305.

And finally, we have once again called upon the services of Karen Valenti at KPAP (see pp47-9) to help us tackle the problem of porter mistreatment. We do, of course, also welcome updates from readers on *any* aspect of the book.

⌨ www.climbmountkilimanjaro.com – the website!

The website that was set up in 2007 to accompany this book is still going strong and is designed – in tandem with the accompanying Twitter and Facebook sites – to keep our readers informed of the latest news and developments on the mountain. The site includes:

● **Updates on the book** From new restaurants in Moshi to route changes on Machame, if we discover something new or altered since the publication of the book, this is where you can find out all about it.

● **Links to weblogs** Compiling a weblog for your Kili climb? Then why not link it to our site so others can follow your progress?

● **Charity climbs** If you're involved in a charity climb or trying to organize one, you'll find space on the website for you to tell the world about your climb.

● **Links to Kili-based websites** Links to sites that we think are worth a look.

● **Kili news** Route alterations, park-fee increases and the tragedies and triumphs that occur on the mountain – we have the latest news.

● **The Kilimanjaro Hall of Fame** Celebrate your achievements with the world by posting photos of yourself and your friends on the summit!

● **Details on the treks we organize** For the past few years we have been arranging treks up the mountain through our company Climb Mount Kilimanjaro (CMK) to see how we compare with the other agencies.

INTRODUCTION

Kilimanjaro is a snow covered mountain 19,710 feet high, and is said to be the highest mountain in Africa. Its western summit is called the Masai 'Ngà'je Ngài', the House of God. Close to the western summit there is the dried and frozen carcass of a leopard. No one has explained what the leopard was seeking at that altitude.

Ernest Hemingway in the preamble to *The Snows of Kilimanjaro*

On 29 September 2010 Kilian Jornet of Spain stood at Umbwe Gate on the southern slopes of Africa's greatest mountain, Kilimanjaro. We can imagine the scene that day, for it's one that's repeated there every day of the year. There would be the noisy, excitable hubbub as porters, guides and rangers packed, weighed, re-packed and re-weighed all the equipment; the quiet murmur of anticipation from Kilian's fellow trekkers as they stood on the threshold of the greatest walk of their lives; maybe there was even a troop of blue monkeys crashing through the canopy, or the scarlet flash of a turaco's under-wing as it glided from tree to tree, surveying the commotion below.

Señor Jornet's main goal that day was no different from the ambitions of his fellow trekkers: he wanted to reach the summit. Unlike them, however, Kilian planned to forego many of the features that make a walk up Kili so special. Not for him the joys of strolling lazily through the mountain's four main eco-zones, pausing frequently to admire the views or examine the unique mountain flora. Nor did Sr Jornet want to experience the blissful evenings spent scoffing popcorn, sharing stories and gazing at the stars with his fellow trekkers. Nor, for that matter, was he looking forward to savouring the wonderful *esprit de corps* that builds between a trekker and his or her crew as they progress, day by day, up the mountain slopes; a sense of camaraderie that grows with every step until, exhausted, they stand together at the highest point in Africa.

It is these experiences that make climbing Kilimanjaro so unique and so special. Yet Kilian had chosen to eschew all of them because, for reasons best known to himself, he had decided to *run* up the mountain. Which is exactly what he did, completing the 21.2km from base to summit in an incredible 5 hours, 23 minutes and 50 seconds – on a trail that takes the average trekker anywhere from five to six days to complete! (For an encore he then ran all the way back down to Mweka Gate, and in doing so set another record for the fastest ascent and descent of Kilimanjaro, completing the round trip in just 7 hours and 14 minutes.)

A mountain for eccentrics

Barking mad though Kilian's exploits may have been, in his defence it must be said that he isn't exactly alone in taking an unorthodox approach to tackling Kilimanjaro. Take the Crane cousins from England, for example, who cycled up to the summit, surviving on Mars bars that they'd strapped to their handlebars. Or the anonymous Spaniard who, in the 1970s, drove up to the summit on a motorbike. Or what about Douglas Adams,

Douglas Adams reached the summit wearing an 8ft rubber rhinoceros costume

author of *The Hitchhikers' Guide to the Galaxy*, who in 1994 reached the summit for charity while wearing an 8ft rubber rhinoceros costume, not to mention the many people who have got to the top and celebrated their achievement by stripping off, posing for summit photos wearing nothing but suncream and a smile. There's also a team of trekkers who, in 2012, climbed barefoot! Then there's the (possibly apocryphal) story of the man who walked *backwards* to the summit in order to get into the *Guinness Book of Records* – only to find out, on his return to the bottom, that he had been beaten by somebody who had done exactly the same thing just a few days previously.

And that's just the ascent; for coming back again we've skiing, a method first practised by Walter Furtwangler way back in 1912; snowboarding, an activity pioneered on Kili by Stephen Koch in 1997; and even paragliding, first attempted by a team back in January 2013.

Don't be fooled

Cyclists, skiers, bikers, boarders and backward walkers: it's no wonder, given the sheer number of people who have climbed Kili over the past century, and the ways in which they've done so, that so many people believe climbing Kili is a doddle. And you'd be forgiven for thinking the same.

You'd be forgiven – but you'd also be wrong. Whilst these stories of successful expeditions tend to receive a lot of coverage, they also serve to obscure the tales of suffering and tragedy that are just as frequent. To give you just one example: for all the coverage of the Millennium celebrations, when over 7000

> **... these stories of successful expeditions ... also serve to obscure the tales of suffering and tragedy that are just as frequent**

people stood on the slopes of Kilimanjaro during New Year's week – with 1000 on New Year's Eve alone – little mention was made of the fact that well over a third of all the people who took part in those festivities failed to reach the summit, or indeed get anywhere near it. Or that another 33 had to be rescued. Or that, in the space of those seven days, three people died.

The reason why most of these attempts were unsuccessful is altitude sickness, brought about by a trekker climbing too fast and not allowing his or her body time to acclimatize to the rarified air. Because Kilian Jornet didn't just set a record by climbing Kilimanjaro in under six hours; he also, unwittingly, set a bad example. For once, statistics give a reasonably accurate impression of just how difficult climbing Kili can be. According to the park

See pp359-60 for more sights and sounds of Kili

authorities, almost one in four people who climb up Kilimanjaro fail to reach even the crater. They also admit to there being a couple of deaths per annum on Kilimanjaro – though independent observers put that figure nearer ten.

There's no doubt the joys of climbing Kili are manifold; unfortunately, so are the ways in which it can destroy you. Because the simple truth is that Kilimanjaro is a very big mountain and, like all big mountains, it's very adept at killing off the unprepared, the unwary or just the plain unlucky. The fact that the Masai call the mountain the 'House of God' seems entirely appropriate, given the number of people who meet their Maker every year on Kili's slopes.

At one stage we were taking a minute to complete thirty-five small paces. Altitude sickness had already hit the boys and two were weeping, pleading to pack up. All the instructors with the exception of Lubego and myself were in a bad way. They were becoming violently ill. It was becoming touch and go. The descent at one stage was like a battlefield. Men, including the porters, lying prone or bent up in agony. Tom and Swato though very ill themselves rallied the troops and helped manhandle the three unconscious boys to a lower altitude.

From the logbook of **Geoffrey Salisbury**, who led a group of blind African climbers up Kilimanjaro, as recorded in *The Road to Kilimanjaro* (1997).

The high failure and mortality rates speak for themselves: despite appearances to the contrary, climbing Kilimanjaro is no simple matter.

'Mountain of greatness'

But whilst it isn't easy, it *is* achievable. After all, no technical skill is required to reach the summit of Africa's highest mountain beyond the ability to put one foot in front of the other; because, unless you go out of your way to find a particularly awkward route, there is no actual *climbing* involved at all – just lots and lots of walking. Thus, anyone above the age of 10 (the minimum legal age for climbing Kilimanjaro) *can*, with the right attitude, a sensible approach to acclimatization, a half-decent pair of calf muscles and lots of warm clothing, make

No technical skill is required to reach the summit of Africa's highest mountain

it to the top. Even vertigo sufferers are not excluded, there being only one or two vertical drops on any of the regular trekking routes that will have you scrabbling in your rucksacks for the Imodium.

Simply put, Kilimanjaro is for everyone. Again, statistics can back this up: with the youngest successful summiteer aged just seven and the oldest, the venerable Vancouver couple Martin and Esther Kafer, aged 85 and 84 respectively, it's clear that Kili conquerors come in all shapes and sizes. Amongst their number there are a few who have managed to overcome enormous personal

Below: Walking down from Kibo Huts towards the Saddle, with Mawenzi in the distance.

disabilities on their way to the summit. Virtually every year there is at least one group of blind trekkers who, incredibly, make it to the top by using the senses of touch and hearing alone. And in January 2004 four climbers who had been disabled on previous expeditions on other mountains all managed to make it to the summit. The party consisted of Australian Peter Steane, who has permanent nerve damage and walks and climbs with the help of two leg braces; his compatriot Paul Pritchard, who has limited control over his right side; Singaporean David Lim, partially disabled in his right leg and left hand after contracting the rare nerve disorder Guillain-Barre Syndrome; and Scotland's Jamie Andrew, an amazing man who had to have his hands and feet amputated after suffering severe frostbite during a climbing expedition near Chamonix, France, in January 1999, and yet who made it to the top of Kilimanjaro with artificial legs and prosthetic arms. There's also Bern Goosen, who has managed to manoeuvre his wheelchair to the summit *twice*, in 2003 and 2007; Erica Davis of Carlsbad, who became the first woman to do so, in 2011; and in 2012 Spencer West, who lost his legs at the age of five due to a rare genetic disorder but managed to ascend entirely on his hands!

In 2012 Spencer West managed to ascend entirely on his hands.

It is this 'inclusivity' that undoubtedly goes some way to explaining Kilimanjaro's popularity, a popularity that saw 57,456 people on the mountain in the 2011-12 season, thereby confirming Kili's status as the most popular of the so-called 'Big Seven', the highest peaks on each of the seven continents.

The sheer size of it must be another factor behind its appeal. This is the Roof of Africa, a massive massif 60km long by 80km wide with an altitude that reaches to a fraction under 6km above sea level. Writing in 1924, one of the pioneers of the coffee industry in Moshi, Charles Dundas, claimed that he once saw Kilimanjaro from a point over 120 miles away. This enormous monolith is big enough to have its own weather system**s** (note the plural) and, furthermore, to influence the climates of the countries that surround it.

The aspect presented by this prodigious mountain is one of unparalleled grandeur, sublimity, majesty, and glory. It is doubtful if there be another such sight in this wide world.
Charles New, the first European to reach the snow-line on Kilimanjaro, from his book
Life, Wanderings, and Labours in Eastern Africa (1873).

But size, as they say, isn't everything, and by themselves these bald figures fail to fully explain the allure of Kilimanjaro. So, instead, we must look to attributes that cannot be measured by theodolites or yardsticks if we are to understand the appeal of Kilimanjaro.

In particular, there's its beauty. When viewed from the plains of Tanzania, Kilimanjaro conforms to our childhood notions of what a mountain should look like: high, wide and handsome, a vast triangle rising out of the flat earth, its sides sloping exponentially upwards to the satisfyingly symmetrical summit of Kibo; a summit that rises imperiously above a thick beard of clouds and is adorned with a glistening bonnet of snow. Kilimanjaro is not located in the crumpled mountain terrain of the Himalayas or the Andes. Where the mightiest mountain of them all, Everest, just edges above its neighbours – and looks less impressive because of it – Kilimanjaro stands proudly alone on the plains of Africa. The only thing in the neighbourhood that can even come close to looking it in the eye is Mt Meru, over 60km away to the south-west and a good 1329m smaller. The fact that Kilimanjaro is located smack bang in the heart of the sweltering East African plains, just a few degrees (330km) south of the equator, with lions, giraffes, and all the other celebrities of the safari world running around its base, only adds to its charisma.

Then there's the scenery on the mountain itself. So massive is Kilimanjaro that to climb it is to pass through **four seasons in four days**, from the sultry rainforests of the lower reaches through to the windswept heather and moorland of the upper slopes, the alpine desert of the Saddle and Shira Plateau and on to the arctic wastes of the summit. There may

Under the canopy in the cloud forest; Marangu Route.

be about 124 higher mountains on the globe but there can't be many that are more beautiful, or more tantalizing.

In sitting down to recount my experiences with the conquest of the "Ethiopian Mount Olympus" still fresh in my memory, I feel how inadequate are my powers of description to do justice to the grand and imposing aspects of Nature with which I shall have to deal.
Hans Meyer, the first man to climb Kilimanjaro, in his book
Across East African Glaciers – an Account of the First Ascent of Kilimanjaro (1891)

Nor is it just tourists who are entranced by Kilimanjaro; the mountain looms large in the Tanzanian psyche too. Just look at their supermarket shelves. The nation's favourite lager is called Kilimanjaro. There's Kilimanjaro coffee (grown on the mountain's fertile southern slopes), Kilimanjaro tea (ditto), Kilimanjaro mineral water (bottled on its western side) and Kilimanjaro honey (again, sourced from the mountain). While on billboards lining the country's highways, Tanzanian models smoke their cigarettes in its shadow and cheerful roly-poly housewives compare the whiteness of their laundry with the mountain's glistening snows. And to pay for all of these things you might just use an old Tanzanian Ts2000 note which just happens to have, on its reverse side, a lion posing in front of the distinctive silhouette of Africa's highest mountain.

It was perhaps no surprise, therefore, that when Tanganyikans won their independence from Britain in 1961, one of the first things they did was plant a torch on its summit; a torch that the first president, Julius Nyerere, declared would '...shine beyond our borders, giving hope where there was despair, love where there was hate, and dignity where before there was only humiliation.'

> **Climbing up Kilimanjaro will be one of the hardest things you ever do. But it will also, without a doubt, be one of the most rewarding.**

To the Tanzanians, Kilimanjaro is clearly much more than just a very large mountain separating them from their neighbour Kenya. It's a symbol of their freedom and a potent emblem of their country. And given the tribulations and hardships willingly suffered by thousands of trekkers on Kili each year – not to mention the money they spend for the privilege of doing so – the mountain obviously arouses some pretty strong emotions in non-Tanzanians as well.

Whatever the emotions provoked in you by this wonderful mountain, and however you plan to climb it, we wish you well. Because even if you choose to walk rather than run, leave the bicycle at home and forego the pleasures of wearing a latex rhino outfit, climbing up Kilimanjaro will still be one of the hardest things you ever do.

But it will also, without a doubt, be one of the most rewarding.

We were in an amiable frame of mind ourselves and, notwithstanding all the toil and trouble my self-appointed task had cost me, I don't think I would that night have changed places with anybody in the world.

Hans Meyer on the evening after reaching the summit, as recorded in
Across East African Glaciers – an Account of the First Ascent of Kilimanjaro (1891)

When to go

The two main trekking seasons for Kilimanjaro correspond with the mountain's two dry seasons (an imprecise term, the weather being often inclement during these periods too) namely January to mid March and June to October. Of course you can walk in the rainy season but not only is there a much higher chance of walking in the rain, your views of Kibo and Mawenzi are likely to be obscured by thick cloud and you may be trudging through thigh-high snow to the summit. Indeed, several agencies even suspend their operations in April and May, deciding that any trek is foolhardy at this time and the rewards for the trekkers considerably less. Curiously, however, Christmas and New Year, when the weather is far from perfect, are actually amongst the most popular times to go. (You can read peoples' experiences of climbing during the rainy season in the box on p98.)

> **The two main trekking seasons for Kilimanjaro are January to mid March and June to October.**

As to the relative merits of the two trekking seasons, the differences are small though significant. The **January to March** season tends to be colder and there is a much greater chance of snow on the path at this time. The days, however, are often clearer, with only the occasional brief shower. It is usually an exceptionally beautiful time to climb and is often a little quieter than the other peak season of **June to October**, which coincides to a large degree with the main academic holidays in Europe and the West. In this latter season the clouds tend to hang around the tree-line following the heavy rains of March to May. Once above this altitude, however, the skies are blue and brilliant and the chance of precipitation is minimal (though still present).

Leaving the Karanga Valley Campsite, with Kibo looming behind.

Although the June to October season tends to be busier, this is not necessarily a disadvantage. For example, if you are travelling independently to Tanzania but wish, for the sake of companionship or simply to cut down on costs, to join up with other travellers for the trek, the high visitor numbers in the June to October peak season will give you the best chance of doing this. And even if you do crave solitude when you walk, it can still be found on the mountain during this peak season. The trails are long, so you can always find vast gaps between trekkers to allow you to walk in peace; a couple of the routes – Umbwe, for example, or the two trails across the Shira Plateau – are quieter than others; indeed Umbwe seldom has more than one or two groups on it at any one time. And besides,

---

❏ **Star gazing**
Having decided when to go you may wish to refine your dates still further by timing your walk so that on the final push to the summit, which is usually conducted at night, you will be walking under the brightness of a **full moon**. The weather is said to be more stable at this time, too – though, of course, the night sky is less spectacular when it's a full moon as fewer stars are visible to the naked eye.

On that subject, stargazers may wish to try to coincide their trip with a major astronomical happening; the views of the night sky from Kili are, after all, quite exceptional. It's good to know that it isn't just the costs of climbing Kilimanjaro that are astronomical; the rewards can be too.

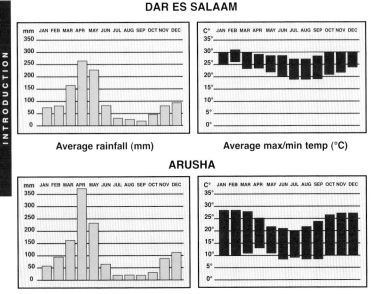

DAR ES SALAAM

Average rainfall (mm)

Average max/min temp (°C)

ARUSHA

Average rainfall (mm)

Average max/min temp (°C)

For statistics and graphs on the weather on Kilimanjaro, please see pp97-100.

Kilimanjaro is just so huge that its presence will dwarf your fellow trekkers to the point where they become, if you wish them to be, quite unnoticeable.

For what it's worth, our favourite times to be on Kilimanjaro are February-March, when the crowds are fewer, the skies clearer and there's less snow than in January; and also mid-September through October, for much the same reasons. Other factors that you may want to consider when deciding the exact date of your trek is whether your final push to the summit will coincide with a full moon (see box, p15); and whether to go mid-week, when the number of people starting their trek should be lower (as many people like to start at the weekend to minimize the amount of time they need to take off work). But having said all that, you may choose to climb on a particular day in order to be on the summit on your birthday/anniversary etc – and that, we think, is as good a reason as any.

● **C1 (Opposite) Top left**: Mount Meru, as seen from Arusha city centre. **Top right**: Trekking to Barafu Campsite with Meru in the distance. **Bottom**: Mawenzi, Kili's second summit, from Simba/Sekimba Camp on the Rongai Route.
● **C2 (Overleaf, clockwise from top) 1**: Marching through the everlastings to the east of the Saddle. **2**: The groundsel forest above Barranco Campsite. **3**: The Breakfast or Barranco Wall. **4**: The top of Kibo from the slopes of Mawenzi.
● **C3** The view east from the summit of Mount Meru with the Ash Cone in the foreground and Kilimanjaro in the background.

C1

C2

With a group or on your own?

INDEPENDENT TREKKING NOT AN OPTION

In 1991, the park authorities made it compulsory for all trekkers to arrange their walk through a licensed agency. Furthermore, they insist that all trekkers must be accompanied throughout their walk by a guide supplied by the agency. Even after these laws were introduced, for a while it was still feasible to sneak in without paying, and many were the stories of trekkers who managed to climb Kilimanjaro independently, tales that were often embellished with episodes of encounters with wild animals and even wilder park rangers.

Fortunately, the authorities have tightened up security and clamped down on non-payees, so these tedious tales are now few in number. Don't try to climb Kilimanjaro without a guide or without paying the proper fees. It's very unlikely you'll succeed and all you're doing is freeloading – indeed, stealing isn't too strong a word – from one of the poorest countries in the world. Yes, climbing Kilimanjaro is expensive. But the costs of maintaining a mountain that big are high. Besides, whatever price you pay, trust us, it's worth it.

WITH FRIENDS . . .

It's Kili time! Time to kick back, relax and take it easy with your friends.
Printed on the labels of Kilimanjaro Beer

So you have decided to climb Kilimanjaro, and have thus taken the first step on the path that leads from the comfort and safety of your favourite armchair to the untamed glory of the Roof of Africa. The second step on this path is to consider with whom you wish to go.

This may not be as straightforward as it sounds, because Kilimanjaro breaks friendships as easily as it breaks records. The tribulations suffered by those who dare to pit themselves against the mountain wear down the most even of temperaments, and relationships are often the first to suffer. Idiosyncrasies in your friend's behaviour that you previously thought endearing now simply become irritating, while the most trivial of differences between you and your chum could lead to the termination of a friendship that, before you'd both ventured onto its slopes, you thought was as steadfast and enduring as the mountain itself. Different levels of stamina, different levels of desire to reach the top, different attitudes towards the porters and guides, even differences in your musical tastes or the colour of your socks: on Kilimanjaro these things, for some reason, suddenly matter.

Then there's the farting. It is a well-known fact that the regular breaking of wind is a sure sign that you are acclimatizing satisfactorily (for more about acclimatization, see pp222-30); while the onset of a crushing headache, combined with loss of sleep and a consequent loss of humour, are all classic symptoms suffered by those struggling to adapt to the rarified atmosphere. Problems occur, of course, when two friends acclimatize at different rates: ie, the vociferous and joyful flatulence of Friend A is simply not appreciated by Friend B, who has a bad headache, insomnia and an ill-temper. Put the two parties together in a remote, confined space, such as that provided by a two-man tent on the slopes of a cold and lonely mountain, and you have an explosive cocktail that can blow apart even the strongest of friendships.

It rained terrible all night, and we put most of the Wachaga porters in our tent. It was rather distressing to the olfactory nerves ... At 4am a leopard visited us but did not fancy our scent.
Peter MacQueen, *In Wildest Africa* (an account of an expedition of 1907, published in 1910)

Of course, the above is just one possible scenario. It may be that both of you adapt equally well/badly to the new conditions and can draw pleasure/comfort from each other accordingly. People from Northern Europe seem particularly good at making the best of the windy conditions: while researching the first edition of this book we encountered a party of four Germans holding a farting competition, and one particularly talented Dutch pair who even managed a quick game of Name that Tune. (It probably won't surprise you to know that all but one of the participants in these events was male.)

And there are plenty of advantages in going with a friend too. There's the companionship for a start. It's also cheaper, because you'll probably be sharing rooms, which always cuts the cost, and if you are planning on booking your climb after you've arrived in Tanzania your bargaining position is so much stronger if there are two of you. Having a companion also cuts the workload, enabling, for example, one to run off and find a room while the other looks after the luggage. It also saves your being paired with someone you don't know when you book with an agency; someone who may snore or blow off more violently than your friend ever would. And, finally, if you *do* both make it to the top, it's good to know there will be somebody to testify to your achievements upon your return.

Climbing Kili with a companion has its problems, but there's no doubting the extra pleasure that can be gained as well. As the graffiti on the walls of the Kibo Huts tells us: '*What does not break us makes us stronger*'. If you are planning on travelling with a friend this, perhaps, should be your motto for the trek.

. . . OR ON YOUR OWN?

Those without friends, or at least without friends willing to climb a mountain with them, should not worry. For one thing, you'll never truly be on your own, simply because the park authorities forbid you from climbing without a guide (see p17) and you'll probably need at least one other crew member to act as porter/cook. Furthermore, planning to go on your own means you can arrange **the trek that you want**; you choose the trail to follow, the time to go and for how long; the pace of the walk, the number of rest-stops, when to go to bed – these are all your decisions, and yours alone. You are the boss; you have nobody else's feelings to consider but your own.

If you want to join up with others, for companionship or simply to make the trek cheaper, that's not a problem (after all, a private trek for one person is always the most expensive option). You can book your trek in your home country with a tour operator (they nearly always insist on a minimum number of participants before the trek goes ahead); or you can book in Tanzania and ask to be put with other trekkers (which will often happen anyway, unless you specifically say otherwise). And even if it does transpire that you are walking alone, you can always meet other trekkers at the campsite in the evening if you so desire.

Trekking by yourself is fun and not the lonely experience many imagine; unless, of course, you enjoy the bliss of solitude and *want* to be alone. That's the beauty of walking solo: everything is up to you.

Budgeting

The most significant cost of your holiday, unless you opt for a few days at one of Tanzania's top-of-the-range safari lodges (US$3000+ per night is the highest – and most ridiculous – rate I've heard for a night's accommodation, though there are probably other, even higher ones), is the walk itself. Set aside US$900-plus for the *absolute cheapest* budget trek (though double this is usual), more if you plan on taking more than the minimum – and not recommended – five days, or if you're ascending by the Lemosho/Shira or Rongai routes (which both have higher transport charges). You will also need to plan to spend more on your trek if you insist on walking without other trekkers. Once on the mountain, however, you won't need to pay for anything else throughout the trek (save, of course, for tips for the crew at the end – see p42-3), especially as the rangers at the huts and campsites along the way are no longer allowed to sell drinks and snacks.

Away from the mountain and the other national parks, by far the most expensive place in Tanzania is Zanzibar. Elsewhere, you'll find transport, food and accommodation, the big three day-to-day expenses of the traveller's life, are pretty cheap in Tanzania and particularly in Moshi and Arusha – it's just unfortunate that Zanzibar and the national parks are pretty much all most visitors want to see of the country!

ACCOMMODATION

Basic tourist accommodation starts at around £5/US$7.50. You can get cheaper, non-tourist accommodation, though this is often both sleazy and unhygienic and should be considered only as a last resort. We have not reviewed these cheap hotels in the book. At the other end of the spectrum, there are hotel rooms and luxury safari camps going for anything up to US$3000 or more per night in the high season.

FOOD

Food can be dirt cheap if you stick to the street sellers who ply their wares at all hours of the day – though dirt is often what you get on the food itself too, with hygiene standards not always the highest. Still, even in a clean and decent low-budget restaurant the bill should still be only around £5/US$8 and in a local place it can be as little as a dollar.

TRANSPORT

Public transport is cheap in Tanzania, though it could be said you get what you pay for: dilapidated buses, potholed roads, inadequate seating and narcoleptic drivers do not a pleasant journey make, but this is the reality of public transport, Tanzanian style. Then again, at around one dollar per hour for local buses and Coasters (the local minibuses that ply the route between Arusha and Moshi; see p184), it seems churlish to complain. That said, given the appalling number of accidents on Tanzanian roads (they say that after malaria and AIDS, road accidents are the biggest killer in the country), if your budget can stretch to it do consider spending it on transport: extra safety and comfort are available on the luxury buses, and at only a slightly higher price.

Booking your trek

With the decision over whether or not to climb independently taken out of your hands, and once you've chosen who is going to join you on this trip of a life-time and when you're going to go, the next thing to decide is which agency will get your business.

The next few pages deal with exactly this matter. This may seem like overkill but booking with the right agency is perhaps **the single most important factor in determining the success or otherwise of your trek**: they are the ones who arrange everything, supply the equipment, and designate somebody to be your guide. So take your time choosing one. Because unless you are a guide, porter, guidebook writer or just plain daft, climbing Kili will be a once-in-a-lifetime experience – and an expensive one too – so it's important that you get it right.

BOOKING WITH AN AGENCY AT HOME

The overwhelming majority of trekkers book their Kilimanjaro climb before they arrive in Tanzania, either through an agency in their home country or via the internet with an agency in Tanzania or abroad. This is only sensible – you will have enough on your plate once you get to Tanzania just trying to get to the top of Africa's highest mountain without having to sort out the whole trek beforehand as well. (That said, there is a fair case to be made for waiting until you arrive in the country before booking, particularly if you are on a tight budget; see p36.)

Booking your trek with an agency in your home country gets rid of the hassle of arranging everything when you arrive. It depends what kind of package you have booked, of course, but few tour companies will sell you a climb up Kilimanjaro and nothing more. Nearly all will include such things as: airport pick-up and drop-off at the start/end of your trip; accommodation in Arusha, Moshi or Marangu for before and after your trek; sightseeing trips; transport to and from the mountain; and maybe even the odd safari or Zanzibar excursion. Pay them some more and they'll throw in the flights and insurance and sort out your visas too. With no need to arrange these things yourself, booking from home will save you a considerable amount of time. It also ensures you know exactly when you'll be walking, rather than having to hang around for a few days as you may have to if you wait until you've arrived in Tanzania before organizing your trek.

Booking with an agency in your country also means you can plan your trek more precisely months in advance, and ask your agent any questions you may have well before you even arrive in Tanzania. Your agency at home will also either have their own guide to lead you up the mountain or, more probably, will be acting on behalf of one of the larger and better trekking operators in Moshi or Arusha, providing you with peace of mind. And, if the trek still turns out to be a disaster, the big advantage of booking from home is that you have a lot more comeback and thus more chance of receiving some sort of compensation.

A run-down of the larger foreign tour operators who arrange treks up Kilimanjaro follows. Before booking with anybody, have a look at *Booking with an agency in Tanzania* on p36, and in particular the advice given in the sections headed *Choosing an agency in Tanzania* (p37) and *Signing the contract* (p39). These contain useful hints that could also be relevant when dealing with agents and operators in your own country.

The agencies

All prices quoted in the following list include park fees unless stated otherwise. For details of the various routes up Kilimanjaro that are mentioned here, please see p53. You'll see a wide range of prices so remember to **ask each agency exactly what is included**. Most companies provide airport transfers and a night or two in a hotel but do make sure this is so. Some prices also include return flights from your home country – we have tried to highlight where this is the case. Some companies specialize in certain routes only; others offer all official routes and, in some cases, have devised (or, rather, the agency they use in Africa has devised) their own route up the mountain.

You should also check each supplier's ethical credentials. A disappointing number of foreign agencies make bold claims about how well they treat their porters, because this is what their Tanzania operator has told them they do. Unfortunately, the foreign agency rarely verifies these claims – so you must. If you can find out the name of the African supplier they use this will be very useful: you can, after all, **read our opinion of the Tanzanian agencies in the reviews in Part 5** (specifically on p185, p210 and p221) and check on the porters' charity KPAP's website (💻 www.kiliporters.org; see pp47-9 for details) to get their opinion. With the suspension of KPAP's partnership program it's no longer straightforward to discern which companies treat their porters fairly; however, I asked KPAP which companies have, over the past few years, consistently complied with their recommendations and can be most trusted to treat their porters fairly in the future. These companies are: **Marangu Hotel**, **Nature Discovery** (the ground operator for Thomson Safaris, see p34), **Good Earth Tours**, **Tanzania Experience**, **Dik Dik Tours** and **Congema Tours**. (They also, in a subsequent email, sang the praises of **Fair Travel Tanzania**; see p189 for details of this new outfit.)

Other advice: if it transpires that two companies use the same African supplier, but charge different amounts for the same trek, don't necessarily opt for the cheaper agency; the more expensive agency may offer extra nights in a hotel, for example, or free one-day tours before or after the trek. You may also

PLANNING YOUR TRIP

❏ So who climbs the most – and on which route?

Once again I am very grateful to KINAPA for supplying the most up-to-date statistics available for this edition on which nationalities climb the most. I'm not sure how reliable they are, but they are the best we can get; plus, to be fair, they do seem to conform to my own impression of which nationalities climb the most.

	2008/9	2009/10	2010/11	2011/12
Tanzanians	1941	2130	974	2597
Australians	1467	1346	2598	2699
Americans	5423	5722	8524	9870
Canadians	1830	2011	3129	3201
British	6080	5930	10,524	8370
Germans	2772	2889	4428	4252
Italians	1126	1353	663	1135
New Zealanders	628	711	565	302
French	1922	2841	2230	2448
Japanese	1398	1758	670	1246
Swiss	1684	1511	1199	1796
Irish	976	1191	1028	928
South Africans	1466	1678	1458	1313
Austrians	1236	1344	1116	1086
Norwegians	1023	1092	1346	1678
Danish	724	678	1556	1156
Swedish	694	586	641	748
Polish	490	506	1023	1317
Dutch		1035	987	
Indians	123	81	273	603
Chinese	67	89	81	772
Others	7639	8740	7635	8952
Total	**40,709**	**44,187**	**52,696**	**57,456**

wish to dismiss the agencies' claims for certain routes – eg that the Marangu Route is easy or Machame is quiet; at the risk of sounding arrogant, trust our descriptions of the trails rather than theirs.

Finally, if you are planning on a safari after your trek, take this into account when choosing which agency to book with: often booking a safari and Kilimanjaro trek with the same company will work out cheaper than booking each leg with a separate company.

Trekking agencies in the UK

● **360 Expeditions** (☎ 020-7183 4360, 🖳 www.360-expeditions.com) Relatively new company using Pristine Trails (see p214) as their ground operator that currently seems to offer treks on the 7-day Rongai Route (with the Mawenzi diversion) only – and only a couple of times a year too. Still, if there's more than six people in the group one of their guides is added to the staff (in addition to the local guides). Prices are currently £2495 including airfare.

● **Aardvark Safaris** (Hants ☎ 01980-849160 or Scotland ☎ 01578-760222, 🖳 www.aardvarksafaris.co.uk) With a name that pretty much guarantees it will always be at the top of any alphabetical list of companies, this agency offers tailor-made

---

I suppose these figures hold few surprises for those who know the mountain. Brits, of course, have a colonial connection to East Africa and are great travellers. In general Americans don't travel as much as Brits but for some reason they love Kilimanjaro, a passion that I can only ascribe, maybe, to the 'Hemingway effect', his books doing much to publicize the mountain in his native country.

The emergence of the new economic superpowers, India and China, appears to be reflected in their figures, too, with both enjoying big leaps in the number of their countrymen climbing the mountain in 2011/12 – a trend we can perhaps expect to continue in the next few years at least?

So which routes do all these climbers use? Once again, my gratitude goes to KINAPA for supplying the following figures for 2011/12:

Machame 22,102	**Rongai** 9464	**Marangu** 17,424
Umbwe 659	**Shira/Lemosho** 7807	

The thing that leaps out at you about these figures is that Machame is now quite significantly the most popular route, a position it has held since 2006/7 when it first knocked Marangu into second place. This won't surprise anybody who's trekked on this trail for the past few years – but will come as a blow to those many foreign agents who still try to hype the 'Whiskey Route' as a wild and untrammelled path. Remember, too, that the Marangu Route gets trekkers all year-round, because people on this route sleep in dormitories in huts rather than under canvas so it still gets trekkers during the rainy season, while the Machame Route is virtually deserted at that time; which means, of course, that during the rest of the year they must get many, many more people than the Marangu Route.

Other points to note? Well, it's interesting how much the Rongai Route has grown in popularity to become the third busiest route (from 4218 in 2005/6), and Lemosho/Shira too (from 4282 in 2005/6).

Finally, I do find it a little surprising to see how unpopular the Umbwe Route continues to be. It's a beautiful route and, being close to Marangu, a convenient one for the agencies to use. But its reputation as the 'hardest' route seems enough to deter most people from taking it.

trips to Africa and is the main agent for Summits Africa (see p191). As such, they specialize in the Machame and Lemosho Route ascents – because that is what Summits Africa do – and have three standards of trek: lightweight, luxury and VIP (the last one includes proper beds, wash tents and also tips for the crew, which saves you the trouble of having to sort them out yourself). For the Machame Route their prices were: 'Lightweight' scheduled trip US$2745 per person; 'Luxury' US$3650pp, VIP US$4725pp. Single supplements (US$110-325 depending on standard of trek) apply. Sterling payments are accepted, with the exact prices calculated according to the exchange rate at the time of booking. We take issue with their claim that Machame is a route that 'few people climb... affording greater peace and exclusivity' – the statistics don't back this up at all – but overall we like Summits Africa so have little against Aardvark. See also p30.

● **Abercrombie & Kent** (☎ 0845-485 1568, 🖳 www.abercrombiekent.co.uk) Upmarket holiday company (they have branches in both Harrods and Monaco!) which will send you big, glossy brochures at the click of a mouse (sadly, with very little information inside, though the photos are nice). You'll have more joy phoning them and the staff do seem pretty knowledgeable, impressively so when you consider how many other types of holiday they sell. They claim that November is a good time to climb, which is a little peculiar, but otherwise they're sound and offer Machame, Umbwe and Rongai with prices starting at £3726 – though as every trek is private and tailor-made, that's a ballpark figure only.

● **Acacia Africa** (☎ 020-7706 4700, 🖳 www.acacia-africa.com) Africa specialist using Springlands as a base (so it looks like Moshi's Zara Tours, see p216, are the local trekking agency here). Prices start at £620 (or £715 including Nairobi transfers) for the basic five-day Marangu trek plus a further US$620 minimum local payment which is collected at the start of the trip. As with most UK travel agents, Acacia offer you the chance to combine your trek with a Zanzibar trip or safari.

● **Action Challenge** (☎ 020-7609 6695, 🖳 www.actionchallenge.com) 'A specialist organizer of challenge events across the globe', Action Challenge's main business is helping with the organization of various charity treks and adventures. Currently they organize a trek a month on the Machame Route. As is often the case with these sorts of charitable expeditions, it can be a terrifically cheap way to climb if you can raise a minimum amount of sponsorship. With Action Challenge, they ask for a deposit (£399-499) to book your place, but then an extra £3800 is required in sponsorship before they allow you on the mountain; alternatively, you can forget trying to raise the sponsorship money and just pay for your trek yourself (trips start at £2199). A UK leader and doctor accompany every trip and the packages include everything, even the flights. Only the Machame, Lemosho and Rongai routes are offered.

● **The Adventure Company** (☎ 0845-004 5023, 🖳 www.adventurecompany.co.uk) Offer trips all over the world including four routes on Kili: Machame Route trips for £1479, Marangu Route packages starting from £1359, an eight-day Lemosho trek for £2399 and Rongai Route jaunts from £1499; each trip lasts about eight days, though only six are actually spent on the mountain. Flights are also available. For 15 years they have used Tropical Trails though as a result of their merger with Intrepid (see p26) it seems quite likely that they will be using Marangu Hotel from now on.

● **Africa Odyssey** (☎ 020-8704 1216, 🖳 www.africaodyssey.com) Very strange – the website looks good but when I contacted them they were very tardy in replying, and when I did chase them up they said they offered only private treks and, in their words, (and I am quoting verbatim), 'start at about $3k per person. Which is a lot! And you can get a good climb for 2ish'. They then went on to recommend Shah Tours (see p214)! Most odd.

● **Africa Travel Resource** (ATR; ☎ 01306-880770, 🖵 www.africatravel resource.com) Often recommended, very reliable and extremely knowledgeable outfit that uses African Walking Company (AWC; see p186) for their climbs. They are also the only agency I know that uses the ALTOX Personal Oxygen Systems (where two bottles of oxygen are fed through cannulas inserted into the nostrils to help clients to the summit; weirdly, their advertised summit success rate is, surprisingly, not as high as some at 87% – though maybe they're just more honest!). ATR's website is a no-nonsense place stuffed with information. Offering only the Rongai and Shira/Lemosho routes as well as AWC's own 'North Route' (essentially a route that begins on the Lemosho Route before heading round the Northern Circuit, then climbing to the summit via the Third Cave and Gillman's Point) they quoted us US$2400 per person for seven days on the Lemosho Route, or US$2000 for six days on Rongai; add a couple of hundred dollars more for a private climb. For the North Route, which is nine days, they charge around US$3200 though they accept private bookings only on this route (ie you can't join a scheduled climb). Recommended.

● **Audley Travel** (☎ 01993-838000, 🖵 www.audleytravel.com) A travel agency with multiple awards to their name that uses Nature Discovery (see p190) as their ground operator and can arrange tailor-made tours. Offer eight days on Lemosho and seven days on Machame as well as a 'Grand Traverse' that combines the Shira Plateau Route with the Northern Circuit and Rongai. With no pretensions to being a budget outfit, they charge from £4135 for this, though flights are included as well as accommodation at lovely Onsea House (see p174). Not cheap – though if you've got the money you could do a lot worse.

● **Charity Challenge** (☎ 020-8346 0500, 🖵 www.charitychallenge.com) This company arranges expeditions to various places in order to raise money for charity. Seeming to concentrate on the Lemosho and Rongai routes only, in order to participate you need to raise a substantial amount of sponsorship – in Kili's case, well over £4000. Fail, and you could be kicked off the trip! Aside from all the fundraising, the cost for climbing Kili is £2699 for Lemosho and £2454 for Rongai – not cheap, though flights are included. Use AWC (see p186) and also Tanzania Travel Company (see p192) as their Kili ground operator.

● **Classic Journeys** (☎ 01773-873497, 🖵 www.classicjourneys.co.uk) Asia specialists who also chuck in the occasional seven-day Rongai Route with the Mawenzi Tarn diversion for their climbs, charging around £1675, excluding flights but including three nights in Moshi, with Tanzania Journeys (see p215) their ground agents.

● **Climb Kili** (☎ 0800-098 8773, 🖵 www.climbkili.com) UK office of Arusha-based company (see p188).

● **Climb Mount Kilimanjaro** (☎ 01424-445837, 🖵 www.climbmountkiliman jaro.com) Company established by the author of this book with the aim of providing high-quality treks for clients at a reasonable price, using the knowledge gained over the past dozen years of researching and writing this book; for more details on our service and the treks we offer, please visit our website.

● **Different Travel** (☎ 0788-169 8623, 🖵 www.different-travel.com) Offer trips all over the world including the (very) occasional foray up Kili, using, we believe, Moshi's Keys Hotel (see p213).

● **Discover Adventure** (☎ 01722-718444, 🖵 www.discoveradventure.com) Organization specializing in expeditions to various far-flung parts of the world, where

you participate on behalf of the charity of your choice. As with many of these charity companies if you manage to raise a certain amount of sponsorship they'll pay for
your climb – about £3950 at least for Kili. Interestingly, they also do a 10-day bike
ride from just outside Nairobi to Ngorongoro Crater, where the trip ends with a safari.
For their Kili climbs they use Ahsante (see p211).

● **Equatours** (☎ 020-3239 3235; 🖳 www.equatours.co.uk) Offers seven-day treks
along the Machame Route from £1995 *including* flights – good value.

● **Exodus** (☎ 0845-287 3545, 🖳 www.exodus.co.uk) Long-standing British company that offers a number of trips including a new Northern Circuit trek (so it's no surprise to find that African Walking Company are the African operator here; see p186).
Also offer plenty of Kili-plus combinations (eg a 17-day Kilimanjaro, Serengeti and
Zanzibar trip for £3799). Regarding their treks, they offer Rongai (six days from
£2069) or Lemosho (eight days, £2399) and the new Northern Circuit route (nine
days, £2849). All prices include return flights from the UK. Laudably, they also run
the Porter Education Project to teach English to the porters during the low season
(Apr-June) and have established three schools in the local area to facilitate this.

● **Explore Worldwide** (☎ 0845-291 4541, 🖳 www.explore.co.uk) Long-established
company offering treks on Lemosho and Rongai, usually in combination with something else (ie a Meru climb, safari or Zanzibar excursion). There's a six-day Rongai
trek with a four-day Meru climb, for example, that starts from £2373. Prices exclude
flights though these can be booked. A *mzungu* (ie Western) guide accompanies every
trip. For Kili they use Ahsante of Moshi (see p211).

● **Footprint Adventures** (☎ 01522-804929, 🖳 www.footventure.co.uk) Offers all
the routes on Kilimanjaro beginning at £910 for a five-day yomp up the Marangu
Route, though all other routes are £935. As they say that these prices include all park
fees, this seems to us to be particularly low – ask carefully what's included before
booking. Uses Zara Tours (p216) as their local trekking agent and thus accommodation away from the mountain is at Springlands (see p203).

● **Gane & Marshall** (☎ 01822-600600, 🖳 www.ganeandmarshall.com) Africa specialists whose co-founder, Richard Gane, was one of the organizers behind 2009's
successful Comic Relief celebrity climb (a UK television charity fundraiser). Treks
offered include regular, open group ones (ie anyone can join) for eight days on Shira
(that's the old Shira Route via the Morum Barrier) for £1606 per person – it's an
unusual take on the route because on day three they divert off to Moir Huts and spend
some time studying the Northern Icefields and the Lent Group, which is a pleasing
change from the standard walk. There's also a six-day, £1246 Rongai climb. Similarly,
they also offer a nine-day Lemosho walk that then diverts off to go round the northern side of Kibo on the Northern Circuit (private treks only; £2453 per person for two
people). All other routes are offered. African Walking Company (see p186) are their
ground operators.

● **Imaginative Traveller** (☎ 0845-867 5870, 🖳 www.imaginative-traveller.com)
Runs small-group overland tours including a fourteen-day Serengeti and Kilimanjaro
trip (£1700) culminating in a six-day jaunt up the Marangu Route.

● **IntoAfrica** (☎ 0114-255 5610, 🖳 www.intoafrica.co.uk) Partner of Maasai
Wanderings, see p190. Costs, as usual, depend on how many people are booking but
for solo travellers they start at US$1995 if joining a scheduled seven-day Machame
trek, rising to US$3385 if undertaking a private expedition and climbing by yourself.

● **Intrepid Travel** (☎ 0800-781 1660, 🖳 www.intrepidtravel.com) Now that
they've merged with The Adventure Company (see p24), Intrepid (whose head office

is actually in Australia) are one of the bigger travel agencies sending people to Kilimanjaro. Offer the Rongai (£1070 plus US$650), Machame (from £1510) and – less common these days – five days on Marangu (from £1024) routes. Nothing unusual there, but what *is* out of the ordinary for such a sizeable operation is their ethical nature, with lots on their website about responsible travel; they also use Marangu Hotel (p221) to ensure their porters are fairly treated. Worth checking out.

● **Jagged Globe** (☎ 0845-345 8848, 🖳 www.jagged-globe.co.uk) Serious mountaineering company established more than a quarter of a century ago that leads about a dozen public climbs up 'trekkable' Kili per year on an eight-day Lemosho Route (£2685 including flights), each led by a UK guide. Prior to all their expeditions they host a weekend in North Wales for their clients both for instruction and to meet their fellow trekkers. Uses Moshi's Keys Hotel (see p213) as their suppliers.

● **Kilimanjaro Tours** (☎ 0800-081 9014, 🖳 www.kilimanjarotours.co.uk) Fairly secretive company (there's no real clue as to who they are, where they're based or even who their local operators are; though given that they use Mountain Inn as their Moshi base, it seems pretty certain that Shah Tours, see p214, are the operators here) who have a hand in organizing the Kilimarathon each year. Kili-wise they offer trips on all the routes and are pretty reasonable at £1285pp for a two-person booking for seven days on Machame, £1130 for six days on Marangu, including airport transfers and two nights at the aforementioned Mountain Inn.

● **KE Adventure Travel** (☎ 01768-773966, 🖳 www.keadventure.com) Worldwide trekking specialists, established for almost thirty years now, running seven-day Rongai (£1495), eight-day Lemosho (£1695) and six-day Machame Route treks, the latter usually combined with a trip up either Mount Kenya (£2395) or Mount Meru (£1995).

● **Outlook Expeditions** (☎ 01248-672760, 🖳 www.outlookexpeditions.com) Company specializing in organizing expeditions for schools to various parts of the world. For Kilimanjaro they offer an unusual three-week itinerary that begins in Dar es Salaam and takes in the Usambara Mountains and a Tarangire safari; the actual Kilimanjaro climb is an eight-day assault on the Machame Route. Uses Duma Explorer (see p189) as their local supplier.

● **Private Expeditions Co** (☎ 0121-288 0388, 🖳 www.privateexpeditions group.com) Trekking specialists who have established three different companies – Private Kilimanjaro (🖳 www.privatekilimanjaro.com), Private Himalaya and Private Machu Picchu – that run the treks in each of the countries concerned. Unusual in that they don't subcontract but actually run the treks themselves from their office in Moshi, they offer open group climbs on Machame and Lemosho (six days from £1149 and eight days from £1449 respectively) and private climbs only on the other routes.

● **Rainbow Tours** (☎ 020-7666 1250, 🖳 www.rainbowtours.co.uk) Smart agency specializing in Africa and Latin America, offering all routes (both scheduled treks and private ones) as well as Mount Meru, with prices fairly reasonable (eg Rongai, six days £1945) and departures every Saturday. Uses AWC (see p186) as their local supplier.

● **RightFoot Adventures** (☎ 01892-750900, 🖳 www.rightfoot-uk.com) Delivers what it calls 'Adventure fundraising', which as far as we can tell from the photos on the website consists solely of climbing Kilimanjaro. Not a regular agency, RightFoot helps charities, companies and individuals with sorting out their climbs – though their website doesn't really clarify what advantages working with them brings. Still, they use recommended AWC so they're doing something right (see p186).

PLANNING YOUR TRIP

● **RJ7 Expeditions** (☎ 0844-264 0001, 🖳 www.rjseven.com) Agency set up by Rhys Jones, one-time record-holder as the youngest person to climb the Seven Summits (hence the company's name). Mainly sells treks on the Machame and 'Lemosho Glades' (ie Lemosho) routes, with each trek led by one of their own guides in tandem with a local operator – in this case the excellent Summits Africa (see p191). When we asked about Machame we were instead (not unreasonably) steered towards Lemosho, for which prices start at £2585; add another £650 if you want their luxury option with sleeping cots etc. Quite expensive, therefore, though to be fair they know their stuff, use one of the best ground operators – and do seem to take porter welfare very seriously.

● **Rock & Rapid Adventure Centre** (☎ 0333-600 6001, 🖳 www.rockandrapid adventures.co.uk) Specializes in outdoor courses and adventures including the occasional Kili climb for charity (£2449 if paying for yourself or you can offset a large proportion of the climb if you manage to raise almost £4500 in sponsorship). Uses, we believe, Moshi's Keys Hotel (see p213).

● **Specialist Tanzania** (☎ 020-7193 2461, 🖳 www.specialisttanzania.com) Offers treks weekly on all routes bar Umbwe with prices beginning at £1175 for six days on Machame (£200 additional charge if travelling alone, £100/50 if travelling in a group of three/four).

● **Tribes Travel** (☎ 01473-890499, 🖳 www.tribes.co.uk) Award-winning, eco-friendly, fair-trade company offering just Machame on private or – a few times a year – group treks. Prices start from £1275 excluding flights but including two nights accommodation; use three different ground operators according to the standard of trek/budget required, with Moshi's Keys Hotel (see p213) one of them.

● **The Ultimate Travel Company** (☎ 020-3355 0941, 🖳 www.theultimate travelcompany.co.uk) Luxury tour operator offering plenty of trips in Africa, including climbs on the Rongai Route (£2385pp based on two sharing, including flights but excluding the hefty airport taxes). Also offers a charity climb with minimum sponsorship of over £4000.

● **Walks Worldwide** (☎ 01962-737 565 or ☎ 0845-301 4737, 🖳 www.walksworld-wide.com) Does pretty much what it says on the tin, offering treks and hikes all over the globe including Shira (from £1699) and Rongai routes (£1299) – so no surprise that AWC (see p186) are the suppliers here. Safaris and Zanzibar excursions can be added too.

● **World Expeditions** (☎ 020-8545 9030, 🖳 www.worldexpeditions.co.uk) See p35 (Australia) for more details.

Trekking agencies in Continental Europe

● **Austria** Clearskies Expeditionen und Trekking (☎ 0512 28 45 61, 🖳 www.clearskies.at); Hauser Exkursionen (☎ 1-50 50 34 6, 🖳 www.hauser-exkur sionen.de) – branch of German agency, see p29; Islaverde Reisen eU (☎ 660 55 52 775, 🖳 www.islaverde.at); Weltweitwandern (☎ 0316-58 35 04-0, 🖳 www.weltweitwandern.at).

● **Belgium** Africa Tours (☎ 051-708 171, 🖳 www.africatours.be); Allibert (☎ 02-526 9290, 🖳 www.allibert-trekking.com; Joker Tourisme (☎ 02-502 19 37, 🖳 www.joker.be); Terres d'Aventure (☎ 02-543 9560, 🖳 www.terdav.com).

● **Denmark** Inter-Travel (☎ 33 15 00 77, 🖳 www.intertravel.dk); Marco Polo Tours (☎ 70 12 03 03, 🖳 www.marcopolo.dk); Profil Rejser (☎ 77 33 55 00, 🖳

www.profil-rejser.dk); **Tanzania Tours** (☎ 61 70 16 10, 💻 www.tanzaniatours.dk) – uses Good Earth (see p190); **Topas** (☎ 86 89 36 22, 💻 www.topas.dk); **Trekking Bureauet** (☎ 46 32 05 32, 💻 trekkingbureauet.dk) – uses Marangu Hotel (see p221).

● **France** **Allibert** (☎ 04 76 45 50 50, 💻 www.allibert-trekking.com); **Huwans Club Aventure** (☎ 04 96 15 10 20, 💻 www.huwans-clubaventure.fr); **Terres d'Aventure** (☎ 08-25 700 825, 💻 www.terdav.com) – uses Corto of Arusha (see p188).

● **Germany** **Chui Tours** (☎ 0611-18249-13, 💻 www.chui-tours.de); **concept reisen** (☎ 030-218 40 53, 💻 www.tanzania-reisebuero.de) – uses Marangu Hotel (see p221) for their treks; **Elefant Tours** (☎ 0761-611667-0, 💻 www.elefant-tours.de) – uses Tanzania Experience (see p215); **Explorer Fernreisen** (💻 www.explorer.de); **Macho Porini** (☎ 080 76/97 07, 💻 www.macho-porini.de) – uses Marangu Hotel (see p221); **Mavia Soul Travel** (☎ 089-242086-786, 💻 www.mavia-reisen.de); **Top Mountain Tours** (☎ 8151 444 1914, 💻 www.top-mountain-tours.de); **Hauser Exkursionen** (München ☎ 089-2 35 00 60, Berlin ☎ 30 88 67 81 03, 💻 www.hauser-exkursio nen.de) – uses Snow Cap of Moshi (see p214); **DAV Summit Club** (☎ 089 64240 196, 💻 www.dav-summit-club.de).

● **Luxembourg** **Bel Africa** (☎ 495 74 38 15, or ☎ 6 33 40 57 73, ☎ 475 31 36 53, 💻 www.belafrica.fr) are agents for Maasai Wanderings (see p190).

● **Netherlands** **7 Summits** (💻 7summits.com) Company run by one-man band Harry Kilkstra that specializes in climbs up each of the continents' highest peaks, with a web-site that has a good FAQ section about Kilimanjaro; uses Zara Tours (see p216). **Explore Tanzania** (☎ 055-533 25 50, 💻 www.exploretanzania.nl) uses African Walking Company (see p186); **Himalaya Trekking** (☎ 052-22 41146, 💻 www.htwan delreizen.nl); **Nederlandse Klim en Bergsport Vereniging** (NKBV; ☎ 0348-409521, 💻 www.nkbv.nl); **Snow Leopard Adventure Reizen** (☎ 070-388 2867, 💻 www.snowleopard.nl); **SNP Reiswinkel** (☎ 024-327 7000, 💻 www.snp.nl); **Kenia en Tanzania online** (☎ 071-516 2035, 💻 www.keniaonline.nl) – agent for Tanzania Journeys (see p215).

● **Norway** **EcoExpeditions** (☎ 90 04 13 30, 💻 www.ecoexpeditions.no); **Explore Travel** (☎ 69 36 18 50, 💻 www.exploretravel.no) uses Marangu Hotel (see p221); **Hvitserk** (☎ 23 21 30 70, 💻 www.hvitserk.no); **Kilroy Travels** (☎ 026 33, 💻 trav els.kilroy.no); **Uhuru** (☎ 41 02 02 78, 💻 www.uhuru.no) – uses Nature Discovery, we believe (see p190).

● **Spain** **A Step Ahead** (💻 www.astepahead.es); **Giroguies** (☎ 972-303 886, 💻 www.giroguies.com).

● **Sweden** **Aventyrsresor** (☎ 08-55 60 69 00, 💻 www.aventyrsresor.se); **Kilroy Travels** (☎ 0771-545769, 💻 travels.kilroy.se).

● **Switzerland** **Acapa Tours** (☎ 056-443 32 21, 💻 www.acapa.ch); **Aktivferien AG** (☎ 052-335 13 10, 💻 www.aktivferien.com); **Allibert** (☎ 022-849 8551, 💻 www.allibert-trekking.com); **b&b travel** (☎ 44-380 4343, 💻 www.bandbtravel.ch); **Kaufmann Trekking** (☎ 041-822 00 55, 💻 www.kaufmanntrekking.ch) – agent for Marangu Hotel (see p221); **Terres d'Aventure** (☎ 022-518 0513, 💻 www.terdav.com).

Trekking agencies in the USA

North American trekking agencies tend to quote land cost only. Also, solo travellers should expect to pay US$150-300 in single supplements on top of the quoted prices.

● **Aardvark Safaris** (☎ toll free in USA 888-776-0888; from outside USA: 1-858-523-9000, 🖳 www.aardvarksafaris.com) Agent for Summits Africa (see p191) so only the Lemosho and Machame Routes are really offered, though with three standard levels, VIP, Lightweight and Luxury. Tours are tailor-made to the individual so prices vary according to specifications.

● **Adventure Center** (☎ 1-800-228-8747, 🖳 www.adventurecenter.com) Offer Rongai and Lemosho routes, as well as a nine-day route that starts on Lemosho but takes in the Northern Circuit (from US$3590). Meru climbs and safari add-ons are also available.

● **Adventures in Good Company** (☎ 877-439-4042, 🖳 www.adventuresingood company.com) Agency specializing in 'adventure holidays' for women including trips up Africa's highest mountain (the only trip they do on the continent), though only every other year *at most* – with 2015 the next scheduled trek; use Marangu Hotel (see p221) as their ground operator.

● **Adventure International** (☎ 1-888-664-3865, 🖳 www.adventure-inter national.com) Using Summits Africa (see p191) as their local outfitter (indeed, one of the guys who founded Summits Africa is also part of Adventure International), this company offers treks on the Rongai, Machame (US$3210 luxury spec, including airport transfers, pillows on the trek, 3-inch thick mattresses and two nights at Blues & Chutney Hotel, see p179) and Lemosho routes as well as an 'Ultimate Kilimanjaro'

It's not just about the climbing – other things to do on and around Kili

There are plenty of other things you can do with Kilimanjaro apart from climbing it. How about entering the **Kilimanjaro Marathon**, for example. Taking place in late February or early March (🖳 www.kilimanjaro marathon.com), the race is run over the standard 26 miles/42.2km and starts by heading out along the road to Dar before returning to Moshi via a climb to Mweka. As such, it doesn't actually enter into the national park at all – though given the levels of exhaustion suffered by your average marathon participant, it's probably just as well that they don't have to climb a mountain too.

A half-marathon is also held at the same time and with prizes of Ts3 million each to the winners of the men's and women's race (Ts1.5 million for the half-marathon, plus prizes for the various disabled categories) this is turning into one of the biggest events in the social calendar in Northern Tanzania.

For those for whom a marathon is not testing enough, there is always the **Kiliman Challenge** (🖳 www.kilimanjaro-man.com). This particular brand of torture begins with a six-day saunter up the Machame Route to Uhuru Peak, followed by a two-day circumnavigation of the base of the Kilimanjaro by mountain bike (around 190km in total), before rounding it all off with participation in the marathon described above. The organizers are at pains to point out that only the last two events are races; with the climb, of course, it's too dangerous to race up. If it all sounds too much, you can opt to take part in just one or two of the activities.

climb that is actually just a standard Lemosho climb but with a couple of days in the West Kilimanjaro corridor tacked on at the start.

● **Adventures Within Reach** (☎ 877-232-5836, 💻 www.adventureswithin reach.com) Award-winning 'adventure company' now working with Moshi's Tanzania Journeys (see p215). Offers all routes, the itinerary of their treks being fairly standard and their prices reasonable: US$2645 for 2-3 people for eight days on Lemosho, for example, or US$1795 for seven days on Machame. Also offer a 'Luxury' option with mess tents, oxygen, dining chairs with backs ... and a whole lot of other stuff that many companies now offer as standard anyway. Still, the basic treks remain reasonably priced and they're very experienced.

● **Africa Adventure Consultants** (☎ 1-866-778-1089, 💻 www.adventures inafrica.com) Another multi award-winning company more famous, perhaps, for its Southern and Western Circuit safaris than Kili, though they offer all the routes save Marangu, with 'budget' climbs on Machame (US$3018 for six days) as well as Lemosho treks (US$4500-7500 for eight days, the exact figure depending on the number of people booking and the time of year). It's good, too, to see Umbwe being offered for a change (US$3070-7024 for six days, the exact price depending on the season and the number of people in your booking). Use Nature Discovery (see p190) for their treks.

● **Africa Travel Resource** (☎ 1-313-744-2871 or tollfree ☎ 1-888-487 5418, 💻 www.africatravelresource.com) American contact of UK company; see p25.

● **African Safari Company** (☎ 1-800-414-3090, 💻 www.africansafarico.com) Offer just the Machame Route, seven days for a private climb, for a reasonable US$2610 per person for 2-3 people, US$2358 if there are 4-8 of you, and US$2130 for a group of nine or more, with Arumeru River Lodge (see p176) and The Bay Leaf

---

Still not exhausted? Then how about taking part in the annual **Kilimanjaro Trail Run** (💻 tanzaniatrailrunning.com), an eight-day, 160-mile slog around the mountain. Led by Simon Mtuy – record holder for a speed ascent on Kili, founder of the highly regarded SENE trekking agency (see p214) and all-round good egg – the trail runs along dirt tracks and footpaths, taking you past lush rainforest and waterfalls, with participants encouraged to plant trees outside the villages where they camp for the night.

Another option is **horseriding**. Makoa Farm (💻 www.makoa-farm.com) near Machame Gate organizes horseback safaris in the West Kilimanjaro Wildlife Management Area, where you stay in permanent luxury camps and mobile camps, farmhouse accommodation next to Kilimanjaro Forest Reserve, comfortable cottages or at the guesthouse on Makoa Farm. Some experience is necessary for most of these rides. Costs are €1920 per person for two people for four days on the Kilimanjaro Wilderness Trail, while for the eight-day West Kilimanjaro Big Game Trail prices rise to €3700pp. It's certainly a unique experience and being on horseback allows you to go where four-wheel drives and mountain bikes never could.

Finally, if all of the above sounds just too, well, energetic, the boss of KINAPA, Mr Lufungulo, revealed that he had plans to build a couple of **luxury lodges on Kilimanjaro**, for those who want to be on the mountain without actually doing anything so exhausting as trekking. The TANAPA website will probably be the best place to look for details on these (💻 www.tanzaniaparks.com).

Hotel (see p179) as their base hotels and Duma Explorer (see p189) as their local supplier.
● **Alpine Ascents International** (☎ 206-378-1927, 🖳 www.alpineascents.com) Highly regarded, very professional and efficient agency that, a little surprisingly, uses Big Expeditions of Arusha (see p187). All their climbs are accompanied by one of their own mountain guides and they do have a very good success rate. Price-wise they charge US$4400 for seven days on the only route they seem to offer – Machame.
● **Climb Kili** (☎ 1-888-589-1884, 🖳 www.climbkili.com) American office of Arusha-based company (see p188).
● **Deeper Africa** (☎ 888-658-7102, 🖳 www.deeperafrica.com) Small company specializing in East Africa and winners of a couple of National Geographic awards down the years. Offer seven-day Machame (from US$4499) and eight-day Lemosho (from US$4599) treks. Not cheap, though their concern for the welfare of porters shines through on their website and they are agents for Africa VIP Travel (see p186).
● **Destination Tanzania Safaris** (☎ 1-888-861-6518, 🖳 www.detasa.com) American office of Arusha-based company (see p188).
● **Embark Adventures** (☎ 503-922-1050, 🖳 embarkadventures.com) A company that claims it was founded on the slopes of Kili, offering just the Machame and Lemosho routes (the latter costing US$3195).
● **Global Adrenaline** (☎ 1-866-884-5622, 🖳 globaladrenaline.com) Offer a twelve-day trip that encompasses an eight-day Lemosho/WesternBreach trek using African Environments (see p185) as their local supplier. Prices vary as each itinerary is custom-made.
● **Global Basecamps** (☎ 866-577-2462, 🖳 www.globalbasecamps.com) Offers treks on the Machame (US$2298 per person for seven days) and Rongai routes via its partner Maasai Wanderings (see p186).
● **Good Earth Tours & Safaris** (☎ 888-776-7173, 🖳 www.goodearthtours.com) American office of Arusha-based company (see p190).
● **International Mountain Guides** (IMG; ☎ 360-569-2609, 🖳 www.mountainguides.com) Long-established company that's conducted almost 200 climbs on Kilimanjaro, each accompanied by one of IMG's American guides (with Moshi's Keys Hotel, see p213, as the local supplier). The climb only – seven days on Machame – costs US$4100-4325 depending on the group size though other routes can be used on request if a private trek.
● **Journeys International** (☎ 734-665-4407, toll-free ☎ 1-800-255-8735, 🖳 www.journeys.travel) Offers treks on the Rongai (six days) and Shira routes (eight days) with prices from US$3535 per person for Rongai, US$3795 for Shira. AWC (see p186) are, according to their Africa desk, just one of several companies they use.
● **Journey to Africa** (☎ 1-877-558-6288, 🖳 www.journeytoafrica.com) Offers a 15-day Kilimanjaro and Wildlife tour utilizing the Machame Route combined with a four-day safari afterwards (US$6380 per person for two people, US$5780pp for four).
● **Kensington Tours** (☎ 1-888-903-2001, 🖳 www.kensingtontours.com) Agent offering fairly luxurious tailor-made trips and cruises and well as three different routes on Kili – Rongai (seven days from US$4222 per person), Machame (six days from US$3186) and, refreshingly, Umbwe (six days from US$3775) – as well as a 12-day Machame climb-safari combo from US$5676pp for 2-4 sharing.
● **Mountain Madness** (☎ 1-800-328-5925, 🖳 www.mountainmadness.com) Founded by the late Scott Fischer, after whom Kili's (now disused) Fischer Campsite is named, the highly regarded Mountain Madness and their sister company African

Environments (see p185) have a long association with the mountain, pioneering Kili's Lemosho Route across the Shira Plateau and boasting a success rate for getting their clients to the top of greater than 90%. These days, while continuing to patronize Lemosho (including an ascent via the Western Breach and a night in Crater Campsite) they also offer an optional jaunt to the Serengeti and, bizarrely, a three-week whirlwind trek up both Kili and Europe's highest peak, Mount Elbrus! Climb-only prices for just Kili are US$5820/US$5575/US$5355 for parties of 3-6/7-10/11-14 respectively on the eight-day Lemosho Route. One of the best.

● **Mountain Gurus** (☎ 1-800-253-4117, 🖳 www.mountaingurus.com) Offer nineday tours of Tanzania including six days on Machame and a three-day safari, a packed schedule with prices from US$2600. More extensive trips that take in a Mount Meru climb and a Serengeti safari are available too. Uses Moshi's Keys Hotel (see p213).

● **Mountain Travel Sobek** (☎ 1-888-831-7526, 🖳 www.mtsobek.com) Upmarket trekking company offering ten-day hikes on the Machame/Western Breach trail (with eight days actually on the mountain), including a night at Crater Campsite, for US$4195/US$4595 per person for 4-8/9-14 members – excluding park fees! Also do a combination trip where you attempt both Kili's Rongai Route and Mount Kenya (US$6395/6895 for 4-6/7-15 participants). Uses African Environments (see p185) as their local supplier.

● **Peak Planet** (☎ 480-463-4058, 🖳 www.peakplanet.com) US agent for African Walking Company (p186). Prices start from US$2100 for six days on the Rongai Route with the Mawenzi Tarn Hut diversion, rising to around US$2850 for eight days on Lemosho and US$3200 for their nine-day Northern Circuit trek.

● **Piper & Heath Travel** (☎ 1-858-598-5559, 🖳 www.piperandheath.com) Uses Duma Explorer (see p189) as their local operator.

● **Rainier Mountaineering Inc Expeditions** (RMI; ☎ 1-888-892-5462, 🖳 www.rmiguides.com) Boasting a 93% success rate for getting clients to Uhuru Peak, these mountain experts operate on all 'seven summits' and charge a whopping US$5900 to trek with them on the busiest route of all, Machame, though you do get a Western guide accompanying you on the trek and a four-day safari on the Northern Circuit at the end. Uses Dik Dik Tours (see p189) as their local supplier.

● **Real Life Adventure Travel** (☎ 925-631-7978, toll free ☎ 877-UGO-KILI, 🖳 www.reallifeadventuretravel.com) American contact of Tanzanian operator (see p214).

● **REI Adventures** (☎ 800-622-2236, 🖳 www.rei.com/adventures) Large and established outfit that's half camping shop, half travel agency with Kili treks on offer too on both Marangu (six days, US$5899) or Lemosho (eight days, US$7199). Significant discounts are available if you become an REI member (though with single supplements too).

● **Serengeti Pride Safaris** (☎ 508-951-1001, 🖳 www.serengetipridesafaris.com) American contact of Tanzanian company based at Usa River, east of Arusha (see p191).

● **Taraji** (☎ 1-703-349-3215, 🖳 www.tarajikilimanjaro.com) Rising from the ashes of the old Kiliwarriors agency (see p35), this is the new agency formed by the American half of the outfit and maintains the rather boastful advertising of its predecessor. Offer both seven-day Machame treks and three different versions of Lemosho: via the Western Breach, a second that follows the regular route via Barafu, and a third, 'Taraji Northern Trail' via the Northern Circuit and Gillman's Point and including a night at Crater Campsite. Offer four comfort options with rates from US$2830 for their cheapest 'Explorer' package for seven days on Machame.

● **Thomson Safaris** (☎ 800-235-0289, 🖳 www.thomsontreks.com) Highly regarded and multi-award-winning outfit that's been operating for more than 30 years. Indeed, they were the first US tour company in Tanzania and one recommended by David Breasher, the director of the IMAX film *Kilimanjaro: To the Roof of Africa* (see p360). Their trekking partner, Nature Discovery (see p190), boasts a good reputation for looking after their porters (the only ones we know of who are fully clad in Gore-Tex!) and are rated by KPAP as one of the top six companies in this field. They offer only three routes but they are interesting ones: a standard six-day Umbwe Route (from US$4290), nine days on the Lemosho Route with a night at Crater Campsite from US$5890 and a great ten-day Grand Traverse from US$8290 that starts on the Shira Plateau and heads east towards Mawenzi Tarn before looping back to School Hut. They are extremely reliable and efficient, offer a great service on and off the mountain with what they boast is the most safety equipment (including Gamow bags and oximeters), 'gourmet' food, highly trained and well-remunerated staff and a very high success rate for getting people to the summit.

● **Travel Beyond** (☎ 800-876-3131, 🖳 travelbeyond.com) Offers adventures all over the planet including a six-day trek on the Marangu Route for US$1827 or seven days on Machame (US$2100) with Marangu Hotel (see p221) as the ground operator.

● **Trek 2 Kili** (☎ 626-253-1151, 🖳 www.trek2kili.com) American contact for joint North American-Tanzanian venture offering all the routes (see p216).

● **Tusker Trail** (☎ toll free 1-800-231-1919, 🖳 tusker.com) Highly recommended, highly regarded and very experienced company that's been operating for over 35 years. Cited by Kilimanjaro Porters Assistance Project for their benevolent treatment of porters (see pp47-9), Tusker claim to have a success rate that hovers around the 98% mark; their guides also receive the best medical training on the mountain and their cooks are trained by the Culinary Institute of America. Offer all routes with trips starting at US$2990 for the Marangu Route (six days) as well as a 'Kili360' tour that begins on the Umbwe Route before heading round the northern side of Kibo to Kibo Huts, a trek of eleven days for US$5980 per person.

● **Ultimate Kilimanjaro** (☎ 312-278-1008, 🖳 www.ultimatekilimanjaro.com) Company that talks a good talk and has one of the most boastful sites on the web, though essentially they are agents for Zara Tours of Moshi (see p216). Offer all the routes: Machame seven days, including two nights' accommodation at Springland, US$1915pp; Marangu, six days, US$1765pp.

● **Wilderness Travel** (☎ 1-800-368-2794, 🖳 www.wildernesstravel.com) Offers an 18-day trip that includes an unusual nine-day version of the 'Shira Plateau' (Lemosho) and Western Breach Route (including a night at Crater Campsite) combined with a Serengeti safari add-on. You can do *just* the climb, however, with prices US$5695/US$5395/$4995 for 4-6/9-11/12-14 members. Uses African Environments (see p185) as their local supplier.

● **Zephyr Adventures** (☎ 888-758-8687, 🖳 www.zephyradventures.com) Hiking, bicycling, skating and multi-sport agency that also does treks on Kili, with lodging at Planet Lodge and the trek organized by Good Earth (see p190). Cost is about US$3100 for seven days on Lemosho.

Trekking agencies in Canada

● **Canadian Himalayan Expeditions** (☎ 1-800-563 8735, 🖳 www.himalayanexpeditions.com) Run private treks (minimum four people) on the five-day Marangu and six-day Machame routes, costing US$1795 and US$1995 respectively.

● **G Adventures** (☎ 1-888-800-4100, ⌨ www.gadventures.com) Huge outfit using agents to sell their tours (rather than their own offices); offer treks on all routes, using Zara (see p216) as the local outfitters.

● **Good Earth Tours** (☎ 1-888-776-7173, ⌨ www.goodearthtours.com) Canadian office of American/Tanzanian agency (see p190).

● **The Heritage Safari Co** (☎ 1-888-301-1713, ⌨ www.heritagesafaris.com) Claims to have a 90% success rate, charging US$2480 for seven days on Machame, Marangu for six days for US$1955pp, with oxygen US$150 extra.

● **Kiliwarrior Expeditions** (☎ 1-800-820-3058, ⌨ kiliwarriorexpeditions.com) When veteran Kili outfitters F&S Kiliwarriors split up the American half went on to form Taraji (see p33) while Wilfred Mollel, the Tanzanian half of the team, kept (most of the) name and built this small agency with a new, Canadian partner. As with the old F&S, they don't offer all routes but just Lemosho or Machame (the former with the Western Breach option too). And as with the old F&S company, they offer two standards of treks, though even their 'Standard package' (from US$3295 per person for two people for seven days on Machame) is very high spec, including a hot shower tent, hot water bottles, solar chargers, a hyperbaric chamber and defibrillator all supplied while on the mountain, two nights at Mount Meru Lodge and one night after the trek at KIA Lodge, and even a free phone call to loved ones back home thrown in too. Nowhere near as large an operation as the old F&S – but still highly efficient, well run, very professional and worth checking out.

● **The Safari Partners** (☎ 1-888-717-2327, ⌨ www.thesafaripartners.com) Offers all routes using Marangu Hotel (see p221) as their local operator.

● **Trek 2 Kili** (☎ 418-608-8831, ⌨ www.trek2kili.com) Canadian contacts for this joint North American-Tanzanian venture offering all the routes (see p216).

● **World Expeditions** (toll free ☎ 1-800-567-2216, ☎ 613 241-2700, ⌨ www.world expeditions.com/ca); also Montreal (toll free ☎ 1-866-606-1721, ☎ 1-514-844-6364, ⌨ www.expeditionsmonde.com). See below (Australia) for more details.

Trekking agencies in Australia

● **Intrepid Travel** (☎ 03-9473 2626, ⌨ www.intrepidtravel.com) Head office of agency with branches in the UK; uses Marangu Hotel (see p221) as their local outfitter.

● **No Roads Expeditions** (☎ 03-9598 8581, ⌨ www.noroads.com.au) Offers four of the routes up the mountain – but not Marangu. The info on their website is a little dated ('25,000 people climbing Kili per year' for example) but overall they seem pretty good, use highly rated Marangu Hotel (see p221) for their treks and also offer expeditions led by an Australian guide.

● **Peregrine Adventures** (☎ 03-8601 4444, ⌨ www.peregrineadventures.com) One of Australia's larger agencies. Offers Rongai and Machame routes with optional Zanzibar/safari add-ons.

● **Pure Adventure** (☎ 08-9303 4710, ☎ 08-9206 5490, ⌨ www.climbingkiliman jaro.com.au) Australian office for Destination Africa Tours (see p36).

● **World Expeditions** (toll free ☎ 1-300 720000, ☎ 02-8270 8400, ⌨ www.world expeditions.com/au, Sydney. Also in Melbourne (☎ 03-8631 3300); Perth (☎ 08-9486 9899); and Brisbane (☎ 07-3003 0954) This company offers a challenging 15-day Twin Peaks Trekking trip encompassing both Mount Kenya and Kilimanjaro (Rongai Route; from A$4290 for both treks), or simple Rongai/Shira treks (A$2490/2990). They also organize a 16-day 'Tanzania on Foot' (A$4990) tour, a combination of safari and trekking including climbs of Meru and Kili. Uses African Walking Company (see p186) for their treks.

Trekking agencies in New Zealand
● **Adventure Consultants** (☎ 03-443 8711, 🖳 www.adventureconsultants.com)
Uses Nature Discovery (see p190) for their climbs and currently offers a Machame
trek (and optional safari) half a dozen times a year as well as a 'luxury' option.
● **Adventure World** (☎ 0800-238 368, 🖳 www.adventureworld.co.nz) Offers six-
day treks on the Marangu Route for NZ$2315 as well as treks on the other routes.
● **Aspiring Guides** (☎ 03-443 9422, 🖳 www.aspiringguides.com)   Partners of
Jagged Globe (see p27).
● **World Expeditions** (☎ 09-368 4161, toll free ☎ 0800 350 354, 🖳 www.worldex
peditions.com/nz). See p35 (Australia).

Trekking agencies in South Africa
● **Acacia Africa** (☎ 21-556 1157, 🖳 www.acacia-africa.com) See p24 (Trekking
agencies in the UK).
● **Destination Africa Tours** (☎ 12-333 7114/5, 🖳 www.climbingkilimanjaro.co.za)
Agency covering all routes that *claims* to have a 96-98% success rate for getting
trekkers to Uhuru. Indeed, their website is one of the most bombastic on the web –
quite surprising, given that they're only another agent for Zara (see p216). Their website includes full-moon dates, Swahili terms, a fitness programme and a typical Kili
menu.
● **Wild Frontiers** (☎ 11-702 2035, 🖳 www.wildfrontiers.com) Organizes regular
trips up Kili and are involved in the annual Kilimarathon. Offers all the routes and,
we believe, still use Keys Hotel as their local supplier (see p213). Prices start at five
days on Marangu for US$1526 per person – though be warned that their advertised
prices *exclude* park fees – one of the very few agencies still to do this.

For a review of **trekking agencies in Tanzania and Kenya**, see p147 (Dar es
Salaam), p158 (Nairobi), p185 (Arusha), p210 (Moshi) and p2210 (Marangu);
and read the following section.

BOOKING WITH AN AGENCY IN TANZANIA

The main advantage of booking with an agency in Tanzania is one of economy:
simply put, you're cutting out the middleman. Many foreign tour operators
don't actually use their own staff to organize and lead the treks but use the services of a Tanzanian tour operator. By booking in Tanzania, therefore, you are
dealing directly with the people who are going to take you up the mountain and
not the Western agent.

So it can be a bit cheaper, particularly if you wait until after you've arrived
in Tanzania to book your trek when you can negotiate face to face. There are
other advantages too. If you ask, there should be no reason why you cannot
meet the guides and porters before you agree to sign up – and even your fellow
trekkers, all of whom have a huge role to play in making your trek an enjoyable
one. You can also personally check the tents and camping equipment before
booking.

Furthermore, the fact that you can book a trek up to 24 hours beforehand
(though see the note on p249) gives you greater flexibility, allowing you to alter
your plans so that you can pick a day that suits you – whereas when booking
with an agency at home you often have to book months in advance, the tour is

usually organized to a pretty tight schedule and altering this schedule at a later date is often impossible. Another point: while the money you spend on a trek may not be going to the most destitute and deserving of Tanzania's population, at least you know that *all* of it is going to Tanzanians, with little if any going into the pockets of a Western company.

Of course, thanks to the internet you don't even need to wait until you arrive in Tanzania before booking: just about every agency in Arusha and Moshi (see p185 and p210) now has online-booking services and while it may seem a bit scary sending a four-figure sum to people in East Africa whom you've never met, the bigger companies at least are used to receiving bookings this way and are trustworthy. What's more, if you go with an agency that's been recommended in this book or by friends, there's no reason why it should be any more risky than if you were booking at home; indeed, there's a slim chance that you might even end up joining a group who *did* book their tour abroad and paid more as a consequence.

Choosing an agency in Tanzania

The best place to look for an agency is either **Arusha** (see p185), which has the greatest number of tour and trekking operators, or **Moshi** (see p210). A third option, **Marangu**, has few agencies (see p221). Agencies in Dar es Salaam and other Tanzanian towns are usually nothing more than middlemen for the operators in Moshi, Arusha or Marangu: book a tour with an agency in Dar, for example, and the chances are you'll still end up on a trek organized by an agency in Moshi or Arusha, only you would have paid more for it. Furthermore, if you book outside of Arusha or Moshi, you have less chance of inspecting the equipment or testing your guide before you set off.

Regarding the **difference between Arusha and Moshi**: in general the former is the home of the more established and larger safari companies/trekking agencies. However, perhaps due to its location, the Arusha-based companies tend to concentrate just as much on safaris in the Serengeti, Ngorongoro and Arusha National Park (including climbs up Meru) as they do on treks up Kilimanjaro. Indeed, some just act as middlemen for one of the agencies in Moshi and don't actually arrange Kili treks themselves. Moshi, on the other hand, is a smaller place and one where the agencies tend to focus more on climbing Kilimanjaro than on safaris. It would also be fair to say that the Moshi-based companies tend to be a little cheaper than those in Arusha, and most budget operators have their offices in Moshi.

Reading the above, therefore, it would seem that you should base yourself in Moshi rather than Arusha if you are in the market for a budget trek. But it's not that simple; for example, if you are thinking of taking a safari before or after your Kili climb, the Arusha-based companies may be able to offer you a better package for both than those in Moshi. It's worth remembering, too, that those companies recommended by KPAP for their fair treatment of porters, the majority are based in Arusha.

Wherever you decide to shop for your trek, check out our reviews of the agencies on p185 (Arusha), p210 (Moshi), p221 (Marangu), which should help in your quest. The golden rule when shopping around is: **stick to agencies that have a licence** and check that licence thoroughly to ensure it covers trekking. If they don't have a licence, or the one they show you looks a bit suspect, or is out of date, take your business elsewhere.

Other advice includes:

● Decide what **sort of trek** you want, what **route** you wish to take, **how long** you wish to go for, and **with how many people**.

● Ask other travellers for their **recommendations** of a good agency.

● **Shop around**. Don't sign up with the first agent you talk to but consult other agencies first to compare.

● Read the section opposite on **signing contracts** and learn it off by heart (or take this book with you!) so you know what to ask the agency.

● Ask about the **number of people** on your trek and the **number of porters** you'll be taking.

● Ask if you can see their **'comments book'**. This is a book where previous clients have written their thoughts on the agency. Many agencies will have one (though it's fair to say in the internet age they are becoming less common, with people often emailing their comments instead; the rule is the same, however: ask to see them!); and if they are any good they will show it to you with little or no prompting. Indeed, if they don't have one, or are reluctant to show you, be suspicious.

● If you have any **dietary requirements** or other **special needs**, ask them if these will be a problem, if it will cost any more, and how exactly they propose to comply with your requirements. For example, if you are a vegetarian, ask the agent what kind of meals you can expect to receive on the trek.

● Ask to see a print-out of the **day-to-day itinerary** (though some, admittedly, will not have this, all agencies should be able to describe the trekking routes and their itineraries without any problem); if you're negotiating with an agency at the upper end of the market, you may even be able to get a preview of the daily menus.

● If you think you've found a good company, ask to see the **equipment** you will be using and make sure the tent is complete, untorn and that all the zips work.

● Check the **sleeping arrangements**, particularly if you're not trekking with friends but have joined a group: are you going to have a tent to yourself, or are you going to be sharing with somebody you've never met before?

● If you are **alone and on a budget**, ask if it is possible to be put with a group, which should make things cheaper. (This is normally done automatically anyway; indeed, if you are travelling alone and were quoted a very low price, you can expect to be put with another group.)

Following on from the last point, many of the operators at the budget end often band together to lump all their customers into one large trekking group, thereby making it cheaper for them as certain fixed costs can be shared. So don't be surprised if, having signed up with one company, you end up being joined by trekkers who booked with another company. Once again, make sure you know in advance about any arrangements like this *before* you sign anything or hand over any money. And if you want to be on your own, tell them.

Finding that you don't have your own tent but have to share with a stranger is just one of the potential hazards of booking with a budget company. Or rather, it's one of the advantages of paying a bit more and going with a company that won't spring any nasty surprises on you. Sign up with a more expensive company and you should also find that they have better safety procedures and emergency equipment and more knowledgeable guides. So unless money is really tight don't look for the cheapest company but the *best-value* one; hopefully our reviews will help you to decide which agencies offer the best deals.

SIGNING THE CONTRACT WITH A TANZANIAN AGENCY

This section is mainly for those who are in Tanzania and dealing with agencies face to face, though much of it is relevant to those booking in their own country – or with a company online – too.

So, you've found a suitable agency offering the trek you want for the required duration at an acceptable price. Before you sign on the dotted line, however, there are a number of questions to be asked, matters to consider and points to discuss with the agency. (And if there is no dotted line to sign on – ie no contract – don't even think about handing over any money or going with them.) What is vitally important is that you **sort out** *exactly* **what is and isn't included in the price of the trek**. Don't just ask what is included in the price: ask what *isn't* included – ie what you yourself will need to pay for as this will give you an idea of exactly how much extra you need to pay in addition to the basic cost of the trek.

The following is a brief checklist of **items that should be included**:
● All park fees (see p40) for both yourself and the porters and guides.
● Hire of porters, assistant guides and guides, their wages and food.
● Food and water for the entire trek. Get a breakdown of exactly how many meals per day you will be getting: normally trekkers are served three main meals per day plus a snack – typically a hot drink with popcorn and biscuits – upon arrival at camp at the end of the day; see p251 for more details on food on the trek.
● Transport to and from the park at the beginning and end of the trek.
● Hire of camping and cooking gear. If you have brought your own gear, you might be able to persuade the agency to reduce the cost of your trek, though it will be only by a small amount.
● Hire of any equipment – torches, ski poles, spare water-bottles etc – that you don't want to bring with you. There will probably be a small surcharge for these – just make sure that whatever you agree is included in the contract.
● Any special dietary requirements or other needs, all of which should be stipulated in the contract.
● Any free night's accommodation at the beginning or end of your trek that the trekking company has agreed to cover.

In addition to the above, clients who are booking from abroad and have agreed that transfers from and to Kilimanjaro Airport are included should again make sure that's stipulated in the contract.

Please note: items that are rarely, if ever, included in the package include cigarettes, soft drinks and the tips you dish out to your crew at the end.

Having sorted that out, you then need to make sure that *everything* the agency has said they will provide, including everything listed above, is **specified in the contract**. This is important because, as you probably already know, a verbal contract is simply not worth the paper it isn't written on. The trekking companies all have standard contracts which should include most of the above but will not include specific things such as the hire of any equipment you need or any free nights' accommodation that you have managed to negotiate into the package. These will need to be written in as well.

THE COST: WHY IS IT ALL SO EXPENSIVE?

With little change from US$1000 for even the cheapest trek, it cannot be denied that climbing Kili is a relatively expensive walk, particularly when compared to other famous treks (the Annapurna Circuit in Nepal, for example, has an 'entry fee' of less than US$30 while the Inca Trail has a fee of around US$50, and it's around US$450 for an all-inclusive tour); with no refund available to those who fail either, even if you are forced to give up after only a few minutes on the mountain, at first sight this trek can seem very bad value too – though to those who successfully reach the summit, of course, the sense of achievement and the enjoyment of the trek makes almost any amount seem worth it.

To give you some idea of where your money goes, the following is a breakdown of fees, wages and other costs incurred on the trek, while the box on p42 is an example of costs for an average trek. Don't forget that, in addition to the official costs outlined below, there is also the matter of **tips** (see p42).

Park fees
● **Rescue fee** US$20 per trip
● **Conservation fee (formerly Park Entry fee)** US$70 per day (US$20 for under 16s; free for under 5s)
● **Hut fee (Marangu Route) only** US$60 per night
● **Camping fee** US$50 per night (US$10 for under 16s; free for under 5s) for routes other than Marangu
● **Crew fees** Ts3500 per crew member per trip (currently just over US$2)

❏ **Discounts on park fees**
There are various discounts available in addition to those enjoyed by under-16-year-olds. Firstly, those who hold a valid resident's permit for East Africa are, under the new regime, supposed to get a 50% reduction on the above park fees; while East African passport holders do even better, with their Conservation fees and Camping fees just Ts10,000 per day each and their hut fees on Marangu Ts5000. This means that they enjoy discounts on the regular fees of at least US$100 less per day.

Do make sure, however, if you're an East African passport holder, or a resident, or under 16, that you furnish your agency with the necessary proof well before your trek, in order that they can apply for these discounts. It will definitely be worth it!

❑ **Possible park fee increase**

At the time of publication, there are rumours that the park fees for the crew will be increasing from Ts3500 per crew member per trek to **Ts3500 per crew member per day**. The change, if it happens, is said to be scheduled for July 2014. Thus, using the Machame Route example in the box on p42, the crew fees would rise from Ts21,000 (US$13) to Ts147,000 (US$91). Thus the cost of the trek will rise by about U$78 – which presumably will be passed on, at least in part, to the client. Normally we don't pay that much attention to the rumours that regularly swirl around Kilimanjaro but this one has some credibility. For one thing, the source is reliable. Secondly, this price increase would tie in with the policies of the boss of KINAPA, Mr Lufungolu, whom I know is concerned about the number of crew on the mountain and the subsequent environmental degradation.

Take a quick look at these figures; already you can see just why the cost of climbing Kilimanjaro is so high. Even if you took the quickest (and thus not recommended) five-day yomp up the Marangu Route, your fees alone still come to US$610 plus porter/guide entrance fees. See p42 for how much a typical trek could cost.

Other costs

The following are the other major expenses involved in an expedition up Kilimanjaro. Note that, unlike park fees, with all of the following the more people in your group, the lower the per-person charge.

Wages (per trip) Wages vary from company to company, of course. Tanzania National Parks (TANAPA) set the following minimum wages way back in 2009; though as I write this almost five years later they are still not being rigidly enforced. The figures they have come up with are as follows:

- **Porters** US$10 per day
- **Assistant guides (and presumably cooks)** US$15 per day
- **Guides** US$20 per day

These wages have been widely criticized by many trekking agencies as simply unsustainable. Perhaps the success of this policy should be measured by the number of agencies who have actually tried to adopt this pay structure – namely about 10 (KPAP's estimate) out of the 150-plus or so companies who operate on the mountain. Instead, the majority of the companies have been observing the minimum wage levels that were set in 2008 and are as follows:

- **Porters** Ts8000 per day
- **Assistant guides** Ts10,000 per day
- **Guide** Ts12,000 per day

Transport A litre of premium petrol at the time of writing costs Ts2133, with diesel slightly cheaper at Ts2073. According to one company's price schedule, the cost of transport from Arusha to Machame is Ts180,000 (around US$110), while for Marangu it's Ts240,000 (US$148), Lemosho Ts330,000 (US$203) and

❏ **AN EXAMPLE: THE MACHAME TREK**

A 7-day Machame trek, taking one guide, one assistant guide/cook and four porters, (assuming they're paid the TANAPA recommended wage), would cost as follows:

Park fees

Rescue fee	US$20
Conservation fee (US$70 x 7 days)	US$490
Camping fee (US$50 x 6 nights)	US$300
Porter/guide entrance fees (approx) Ts21,000:	US$13*

* Using exchange rate at time of going to press

Wages

Four porters (assuming a wage of US$10 per day)	US$280
Assistant guide/cook (assuming US$15 per day)	US$105
Guide (assuming US$20 per day)	US$140

Food

One person plus crew (Ts360,000)	US$220

Transport

Estimate per person (Ts180,000)	US$110
TOTAL US$823 + US$525 + US$220 + US$110 =	**US$1678**

Obviously if there are more of you some costs, such as food, wages and transport, can be divided between the group, thus making it cheaper. Nevertheless, the above example gives you an idea of just how quickly the costs add up. Any excess over these costs goes straight to the agency but they have significant costs of their own, including an annual licence fee of US$2000, not to mention tax that amounts to nearly 30%. Remember, too, when working out your budget, to add on **tips** for your crew; see below for details.

Rongai Ts480,000 (US$295) – which is why the latter two routes are usually the most expensive to climb. Of course, the per-person charge may change dramatically if you need to hire a second vehicle for your crew.

Food Your total bill has to cover not only *your* food but the food of the porters and guides too. One agency boss told me that a rough estimate for a seven-day climb of the cost of food for one person (excluding cooking fuel) is Ts360,000, while for two it's Ts211,000 per person and for three or more it's around Ts160,000pp.

TIPPING

Like a herd of elephants on the African plains, the subject of tipping is a bit of a grey area. What is certain is that, in addition to the cost of booking your trek, you will also need to shell out tips to your crew at the end. The gratuity system on Kilimanjaro follows the American style: that is to say, a tip is not so much a bonus to reward particularly attentive service or honest toil as a mandatory payment to subsidize the poor wages the porter and guides receive. In other words, **tipping is obligatory**.

To anybody born outside the Americas this compulsory payment of gratuities seems to go against the very spirit of tipping. Nevertheless, it is very hard to begrudge the guides and porters a decent return for their labours – and depriving your entourage of their much-needed gratuities is not the way to register your protest against this system.

As to the **size of the remuneration**, there are no set figures or formulas, though we do urge you to let your conscience instruct you on this matter as much as your wallet. The best advice I have found is on the KPAP website (🖳 www .kiliporters.org), which I have reproduced here. They suggest – assuming the company you are with does not pay the minimum wage – that **guides should receive US$20-25 per day**, **assistant guides US$15-20 per day**, **cooks US$12-15 per day** and **porters US$8-10 per day**. Pretty reasonable, we think – though of course it assumes you know that your company is paying below the minimum wage, which is often impossible to determine with any certainty!

They give a few examples of how this might work in practice on their website but we think their figures for the number of porters you will need are gross under-estimates (they suggest that one trekker would require just one porter whereas you will probably need at least five) so we have adapted their table and present it here (note that, as with KPAP's example, we have assumed we are talking about a **six-day trek**):

No of trekkers	Guide (US$)	Assistant Guide (US$)	Cook (US$)	Porter (US$)	Total (US$)	Total per trekker (US$)
1	140	–	84	56 x 5	504	504
2	140	105	84	56 x 8	777	388.50
3	140	105	84	56 x 11	945	315
4	140	105 x 2	84	56 x 12	1106	276.50

These are mere guidelines; you may wish to alter them if you feel, for example, a certain porter is deserving of more than his normal share or if your trek was particularly difficult.

Having collected all the money, the usual form is to hand out the individual shares to each porter and guide in turn. **Do not hand all your tips to the guide** unless you are happy that the distribution of the tips will be fair and honest; sadly, no matter how much respect and affection you have towards your guide, often he'll end up trousering most of it.

A survey by KPAP among their former partner companies back in 2011 (the last set of data we have before KPAP were banned from the park) found that while porters received an average of Ts8661 in tips per day when the tourists gave it to them individually, that figure dropped to Ts5359 if the guide distributed them instead.

For more details on this, see the KPAP box on pp47-49.

The crew

PORTERS

My guide was as polite as Lord Chesterfield and kindly as the finest gentleman of the world could be. So I owe much to the bare-footed natives of this country, who patiently for eight cents a day bear the white man's burden. **Peter MacQueen** *In Wildest Africa* (1910)

The wages may have gone up – a porter today could earn around US$10 per day if the minimum wages are enforced – and all now have footwear of some description, but the opinion expressed back at the beginning of the 20th century by the intrepid MacQueen is much the same as that voiced by thousands of trekkers at the beginning of the 21st century.

These men (and the ones hired by trekkers are nearly always male, though female porters are occasionally seen on the mountain) never fail to draw both gratitude and, with the amount they carry and the minimum of fuss they make about it, admiration from the trekkers who hire them. Ranging in age from about 18 (the minimum legal age, though some look a good deal younger) to 50 (and occasionally beyond this), porters are amongst the hardest workers on Kilimanjaro. To see them traipsing up the mountain, water in one hand, cooker in another, rucksack on the back and picnic table on the head, is staggering to behold. And though they are supposed to carry no more than 20kg (plus 5kg of their own luggage), many, desperate for work in what is an over-supplied market, manage to bypass KINAPA's own weight checks at the gates to carry much more.

And if that isn't enough, while at the end of the day the average trekker spends his or her time at camp moaning about the hardships they are suffering – in between cramming down mouthfuls of popcorn while clasping a steaming hot cup of tea – these hardy individuals are putting up the tents, helping with the preparation of the food, fetching more water and generally making sure every trekker's whim is, within reason, catered for.

Yet in spite of appearances, porters are not indestructible. Though they rarely climb to the summit themselves, a few still die each year on the slopes of Kilimanjaro. The most common cause of death, perhaps unsurprisingly given the ragged clothes many wear, is exposure. For this reason, if you see a porter dozing by the wayside and it's getting a bit late, put aside your concerns about depriving him of some much needed shut-eye and wake him up: many are the tales of porters who have perished on Kilimanjaro because they took forty winks and then couldn't find their way back to camp in the dark. It's this kind of horror story that has caused so much concern over recent years and led to the formation of organizations such as the Kilimanjaro Porters Assistance Project (see pp47-9).

How many . . .

As a general rule, the larger the number of trekkers, the fewer porters per person are required and, if you take the Marangu Route (where no tent is needed), you can probably get away with as few as two per trekker. On other routes, where tents are necessary, around three porters or more per person is the norm. (Just for the record, and just in case taking porters up a mountain makes you feel a little less virile, you may like to know that the great Count Teleki – see p115 – took no fewer than 65 porters up the mountain with him!) Those looking to save every last shilling often ask the agency to cut down on the number of porters. But this is neither easy nor – given that the cost of a porter's wages is a relatively minor part of the overall cost – a particularly brilliant idea.

Remember that even if you do carry your own rucksack, there is still all the food, cooking equipment, camping gear and so forth to lug up the mountainside. What's more, you're also tempting the agency to overload each porter in order to reduce their total number – leading to the kind of illegal practices described in the box on p47-9. So, in general, accept the agency's recommendations as to the number of porters on your expedition and make sure that they're not overloaded.

. . . and how much?

The porters' wages are paid by your agency. All you need to worry about is how much to give them as a **tip** at the end of the trek. Given the privations they suffer over the course of an average trek and their often desultory wages, their efforts to extract as much money as possible from the over-privileged *mzungu* (Swahili for 'white person') are entirely forgivable. One elaborate yet surprisingly common method is for the porters to pretend there are more of them than there actually are; which, given the vast numbers of porters running around each campsite and the fact you don't actually walk with them on the trail, is a lot easier to achieve than you may think.

It's a technique hinted at by John Reader in his excellent 1982 book *Kilimanjaro*:

> *I hired four porters for part of my excursion on Kilimanjaro. The fourth man's name was Stephen, or so the other three told me. I never met Stephen himself. Our gear seemed to arrive at each campsite without his assistance and I am not aware that he ever spent a night with us. I was assured that he was engaged elsewhere on tasks essential to the success of my journey, but I occasionally wondered whether Stephen actually existed. I was particularly aggrieved when he failed to collect his pay in person at the end of the trip. The other guides collected it for him. They also collected his tip.*

The practice is common enough to have been given a name – *kirunje*, which is Swahili for 'shadow'. This sort of thing shouldn't happen if you're with a reputable company but it's a good idea anyway to **make sure you meet your team at the start of the trail before you set off**. This will help to prevent this sort of scam and it's good manners too. While at the end, to ensure each porter gets his fair share, dish the tips out yourself – *do not* give them to your guide to hand them out on your behalf unless you are sure your agency has systems in place to prevent the guide taking it all for himself; see the box on pp47-9 for why this is so.

Please note that however much money and equipment you lavish on them at the end, the porters' reaction will usually be the same. Simply put, porters are not above play-acting, in the same way that the sea is not above the sky. On being given their gratuity some porters will grimace, sigh, tut, shake their head, roll their eyes in disgust and stare at the money in their hand with all the enthusiasm and gratitude of one who has just been handed a warm jar of the contents of the Barranco Camp toilets. Several of the more talented ones may even manage a few tears. Nevertheless, providing you have paid a reasonable tip (and for guidance over what is the correct amount, see pp42-3), don't fall for the melodramatics but simply thank them warmly for all their endeavours over the course of the trek. Once they realize your conscience remains unpricked it will all be handshakes and smiles and, having pocketed the money, they'll soon trot off happily enough.

GUIDES

If portering is the first step on the career ladder of Kilimanjaro, it is the guides who stand proudly on the top rung. Ornithologist, zoologist, botanist, geologist, tracker, astronomer, butler, manager, doctor, linguist and teacher, a good guide will be all of these professions rolled into one. With luck, over the course of the trek they'll also become your friend.

The metamorphosis from porter to guide is a lengthy one. Having served one's apprenticeship by lugging luggage as a porter, a few talented and ambitious ones are eventually promoted to the position of **summit porter**. In addition to carrying their fair share of equipment, they are also expected to perform many of the duties of a fully fledged guide – including, most painfully of all, escorting trekkers on that final, excruciating push to the summit.

From there the next logical step is to become a fully fledged guide – though standing between them and a licence is a period of intensive training conducted by the park authorities. This mainly involves a two- to three-week tour of the mountain, during which time they are supposed to cover every designated route up and down Kilimanjaro. On this course they are also taught the essentials of being a guide, including a bit about the fauna and flora of Kili, how to take care of the mountain environment, how to spot the symptoms of altitude sickness in trekkers and, just as importantly, what to do about it.

Training complete, they receive their licences and are free to tout themselves around the agencies looking for work. While a few of the better guides are snapped up by the top agencies and work exclusively for them, the majority are freelance and have to actively seek work in what is already an over-supplied market. This helps to explain why a newly qualified guide will probably have to settle for being an **assistant guide** in order to secure work, for which they'll receive a higher wage than a porter and a commensurately greater proportion of the tips – though not as much as they would receive if leading the climb themselves.

A PORTER'S LOT IS NOT A HAPPY ONE

Nobody should underestimate the achievement of reaching the summit of Kilimanjaro. For five days or so you've dragged yourself up around 4000m of vertical height, through four different seasons, on terrain that may be as alien to you as the moon. Imagine then, trying to do the same trek while eating only one square meal a day, with nothing but a pair of secondhand plimsolls on your feet and tatty cast-offs for clothes; that your days on the mountain are spent carrying up to 30kg on your back or head, while your nights are spent sharing a draughty four-man tent with up to nine other people, often with no ground mats and inadequate sleeping bags. And that, should anything go wrong – which, given the conditions you're expected to work in, they very well might – there'll be no insurance to cover you.

Imagine, furthermore, climbing not out of desire to be on Africa's highest mountain, but out of necessity; for if you don't submit yourself to these deprivations you won't be able to fund yourself through college (which costs about US$350 per year) or feed your children. Imagine, too, that your reward for putting up with such conditions is somewhere around Ts8300 per day (the average wage in 2011 for those companies that *weren't* part of the now-suspended KPAP partnership program); and that, out of this, you have to pay for your transport to and from the mountain (Ts6000 each way from Arusha to Marangu Gate), your food whilst on the mountain (which is why you eat only once a day) and even have to bribe the guide (at least Ts10,000-20,000) in order to be allowed on the mountain in the first place. No wonder you often end up relying on tips from tourists in order to take home any money from your labours. Tips that, if you're unlucky, may end up in the pocket of that same guide you bribed in order to get a job in the first place.

Such is the lot for many porters on Kilimanjaro: a precarious existence that, at best, involves hardship and indignity, and at worst can lead to death, as happens every year on the mountain. It is these kinds of conditions that various organizations are now trying to improve. Foremost amongst these, without a doubt, is KPAP.

The Kilimanjaro Porters Assistance Project (KPAP)

Registered at the beginning of 2003, KPAP (🖥 www.kiliporters.org) is an initiative of the American-based International Mountain Explorers Connection (IMEC; 🖥 www.mountainexplorers.org), which fights for porters' rights worldwide including those working in other tourist hotspots such as Nepal's Annapurna Sanctuary. With offices (open roughly Mon-Sat 8am-1pm, though occasionally later) just round the corner from the Coffee Shop in Moshi, KPAP has been run for the past few years with both passion and bravery by American Karen Valenti.

According to their manifesto, the organization's focus is on improving the working conditions of the porters on Kilimanjaro. They do this in three main ways:

● Lending trekking equipment and clothing at no charge. KPAP have a couple of wardrobes full of good-quality trekking gear, much of it donated by American skiing companies and couriered over by trekkers. For a returnable deposit (which can be anything from a school certificate to a mobile-phone charger) the porter can borrow items of clothing such as fleeces, boots etc. (*continued overleaf*)

❏ A PORTER'S LOT IS NOT A HAPPY ONE

The Kilimanjaro Porters Assistance Project (KPAP) *(continued from p47)*

(KPAP manifesto *continued*) ● Providing classes on English, first-aid, HIV awareness and money management for the benefit of porters.

● Educating the climbers and general public on proper porter treatment.

The partnership scheme and why it's been suspended

KPAP also tried to encourage the trekking agencies to improve the way they treated their crew via the '**Partner for Responsible Travel**' scheme. Established in 2006, the partner program was created to recognize and highlight those tour operators committed to fair treatment of the mountain crew.

In order to join the scheme, companies had to conform to certain guidelines issued by KPAP. These included directives on porters' wages, a limit on the amount the porters were required to carry, the amount of food and water they received on the mountain, what the sleeping conditions were like and how they were treated in the event of an accident or sickness. In order to be considered as a partner, the trekking agency not only had to adhere to these guidelines but also had to allow KPAP to monitor them, too, to make sure they stuck to them. If the trekking agency managed to fulfil all these criteria the benefits, in terms of increased marketing opportunities and the extra demand that came from being known as a Partner for Responsible Travel, could have been considerable.

Unfortunately, KPAP have been forced (temporarily, we hope) to suspend the scheme for the simple reason that, since August 2012, they have been banned from working in the park. The ban is obviously a severe setback to their ambitions. In the last edition we wrote that we believed KPAP to be 'the only organization that... properly monitors what is happening on the mountain, and as such their opinions should be relied upon to an even greater extent than more established campaign groups such as Tourism Concern.' We still maintain that KPAP is a fantastic charity, working on a shoestring and fighting for the rights of porters, despite opposition from several large agencies and, as we now see, even the authorities.

However, being unable to monitor the actions of their partner companies as closely as they would hope, KPAP decided they could not in all conscience recommend certain agencies, given that the policies of these agencies towards their mountain crews can change at a moment's notice.

At the time of writing Karen and her team still hope that the ban is temporary; after all, it has never been properly explained to them why they were barred from the park in the first place!

So how can you help?

There are many things trekkers can do to help the campaign. Obviously, if the partnership program is one day reinstated, signing up for a trek with one of the partner companies is important. In addition, KPAP recommend the following:

● **1 Make sure your porters are outfitted with appropriate clothing** Porters need adequate footwear, socks, waterproof jackets and trousers (pants), gloves, hats, sunglasses, etc. Clothing can be borrowed at the KPAP office in Moshi – make sure your porters know this.

● **2 Fair wages should be paid to the porters** See p41 for the minimum wages KINAPA are proposing to introduce and enforce. Ask your porters how much they are paid and if it includes food. Showing that you care about such things will encourage all operators and guides to treat their porters fairly.

● **3 Make sure porters have proper food and water** If they are required to purchase their own food, wages should be increased accordingly.

● **4 Check the weights of porters' loads** Kilimanjaro National Park has a maximum carrying weight per porter of 25kg, which includes the porter's personal gear which is assumed to be 5kg. Thus the load they carry for the company should not exceed 20kg. If you can, be there at the weighing of the luggage at the start of the trek to make sure no funny business is going on.

If additional porters need to be hired, do ensure that the tour company is paying each porter their full wage when you return.

● **5 Count the number of porters every day** Know the number of people in your crew. After all, you are paying for them. If there are any missing, ask where they are. If they've been sent down the mountain, ask why, and whether they will still receive both a fair wage and their share of the tips.

● **6 Make sure your porters are provided with proper shelter** Where no shelter is available (ie on all routes other than Marangu), porters need proper accommodation: that means their own tents and sleeping bags.

● **7 Ensure your porters are given the tips you intend for them** Give your tips to the guide and you run the risk that they won't pass on the full amount to your crew. Tipping directly to each individual crew member ensures they receive their fair share. Alternatively, see that your tour company has a transparent method of distributing tips.

● **8 Make sure any sick or injured porters are properly cared for** Porters deserve the same standard of care as their clients. Sick or injured porters need to be sent back with someone who speaks their language and understands the problem.

● **9 Get to know your porters and thank them** Some porters speak English and will appreciate your making an effort to speak with them. The Swahili word *pole* (pronounced 'polay') – which translates loosely as 'I'm sorry for you' – shows respect for porters after a hard day carrying your bags. *Ahsante* ('asantay') means 'Thank you'.

● **10 Report any instances of abuse or neglect** To both the trekking agency concerned and, more importantly, to KPAP on 🖳 info@kiliporters.org.

● **11 Complete the post-climb survey** This is perhaps the most important and easiest thing you can do. Before heading off up the mountain, pick up a questionnaire from the KPAP office or the website (🖳 www.kiliporters.org), as this will remind you of what to look out for on the mountain. By providing KPAP with your feedback regarding the tour company's treatment of its staff, they will be able to share with the company any problem areas that need to be corrected.

● **12 Buy the book!** *Cameras of Kilimanjaro* is a collection of photos taken by porters on Kilimanjaro as well as interviews, statistics and facts about their life on the mountain, with a proportion of the proceeds going to KPAP. You can pick up a copy by following the links from the KPAP website (see below) or visiting 🖳 www.porter photoproject.com.

Further details
● **Kilimanjaro Porters Assistance Project (KPAP)** 🖳 www.kiliporters.org
● **International Mountain Explorers Connection** 🖳 www.mountainexplorers.org
IMEC is the umbrella organization of which KPAP is a part
● **International Porter Protection Group (IPPG)** 🖳 ippg.net.

The remarkable Mr Lauwo

Mzee Yohana Lauwo, the porter guide who accompanied the first Europeans up the Kilimanjaro Mountain a century ago, was the centre of attention in a commemorative ceremony in Moshi on Friday. Mzee Lauwo, now over 118 years, was presented with a prize in cash. The Deputy Minister for Lands, Natural Resources and Tourism, Ndugu Chabanga Hassan Dyamwalle, suggested that Mzee Lauwo also be given a house to be built in his own village.

The ambassador to the Federal Republic of Germany (FRG) to Tanzania, Christel Steffler, presented Mzee Lauwo with a letter which expressed gratitude for his service in cementing German-Tanzanian relations. She said it was high time porters and guides were given the recognition they deserved for their work.

Press cutting from a local newspaper, found stuck on the wall of Kibo Hotel, Marangu

In 1989, celebrations for the centenary of Hans Meyer's first-ever ascent of Kilimanjaro were organized. As the committee in charge of arranging the festivities looked at some old photos taken at around the time of Meyer's ascent, the members were struck by the similarity of one of the locals pictured to a very elderly man who still lived in Marangu village. That man was Mr Yohana Kinyala Lauwo, known to his friends and family as Kinyala. Could it really be that somebody who was on Meyer's conquest of Kilimanjaro was actually still alive?

The committee decided to visit Mr Lauwo in the hope that he would be able to tell them whether it was him in those photos or not. Unfortunately, when they pointed to the person in the photographs, even Mr Lauwo was rather vague as to whether it was really him. While claiming to have climbed Kili at least three times before World War I – and, according to the legend that grew up around him, for seventy years in total – he did not recall either Meyer or Purtscheller. He did, however, remember an expedition involving a 'Dutch doctor' that he worked on, the experience perhaps being particularly memorable as he didn't wear shoes for the entire eight days! Could Mr Lauwo's memory be slightly hazy on this matter and the Dutch doctor actually be a German one?

The committee certainly thought so and not only decided that 'Kinyala' was part of the team that climbed Kili with Meyer – but even claimed, using other evidence that they had come by, that he was the main guide who led them up! Their story about how Lauwo became the head guide on the most-celebrated climb of Kilimanjaro goes something like this: In 1889 the Germans were beginning to build highways in the area to assert and secure their domination of the region, coercing the local village chiefs into supplying the labour to work on the roads. Kinyala was one of those who tried to avoid being enlisted but he was arrested and taken to the local chief or *Mangi*, Marealle, for punishment. As luck would have it, however, Meyer and Purtscheller arrived at the same time at the court of Mangi Marealle to ask for porters and guides to help with their expedition.

Tall, lithe, loose-limbed and from the mountain village of Marangu, Kinyala Lauwo fitted the bill as a mountain guide, his relative youth notwithstanding. He would have known at least the lower slopes of Kili very well for the forest would have been a happy hunting ground for collecting honey, plants for medicine, colobus monkey skins for ceremonial clothing and ivory for trading with the Swahili traders from the coast.

But can we be certain all this is true and, more importantly, that the elderly Mr Lauwo who resided in Marangu all his life is the same man in the photos taken from Meyer's time? And was he really the main guide?

Getting to Kilimanjaro

One of the gladdest moments in life, methinks is the departure upon a distant journey into unknown lands. Shaking off with one mighty effort the fetters of habit, the leaden weight of routine, the cloak of many cares and the slavery of home, man feels once more happy... The blood flows with the fast circulation of childhood ... afresh dawns the morn of life.
Diary entry of **Richard Burton** (the explorer, not the actor), 2 December 1856

BY AIR

Tanzania has four major international airports: Dar es Salaam, Zanzibar, Mwanza and Kilimanjaro. The latter, as you may expect, is the most convenient for Kilimanjaro, standing only 43km away from the mountain town of Moshi and 50km from Arusha. Information about international flights to and from KIA (the acronym for Kilimanjaro International Airport, though the three-letter international airport code is JRO) can be found on p349.

And if so, how far up did he go with them? To the summit? Unfortunately, Meyer himself is very unhelpful on this matter, for while he was full of admiration for the guides he hired on the coast of Tanzania and refers to them throughout his account, he only briefly mentions a local Chagga guide – and never by name. This could be due to the contempt with which Meyer clearly felt for this guide:

As on a former occasion (1887), our guide tried hard to persuade us to camp in this very inviting neighbourhood, although it was still comparatively early; but now, as then, I turned a deaf ear to all his representations, and after a short rest pushed onward and upward to where the forest loomed ahead. The guide protested volubly and forcibly, and capered about like a madman; but we paid no heed to his frantic demonstrations, and left him to follow when he should have danced himself back to his ordinary senses.

It is, of course, highly unlikely we'll ever find out whether Kinyala really was part of that first successful climb of Kili; and if he was, we'll probably never know in what capacity he served – and if it was as the head guide, how far he actually ventured up the mountain with them. There are those who seem convinced by his claim; while others will always view the evidence that backs up his claim as circumstantial at best. They will also, not unreasonably, point to the fact that if Mr Lauwo really did climb as an 18 year old with Meyer's team back in 1889, he would have been around 125 years old when he died in 1996, which means that he would have set all kinds of longevity records! But even if it isn't true, there seems little doubt that Mr Lauwo did work as a guide for many decades (if not quite the 70 years that is claimed), beginning at a time when the locals wore little more than blankets to protect them from the cold. Furthermore, he isn't the only person in his family who took part in a famous ascent of Kili; by chance a nephew of Mr Lauwo's, Emmanuel Petro Minja, guided Lieutenant Alexander Nyirenda on his trek to the summit on December 9, 1961, and carried the torch that the lieutenant planted there to celebrate Tanzania's independence (see p121).

It used to be the case that only a few airlines served Kilimanjaro. KLM, Ethiopian Airlines, Kenyan Airways and local operators fly540 and Precision were for several years the only carriers using the runway. The resulting lack of competition meant that airfares for flights in and out of JRO were relatively high – to such an extent that many trekkers would fly into Nairobi instead and catch a bus down in order to save themselves a hundred dollars or more. The situation has improved recently, however, with the introduction of regular services from both Turkish Airlines and Qatar Airways. So, while Nairobi (Kenya) and to a lesser extent Dar es Salaam remain the main regional hubs and airfares to these destinations are, on the whole, still lower, the saving is seldom sizeable and nowadays most people prefer to fly direct to Kilimanjaro, particularly as Nairobi and Dar are a minimum of six and ten hours away respectively by bus from Arusha.

You will find brief guides in this book to Dar es Salaam (p144) as well as Nairobi (p153) and Kilimanjaro International Airport (p162).

From the UK

A flight to Kilimanjaro from London with KLM via Amsterdam will set you back a minimum of £550, or £750 in the July-August high season, though depending on when you book your tickets – and from whom – the fare may well rise to £1100 or more.

There are a number of websites specializing in flights of which you'll probably already be aware, one of the more popular being **Cheapflights** ▣ www.cheapflights.co.uk, which gives a summary of the flight offers to your destination from several different agents. Other online agencies to recommend are **DialAFlight** (▣ www.dialaflight.com, ☎ 0844-811 4444), **Netflights** (▣ www.netflights.com) and **Expedia** (▣ www.expedia.co.uk), while **lastminute** (▣ www.lastminute.com) is useful in that it provides a table which shows the price of flights using various arrival and departure dates (so if you're flexible as to when you want to fly, you could save yourself a couple of hundred pounds by flying on dates when the price is lower). High-street travel agents (all of which have a considerable online presence too) include **STA Travel** (☎ 0333-321 0099; ▣ www.statravel.co.uk), **Flight Centre** (☎ 0844-800 8660; ▣ www.flightcentre.co.uk) and **Trailfinders** (☎ 020-7368 1200; ▣ www.trailfinders.com), all with branches countrywide.

From North America

Try **Flight Center** (USA ▣ www.flightcenter.com; ☎ 877-409-8782; Canada ▣ www.flightcentre.ca, ☎ 1-877-967-5302), **Travel Cuts** (Canada ▣ www.travelcuts.com; ☎ 1-800-667-2887) and **STA Travel** (▣ www.statravel.com; ☎ 1-800-781-4040).

From Australia and New Zealand

Try **Flight Centre** (Aus ▣ www.flightcentre.com.au, ☎ 133 133; NZ ▣ www.flightcentre.co.nz, ☎ 0800 2435 44) and **STA Travel** (Aus ▣ www.statravel.com.au, ☎ 134 782; NZ ▣ www.statravel.co.nz, ☎ 0800-474 400).

OVERLAND

A big country lying at the heart of East Africa, Tanzania has borders with many countries including Burundi, Kenya, Malawi, Mozambique, Rwanda, Uganda and Zambia.

There are several border crossings between Tanzania and **Burundi** including a sailing on the venerable old *MV Liemba* that traditionally journeys to Kigoma, cutting across the northern corner of Lake Tanganyika from the Burundi capital Bujumbura. However, it's important to check on the current situation with regard to both the state of the *Liemba* – it's often out of action – and the security situation in Burundi.

The borders with **Rwanda** (at the Rusumo crossing), **Uganda** (most commonly crossed at Mutukula, north-west of Bukoba), **Zambia** (main crossing Tunduma/Nakonde), **Mozambique** (over the Unity Bridge across the Ruvuma), **Malawi** (Songwe River Bridge) and **Kenya** (see p161 for details on the border crossing at Namanga; Tarakea, north-east of Kili, may become another official crossing point soon) are all relatively straightforward and served by public buses.

Tanzania and Zambia are also linked by express train, running twice weekly between Dar es Salaam and Mbeya.

The routes up Kilimanjaro

GETTING TO THE MOUNTAIN

This book aims to take you from your armchair to the summit of Africa's highest mountain. If you have booked a package from home, of course, your transport to and from the mountain will already have been sorted out and you needn't worry. But if you haven't then this book will tell you about the city you are flying to and the towns of Arusha, Moshi and Marangu that lie nearest to the mountain. It also goes into some detail about which local trekking company to book with and where you can find them; and having booked your trek with a company in Tanzania, you will invariably find that it includes transport to and from the Kilimanjaro National Park gates.

From there, it's all about the walking...

GETTING UP THE MOUNTAIN   [See colour map inside back cover]

Kilimanjaro has two main summits. The higher one is **Kibo**, the glacier-clad circular summit that stars on all the pictures of Kilimanjaro. While spiky **Mawenzi**, to its east, is impossible to conquer without knowledge of advanced climbing techniques and no small amount of courage, it is possible to *walk* up

to the top of Kibo at a height of 5895m above sea level.

Look down at Kilimanjaro from above and you should be able to count **seven paths** trailing like ribbons up the sides of the mountain. Five of these are ascent-only paths (ie you can only walk *up* the mountain on them; you are not allowed to come down on these trails); one, Mweka, is a descent-only path, and one, the Marangu Route, is both an ascent and descent trail. At around 4000m these trails meet up with a path that loops right around the Kibo summit. This path is known as the Kibo Circuit, though it's often divided into two halves known as the Northern and Southern circuits. By the time you reach the foot of Kibo, only three paths lead up the slopes to the summit itself. For a *brief* description of the trails and a look at their relative merits, read on; for a map, see inside back cover, while for further details check out the **full trail descriptions**, beginning on p248. Note that some trekking agencies vary the routes slightly, particularly those routes that cross the Shira Plateau, though any agency worth its salt will provide you with a detailed itinerary so you can check exactly which path you'll be taking each day.

Ascending Kilimanjaro: the options

There are six ascent trails leading up to the foot of Kibo peak. These are (running anti-clockwise, beginning with the westernmost trails): the little-used **Shira Plateau Route**, **Lemosho Route**, **Machame Route**, **Umbwe Route**, **Marangu Route** and, running from the north-eastern side, the **Rongai (Loitokitok) Route**. Each of these eventually meets with a path circling the Kibo cone, a path known as either the **Northern Circuit** or the **Southern Circuit** depending on which side of the mountain you are. (It is possible and very worthwhile to walk right around Kibo on this path, though this needs to be arranged beforehand with your agency, takes a long time, and permission from KINAPA may need to be sought before embarking on such an expedition.)

The trails mix and merge at this point, so that by the time you reach Kibo just three trails lead up to the Crater Rim: the **Western Breach Route** (aka the **Arrow Glacier Route**), **Barafu Route** and the nameless third path which runs up from Kibo Huts to Gillman's Point, which we shall call the **Kibo Huts Route**. Which of these you take to the summit will depend upon which path you took to get this far: the Shira, Lemosho, Machame and Umbwe routes can use either the difficult Western Breach Route or the easier (but longer) Barafu Route, while the Marangu and Rongai trails use the Kibo Huts Route. You can deviate from this rule – and many of the larger agencies make a habit of doing so – and design your own combination of trails but you may require permission from KINAPA and the agencies may well charge more to organize such a trek.

The minimum number of days for each route is written below. Note these refer to the total time it takes from the gate to the summit and back again to the gate. In other words, **they also include the descent from Uhuru Peak to the gate**. This is nearly always a day and a half, ie you begin to descend from the summit (usually, and assuming you climbed to the summit during the night) at about 7am, and, all being well, you don't reach the gate until lunchtime the next day. Note, too, that when we say 'minimum', we mean it – treks typically last at least a day longer than these minimum durations.

A brief description of each of the six main trails follows:

The Marangu Route (minimum five days) The oldest and traditionally always seen as the most popular trail on the mountain (though see the statistics p22 for the current story). The Marangu Route also has the dubious honour of having the lowest success rate for getting trekkers to the summit, presumably because it is one of the three routes where you can pay to be on the mountain for just five days – where other routes require you to pay for a minimum of six. It is also the one that comes closest (though not very) to the trail Hans Meyer took in making the first successful assault on the summit. Furthermore it is the only ascent trail where camping is not necessary, indeed not allowed, with trekkers sleeping in dormitory huts along the way. From Kibo Huts, trekkers climb up to the summit via Gillman's Point. The trail should take a minimum of five days and four nights to complete, though an extra night is usually taken after the second day to allow trekkers more time to acclimatize.

The Machame Route (minimum six days) This has now overtaken Marangu as the most popular trail. It's certainly the one the majority of guides consider the most enjoyable. Though widely regarded as more difficult than the Marangu Route, the success rate on this trail is higher, possibly because it is a day longer at six days and five nights (assuming you take the Barafu Route to the summit), which gives trekkers more time to acclimatize; most trekkers also take an extra acclimatization day in the Karanga Valley (thereby making it seven days in total). You can also take the more difficult Western Breach Route though this shortens the trek by a day or two; it would thus be wise to build in acclimatization days if taking this option.

The Shira Plateau and Lemosho routes (minimum six days) Both of these routes run from west to east across the centre of the Shira Plateau. The **Shira Plateau Route** is the original plateau trail though it is seldom used these days, for much of it is now a 4WD track for emergency vehicles. Walkers embarking on this trail often begin their trek above the forest in the moorland zone. After traversing the plateau the trekker has a choice of climbing Kibo via the Western Breach/Arrow Glacier Route or the longer and easier Barafu Route. If opting for the former, expect the trek to last a total of six days and five nights. By the latter trail the walk should last eight days if extra overnight stops on the plateau and in the Karanga Valley are taken – if not, seven days is more likely.

The **Lemosho Route** (aka the **Lemosho Glades Route**) improves on the Shira Plateau Route by starting below the Shira Ridge, thus providing trekkers with a walk in the forest at the trek's start, giving them more time to acclimatize and enabling them to enjoy, in this author's opinion, the best forest on the mountain. As with the Shira Plateau Route, you can ascend Kibo either by the Western Breach or by the Barafu Route; allow five nights for the former (though this is *too fast* for such a long trail) or a recommended seven nights for the latter.

Note: It's common for trekking agencies to refer to the Lemosho Route as the Shira Route, which is of course confusing. If you have already booked your 'Shira' trek and want to know what route you will actually be taking, one way to check is to see where your first night's campsite will be; if it's the Big Tree Campsite – or Mti Mkubwa in Swahili – you'll be using the Lemosho Route.

The topography of Kilimanjaro

And surely never monarch wore his royal robes more royally than this monarch of African mountains, Kilimanjaro. His foot rests on a carpet of velvety turf, and through the dark green forest the steps of his throne reach downward to the earth, where man stands awestruck before the glory of his majesty. Art may have colours rich enough to fix one moment of this dazzling splendour, but neither brush nor pen can portray the unceasing play of colour – the wondrous purples of the summit deepening as in the Alpine afterglow; the dull greens of the forest and the sepia shadows in the ravines and hollows, growing ever darker as evening steals on apace; and last, the gradual fading away of all, as the sun sets, and over everything spreads the grey cloud-curtain of the night. It is not a picture but a pageant – a king goes to his rest. **Hans Meyer** *Across East African Glaciers* (1891)

Kilimanjaro is not only the highest mountain in Africa, it's also one of the biggest volcanoes on the entire planet, covering an area of approximately 388,500 hectares. In this area are three main peaks that betray its origins as the offspring of three huge volcanic eruptions.

The oldest and lowest peak, known as **Shira**, lies on the western edge of the massif. This is the least impressive of the three summits, being nothing more than a heavily eroded ridge, 3962m tall at its highest point, **Johnsell Point**. This ridge is, in fact, merely the south-western rim of the original Shira crater, the northern and eastern sides being covered by later material from Kibo (see p92). The Shira Ridge separates the western slopes from the **Shira Plateau**. This large rocky plateau, 6200ha in size, is one of Kilimanjaro's most intriguing features. It is believed to be the *caldera* (a collapsed crater) of the first volcano that was subsequently 'filled in' by lava from later eruptions which then solidified and turned to rock.

The plateau rises gently from west to east until it reaches the youngest and main summit, **Kibo**. This is the best-preserved crater on Kilimanjaro; its southern lip is slightly higher than the rest of the rim, and the highest point on this southern lip is **Uhuru Peak** – at 5895m the highest point in Africa and the goal of just about every Kilimanjaro trekker.

Kibo is the only one of the three summits which is permanently covered in snow or ice, thanks to the large **glaciers** that cover much of its surface. Kibo is also the one peak that really does look like a volcanic crater; indeed, there are three concentric craters on Kibo. Within the inner **Reusch Crater** (1.3km in diameter) you can still see signs of volcanic activity, including fumaroles, the smell of sulphur and a third crater, the **Ash Pit**, 130m deep by 140m wide.

The outer **Kibo Crater** (1.9 by 2.7km) is not a perfect, unbroken circle. There are gaps in the circumference where the walls have been breached by lava flows; the

The Rongai Route (minimum five days) This is the only trail to approach Kibo from the north. Indeed, the original trail began right against the Kenyan border, though recently it shifted eastwards and now starts at the Tanzanian town of **Loitokitok** after which the new trail has been named (though everybody still refers to it as the Rongai Route; it is also sometimes called the **Nalemuru Route**, after the nearby river). For the final push to the summit, trekkers take the Kibo Huts Route, joining it either at the huts themselves or just below Hans Meyer Cave. In theory the trek can be completed in five days and four nights though really you need six or even seven, especially if taking the detour to camp beneath Mawenzi peak which adds a day.

most dramatic of these is the **Western Breach**, through which some climbers gain access to the summit each year. The crater has also subsided a little over time, leading to a landslide 100,000 years ago that created the **Barranco** on Kibo's southern side. On the whole, though, Kibo's slopes are gentle, allowing trekkers as well as mountaineers to reach the summit. (For more on the Kibo summit, see p344.)

Separating Kibo from Kilimanjaro's second peak, Mawenzi, is the **Saddle**, at 3600ha the largest area of high-altitude tundra in tropical Africa. This really is a beautiful, eerie place — a dusty desert almost 5000m above sea level, featureless except for the occasional parasitic cone dotted here and there, including the **Triplets**, **Middle Red** and **West Lava Hill**, all running south-east from the south-eastern side of Kibo. (A *parasitic cone* is a mini cone on the side of a volcano caused by a later, minor eruption; amazingly, there are said to be some 250 parasitic cones on Kilimanjaro!)

Nothing could be more marked than the contrast between the external appearance of these two volcanoes – Kibo, with the unbroken, gradual slopes of the typical volcanic cone – Mawenzi with its bewildering display of many-coloured lavas and its fantastically carved outlines, the result of long ages of exposure, combined with the tendency of its component rocks to split vertically rather than horizontally. The hand of time has left its impress upon Kibo too, but the havoc it has wrought is not to be detected at a distance. **Hans Meyer** *Across East African Glaciers* (1891)

Seen from Kibo, **Mawenzi**, the second summit, looks less like a crater than a single lump of jagged, craggy rock emerging from the Saddle. This is merely because its western side also happens to be its highest and hides everything behind it. Walk around Mawenzi, however, and you'll realize that this peak is actually a horseshoe shape, with only the northern side of the crater having been eroded away. Its sides too steep to hold glaciers, there is no *permanent* snow or ice on Mawenzi, and the gradients are enough to dissuade all but the bravest and most technically accomplished climbers.

Mawenzi's highest point is Hans Meyer Peak at 5149m but so shattered is this summit, and so riven with gullies and fractures, that there are a number of other distinctive peaks including Purtscheller Peak (5120m) and South Peak (4958m). There are also two deep gorges, the Great Barranco and Lesser Barranco, scarring its northeastern face.

Few people know this but Kilimanjaro does actually have a crater lake. **Lake Chala** (aka Jala) lies some 30km to the south-east, lying right across the Tanzanian and Kenyan border, and is said to be up to 2½ miles deep. For details on how exactly Kilimanjaro came to be this shape, see pp91-7.

The Umbwe Route (minimum five days)   The hardest and statistically the least popular trail, this involves a tough vertical slog through the jungle, in places using the tree roots as makeshift rungs on a ladder. Having reached the Southern Circuit, trekkers traditionally continue north-west to tackle Kibo from the west and the more difficult Arrow Glacier/Western Breach Route, though you can also head east round to Barafu and approach the summit from there. The entire walk up and down takes a minimum of five days if going via Barafu Campsite (though this is far too rapid). Going via the Western Breach is even shorter, though again the five-day minimum rule applies and six or seven days is much more sensible for acclimatization purposes.

Descending Kilimanjaro: the designated descents

In an attempt to control the number of people walking on each trail, and thus limit the amount of soil erosion on some of the more popular routes, KINAPA introduced regulations regarding the descent routes and which ones you are allowed to take. In general, the main rule is as follows: those ascending Kilimanjaro from the west, south-west or south (ie by taking the Machame, Umbwe, Lemosho or Shira Plateau routes) must take as their descent route the **Mweka** trail; whereas if you have climbed the mountain from the south-east or north (ie on the Marangu or Rongai/Loitokitok trails) you must descend by the **Marangu Route**. See p334 for descriptions of these trails.

Those trekkers who wish to **deviate from these rules** should first seek permission from KINAPA; begin making contact with them well in advance of your trek, as the process can take a long time.

Day trips

If for some reason you cannot climb all the way to the top but nevertheless wish to experience the pleasure of walking on Africa's most beautiful mountain, it is possible to enter the park for one day only. There are some advantages in doing this. It's safer for one thing, for few will get beyond 3000m altitude in one day so altitude sickness shouldn't be an issue. With no camping or rescue fees, porters' wages or food to pay, it will work out much cheaper too: just US$70 per day entry fee plus a wage for the compulsory guide, transport to and from the mountain and a packed lunch, the whole package can cost as little as US$100. And as well as being wonderfully pleasant, if you're fit and start out early enough there's no reason why you can't climb above the treeline to the heathland, thereby covering two vegetation zones and giving yourself a good chance of a reasonably unhindered view of Kibo and Mawenzi. There are even designated picnic spots on the way.

Marangu Gate has a **3-hour nature loop** through the cloud forest which is lovely and from which you can descend either via the trekkers' trail or the less scenic but faster porters' route. There are also a number of seldom-visited waterfalls in the area. The ambitious can attempt to reach the Mandara Huts (p256) and descend again in one day. Furthermore, just 15 minutes beyond the Mandara Huts through a small patch of forest alive with monkeys is Maundi Crater (p256), with excellent views of Kibo and Mawenzi to the north-west and the flat African plains stretching away to the east.

The other place where day trips are allowed is on the Shira Plateau, where your chances of spotting big game are much greater (though still very, very small). However, the time taken in entering the park from the west deters most day-trippers.

What to take

CLOTHES

The best head-gear for all weathers is an English sun-helmet, such as are supplied by Messrs. Silver & Co., London; while a soft fez or smoking cap should be kept for wearing in the shade – one with flaps for drawing down over the ears on a cold night to be preferred.
Hans Meyer *Across East African Glaciers* (1891)

According to his book *Life, Wanderings, and Labours in Eastern Africa*, when Charles New attempted to climb Kili in 1861 he took 13 porters, all of whom were completely naked. New and his crew became the first to reach the mountain's snow-line, which is a rather creditable effort considering their lack of suitable apparel. Assuming your goal is to reach more than just snow, however, you will need to make sure you (and indeed your porters) are appropriately attired for the extreme conditions.

The fact that you will be paying porters to carry your rucksack does, to some degree, make packing simpler – allowing you to concentrate on warmth rather than weight. However, packing for warmth does not mean packing lots of big jumpers. The secret to staying warm is to **wear lots of layers**. Not only does this actually make you warmer than if you just had one single, thick layer – the air trapped between the layers heats up and acts as insulation – but it also means you can peel off the layers one by one when you get too warm, and put them on again one by one when the temperature drops.

A suitable mountain wardrobe would include:

● **Walking boots** Mountaineering boots (ie ones with stiff soles that take a crampon) are unnecessary unless you're taking an unusual route or trekking in the low season when crampons may be required. If you're not, a decent pair of trekking boots will be fine.

The important thing about boots is comfort, with enough toe room: on the ascent up Kibo you might be wearing an extra pair or two of socks, and on the descent your toes will be shoved into the front of the boots with every step. Remember these points when trying on trekking boots in the shop. Make sure they are also sturdy, waterproof, durable and high enough to provide support for your ankles. Finally, ensure you break them in *before* you go to Tanzania, so that if they do give you blisters, you can recover before you set foot on the mountain.

● **Socks** Ahhh, the joy of socks ... a couple of thick thermal pairs and some regular ones should be fine; you may stink but you'll be comfortable too, which is far more important. Some people walk in one thick and one thin pair of socks, changing the thin pair regularly, rinsing them out in the evening and tying them to their pack to dry during the day.

● **Down jacket** Not necessary if you have enough fleeces but nevertheless wonderfully warm, light, compact – and expensive. Make sure it is large enough to go over all your clothes.

● **Fleece** Fleeces are light, pack down small, dry quickly and can be very, very warm. Take at least two: one thick 'polar' one and one of medium thickness and warmth. Make sure that you can wear the thinner one over all the T-shirts and shirts you'll be taking, and that you can wear your thick one over all of these – you'll probably need to on the night-walk up Kibo.

● **Thermals** The value of thermal underwear lies in the way it draws moisture (ie sweat) away from your body. A thermal vest and long-johns are sufficient.

● **Trousers** Don't take jeans, which are heavy and difficult to dry. Instead, take a couple of pairs of trekking trousers, preferably one light and one heavy.

● **Sunhat** One reader wrote in to say that, because he wears glasses, a baseball cap or similar was much more useful than a regular sunhat as it kept the rain off his spectacles. This is a good idea but do make sure you have something to cover the back of your neck too. Whatever you choose, headgear is essential as it can be hot and dazzling on the mountain ...

● **Woolly/fleecy hat** ... but it can also be very cold. Brightly coloured bobble hats can be bought very cheaply in Moshi; or, better still, invest in one of those **balaclavas** which you can usually find on sale in Moshi, which look a bit like a knitted miniature pizza oven but which will protect your face from the biting summit wind.

● **Bandanna (aka 'buff')** For keeping the dust out of your face when walking on the Saddle, to use as an ear-warmer on the final night, and to mop the sweat from your brow on those exhausting uphill climbs. Also useful for blocking out odours when using the public toilets at the campsites.

● **Gloves** Preferably fleecy; many people wear a thin thermal under-glove too.

● **Rainwear** While you are more likely to be rained on during the walk in the forest, where it should still be warm, once you've got your clothes wet there will be little opportunity to dry them on the trek – and you will not want to attempt to climb freezing Kibo in wet clothes.

A **waterproof jacket** – preferably made from Gore-Tex or a similar breathable material, hopefully with a warm or fleecy lining too, and big enough to go over all your clothes so you can wear it for the night-walk on Kibo – is ideal; **waterproof trousers** are a necessity too. Alternatively, one reader suggests a cheap waterproof **poncho** 'from a dollar store', preferably one that goes over your backpack as well as yourself.

● **Summer clothes** T-shirts and shorts are the most comfortable things to wear under the humid forest canopy. You are strongly recommended to take a shirt with a collar too, to stop the sun from burning the back of your neck.

OTHER EQUIPMENT

Any trekking agency worth its licence will provide a **tent**, as well as **cooking equipment**, **cutlery** and **crockery**. You will still need to pack a few other items, however, if you don't want to return from your trek as a sunburnt, snow-blinded, dehydrated wretch with hepatitis and hypothermia. Some of these items can be bought or rented in Moshi or Arusha. Your agency can arrange equipment rental, which is the most convenient way, though you may well find it cheaper to avoid going through them as they will, of course, take their cut. Note that the following lists concern the trek only; it does not include items necessary for other activities you may have planned on your holiday, such as binoculars for your safari or a bucket and spade for Zanzibar.

Before buying or renting all of the following, check to see what your agency will supply as part of their trekking package. Many will provide mattresses and water purifiers, for example, which will save you a little.

Essentials

● **Sleeping bag** The warmest you've got. Four- (and even five-) season bags are obviously best but for many people a three-season bag (up to -10°C) is probably the most practical, offering a compromise between warmth and cost; team this with a **thermal fleecy liner**, which is available in camping shops back at home for about £20-30/US$30-45, to provide further insurance against the cold.

● **Sleeping mat** Essential unless you're following the standard Marangu Route as you'll be sleeping in huts. Trekking agencies sometimes supply these – check to see if yours does.

● **Water bottles/Platypus Hoser/Camelbak system** On that final push up Kibo you'll need to carry three litres of water *at the very least*; many people take enough bottles to carry four litres. It's certainly good to take a lot of water, though do remember you've got to carry it with you and four litres of water weighs four kilos.

Make sure your bottles are **thermally protected** or they will freeze on the summit. Regular army-style water bottles are fine, though these days many trekkers prefer the **Platypus Hoser-style systems** (aka **CamelBaks**), a kind of soft, plastic bladder with a long tube from which you can drink as you walk along. We think they're great and they have several advantages over regular bottles; not the least of which being that they save you fiddling about with bottle tops and you can keep your hands in your pockets while you drink – great on the freezing night-time walk to the summit. But while they encourage you to drink regularly, which is good for dealing with the altitude, they discourage you from taking a break, which is bad. What's more, these systems nearly always freeze up on the way to the summit, especially the hose and mouthpiece. One way to avoid this – or at least delay it – is to **blow back into the tube** after you have taken a drink to prevent water from collecting in the tube and freezing. (One reader suggested adding Dioralyte which also helps to delay freezing.) So, if you are going to bring one of these, make sure it's fully insulated – and don't forget to take frequent breaks!

● **Water purifiers/filter** Also essential, unless you intend to hire an extra porter or two to transport your drinking water up from the start, or if your agency has stated they will purify your water for you (many now do). While you can get your cooking crew to boil you some water at the end of every mealtime, you'll still find purifiers and/or a filter essential if you're going to drink the recommended 3-4 litres every day, for which you may have to collect water from the mountain streams. Of the two, **purifying tablets** such as iodine are more effective as they kill everything in the water, though they taste awful. A cordial

A Kilimanjaro washbag

Hygiene is very, very important on Kilimanjaro. The last thing you want is a stomach bug due to the poor hygiene regime of one of your fellow trekkers – or, indeed, yourself. The trouble is, of course, that opportunities to wash are minimal on the mountain and water is limited the further up you go. Put the following in your washbag, however, and you should be able to maintain some sort of standard:

● **Bacterial handwash** This stuff is very effective and though you won't find it on most kit lists, I think it's essential. Giving some to your cook before they prepare meals is a good idea too!

● **Moist toilet tissues (Wet-wipes)** For mopping brows, mainly; use several at the end of the day and it's the closest thing to a shower on the mountain on most treks.

● **Toothbrush and toothpaste** Ensure your dental checks are up to date; if there is one thing more painful than climbing to the summit of Kili, it's climbing to the summit of Kili with toothache.

● **Toilet paper**

● **Soap** Though you won't get through much of it on the mountain and your trekking agency should provide some for you.

● **Tampons/sanitary towels**

● **Contraceptives** For those with too much energy. But gentlemen be warned: if she says she has a headache on the mountain, the chances are she *really does have* a headache.

You should also bring a **towel**. The controversy here is over which sort of towel to have. Many just bring one enormous beach towel because they plan to visit Zanzibar after the trek and don't see the point of packing two towels.

At the other extreme there are the tiny so-called 'travel towels', a sort of chamois-cloth affair sold in camping shops and airport lounges the world over. Some people swear by these things but others usually end up swearing at them, finding that they have all the absorbency of your average block of volcanic stone. Nevertheless, we grudgingly admit that they do have their uses on Kilimanjaro, where opportunities to wash anything other than face and hands are minimal. You can dry your towel by attaching it to the outside of your rucksack during the day.

will help to mask this taste; you can buy packets of powdered flavouring in the local supermarkets. **Filters** are less effective and more expensive, though the water they produce tastes much better.

There's now a third option, the **Steripen** (🖥 www.steripen.com), which kills waterborne microbes by using ultraviolet light. The pen is simple to use: simply hold it in a litre of water for 30 seconds and ... that's it. I've seen one of these in action on the mountain and I have to say I found it a very impressive bit of kit. My only quibble was that you can use it on only one litre of water at a time, so it can be awkward if you have, for example, a three-litre bottle.

● **Torch** A **head-torch**, if you have one and don't find it uncomfortable, is far more practical than a hand-held one, allowing you to keep both hands free; on the last night this advantage is pretty much essential, enabling you to keep your hands in your pockets for warmth.

● **Sunscreen** High factor (35-40) essential.

● **Sunglasses** Essential for the summit where the light on Kibo can be really painful and damaging and cause snow-blindness.

● **Ice axe/crampons Ice axes** are only really useful if you are taking a highly unusual route on the mountain (ie none of the official ones) where you have to cross glaciers, or, possibly, if you're travelling out of season when snow and ice can be heavy. **Crampons**, too, would be useful on these occasions, though ask your agency first if they will be necessary before bringing them. Otherwise leave them, your snow boots, rope, karabiners and all that other mountaineering gear at home.

● **Glasses/contact lenses** For those who need them, of course. **Contact lenses** are fine but super-expensive ones should be avoided on the final assault to the summit as there's a risk that when the strong cold wind blows across the Saddle

---

A Kilimanjaro medical kit

According to Meyer, the Chagga treated their cuts and scars with the liberal application of cow dung. We advise, however, that you don't. Instead,
if you're going on a cheap trek, take a medical kit with you as few of the
budget agencies will have one. (And even if you're going with a more luxurious operator, check to see what they pack in the way of medication, bandages etc.)

A medical kit should include:

● **Antiseptic cream and plasters** For small cuts and grazes.
● **Bandages** Useful for twists and sprains as well as for larger flesh wounds.
● **Compeed** For blisters.
● **Elastic joint supports** For steeper gradients if you have knee/ankle problems.
● **Ice packs** One of my clients brought 'Ice Paks'; these turn icy cold when 'snapped' and provide great relief for painful joints. Can be bought online, are very reasonable – and are ideal if you know that your knees or ankles will play up on the mountain.
● **Anti-malarials** You won't catch malaria on the mountain but if you're on a course of anti-malarials you should continue taking them. Be warned, however, that there is a rumour circulating among guides that the popular anti-malarial drug Malarone interferes with the efficacy of the anti-altitude sickness drug Diamox. Speak with your guide/doctor to get their opinion on this.
● **Aspirin/Paracetamol** Or other painkillers, though do read the discussion on AMS (p366) and the medical indications in the packet before scoffing these.
● **Imodium** Stops you going when you don't want to go, which could come in handy.
● **Rehydrating powders** Such as Dioralyte. Usually prescribed to people suffering from diarrhoea but useful after a hot day's trekking as well.
● **Lip salve or chapstick/vaseline** See under *Highly desirables*, p65.
● **Throat pastilles** Useful, as the dry, dusty air causes many a sore throat.
● **Any current medication you are on** Bring all your needles, pills, lotions, potions and pungent unguents.
● **Diamox** Diamox is the brand name for Acetazolamide, the drug that fights AMS and which many people use prophylactically on Kilimanjaro. See the box on p228 to help you decide whether you want to bring a course of these with you.
● **Sterile needles** If you need an injection in Tanzania, insist that the doctor uses your new needles.

Carry everything in a **waterproof bag or case** and keep at least the emergency stuff in your daypack – where hopefully it will lie undisturbed for the trek's duration.

the lenses can dry, go brittle very quickly and fall out of your eye. I suggest affordable disposable lenses be worn but that spare **glasses** be carried, especially during the assault on the summit. Obviously you'll need to be extra careful to keep your hands super clean and dry when putting lenses in.

Highly desirables
● **Plastic bags** Useful for segregating your wet clothes from the rest of your kit in your rucksack and for collecting rubbish to take off the mountain.
● **Trekking poles** If you've done some trekking before you'll know if you need trekking poles or not; if you haven't, assume you will. While people often use

Cameras and camera equipment
It's important to prepare properly when it comes to taking a camera on Kilimanjaro. After all, it's likely that your camera will not have spent seven days in constant use before and almost certainly not in the dusty and/or humid conditions one finds on Kili, with its extremes of temperature and weather.

The first thing to do is to make sure you have enough **memory cards**; I take an average of 400-600 shots each time I spend a week on Kilimanjaro and while that's probably a bit extreme, if you like taking photographs you could well match or even surpass these figures. Indeed it may feel as if you've spent the entire trip with your camera attached to your face, such is the frequency with which you find something worth photographing.

Bring at least one **spare battery** and make sure all rechargeable batteries are fully charged before you set off on the mountain. More and more photographic equipment is becoming available for sale in Arusha and, to a lesser extent, Moshi, but I certainly wouldn't rely on them having the battery you require for your camera. And for goodness sake don't forget to bring the **charger**, so you can charge your batteries the night before you head off onto the mountain.

For those with an SLR, regarding **lenses**, I always take a couple of zooms: a wide-angle (around 18mm-135mm) and a telephoto. This latter is far less useful on Kilimanjaro, of course, as panoramic shots of the mountain and stunning wide-angle views are the order of the day but occasionally it's nice to zoom in on a bird of prey or a particular part of the mountain. A telephoto zoom also comes into its own if you're going on safari after your trek (I suggest a 300m minimum for this).

Other useful equipment includes: a **polarizing filter** to bring out the rich colours of the sky, rocks and glaciers. A **tripod** is useful for those serious about their photography, in order to keep the camera steady and allow for maximum depth of field – though remember, you're the one who's going to have to carry it if you want to use it during the day (though you could ask your agency to provide a porter for this task); a bean-bag, or one of those new, bendy 'gorillas', would be a more portable alternative. One other essential investment is a **camera-cleaning kit**. Your camera goes through a lot of hardship on Kili, not least because of the different vegetation zones you pass through, from the humidity of the forest to the dusty desert of the Saddle. Either buy a ready-made kit from a camera shop or make one yourself by investing in a soft cloth, cotton buds, a blow brush and tweezers.

Many people with expensive SLR cameras also bring a cheap point-and-shoot **compact**; this is not a bad idea, as it doubles your chances of getting some photographic record of your journey.

them the whole way, poles really come into their own on the descent where they minimize the strain on your knees as you trudge downhill. Telescopic poles can be bought from trekking/camping outfitters in the West, or you can invest in a more local version – a Masai 'walking stick' – from souvenir shops in Moshi or Arusha.

● **Boiled sweets/chocolate** For winning friends and influencing people. Good for energy levels too. And morale. If you can bring them from home so much the better; sweets sold in Tanzania may look similar to those at home – but they seldom taste the same.

● **Chapstick/lip salve or vaseline** The wind on the summit will rip your sunburnt lips to shreds. Save yourself the agony by investing in a chapstick, available in strawberry and mint flavours from pharmacists in Moshi and Arusha.

● **Camera and equipment** See box opposite.

Usefuls

● **Earplugs** Some porters have stereos and mobile phones and they love advertising this fact by playing the former and speaking into the latter extremely loudly at campsites. A set of earplugs will reduce this disturbance.

● **Gaiters** For every edition of this book we put these in the 'Useful' category; and every edition at least one trekker writes in to tell me that they should be in the 'Essentials' category. I've never worn them on Kili, though I can see the

---

❏ **GPS waypoints**

If you have a handheld GPS receiver you will be able to take advantage of the waypoints marked on the maps and listed on pp361-5 of this book. Essentially a GPS calculates your position on the Earth using a number of satellites and the results should be accurate to a few metres. It is, of course, not essential that you use a GPS; your chances of getting lost on the mountain are very slim, given that you will be accompanied at every step by a guide who may have climbed on your route a hundred times or more.

If you do decide to use a GPS unit in conjunction with this book don't feel that you need to be ticking off every waypoint as you reach it; you'll soon get bored with that method. But if you look it occasionally – when you stop for lunch, for example – it will give you an idea both of where you are on the trail, and also how far you have to go.

You have two ways of inputting the waypoints into your receiver. You can either manually key the nearest presumed waypoint from the list in this book on p361-5 as and when the need arises. Or, much less laboriously, and with less margin for keystroke error, download the complete list (but not the descriptions) for free from our website at 🖳 www.climbmount kilimanjaro.com.

point of them and they are pretty vital if you don't have waterproof trousers, as they perform a similar function. To be fair, many of the guides I have trekked with feel naked without them. So it's a matter of preference, really, and they are particularly useful on the slopes of Kibo and the dusty Saddle to prevent small stones from entering one's shoes.

● **Aluminium sheet blanket** Provides extra comfort if your sleeping bag isn't as warm as you thought, though they do cause condensation overnight that can leave your sleeping bag feeling damp.

● **Sandals/flip-flops** Useful in the evenings at camp, but make sure they are big enough to fit round a pair of thick socks.

● **Candles** But don't use them in the tent and keep them away from everybody else's tent too. Usually supplied by the trekking company for use in the mess tent.

● **Bootlaces/string**

● **Clothes pegs** Useful for attaching wet clothes to the back of rucksacks to allow them to dry in the sun while you walk; a reader wrote in to recommend **binder clips** (also known as bulldog or office clips) as a smaller, stronger alternative.

● **Penknife** Always useful, if only for opening beer bottles at the post-trek party.

● **Matches** As with the penknife, always useful, as any Boy Scout will tell you.

● **Sewing kit** For repairs on the trail.

● **Insulating tape** Also for repairs – of shoes, rucksacks, tents etc, and as a last resort for mending holes in clothes if you have forgotten your sewing kit or are incapable of using it.

● **Watch** Preferably cheap and luminous for night-time walking.

● **Compass** Not essential, but useful when combined with ...

● **Map** See p353 for a list of our preferred maps; again not essential but will, in combination with a compass, help you to determine where you are on the mountain, and where you're going.

● **GPS receiver** See box p65.

● **Trowel** If you envisage needing to defecate along the trail at places other than the designated toilet huts, this will help to bury the evidence and keep the mountain looking pristine; see p234.

● **Whistle** It's difficult to get lost on Kilimanjaro but if you're taking an unusual route – on the northern side of the mountain, for example, or around Mawenzi – a whistle may be useful to help people locate which ravine you've fallen into. The international distress (emergency) signal is six blasts on a whistle.

● **She-wee** AKA the Miss Piss, this is for ladies who want to wee without the bother of removing layers or getting out of the tent at night. According to some, the 'female urinal' is cheaper and better. Men, by the way, usually make do with an empty mineral water bottle.

Luxuries

● **Mobile phone** You can get reception on much of the mountain now – including, so it is said, on the summit. What better place could there be from which to phone friends stuck behind their desks at work on a rainy day back home? We point out where you can get reception for each trail.

❑ **What to put in your daypack**
Normally you will not see your backpack from the moment you hand it to the porter in the morning until lunchtime at least, and maybe not until the end of the day. It's therefore necessary to pack everything you may need during the day in the bag you carry with you. Some suggestions, in no particular order:

- sweets
- water
- water purifiers
- toilet paper and plastic bag for packing used paper to the next camp; see p234 for toilet etiquette
- trowel

- this book/maps
- camera and spare batteries
- sunhat/sunglasses and suncream
- rainwear
- walking sticks/knee supports
- medical kit, including chapstick
- lunch (supplied by your crew)

● **Hot water bottle** Several people have suggested this; indeed a number of trekking companies now supply them as standard. Get your crew to fill it with hot water before bedtime and use the water in the morning to wash with or drink.
● **Pillow** One luxury I have never used on the mountain but would love to is a pillow; not one of those inflatable travel ones but a proper, plump, goose-down number. Bulky and a pain to carry, of course – but so much nicer than resting one's weary head on a scrunched-up fleece at the end of the day.
● **MP3 players** and **iPods** While some find the idea abhorrent, many trekkers bring their tunes on the trek. There is nothing wrong with a little mountainside music, of course, but do remember that while you may think you've found the perfect soundtrack for climbing up Kili, others may disagree: bring headphones, so as not to disturb.
● **Diary/reading material** A list of appropriate reading matter can be found on pp354-8. Note that more than one client has said that books and other forms of entertainment are essential to while away the hours in camp, whereas others say it's all unnecessary; it depends who you're climbing with, I suppose, and how well you're all getting along.
● **Champagne** For celebrating, of course, though don't try to take it up and open it at the summit – the combination of champagne and altitude sickness could lead to tragedy and, besides, the glass could well crack with the cold.

WHAT TO PACK IT IN

You'll need two bags: a **rucksack** – a 70-litre one is the absolute minimum, with 90 litres more practical for carrying all the equipment necessary for most climbs – and a smaller, lighter **daypack**. While trekkers usually spend a long time finding the rucksack that's most comfortable for them, few bother to spend as long when choosing a daypack. However, on Kili it is the porters who traditionally carry your rucksack (usually on their heads, and often inside a rice sack or similar outer layer to protect it from getting wet or damaged), while you will carry your daypack. So make sure you **choose your daypack with care** and that it is both comfortable and durable. It also needs to be big enough to hold everything you may need when walking. See box above for a possible list of these things.

Two more points. Firstly, **don't leave valuables in your rucksack**. Though porters are very trustworthy, it's only fair that you do not put temptation in their path. Secondly, **put everything in plastic bags** (or **bin bags**) inside your backpack and daypack to keep everything dry.

Fitness, inoculations and insurance

FITNESS

I ascribe the almost perfect health I have always enjoyed in Africa to the fact that I have made every step of my journey on foot, the constant exercise keeping my bodily organs in good order. **Hans Meyer** *Across East African Glaciers* (1891)

There's no need to go overboard with fitness preparations for climbing Kili. The main reason why people fail to reach the summit is altitude sickness rather than lack of necessary strength or stamina. But while the trek will obviously be more enjoyable for you the fitter you are, so anything you can do in the way of training can only help (see box p70).

A weekend (or several) of walking would be a good thing to do; it won't improve your fitness to a great degree but it will at least confirm that you can walk for more than a few hours at a time, and for more than one day at a time too. Wear the clothes you plan to take to Kilimanjaro – particularly your boots and socks – and the daypack that you hope to be carrying all the way to the top of Kibo, too.

INOCULATIONS

Sort out your vaccinations a few months before you're due to fly. Note that **it is compulsory to have a yellow-fever vaccination in order to enter Tanzania if you're coming from a country where the disease is endemic** (even if you were only transiting there, assuming you left the airport in that country for more than 12 hours); see p81 for further details.

In the UK the jab costs about £50-80 including a certificate (and from what I understand it's about US\$80 in the States) to prove you've been vaccinated. Other recommended inoculations include:

● **Typhoid** This disease is caught from contaminated food and water. A single injection lasts for three years. Available on the NHS in the UK. There is also a typhoid vaccine that is combined with one for...

● **Hepatitis A** This debilitating disease of the liver is spread by contaminated water, or even by using cutlery that has been washed in this water. The latest inoculation involves two injections; the first will protect you for a year, the second, taken six to twelve months later, will cover you for 20 years. (These times may vary if you're taking the combined Hep A/typhoid vaccine).

● **Polio** The polio vaccine used to be administered by sugar-lump, making it one of the more pleasant inoculations, though these days it's nearly always injected. The vaccine lasts for ten years and there's a high chance you may already have been immunized for life if you had a course of inoculations during childhood – which if you were born after 1958 you probably will have done (in the UK at least).

● **Tetanus** Tetanus vaccinations last for ten years and are absolutely vital for visitors to Tanzania. The vaccination is usually given in combination with one for **diphtheria**. Once you've had five injections, you're covered for life. Once again, the chances you were immunized for good against this at childhood is high. If you need a booster, it should last for five years.

● **Meningococcal meningitis** This disease of the brain is often fatal though the vaccination, while not free, is safe, effective and lasts for three to five years.

● **Rabies** If you're spending some time with animals or in the wilderness, it's also worth considering having a course of **rabies** injections, consisting of three injections spread over one month, though it isn't pleasant.

Malaria
Malaria is a problem in Tanzania, which is considered one of the highest risk countries in the world. While you are highly unlikely to contract malaria on Kilimanjaro, which is too high and cold for the anopheles mosquito (the species that carries malaria but which is rarely seen above 1200m – much lower than your starting point on Kili), it is rife in coastal areas and on Zanzibar. It's also present in Moshi and, despite an altitude above 1200m, in Arusha too.

When beginning a course of **anti-malarials**, it is very important to begin taking them before you go; that way the drug is established in your system by the time you set foot on Tanzanian soil and it will give you a chance to see if the drug is going to cause a reaction or allergy. Once started, complete the full course, which usually runs for several weeks after you return home.

Which anti-malarial you need depends on which parts of Africa you are visiting and your previous medical history. Your doctor will be able to advise on

---

High-altitude health
Before you go, if you suffer from heart or lung problems, high blood pressure or are pregnant, you must visit your doctor to get advice on the wisdom of climbing up Africa's highest mountain; many of the deaths on the mountain are due to pre-existing conditions that have gone undetected before.

The illness you are most likely to suffer from is altitude sickness; indeed, it's a rare trekker on Kilimanjaro who doesn't to some degree. Altitude sickness is caused by the body's inability to adapt quickly enough to the thinner mountain air present at high altitudes. It can be fatal if ignored or left untreated but is also often preventable. For a run-down on the causes, symptoms and treatments of altitude sickness, read the section on pp222-30 carefully.

One more thing: if you're planning on relying on it on the mountain, try Diamox (see p228) before you go to make sure you have no severe adverse reaction to it.

A FITNESS REGIME

Though altitude sickness is the main reason why people fail to reach the summit – and this can strike you regardless of whether you are fit or not – there's no doubt that you *do* need to be in reasonable condition to tackle Kilimanjaro, and will have a much more pleasant time on the mountain if you are fit and healthy.

For this reason, and to answer the many emails we get from people who want to undertake some sort of fitness regime before their trek, here is a typical daily exercise programme for Kilimanjaro. It should be started about four months (three minimum) before the climb. This should help to reduce body fat, improve aerobic fitness and also strengthen the muscles in the places where it really matters: your legs.

We think it helps to concentrate on aerobic exercises one day (say three times a week) alternating with leg-strengthening exercises for the other three days – then follow God's example and rest on the seventh day.

Aerobic exercise

Aerobic exercise is designed to improve oxygen consumption in the body. Thirty minutes to an hour of jogging, cycling, climbing stairs or even just brisk walking are all good aerobic exercise. Aim to exercise at 70% of your maximum heart rate for the best results.

Leg strengthening

Go to any gym and you'll come across plenty of contraptions designed to increase the strength of your calves, thighs, hamstrings and buttocks. These are fine though the usual warnings apply: always read the instructions carefully before using any machine and never be too ambitious and overload the machine with too much weight. Either course of action could lead to serious injury and the cancellation of your trek altogether.

If you don't have access to gym equipment, however, don't worry: there are exercises you can do without the need for machines. **Lunges**, where you take an exaggerated step forward with one leg, dropping your hips as low as possible while keeping your torso upright, are great for thighs, hamstrings and buttocks. A **reverse lunge**, which is the same as a regular lunge only you take a step *backwards*, until your forward thigh (ie the one you didn't take a step backwards with) is parallel to the floor, is also good, particularly for your hamstring. **Calf raises**, where you position yourself with the front half of your feet on a platform, then gently raise and lower yourself on your toes so your heel is alternately higher and lower than the toes, is also useful.

Smoking and other preparations

While the above exercises certainly provide many benefits, we still maintain that nothing is better preparation than **going for a long walk**! A walk provides excellent aerobic exercise, is great for strengthening leg muscles and if the walk is long enough and involves plenty of uphills, can be great for improving stamina too. Find walks in your area or take a walking weekend or holiday. You never know, you may even enjoy it too.

Finally, you can always take up **smoking**. I'd long heard the rumour that smokers have a better chance of reaching the summit, apparently due to the fact that their bodies are used to less oxygen because of the reduced functioning of their lungs – and certainly my experiences of taking smokers up the mountain bear this bizarre idea out. While those of my clients who've led a blameless, tobacco-free life frequently struggle with the altitude, long-term smokers tend to saunter up. Breathless, certainly, and often wheezing – but headache-free and happy. Of course, we're not seriously suggesting you take up smoking – but it's interesting, isn't it?

what drug is best for you. With Tanzania in the highest risk category, the chances are you will be recommended either Lariam (the brand name for mefloquine), Doxycycline or Malarone, which is supposedly free of side effects but very expensive.

Stories of Lariam causing hallucinations, nightmares, blindness and even death have been doing the rounds in travellers' circles for years now but if you feel no adverse reaction – and millions don't – carry on taking it and don't worry.

Of course the best way to combat malaria is not to get bitten at all. A **repellent** with 30% Diethyltoluamide (DEET) worn in the evenings when the anopheles mosquito is active should be effective in preventing bites. Some use it during the day too, when the mosquitoes that carry yellow and dengue fevers are active.

Alternatively, you could just keep covered up with long sleeve shirts and long trousers, sleep under a **mosquito net** and burn **mosquito coils**; these are available within Tanzania.

Travellers' medical clinics (UK)
For all your jabs, malaria advice and anything else you need to know regarding health abroad, visit your doctor or one of the following clinics:
● **Trailfinders Travel Clinic** (☎ 020-7938 3999; 🖥 www.trailfinders.com/trav elessentials/travelclinic.htm) 194 Kensington High St, London.
● **Nomad Travellers Store and Medical Centre** (☎ 0845-260 0044; 🖥 www. nomadtravel.co.uk) has several branches in London as well as Bristol (☎ 0117-922 6567), Manchester (☎ 0161-832 2134), Southampton (☎ 023-8023 4920), Loughton (☎ 020-8508 6626) and Bishops Stortford (☎ 01279-653694).
● **MASTA** (Medical Advisory Services for Travellers Abroad; 🖥 www.masta-travel-health.com) has branches throughout the country.

Also worth looking at is the website of the **US Center for Disease Control** (🖥 www.cdc.gov); it's packed full of advice and the latest medical news Stateside.

INSURANCE

When buying insurance you must make clear to the insurer that you'll be trekking to the top of a very big mountain. If you are taking an unusual route and will be using ropes you need to tell them that too. Telling them that you're climbing Kili is usually enough to double the premium and may even exclude you from being covered altogether. But if you don't make this clear and pay the lower premium you'll probably find, should you try to make a claim, you aren't actually covered at all.

Remember to **read the small print** of any insurance policy before buying and shop around, too, for each insurance policy varies slightly from company to company. Details to consider include:
● How much is the deductible if you have to make a claim?
● Can the insurers pay for your hospital bills etc immediately, while you are still in Tanzania, or do you have to wait until you get home?
● How long do you have before making a claim and what evidence do you require (hospital bills, police reports etc)?

Remember the premium for the entire trip will probably double when you mention you are climbing above 4000-5000m, even though you will actually be on the mountain for only a few days. However, you will need to be covered for your entire trip: there are just as many nasty things that can happen – indeed, many more – when off the mountain than on it; theft becomes a much bigger issue too.

One other thing to note. There is currently no helicopter rescue on Kilimanjaro. If you have insurance that includes some sort of helicopter rescue the chances are that they will land in the foothills somewhere and evacuate you from there – so you'll probably still have some sort of lengthy and uncomfortable descent from Kili first.

For UK residents, the following companies offer insurance up to 6000m:
- **British Mountaineering Council** (🖳 www.thebmc.co.uk; ☎ 0161-445 6111)
- **ihi Bupa** (🖳 www.ihi.com)
- **Insure and Go** (🖳 www.insureandgo.com; ☎ 0844-888 2787)

For American trekkers the following have been recommended by readers:
- **Travel Guard** (🖳 www.travelguard.com) have an 'Adventure package' upgrade that currently covers trekkers on Kilimanjaro.
- **HTH** (🖳 www.hthtravelinsurance.com; ☎ 888-243-2358)
- **International Plan** (🖳 www.internationalplan.com; ☎ 480-248-2179) We sent an email to these people asking if they offered insurance for those climbing Kilimanjaro but failed to get a reply. Still, they were recommended by several clients so it would be worth checking with them.
- **World Nomads** (🖳 www.worldnomads.com) Note that the policy details change depending on where you reside. For example, a Florida resident is excluded from Security Evacuation coverage entirely, which the general policy indicates covers a person for up to US$500,000; while for a New Jersey resident that is not the case. So do check the small print carefully!

❑ My favourite piece of advice on Kilimanjaro

'**WARNING** Due to the rise in the frequency and severity of human-leopard encounters, the Ministry of Tourism, Kilimanjaro Branch, Tanzania, is advising trekkers and anyone else that uses Kilimanjaro for recreational or work-related purposes to take extra precautions while on the mountain.

In particular, we advise that all trekkers wear little bells on their clothing. This will give advanced warning to any leopards that might be close by and thereby prevent you from taking them by surprise. We also advise anyone visiting Kilimanjaro to carry pepper spray with him or her in case of an encounter with a leopard.

Visitors should also be on the watch for any fresh leopard activity, and be able to tell the difference between leopard cub shit and big leopard shit:
Leopard cub shit is smaller and contains lots of berries and fur.
Big leopard shit has bells in it, and smells like pepper.
Enjoy your stay in Tanzania!'

This was sent to me by a friend via Facebook and caught me so much by surprise that I snorted tea out of my nose. Hope it had a similar effect on you. (In case you're wondering, it *is* a joke – and leopard-human encounters are pretty much unheard of today!)

TANZANIA

2

> '*Strange country isn't it?*'
> '*Yes. It seems so cruel one moment, then suddenly kind and very beautiful.*
> *Maybe there are parts God forgot about – he meant it all to be like this.*'
> **Robert Taylor** and **Anne Aubrey** discuss the land we now call Tanzania in
> the 1959 swashbuckling classic *Killers of Kilimanjaro*

Although this book concentrates specifically on Kilimanjaro, some background knowledge of the country in which it stands, Tanzania, is necessary. For the chances are that climbing Kilimanjaro forms only one part of your trip to Tanzania, and as such you are going to need to know what this beautiful country is like and how you are going to negotiate travelling around it. With this in mind, the following chapter is divided into two parts. The first provides a background of the country by looking at the history, economy, culture etc. This should both increase your enjoyment of visiting Tanzania and serve to put Kilimanjaro in its national context. The second half deals with the more practical side of things, offering advice and tips to help the visitor.

Facts about the country

GEOGRAPHY

Tanzania occupies an area of 945,087 sq km – a little over twice the size of California – made up of 886,037 sq km of land (including the offshore islands of Pemba, Mafia and Zanzibar) and 59,050 sq km of water. This makes it the largest country in the geo-political region of East Africa. It is bounded to the north by Uganda and Kenya, to the west by the Democratic Republic of Congo (DRC), Burundi and Rwanda, to the south by Mozambique, Malawi and Zambia, and to the east by the Indian Ocean. The terrain in that 886,037 sq km of land includes a wide, lush coastal plain and a large and dusty central plateau flanked by the eastern and western branches of the **Great Rift Valley** (see p92). There are highlands in both the north and south of the country and in the centre of the plateau are some volcanic peaks which again owe their existence to the Rift Valley. Interestingly, over a quarter of the country is given over to national parks or nature reserves.

Tanzania is also a land of extremes, housing Africa's largest game reserve, the **Selous** (covering approximately 55,000 sq km, and with an approximately equal number of elephants), and the **Serengeti**, the park with the greatest concentration of migratory game in the world. Its borders also encompass a share in the continent's largest lake, **Lake Victoria**, and part of **Lake Tanganyika**, the longest and, after Lake Baikal in Siberia, deepest freshwater lake in the world. The third largest lake in Africa, **Lake Malawi**, also forms one of Tanzania's borders. These lakes were formed when the Great Rift Valley, which runs through the heart of the country, opened up about 30 million years ago. As a direct result of the formation of this valley, Tanzania contains Africa's lowest point, the floor of Lake Tanganyika, some 350m below sea level. It is also, of course, the proud owner of Africa's highest...

Beautiful as this country undoubtedly is, it is also beset by enormous environmental problems, from deforestation to desertification, soil degradation, erosion and reef bombing. Significant damage has already occurred, and is still occurring, with added pressures on the land caused by the meteoric rise in tourism over the past couple of decades. For details of how you can minimize your impact on the environment of Kilimanjaro, see p233.

CLIMATE

Tanzania's climate varies greatly, and you'll be encountering just about all of the variations in the four or five days it takes you to walk to the top of Kilimanjaro. For more about this, see the Kilimanjaro climate section on p97.

Away from the mountain, the narrow coastal strip tends to be the hottest, most humid and tropical part of the country, with the inland plateau being of sufficient elevation to offer some cooler temperatures and respite from the heat. On the coast the average temperature during the day is a sticky 27°C; luckily the sea breezes temper this heat and make it bearable. On the inland plateau you're looking at an average temperature of around 20-26.5°C during the cooler months of June to August, up to a roasting 30°C between December and March.

The **rainy seasons** extend from November to early January (the short rains), and from mid March to May (the long rains). On the coast the average annual rainfall is around 1400mm; inland it is a much drier 250mm, though in mountainous areas it can be a magnificent 2000mm; unsurprisingly, flooding can be a problem at this time.

HISTORY

We, the people of Tanganyika, would like to light a candle and put it on the top of Mount Kilimanjaro, which would shine beyond our borders, giving hope where there was despair, love where there was hate, and dignity where before there was only humiliation.
  Julius Nyerere in a speech to the Tanganyika Legislative Assembly in 1959. Following independence in 1961, his wish was granted and a torch was placed on Kili's summit.

The discovery of the 1,750,000-year-old remains of an early hominid, **Australopithecus Zinjanthropus Boisei**, at Olduvai Gorge in the Ngorongoro Crater (near hominid footprints that could be as much as three-and-a-half million years old), suggest that Tanzania has one of the longest histories in the world. We are now going to cram these three and a half million years into the next three and a half pages – a task made considerably simpler by the fact that this history has, until the last 200 years or so, been unrecorded. (By the way, for a detailed history of Kilimanjaro, see p100.)

We know that **Khoisan speakers** (from southern Africa) moved into the area of modern Tanzania around 10,000 years ago, to be joined between 3000BC and 1000BC by Cushitic speakers from the Horn of Africa (Ethiopia and Eritrea), who brought with them more advanced agricultural techniques. Over the next few hundred years **Bantu speakers** from West Africa's Niger Delta and Nilotic peoples from the north and Sudan also migrated to the area we now know as Tanzania.

By 400BC merchants from Classical Greece knew about and traded with the coast of East Africa, which they called **Azania**. Some of them eventually settled here to take advantage of the trading opportunities, to be joined later by **traders from Persia** and, by the end of the first millennium AD as trade routes stretched into China, merchants from **India**. The majority of immigrants, however, proved to be the seafaring **traders from Arabia**, and soon the Swahili language and culture, an amalgamation of the cultures of Arabia and the Bantu speakers who had also settled on the coast, began to emerge there.

Portuguese, Arabs, Germans and British

Life on the coastal strip of what is now Tanzania continued, as far as we know, pleasantly enough for a number of centuries, a fairly idyllic existence that was rudely shattered by the arrival of the **Portuguese** following Vasco da Gama's legendary expedition at the end of the 15th century. As greedy as they were intrepid, they built the coastal village of Kilwa Kisiwani into a major trading port which, in typical Portuguese style, they later sacked. Understandably unpopular, the Portuguese nevertheless held on grimly and gamely to their East African possessions for almost 200 years until the end of the 17th century. That they managed to survive for so long is largely due to a lack of a united opposition, which didn't arrive until 1698 in the form of **Omani Arabs**, summoned to help by the long-suffering traders of Kilwa Kisiwani. Unlike the Portuguese, the Omani Arabs were keen to forge trading links with the interior. They pushed new routes across the plains to Lake Tanganyika, thereby facilitating the extraction of gold, **slaves** and ivory from deep within the continent. The Arabs grew inordinately wealthy from the fat of Africa's land to the extent that the Omani sultan decided to pull up his tent pegs from the desert sands of Arabia and relocate, establishing his new capital at Stonetown on Zanzibar.

While this was going on, the Europeans returned to Africa. Initially it was just a trickle of **missionaries** and **explorers**, hell-bent (if that's the right term) on making converts and mapping continents respectively. Indeed, one man who famously combined both vocations, Dr David Livingstone, spent a while in Tanzania as part of his efforts to find the source of the Nile, and it was at the village of Ujiji, on the Tanzanian side of Lake Tanganyika, that HM Stanley is believed to have finally caught up with him and uttered those immortal words 'Dr Livingstone, I presume'.

With intrepid, independent Europeans now roaming all over the continent, it could only be a matter of time before one European country or another would come up with the idea of full-scale colonization. By the late **1880s** Britain had already secured a dominant role on Zanzibar. But over on the mainland it was Germany who was making the most progress.

Or rather, one German, for it was **Carl Peters** who, acting independently of his government, established German influence on the mainland at this time, negotiating treaties with local chiefs in order to secure a charter for his **Deutsch-Ostafrikanische Gesellschaft** (DOAG, the German East Africa Company). A few years later and with his homeland's government now supporting his work, Peters' DOAG was formally given the task of administering the mainland. This left the British on Zanzibar fuming – and not a little scared – at the German's impertinence, and war was averted between the two superpowers only with the signing of an accord in 1890 in which Britain was formally allowed to establish a protectorate over her Zanzibar territories. One year and further negotiations later and the land we now know as Tanzania (Zanzibar excluded) officially came under direct German control as **German East Africa**.

The Germans brought a Western education, a rail network, and a higher level of healthcare with them to Africa. They also brought harsh taxes, suppression, humiliation and no small amount of unrest. They were eventually replaced as colonial overlords after World War One by the **British** following a League of Nations mandate. The territory was renamed Tanganyika at this time. After World War Two a near bankrupt Britain clung on to administrative control, though officially Tanganyika was now a 'trust territory' of the fledgling United Nations.

Independence

Life under the British was marginally better than under the Germans, with greater political freedom and an improved economy thanks to the cultivation of export crops; but it was only marginal and soon political groups were springing up all over the country with each campaigning for the same thing: independence. The most important of these was the Dar es Salaam-based Tanganyika Africa Association which, in 1953, elected teacher **Julius Nyerere** as its president. Pressure from Nyerere and his party (now known as TANU, or the Tanganyika African National Union) forced Britain to agree to the formation of an internal self-government. Indeed, so impressed was Britain with Nyerere that the only condition they placed on the establishment of this new regime of self-government was that he should be its first chief minister.

Now a mere formality, **independence** for Tanganyika was eventually declared on 9 December 1961, with Nyerere, as Britain had hoped, as prime minister. Exactly one year later it was formally established as a **republic**, with Nyerere promoted to president.

On **Zanzibar**, meanwhile, things were going less smoothly. Whilst the Zanzibaris won their independence not long afterwards (December 1963), the two parties that formed the first government did not enjoy popular support but instead had been thrust into power by the departing British because of their pro-British leanings. With a tenure that was decidedly shaky, it came as no surprise when they were toppled in a revolution just a month later. In their place came the popular, radical Afro Shirazi Party (ASP).

Less than a year after independence, on 26 April 1964 the ASP leader, Abeid Karume, was signing an act of union with his mainland neighbours and the **United Republic of Tanganyika** was formed. In October of the same year the name was changed to the **United Republic of Tanzania**, the name being a neat combination of the two former territories. The two maintained separate governments, however, even after 1977 when ASP and TANU were combined by Nyerere to form **Chama Cha Mapinduzi** (Party of the Revolution), or **CCM**, the party which maintains political control of Tanzania to this day.

Modern history

From 1967 to the late 1980s Nyerere and his party followed a socialist course; the economy was nationalized, the tax regime was deliberately aimed at redistributing wealth and new villages were established in order to modernize the agricultural sector and give the rural poor greater access to social services. Unfortunately, the 20-year experiment was eventually deemed a flop, with the economy in seemingly perpetual decline. By 1992 things had got so desperate that the CCM took the unprecedented step of legalizing opposition parties after pressure from Western donors for more democracy in the country.

Curiously, this move seems to have done little to achieve this. Three years after the legalization of political opponents, the first democratic elections were held and the CCM, now under the leadership of **Benjamin Mkapa** following Nyerere's resignation in 1985, emerged once again as the major force in Tanzanian politics. The elections in late 2000 confirmed their dominance with over 95% of parliamentary seats won by CCM candidates. While they undoubtedly remain Tanzania's most creditable political party, the scale of the victory suggests that proper political debate is all but impossible, a prediction that the election of **Jakaya Kikwete** in 2005 (and re-election in 2010), another CCM candidate, did little to dispel.

On semi-autonomous **Zanzibar**, things, as usual, have been a little more explosive. In 1995 the incumbent CCM president, Salmin Amour, was returned to office after an election that many believe was rigged. Fresh elections in 2000 resulted in yet more controversy, with widespread reports of ballot rigging and intimidation of opposition leaders. In January 2001, 27 protesters were shot dead in Pemba as they marched through the streets protesting against these voting irregularities. And though the situation has quietened a little since then, Jakaya Kikwete has admitted that the unrest on Zanzibar would be his biggest problem in his first term as president, and it continues to simmer to this day in the middle of his second term.

The future

In some ways Tanzania is a model African nation, garnering international acclaim for its fight against corruption and its efforts to reform itself peacefully – as exemplified by the move towards democracy in the 1990s. The government of President Jakaya Kikwete, who was brought to power with over 80% of the vote in 2005, provided further evidence that Tanzania is one of the more enlightened nations with the promotion of female ministers to key finance and foreign posts.

The outlook for the economy also seems rosy: in the same year that Kikwete was re-elected, Tanzania joined its neighbours in forging an East African Common Market. In 2012 huge gas reserves were discovered off the Tanzanian coast. The Chinese, too, have invested heavily in the country, as anybody who has witnessed the growth of Arusha over the last few years will testify with its gleaming new towers and tarmac roads. It remains, however, a nation beset by problems. The usual African ailments – poverty, AIDS, and a lack of clean water, basic healthcare and decent education – are as prevalent in Tanzania as they are over much of the continent. Kikwete's attempts to root out corruption have only been partially successful, too; in 2012 six ministers were sacked for the 'rampant misuse of funds'.

In addition to those pan-African ailments, however, Tanzania has other local problems to contend with, from a lack of credible opposition to the main autocratic CCM party to the secessionist grumblings of many on Zanzibar who were never happy with the union with the mainland – a dissatisfaction that four subsequent decades and more of turmoil have done little to dispel. The influx of refugees from neighbouring Burundi and Congo has also put added pressure on the country, particularly in the west around lakes Victoria and Tanganyika. It remains to be seen whether the moderate line Tanzania has taken throughout its independence will continue into the future; and whether this thoughtful, conservative (with a small 'c') attitude will be enough to help it to overcome the enormous difficulties it still faces.

ECONOMIC AND POPULATION STATISTICS

Tanzania is one of the world's poorest countries, in the bottom 10% of nations in terms of per capita income. Its per capita GDP stands at a modest US$1600 (2011 estimate) and just over 36% live below the poverty line. (Nevertheless, these are significant improvements on the figures recorded in the first edition of this book when GDP per capita was US$264 and over 50% lived below the poverty line.) Other statistics also suggest that Tanzanians are better off than they were in 2001 when the first edition of this book was published. Infant mortality stands at a level of 65.74 per 1000 births (down from 85 per 1000 in 2001 and from 98 in 2005), and life expectancy is now 53.14, up from 45.2 in 2005 and 49 in 2001. Presumably some of this improvement can be put down to the decrease in HIV infection, with 4.6% of the population now estimated to be infected, down from 6.2% in 2009 and 8.8% of the population in 2005 (though that 4.6% still represents over 1.4 million people).

It's early days yet but the economy is starting to show some positive signs too. Growth in real GDP, for example, was 6.4% in 2011, though this has in turn led to inflationary pressures, with the Consumer Price Index rising to a worrying 12.10% in December 2012. These figures are a bit surprising given that Tanzania is still largely an **agricultural** country. The style of agriculture is mainly traditional, the large collective farms introduced under Nyerere's socialist experiment having been rejected on the whole in favour of the age-old system whereby each farmer cultivates a small plot of land called a *shamba*. The most popular home-grown crops are cotton, rice, sorghum, sugar, bananas and coconuts; sisal, coffee and tea are produced principally for the export market, while cloves and other spices are still grown on Zanzibar and the coast. Agriculture accounts for over a quarter of Tanzania's GDP and employs 80% of the workforce.

Tanzania also has a solid **mining** base with oil, tin, iron, salt, coal, gypsum, phosphate, natural gas, nickel, diamonds and, of course, tanzanite all extracted in the country. Tourism is now a major contributor to the GDP of the country and is a vital source of much-needed foreign currency, particularly in the north.

THE PEOPLE

With 46,912,768 people (CIA world factbook estimate July 2012) split into more than a hundred ethnic groups, numerous local languages and dialects and three main religions, Tanzania is something of an ethnic and cultural hotchpotch. It is a credit to the country that they exist largely in harmony, without succumbing to the sort of ethnic hatred that has riven many other countries around these parts. Native Africans make up 99% of the population; of these, the vast majority (estimated at 95%) are of Bantu origin, though even here there are over 130 tribes. The other 1% are of European, Arabian or Indian origin. Around Kilimanjaro it is the Chagga people, one of the more wealthy and powerful groups in Tanzania, who dominate.

The **religious** division is a lot more equal. The (slight) majority (35%) are now Muslim (less than ten years ago it was Christian), with 30% now professing the Christian faith and traditional indigenous beliefs accounting for the other 35%. These figures exclude Zanzibar, which is 99% Muslim. Presumably adherents of the Hindu and Sikh faiths are too small in number to register in the statistics, though they are undoubtedly a highly visible presence in Tanzania with some large, ostentatious Hindu temples in Dar, Arusha and Moshi.

The Chagga people around Kilimanjaro are largely Christian; you can read more about them, their culture and their beliefs on p141.

Language

The first and most common language in Tanzania is **Swahili**, the language originally used by traders on the coast and thus based on Arabic and various Bantu dialects. Zanzibar is still known as the home of Swahili, where the purest form of the language is spoken. A few words of Swahili will go a long way in Tanzania; although the prefixes and suffixes used in the language can be a little tricky to grasp, any efforts to speak a few words will endear you to the local people. See p348 for an introduction to Swahili.

Around Kilimanjaro, however, it is not Swahili but the language of the **Chagga** people, a tongue sometimes known as **Kichagga**, that predominates, though there are several different dialects. See p138 for a brief introduction.

Practical information for the visitor

DOCUMENTS AND VISAS

Rumours are once again afoot – as they periodically are – that there will soon be a visa that covers the five East African countries (Kenya, Uganda, Tanzania, Rwanda and Burundi); many are hopeful that by the end of 2013 this long-held ambition might finally have been realized. But for the moment separate visas still need to be bought for each country. See also pp351-2.

For Tanzania
Visitors from most countries (including pretty much every country in Europe, as well as Canada, Australia and New Zealand) must pay US$50 for their visa; visitors from Ireland and the United States, however, must fork out US$100. Chinese citizens and East African passport holders currently don't require visas.

A visa is typically valid for 90 days from the **date of issue** (and not the day you arrive in Tanzania, though I have to say many officials don't seem to recognize this!). It used to be the case that, unless you were coming from a country without Tanzanian representation, officially you had to buy your visa at the consulate/embassy beforehand. That law was never really enforced, however, and the latest news we have is that everyone can seemingly now buy their visa at the airport *except* for the following:

Afghanistan, Algeria, Bangladesh, Benin, Burkina Faso, Cameroon, Chad, Egypt, Eritrea, Ethiopia, Gabon, Ghana, Gambia, Iran, Iraq, Jordan, Kuwait, Lebanon, Liberia, Libya, Mali, Morocco, Niger, Nigeria, Pakistan, Saudi Arabia, Senegal, Sri Lanka, Somalia, Sudan, Syria, Togo, Tunisia, Turkey and Yemen.

❑ **Visas for Kenya**
Remember that, if you're flying in and out of Kenya rather than Tanzania you will need a **Kenyan visa** too (typically US$50). If you plan to fly to Kenya and cross into Tanzania from there, you can return to Kenya using the same single-entry visa you arrived with *providing* your visit to Tanzania lasted for less than two weeks and that your Kenyan visa has not expired. Apparently, you can do this only once (ie it's a double-entry visa, not a multiple-entry one), or so we were told at the Kenyan border. Otherwise, you will need to buy a multiple-entry visa. (As mentioned elsewhere, by the time you read this there is a fair chance that the whole of East Africa will be covered by a single visa. Do check this out if you are visiting more than one country in the region.)
For a list of addresses of Kenyan embassies abroad, see p352.

A list of the addresses of some of the more popular Tanzanian embassies and consulates is given on p351, for those who need or want to buy their visa beforehand.

With all **applications** you will need to present a passport that's valid for at least six months together with two passport photos. If applying in person, some consulates/high commissions (including the ones in London and Washington DC) insist that you pay in cash. Note that photos are not usually required at the airport.

You can pick up a visa at one of the **four border controls**: Dar es Salaam International Airport, Kilimanjaro International Airport, Zanzibar International Airport and the Namanga border crossing between Tanzania and Kenya. (With the upgrading of the road between Marangu and the border crossing at Loitokitok, by the start of Kilimanjaro's Rongai Route, there is some hope that this too will become an official crossing point. But for the moment, though a few adventurers – after some pretty intense negotiations – are getting through, this crossing remains officially closed to Westerners.)

Yellow-fever vaccination certificate It seems that once again it is compulsory for visitors to Tanzania to show evidence that they have been vaccinated against yellow fever if coming from a country where the disease is endemic and assuming that they actually left the airport in that country rather than just transiting for less than 24 hours.

Given that airport staff in Tanzania have in the past asked to see proof of inoculation whether you require the jab or not, it's probably best to play it safe and get one anyway. The certificate can be picked up from your doctor after you have received the inoculation and is usually free, though the jab itself is not.

Airport tax
Airport tax is currently US$40 for international flights (US$25 from Zanzibar) though this I believe is always included in the fare. Internal flights are subject to airport taxes (and a security fee) of (usually) US$9 – again, it seems to be just about always included in the ticket price now.

MONEY AND BANKS
Currency
Once again, noises are being made that the member states of the East African Community might eventually have some sort of monetary union with a single currency legal tender in all five states. The obstacles they will need to overcome in order to introduce this, however, are both massive and manifold, so for the time being the **Tanzanian shilling (Ts)** remains the national currency. It's fairly stable but cannot be imported except by residents of Tanzania, Kenya and Uganda and cannot be exported.

Cash Foreign currency can be imported and exported without limit. **Dollars** and, to a lesser extent, **sterling** and **euros** are the best currencies to bring.

The question is: in what form should you take your money to Tanzania, ie: should you just bring cash? Or should you rely solely on your credit/debit cards

❏ Exchange rates

To get the latest exchange rates visit 🖥 www.xe.com/ucc. At the time of writing they were:

UK£1	Ts2580
€1	Ts2167
US$1	Ts1602
Can$1	Ts1532
A$1	Ts1508
NZ$1	Ts1338
SwissFr1	Ts1761
KenyaS1	Ts18.60
Japan ¥1	Ts16.04
S Africa R1	Ts157.4
Norway NOK1	Ts263.8
Sweden SEK1	Ts242.6
Poland PLN1	Ts519.8

and use the latter to get money out of cashpoints in Tanzania? (We can forget about travellers' cheques nowadays, as banks no longer seem to accept them.) Overall, we advocate bringing credit/debit cards, with a few hundred US dollars in cash as back-up in case you can't find a cashpoint that will take your card.

Tanzanian banks prefer cash (US dollars are the only widely accepted currency) for currency exchange. Dollars are also very useful for those occasions when the Tanzanian shilling is not accepted, such as when paying for upmarket hotel rooms and air tickets, both of which, officially at least, must be paid for in hard currency. The downside of cash is, of course, that it is also the riskiest way to carry money. How many dollars you bring, of course, depends on how much of your trip you've paid for in advance, how long you're staying, and what you hope to do while there.

You will need cash for **tipping**. For a rough guide as to how much you should take, see p43 – then add a few dollars, just in case.

One more thing: when it comes to bringing dollars, **make sure they are new notes** – notes printed before 2003 are seldom accepted.

Credit/debit cards Using a credit/debit card is now the most popular option. **Credit cards** are useful in major tourist hotels, restaurants, gift shops and airline offices and their usefulness is growing every day. Both **debit and credit cards** enable you to withdraw cash from an ATM; Visa is probably the more useful card in that you can withdraw money from more ATMs than with MasterCard. However, do note that credit cards tend to be more expensive as you get charged interest from the moment that you withdraw money (unless you 'pre-load' your card so it is in credit and remains so even after you've withdrawn money). Of course, you run the risk that the cash machines will reject your card or, worse, swallow it, leaving you stuck in Africa with no means of support. So, we recommend you bring one Visa and one MasterCard, to increase your chances of being able to withdraw cash from an ATM.

❏ Tourist information offices

Dar es Salaam (see p147) and **Arusha** (see p167) are the only cities with tourist information offices.

Outside Tanzania there's a tourist office in New York (☎ 212-447 0027), 347 Fifth Ave, Suite 1205, New York, NY 10016. Consulates and embassies around the world (see p351) also have the odd brochure, or you can look at the online information services with 🖥 www.tanzaniatouristboard.com the official site.

Banks, ATMS and moneychangers

Banking hours are typically 8.30am-4pm Monday to Friday, and 8.30am-1pm on Saturday. However, these days many banks no longer change money and if they do the queues for a cashier can be long. As such, most people visit a moneychanger these days to swap their currencies. **Moneychangers** are fairly ubiquitous (though less so now that ATMs are increasing in number) and we have pointed out some of them in the city/town guides.

As a general rule, you get a better rate for large denomination bills (US$50 and $100 bills) than small ones. Keep your **exchange receipts** so that when you leave the country you can change your spare shillings back into hard currency. They rarely check, but you never know.

There are **ATM**s ('**cashpoints**') in every town in Tanzania and Kenya. Not only are they getting more numerous, they are also becoming more reliable; most people have no trouble finding a machine that is reliable.

GETTING AROUND

Public transport in Tanzania is unreliable, uncomfortable, slow, and not recommended for those with either long legs or haemorrhoids. It is also dangerous. A little-known but highly pertinent fact about Tanzania's transport system is that 8% of deaths in Tanzanian hospitals are road-accident victims. According to official sources, between June 2008 and July 2012 Tanzania suffered an average of 3875 road deaths per year – and these are just the ones the authorities know about. Reckless driving is by far and away the biggest cause of most of these accidents, with poor maintenance of roads and vehicles also significant contributors.

That said, Tanzanian transport is cheap, convenient and, it must be said, cheerful: conversation usually flows pretty easily on a bus or dalla-dalla (providing you can make yourself heard above the noise of the stereo). And while the average road is little more than a necklace of potholes strung together with tyre tracks, the main roads between towns are splendid, well-maintained tarmac strips – with speed ramps to deter drivers from going too fast.

By bus

The most luxurious form of ground transport is provided by the **express bus** companies; a few of them, such as Dar Express, deserve their reputation for safety and comfort; you may want to ask your hotel or a local which bus company is currently the most reliable. These express buses run to a fixed timetable and will leave without you if you're late. Buy your ticket in advance.

The cheaper alternative is the ordinary buses or **Coasters** – minibuses which leave when full. These are cheap but you definitely get what you pay for. As with all forms of local transport, ask your fellow passengers what the correct fare is before handing any money over to the 'conductor'; rip-offs are the rule rather than the exception on many journeys. In addition there are the indigenous **dalla-dallas**: minibuses (smaller than Coasters) plying routes around and between neighbouring towns. They're usually a tight squeeze as

TANZANIA

drivers pile in the customers to maximize their takings. If you're being pushed into one that looks full-to-bursting, simply refuse to enter; there'll be another along in a minute. In Kenya these minibuses are known as **matatus**.

Finally, there are the **shuttle buses** that convey passengers from Nairobi to Arusha/Moshi and back. Comfy and reasonably priced, they're by far the best way of crossing the border overland. See the relevant chapter for more details.

By car

You can **hire a car** in Dar es Salaam and from many of the bigger tour and trekking agencies in Moshi and Arusha – usually with driver included. Make sure you choose a vehicle that is suitable for your requirements. Don't, for example, be tempted to conduct your own off-road safari in a two-wheel drive.

You can **hitch** around the country, though payment will often be expected from a Western tourist; it is, of course, wiser not to hitch alone.

By train

Tanzania has only a skeleton train service; services to Arusha and Moshi have long since stopped, though the stations and tracks are still there in both towns and are interesting places to look around if you're very bored.

By air

Flying is an efficient way to cover the vast distances of Tanzania, and there are several small chartered and scheduled airlines including Coastal Air, Precision Air, Air Excel, fly540, ZantasAir, ZanAir and the new budget airline Fastjet. For details of airlines flying to Kilimanjaro, see p349.

ACCOMMODATION

Tanzania's guesthouses and hotels can be split into three sorts: those that welcome tourists, those that accept them, and those that refuse them altogether. The latter are usually the cheapest, double as brothels, have minimum security and advertising and can safely be ignored.

Room rates for the other two start at about Ts12,000/18,000 per night for a single/double; dorms are a rarity (though where you can find them they're about Ts10,000 per night). Bear in mind that many hotels still have two tariffs, one for locals and people living in Tanzania (commonly known as the 'residents' rate') and a more expensive one for foreigners. If business is slow, it doesn't take much effort to persuade some of the smaller hotels to charge you the residents' rate, regardless of whether you live in Tanzania or not.

Always take your time when choosing a hotel, particularly in the towns featured here where there are lots of options. **Standards** vary widely but you'll probably be surprised at how pleasant some of them can be, with mosquito nets and attached bathrooms and maybe even a telly.

In Nairobi, safety is a concern in some of the hotels, though the ones we have chosen to recommend in this book were fine. Accommodation on Zanzibar, incidentally, is generally much more expensive. Note, too, that in Swahili *hotel* or *hoteli* sometimes means restaurant rather than accommodation (*mazate*).

For details of **accommodation on the mountain**, see p250.

ELECTRICITY

Tanzania is powered by 250V, 50 cycles, AC network. Those bringing electrical items from home may wish to invest in a power breaker: Tanzania's electricity supply can be erratic on occasions and power surges could seriously impair the efficacy of your electrical instruments, if not melt them altogether. Plugs and sockets vary in style, though by far the most common are the British three-square-pin or, less common, European two-round-pin style.

TIME

Tanzania is **three hours ahead of GMT** and thus two hours ahead of Western Europe, eight ahead of New York, eleven ahead of San Francisco, one ahead of Johannesburg, seven hours behind Sydney and nine behind Wellington.

A point of endless confusion for travellers, and with the potential to cause major problems for the uninitiated, is the concept known as **Swahili time**, used throughout much of East Africa where Swahili is the *lingua franca*. Swahili time begins at dawn, or more precisely at 6am. In other words, 6am is their hour zero (and thus equivalent to our midnight), 7am in our time is actually one o'clock in Swahili and so on.

To add further confusion, this system for telling the time is not prevalent everywhere in Tanzania, with most offices, timetables etc using the standard style for telling the time. Whenever you're quoted a time it should be obvious which clock they are using but always double check.

BUSINESS HOURS

These are typically 8am-noon and 2-4.30pm Monday to Friday, and 8am-12.30pm for some private businesses on Saturdays.

POST AND TELECOMMUNICATIONS

Telephone

The incredible rise in popularity of **mobile phones** in Tanzania means that the old Yellow TTCL **cardphones** are obsolete these days, though the offices – and the phones themselves – are still present. If you're staying in

> The telephone country access code for Tanzania is ☎ 255.

Tanzania for some time you'll find it far easier and often cheaper to invest in a Tanzanian mobile phone or at least a **Tanzanian SIM card** (Ts2000) and a pay-as-you-go voucher (available just about everywhere).

If your existing phone is unlocked you can put the SIM card straight in there; if not, you can pick a phone up cheaply in Tanzania or see if you can get your phone unlocked (Bensons in Arusha offer this service – see p171 – but when I checked they were asking for US$200 to unlock my iPhone4, and said it would take five days; so I bought an old mobile from the street instead for Ts25,000). Buying a SIM in Tanzania can save you a small fortune in bills compared to using a mobile and SIM from your home country. That said, telephoning in Tanzania has always been a hit-and-miss affair, and sometimes it's an illogical one too. Phone a Tanzanian landline from a Tanzanian mobile, for example, and you often still have to dial Tanzania's international dialling code (+255). Furthermore, if you are having trouble ringing home, try tacking an extra '0' on to the front of the international dialling code: for example, if you wish to ring the UK but the phone continues to bar your call, dial ☎ 00044 (or ☎ 000144) rather than just ☎ 0044 (or ☎ 00144). But even if you follow these rules, there are still occasions when it's impossible to get any sort of connection.

Of course the best and cheapest way of ringing abroad is **via Skype and the internet**; most hotels now offer some sort of internet service. If the speed is fast enough it's possible to have a reasonably fluent conversation; though this does mean of course that you'll need to have, or borrow, some sort of laptop/iPad/computer to facilitate this.

Internet access

In contrast to the phones, Tanzania's **internet cafés** are havens of efficiency and value, charging about Ts2000 per hour. Some of the equipment is a little dated, as you'd probably expect, and the speed of the connection can be a little slow (though since the arrival of broadband the situation has improved markedly).

If you've already tried to make a phone call or post a letter here, you'll come to regard the internet with something approaching affection: it's your best chance of keeping in regular touch with home. Furthermore, it's a rare hotel/restaurant/café that doesn't offer its guests some sort of wi-fi connection. In the city guides we have picked out some of the better internet cafés for those who don't have their own laptop etc with them.

Post

Thanks to the presence of the English missionaries, matters have already advanced so far in Jagga that the Europeans stationed there get their letters and newspapers not more than a month old. **Hans Meyer** *Across East African Glaciers* (1891)

The postal system in Tanzania has improved since Meyer's day but not massively. Reasonably reliable and reliably sluggish, things do occasionally get 'lost in the post' but most gets through… eventually. You should allow about two weeks for letters to reach their destinations from Dar, a day or two longer from regional post offices. The much-loved **poste restante** system has pretty much disappeared.

Media

You'll find that **BBC World** and **CNN** are both popular in Tanzania and often fill air-time on the national channels during the day (one national station, ITV, for example, switches to CNN at 8am every morning). **Channel O** is Africa's MTV equivalent and a favourite with waitresses who often have it blaring out in the restaurant while you're trying to eat. **EA TV** is the latest and trendiest station, broadcasting all over East Africa.

The rise in the popularity of television – particularly since satellite TV from the Middle East and elsewhere started to become available – has led to an equivalent fall in the popularity of radio, though **Radio Free Africa**, **Kiss FM** and **Radio 1** all have reasonable audiences.

❏ **HOLIDAYS AND FESTIVALS**

The following are **public holidays** in Tanzania; note that some (eg Zanzibar's Revolutionary Day) are not held nationwide but are celebrated locally only.

1 Jan	New Year	**7 July**	Industrial Day
12 Jan	Zanzibar Revolutionary Day	**8 Aug**	Farmers' Day
April	Good Friday/Easter	**9 Dec**	Independence/Republic Days
26 April	Union Day (National Day)	**25 Dec**	Christmas Day
1 May	International Labour Day	**26 Dec**	Boxing Day

Islamic holy days

The dates of the following holidays are determined according to the Islamic lunar calendar and as such do not fall on the same date each year. Their **approximate** dates for the next few years are given. The extent to which these days are celebrated and whether these celebrations will impact on your holiday depends to a great extent on where you are in Tanzania; remember that around Kilimanjaro the people are largely Christian so the impact tends to be minimal, though some shops and businesses close.

● **Id al Fitr** (End of Ramadan – a two-day celebration) approx dates: 28 July 2014, 17 July 2015, 5 July 2016
● **Eid El-Hajj** (also known as Eid El-Adha or Eid Al-Kebir) approx dates: 4 October 2014, 23 September 2015, 11 September 2016

The *Guardian* is the pick of the **English-language newspapers** for world events, while the *Daily News* is more Tanzania-centric (and the country's oldest paper). The weekly *Arusha Times* covers local news stories in its own inimitable fashion. There are a couple of Kenyan newspapers such as the *East African* which feel more professional and sophisticated and are worth checking out.

FOOD

The native foods do not offer much variety, though they do differ widely in different districts; but if the traveller is not too dainty and is prepared to make the best of what is to be had, it is wonderful what can be done. **Hans Meyer** *Across East African Glaciers* (1891)

Tanzanian food is, on the whole, unsubtle but tasty and filling. If there's one dish that could be described as quintessentially East African, it would be *nyama choma* – plain and simple grilled meat. If the restaurant is any good they'll add some sauces – often curry and usually fiery – to accompany your meat and the whole lot will usually come with rice, chips, plantains or the ubiquitous *ugali* (a stodgy cornmeal or cassava mush). Usually served in a single cricket-ball-sized lump that you can pick up with your fork in one go, ugali has the consistency of plasticine and gives the impression of being not so much cooked as congealed. A bit bland, it nevertheless performs a vital role as a plate-filler and acts as a soothing balm when eating some of the country's more thermogenic curries.

The food of the dominant tribe of the Kilimanjaro region, the Chagga, is dominated by bananas, which you'll see growing all over the lower slopes of the mountain. Not only do they brew their own beer from them (see p88) but the fruit (and its cousin the plantain) crop up in dishes such as *mchemsho*, a kind of banana and meat stew.

Aside from the Chagga's bias for the banana, the indigenous cuisine of Tanzania caters mainly for carnivores, allowing the country's significant Indian minority to corner the market for vegetarian fare. Indian restaurants abound in Dar, Moshi, Arusha (and Nairobi), catering mainly for the budget end of the market; that said, the cuisine at a top-notch Indian restaurant in Tanzania is amongst the best served outside Britain or India.

A good website that includes a section on Tanzanian dishes is 🖥 www.food bycountry.com. For details about food on the trail, see p251.

DRINKS

The usual world-brand **soft drinks** are on sale in Tanzania. Juices are widely available and pretty cheap, though be warned: a lot of upset stomachs are caused by insanitary juice stalls. Coconuts are far safer and are ubiquitous at the coast and on Zanzibar. **Alcoholic** drinks include a range of beers including the tasty Serengeti (our favourite), Ndovu (a pretty close second), Safari and Kilimanjaro from Tanzania, Tusker from Kenya, and the potent Chagga home-brew *mbege*, or banana beer. You'll usually be offered this if you take a stroll around Marangu (or indeed any Chagga village), particularly if it's market day when the world (or at least the male half of it) seems to be intent on obliterating itself by imbibing vast quantities of the stuff from jerrycans.

THINGS TO BUY

kíRìmíyà – A Chagga term meaning a treat brought home by mother to kids upon completion of a successful day at market From **University of Oregon**'s *Word of the Week* website

Tanzania has the usual supply of weavings and woodcarvings, T-shirts, textiles and trinkets. The shops in Arusha in particular are becoming more sophisticated and expert at appealing to Western tastes. Amongst the T-shirts, at least in Moshi, are a number of variations on the 'I climbed Kili' motif. Witchcraft items, battle shields, Masai beads and necklaces as well as bows and

About bargaining

I promise this is the first and last time I will lecture you on how to behave. But I just have one simple message: **please don't bargain too hard**.

I used to take a certain amount of pride in how cheaply I could obtain various goods and services in the country and how tenaciously I would stick to my price until, out of sheer desperation (probably to get rid of me as much as anything else) the vendor would relent and give me the price I demanded. (Not asked, note, but demanded.)

It is only recently, having now spent a fair bit of time there, that I am able to see the living conditions of many people in this country – and I realize how wrong my approach to bargaining has been. Sure, nobody wants to get ripped off and if you think you're being taken for a sucker it's important that you stand up for yourself. Furthermore, it is the culture to haggle in this country and you will be expected to engage in some sort of a 'discussion' about how much you're willing to pay for something. But do it with a smile and treat the process as a bit of a game rather than a war to be fought to the death. Because if you've just spent 20 minutes haggling over some item in order to save yourself the equivalent of 40p, it's not just the price that will have been reduced – you'll probably find your self-respect has shrunk too.

arrows are up for grabs in the high streets of Moshi and Arusha. Kilimanjaro **coffee** makes for a good and inexpensive present for the person who's been feeding your cat while you've been away; buy it in a wooden box or velvet bag in a souvenir store, or pick a simple bag of it up for a third of the price in a supermarket. Though not grown on the slopes of Kilimanjaro, the organic Africafe has been described by one enthusiastic reader as the best instant coffee in the world and makes an affordable souvenir.

Another popular souvenir is the *kanga*, the typical Tanzanian woman's dress that usually has a message or motto running through the print, or the similar but smarter and message-less *kitenge*.

It depends on your taste, of course, but Zanzibar is widely reckoned to have a better selection and higher quality of souvenirs (though I think the shops of Arusha are catching up; check out Blue Heron Café, for example, or the souvenir/furniture outlets by Shoprite in the TFA complex). Some of the items in Zanzibar, particularly the carved door jambs and furniture, are lovely, though difficult to get home; furthermore, these people are extremely tough negotiators, know the true price of everything and bargains are few.

In the afternoon I bought some small capes made of hyrax skins, of a style formerly much in vogue, and two long spears of the most modern narrow-bladed pattern, which were quite works of art. **Hans Meyer** *Across East African Glaciers* (1891)

SECURITY

Tanzania is a pretty safe country, at least by the standards of its neighbours. That said, the standards of its neighbours are very, very low indeed – as anybody who has already been to Kenya's capital, known to many travellers as 'Nairobberi', will testify – so do take care. Violent crime is relatively rare during the day but

not unknown, especially in Dar es Salaam and Arusha, while pickpockets are common throughout the country and reach epidemic proportions in busy areas such as markets and stations. The best (if somewhat contradictory) advice is:
● Keep a close eye on your things.
● Don't walk around after dark but take a taxi (particularly in Arusha, and particularly by the bridges over the Themi River along the Nairobi–Moshi Highway, Sokoine Rd where it crosses the Goliondoi River and Nyerere Rd just east of the clock tower, all of which are notorious hotspots for muggers).
● Wear a moneybelt and don't flaunt your wealth.
● Be on your guard against scams and con merchants...

... but at the same time don't let a sense of paranoia ruin your holiday and remember that the vast majority of travellers in East Africa spend their time here suffering no great loss beyond the occasional and inevitable overcharging. If you are unfortunate enough to become the victim of a mugging, remember that it's your *money* they're after, so hand it over – you should be insured against such eventualities anyway. Report the crime as soon as possible to the police, who are generally quite helpful, particularly when the victim is a tourist. This will help to back up your claim from the insurers and may prevent further crimes against tourists in the future.

HEALTH

Diarrhoea is often symptomatic of nothing more than a change of diet rather than any malignant bacteria, so if you get a vicious dose of the runs and your sphincter feels like a cat flap in the Aswan Dam, don't panic and assume you've got food poisoning. That said, there are problems with hygiene in Tanzania, so it's wise to take certain precautions. Take heed of that old adage about patronizing only places that are popular – so food doesn't have a chance to sit around for long – as well as that other one about eating only food that has been cooked, boiled or peeled. Stick to **bottled**, **purified** or **filtered water** and avoid ice unless you're certain it has been made from treated water. Washing fruit, vegetables and your hands and ensuring food is thoroughly cooked can all prevent food poisoning. Shellfish, ice cream from street vendors and under-cooked meat should all be avoided like the plague, or you could end up feeling like you've got it. Slathering yourself in an **insect repellent** to prevent you from being eaten alive by the smaller members of Tanzania's animal kingdom is a good idea too.

We could go into a detailed examination here of all the dreadful diseases you could catch in Tanzania. But the truth is that for most of the worst ones you should have already had an inoculation or be taking some sort of prophylactic. Besides, it's unlikely that you'll suffer anything more in Tanzania than a dose of **the runs**, some **altitude sickness** or, if you're careless, a touch of **sunstroke**. If you've got the first, just rest up and take plenty of fluids until you recover; to protect against the last wear a high-factor sun lotion and a hat and again drink a lot of fluids – maintaining a reasonable salt intake will also help to prevent dehydration. As for altitude sickness, which the majority of trekkers on Kili suffer from to some extent, as well as other ailments that you may contract on the trail, read the detailed discussion on pp222-232.

KILIMANJARO

Geology

Our geological work was especially delightful... Every rock seemed to differ from another, not only in form but in substance. In half-an-hour it was no uncommon thing for us to pick up specimens of as many as two-and-twenty different kinds. **Hans Meyer** *Across East African Glaciers* (1891)

Rising 4800m above the East African plains, 270km from the shores of the Indian Ocean and measuring up to 40km across, Kilimanjaro is a bizarre geological oddity, the tallest freestanding mountain in the world and one formed, shaped, eroded and scarred by the twin forces of fire and ice. It is actually a volcano, or rather three volcanoes, with the two main peaks, **Kibo** and **Mawenzi**, the summits of two of those volcanoes. The story of its creation goes like this:

About three-quarters of a million years ago (making Kilimanjaro a veritable youngster in geological terms) molten lava burst through the fractured surface of the **Great Rift Valley**, a giant fault in the earth's crust that runs through East Africa (see box p92; actually, Kilimanjaro lies 50 miles from the East African Rift Valley along a splinter running off it, but that need not concern us here). The huge pressures behind this eruption pushed part of the Earth's crust skywards, creating the **Shira volcano**, the oldest of the volcanoes forming the Kilimanjaro massif. Shira eventually ceased erupting around 500,000 years ago, collapsing as it did so to form a huge *caldera* (the deep cauldron-like cavity on the summit of a volcano) many times the size of its original crater.

Soon after Shira's extinction, **Mawenzi** started to form following a further eruption within the Shira caldera. Though much eroded, Mawenzi has at least kept some of its volcanic shape to this day. Then, 460,000 years ago, an enormous eruption just west of Mawenzi caused the formation of **Kibo**. Continual subterranean pressure made Kibo erupt several times more, forcing the summit ever higher until reaching a maximum height of about 5900m. A further huge eruption from Kibo 100,000 years later led to the formation of Kilimanjaro's characteristic shiny black stone – which in reality is just solidified black lava, or **obsidian**. This spilled over from Kibo's crater into the Shira caldera and around to the base of the Mawenzi peak, forming the so-called Saddle. Later eruptions created a series of distinctive mini-cones, or **parasitic craters**, that run in a chain south-east and north-west across the mountain, as well as the smaller **Reusch Crater** inside the main Kibo summit. The last volcanic activity of note, just over 200 years ago, left a symmetrical inverted cone of ash in the Reusch Crater, known as the **Ash Pit**, that can still be seen.

Today, **Uhuru Peak**, the highest part of Kibo's crater rim and the goal of most trekkers, stands at around 5895m. The fact that the summit is now around five metres shorter than it was 450,000 years ago can be ascribed to the simple progress of time and the insidious glacial erosion down the millennia. These glaciers, advancing and retreating across the summit, created a series of concentric rings like **terraces** near the top of this volcanic massif on the western side. The Kibo peak has also subsided slightly over time, and about 100,000 years ago a landslide took away part of the external crater, creating **Kibo Barranco**, or the **Barranco Valley** (see p277). The glaciers were also behind the formation of the valleys and canyons, eroding and smoothing the earth into gentle undulations all around the mountain, though less so on the northern side where the glaciers on the whole failed to reach, leaving the valleys sharper and more defined.

While eruptions are unheard of in recent times, Kibo is classified as being dormant rather than extinct, as anybody who visits the inner **Reusch Crater** can testify. A strong sulphur smell still rises from the crater, the earth is hot to touch, preventing ice from forming, while occasionally *fumaroles* (a small hole or opening through which sulphurous gases escape) emerge from the Ash Pit that lies at its heart. Indeed, according to the 2003 Nova documentary *Volcano Above the Clouds*, scientists say that Kibo is actually becoming more active again and that, using estimates based on the temperature of some of the

The Great Rift Valley

According to the theory of plate tectonics, the Earth's exterior is made up of six enormous plates that 'float' across the surface of the planet. Occasionally they collide, causing much buckling and crumpling and the creation of huge mountain ranges such as the Himalayas. At other times, these plates deteriorate and break up because of the massive forces bubbling away in the earth's interior. When this happens, valleys are formed where the Earth fractures.

The Great Rift Valley, whose origins are in Mozambique but which extends right across East Africa to Jordan, is a classic example of a fracture in the Earth's surface caused by the movement of these plates. The same monstrous internal forces that two million years ago caused the disintegration of the tectonic plate and the formation of the Rift Valley are also responsible for the appearance of volcanoes along the valley, as these forces explode through the surface, pushing the Earth's crust skywards and forming – in the case of Kilimanjaro – one huge, 5895m-high geological pimple.

Of Africa's sixteen active volcanoes, all but three belong to the Rift Valley. Kili was just one of a number of volcanic eruptions to hit the valley; others included Ol Molog (to the north-west of Kilimanjaro) and Kilema (to the south-east).

By the way, don't be misled into thinking that these kinds of major tectonic shifts happened millions of years ago and have little relevance to the present day: the earthquake in Arusha in 2007 shows that this 'active rifting' is still occurring, and even minor movements can have major repercussions.

fumaroles, magma lies only 400m below the surface and a cataclysmic landslide, similar in magnitude to the one that led to the formation of the Western Breach, could happen any day!

THE GLACIERS

It is now time to consider the discovery on which Mr Rebmann particularly prides himself, namely, that of perpetual snow. **W D Cooley** *Inner Africa Laid Open* (see box p107)

At first glance, Kilimanjaro's glaciers look like nothing more than big smooth piles of slightly monotonous ice. On second glance they pretty much look like this too. Yet there's much more to Kili's glaciers than meets the eye, for these cathedrals of gleaming blue-white ice are dynamic repositories of climatic history – and they could also be providing us with a portent for impending natural disaster.

You would think that with the intensely strong equatorial sun, glaciers wouldn't exist at all on Kilimanjaro. In fact, it is the brilliant white colour of the ice that allows it to survive as it reflects most of the heat. The dull black lava rock on which the glacier rests, on the other hand, *does* absorb the heat; so while the glacier's surface is relatively unaffected by the sun's rays, the heat generated by the sun-baked rocks underneath leads to glacial melting.

As a result, the glaciers on Kilimanjaro are inherently unstable: the ice at the bottom of the glacier touching the rocks melts, the glaciers lose their 'grip' on the mountain and 'overhangs' occur where the ice at the base has melted away, leaving just the ice at the top to survive. As the process continues the ice fractures and breaks away, exposing more of the rock to the sun... and so the cycle begins again. The sun's effect on the glaciers is also responsible for the spectacular structures – the ice columns and pillars, towers and cathedrals – that are the most fascinating part of the upper slopes of Kibo.

You would have thought that, after 11,700 years of this melting process, (according to recent research, the current glaciers began to form in 9700BC) very little ice would remain on Kilimanjaro. The fact that there are still glaciers is due to the prolonged 'cold snaps', or ice ages, that have occurred down the centuries, allowing the glaciers to regroup and reappear on the mountain. According to estimates, there have been at least eight of these ice ages, the last a rather minor one in the 15th and 16th centuries, a time when London's River Thames frequently froze over and winters were severe. At these times the ice on Kilimanjaro would in places have reached right down to the treeline and both Mawenzi and Kibo would have been covered. At the other extreme, before 9700BC there have been periods when Kilimanjaro was completely free of ice, perhaps for up to 20,000 years.

The woes of Kilimanjaro – where have all the glaciers gone?

Of the 19 square kilometres of glacial ice to be found on Africa, only 2.2 square kilometres can be found on Kilimanjaro. Unfortunately, both figures used to be much higher: Kili's famous white mantle shrunk by a whopping 85%-plus between the first survey of the summit, in 1912, and 2011. Even since 1989, when there were 3.3 square kilometres, there has been a decline of over 33%;

and indeed in the seven years between 2000 and 2006 the mountain lost a quarter of its remaining ice. At that rate, say the experts, Kili will be completely ice-free in just a few decades.

So how high is it then?

Ever since Hans Meyer ambled down from the summit of Kibo and told anybody who'd listen that he'd reached 19,833ft above sea level (**6045m**), an argument has been raging over just how high Africa's highest mountain really is. For though Meyer's estimate is now unanimously agreed to be a wild over-estimate (an inaccuracy that can be ascribed to a combination of the imprecise 19th-century instruments that he had at his disposal, and perhaps a touch of hubris), finding a figure for the height of Kili that meets with a similar consensus of opinion has proved altogether more difficult.

For years the accepted height of Kilimanjaro was **5892m**, that being the figure set by the colonial German authorities some five years after Meyer's ascent. You'll see this figure crop up time and again in many a 20th-century travelogue as well as on pre-World War Two maps of the Kilimanjaro region. Not many people at the time bothered to question this estimate; the few dissenting voices almost invariably belonged to climbers whose own estimates (which were, perhaps unsurprisingly, nearly always over-estimates, ranging from 5930m to 5965m) are today regarded as even more inaccurate than the Germans' figure.

Under British rule the figure was revised to **5895m** following the work of the cartographers of the Ordnance Survey (OS), who mapped Kilimanjaro in 1952; it is this figure that those trekkers who reach the summit will find written on the sign at the top, as well as on the certificates they receive from KINAPA and on the souvenir T-shirts on sale back in Moshi.

The trouble was, of course, that whereas the OS's techniques and equipment may have been state of the art in the 1950s, so were vinyl records and the transistor radio. Technology has moved on a couple of light years since then. The OS's readings for Kilimanjaro had been taken from a distance of over 55km away from the mountain; as such, the probability that the OS's figure was not entirely accurate was rather high.

So in 1999 a team of specialists at University College of Land and Architectural Studies in Arusha together with experts from Karlsruhe University in Germany set out to measure the precise altitude using a technique involving GPS (Global Positioning Satellites) that had previously been used on Everest, and which resulted in that mountain shrinking by a couple of metres to 8846.10m.

The result of their findings in Africa? Kilimanjaro was now a full 2.45 metres shorter than the traditionally accepted figure, at **5892.55m**.

That wasn't the end of the story, however, for in 2008 a team of 19 boffins from six countries decided that even this measurement wasn't accurate enough, for reasons too complicated for a layman to understand (and I include myself in this category), and by combining GPS data with gravimetric observations (where variations in a gravitational field are measured) they came up with a figure of **5890.79m** for the orthometric height (ie the distance above the mean sea level).

So is Kilimanjaro shrinking? Or was the old estimate of 5895m just plain inaccurate? Unfortunately, the scientists have yet to tell us that. And while they have every confidence in the accuracy of their latest readings, the old figure of 5895m is still the official figure and the one you'll hear bandied about by tour operators, guides, porters and anybody else you care to speak to; and until we are told otherwise, 5895m is the one we're using in this book too.

'We found that the summit of the ice fields has lowered by at least 17 metres since 1962,' said Professor Lonnie Thompson of Ohio State University. 'That's an average loss of about a half-metre (a foot and a half) in height each year.'

The big question, therefore, is not whether they are shrinking, but why – and should we be concerned? Certainly glacial retreats are nothing new: Hans Meyer, the first man to conquer Kilimanjaro, returned in 1898, nine years after his ascent, and was horrified by the extent to which the glaciers had shrunk. The ice on Kibo's slopes had retreated by 100m on all sides, while one of the notches he had used to gain access to the crater in 1889 – now called Hans Meyer Notch – was twice as wide, with the ice only half as thick. Nor are warnings of the complete disappearance of the glaciers anything new: in 1899 Meyer himself predicted that they would be gone within three decades and the top of Kili would be decorated with nothing but bare rock.

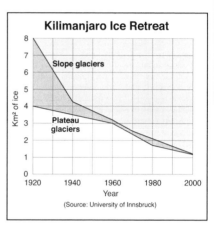

Kilimanjaro Ice Retreat

Km² of ice

Slope glaciers

Plateau glaciers

Year

(Source: University of Innsbruck)

What concerns today's scientists, however, is that this current reduction in the size of Kili's ice-cap does seem to be more rapid and more extensive than previous shrinkages. But is it really something to worry about, or merely the latest in a series of glacial retreats experienced by Kili over the last few hundred years?

Professor Thompson and his team attempted to find answers to all these questions. In January and February 2000 they drilled six ice cores through three of Kibo's glaciers in order to research the history of the mountain's climate over the centuries. A weather station was also placed on the Northern Icefield to see how the current climate affects the build-up or destruction of glaciers.

Their conclusions were not good. In a speech made at the annual meeting of the American Association for the Advancement of Science in February 2001, the professor declared that while he cannot be sure why the ice is melting away so quickly, what is certain is that if the glaciers continue to shrink at current rates, the summit could be completely ice-free by 2015. Other, later calculations have extended this figure to 2040 or so: Austrian scientist Georg Kaser, who together with Thomas Moelg has been studying new glacial data, said in 2007 'We have done different kinds of modelling and we expect the plateau glaciers to be gone roughly within 30 or 40 years from now, but we have a certain expectation that the slope glaciers may last longer.'

But whatever estimates you believe, there can be no doubt that the glaciers are in serious trouble. This doesn't surprise locals who live in the shadow of Kilimanjaro, some of whom believe they know why the ice is disappearing.

Another inconvenient truth

In 2007 Kilimanjaro's disappearing glaciers became *the* symbol of global warming when it featured in Al Gore's film *An Inconvenient Truth*. His use of Africa's highest mountain seemed both an obvious and potent choice: everybody marvels at Kilimanjaro's snowy summit and the thought of it being bare by 2020 is a distressing one. Indeed, Al Gore wasn't the only one to use Kilimanjaro's glaciers as a microcosm of man's deleterious effect on the environment: Greenpeace even held a satellite news conference from the summit in order to highlight the decline of Africa's largest collection of glaciers due to climate change.

However, there are several groups who think that it was wrong to use Kilimanjaro as a poster-child for global warming. Among their number are those who deny altogether that anything is wrong. It may not surprise you to find that the then minister in charge of tourism in Tanzania, Ms Shamsa Mwangunga, claimed in July 2008 that the snows of Kilimanjaro will be with us in perpetuity, citing eyewitness evidence that the glaciers were, contrary to all scientific opinion, actually growing. Nor was she the first minister to hold these opinions: one of her predecessors, Ms Zakhia Meghji, expressed similar sentiments when she held office in 2002.

While most dismissed Ms Mwangunga's sentiments as those of someone who clearly has a vested interest in telling the world that the snows aren't melting, there are others who remain uneasy at Kilimanjaro being used by the green lobby in this way. The main concern is that the mountain is a bad example to use when discussing global warming. As we said earlier, Kilimanjaro's glaciers have been shrinking for the best part of a century, long before humans began pumping large amounts of carbon dioxide into the atmosphere. Indeed, it is believed that they have been expanding and contracting regularly over the past few thousand years – and separating this natural contraction from the reduction caused by man's effect on the climate is no simple matter. Furthermore, recent data from Kilimanjaro show temperatures never rise above freezing on the summit – so how can a warmer climate be responsible for melting glaciers?

The Austrian Georg Kaser, who has studied the glacial decline on Kilimanjaro for several years (see p95), is one who believes that global warming is *not* melting the ice on Kilimanjaro. Instead, he concluded that the loss of ice was driven by a lack of snowfall and sublimation (this is when ice essentially skips the melting step and simply evaporates, and is caused by exposure to sunlight and dry air), with melting having only a negligible effect. And while climate change could have led to a decline in precipitation (snowfall) that replenishes the glaciers – after all, there have been droughts in much of Tanzania in the past few years – contrary to popular wisdom the glaciers, while undoubted shrinking by about a metre a year, aren't actually melting. Indeed, if the current climate models are correct, global warming should actually *increase* rainfall in Eastern Africa. This should mean greater snowfall on the summit of Kilimanjaro, and thus, perversely, could be the thing that saves Kilimanjaro's snows!

And it is this last point that worries those who believe in the reality of global warming but are uneasy about Kilimanjaro being used by Al Gore and his supporters in this way: that global warming *is* responsible for the decline of many other glaciers in the world – but *not* on Kilimanjaro. And that by citing Kilimanjaro's shrinking glaciers as an example of the effects of global warming, they are allowing climate-change sceptics the chance to prove, justifiably, that it isn't so – which could then open the door to them dismissing other climate-change trends that *are* true, thereby diluting the climate change lobby's arguments.

According to an AllAfrica.com news report, a 50-year-old native of Old Moshi, Mama Judith Iyatuu, reckons that it's the evil eyes of the white tourists which are melting the ice, while 65-year-old Mzee Ruaici Thomas from Meela village believes that the ice is disappearing because God is unhappy with mankind.

Whatever the reasons, if Kilimanjaro were to lose its snowy top, the repercussions would be extremely serious, particularly for those villagers who live on the mountain slopes and for whom the glaciers are a source of water.

But many reckon it is more than just a local problem. For if the scientists are to be believed, what is happening on Kilimanjaro is a microcosm of what could face the entire world in the future. Even more worryingly, more and more scientists are now starting to think that this future is probably already upon us.

For an excellent (and refreshingly readable) summary of Kilimanjaro's glaciers as at 2011, check out Douglas Hardy's entry for the mountain in the *Encyclopedia of Snow, Ice & Glaciers*, available online at:

💻 www.geo.umass.edu/climate/tanzania/pubs/hardy_2011_encyclo-sig.pdf.

Climate

Kilimanjaro is big enough to have its own microclimates. The theory behind this pattern is essentially very simple. Strong winds travel across the oceans, drawing moisture up as they go. Eventually they collide with a large object – such as a mountain like Kilimanjaro. The winds are pushed upwards as they hit the mountain slopes, and the fall in temperature and atmospheric pressure leads to precipitation or, as it's more commonly called, snow and rain.

In one year there are two rain-bearing seasonal winds buffeting Kilimanjaro. The south-east trade wind bringing rain from the Indian Ocean arrives between March and May. Because the mountain is the first main obstacle to the wind's progress, and by far the largest, a lot of rain falls on Kili at this time and for this reason the March-to-May season is known as the **long rains**. This is the main wet season on Kilimanjaro. As the south-east trade winds run into the southern side of Kili, so the southern slopes tend to be damper and

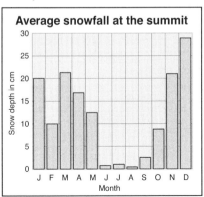

Adapted from DR Hardy's *Kilimanjaro snow* in: AM Waple & JH Lawrimore (eds.) *State of the Climate in 2002*, Bull. Am. Meteorol. Soc., 84, S48

as a consequence more fertile, with the forest zone much broader than on the northern slopes.

Then there are the dry **'anti-trade' winds** from the north-east which carry no rain and hit the mountain between May and October. These anti-trade winds, which blow, usually very strongly, across the Saddle (the broad valley between Kilimanjaro's two peaks), also serve to keep the south-east trade winds off the upper reaches of Kilimanjaro, ensuring that the rain from the long monsoon season stays largely on the southern side below 3000m, with little falling above this. Which is why, at this time of year, the first day's walk for trekkers on the Marangu, Umbwe or Machame routes is usually conducted under a canopy of cloud, while from the second day onwards they enjoy unadulterated sunshine.

A second seasonal rain-bearing wind, the north-east monsoon, having already lost much of its moisture after travelling overland for a longer period, brings a **short rainy season** between November and December. While the northern side receives most of the rain to fall in this season, it is far less than the rain brought by the south-east trade winds and as a result the northern side of Kili remains on the whole drier and more barren than the southern side. Once again, the rain falls mainly below 3000m.

❑ Trekking in the rainy season

For those who absolutely have no choice but to walk during the rainy season, don't get too downhearted. For one thing, it's not uncommon for the rains not to come at all – devastating for the local farmers, of course, but good news for your average trekker. (We were on the mountain in late November once and didn't see a drop of rain the whole time we were there.) And even when there is rain, it doesn't necessarily make for a dreadful trek. We have had letters from several readers who positively recommend the experience. For example, take Jack Hollinghurst from the UK who wrote the following way back in 2006:

'...*I do think that you don't give enough encouragement to walking in the rainy season. I was forced to walk at this time by holiday dates and thought it excellent. Due to the hugely reduced numbers of trekkers on the mountain me and my friend were given our own room at all of the huts (including Kibo, where it is about 12 beds to a room) and* [your] *advice about having dinner early at Horombo is irrelevant as there were about five other groups there at the most.*

'...*the walking is* [also] *much more enjoyable when you have some peace and quiet...Maybe you should advise walkers to wear waterproof trousers at this time of year (although I didn't take any and was fine) but otherwise I wouldn't walk at any other time of year.'*

His sentiments were endorsed by Martin Fehr from Denmark, who wrote to me early in 2009:

'*Don't be afraid to recommend climbing the mountain* [at the end of] *April. Our porters were so happy to have work in low season, we didn't get a lot of rain, and there were absolutely no climbers on the mountain besides us, which made our climb exceptionally great! Plus the top of the mountain was all covered in snow – a challenge, but soooo beautiful (and it was great to be able to "sleigh" down the mountain as well).*

This theory seems fine in principle but it does pose a tricky question: if the precipitation falls below 3000m, how did the snow and ice on the summit of Kibo get there in the first place? The answer, my friend, is blowing in the (anti-trade) wind: though these winds normally blow very strongly, as those who walk north across the Saddle will testify, they occasionally drop in force, allowing the south-east trade winds that run beneath them to climb up the southern slopes to the Saddle and on to the summit. Huge banks of clouds then develop and snow falls.

This, at least, is the theory of Kilimanjaro's climate. In practice, the only predictable thing about the weather is its unpredictability. What is certain is that, with rain more abundant the further one travels down the mountain slopes, life, too, becomes more abundant – as the Fauna and Flora section on p124 illustrates.

The temperature at the summit: bikinis – or brass monkeys?

It's a question many trekkers want to know the answer to: just how cold is it on the summit of Kilimanjaro? Well, there is an old mountaineer's saw that says that, above 4000m, for every 150 metres you ascend the temperature drops by 1°C. Given that the average temperature at around 4000m is 0°C, by the time

However, Martin does go on to warn: *'Of course, by climbing the mountain during the low season you are very much at the mercy of the elements – and conditions can be quite extreme at this time.'*

Martin's experience – and his opinion of walking in the low season – seems similar to that of Tom Stoa, another reader and Kili conqueror who sticks up for the rainy season:

'I went in April, 2008, despite the recommendations of you and everyone else to avoid April due to weather, simply because that is when I could go. No regrets. I chose the Marangu route, 6 days, because of the huts – I figured that despite the rain, we would be warm, dry and comfortable in the huts at least. And that was correct (and we were lucky, it mostly just rained at night). Being the off season, my son and I had a hut to ourselves each night, and the big dining hut was also nearly empty.

We made the summit just fine. My only regret was not having crampons for the big icy snowfield between Hans Meyer Cave and before Gillman's Point. We were gingerly kicking steps in the snow, or trying to step in the steps of others. Having some alpine climbing experience, I know that a slip would have resulted in a nasty, long slide with a crash onto the rocks below. I know that crampons are not customary on Kili, but for that route, on that day, they would have made all the difference between a very sketchy and slow slog, versus an "easy" and safe walk up.'

So there you have it. It would seem that if you have an adventurous spirit, maybe consider the Marangu Route (the only route on the mountain where you sleep in huts rather than under canvas), have crampons and/or ice axes, can put up with some pretty extreme conditions and are prepared for some possibly treacherous walking – the low season is a fine time to climb!

For predictions of what the weather will be like in the immediate future, visit 💻 www .mountain-forecast.com – the best website we found for Kili's immediate climbing conditions.

KILIMANJARO

you reach the summit you would have ascended through about 13 lots of 150m. In other words, the temperature would be around -13°C. Pretty chilly you may think, but bearable. But this, of course, fails to take into consideration the wind-chill factor which can push that figure even further downwards, to around -30°C – though these extremes are rare, as you can see in the graph. This shows the average month-ly air temperatures over the year at weather stations at 2340m, 3630m, 4570m and 5800m. It gives you an idea of how much the temperature drops as you ascend through

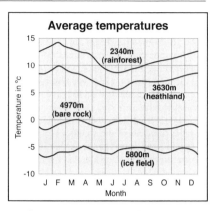

Temperature graph adapted from *General Characteristics of Air Temperature and Humidity Variability on Kilimanjaro, Tanzania* by WJ Duane, NC Pepin, ML Losleben and DR Hardy

the various vegetation zones: montane rainforest (2340m), heathland (3630m), alpine desert (4570m), and on an icefield at 5800m, just 95m below Uhuru Peak. You can see that even in the warmest month the mean temperature does-n't rise above -5°C at the top; the mean temperature at the summit, by the way, is -7.1°C. We have also mapped mean precipitation (ie rain – or, at this altitude, snow) at this higher weather station.

It is beyond the scope of this book to go into Kili's climates and weather patterns in any further detail, so instead I'll just point you in the direction of the University of Massachusetts' geoscience website ⌨ www.geo.umass.edu/cli mate/kibo.html which summarizes data from their summit weather station. You can also find on this website the fascinating *General Characteristics of Air Temperature and Humidity Variability on Kilimanjaro, Tanzania* by WJ Duane, NC Pepin, ML Losleben and DR Hardy, from which much of the material in this section was taken. While for the latest on the readings from the weather stations and other news, do visit their blog at ⌨ kiboice.blogspot.co.uk.

The history of Kilimanjaro

EARLY HISTORY

Thanks to several primitive **stone bowls** found on the lower slopes of Kilimanjaro, we know that man has lived on or around the mountain since at least 1000BC. We also know that, over the last 500 years, the mountain has at various times acted as a navigational aid for traders travelling between the interior and the coast, a magnet for Victorian explorers, a political pawn to be traded between European superpowers who carved up East Africa, a battlefield for these same superpowers, and a potent symbol of independence for those who wished to rid themselves of these colonial interlopers. Unfortunately, little is known about the history of the mountain during the intervening 2500 years.

It's a fair bet that Kilimanjaro's first inhabitants, when they weren't fashioning bowls out of the local terrain, would have spent much of their time hunting and gathering the local flora and fauna, Kilimanjaro being a fecund source of both. Add to this its reputation as a reliable region both for fresh drinking water and materials – wood, stones, mud, vines etc – for building, and it seems reasonable to suppose that Kilimanjaro would have been a highly desirable location for primitive man and would have played a central role in the lives of those who chose to take up residence on its slopes.

Unfortunately, those looking to piece together a comprehensive history of the first inhabitants of Kilimanjaro rather have their work cut out. There are no documents recording the life and times of the people who once lived on the mountain; not much in the way of any oral history that has been passed down through the generations; and, stone bowls apart, little in the way of archaeological evidence from which to draw any inferences. So, while we can *assume* many things about the lives of Kilimanjaro's first inhabitants, we can be certain about nothing: and if Kilimanjaro did have a part to play in the pre-colonial history of the region, that history, and the mountain's significance within it, has, alas, now been lost to us.

And so it is to the notes of foreign travellers that we must turn in order to find the earliest accounts of Kilimanjaro. These descriptions are usually rather brief, often inaccurate and more often than not based on little more than hearsay and rumour rather than actual first-hand evidence.

One of the first-ever descriptions of East Africa is provided by *Periplus of the Erythraean Sea*, written anonymously in AD45. *Periplus* – a contender for the title of the world's first-ever guidebook – is a manual for seafarers to the ports of Africa, Arabia and India and includes details of the sea routes to China. In it the author tells of a land called Azania, in which one could find a prosperous market town, Rhapta, where 'hatchets and daggers and awls ... a great quantity of ivory and rhinoceros horn and tortoise shell' were all traded. Yet interestingly, there is no mention of any snow-capped mountain lying nearby; indeed, reading *Periplus* one gets the impression that the author considered Rhapta to be just about the end of the world:

Beyond Opone [modern-day Ras Harun on the Somalian coast] *there are the small and great bluffs of Azania ... twenty-three days sail beyond there lies the very last market town of the continent of Azania, Rhapta ...*

Just over a hundred years later, however, **Ptolemy of Alexandria**, astronomer and the founder of scientific cartography, wrote of lands lying to the south of Rhapta where barbaric cannibals lived near a wide shallow bay and where, inland, one could find a '**great snow mountain**'. Mountains that wear a mantle of snow are pretty thin on the ground in Africa; indeed, there is only one real candidate – and that, of course, is Kilimanjaro.

How exactly Ptolemy came by his information is unknown, for he almost certainly never saw Kilimanjaro for himself. Nevertheless, based on hearsay though it may have been, this is the earliest surviving written mention of Africa's greatest mountain. It therefore seems logical to conclude that the outside world first became aware of Africa's tallest mountain in the years between the publication of *Periplus* in AD45, and that of Ptolemy's work, sometime during the latter half of the 2nd century AD.

THE OUTSIDERS ARRIVE
Arabs, an anonymous Chinaman and some Portuguese
Following Ptolemy's description, almost nothing more is written about Kilimanjaro for over a thousand years. The Arabs, arriving on the East African coast in the 6th century, must have heard something about it from the local people with whom they traded. Indeed, the mountain would have proved essential to the natives as they travelled from the interior to the markets on the East

---

Kilimanjaro – the name
The meaning of the name Kilíma Njáro, if it have any meaning, is unknown to the Swáhili... To be analysed, it must first be corrupted. This has been done by Mr Rebmann, who converts Kilíma Njáro into Kilíma dja-aro, which he tells us signifies, "Mountain of Greatness." This etymology... is wholly inadmissable for the following reasons: 1st. It is mere nonsense...

So said **W D Cooley** (see p107), leading British geographer during the mid 19th century in his book *Inner Africa Laid Open*. Nonsense Rebmann's suggestion may have been but in the absence of better alternatives the translation is as valid as any other. For the fact of the matter is that despite extensive studies into the etymology of the name Kilimanjaro, nobody is sure where it comes from or exactly what it means.

When looking for the name's origin, it seems only sensible to begin such a search in one of the local Tanzanian dialects, and more specifically, in the language spoken by those who live in its shadow, namely the Chagga people. True, the name Kilimanjaro bears no resemblance to any word in the Chagga vocabulary; but if we divide it into two parts a few possibilities present themselves. One is that Kilima is derived from the Chagga term *kilelema*, meaning 'difficult or impossible', while *jaro* could come from the Chagga terms *njaare* ('bird') or *jyaro* ('caravan'). In other words, the name Kilimanjaro means something like 'That which is impossible for the bird', or 'That which defeats the caravan' – names which, if this interpretation is correct, are clear references to the sheer enormity of the mountain.

Whilst this is perhaps the most-likely translation, it is not, in itself, particularly convincing, especially when one considers that while the Chagga language would seem the most logical source for the name, the Chagga people themselves do not actually have one single name for the mountain! Instead, they don't see Kilimanjaro as a single entity but as two distinct, separate peaks, namely Mawenzi and Kibo. (These two names, incidentally, are definitely Chagga in origin, coming from the Chagga terms *kimawenzi* – 'having a broken top or summit' – and *kipoo* – 'snow' – respectively.)

African shore: as one of the few unmissable landmarks in a largely featureless expanse of savannah and scrub, and with its abundant streams and springs, the mountain would have been both an invaluable navigational tool and a reliable source of drinking water for the trading caravans. But whether the merchants from the Middle East actually ventured beyond their trading posts on the coast to see the mountain for themselves seems doubtful, and from their records of this time only one possible reference to Kilimanjaro has been uncovered, written by a 13th-century geographer, **Abu'l Fida**, who speaks of a mountain in the interior that was 'white in colour'.

The Chinese, who traded on the East African coast during the same period, also seemed either ignorant or uninterested in the land that lay beyond the coastline and in all their records from this time once again just one scant reference to Kili has been found, this time by an anonymous chronicler who states that the country to the west of Zanzibar 'reaches to a great mountain'.

After 1500 and the exploration and subsequent conquest of the African east coast by Vasco da Gama and those who followed in his wake, the Arabs were replaced as the major trading power in the region by the Portuguese. They

---

Assuming Kilimanjaro isn't Chagga in origin, therefore, the most likely source for the name Kilimanjaro would seem to be Swahili, the majority language of the Tanzanians. Rebmann's good friend and fellow missionary, Johann Ludwig Krapf, wrote that Kilimanjaro could either be a Swahili word meaning 'Mountain of Greatness' – though he is noticeably silent when it comes to explaining how he arrived at such a translation – or a composite Swahili/Chagga name meaning 'Mountain of Caravans'; *jaro*, as we have previously explained, being the Chagga term for 'caravans'. Thus the name could be a reference to the many trading caravans that would stop at the mountain for water. The major flaw with both these theories, however, is that the Swahili term for mountain is not *kilima* but *mlima* – *kilima* is actually the Swahili word for 'hill'!

The third and least-likely dialect from which Kilimanjaro could have been derived is Masai, the major tribe across the border in Kenya. But while the Masai word for spring or water is *njore*, which could conceivably have been corrupted down the centuries to *njaro*, there is no relevant Masai word similar to *kilima*. Furthermore, the Masai call the mountain *Oldoinyo Oibor*, which means 'White Mountain', with Kibo known as the 'House of God', as Hemingway has already told us at the beginning of his – and this – book. Few experts, therefore, believe the name is Masai in origin.

Other theories include the possibility that *njaro* means 'whiteness', referring to the snow cap that Kilimanjaro permanently wears, or that Njaro is the name of the evil spirit who lives on the mountain, causing discomfort and even death to those who climb it. Certainly the folklore of the Chagga people is rich in tales of evil spirits who dwell on the higher reaches of the mountain and Rebmann himself refers to 'Njaro, the guardian spirit of the mountain'; however, it must also be noted that the Chagga's legends make no mention of any spirit going by that name.

So we are none the wiser. But in one sense at least, it's not important: what the mountain means to the many thousands who walk up it every year is far more meaningful than any name we ascribe to it.

proved to be slightly more curious about what lay beyond the coast than their predecessors, perhaps because their primary motive for being there was as much colonial as commercial. A vague but once again unmistakable reference to Kilimanjaro can be found in a book, *Suma de Geographia*, published in 1519, an account of a journey to Mombasa by the Spanish cartographer, astronomer and ship's pilot **Fernandes de Encisco**:

West of Mombasa is the Ethiopian Mount Olympus, which is very high, and further off are the Mountains of the Moon in which are the sources of the Nile.

Amazingly, in the 1400 years since Ptolemy this is only the third reference to Kilimanjaro that has been found; with the return of the Arabs in 1699, it was also to be the last for another hundred years or so. Then, just as the 18th century was drawing to a close, the Europeans once more cast an avaricious eye towards East Africa.

THE 1800s: PIONEERS . . .

With British merchants firmly established on Zanzibar by the 1840s, frequent rumours of a vast mountain situated on the mainland just a few hundred miles from the coast began to reach their ears. British geographers were especially intrigued by these reports, particularly as it provided a possible solution to one of the oldest riddles of Africa: namely, the precise whereabouts of the source of the Nile. Encisco's 16th-century reference to *the Mountains of the Moon in which are the sources of the Nile* (see above) is in fact a mere echo of the work of Ptolemy, writing 1400 years before Encisco, who also cites the Mountains of the Moon as the true origin of the Nile.

But while these Mountains of the Moon were, for more than a millennium, widely accepted in European academia as the place where the Nile rises, nobody had actually bothered to go and find out if this was so – nor, indeed, if these mountains actually existed at all.

Interest in the 'dark continent' was further aroused by the arrival in London in 1834 of one Khamis bin Uthman. Slave dealer, caravan leader and envoy of the then-ruler of East Africa, Seyyid Said, Uthman met many of Britain's leading dignitaries, including the prime minister, Lord Palmerston. He also met and talked at length with the leading African scholar, **William Desborough Cooley**. A decade after this meeting, Cooley wrote his lengthy essay *The Geography of N'yassi, or the Great Lake of Southern Africa Investigated,* in which he not only provides us with another reference to Kilimanjaro – only the fifth in 1700 years – but also becomes the first author to put a name to the mountain:

The most famous mountain of Eastern Africa is Kirimanjara, which we suppose, from a number of circumstances to be the highest ridge crossed on the road to Monomoezi.

Suddenly Africa, long viewed by the West almost exclusively in terms of the lucrative slave trade, became the centre of a flurry of academic interest and the quest to find the true origins of the Nile became something of a *cause célèbre* amongst scholars. Long-forgotten manuscripts and journals from Arab traders and Portuguese adventurers were dusted off and scrutinized for clues to the whereabouts of this most enigmatic river source. Most scholars preferred to conduct their research from the comfort of their leather armchairs; there were others, however, who took a more active approach, and pioneering explorers such as Richard Burton and John Hanning Speke set off to find for themselves the source of the Nile, crossing the entire country we now know as Tanzania in 1857. This was also the age of Livingstone and Stanley, the former venturing deep into the heart of Africa in search of both knowledge and potential converts to Christianity; and the latter in search of the former.

David Livingstone preaching near Lake Tanganyika. (HG Adams, 1873)

. . . AND PREACHERS

Yet for all their brave endeavours, it was not these Victorian action men but one of the humble Christian missionaries who arrived in Africa at about the same time who became the first European to set eyes on Kilimanjaro. **Johannes Rebmann** was a young Swiss-German missionary who arrived in Mombasa in 1846 with an umbrella, a suitcase and a heart full of Christian zeal. His brief was to help **Dr Johann Ludwig Krapf**, a Doctor of Divinity from Tubingen, in his efforts to spread the Christian faith among East Africa's heathen. Krapf was something of a veteran in the missionary field, having previously worked for the London-based Church Missionary Society in Abyssinia. Following the closure of that mission, Krapf sailed down the East African coast to Zanzibar and from there to Mombasa, where he hoped to found a new mission and continue his evangelical work.

Instead, his life fell apart. His wife succumbed to malaria and died on 9 July 1844. His daughter, born just three days previously, died five days after her mother from the same disease, while Krapf too fell gravely ill with the same; and though he alone recovered, throughout the rest of his life he suffered from sporadic attacks that would lay him low for weeks at a time.

But though his body grew weak with malaria, his spirit remained strong, and, following the death of his wife, over the next six months Krapf both translated the New Testament into Swahili and devised a plan for spreading the gospel throughout the interior of Africa. Estimating that the continent could be crossed on foot from east to west in a matter of 900 hours, Krapf believed that establishing a chain of missions at intervals of one hundred hours right across the continent, each staffed by six 'messengers of peace', would be the best way to promulgate the Christian religion on the dark continent.

Unfortunately for Krapf, Islam had got there first, which made his job rather tougher; indeed, in the six months following his arrival in Mombasa, the total number of successful conversions made by Krapf stood at a nice round figure: zero. Clearly, if the faith was to make any inroads in Africa, fresh impetus was required. That impetus was provided by the arrival of Rebmann in 1846. Having recovered from the obligatory bout of malaria that all but wiped him out for his first month in Africa, Rebmann set about helping Krapf to establish a new mission at Rabai-mpia (New Rabai), just outside Mombasa. The station lay in the heart of Wanika territory, a tribe who from the first had proved resistant to conversion. Even the founding of a mission in their midst did little to persuade the Wanika to listen to their preaching: by 1859, 14 years after Krapf first arrived, just seven converts had been made.

It was clear early on that they would have little success in persuading the Wanika to convert. So, almost from the start the proselytizing pair began to look to pastures new to find potential members for their flock. In 1847 they founded a second mission station at Mt Kasigau, three days' walk from Rabai-mpia – the first in their proposed chain of such stations across the African continent – and later that same year they began to plan the establishment of the next link, at a place called **Jagga** (now spelt Chagga). Rebmann and Krapf had already heard a lot about Jagga from the caravan leaders who earned their money transporting goods between the interior and the markets on the eastern shore and who often called into Rabai-mpia on the way. A source of and market for slaves, Jagga was renowned locally for suffering from extremely cold temperatures at times, a reputation that led Krapf to deduce that Jagga was probably at a much higher altitude than the lands that surrounded it. This hypothesis was confirmed by renowned caravan leader Bwana Kheri, who spoke to Krapf of a great mountain called 'Kilimansharo' (this, incidentally, being the sixth definite reference to Kilimanjaro). From other sources, Krapf and Rebmann also learned that the mountain was protected by evil spirits (known in the Islamic faith as *djinns*) who had been responsible for many deaths, and that it was crowned with a strange white substance that resembled silver, but which the locals simply called 'cold'.

Following protracted negotiations, Bwana Kheri was eventually persuaded to take Rebmann to Chagga in 1848 (Krapf, being too ill to travel, remained in Rabai-mpia). The parting caused great distress to both parties, as detailed in Krapf's diary:

Here we are in the midst of African heathenism, among wilful liars and trickish men, who desire only our property... The only earthly friend whom I have, and whom he has, does at once disappear, each of us setting our face towards our respective destinations while our friends at home do not know where we are, whither we go and what we are doing.

Rebmann's journey and the discovery of snow

And so, armed with only his trusty umbrella – along a route where caravans typically travelled under armed escort – Rebmann, accompanied by Bwana Kheri and eight porters, set out for Chagga on 27 April 1848. A fortnight later, on the morning of 11 May, he came across the most marvellous sight:

At about ten o'clock, (I had no watch with me) I observed something remarkably white on the top of a high mountain, and first supposed that it was a very white cloud, in which supposition my guide also confirmed me, but having gone a few paces more I could no more *rest satisfied with that explanation; and while I was asking my guide a second time whether that white thing was indeed a cloud and scarcely listening to his answer that **yonder** was a cloud but what that white was he did not know, but supposed it was **coldness** – the most delightful recognition took place in my mind, of an old well-known European guest called **snow**. All the strange stories we had so often heard about the gold and silver mountain Kilimandjaro in Jagga, supposed to be inaccessible on account of evil spirits, which had killed a great many of those who had attempted to ascend it, were now at once rendered intelligible to me, as of course the extreme cold, to which poor Natives are perfect strangers, would soon chill and kill the half-naked visitors. I endeavoured to explain to my people the nature of that 'white thing' for which no name exists even in the language of Jagga itself...*   **Johannes Rebmann** from his account of his journey, published in Volume I of the *Church Missionary Intelligencer*, May 1849

An extract from the next edition of the same journal continues the theme:

The cold temperature of the higher regions constituted a limit beyond which they dared not venture. This natural disinclination, existing most strongly in the case of the great mountain, on account of its intenser cold, and the popular traditions respecting the fate of the only expedition which had ever attempted to ascend its heights, had of course prevented them from exploring it, and left them in utter ignorance of such a thing as 'snow', although not in ignorance of that which they so greatly dreaded, 'coldness'.

WD Faulty? – The great snow debate

The most relentless critic was a redoubtable person, for long years a terror to real explorers, Mr Desborough Cooley, a kind of geographical ogre, who used to sit in his study in England, shaping and planning out the map of Africa (basing his arrangements of rivers, lakes and mountains on ridiculous and fantastic linguistic coincidences and resemblances of his own imagination), and who rushed out and tore in pieces all unheeding explorers in the field who brought to light actual facts which upset his elaborate schemes.
   HH Johnston *The Kilima-njaro Expedition – A Record of Scientific Exploration in Eastern Equatorial Africa* (1886)

Though Rebmann's accounts of Kilimanjaro caused a minor sensation amongst the wider reading public when first published in the *Church Missionary Intelligencer* of May 1849, the response it elicited from academic circles back in Europe was initially as cool as the top of Kibo itself. Leading the sceptics was one **William Desborough (WD) Cooley**. Cooley was widely regarded in his day as one of Britain's leading geographers and something of an expert on Africa (though he never actually ventured near the continent throughout his entire life). Indeed, Cooley had already added to the stock of knowledge about the mountain way back in 1845, a full four years before Rebmann's essay was published, by providing the world with a description of Kilimanjaro that he had managed to construct from details furnished to him by the slave dealer-cum-ambassador Khamis bin Uthman (see p104). But if he is remembered at all today it is as the man who refused to believe that Kilimanjaro could be topped with snow, as this response to Rebmann's first account (see p106) makes clear:

I deny altogether the existence of snow on Mount Kilimanjaro. It rests entirely on the testimony of Mr Rebmann... and he ascertained it, not with his eyes, but by inference and in the visions of his imagination.   *Athenaeum*, May 1849

(continued on p108)

KILIMANJARO

Still bent on spreading Christianity, and undeterred (indeed ignorant) of the scepticism with which his reports in the *Intelligencer* were about to be met back in Europe (about which, see the box below), Rebmann returned to Rabaimpia but continued to visit and write about Kilimanjaro and the Chagga region for a few more years.

His second trip, made in November of the same year, was blessed by favourable weather conditions, providing Rebmann with his clearest view of

❏ **WD Faulty? – The great snow debate**   *(continued from p107)*

Absurd as it seems now, Cooley's reputation in intellectual circles at that time was as high as Kili itself, and such was the reverence with which his every pronouncement was received in the mid 19th century that it was his version of reality that was the more widely accepted: as far as people in Europe were concerned, if Cooley said Kilimanjaro did not have snow on it, it did not have snow on it.

A second report by Rebmann, following his trip to the Chagga lands in November 1848, did little to stem the scepticism, even though he – perhaps now aware of the controversy his first account had caused back home – went to great lengths to back up his earlier report:

.. during the night, I felt the cold as severely as in Europe in November; and had I been obliged to remain in the open-air, I could not have fallen to sleep for a single moment: neither was this to be wondered at, for so near was I now to the snow-mountain Kilimandjaro (Kilima dja-aro, mountain of greatness), that even at night, by only the dim light of the moon, I could perfectly well distinguish it.

If Rebmann hoped to persuade his critics, however, he was sadly mistaken: if he was capable of making a mistake once, they countered, then surely he could be wrong a second and third time too. And so for much of the next two years Rebmann's account of his time on Kili was treated with equal parts suspicion and derision.

Indeed, it wasn't until 1850 and the publication of an account by Rebmann's friend and mentor, Dr Krapf, that doubts began to be cast on Cooley's ideas. In an edition of the *Church Missionary Intelligencer* in which he recounts his own experiences working in the Ukamba region immediately to the north of Kilimanjaro, Krapf baldly states that:

All the arguments which Mr Cooley has adduced against the existence of such a snow mountain, and against the accuracy of Rebmann's report, dwindle into nothing when one has the evidence of one's own eyes before one; so that they are scarcely worth refuting.

Suddenly it became that much harder to deny the existence of snow on Kili: after all, there were now two Europeans who had seen the mountain for themselves – and both of them had insisted that they'd seen snow there.

Yet Cooley remained adamant in his convictions and, thanks to the support of some pretty influential friends to back up his arguments, enjoyed popular public support. No less a figure than the President of the Royal Geographical Society, **Sir Roderick Murchison**, said that the idea of a snow-capped mountain under the equator was to *'a great degree incredulous'* (even though there are other snow-capped mountains in the Andes and Papua New Guinea that fall 'under the equator', and which were already known about by the mid 19th century).

Kilimanjaro, and the outside world with the most accurate and comprehensive description of the mountain that had yet been written:

There are two main peaks which arise from a common base measuring some twenty-five miles long by as many broad. They are separated by a saddle-shaped depression, running east and west for a distance of about eight or ten miles. The eastern peak is the lower of the two, and is conical in shape. The western and higher presents the appearance of a magnificent dome, and is covered with snow throughout the year, unlike its eastern neighbour, which loses its snowy mantle during the hot season.

Even those who *had* been to Africa for themselves had serious reservations about the missionaries' claims. The esteemed Irish explorer **Richard Burton**, for example, having listened to Krapf give a talk on Kilimanjaro in Cairo, declared that *'These stories reminded one of a de Lunatico'*; while **David Livingstone**, recently returned from his latest adventures in Africa, lent further weight to Cooley's arguments during an address to the Royal Geographical Society. In it, Livingstone related a story about some mountains in the Zambezi Valley which were described to him by locals as being of a *'glistening whiteness'*. Livingstone initially believed that these mountains must be covered by snow, until, having seen the mountains for himself, he realized that they were in fact composed of *'masses of white rock, somewhat like quartz'*.

As if to drum home the point of the tale, Sir Roderick Murchison later declared at the same meeting that Livingstone's account:

...may prove that the missionaries, who believed that they saw snowy mountains under the equator, have been deceived by the glittering aspect of rocks under a tropical sun.

The next broadside fired by either side occurred in 1852 and the publication of Cooley's grandly (but inaccurately) titled *Inner Africa Laid Open*. This, Cooley clearly hoped, was to be his masterpiece: the culmination of a lifetime's armchair studying, this was the opus that would secure his reputation during his lifetime and ensure his name lived on in perpetuity as one of the great intellectual heavyweights of the 19th century. As it transpired, the book did indeed serve to preserve Cooley's name for posterity – though presumably not in the way that he had hoped.

To read the book now, it is clear that Cooley hoped it would once and for all dismiss all this nonsense about snow on Kilimanjaro. Within the first few pages almost every part of Rebmann's account is called into question, with the claim of snow on Kilimanjaro being treated with particularly vehement derision:

... it is obvious that the discovery of snow rests much more on 'a delightful mental recognition' than on the evidence of the senses... But in his mind the wish was father to the thought, the 'delightful recognition' developed with amazing rapidity, and in a few minutes the cloudy object, or 'something white,' became a 'beautiful snow mountain', so near to the equator.

Later in the book Cooley forgets the conduct becoming of an English gentleman and the attacks on Rebmann border on the personal, starting with an attack on his eyesight:

Various and inconsistent reasons have been assigned for this failure [by Rebmann to see Kilimanjaro from a nearby hill], *but the only true explanation of it is contained in Mr Rebmann's confession that he is very short-sighted. He was unable to perceive, with the aid of a small telescope, Lake Ibe, three days distant to the south, which his followers could discern with the naked eye; nor could he even see the rhinoceroses in his path.*

(continued on p110)

On this second trip Rebmann was also able to correct an error made in his first account of Kilimanjaro: that the local 'Jagga' tribe were indeed familiar with snow and did have a name for it – that name being 'Kibo'!

A third and much more organized expedition in April 1849 – at the same time as the account of his earlier visits to Kilimanjaro was rolling off the presses in Europe – enabled Rebmann, accompanied by a caravan of 30 porters (and, of course, his trusty umbrella), to ascend to such a height that he was later to boast that he had come 'so close to the snow-line that, supposing no impassable

---

❏ **WD Faulty? – The great snow debate**   (*continued from p109*)

And he goes on to finish his onslaught with this rather uncompromising, hysterical summary of Rebmann's accounts:

... betraying weak powers of observation, strong fancy, an eager craving for wonders, and childish reasoning, could not fail to awaken mistrust by their intrinsic demerits, even if there were no testimony opposed to them.

To further back up his argument, Cooley was able to point out a number of inconsistencies between Rebmann's and Krapf's accounts, such as the postulation by Krapf that the mountain is 12,500ft (3810m) high – this after Rebmann had estimated the height to be closer to 20,000ft (6096m, a pretty good guess by the myopic Rebmann).

Cooley's desire to prove Rebmann wrong was fuelled by more than just a desire to crush a young upstart in a field in which he considered himself the ultimate authority. He was also frightened that the existence of snow on Kilimanjaro would provide support for his rivals' theories at the expense of his own. In the big debate that raged in academic circles in the mid 1800s on the exact location of the source of the Nile, Cooley was firmly of the opinion that the river started from a large lake in Central Africa called Lake N'yassi. (Indeed, in the 1830s he even organized an expedition to prove his theory, though unfortunately it failed abysmally for reasons that remain rather obscure.)

Aligned against Cooley were opponents such as the geographer **Charles Beke**, who preferred the idea that the Nile had its source in a mountain range in the interior – possibly, as Encisco (p104) had stated in the 16th century, the legendary Mountains of the Moon – and looked upon the discovery of snow on an East African mountain as evidence to back up their theories. Indeed, when Rebmann and Krapf's accounts first reached Britain, Beke was only too keen to accept their every word as gospel and even went so far as to suggest that Kilimanjaro was now the most likely source of the Nile.

And that, for the next decade or so, was that: Rebmann and Krapf continued to visit Kilimanjaro and continued to see snow, while Cooley and the gang back in England continued to refute their every utterance and enjoy the majority of public opinion.

Then in 1862, **Baron Carl von der Decken** made his second and more successful attempt on Kilimanjaro (see p112), this time with his friend Dr Otto Kersten who had replaced Thornton for this second expedition to the region. In reaching a reported 14,200ft (4328m) von der Decken and Kersten came as close to the snow as any European ever had, and the brave baron's subsequent account of the expedition exploded Cooley's theories once and for all:

During the night it snowed heavily and next morning the ground lay white all around us. Surely the obstinate Cooley will be satisfied now.

abyss to intervene, I could have reached it in three or four hours'. After Rebmann's pioneering work it was the turn of his friend Krapf, now risen from his sickbed, to see the snowy mountain his friend had described in such detail. In November 1849 he visited the Ukamba district to the north of Kilimanjaro and during a protracted stay in the area Krapf became the first white man to see Mount Kenya. Perhaps more importantly, he was also afforded wonderful views of Kilimanjaro, and was able to back up Rebmann's assertion that the mountain really was adorned with snow (see box p107 for quote).

There was now a third eyewitness claiming to have seen snow on Kilimanjaro, and a baron at that; Cooley's position as a result began to look increasingly untenable, and his support began to ebb quietly away.

If the baron really believed his testimony alone would persuade Cooley, however, he was much mistaken:

So the Baron says it snowed during the night...In December with the sun standing vertically overhead! The Baron is to be congratulated on the opportuneness of the storm. But it is easier to believe in the misrepresentations of man than in such an unheard-of eccentricity on the part of nature. This description of a snowstorm at the equator during the hottest season of the year, and at an elevation of only 13,000 feet, is too obviously a 'traveller's tale', invented to support Krapf's marvellous story of a mountain 12,500 feet high covered with perpetual snow.

But the redoubtable Cooley was fighting a lonely battle now. The Royal Geographical Society withdrew their backing, with Sir Roderick Murchison – presumably between mouthfuls of humble pie – finally admitting that Rebmann and Krapf were probably right after all. As if to add insult to Cooley's injured pride, the Society even awarded their Gold Medal in 1863 to von der Decken for his contributions to the sum of geographical knowledge of Africa. (Incidentally, in addition to his account of Kilimanjaro, von der Decken was also the first European to see and describe Mount Meru.)

Fourteen years after Rebmann had first announced that there was snow on the equator, the world was finally listening to him. Cooley meanwhile, resolutely refused to believe in the existence of snow on Kilimanjaro, carrying his scepticism with him to the grave and leaving behind a reputation for stubbornness and ignorance that has survived to this day.

In Cooley's defence, one has to remember just how little was known about the continent at that time: few people from Europe had ever visited Africa; fewer still had penetrated beyond the coast; and of those who had, even fewer had survived to tell the tale. So the armchair scholars of Europe were forced to rely upon the sketchy mentions of Kili in historical records for their information; and of those descriptions, none since Ptolemy mentions anything about snow.

As some compensation, perhaps, Cooley at least had the satisfaction of knowing that, while defeated in this particular battle, he gained at least a partial victory in the wider war: in 1858 a large body of water in the heart of central Africa was discovered and was named **Lake Victoria** after Britain's sovereign. This lake would later be proved to be one of the sources of the Nile. Cooley may have got the name and location of this body of water wrong, but his supposition that the Nile had a lake as its source, and not a mountain, had been proved correct after all.

FIRST ATTEMPTS ON THE SUMMIT

Baron von der Decken and Charles New

After the missionaries came the mountaineers. In August 1861 Baron Carl Claus von der Decken, a Hanoverian naturalist and traveller who had been residing in Zanzibar, accompanied by young English geologist Richard Thornton, himself an explorer of some renown who had accompanied (and been sacked by) Livingstone during the latter's exploration of the Zambezi, made the first serious attempt on Kilimanjaro's summit. Initially, despite an entourage of over fifty porters, a manservant for von der Decken and a personal slave for Thornton, their efforts proved to be rather dismal and they had to turn back after just three days due to bad weather, having reached the rather puny height of just 8200ft (2499m). Proceeding to the west side of the mountain, however, the pioneering baron did at least enjoy an unobstructed view of Kibo peak on the way:

Bathed in a flood of rosy light, the cap that crowns the mountain's noble brow gleamed in the dazzling glory of the setting sun... Beyond appeared the jagged outlines of the eastern peak, which rises abruptly from a gently inclined plain, forming, as it were, a rough, almost horizontal platform. Three thousand feet lower, like the trough between two mighty waves, is the saddle which separates the sister peaks one from the other.

Von der Decken also provided the most accurate estimate yet for the height of both Kibo – which he guessed was between 19,812 and 20,655ft (6038.7m to 6295.6m) – and Mawenzi (17,257-17,453ft, or 5259.9-5319.7m). Thornton, for his part, correctly surmised that the mountain was volcanic, with Kibo the youngest and Shira the oldest part of the mountain.

The following year von der Decken, now accompanied by Dr Otto Kersten who had replaced Thornton as the baron's travelling and climbing companion, reached a much more respectable 14,200ft (4328m) and furthermore reported being caught up in a snowstorm (see box p110). On his return to Europe, the baron described Kibo as a 'mighty dome, rising to a height of about 20,000 feet, of which the last three thousand are covered in snow'.

Following this second attempt, von der Decken urged **Charles New** (1840-75), a London-born missionary with the United Free Methodist Church in Mombasa, to tackle the mountain, and in 1871 New made a laudable attempt to reach the summit. That attempt failed, as did a second attempt in August of the same year; nevertheless, by choosing on the latter occasion to climb on the south-eastern face of Kibo where the ice cap at that time stretched almost to the base of the cone, New inadvertently wrote himself into the history books as the first European to cross the snow-line at the African Equator:

The gulf was all that now lay between myself and it, but what an all! The snow was on a level with my eye, but my arm was too short to reach it. My heart sank, but before I had time fairly to scan the position my eyes rested upon snows at my very feet! There it lay upon the rocks below me in shining masses, looking like newly washed and sleeping sheep! Hurrah! I cannot describe the sensations that thrilled my heart at that moment. Hurrah!

On this second expedition New also discovered the crater lake of Jala, the mountain's only volcanic lake, to the south-east of Mawenzi.

New's experiences on Kilimanjaro fanned his passion for the mountain and two years later he was back preparing for another assault on the still-unconquered peak. Unfortunately, the volatile tribes living at the foot of the mountain had other ideas and before New had even reached Kilimanjaro he was forced to return to the coast, having been stripped of all his possessions by the followers of the Chief of 'Moji' (Moshi), a highly unpleasant man by the name of Mandara (see p258). Broken in both health and spirits, the unfortunate New died soon after the attack.

As rumours of New's demise trickled back to Europe, enthusiasm among explorers for the still unconquered Kilimanjaro understandably waned and for the next dozen years the mountain saw few foreign faces. Those that did visit usually did so on their way to somewhere else; people such as **Dr Gustav A Fischer** in 1883, who stopped in Arusha and visited Mount Meru on his journey to Lake Naivasha and declared Kilimanjaro to be fit for 'European settlement', a statement that would have greater resonance later on in the century; and the Scottish geologist, **Joseph Thomson**, who became one of the first to examine properly the northern side of the mountain during an attempt to cross the Masai territories. He also attempted a climb of Kili, though having allowed himself only one day in which to complete the task his attempt was always doomed to failure; in the end he reached no higher than the tree-line at about 2700m. (Failure though he may have been in this instance, his name lives on as a species of gazelle.)

The first European to venture back to the region with the specific intention of visiting Kilimanjaro arrived in the same year, 1883. In an expedition organized by the Royal Geographical Society, **Harry Johnston** arrived in East Africa with the aim of discovering and documenting the flora and fauna of Kilimanjaro. Though his work did little to further our understanding of the mountain, Johnston's trip is of anecdotal interest in that he later claimed in his biography that he was actually working undercover for the British Secret Service.

No documentary evidence has ever turned up to back this claim (though there is a letter written by him to the Foreign Office in which he asks for 40 men and £5000 for the purpose of colonizing Kilimanjaro). Much doubt has been cast, too, upon his boast that he reached almost 5000m during his time on the mountain; while his suggestion that Kilimanjaro was 'a mountain that can be climbed even without the aid of a walking stick' was widely ridiculed when first broadcast later that year.

But, whatever the inaccuracies and falsehoods of Johnston's recollections, his journey did at least assure other would-be Kilimanjaro visitors from Europe that the region was once again safe to visit. His visit also served to bring the mountain to the attention of European powers...

KILIMANJARO

COLONIZATION

... a country as large as Switzerland enjoying a singularly fertile soil and healthy climate, ... within a few years it must be either English, French or German ... I am on the spot, the first in the field, and able to make Kilima-njaro as completely English as Ceylon.

HH Johnston *The Kilima-njaro Expedition – A Record of Scientific Exploration in Eastern Equatorial Africa* (1886)

In describing the mountain thus, HH Johnston brought Kilimanjaro to the attention of the world's leading powers. Soon the two great colonizers in East Africa, Germany and Britain, were jockeying for position in the region. British missionaries were accused of putting the temporal interests of their country over the spiritual affairs of their flock, while for their part certain German nationals made no secret of the fact they wished to colonize Kilimanjaro. In 1884, the **Gesellschaft für Deutsche Kolonisation** (GDK), a political party founded by the 28-year-old **Dr Carl Peters** with the ultimate goal of colonizing East Africa, persuaded a dozen local chiefs to throw off the rule of the (British controlled) **Sultan of Zanzibar** and, furthermore, to cede large sections of their territory to the German cause; one of Dr Peters' envoys, Dr Juhlke, even managed to establish a protectorate over Kilimanjaro in 1885. The British fought fire with fire in response, forcing two dozen chiefs (including some of those who had sided with the Germans) to swear allegiance to the sultan – and therefore indirectly to them.

The situation was becoming dangerously volatile, with war looking increasingly likely. After further bouts of political manoeuvring, in October 1886 the two sides met in London and Berlin to define once and for all the boundary between British- and German-controlled East Africa and head off the possibility of war: the border between British-ruled Kenya and German East Africa was now in place.

The first period of German rule over Kilimanjaro proved to be exceptionally harsh, and many Germans soon felt uneasy about the excesses of Dr Peters and his followers. In 1906 an enquiry opened in the Reichstag into the conduct of the doctor and his men, in which an open letter by a Herr Eltz (about whom very little is known) was read out to the court. Its contents give an idea of the hatred that the doctor and his men aroused in the locals:

What have you achieved by perpetual fights, by acts of violence and oppression? You have achieved, Herr Doctor, I have it from your own mouth in the presence of witnesses – that you and the gentlemen of your staff cannot go five minutes' distance from the fort without military escort. My policy enables me to make extensive journeys and shooting trips in Kilimanjaro and the whole surrounding country with never more than four soldiers. You have cut the knot with the sword and achieved that this most beautiful country has become a scene of war. Before God and man you are responsible for the devastation of flourishing districts, you are responsible for the deaths of our comrades Bulow and Wolfram, of our brave soldiers and of hundreds of Wachagga. And now I bring a supreme charge against you: Necessity did not compel you to this. You required deeds only in order that your name might not be forgotten in Europe.

Soon German soldiers were being attacked and killed and, with opposition to their rule growing stronger and more organized, they suffered a massive defeat at Moshi at the hands of the Chagga, led by Meli, Mandara's son (see p258).

The biggest present ever?
There is a widely believed story that the kink in the border between Kenya and Tanzania near Kilimanjaro was created to satisfy the whim of Queen Victoria, Britain's reigning monarch at the time the border was first defined. According to the story, she magnanimously decided to give Kilimanjaro to her grandson, the future Wilhelm II, as a birthday present, following a complaint from him that while Britain had two snowy mountains in her East African territories (Mounts Kili and Kenya), Germany was left with none. In order to effect the transfer of such a generous gift, the border had to be redrawn so that Kili fell to the south of the boundary in German territory, which is why the border has a strange kink to the east of the mountain.

Alas, however romantic the story, it is simply not true. The kink is there not because of Victoria's largesse, but as part of the agreement struck between Germany and Britain, and it exists not because of Kili, but Mombasa. Britain's territories in East Africa needed a port: the Germans already had Dar, and if the border between the two was to continue on the same bearing as it had taken to the west of Kilimanjaro the Germans were going to end up with Mombasa too. So a kink was placed in the border to allow Mombasa to fall in British territory.

Though the Germans regained control, it was clear to them that a more benevolent style of government was required if they were to continue ruling over their East African territories. This new 'caring colonialism' paid off and for the last few years of their rule the Germans lived largely at peace with their subjects and even forged a useful alliance with the Chaggas during the Germans' push against rebellious Masai tribes. The Germans also started the practice of building public huts on Kilimanjaro, establishing one at 8500ft (2591m), called **Bismarck Hut**, and one at 11,500ft (3505m) known as **Peters' Hut**, after Dr Carl.

KILIMANJARO CONQUERED

While all this was going on, attempts to be the first to conquer Kilimanjaro continued apace. In 1887, **Count Samuel Teleki** of the Austro-Hungarian Empire made the most serious assault on Kibo so far, before 'a certain straining of the membrane of the tympanum of the ear' forced him to turn back. Then the American naturalist, **Dr Abbott**, who had come primarily to investigate the fauna and flora of the mountain slopes, made a rather reckless attempt. Abbott was struck down by illness fairly early on in the climb but his companion, Otto Ehlers of the German East African Company, pushed on, reaching (according to him) 19,680ft (5998.5m). Not for the first time in the history of climbing Kilimanjaro, however, this figure has been sceptically received by others – particularly as it is over 100m above the highest point on the mountain! (By way of compensation, however, it was on Kilimanjaro that Abbott first identified and collected the species of duiker that now bears his name.)

In spite of their relative failures, both Teleki and Abbott played a part in the success of the eventual conqueror of Kilimanjaro, **Dr Hans Meyer**: Teleki, by providing information about the ascent to Meyer in a chance encounter during

Meyer's first trip to the region in 1887; Abbott, by providing accommodation in Moshi for Meyer and his party during their successful expedition of 1889.

Hans Meyer was a geology professor and the son of a wealthy editor from Leipzig (he himself later joined the editorial board and became its director, retiring in 1888, one year before the conquest of Kili, to become professor of Colonial Geography at Leipzig University). In all he made four trips to Kilimanjaro. Following the partial success of his first attempt in 1887, when he managed to reach 18,000ft (5486.4m), Meyer returned the following year for a second assault with experienced African traveller and friend Dr Oscar Baumann. Unfortunately, his timing couldn't have been worse: the **Abushiri War**, an Arab-led revolt against German traders on the East African coast, had just broken out and Meyer and his friend Baumann were captured, clapped into chains and held hostage by Sheikh Abushiri himself, the leader of the insurgency. In the end both escaped with their lives, but only after a ransom of ten thousand rupees was paid.

However, on his third attempt, in 1889, Meyer finally covered himself in glory. Though no doubt a skilful and determined climber, Meyer's success can largely be attributed to his recognition that the biggest obstacle to a successful assault was the lack of food available at the top. Meyer solved this by establishing camps at various points along the route that he had chosen for his attempt, including one at 12,980ft (3956.3m; Abbott's camp); one, Kibo camp, 'by a conspicuous rock' at 14,210ft (4331.2m); and, finally, a small encampment by a lava cave and just below the glacier line at 15,260ft (4651.2m). Thanks to these intermediary camps, Meyer was able to conduct a number of attempts on the summit without having to return to the foot of Kili to replenish supplies after each; instead, food was brought to the camps by the porters every few days.

He also had a considerable back-up party with him, including his friend and climbing companion, Herr Ludwig Purtscheller – a gymnastics teacher and alpine expert from Salzburg – two local headmen, nine porters, three other locals who would act as supervisors, one cook and one guide supplied by the local chief, Mareale, whom he had befriended during his first trip to the region. These men would help to carry the equipment and man the camps, with each kept in order by Meyer's strict code of discipline, where minor miscreants received ten lashes and serious wrongdoers twenty.

The size of his entourage, however, shouldn't detract from the magnitude of Meyer's achievement: as well as the usual hardships associated with climbing Kilimanjaro, he also had to contend with deserters from his party, the lack of a clear path, elephant traps (large pits dug by locals and concealed by ferns to trap the unwary pachyderm), as well as the unpleasant, rapacious chief of Moshi, Mandara (see p258). Furthermore, Meyer did not begin his walk *on* the mountain, as today's visitors do, but in Mombasa, 14 days by foot, according to Meyer, from the Kilimanjaro town of Taveta!

Then there was the snow and ice, so much more prevalent in the late 1800s on Kili than it is today. Above 4500m Meyer had to trek upon snow for virtually the whole day, even though his route up Kibo from the Saddle is not too dissimilar to that taken by thousands of trekkers every year – and today there is no snow on the route. The added difficulties caused by the snow are well described in Meyer's book *Across East African Glaciers*. Rising at 2.30am for their first assault on the summit, Meyer and Purtscheller spent most of the morning carving a stairway out of a sheer ice-cliff, every stair laboriously hewn with an average of 20 blows of the ice axe. (The cliff formed part of the now extinct Ratzel Glacier, named by Meyer after a geography professor in his native Leipzig.) As a result, by the time they reached the eastern lip of the crater, the light was fading fast and the approach of inclement weather forced them to return before they could reach the highest point of that lip.

On their second attempt, however, three days later on 6 October 1889, and with the stairs in the ice still intact from the first ascent, they were able to gain the eastern side of the rim by mid-morning; from there it was but a straightforward march to the three small tumescences situated on the higher, southern lip of the crater, the middle one of which was also the highest point of the mountain.

The conquest of Kilimanjaro
Taking out a small German flag, which I had brought with me for the purpose in my knapsack, I planted it on the weather-beaten lava summit with three ringing cheers, and in virtue of my right as its discoverer christened this hitherto unknown and unnamed mountain peak – the loftiest spot in Africa and the German Empire – Kaiser Wilhelm's Peak [now known as Uhuru Peak]. *Then we gave three cheers more for the Emperor, and shook hands in mutual congratulation.* **Hans Meyer**
Across East African Glaciers

Meyer's route to the top and the modern trails: a comparison
While no modern path precisely retraces Hans Meyer's original route to the summit, some of today's paths do occasionally coincide with the trail he blazed. For instance, Meyer and his climbing partner, Purtscheller, began their assault on Kilimanjaro, on 28 September 1889, from **Marangu** village. From there they headed due north up through the trees, arriving two days later at the very upper limits of the forest, where they made camp.

Trekkers on the Marangu trail follow a similar itinerary today, though their starting point is a good deal higher than Meyer's at Marangu Gate, rather than Marangu village – which explains why trekkers today need only one day to reach the upper edge of the forest, while Meyer took two. It is also worth noting that, according to the beautifully drawn maps by Dr Bruno Hassenstein in Meyer's book *Across East African Glaciers*, his camp on this second night lay to the south-west of Kifunika Hill at an altitude of 8710ft (2654.8m), whereas the Mandara Huts lie a couple of hours' walk to the east of Kifunika, at a loftier 2743m. *(continued on p118)*

AFTER MEYER

Mawenzi, Pastor Reusch and a frozen leopard

In the decades following Meyer's successful assault on Kili, few followed in his footsteps. Meyer climbed again in 1898, though this time he got only as far as the crater rim. In 1909 surveyor M Lange climbed all the way to Uhuru Peak, and in doing so became only the third (after Meyer and Purtscheller) to reach the summit of Kilimanjaro – a full 20 years after the first two.

The conquest of the last remaining peak on Kilimanjaro, that of the summit of Mawenzi (called, somewhat perversely, Hans Meyer Peak), was achieved by

---

❑ **Meyer's route to the top and the modern trails: a comparison**
(Continued from p117) On the third day, Meyer struck a westerly course, crossing the Mdogo (lesser) and Mkuba (greater) streams before making camp at an altitude of 9480ft (2889.5m). This was the all-important **Halfway Camp**, the intermediate station that Meyer would use as his base for tackling Kibo. In the history of climbing Kibo, no single spot on the entire mountain, save Uhuru Peak itself, has played a more prominent role: Harry Johnston had built some huts nearby during his reconnaissance mission of 1883; Meyer himself had camped here during his first expedition on the mountain, with Baron von Eberstein in 1887, and Abbott and Ehlers had also camped nearby in 1889, just a few months before Meyer and Purtscheller arrived. There's even evidence to suggest Count Teleki had also stopped here in 1887; in his account of their attempt on Kili in *Discovery by Count Teleki of Lakes Rudolf and Stefanie*, Lieutenant Ludwig von Höhnel speaks of making camp at 9390ft (2862m) by a brook, near some old huts built originally by HH Johnston.

So where is this spot? There are plenty of clues. It is no coincidence, for example, that all these different parties chose to make camp at this site. Then, as now, campsites would have been chosen largely for their proximity to water and other amenities, so we can guess that a mountain stream or brook must run nearby. We also know that Meyer headed almost due west from his camp of the night before, and that the spot lies at around 2862m, above the tree-line. No modern campsite exactly fits this description – the Horombo Huts, the second night's accommodation on the Marangu trail, are too high up at 3657m. Rau Campsite, however, on the sadly now defunct Alternative Mweka/Kidia Route, seems a more plausible candidate: though this campsite is too high at 3260m, just below it is a glorious stretch of grasslands bordering the forest and near a mountain stream that would appear to fit the description given by Meyer. If the 19th-century explorers really did camp around there, they are to be congratulated on choosing one of the most beautiful places on the mountain.

Leaving most of his porters behind at this site – it would be their duty from now on to ferry supplies up to the camp from Marangu – Meyer struck due north up to the Saddle, past the **Spring in the Snow**, or Schneequell (12,910ft/3935m) and on to **Abbott's Camp** at 12,980ft (3956.3m), so-called by Meyer because he found an empty Irish stew tin and a sheet of the Salvation Army newspaper *En Avant* at this spot and guessed that this must have been where his missionary friend Dr Abbott had camped a few months previously. As to their location, according to the maps in Meyer's book the Schneequell lies almost exactly due south of East Lava Hill, the easternmost of the parasitic cones on the Saddle, and would seem to tie in fairly neatly with the Last Water Point, the Maua River, that lies below Zebra Rocks on the Marangu Route (see p261). Abbott's Camp, meanwhile, lies to the north-north-west of here, at a point between the two Marangu Route paths to the Saddle. From here,

the climbers **Edward Oehler** and **Fritz Klute** on 29 July 1912. Thus, 64 years after the first European had clapped eyes on Kilimanjaro, both of its main peaks had been successfully climbed. As an encore, Oehler and Klute made the third successful expedition on Kibo and the first from the western side. In the same year, **Walter Furtwangler** and **Ziegfried Koenig** achieved the fourth successful climb and became the first to use skis to descend. Two more successful assaults occurred before the outbreak of World War One, and **Frau von Ruckteschell** kept up the German's impressive record on Kilimanjaro by becoming the first woman to reach Gillman's Point.

Meyer's path and the Marangu Route diverge for good. Where Marangu trekkers head roughly north across the Saddle, keeping Kibo to their left, in 1889 Meyer and his two companions, the alpine expert Purtscheller and Mwini Amani, their guide, set off directly for the summit in a more westerly direction, stopping for the night by a prominent rock at 14,200ft (4328.1m). This is **Viermannstein**, the Rock of Four Men, a place popular with Kili explorers in the 19th century. Unfortunately, because it lies far from any trail today, the site rarely features on modern trekking maps; for an approximate location, draw a line running east from Barafu Campsite, and a second due south from the easternmost Triplet: the rock stands near to where they coincide.

Meyer's aim in 1889 was **Ratzel Glacier**, on the south-eastern rim of Kibo. The glacier has now, alas, disappeared, though we know from maps where it was: if walking up to the summit from Barafu Campsite, it would have been on your right when approaching Stella Point. In Meyer's day the glacier covered the entire south-eastern lip of Kibo; it was into this glacier that Meyer and Purtscheller, on 3 October, carved a series of steps that led all the way to the crater rim and a height of 19,260ft (5870.4m).

On this occasion, considerations of time and weather forced them to withdraw back down to camp, having seen – but not scaled – the highest point on Kibo. After a day's rest and contemplation, however, and having decided to bivouac at **Lava Cave** on the slopes of Kibo at 15,960ft (4864.6m), the duo were ready for another assault on the summit. From there, at 3am on a cold October morning, they set off. At dawn they were at the foot of the glacier where, to their delight, they found the glacial stairway that they'd built two days previously was still there. By 8am they had reached and crossed a large crevasse, the only serious obstacle on the way to the summit. Just 45 minutes later they were back standing on the crater rim, the limit of their achievements two days previously.

On this occasion, however, both time and weather were on their side. Walking around the southern rim of Kibo, they climbed three small hillocks, the middle of which they found by aneroid to be the highest by some 40ft or more. Thus at 10.30am on 6 October 1889, Meyer and Purtscheller wrote themselves into the history books as the first to make it to the highest point in Africa.

So where exactly did they gain **access to the crater**? According to Dr Hassenstein's maps, the Lava Cave lies at the northern end of the large South-East Valley, due west of the middle of the three triplets. That puts it somewhere to the north-east of Barafu Campsite, and more than 150m higher, on one of the rocky spurs that run south-east down from Kibo. Where it certainly is *not*, though many a guide will tell you otherwise, is Hans Meyer Cave on the Marangu Route, which at 5151m is simply too high and too far north. The notch by which they gained access to the crater lay almost exactly north-west of this Lava Cave Camp. *(continued on p120)*

Fresh attempts on Kilimanjaro were suspended for a while during World War One. The countryside around Kilimanjaro became the scene of some vicious fighting, including Moshi itself, which was attacked by British forces in March 1916. Paul von Lettow Vorbeck, the German commander, went down in military history at this time as the man who led the longest tactical retreat ever. With the Germans' defeat, however, Kilimanjaro, along with the rest of German East Africa, reverted to British rule.

❏ **Meyer's route to the top and the modern trails: a comparison**
(Continued from p119) Though again this is pure guesswork, all the evidence does seem to point to the fact that Meyer and Purtscheller on this particular occasion passed into the crater rim from a spot very near to **Stella Point** (5745m); the difference in height (Meyer estimated the height at this point on the crater to be 5778m) can possibly be ascribed to the fact that Meyer's estimates tend to be over-estimates (his height for Uhuru Peak, for example, is over 6000m) – perhaps because in Meyer's day there was a lot more ice at the summit, which would have raised the altitudes.

Having christened the summit after their Kaiser and taken the topmost stone from the summit as a souvenir (a stone that Meyer later gave to the Kaiser, who used it as a paperweight), the pair then hurried back to Abbott's camp on the Saddle. The next few days were spent trying to conquer **Mawenzi** but with no success, the mountain peak defeating them wholly on the first occasion on 13 October, and an attack of colic brought on by some over-ripe bananas stalling their second attempt two days later. Before returning to civilization, however, they spent five more days revisiting Kibo: on 17 October they headed to the crater's northern side. There they reached 5572m before confronting a sheer wall of ice that forced them to retreat; and then finally, on the 18th, they approached the crater from the east.

The path Meyer took up to the crater on this occasion is not too dissimilar to the trail up to Gillman's from the Kibo Huts. Meyer and Purtscheller on this final climb bivouacked at a location they called **Old Fireplace** because, to their considerable surprise, they found the remains of a recent campfire there, along with the bones of an eland and some pieces of banana matting. This camp, according to Meyer, sat at an altitude of 15,390ft (4690.9m). It's just possible, therefore, that the Old Fireplace is in fact the site we now call **Jiwe La Ukoyo**, which many local mountain guides insist was once a popular hunters' campsite. From the Old Fireplace, Meyer and Purtscheller climbed up the snow-clad slopes of Kibo once more, gaining access into the crater via a cleft in the rim that is now known as **Hans Meyer Notch**, and which lies just a few hundred metres to the north of Gillman's Point. Though they failed in their attempts to reach the inner cone of the volcano, they were at least able to confirm that the floor of the crater was made up of a mixture of mud and ashes. They were also startled when, peering into the first cone, they came across the carcass of an antelope (which possibly explains what the leopard, whose frozen body was found up here many years later, was doing at this altitude).

After one more unsuccessful attempt on Mawenzi, Meyer and Purtscheller finally decided to call it a day and, on 22 October, they said goodbye to the Saddle for the last time. The pair had spent 16 days between 15,000 and 20,000ft. During this time they had made four ascents of Kibo, reaching the crater three times and the summit once, and three sorties on Mawenzi, reaching the 5049m summit of Purtscheller's Spitze (Point) but failing to reach the very top.

After the war, attention turned away from Kibo to the lesser-known Mawenzi. In 1924 **George Londt** of South Africa became, by accident, the first to climb South Peak (he was aiming for Hans Meyer Peak but got lost); the peak (4958m), was named after him. Three years later three English mountaineers climbed Mawenzi, including 22-year-old **Sheila MacDonald**, the first woman to do so; the trio then climbed Kibo, with Ms MacDonald writing her name into the record books again as the first woman to complete the ascent to Uhuru Peak. In 1930 two British mountaineers, HW Tilman and Eric Shipton, names more usually associated with Everest, climbed Mawenzi's Nordecke Peak – again, like Londt, by accident.

While all this was happening on Mawenzi, over on Kibo another man was writing himself into the history of Kili: **Pastor Richard Reusch**. Missionary for the Lutheran Church, former officer in the Cossack army and long-time Marangu resident, Reusch is said to have climbed the mountain on no fewer than 65 occasions. During his first assault on the summit in 1926 he found the frozen leopard on the crater rim that would later inspire Hemingway (Reusch cut off part of an ear as a souvenir), while on another sortie the following year he became the first to gaze down into the inner crater, a crater to which he would later give his name. Later work by mountaineer **HW Tilman** and vulca-nologist **JJ Richard** led to confirmation, in 1942, that Kilimanjaro was still active, and while this led to some local panic, in 1957 the Tanganyika Geological Survey and the University of Sheffield were able to allay fears by declaring the volcano to be dormant and almost extinct.

KILIMANJARO TODAY

The 20th century witnessed the inevitable but gradual shift away from explo-ration towards tourism. The most significant change occurred in 1932 with the building of Kibo Hut; name plates and signs were put up too as the mountain was gradually made more tourist-friendly. With a ready base for summit assaults now established, tourists began to trickle into Tanzania to make their own attempt on Africa's greatest mountain.

In 1959 the mountain became the **focus for nationalist feelings** and a sym-bol of the Tanganyikans' independence aspirations following Julius Nyerere's speech to the Tanganyika Legislative Assembly (see p74 for quote). Nyerere eventually got his wish and, after independence was granted in 1961, a torch was indeed placed on the summit of Kilimanjaro. Independence also provided Tanganyika with the chance to rename many of the features of the mountain; in particular, the very summit, dubbed Kaiser Wilhelm Peak by Hans Meyer, was renamed Uhuru Peak – Uhuru meaning, appropriately, 'Freedom' in Swahili.

Since this mountain's moment of patriotic glory, the story of Kilimanjaro has largely been about **tourism**. The early trickle of tourists of 70 years ago is nowa-days more akin to a flood, with visitor numbers increasing exponentially from fewer than 1000 in the late 1950s to 11,000 in the 1990s, to the 50,000-plus we see today. What has been an economic boon to the people of Kilimanjaro, how-ever, has brought little benefit to the mountain itself. With the increase in the number of trekkers comes commensurately greater numbers of pressures and problems. Its soil is being eroded, its vegetation is being burnt or chopped, its wildlife is disappearing and its glaciers are melting. Along with these **environmental pressures** come challenges to its dignity, as climbers dream up ever more bizarre ways of climbing to the top, whether riding up by motorcycle or walking in fancy dress, as discussed in the introduction to this book.

Then there's the problem of **fire**. In February 1999, fires raged for five days and 70 hectares were destroyed, the blaze finally being brought under control thanks to the combined efforts of 347 villagers, park rangers and 40 soldiers of the 39th Squadron of the Tanzanian People's Defence Force. Further fires on Shira Plateau in 2001, on the Rongai Route before Kikelelwa Campsite in 2007, in October 2008 on the Marangu Route between the Mandara and Horombo Huts, and on the northern side of the mountain in July 2013, have caused yet more damage. Depressingly but unsurprisingly, human activity is believed to have been behind the fires.

Twenty-two squatters from the Kamwanga and Rongai districts who were living illegally in the protected areas of the national park were arrested for the 1999 fire, having been identified as the culprits by 600 villagers in a secret

---

❏ **For the record**

● **Fastest ascent of Kilimanjaro** In September 2010 Spanish mountain runner Kilian Jornet, aged just 22, ran to the 5895m summit in 5 hours 23 minutes and 50 seconds, thereby beating by a minute the ascent-only record of Kazakh runner Andrew Puchinin, set the previous year.

● **Fastest ascent and descent** That's not the end of the story, however, for Kilian then trotted back down to base camp in a total time of 7 hours 14 minutes, thus destroying Simon Mtuy's six-year-old record (8 hours and 27 minutes) for the fastest ascent and descent.

● **Fastest ascent and descent – unaided** Simon Mtuy (Tanzania) still holds one record, however, for on 22 February 2006 he climbed from Umbwe Gate to the summit and back in 9 hours 19 minutes. In doing so, he achieved the fastest ever unaided ascent and descent (by unaided, they mean that he carried his own food, water and clothing). This despite suffering from a nasty bout of diarrhoea, as well as taking a three-minute break at the top to video himself, plus two further breaks to vomit!

I should also mention that Simon, who runs Summit Expeditions and Nomadic Experience trekking agency in Moshi, was there to greet Kilian as he finished his record-breaking feat – proving he is a gentleman as well as an extraordinary athlete!

● **Fastest ascent (female)** On 4 September 2011 Debbie Bachmann, originally from Zimbabwe but now a resident of Tanzania where she works as a guide on Kilimanjaro, recorded a time of 11 hours and 51 minutes on reaching Uhuru Peak via the Umbwe Route and Western Breach. Debbie, a mother of two, was aged 34 at the time and it was her 27th time at the summit. She then ran down, reaching the bottom in 18 hours and 31 minutes – though this includes half-an-hour's delay at Mweka Camp as the warden was reluctant to let her continue as it was late in the day!

● **Youngest person to reach the summit** On 21 January 2008 Keats Boyd from Los Angeles successfully hauled his 7-year-old body up to the summit of Africa's highest

ballot. A cigarette butt discarded by one of them is said to have started the blaze, though others have pointed an accusing finger at local farmers who like to clear their farms by fire before the start of the annual rains.

Other possible culprits include honey collectors, who make fires to smoke out the bees; we've even heard accusations that those in charge of the park, KINAPA, start fires in order to extract more money from TANAPA, the body that oversees the administration of all of the country's reserves and parks – though we think this has more to do with the Tanzanians' love of a good conspiracy theory than any basis in reality. Needless to say, we don't endorse any of these accusations.

Yet no matter what indignities are heaped upon it, Kilimanjaro continues to inspire both awe and respect in those who gaze upon it. And while man will continue to visit in droves and in his clumsy way will carry on defacing and demeaning it, setting it ablaze and covering it with litter, the mountain itself remains essentially the same powerful, ineffably beautiful sight it always was; perhaps because, while we throw all that we can at it, the Roof of Africa does what it always has done – and what it does best: it simply rises above it all.

mountain – and in doing so became the youngest person ever to reach the top of Kilimanjaro. An impressive feat, not least because in breaking the record Keats must also have broken all sorts of rules, including the one that says you have to be at least 10 to climb Kili! That record was challenged in 2013 by Aaryan Balaji, a Grade 2 student of Mahatma Gandhi International School in Port Blair, India, who was also seven; however, despite extensive research we have been unable to find out his *exact* age and thus determine who was the youngest. The youngest person to climb Kilimanjaro who *was* above the minimum age was Jordan Romero of Big Bear Lake, California, who achieved the summit on 23 July 2006 at the tender age of 10 years and 11 days.

● **Oldest person to reach the summit** Perhaps surprisingly, this is the record that has changed hands most frequently over the past few years. Currently the record for the oldest man and oldest woman to climb Kili is held by the same couple, Martin and Esther Kafer, from Vancouver, Canada, who have been married since 1953 and who reached the summit in September 2012 aged 85 and 84 respectively. Esther was just a year older than Bernice Buum, who reached the summit aged 83 in September 2010; while Martin's achievement pipped those of farmer Richard Byerley from Washington, USA, who in October 2011 reached the summit of Africa's highest mountain at the ripe old age of 84 years and 71 days – and who in turn had eclipsed British grandad George Solt, a retired professor from Olney, Buckinghamshire, who the previous summer had summited at the age of 82.

Those Kilimanjaro-buffs among you will note that Mr Kafer is in fact two years younger than Valtée Daniel, the mysterious Frenchman who at 87 is accepted by some as the oldest man on the summit. But Mr Daniel's climb has never been recognized by the *Guinness Book of Records*, who insist that any record attempt is verified by independent witnesses and must be filmed, photographed and meticulously documented in a log book.

KILIMANJARO

Fauna and flora

Kilimanjaro is often called 'The Island Above the Clouds' because it boasts more unique species than many small countries. Many happy years could be spent studying and writing about this mountain's fascinating flora and fauna. The following, therefore, is but a small introduction to the nature of Kilimanjaro.

FAUNA

In order to see much in the way of fauna, you have to be either very lucky or, it would seem, an author of a book on Kilimanjaro. When Hans Meyer was coming down from the mountain in 1889 he spotted an elephant on the slopes. In 1926 a leopard was found frozen in the summit ice at a place we now call Leopard Point – providing Hemingway with the inspiration for *The Snows of Kilimanjaro*. The mountaineer, HW Tilman, saw 27 eland on the Saddle when he passed this way in 1937, with each, according to him, especially adapted for the freezing conditions with thicker fur. In 1962, renowned travel writer Wilfred Thesiger and two companions were accompanied to the summit by five wild dogs (aka African hunting dogs). Though the dogs then turned round and disappeared after the three men made the summit, paw-prints in the ice proved that this wasn't the first time they had climbed to the top. More recently, Rick Ridgeway claimed he saw a leopard on his ascent, as did Geoffrey Salisbury while leading his group of blind climbers to the summit; and in 1979 a local guide called David was savaged by a pack of wild dogs above the Mandara Huts and lost a finger.

We mention these stories to demonstrate that the more exotic fauna of East Africa does occasionally venture onto the mountain. It just doesn't happen very often, with most animals preferring to be somewhere where there aren't 50,000-plus trekkers (not to mention their crews) marching around every year.

The decline of fauna on Kilimanjaro is perhaps best illustrated by these random quotes I have drawn from

Baboons in the branches of a Dum palm
(from *Across East African Glaciers,* Hans Meyer, 1891)

Tanganyika Notes and Records: Kilimanjaro, an excellently informative book published in March 1965. It's depressing to see how abundant the wildlife appeared even then, less than fifty years ago.

'Millard considers that the elephant population of Kilimanjaro is of the order of 1,500 and from personal observation this appears to be a very reasonable estimate.'
'Giraffe have been seen by Millard in heavy forest within the montane forest belt.'
'Up to about 1950, Rhinoceros were often encountered in the forest above Marangu...They are still to be found from West Kilimanjaro where their position is fairly good around to Kitenden where their numbers have been considerably reduced.'
'Wild Dogs have been seen in the Mandera [sic] *(Bismark) hut area and in the country to the south of Mawenzi (Forest Division).'*

Just for the record, elephants do still wander up the slopes of Kilimanjaro, particularly from Amboseli and from the West Kilimanjaro corridor, though in nothing like the numbers recorded above; giraffe are seldom if ever recorded on the mountain now, though it's feasible that they too may wander up the northern and western slopes; the total population of rhino in the whole of Tanzania is now less than fifty, with the nearest to Kilimanjaro now well over 100km away in Ngorongoro Crater to the west or Mkomazi National Park to the south-east; while wild dogs are so rare now in Tanzania that a website has even been set up so that those fortunate enough to spot one can tell the world about it!

So in all probability you will see virtually nothing during your time on the mountain beyond the occasional monkey or mouse. Nevertheless, keep your mouth shut and your eyes open and you never know...

Forest and cultivated zones

Animals are more numerous down in the forest zone than anywhere else on the mountain; unfortunately, so is the cover provided by trees and bushes, so sightings remain rare. As with the four-striped grass mice of Horombo (see p258), it tends to be those few species for whom the arrival of man has been a boon

Protecting Kilimanjaro

Kilimanjaro has enjoyed some form of protection since the early years of the 20th century under German rule, when the mountain and surrounding area were designated as a game preserve. In 1921 this status was upgraded to become a forest and game preserve, thereby protecting the precious cloud forest that beards Kili's lower slopes.

Another change in 1957 saw Tanganyika National Parks Authority propose that the mountain become a national park, though this wasn't actually realized until 1973, when **Kilimanjaro National Park (KINAPA)** was formed; a park that, for simplicity's sake, the authorities decided would include all land above 2700m. KINAPA didn't actually officially open until 1977; 12 years later, in 1989, the park was declared a **World Heritage Site** by UNESCO. In 2013 it was also honoured as **one of the Seven Natural Wonders of Africa**, along with its neighbours the Ngorongoro Crater and Serengeti migration. Thus Northern Tanzania plays host to three of the seven (the Serengeti migration being shared with Kenya), with the others being the Nile River, Sahara Desert, Red Sea Reef and the Okavango Delta.

KILIMANJARO

> ❏ 'URGENT MESSAGE:
> *Location: Amboseli Game Park, Kenya*
> *Human population: 150*
> *Baboon population: 90,000*
> *Meteorological conditions: Severe drought*
> *Water supplies: Nil*
> *Situation: Mutilated bodies discovered.*
> *Baboons have turned into man-eating pri-*
> *mates – POSITION DESPERATE!'*
>
> Taken from the back cover of terrible 1980s'
> horror film *In the Shadow of Kilimanjaro*,
> supposedly based on a true story. You may
> like to consider this when walking past a
> troop of them on your Meru climb.

rather than a curse that are the easiest to spot, including **blue monkeys**, which appear daily near the Mandara Huts and which are not actually blue but grey or black with a white throat. These are the plainer relatives of the beautiful **colobus monkey**, which has the most enviable tail in the animal kingdom; you can see a troop of these at the start of the forest zone on the Rongai and Lemosho routes, and near the Mandara Huts, where a couple are semi-tame. Strangely, despite their beauty, their name is actually derived from the Greek for 'mutilated' as unlike other primates they don't have a proper opposable thumb but a mere stump. This 'deformity' is even more bizarre when one considers that they are amongst the most arboreal of monkeys; in other words, they very rarely drop down to the ground, preferring instead to spend their time in the trees – where you would have thought a proper opposable thumb would be an advantage for grabbing hold of branches etc. Indeed, so rarely does it drop down to the ground that it would normally be rather difficult to spot were it not for its flamboyant coat and its strange, frog-like croak.

Olive baboons, **civets**, **leopards**, **mongooses** and **servals** are said to live in the mountain's forest as well, though sightings are extremely rare; here, too, lives the **bush pig** with its distinctive white stripe running along its back from head to tail.

Then there's the **honey badger**. Don't be fooled by the rather cute name, for as well as being blessed with a face only its mother could love, these are the most powerful and fearless carnivores for their size in Africa. Even lions give them a wide berth. You should too: not only can they cause a lot of damage to your person but the thought of having to tell your friends that, of all the bloodthirsty creatures that roam the African plains, you got savaged by a badger, is too shaming to contemplate. Of a similar size, the **aardvark** has enormous claws but unlike the honey badger this nocturnal, long-snouted anteater is entirely benign. So fear not: as the old adage goes, aardvark never killed anyone. Both aardvarks and honey badgers are rarely, if ever, seen on the mountain. Nor are **porcupines**, Africa's largest rodents. Though also present in this zone, they are both shy and nocturnal and your best chance of seeing one is as roadkill on the way to Nairobi.

Further down, near or just above the cultivated zone, **bushbabies** or galagos are more easily heard than seen as they come out at night and jump on the roofs of the huts. Here, too, is the **small-spotted genet** with its distinctive black-and-white tail, and the noisy, chipmunk-like **tree hyrax**.

One creature you definitely won't see at any altitude is the rhinoceros. Over-hunting has finally taken its toll of this most majestic of creatures – Count Teleki (see p115), for example, is said to have shot 89 of them during his time in East Africa, including four in one day – and, as we said earlier, there are none on or anywhere near Kilimanjaro today.

Heath, moorland and above

Just as plant-life struggles to survive much above 2800m, so animals too find it difficult to live on the barren upper slopes. Yet though we may see little, there are a few creatures living on Kilimanjaro's higher reaches.

Above the treeline you'll be lucky to see much. The one obvious exception to this rule is the **four-striped grass mouse**, which clearly doesn't find it a problem eking (or should that be eeking?) out an existence at high altitude; indeed, if you're staying in the Horombo Huts on the Marangu Route, one is probably running under your table while you read this, and if you stand outside for more than a few seconds at any campsite you should see them scurrying from rock to rock. Other rodents present at this level include the **harsh-furred** and **climbing mouse** and the **mole rat**, though all are far more difficult to spot. (Your best chance of seeing the harsh-furred mouse is probably on Shira Plateau, particularly amongst the heather by the toilets near the caves at Shira Caves Campsite and, less often, at Shira 1 Campsite on the Lemosho Route.)

For anything bigger than a mouse, your best chance above 2800m is either on the Shira Plateau, where **buffaloes and other grazers** are said to roam occasionally, or on the northern side of the mountain on the Rongai Route. Kenya's Amboseli National Park lies at the foot of the mountain on this side and many animals, particularly **elephants**, amble up the slopes from time to time. **Grey** and **red duikers**, **elands** and **bushbucks** are perhaps the most commonly seen animals at this altitude, though sightings are still extremely rare.

None of these larger creatures lives above the tree-line of Kilimanjaro permanently, however, and as with the **leopards** that occasionally make their way up the slopes, they are, like us, probably no more than day-trippers.

On Kibo itself the entomologist George Salt found a species of **spider** that was living in the **alpine zone** at altitudes of up to 5500m. What exactly these high-altitude arachnids live on up there is unknown – though Salt reckoned it was probably the flies that blew in on the wind, of which he found a few, and which appeared to be unwilling or unable to fly. What is known is that the spiders live underground, better to escape the rigours of the weather. We've also seen a white butterfly on the way up to Mawenzi Tarn Huts at 4122m; once again, we can only assume that it has been blown up the slopes from the moorland or forest zone.

AVIFAUNA

Kilimanjaro is great for birdlife. The cultivated fields on the lower slopes provide plenty of food, the forest zone provides shelter and plenty of nesting sites, while the barren upper slopes are ideal hunting grounds for raptors.

KILIMANJARO

Hartlaub's turaco

In the **forest**, one of the easier birds to spot is the dark green **Hartlaub's turaco**, partly because of its noisy, monkey-like call, and partly because when it flies, viewers are treated to flashes of bright red under-wings. If you're lucky you may also come across **silvery-cheeked hornbills**, though to be honest you're more likely to see them on Meru, and even in Arusha near Jacaranda Hotel, than on Kilimanjaro. **Montane white-eyes** – small green birds with distinctive white circles around their eyes – can be found around Machame Huts and occasionally elsewhere on the mountain; another habitué of the Machame Huts is the **common stonechat**, a relative of the more common alpine chat but slightly more striking in appearance, with a white stripe on its black wings and a chestnut patch on its breast. Other small birds said to live in the forest include the **speckled mousebird** that hang around the fruit trees, and the **trogon** which, despite a red belly, is difficult to see because it remains motionless in the branches. Smaller birds include the **Ruppell's robin chat** (black and white head, grey top, orange lower half) and the **common bulbul**, with a black crest and yellow beneath the tail.

Tropical boubou

Further up the slopes, the noisy, scavenging, garrulous **white-necked raven** is a constant presence on the mountain during the day, eternally hovering on the breeze around the huts and lunch-stops on the lookout for any scraps. Smaller but just as ubiquitous is the **alpine chat**, a small brown bird with white side feathers in its tail, and the **streaky seed-eater**, another brown bird (this time with streaks on its back) that often hangs around the huts. The **alpine swift** also enjoys these misty, cold conditions. The prize for the most beautiful bird on the mountain, however, goes to the dazzling **scarlet-tufted malachite sunbird**. Metallic-green save for a small scarlet patch on either side of its chest, this delightful bird can often be seen hovering above the grass, hooking its long beak in to reach the flies sheltering in the lobelias.

Speckled mousebird

Climbing further, we come to raptor territory. You'll rarely see these birds up close as they spend most of the day gliding on the currents looking for prey. **Augur buzzards** are very occasionally spotted hovering in the breeze; these are impressive birds in themselves – especially if you're lucky enough to see one up close – though not as large as the **crowned eagle** and the rare **lammergeyer**, a giant vulture with long wings, a wedge tail and a tufty beard beneath the beak.

Blue monkey

Colobus monkey

Vervet monkeys (Meru)

White-necked raven

Skink or grey lizard

Four-striped grass mouse

Streaky seed eater

Malachite sunbird

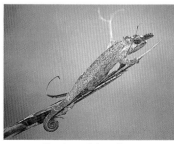

Two-horned chameleon

Lammergeyer

FLORA

It is said that to climb up Kilimanjaro is to walk through **four seasons in four days**. It is true, of course, and nowhere is this phenomenon more apparent than in its flora. The variety of flora found on Kilimanjaro can be ascribed in part to the mountain's tremendous height and in part to its proximity to both the equator and the Indian Ocean. Add to this the variations in climate, solar radiation and temperature from the top of the mountain to the bottom (temperatures are estimated to drop by 1°C for every 150m gain in altitude), and you end up with the ideal conditions for highly differentiated and distinctive vegetation zones. In all, **Kilimanjaro is said to have between four and six distinctive zones**, or 'seasons', depending on what you read.

Cultivated zone and forest (800m-2800m)

The forest zone, along with the cultivated zone that lies below it, together receive the most rainfall – about 2300mm per year – of any part of the mountain. The forest also houses the greatest variety of both fauna (see p124) and flora.

For the layman, it may be difficult at first to identify the individual species of **tree**, though some do stand out. On the Marangu Route the first trees you'll possibly notice – and Antipodeans should recognize – are actually non-native: the pale-barked **eucalyptus** was planted by the first park warden of Kilimanjaro, though it is now a tree that his successors are trying to eradicate as it takes so much water from the land. Enormous **camphorwoods** also flourish at this altitude, as do **fig** trees and *talamontana*, or **wild mango**. Further up the slopes towards the upper limit of the zone, the smooth grey **African holly** (*Ilex mitis*), with its characteristic red and yellow fruit, becomes the dominant tree.

Seradoxus
Fireball lily

Trifolium usambarensis

Podocarpus (left) and *juniper* (right)

African redwood (*Hagenia abyssinica*), though nothing like as common, is perhaps more recognizable with its enormous, blousy, pink-flowered panicles – it's quite the campest tree on the mountain.

Another instantly recognizable species is the giant fern, *Cyathea sp*, which clearly enjoys the damp conditions, as does *Usnea sp* or **old man's beard**, which lies draped over most of the branches at the upper limit of the forest zone. At about the same altitude is the **podocarpus**, with its slender-finger leaves, and the **juniper** whose leaves, at least when gazing up at the canopy, look similar; put examples of each side by side, however, and you can clearly see the difference between them as the photo (see p130) clearly demonstrates. Incidentally, with the drier climate the trees of the northern slopes are slightly different, with **olive trees** now abundant and one species, ***Olea kilimandscharica***, indigenous to the mountain. What catches the eyes of most trekkers is not these giants, however, but the small splashes of colour that grow in their shade: the **flowers**. The star of the montane forest zone is the beautiful flower ***Impatiens kilimanjari***, an endemic fleck of dazzling red and yellow in the shape of an inch-long tuba. You'll see them by the side of the path on the southern side of the mountain. Vying for the prime piece of real estate that exists between the roots of the trees are other, equally elegant flowers including its relatives, *Impatiens pseudoviola* and *Impatiens digitata*, and the

beautiful **African violet**, *Viola eminii*. Hanging from the trees is the ***Begonia meyeri johannis***, with sweet-smelling white and pink flowers that often litter the path like confetti. There's a **lobelia**, too, with blue or pink, distinctive, three-lobed flowers, that thrives in both the forest and the heath zone above. It's very similar to the ones you'll find in the hanging baskets of Europe (though it bears very little resemblance to the lobelias you will see further up the mountain). For that matter, it also bears little resemblance to *Lobelia gibberoa*, a giant lobelia almost 5m tall with a whorl of large leaves at its top and a very tall flower spike; these tend to love water and you'll usually find them growing on the banks of streams. **Orchids** also enjoy the dark moist conditions of the montane forest, in particular *Polystachyus*, with flowers that always resemble, to me at least, insects in flight.

Perhaps the most unusual aspect of Kilimanjaro's forest zone, however, is not the plants and trees that it *does* have but one that it doesn't. Kili is almost unique in East Africa in

Impatiens kilimanjari

Impatiens pseudoviola

Begonia meyeri-johannis

Impatiens digitata

Lobelia gibberoa

Polystachyus (orchid)

*Parochaetus
communis*

Kniphofia thomsonii
Red hot poker

Hypericum revolutum
St John's Wort

Protea kilimandsharica
(with malachite
sunbird)

not having any bamboo at the upper limit of the forest zone, possibly because it is one of the driest mountains and cannot support bamboo stands the way other African mountains can. As a result, the forest zone ends suddenly, with little warning, throwing us immediately into the less shady trails of the ...

Heath and moorland (2800m-4000m)

These two zones overlap, and together occupy the area immediately above the forest from around 2800m to 4000m – known as the **low alpine zone**. Temperatures can drop below 0°C up here and most of the precipitation that does fall comes from the mist that is prevalent at this height.

Immediately above the forest zone is the **alpine heath**. Rainfall here is around 1300mm per year. Both the **giant heather** *Erica excelsa* and the similar but less bushy *Erica arborea* grow in abundance. The latter also exists in the upper part of the forest zone, where it can grow to 10 metres or more; the higher you go, however, the less impressive the specimens, with many refusing to grow beyond 2.5-3m. **St John's wort**, *Hypericum revolutum*, with its distinctive yellow flowers, also grows at this level, and occasionally at the upper reaches of the forest too. Most people will know this flower thanks to its anti-depressant properties.

Grasses now dominate the mountain slopes, picked out here and there with some splendid wild flowers including the yellow-flowered *Protea kilimandscharica*, an indigenous rarity that can be seen on the Mweka and Marangu trails and, so we've been told, around Maundi Crater – the best place for botanists to spot wild flowers. A whole raft of *Helichrysum* species make their first appearance here too, though certainly not their last; see box p135.

A plant that most readers will recognize instantly is the back-garden favourite *Kniphofia thomsonii*, better known to most as the **red-hot poker**. Climbing higher, you'll begin to come across **sedges** such as *Mariscus kerstenii* with, like most sedges, a triangular stalk. Keep your eyes peeled and if you're extremely lucky you may also spot an orchid, *Disa stairsii*, a short flower with a spike of small pink flowers. Also growing in the grass here is a pretty, delicate **anemone**, *Anemone thomsonii*, with white flowers; a **scabious**, *Scabiosa columbaria*; and, occasionally, a vivid red **gladiolus** that's simply gorgeous, *Gladiolus watsonides*, which you can also find living in the upper reaches of the forest belt.

The shrubs are shrinking now: *Philippia trimera* is the most common of them, along with the gorse-like *Adenocarpus* beside which it often grows; the prettiest shrub in the upper reaches of the heath zone is the pink-flowered *Blaeria filago*. Growing in abundance in patches at this altitude is **African wormwood** (*Artemisia afra*), a waist-high plant that is more easily distinguished by its pungent aroma that perfumes the air for entire sections of the trail than by its rather dreary grey-green leaves. Known to the Chagga as *kichachayia* (my spelling), the wormwood, when placed in hot water and drunk as tea, is said to have medicinal properties and is a good cure for a bad stomach.

Climbing ever further, you'll soon reach the imperceptible boundary of the moorland zone, which tends to have clearer skies but an even cooler climate. Average per annum precipitation is now down to 525mm. At this altitude, perhaps the weirdest plant on the mountain is the strange *lobelia deckenii*, another endemic species. These curious, phallic- and cabbage-shaped plants take eight years to flower (the blue flowers are hidden inside the leaves to protect them from frost), and enjoy a symbiotic relationship with *Nectarinia johnstoni*, the dazzling green malachite sunbird. It is said that any insects at

Gladiolus watsonides

Anemone thomsonii

Artemisia afra
African wormwood

Adenocarpus mannii

Disa stairsii
(orchid)

Bidens kilimandsharica

Lobelia deckenii

Thunbergia alata

Bearded lichen

Carduus keniensis

Lobelia deckenii flowers

Leonotis nepetifolia

Dierama pendulum

this altitude are attracted by the purple flowers of the lobelia and by the warmth and shelter that the velvet leaves supply. This in turn attracts the sunbirds who feed on the flies – and in doing so pollinate the flower. The lobelias are at their best in February and March.

Sharing the same cold, bleak environment are the most distinctive plants on the entire mountain: the giant **tree groundsel**, or **dendrosenecio** (until recently called simply 'senecio', a name that you will see crop up in most books and is used by all the guides too). Even without the name change the literature on these plants is most confusing so I am grateful to Mr Eric Knox, director of Indiana University Herbarium and the leading authority on these plants, for helping me.

There are two main dendrosenecio species on Kilimanjaro. The first is *Dendrosenecio kilimanjari*, which has two subspecies: *D. kilimanjari ssp cottonii* is found only above 3600m and has dull, mustard-coloured flowers. They

Dendrosenecio kilimanjari (tree groundsel) *ssp kilimanjarii*

Dendrosenecio kilimanjari (tree groundsel) *ssp cottonii*

cleverly protect themselves from the cold by using their dead leaves (which are like felt) to insulate their trunk. These groundsels are slow growers; according to some guides, you can estimate the age of a groundsel by counting the number of 'cabbages' or rosettes, with each 'cabbage' representing about 25 years growth. They tend to favour the damper, more sheltered parts of the mountain, which is why you'll see them in abundance near Barranco Campsite as well as other, smaller valleys and ravines. The second subspecies, *D. kilimanjari ssp kilimanjarii*, thrives further down the slopes, can grow up to 5m high, and on the rare occasion it flowers the petals themselves are yellow and grow from a one-metre-long spike. Even further down, at a range of between 2750 and 3350 metres at the fringes of the montane forest, we get the second dendrosenecio species, *Dendrosenecio johnstonii*. Your best chance of seeing these giants is along the Machame Route where they form surprisingly big trees.

Alpine desert (4000m-5000m)

By the time you reach this altitude, only three species of tussock grass and a few everlastings can withstand the extreme conditions. This is the alpine desert, where plants have to survive in drought conditions (precipitation here is less than

❏ Identifying helichrysums (everlastings)

Perhaps the most prolific plants on the mountain, and ones that make their appearance just above the forest and continue up to the foot of Kibo (and even, on occasions, on it), are the helichrysums, also known as everlastings; those dry-looking flowers that resemble living pot pourri and grow in clumps all over the moorland (as well as above and below it). Members of the daisy family, the identification of individual helichrysums is complicated by three factors: there are many **different subspecies**; secondly they change their appearance the further up the mountain they go in order to adapt to the conditions; and thirdly they all look much the same. So how do you distinguish between different types of helichrysums? Well, the easiest one to recognize is

Helichrysum meyeri-johanis, named after the first man to climb Kilimanjaro, which has a pinkish tinge to its petals. The others, however, require a little more detective work. *Helichrysum kilimanjari* differs from *H meyeri-johanis* in that its flowers are yellow/brown, and when you crush its leaves they give off a distinctive lemon smell. Those two tend to remain in the moorland zone, but as you move up to the high desert other species appear. *Helichrysum cymosum* and *Helichrysum splendidum* both bear tight clusters of small yellow flowers, the former being distinguishable by its leaves that hug the main stem tightly in order to protect it from the cold. *Helichrysum citrispinum* also has leaves that perform this function, though its flowers are larger, white, dry, and don't grow in tight clusters. Also present at this altitude is *Helichrysum newii*, named after Charles New, the first man to reach the snowline on Kilimanjaro. A truly remarkable plant, this was the helichrysum that was found surviving at

Helichrysum meyeri-johanis

Helichrysum kilimanjari

Helichrysum citrispinum

Helichrysum splendidum

Helichrysum cymosum

Helichrysum newii

5670m near the eastern fumarole in the crater – a record on the mountain. It is believed that the heat from the fumarole allowed this plant to survive the extreme cold.

Ranunculus oreophylus
Yellow star

Arabis alpina
Alpine rock cress

200mm per year), and put up with both inordinate cold and intense sun, usually in the same day. The **everlastings** continue to dominate, though they are shorter and stumpier now, presumably huddling nearer to the ground to protect themselves from the wind. At this altitude flowers need special strategies to cope. The striking **yellow star**, *Ranunculus oreophylus*, and *Haplocarpha rueppellii* both do so by hugging the ground, better to avoid the wind and feed on what little warmth the ground can provide. The other yellow flowers at this altitude are the straggly **senecio species**, usually found surviving – if not exactly thriving – in the lee of the rocks and boulders. The shy white *Arabis alpina* or **Alpine rock cress** also clings on to survival at this chilly altitude by sheltering behind rocks.

Ice cap (5000m-5895m)

On Kibo, almost nothing lives. There is virtually no water. On the rare occasions that precipitation occurs, most of the moisture instantly disappears into the porous rock or is locked away in the glaciers. That said, specimens of *Helichrysum newii*, an **everlasting** that truly deserves its name, have been found in the crater (see p135), and **moss and lichen** are said to exist almost up to the summit. While these mainly orange lichens may not be the most spectacular of plants, it may interest you to know that their growth rate on the upper reaches of Kilimanjaro is estimated to be just 0.5mm in diameter per year; for this reason, scientists have concluded that the larger lichens on Kilimanjaro could be amongst the oldest living things on earth, being hundreds and possibly thousands of years old!

The People of Kilimanjaro: the Chagga

With regard to the Chagga people, they are a fine, well-built race. Their full development of bone and muscle being probably due to the exercise they all have to take in moving about on steep hills: they seem intellectually superior to the general run of coast Natives, and despite their objectionable traits (almost always present in the uneducated Native), such as lying, dirty habits, thieving, &c., they are certainly a very nice and attractive race.
Rev A Downes Shaw *To Chagga and Back – An Account of a Journey to Moshi, the Capital of Chagga, Eastern Equatorial Africa*, 1924

Kilimanjaro is the homeland of the Chagga people, one of Tanzania's largest ethnic groups. It is fair to say that when you are in Moshi, Marangu or Machame, there is little indication that you are in a 'Chagga town'. Yet in the smaller villages, though waning year by year, traditional Chagga culture remains fairly strong and occasionally a reminder of the past is uncovered by today's tourist, particularly when passing through the smaller villages on the less-visited eastern side of Kilimanjaro. Such finds make visits to these villages truly fascinating.

Do not, however, come to Kilimanjaro expecting to witness some of the more extreme practices described in this section. This point needs emphasizing: the Chaggas' traditional way of life has been eroded by the depredations of Western culture and, as far as we know, is now largely extinct. Indeed, much of the material on which the following account is based is provided by the reports of the 19th- and early 20th-century Europeans who visited the area; in particular, Charles Dundas's comprehensive tome, *Kilimanjaro and its People*, which was first published way back in 1924. (Incidentally, you can see a portrait of Dundas in Moshi's Union Café, where he's celebrated as the first boss of the Kilimanjaro Native Cooperative Union, KNCU, see p205.)

This, of course, begs the question: why have we included in a modern guide to Kilimanjaro descriptions of obsolete Chagga practices and beliefs that were largely wiped out almost 100 years ago? Well, research revealed the relevance of this inclusion since there are still faint echoes of their traditional way of life that have survived into the present day. Reading this admittedly brief account of the Chagga and how they lived and thought could provide you with a better understanding – and thereby some insight – into the mind, beliefs and behaviour of the people who live in Kilimanjaro's shadow today.

ORIGINS

The Chagga are believed to have arrived between 400 and 250 years ago from the north-east, following local upheaval in that area. Logically, therefore, the eastern side of the mountain would have been the first to have been settled.

(Opposite) Traditional Chagga 'beehive' hut and raised granary.

Upon their arrival these new immigrants would have found that the mountain was already inhabited. An aboriginal people known as the Wakonyingo, who were possibly pygmies, were already living here, as indeed were the Wangassa, a tribe similar to the Masai, and the Umbo of the Usambara mountains. All of these groups were either driven out or absorbed by the Chagga.

Initially, these new immigrants were a disparate bunch, with different beliefs, customs and even languages. With no feelings of kinship or loyalty to their neighbour, they instead settled into family groups, or **clans**. According to Dundas, in his day some 732 clans existed on Kilimanjaro; by 1924, however, when his book was published, some of these clans were already down to just a single member.

These family ties were gradually cut and lost over time as people moved away to settle on other parts of the mountain. Thus, in place of these blood ties, people developed new loyalties to the region in which they were living and to the neighbours with whom they shared the land. Out of this emerged 20 or so states or chiefdoms, most of them on a permanent war footing with the other 19. Wars between the tribes and indeed between villages in the same tribe were commonplace, though they usually took the form of organized raids by one village on another rather than actual pitched battles. Slaves would be taken during

---

Chagga/Kichagga language – a quick introduction

The language of the Chagga, Kichagga, is classified as a Niger-Congo language and has various **dialects** including Vunjo, Rombo, Machame, Huru and Old Moshi. The following is a very brief introduction to that dialect spoken in Marangu. As Chagga is rarely written down, compiling this 'phrase-book' wasn't easy; indeed, many of the spellings below are nothing more than phonetic guesswork. For their help with this box I am indebted to my Chagga chums, Amina Malya and Vincent Munuo; and especially Frank Mtei, who came up with the first draft of the translations below; and Alex Minja for his expert help too.

1	*kimu*	2	*shiwi*	3	*shiraru*	4	*shina*	5	*shitanu*
6	*shirandaru*	7	*mfungare*	8	*nyanya*	9	*kenda*	10	*ikumi*

Yes / No	*Ye'e / Ote*	I have a headache	*Ngiwawiyo mrue*
Please	*Ngakuterewa*	I feel sick	*Ngiwawiyo*
Thank you	*Aika*	I am very cold	*Ngiichoo mbeo*
How are you?	*Shimbonyi shapfo?*	Will you carry me?	*Ochirima ingiira*
Very well, thank you	*Nashicha kapisa, aika*	I do not like porridge	*Ngikundi msopfo*
How old are you?	*Nuore maka inga?*	I cannot feel my fingers	*Ngiichue shimnue shewaawaa*
I am British	*Inyi nyimwingeresa*		
I am American	*Inyi nyimwamerikany*	There is an elephant sleeping in my tent	*Kuwore njofu eela itentiny lyako*
Don't mind	*Molaswe*		
How far is it to the camp?	*Ngeshika masaa yenga handun gendelaa?*	A leopard is biting my leg	*Kuwore rung'we ilya kurende koko*
How many times have you climbed the mountain?	*Ni mara tsinga ulemro msari?*	We are together!	*Luilose!*

these raids, cattle rustled and huts burned down, though there was often little bloodshed – the weaker party would merely withdraw at the first sign of approaching hostilities and might even try to negotiate a price for peace.

Eventually the number of groups was whittled down to just six tribes, or states, with each named after one of the mountain's rivers. So, for example, there are the Wamoshi Chaggas (after the Moshi River) and the Wamachame Chaggas who settled near Machame River. With all this intermingling going on, a few words inevitably became used by all the people living on the mountain – and from this unlikely start grew a common language, of which each tribe had its own dialect. Similar customs developed between the tribes, though as with the language they differed in the detail. However, it was only when the Germans took control of the region during the latter part of the 19th century and the local people put aside their differences to present a united front in disputes with their colonial overlords that a single ethnic group was identified and named the Chagga. From this evolved a single, collective Chagga consciousness.

Today the Chaggas, despite their diverse origins, are renowned for having a strong sense of identity and pride. They are also amongst the richest and most powerful people in Tanzania, thanks in part to the fertile soils of Kilimanjaro, and in part to the Western education that they have been receiving for longer than almost any other tribe in East Africa, Kilimanjaro being one of the first places to accept missionaries from Europe. Take a tour around Tanzania and you will also find the Chagga people to be one of the most widespread of all the tribes, seemingly able to settle in even the furthest-flung corners of the land, and – thanks to their talent for trade and politics – to thrive and prosper too.

SOCIAL STRUCTURE AND VILLAGE LIFE

Hans Meyer notes in his book that the biggest Chagga settlement when he visited in 1889 was Machame, with 8000 people. 'Moji' (Moshi) had 3000, as did Marangu. Each family unit, according to him, lived in two or three extremely simple thatched huts in the shape of beehives, with a granary and small courtyard attached. There are several examples of these **'beehive' huts** still dotted around Kilimanjaro's slopes. Only the **chief**, the head of village society and its lawmaker, lived in anything more extensive. The chief of every village was often venerated by his subjects and to meet him required going through an elaborate ceremony first. According to his report in the *Church Missionary Intelligencer*, Johannes Rebmann, the first white man to see Kilimanjaro, had to be sprinkled with goat's blood and the juice of a plant and was then left waiting for four days before being granted an audience with Masaki, the chief of Moshi. While modern society has reduced his role to a largely ceremonial one, the chief is still a widely respected person in village life today – though thankfully there is now less ceremony involved when paying him a visit.

There are other similarities between the Chagga society of yesterday and today. The economy was, then as now, largely agricultural, using the environmentally destructive slash-and-burn technique for clearing land. **Bananas** were once the most common crop, and though banana bushes were largely

THE CHAGGA VIEW OF KILIMANJARO

The summit of Kilimanjaro is and always has been as enchanting to the Chagga as it has been to visitors. According to Dundas, the Chagga view the Kibo summit as something beautiful, eternal and strengthening, its snows providing streams that support life, while the clouds that gather on its slopes provide precious rainfall. By comparison, the plains that lie in the opposite direction are seen as oppressively hot, where famine stalks, drought and malaria are rife and large creatures such as crocodiles and leopards prey on man. Indeed, so venerated is Kilimanjaro that the Chagga dead are traditionally buried facing towards Kibo, and the side of the village facing the summit is known to be the honourable side, where meetings and feasts are held and chiefs are buried. Furthermore, when meeting somebody, he who comes from higher up the slopes of Kilimanjaro should traditionally greet the other first, for it is he who is coming from the lucky side.

Intriguingly, some Chagga myths about Kilimanjaro are remarkably accurate. In particular, the Chagga traditionally believed that the mountain was formed by a volcano – even though the main eruption that formed Kibo occurred around half a million years ago, way before the arrival of man. What's more, there is a story in Chagga folklore concerning the twin peaks of Mawenzi and Kibo, in which Mawenzi's fire burns out first, and the Mawenzi peak is forced to go to Kibo, whose fire was still burning. Parallels between this story and what scientists now believe really happened – with Kibo continuing to erupt long after Mawenzi expired – are remarkable.

Did the Chagga climb to the top of Kilimanjaro before the Europeans?

The answer is: probably not. The quote on p107 by Rebmann in which he talks about '*the popular traditions respecting the fate of the only expedition which had ever attempted to ascend its heights*' suggests that he had information that they had tried only once – and failed. True, they definitely seem to have reached the snowline before the *mzungu* (white man) arrived: their belief that Kibo was covered in a magic silver which melted on the way down suggests as much. Furthermore, Rebmann's guide refers to the snow on the summit of Kilimanjaro as 'coldness' (see p107), and later on Rebmann discovers the Chagga have a word for snow: Kibo. What's more, Meyer found traces of a hunting expedition on the Saddle. All of which seem to confirm that they had climbed Kilimanjaro and had some experience of snow. But the fact that Charles New's entourage of porters and guides were buck naked when they climbed up to the snow-line suggests that they were, on the whole, unused to the conditions on Kibo; that, and the fact that the name Kilimanjaro, if it is of Chagga origin (about which, see box p102), roughly translates as 'That which is impossible for birds', suggests they thought that it was therefore impossible for man to reach the top.

Charles Dundas is equally sceptical of the notion that the Chagga climbed Kilimanjaro before Meyer:

It is inconceivable that natives can ever have ascended to the crater rim, for apart from cold, altitude and superstitious fears, it is a sheer impossibility that they could have negotiated the ice. Nor is there any tradition among the natives that anyone went up as high... Rebmann tells us that Rengwa, great-grandfather of the present chief of Machame, sent an expedition to investigate the nature of the ice, which descends very low above Machame, but is impossible to scale. Only one of the party survived, his hands and feet frozen and crippled for life; all the rest were destroyed by the cold, or by evil spirits, as the survivor reported.

replaced by **coffee** plantations in the early 20th century, both are still grown today.

When it came to trading these bananas and coffee in former times, instead of the Tanzanian shilling people used red and blue glass beads as currency, or lengths of cloth known as *doti*. One hundred beads were equal to one *doti*, with which you could buy, for example, twenty unripe bananas; twelve *doti* would get you a cow.

RELIGION AND CEREMONIES

Unsurprisingly for a people that has been subjected to some pretty relentless missionary work for over a century, most Chagga are today **Christian**. Traditional beliefs are still held by some, though the intensity of the beliefs and the excesses of many of the rituals have largely disappeared. Superstition played a central role in traditional Chagga religion: witchcraft (*wusari* in Chagga) formed a major part, **rainmakers** and rain-preventers were important members of society and dreams were infallible oracles of the future; indeed, many Chagga were said to have dreamt of the coming of the white man to Kilimanjaro.

The traditional faith was based around belief in a god called **Ruwa**. Ruwa was a tolerant deity who, though neither the creator of the universe nor of man, nevertheless set the latter free from some sort of unspecified incarceration. Ruwa had little to do with mankind following this episode, however, so the Chagga instead **worshipped their ancestors**, whom they believed could influence events on Earth. Chagga mythology had many parallels with stories from the Bible, including one concerning the fall of man (though in the Chagga version, a sweet potato was the forbidden fruit, and it was a stranger rather than a serpent that persuaded the first man to take a bite); there are also stories that bear a resemblance to the tales of Cain and Abel, and the great flood.

The Chagga faith also had its own **concept of sin** and their own version of the Catholic practice of confession. In the Chagga religion, however, it is not the sinner but the person who is sinned against who must be purified, in order that the negative force does not remain with him or her. This purification would be performed by the local medicine man, with the victim bringing along the necessary ingredients for performing the 'cleansing'. These included the skin, dung and stomach contents of a hyrax (the small tree-dwelling mammals that live on Kilimanjaro); the shell and blood of a snail; the rainwater from a hollow tree and, as with all Chagga ceremonies, a large quantity of banana beer for the medicine man. These ingredients would then be put into a hole in the ground lined with banana leaves and with a gate or archway built above, which the victim would then have to pass through. This done, the victim would be painted by the medicine man using the mixture in the hole. This entire ceremony would be performed twice daily over four days.

Medicine men did more than care for one's spiritual health; they looked after one's physical well-being too. For the price of a goat and, of course, more banana beer, the medicine man would be able to cure any affliction using a whole host of methods – including spitting. If you were suffering from a fever, for instance, you could expect to be spat upon up to 80 times by the medicine man, who would finish off his performance by expectorating up your nostrils and then blowing hard up each to ensure the saliva reached its target. For this particular method, the traditional payment was one pot of honey – and probably some more banana beer.

Chagga warriors
(from *Across East African Glaciers,* **Hans Meyer**, 1891)

The Ngasi

The Ngasi was a brutal rite-of-passage ceremony that marked the passing of boys into adulthood. The ceremony was presided over by the so-called King of Ngasi, a man who had the authority to viciously flog any boy taking part in the ceremony who displeased him.

Before the Ngasi started, the boys who were to take part were summoned from their houses by the singing of lugubrious songs at the gate of their homes. From there they were taken to the place of ceremony deep in the forest and the proceedings began. **Hunting** formed a large part of the Ngasi; boys were tested on their ability to track down and kill game, the animals caught being smeared with the novices' excrement. Another test they had to undergo was to climb a tree on the riverbank and cross the river by clambering along its branches to where they intertwined with the branches of the trees on the other side. After this, a chicken would be sacrificed and the boys ordered to lick the blood.

The final part of the initial stage was the most brutal, however: orders were secretly given to the boys to slay a crippled or deformed youth amongst their number. Traditionally, the victim was killed in the night. The parents were never actually told what had happened to their son and, as all present at the Ngasi ceremony were sworn to silence, they rarely found out the whole story. The boys then moved to a new camp. They were now called Mbora, and were free to collect the old clothes that they had shed at the start of the Ngasi (one set of boy's clothes, of course, was left unclaimed). They then repaired to the chief's house for a feast, from where they headed home.

After the tribulations of the ceremony, the boys were allowed a month's holiday, before they returned to the chief's house to participate in the sacrificing of a bull. They were then free to head back to their homes, raping any young women they chanced to meet on the way; the poor women had no redress. The Ngasi was now at an end; the boys who successfully completed the ceremony were now men.

Matrimony

Ver hard on Wachaga to get wife, but when he get her she can make do plant corn, she make wash and cook and make do work for him. Ingreza [English] man very much money to spend. She wife no can wash, no plant corn, herd goats or cook. All money, much merkani (cloth), heap money, big dinner. She eat much posho. She no can cook dinner. She only make 'Safari' and look. Porr, porr Ingreza man. A local's view of matrimony as recorded in **Peter MacQueen**'s book *In Wildest Africa*, published in 1910

After the Ngasi, boys were free to marry. **Marriage** was arranged by the parents, though the boy and girl involved were allowed to voice their opinions – and unless the parents were particularly inflexible, these opinions would count for something. Furthermore, in order for the boy to stand a chance with his potential suitor, he had to woo her. The Chaggas' **courtship** process involved, as elsewhere in the world, a lot of gift-giving, though the gifts followed a strict set of rules: spontaneity played little part in this process. The first gift, for example, from the man to the woman, was always a necklace. The Chagga male would be well rewarded for his generosity, for traditionally in return the girl would dance naked all day with bells attached to her legs by her mother. Over the following days other gifts were exchanged until the time came when the girl, having visited all her relatives, would be shut away for three months. No work would be done by the girl during this time and she would be given fattening food and kept in a cage. At the end of this period a **dowry** would be paid, the marriage ceremony performed and the bride would be carried on the back of the Mkara (the traditional Chagga equivalent of the best man) to her new husband's house.

KILIMANJARO ECONOMY

Tourism is the biggest earner in the region, though **agriculture** is still very much part of the local economy. The volcanic soil of the mountain slopes, so rich with nutrients, is amongst the most fertile in East Africa. Thanks to the regular and reliable rainfall blown in from the Indian Ocean (see p97) and the proliferation of springs trickling forth from the bare rock, Kilimanjaro is also one of the damper parts of the region, and the south-eastern slopes particularly so, thus increasing still further the agricultural fecundity of the mountain.

On the lower slopes of Kilimanjaro annual staple crops such as beans, maize and millet are grown, while cash-crops such as Arabica coffee are planted in the *kihamba* land further up the mountainside. Bananas are also grown at this altitude, their leaves and stems providing both a nutrient-rich mulch for the coffee trees and fodder for the livestock that are traditionally grazed at this height. In Chagga society it is customary for a farmer's land to be divided between his sons on his death; whilst this may seem a fair way of dividing land, it also means that a farmer's landholdings diminish in size with every generation, and many farms are now less than a hectare in size.

The Chagga are also keen bee-keepers, the hives being hollow sections of a tree trunk closed at both ends and left to hang in trees; you may see these hives placed (illegally) in Kilimanjaro's forests or by the side of the Arusha–Marangu road. Once the swarm has taken possession and completed the combs the bees are smoked out and the honey collected.

4 ARRIVING IN EAST AFRICA: DAR ES SALAAM & NAIROBI

The following chapter is devoted to helping you take your first few steps in East Africa. It contains guides to the two cities you are most likely to fly into — namely **Dar es Salaam** (Tanzania) and **Nairobi** (Kenya). The guides to the two cities are deliberately rather brief but they should be adequate for finding your way around and for choosing somewhere to sleep and eat, as well to experience something of metropolitan East Africa.

We explain, at the end of each description, how to get to Kilimanjaro. **Kilimanjaro International Airport** is, of course, the most convenient airport for the mountain and with more and more airlines flying there this chapter may be surplus to requirements in the future; details about it can be found on p162.

Dar es Salaam

Dar es Salaam (commonly called Dar) is a city with a bit of an identity crisis: a large metropolis (population 2.2 million) which behaves as if it were a small and sleepy seaside town; a city that was at the forefront of the country's struggle for independence in the 1950s yet still contains the finest collection of dusty old colonial buildings in possibly the whole of East Africa; and a place that everybody thinks is the administrative capital of Tanzania – but isn't.

It *is* the commercial heart of the country, however, and has been almost since its inception in the 1860s by Sultan Sayyid Majid of Zanzibar. Intended as a mainland port for many of the goods and spices being traded on his island, the sultan, clearly a man of poetic bent, named his new city Dar es Salaam (Haven of Peace). And peacefully was how it spent its first few years, too, as the sultan died soon after founding the city, allowing Bagamoyo, a dhow port to the north, to emerge as the pre-eminent harbour on this particular stretch of the east coast.

Missionaries from Europe added fresh impetus to Dar with their arrival in the 1880s but it was the coming of the Germans in 1891 that really gave this city a fillip, the colonials feeling that the harbour here was more suitable to their steam-powered craft than Bagamoyo.

Having made Dar their seat of power, it remained the capital until 1973 when the Tanzanian government decided to move the legislature to Dodoma, smack in the geometric heart of the country – which probably seemed like a good idea at the time, until somebody pointed out the shortage of water and other basic amenities there.

So, while the capital may be Dodoma, much of the politicking and indeed everything else of importance takes place here in Dar. For tourists, there's nothing particularly special to warrant a long stay in this city; but by the same token, don't fret too much if you do have to spend some time in Dar: it's pleasant, it's laid back and, compared to Nairobi, it's a whole lot saner too.

A TOUR OF THE CITY

None of Dar's attractions is going to make your eyes pop out on springs from their sockets but the following half-day tour is fine for those with time to kill in the city and a cursory interest in the place. For those in a hurry, the **National Museum** (see box p146) at least is worth seeing, being the most absorbing and, for Kili-bound trekkers, the most relevant attraction in Dar. One word of warning: if any of the streets listed below seem unhealthily deserted – the lanes around State House and Ocean Rd, in particular, can be a little *too* quiet at times – consider taking an alternative and safer route.

Your tour begins around the back of the **Azania Front Lutheran Church**, built on the seafront at the turn of the century by German missionaries. Heading east along the promenade past many old **colonial buildings** now used by the Tanzanian authorities to house various **ministries**, walk round the south-eastern tip of the peninsula past **Kigamboni Ferry Terminal** and on to the **fish market**, Dar's most vibrant attraction. Having ensured all your money and valuables are securely tucked away, feel free to take a wander around – it's at its best early in the morning – and see what the local fishermen have managed to catch overnight.

Returning to the main road, take the first turning on the left (west) up Magogoni St. Surrounded by spacious, peacock-filled grounds, **State House**, built by the British in the years following World War One, stands to your right; you will get your best view of the house at the junction with Luthuli St. Hurdling the chains lining the road, cross this junction and continue straight on along Shaban Robert St where, to your right, you come to the **National Museum** (see the box on p146).

A right turn after that will land you on one of the prettier roads in central Dar, the eastern end of Samora Avenue, with the **botanical gardens** to your left and, on the opposite side towards the end of the street, steeple-topped **Karimjee Hall**, where Nyerere (see p76) was sworn in as Tanzania's first president.

Facing the end of the street and hidden behind high walls is the now-defunct **Ocean Road Hospital**, another German building dating back to the last years of the 19th century. Stroll round to the sea-facing front of the hospital to study the rather curious architecture, a hybrid of Arabic and European styles, and to view the curious spiked mace that sits atop the hospital roof.

From here you have two choices: one is to continue your walk along the coast road back to the fish market and on to the church; the other is to return to the junction behind the hospital, turn south for 100m then right and amble along attractive, tree-shaded Sokoine Drive back to the cathedral.

National Museum

It still holds true – even after the current revamp – that the National Museum (⌨ www.houseofculture.or.tz; daily 9.30am-6pm; Ts6500), Tanzania's best, still fares badly when compared to Kenya's version. Indeed, other than attaching a lot of empty buildings to the original structure, one is forced to wonder in what way the actual museum has improved at all? Nevertheless, the exhibits themselves remain mildly diverting at times and the buildings are a cool escape from the heat of the day. And if you manage to avoid the marauding school parties you may well have the entire complex to yourself, with only the cleaner for occasional company.

Most of the more interesting exhibits can be found in the first couple of rooms, located upstairs from the ticket desk. The **Hall of Human Origins** is absorbing, describing as it does our evolution through the millennia, with the help of some apposite objects from Leakey's discoveries at **Olduvai Gorge**. Next door, the **History Gallery** maps out in pretty concise and thorough detail the story of Tanzania, including some interesting articles on the early explorers as well as – inevitably – a lengthy discourse on Tanzania's fight for independence. The third room is even more interesting (we only hope that it remains for we fear it may be but a temporary exhibition that is due to travel onwards), an exhibition devoted to **African Rock Art** with detailed descriptions and photographs of primitive and prehistoric carvings and paintings from all over the continent, from the Sahara to southern Africa. Take your time wandering around – it's fascinating.

Returning downstairs, a small courtyard plays host to half-a-dozen **historic cars** and a small **memorial garden** dedicated to the 12 victims who perished in the US Embassy bombing in Dar on 7 August 1998. Similar in style to the one in Nairobi (see p154), the **sculpture** here includes twisted metal, a rusting motorbike and a window pane shattered by the blast.

The **original museum building** that stands beyond is of only minor interest with its displays of zoological and ethnographic items. Upon entering the building there are two exhibits we found interesting: the first is a bust of Clemens Gillman, once the acting general manager of the railways, then the first chairman of the museum, appointed in 1937, and nowadays better known as the man after whom a point is named on the crater rim of Kilimanjaro. Before it, even more bizarrely, is the country's first ATM, established in 1997 and looking pretty much like any other ATM you see today. It's not plugged in, by the way, so don't try feeding your card into it. If you hunt around one of the two rooms beyond you'll find a couple of old Chagga storage baskets and grinding stone, a traditional 'container' used by the Chagga to hold their *mbege* (the potent banana-based beverage), a huge metal Maasai necklace and some interesting old photos of tribal customs; while in the other room there are some wildlife photos from Dick Peddersen – though nothing like the quantity you'll find in the Natural History museum in Arusha (see p165); overall there's nothing to keep you in the musty old building for too long.

ARRIVAL
By air
Though safer than arriving in Nairobi, it still pays to be on your guard when landing in Dar: like a recently hatched turtle taking to the ocean for the first time, you are at your most vulnerable when you land in a new country – and even in the 'Haven of Peace' there are still plenty of sharks out there.

Joseph Nyerere International Airport is about 12km west of the city centre and it has two terminals, about 700m apart from each other. Whether arriving from overseas or within Tanzania, the chances are you will land at **Terminal Two**, the busier of the two.

The **taxi counter** has a set rate of Ts30,000 to take you into the centre (don't let them gouge you for US$30, though they'll try), or you could try to negotiate a lower rate with the drivers themselves. You could also walk to the main road (around 500m) and take a **dalla-dalla** into town for Ts300-500, though this is not really practical if you have a lot of luggage.

Overland
If arriving by bus you'll fairly certainly be dropped at Ubungo Bus Station. A taxi to the centre will cost around Ts15,000-20,000.

ORIENTATION & GETTING AROUND
Navigating your way around central Dar is no easy task. Things are fairly straightforward on the coast, where Kivukoni Rd/Ocean Rd follows the shore from the railway station to Ocean Road Hospital and beyond. But step back from the shore and you find yourself in a labyrinth of small streets, many of which curve imperceptibly but dramatically enough to confuse and disorientate.

Keep the map on p151 with you, using it first to help you find your way to the tourist office (see opposite) where they have a photocopied map of the city. They will also be able to help you out with the city's **public transport** system, which can also be rather confusing. Buses and dalla-dallas ply all the main routes, though finding where they start and stop can be difficult. Ask locals, your hotel, or take a cab. Fortunately, central Dar is compact enough to walk around.

SERVICES
Tourist information
There's a tourist information office (Mon-Fri 8am-4pm, Sat 8.30am-12.30pm; ☎ 022-213 1555, 🖥 ttb2@ud.co.tz) in Matasalamat Building on Samora Avenue. It depends who is working there when you call in but we found the staff to be helpful, knowledgeable and patient.

Banks
There are **cashpoints** everywhere. To change cash, try the moneychangers down Samora Avenue west of Ohio St. The AMEX rep is Rickshaw Travels in Serena Hotel.

Communications
The main **post office** (Mon-Fri 8am-4.30pm, Sat 9am-1pm) is on Maktaba/Azikiwe St. The **telephone office** (Mon-Fri 8am-4.30pm, Sat 9am-12.30pm) is on Bridge St.

You won't have any trouble finding an **internet café** in Dar; they are everywhere. Those staying in the YMCA or YWCA who want wi-fi should head to Mokka City Café (see p150) – the service is speedy, the staff friendly and the drinks good.

Trekking/travel agencies
You *can* organize your Kili trek from here, though unless there are mitigating circumstances you'd be daft to do so, it being far easier, safer and cheaper to travel to Moshi and arrange it from there. The following travel agents, however, will be able to help you out with other aspects of your trip; at

---

Dar's area code is ☎ 022. If phoning a landline from outside Tanzania dial ☎ +255-22. We have included the area code in the phone numbers of this chapter.

least two of them also have offices in Arusha.

● **Easy Travel & Tours** Raha Tower, corner of Bibi Titi Mohamed St & Maktaba St (☎ 0784-602151, ☎ 022-2121747, 🖳 www.easytravel.co.tz).

● **Kearsley Travel & Tours** Now in new offices on Zanaki St (☎ 022-2137713-8, 🖳 www.kearsleys.com).

● **Leopard Tours** Serena Hotel (☎ 022-260 2835, 🖳 www.leopard-tours.com).

● **Rickshaw Travels** Serena Hotel (☎ 022-213 7275, 🖳 rickshawtravels.com).

Airline offices

Note this list is far from complete but we hope it has the most useful airlines for Kili trekkers. See also p349.

● **Air Tanzania** Ohio St (☎ 022-211 7500, 0782-737730; Mon-Fri 8am-5pm, Sat 9am-2pm).

● **Coastal Aviation** Upanga Rd (☎ 022-2602 430; Mon-Fri 7.30am-5pm, Sat 8.30am-1pm).

● **Egyptair** Serena Hotel (☎ 022-213 6665; Mon-Fri 9am-5pm, Sat 9am-1pm).

● **Emirates** 6th Floor, Haidery Plaza, Ali Hassan Mwinyi Rd (☎ 022-2116100).

❏ Diplomatic missions in Dar es Salaam

● **Australia** Plot No 431, Mahando St, Msasani Peninsular; ☎ 022-2602 584

● **Belgium** 5 Ocean Rd; ☎ 022-211 2688; 🖳 countries.diplomatie.belgium.be

● **Burundi** Lugalo Rd, Plot No 1007, Upanga East; ☎ 0742-767006

● **Canada** 38 Mirambo St, Garden Ave; ☎ 022-216 3300

● **Democratic Republic of Congo** 438 Malik Rd, Upanga; ☎ 022-215 0282

● **Denmark** Ghana Ave; ☎ 022-216 5200-1; 🖳 tanzania.um.dk

● **Egypt** 24 Garden Ave; ☎ 022-211 3591/211 7622

● **Finland** Mirambo St, Garden Ave; ☎ 022-2196 565

● **France** Ali Hassan Mwinyi Rd; ☎ 022-219 8800, 🖳 www.ambafrance-tz.org

● **Germany** Umoja House, Garden Avenue & Mirambo St; ☎ 022-211 7409/15; 🖳 www.daressalam.diplo.de

● **Ireland** 353 Toure Drive, Oysterbay; ☎ 022-260 2355; 🖳 www.embassyof ireland.or.tz

● **Italy** Lugalo Rd (Upanga); ☎ 022-211 5935/6; 🖳 www.ambdaressalaam .esteri.it

● **Japan** Plot 1018, Ali Hassan Mwinyi Rd; ☎ 022-211 5827/29; 🖳 www.tz .emb-japan.go.jp

● **Kenya** Ali Hassan Mwinyi/Kaunda Drive Junction, Oysterbay; ☎ 022-266 8285, 🖳 kenyahighcomtz.org/

● **Malawi** 1st Floor, Zambia House, Ohio/Sokoine Drive; ☎ 022-212 4623

● **Norway** Mirambo St/Garden Ave junction; ☎ 022-216 3100; 🖳 www.nor way.go.tz

● **Poland** 63 Aly Khan Rd, Upanga; ☎ 022-211 5271

● **Russian Federation** Plot 73 Ali Hassan Mwinyi Rd; ☎ 022-266 6005/6

● **Rwanda** Plot 32 Ali Hassan Mwinyi Rd; ☎ 022-212 0703

● **South Africa** Plot 1338/39 Mwaya Rd, Masaki; ☎ 022-260 1800

● **South Korea** Tanzania Plot 97, Msese Rd, Kinondoni; ☎ 022-266 8788

● **Spain** Plot 99B Kinondoni Rd; ☎ 022-266 6018/266 6936

● **Sudan** 64 Upanga Rd; ☎ 022-211 7641

● **Sweden** Mirambo St, Garden Ave; ☎ 022-219 6500

● **Switzerland** Plot 79, Kinondoni Rd; ☎ 022-266 6008

● **Uganda** 25 Msasani Rd, Oysterbay; ☎ 022-266 7391

● **UK** Umoja House, Garden Ave; ☎ 022-229 0000

● **United States** 686 Old Bagamoyo Rd, Msasani; ☎ 022-229 4000; 🖳 tanzania .usembassy.gov

● **Zambia** Plot 5 & 6, Junction Ohio/Sokoine Drive; ☎ 022-211 2977

● **Zimbabwe** 6th Fl, New Life House, Sokoine Drive; ☎ 022-8382156-59

● **Flightlink** Sea Cliff Village, Masaki (☎ 0782 354 448/9/50).

● **Gulf Air** Raha Towers, Bibi Titi Mohamed St/Maktaba St (☎ 022-211-0827).

● **Kenya Airways** Corner of Upanga Rd & Bibi Titi Mohamed St (☎ 0746-444525; Mon-Fri 8.30am-5pm, Sat 8.30am-12.30pm). Shares its office with...

● **KLM** Corner of Upanga Rd & Bibi Titi Mohamed St (☎ 022-216 3914; Mon-Fri 8.30am-5pm). Note: unlike Kenya Airways they are closed on Sat.

● **Precision Air** NIC building ground floor, Pamba Rd (☎ 022-212 1718; Mon-Fri 8am-5pm, Sat 9am-1pm).

● **Qatar Airways** Elia Complex, Ground Floor, Junction of Zanaki & Bibi Titi Mohamed St (☎ 022-219 8300; Mon to Fri 8.30am-5pm, Sat 8.30am-1pm).

● **South African Airways** Raha Tower, corner of Bibi Titi Mohamed St & Maktaba St (☎ 022-211 7044; Mon-Fri 8.30am-4.30pm, Sat 8.30am-12.30pm).

WHERE TO STAY (see map p151)

The following are listed in **price order**, with the **cheapest first**. For details of the abbreviations, see box below.

● *YWCA* (☎ 0713-622707; 🖳 ywca.tanzania@africaonline.co.tz; just off Azikiwe St; sgl/dbl Ts10,000/20,000) Perhaps the most popular budget hostel currently operating in Dar, the YWCA has pretty basic accommodation but it's clean and has a good location by the post office – from where you can catch a dalla-dalla to Ubungo bus station. Oh, and in case you're wondering, you needn't be either young, female or a Christian to stay here, as this author, an agnostic middle-aged male, can verify. Even if the singles are full it's worth getting a double here (Ts15,000 for single occu-

pancy) as it's still cheaper than anywhere else in town.

● *YMCA* (☎ 022-213 5457; 🖳 www.tymca.co.tz; Upanga Rd; sgl/dbl/tpl Ts25,000/28,000/39,000) The fallback place should the above be full, the YMCA is only a minute's walk away from its sister – but miles apart in terms of friendliness and value for money. But it's still reasonably cheap by Dar standards (save for the overpriced singles), clean(ish) and safe-ish too.

● *Safari Inn* (☎ 022-213 8101; 🖳 safariinn.co.tz; Band St, off Libya St; s/c sgl/dbl Ts24,000/30,000, or Ts28,000/35,000 with air-con) Still a popular budget choice and all the rooms are en suite, though some are a bit gloomy with many lacking windows. However, there is free internet and the room rates include something that resembles a breakfast, only smaller.

● *Econolodge* (☎ 022-211 6048; 🖳 www.econohotel.8m.com; Libya St; s/c sgl/dbl/tpl Ts22,000/30,000/40,000, or Ts35,000/40,000/47,000 with air-con) Not quite as 'Econo' as it makes out, this is the smartest in the huddle of hotels around Libya St. All the rooms are spacious and come with a bathroom. Pretty good value, if a little characterless.

● *Starlight Hotel* (☎ 022-211 9387; 🖳 www.starlighthotelltd.com; Bibi Titi Mohamed St; s/c sgl/dbl US$35/40) Catering mainly for local businessmen and warranting a mention largely due to its position in the mid-range price bracket, the Starlight looks impersonal and gloomy but is friendly, central and – with all 150 rooms equipped with air-con, hot water, wi-fi, TV and fridge – fair value too. Starting to look a little lacking in guests, however, and the only hotel in this section to reduce its prices since the last edition.

❏ **Abbreviations**

Throughout this book we have used the following abbreviations when writing about accommodation: **pp** means per person; **s/c** is short for self-contained, a local term meaning that the room comes with a bathroom (ie the room is en suite or a bathroom is attached); while **sgl/dbl/tpl** means single/double/triple rooms. So, for example, where we have written 's/c sgl/dbl/tpl US$35/40/45', we mean that a self-contained single room costs US$35 per night, a self-contained double costs US$40 and a self-contained triple costs US$45.

● *New Avon Hotel* (☎ 022-212 6721, ☎ 0768-002866; 🖳 www.newavonhotel.com; Aggrey St; s/c sgl/dbl US$60/75 rising to US$145 for the suite) A new place in a good location to the west of the city centre, currently all polished and shiny and with well-equipped self-contained rooms featuring flat-screen TV, telephone, internet and hairdryer.

● *Peacock Hotel* (☎ 022-211 4126; 🖳 www.peacock-hotel.com; Bibi Titi Mohamed St; s/c sgl/dbl US$110/130; bigger s/c sgl/dbl rooms with sofas (!) US$135/160) Refreshingly free of any pretension, this ugly but friendly establishment is seeing more and more tourists. It's OK, with all the facilities you'd expect from a hotel of this class and it's so nice to be welcomed by receptionists who seem genuinely glad you've dropped in.

● *New Africa Hotel* (☎ 022-211 7050; 🖳 www.newafricahotel.com; corner of Azikiwe St & Sokoine Drive; s/c sgl/dbl from US$190/210) In a better location than the Serena Hotel (see below), its nearest rival, though not with quite the same level of sophistication, the New Africa stands on the site of the Germans' original Kaiserhof. Home to Dar's main casino as well as a host of bars and restaurants, the New Africa's rooms have everything you'd expect from a hotel of this calibre, including mini-bar, satellite TV, telephones with internet hook-up and so on. If you're willing to pay over a hundred dollars for all this, you may as well pay the extra for one of the rooms with a sea view.

● *Dar es Salaam Serena Hotel* (☎ 022-211 2416, 🖳 www.serenahotels.com; Ohio St; s/c rooms US$220 up to US$800 for the presidential suite, depending on demand) This place has changed hands a couple of times since the first edition of this book and used to be the top place in the town centre before the arrival of the Kempinski (now the Hyatt Regency). It's still a fine establishment, boasting a swimming pool, gym and all mod-cons, as well as being the base for British Airways, the AMEX representative Rickshaw Travels, the safari experts Leopard Tours (see p148) and a bureau de change. Even if you're not staying here, do

call in to have a peek at the photos by John Cleare during the first ascent of Kili via the Kersten Glacier that adorn the shopping walkway, or simply to take advantage of their fierce air-con.

● *Hyatt Regency Dar es Salaam: The Kilimanjaro* (☎ 0765-701234; 🖳 www.daressalaam.kilimanjaro.hyatt.com; Kivukoni Rd; rooms sgl/dbl US$295/320, rising to US$2500 for the Royal Suite) Yet another luxury hotel that's changed hands (it was previously called the Kilimanjaro Kempinski), you won't find a more refined or, given its name, *appropriate* place to stay. Actually, the hotel's association with Kili is tenuous, other than the fact that you need a bank balance the size of a mountain to be able to stay here. However, it *is* a gorgeous, fountain-filled haven, sophisticated and shiny and the rooms feature what they describe as 'elegantly tropical' interiors, wood floors, high-speed internet access and wi-fi, international satellite LCD TV with movie channels, multilingual telephone voicemail and all the other bits 'n' bobs you'd expect of a hotel of this standard. The location overlooking the Indian Ocean is great, too.

WHERE TO EAT AND DRINK

Many eateries in Dar close on Sundays. One that doesn't, and which has for many years been the most popular place in town amongst travellers – and indeed just about everyone else to judge by the frenetic 'busy-ness' of the place – is *The Chef's* (formerly *Chef's Pride*; daily noon-11pm) on Chagga St. It is a popularity that is well deserved: tasty, huge portions of food, fair prices (mains Ts4000-20,000, with most for Ts8000-12,000), a location close to the cheaper hotels and English football on the telly is a combination that for some is hard to resist, and many travellers, having eaten here once, venture nowhere else in the city. Just be prepared to share a table, however – it gets that busy.

Another place that's winning over the travellers, particularly those staying at the YWCA or its brother and who are seeking a good wi-fi/internet connection, is the swish *Mokka City* (🖳 www.mokkacity.com;

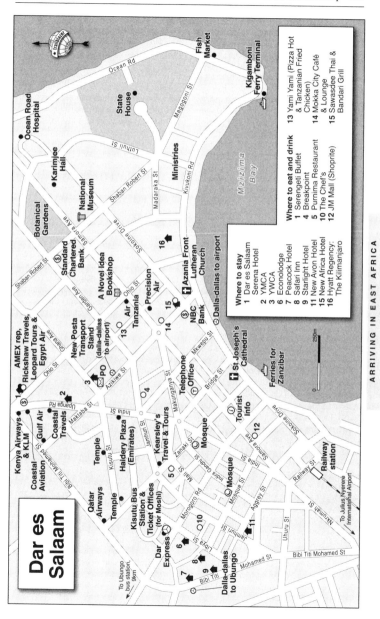

Dar es Salaam

Ocean Rd

Ocean Road Hospital

Karimjee Hall

Botanical Gardens

National Museum

State House

Fish Market

Kigamboni Ferry Terminal

Mzizima Bay

Luthuli St

Shaban Robert St

Standard Chartered Bank

A Novel Idea Bookshop

Sokoine Drive

Madaraka St

Kivukoni Rd

Magogoni St

Ministries

Shaban Robert St

Garden Ave

16

Precision Air

Azania Front Lutheran Church

Dalla-dallas to airport

Ohio St

NBC Bank

Chagga Ave

AMEX rep, Rickshaw Travels, Leopard Tours & Egypt Air

New Posta Transport Stand (dalla-dallas to airport)

Ohio St

13 Air Tanzania

15

14

St Joseph's Cathedral

Ferries for Zanzibar

PO

Azikiwe St

3

Mkwepu St

Telephone Office

Bridge St

Makunganya St

4

Kenya Airways & KLM

Gulf Air

Coastal Aviation

Upanga Rd

Maktaba St

2

India St

Haidery Plaza (Emirates)

Jamhuri St

Kearsley's Travel & Tours

Zanaki St

Mosque

Samora Ave

Tourist Info

12

Sokoine Drive

Railway station

Coastal Travels

Qatar Airways

Temple

Kisutu St

Temple

Mali St

India Gandhi Rd

Mosque

5

India St

Mosque St

Aggrey St

To Julius Nyerere International Airport

Kisutu Bus Station & Ticket Offices (for Moshi)

Morogoro Rd

Jamhuri St

Railway St

Dar Express

10

Libya St

Mosque St

11

Nkrumah St

Uhuru St

6

8

7

Bibi Titi

Dalla-dallas to Ubungo

Mohamed St

Bibi Titi Mohamed St

To Ubungo bus station, 9km

250m

0

Where to stay
1 Dar es Salaam Serena Hotel
2 YMCA
3 YWCA
6 Econolodge
7 Peacock Hotel
8 Safari Inn
9 Starlight Hotel
11 New Avon Hotel
15 New Africa Hotel
16 Hyatt Regency: The Kilimanjaro

Where to eat and drink
1 Serengeti Buffet
4 Breakpoint
5 Purnima Restaurant
10 The Chef's
12 JM Mall (Shoprite)
13 Yami Yami (Pizza Hot & Tanzanian Fried Chicken)
14 Mokka City Café & Lounge
15 Sawasdee Thai & Bandari Grill

ARRIVING IN EAST AFRICA

daily 7am-8.30pm), a café in the centre with a great selection of breakfasts (Ts5000-15,000), including everything from a simple fruit salad to the full fry-up, as well as fast food, sundaes and waitresses who smile (though the service can be a tad tardy). Recommended.

For truly cheap-eats the Indian quarter of central Dar, particularly around the temple-laden Kisutu St (and its extension Pramukh Swami St) and the junction of Indira Gandhi and Zanaki streets, is as good a place as any to start looking. *Purnima* (Mon-Fri 9am-6pm, Sat & Sun 8am-1pm), on Zanaki St, is a great little place, where a vegetarian thali will make you poorer by only Ts5000. There are plenty of other similar places around here – follow your nose to find them.

For more African offerings, the lively *Breakpoint Outdoor Catterers* (sic) is a huge and hugely popular al-fresco joint serving cold beer and Tanzanian staples such as *nyama choma*, all accompanied by a music system thumping out the latest African tunes and a screen showing the latest Hollywood blockbuster. Turn up here on your own in the evening, particularly at the weekend, and you could feel a bit of a Billy No Mates. Still, four *mishkaki* (kebabs), a plate of chips and a cold beer is only Ts11,500 and it's always fun watching the locals at play. A more sanitized, Western version of this can be found on the other side of Azikiwe St on Pamba St at **Yami Yami**, home to several restaurants set in an outdoor eating area – though there's no beer and the whole place is disappointingly more genteel. Still, it's always good to see the locals ripping off successful Western chains, in this case *Pizza Hot* and *TFC* (Tanzanian Favourite Chicken). Expect to pay Ts10,000 for a basic margherita pizza.

For more refined cuisine in plusher surroundings, try the restaurants in the upmarket hotels, including *Sawasdee Thai* or the Indian *Bandari Grill*, both at the New Africa (see p150), and *Serengeti Buffet Restaurant* at the Serena (see p150). Your bank manager won't thank you for dining here but your stomach certainly will.

MOVING ON – TO KILIMANJARO
By bus to Moshi and Arusha
The **Dar Express** office is located in the old Kisutu bus station in the heart of downtown on Libya St. Tickets are Ts28,000-30,000 to either destination; the journey is around 10 hours to Moshi, 12 to Arusha. Unfortunately, the buses do not depart from their office but from Ubungo bus station, a fair distance out of town. A taxi from Kisutu to Ubungo will set you back about Ts12,000-15,000 (though they'll try for Ts20,000); you can try to catch a dalla-dalla from outside the Peacock on Bibi Titi Mohammed St or by the main post office but it's not easy.

If you don't want to travel with Dar Express for some reason do at least choose your bus company carefully: despite the presence of speed ramps and traffic police, the Dar to Moshi highway is notorious for accidents and often it's the same few bus companies that are involved. Unfortunately, the number of touts operating at both of Dar's stations means that it can be difficult to buy the ticket you want. Be persistent and insistent and take anything the touts say with a pinch – no, make that a huge bucket – of salt.

By air
The national carrier **Air Tanzania** have their main office on Ohio/Garden St and still operate the occasional local flight, and are rumoured to be starting flights between Dar and Arusha again soon.

A better bet would be to book with **Precision Air** who fly three times daily to Kilimanjaro from Dar and three times a day to Arusha Airport too.

Air Excel have two flights daily to Arusha Airport (currently at 9.15am and 4.20pm; 2hr 10 mins flying time), while **Coastal Aviation**, on Upanga Rd, have a daily direct flight from Dar to Arusha at 9am, arriving at 11am, and a less direct one 15 minutes later via Saadani, Pangani and Moshi that takes three hours to reach Arusha. Finally, the budget airline **Flightlink** began operating flights to Arusha via Zanzibar in June 2013, the cost currently US$125 for non-residents.

Going to the airport, look for the dalla-dalla signed either 'airport' or 'U/Ndege' (short for Uwanja wa Ndege, Ts400) that departs from the seafront; leave in plenty of time – it can take well over an hour and drops you a 10-minute walk away. At around Ts20,000 a taxi's a little cheaper from town than from the seafront.

Nairobi

As rough as a lion's tongue, East Africa's largest city has come quite a long way since its inception in May 1899 as a humble railway supply depot on the Mombasa to Kampala line. It is a city that has suffered much from plagues, fire and reconstruction – and that was just in its first 10 years – yet it has obstinately continued to prosper and grow, rising from a population of approximately zero in 1898 to around three million today.

Official recognition of the city's increasing importance arrived in 1907 when the British made it the capital of their East African territories, and you can still find the occasional colonial relic in the city, from the Indian-influenced architecture of a few downtown buildings (shipped over from the subcontinent; Indians supplied much of the labour force used in building the railway) to some distinctly elegant hotels and orderly public gardens (including one, just to the north of Kenyatta Avenue, which still bears a statue of Queen Victoria). But if you came with the specific purpose of seeing a faded colonial city you'd be disappointed: because as the capital of the Kenyan republic and the UN's fourth official 'World Centre', Nairobi is East Africa's most modern, prosperous and glamorous metropolis. It is also, first and foremost, black Africa at its loudest and proudest.

A TOUR OF THE CITY

The number one sight in Nairobi is the National Museum; details of it can be found in the box on p154.

As for Nairobi's other sights, they can be seen as part of a half- to full-day walking tour. This is best done on a Sunday morning, when the hassle from touts is at its lowest and the gospel choirs are out in force on the streets and in the parks. The tour begins at the **Railway Museum** (💻 www.krc.co.ke; daily 8am-5pm; Ks400). To reach it, from the railway station head west for 5-10 minutes along the road running parallel to the tracks. The museum is a gem. If it's possible to feel nostalgia for a time that one never knew and a place one has never visited before, this is the museum that will prompt those feelings with its fading photos of British royalty riding in the cow-catcher seats at the front of the train and its old posters advertising the newly opened Uganda Railway. This is an endearing little museum and the rusty locomotive graveyard out front is a diverting place for a nose around too.

Returning to the station, head north along Moi Avenue. At the junction with Haile Selassie Avenue is the **former site of the American Embassy**, blown up on 7 August, 1998, by Al-Qaeda. The site has now been landscaped into a very small **remembrance garden** (daily 8am-6pm; Ks20), at the back of which is a **Visitor Centre** (Mon-Sat 9am-6pm, Sun 1-6pm; Ks100) which explains in greater detail what happened that day including a video reconstruction of the events, *Seconds From Disaster*. The garden is worth a visit; you'll find a memorial bearing the names of the Kenyan victims (who constituted all but 12 of the 263 who died), while at the back of the enclosure is a pyramid sculpture containing some of the debris from that day, namely some twisted metal, a lump or two of concrete and a door handle. It's a busy junction, and the Co-op building behind – also badly damaged in the blast – is from the eyesore school of architecture; yet still the park is suffused with an atmosphere of the deepest poignancy. Sadly, one presumes a similar memorial will be built in the near future for the victims of the Westgate Shopping Mall atrocity.

Continuing north along Moi, City Hall Way runs parallel to Haile Selassie Ave, two blocks north. The **hall** itself lies about 400m along the road on the right (north). Opposite, to your left, is a **statue** of first president Jomo Kenyatta, sitting regally overlooking the city square with his back to the **law courts**. To Kenyatta's left, rising imperiously from fountains, are the **Kenyatta International Conference Centre**, like a giant water-lily bud on the verge of opening, and the vertiginous **KANU Tower**, formerly the tallest building in the city and still one of the ugliest – though most locals would probably take issue

---

National Museum
(🖥 www.museums.or.ke; Off Museum Hill, near Uhuru Highway; daily 8.30am-5.30pm; Ks800, Ks1200 with snake park) If you have time to see only one sight in Nairobi, this is definitely the one to head for, an institution that is not only almost as old as the city itself (having been established way back in 1910) but which effortlessly manages the difficult feat of justifying the whopping great entrance fee.

Virtually every gallery in the museum holds something of interest for the visitor. True, the first couple of rooms, where many of Kenya's creatures – including every species of Kenya's avifauna – has been stuffed and put on display, may feel a little old-fashioned; though even here there are some highlights, including the skeleton (and, in the courtyard, a model, faithfully cast in fibreglass) of the **nation's favourite pachyderm**, Ahmed, an elephant so huge its tusks alone weighed an incredible 65kg each. The next couple of galleries are our favourite, however, which study in great detail (but never tediously so) the different theories as to the evolution of man, illustrated by many of the actual skulls and other fossils that helped to shape these theories.

Heading upstairs more treats await including a room devoted to the history of Kenya and another that studies the cultures, art and festivals of the nation's tribes, with particular focus on how they celebrate the various rites of passage of their members' lives. This floor is also where you'll find rooms that are mainly given over to contemporary photographic and art exhibitions which we find are usually well worth seeing and a pleasant respite from the more serious, educational exhibits elsewhere.

with this opinion. (KANU, incidentally, are the most powerful party in Kenya and have dominated the political arena since independence.)

Strolling along City Hall Way – past **Holy Family Cathedral**, neatly juxtaposed with the casino directly opposite – you'll find to the left of the road, lined with flags and guarded by two black lion statues and several bored-looking guards in neo-colonial ceremonial livery, the object of the Kenyatta statue's gaze: his **mausoleum**. Next door and adorned with a rather quaint clock tower is the Kenyan **Parliament**.

Heading back north along Uhuru Highway, in about 10 minutes you'll come to a large roundabout and the centre of worship in the city, surrounded as it is by a **synagogue** (to the north-east) and no fewer than **four churches** (St Paul's Catholic Chapel to the north-west, with St Andrew's behind it up the hill, the First Church of Christ Scientist further along the same road and the city's main Lutheran church on the roundabout's south-western edge).

From the roundabout you can continue north for 15 hot, dusty minutes along the highway to the **National Museum** (see box p154), or turn east along University Way, taking a right turn south through the business heart of Nairobi along Muindi Mbingu St. On the way you might wish to take a short detour to see the **indoor market**, or **Jamia Mosque** (Nairobi's most impressive mosque but closed to infidels), before rejoining Kenyatta Avenue. Take a left here, pausing on the way at one of the street vendors to pick up some reading material to peruse at your table, and after a couple of hundred metres you'll come to the final port of call on this walk, the Thorn Tree Café with its overpriced but wonderfully cold beer.

PRACTICAL INFORMATION

SECURITY
Nairobi has been the venue of a couple of horrific terrorist attacks in recent years, with 2013's atrocity at the Westgate Mall, when 72 people were killed by Somali fundamentalists, coming on top of the 1998 attack on the US Embassy (see p154) in which 263 people perished. There is little you can do to avoid these – thankfully rare – tragedies. However, these major events are not the only dangers facing tourists in Kenya's capital. A few years back some inspired wag dubbed Kenya's capital 'Nairobberi', and less-inspired wags have been retreading that joke ever since. Tired as the gag may be, however, it does still have relevance, for Nairobi's reputation as East Africa's Capital of Crime is well founded.

To be fair, the authorities are trying to improve matters, at least in the centre, blocking off many of the darker backstreets. There seem to be fewer beggars and touts populating the centre too. There is also a 'beautification' programme going on, which seems to involve a lot of tree-planting.

Nevertheless, the need to be wary when out on the streets of Nairobi remains paramount. The **most notorious hotspot** is the area immediately to the east of Moi Avenue, including River Rd and the bus stations, a popular location with travellers because of the cheap hotels there. During the day violent robbery is rare though certainly not unheard of, simply because it's so packed with people; pickpocketing, on the other hand, is rife at this time, probably for the same reason. At night, both techniques are common.

To avoid becoming another victim, **be vigilant**, leave valuables at your hotel (having first checked their security procedures) and make sure they give you a receipt for any goods deposited. Furthermore, tuck moneybelts under your clothing and don't walk around at night but take a taxi, even if it's for just a few hundred metres.

It can only be to your advantage if you are over-cautious for your first couple of days in the capital. After that, if you're still staying here, you can begin to appreciate Nairobi's charms – which do exist, and are not entirely inconsiderable – and can begin to moan, like the rest of the travellers here, about how unfair guidebook writers are about Kenya's capital.

ARRIVAL
By air
A fire in August 2013 destroyed a large number of buildings at **Jomo Kenyatta Airport** (18km from the centre of Nairobi), including the international terminal. For the time being international flights are using the domestic terminal. But hopefully a new international terminal will have been built by the time you read this. If you haven't already got a **visa** you should get one before passing through passport control (this takes time!). Payment is accepted in US dollars, euros or pounds sterling only.

Passing through immigration, luggage collection is straight down the stairs. Once again be vigilant and, having retrieved your bags, check that they don't look to have been opened: when climbing Kilimanjaro, there are few things more annoying than finding that the thermally insulated mountain hat you thought was safely tucked away in the side-pocket of your rucksack had in fact been taken by a light-fingered baggage handler and is now being used as a makeshift tea cosy in the staffroom of Jomo Kenyatta Airport. Entering the arrivals' hall after customs, to your right is a money-changer offering, as moneychangers are wont to do at airports worldwide, dismal rates, and an ATM that accepts Visa cards – your best bet for a fair rate at the airport, though you could pay for your cab in dollars and wait to change money in town.

You have a number of choices in tackling the journey from the airport to the centre of Nairobi. Taxis cost about Ks1100-1500 with bargaining, or before 8pm you can take the No 34 bus that runs down River Rd with a stop on Moi Avenue (Ks40). Remember to be careful of pickpockets on this route.

❏ **Nine useful things to know about Kenya**
● Citizens of most countries need a **visa**, including Britain and the US. Get your visa before leaving home or you can buy one at Nairobi's Jomo Kenyatta Airport, though this usually involves queuing.
● One thing to remember: as long as you remain in East Africa there is no need to buy a multiple-entry Kenyan visa if you are flying into Kenya but wish to visit Tanzania or Uganda too, as long as you stay in those countries for less than two weeks and providing, of course, your Kenyan visa has not expired by the time you return to Kenya.
● The official **language** is Swahili. For a quick guide to Swahili, see p348. In addition, many Kenyans speak both their own tribal language and English, which is widely spoken everywhere.
● As with Tanzania, Kenya is **three hours ahead of GMT**. Note that, in addition to standard time, many locals use **Swahili time**, which runs from dawn to dusk (or 6am to 6pm to be precise). See p85 for details on how to convert between East African time and Swahili time.
● The Kenyan **currency** is the shilling (Ks). At the time of writing, €1=Ks117.6, US$1=Ks86.6, UK£1=Ks141.6. Don't change money on the street.
● Kenya's **electricity supply** uses the British-style three-pin plugs on 220-240V.
● The **international dialling code** is ☎ 254; the Nairobi code is 020 and numbers starting 07 are for mobiles.
● The **emergency telephone number** is ☎ 999.
● **Opening hours** are typically 8am to 5 or 6pm with some establishments shutting on Sundays. Banks, post offices etc have their own hours, see p85.

By bus
Arrive in Nairobi by **shuttle bus** from Arusha/Moshi and, if they don't drop you off at your hotel, you'll probably be dropped off by Jevanjee Gardens right in the heart of the action. The exception to this is passengers on the Impala Shuttle, see p161, who will be dropped off at Silver Springs Hotel – useful for those staying there or at either Upper Hill or Wildebeest Eco Camp, though to be honest you've still got a fair way to go to get to either of these (and particularly the last). Arrive by **'ordinary' bus**, on the other hand, and you could well be dropped off near the infamous River Rd, home to several hotels but also a significant minority of ne'er-do-wells – take care!

ORIENTATION & GETTING AROUND
Despite decades of unplanned growth, a mass of sprawling suburbs and a wholesale aversion to street numbers, central Nairobi is actually very easy to navigate, with nearly everything of interest to the traveller within walking distance of Kenyatta Avenue.

A couple of obvious landmarks are the enormous **KANU Tower**, to the south of City Hall, and the even more enormous **Nation Centre**, a red Meccano-type structure nestling between two giant cylindrical towers just off the eastern end of Kenyatta Avenue. Central Nairobi is fairly compact and the fit will be able to walk everywhere. Buses and *matatus* (Kenyan minibuses) run from early morning to late at night, though **we strongly advise you to take taxis after**

dark. During the day things are much safer, though keep your wits about you.

SERVICES
Banks
Banks are usually open Monday to Friday 9am-3pm, Saturday 9-11am; foreign exchange bureaux open later though on Saturday often they too close early (usually noon). Many of the banks have **ATM**s (cash machines) as well, with most accepting Visa cards. Be on your guard for onlookers when withdrawing money from an ATM.

Communications
Big, bright and gleaming, the **post office** (Mon-Fri 7.30am-6pm, Sat 9am-1pm) occupies a fairly large slice of valuable real estate at the western end of Kenyatta Avenue. Registered, recorded and normal deliveries can be made here and there's a poste restante counter (No 15).

If you're staying a while in Kenya, the best way to use a **phone** is to get hold of a local SIM card – visit the Orange shop one block south of the post office or similar outlets around town. The card costs around Ks100, you need to go through the two-minute registration process (bring some form of ID), and insert it into your existing phone; you'll find you save yourself a fortune this way, particularly if you are phoning abroad though if you're heading to Tanzania it's better to wait and get a local SIM card there (see p85). Just make sure you get the right-sized card for your phone

ARRIVING IN EAST AFRICA

❑ **Diplomatic missions in Nairobi**
Australia Riverside Drive, 400m off Chiromo Rd; ☎ 020-427 7100; 🖳 www .kenya.embassy.gov.au; **Belgium** Limuru Rd, Muthaiga, ☎ 020-712 20 11; 🖳 coun tries.diplomatie.belgium.be/en/kenya; **Canada** Limuru Rd, Gigiri, ☎ 020-366 3000; **Denmark** 13 Runda Drive, Runda; ☎ 020-425 3000; 🖳 kenya.um.dk; **France** Barclays Plaza, 9th Floor, Loita St; ☎ 020-277 8000; 🖳 www.ambafrance-ke.org; **Germany** 113 Riverside Drive; ☎ 020-4262 100; 🖳 www.nairobi.diplo.de; **Japan** Mara Rd, Upper Hill; ☎ 020-289 8000; 🖳 www.ke.emb-japan.go.jp; **South Africa** 3rd Floor, Roshanmaer Place, Lenana Rd; ☎ 020-2827100; 🖳 south-africa .embassies.nairobi.tel/; **Thailand** Rose Ave, off Denis Pritt Rd; ☎ 020-291 9100; 🖳 www.thaiembassy.org/nairobi; **UK** Upper Hill Rd; ☎ 020-284 4000; **United States** United Nations Av; ☎ 020-363 6000; 🖳 nairobi.usembassy.gov

(iPhones, for example, use smaller SIM cards) and that your phone is unlocked and can take other cards. If you're staying only for a night or two, it's probably not worth the hassle and instead use the (more expensive) hotel phone, Skype – or remain incommunicado until you leave Kenya.

You'll have no trouble finding an **internet café** in the centre. Surf City, just off Jevanjee Gardens (Ks0.50 per minute), is reliable though there are doubtless others closer to you that are just as competent and speedy. **Wi-fi** is available in most hotels now and is usually free.

Trekking agencies

It's a lot cheaper to book your trek in Tanzania. Still, some people like to see what's on offer here and there is a good company operating out of Nairobi. **Kibo Slopes Safaris** (PO Box 58064; ☎ 020-213 9981; 🖳 www.kiboslopessafaris.com) a smart and professionally run agent offering Kilimanjaro treks combined with a Kenyan safari. Using their own climbing outfit in Tanzania, (Kibo Slopes Tanzania), in Arusha, their prices for a Kili climb are steep, however, at US\$5204 for a 10-day itinerary for one person on the Lemosho Route, US\$3712 each for two people (both starting from Nairobi); Machame and Marangu treks are also available. You can find a branch of their office in the compound of Silver Springs Hotel where the Impala Shuttle (see p161) pulls up.

WHERE TO STAY

The following list of hostels and hotels is arranged with the cheapest first. Those intending to **camp** should check out either Upper Hill (Ks600 per person) or, better still, Wildebeest Eco Camp (Ks1000pp, Ks1250 if using one of their tents), listed below. River Rd remains the cheapest area in the centre, though tourist-friendly hostels are slowly disappearing from the area and those that remain are distinctly scruffy. For details of abbreviations see box p149.

In Nairobi, safety is a concern in some of the hotels, though the ones we have chosen to recommend in this book were fine.

● **Wildebeest Eco Camp** (☎ 0734-770733; 🖳 www.wildebeestecocamp.com; Moko-yeti Road West, Langata; rates are Ks1250 in a dorm, Ks3000/4500 sgl/dbl with shared facilities; tents Ks4500/5500 sgl/dbl with shared facilities, luxury tents Ks9000/11,000/13,000 sgl/dbl/tpl) Simply put, this is a wonderful place, efficiently built, owned and run by an Australian family who relocated here after leaving their previous premises to the west of Uhuru Park. The **private rooms** are clean and pleasant but it's the fragrant, bird-filled tropical grounds and frog-filled pond that truly steal the show, bordered as they are by **de luxe en suite safari tents** that provide some of the most appealing accommodation in the capital, with cotton sheets and full electricity. There are also **dorms**, a **campsite** and a **restaurant** with **wi-fi** too. All in all it's worth the very lengthy trip out of town (it lies about 15km from the centre, or about an hour given the usual traffic), whatever your budget. Just blissful.

● **New Kenya Lodge** (☎ 020-222 2202; 🖳 www.nksafari.com; River Rd opposite the end of Latema Rd; rates are Ks600 in a dorm, Ks700 sgl, Ks1200 dbl) Another scruffy, old-style backpacker place with a few (equally scruffy) private rooms redeemed by the friendliness of Nicholas the receptionist. Might be an idea to ring ahead. Like most such places, New Kenya also has a safari operation.

● **Upper Hill Campsite** (☎ 020-250 0218, ☎ 0721-517869; 🖳 www.upperhillcampsite.com; Othaya Rd, Lavington; Ks840 in a dorm, Ks840/1560 sgl/dbl in a small safari tent, private cabin/room Ks2640/Ks3000 for both sgl and dbl, en suite Ks4200) The nearest rival to Wildebeest and in a more convenient location, just 6km west of the centre, where it's been since its inception in 1995. The **Drunken Geko Bar** here is one of the main meeting places for travellers in the city and the whole place is tidy and tranquil, with wi-fi now installed too.

● **YMCA** (☎ 0729-152816; 🖳 www.kenyaymca.com; State House Rd; non s/c dorm/sgl/dbl Ks1000/1400/2100; s/c dorm/sgl/dbl Ks1100/2000/3100; add Ks600 for half-board, Ks1200 full-board) Despite the

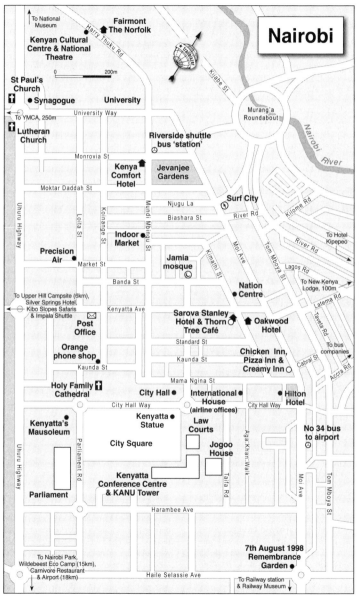

name, women, atheists and the elderly are all welcome at this friendly, secure hostel, a fair choice for those on a budget who don't fancy their chances in the hurly-burly of the River Rd area but still want to be reasonably close to town. The real clincher, however, is the pool (Ks150 for non-residents).

● *Hotel Kipepeo* (☎ 0710 207162; ☐ www .hotelkipepeo.com; River Rd; s/c sgl/dbl/tpl Ks3400/4100/5400) Probably the best of the places left in the River Rd area, the safe and friendly Kipepeo boasts clean self-contained rooms with hot water, mosquito nets, TV and wi-fi – and the rates are fair.

● *Kenya Comfort Hotel* (☎ 0720/722-608 866; ☐ www.kenyacomfort.com; Jevanjee Gardens; rates start at US$25/45/65 for dorm/sgl/dbl for bed only rising to US$65/85 sgl/dbl if you want air-con and TV) Superbly situated just five minutes north of Kenyatta Avenue – and, more importantly, right next to where the shuttle buses pull in, which could be very handy if you've taken the afternoon shuttle and arrived after dark. Though it looks fairly petite, features include a sauna and steam room, internet and 91 bedrooms. All in all this is not a bad deal for central Nairobi and one of the better lower mid-range choices.

● *Oakwood Hotel* (☎ 0735-478924; ☐ www.madahotels.com/oakwood; Kimathi St; s/c sgl/dbl/tpl US$80/90/100 inc breakfast) Wooden floors, wooden walls, wooden ceiling and wooden doors – spending a night at the Oakwood can make you feel like Charles II hiding from Parliament. The Oakwood's strengths are its location opposite Thorn Tree Café, its elegant antique lift, the digital satellite TV and video in each room, wi-fi in the bar and the vague whiff of colonial charm. Its main drawback is the casino that occupies much of the ground floor, desecrating the once-charming façade. Nevertheless, though not spectacular this 1940s' hotel is convenient and reasonable enough value.

● *Silver Springs Hotel* (☎ 020-272 2451; ☐ www.silversprings-hotel.com; out of town near the hospital; rates start at sgl/dbl Ks15,000/18,000, rising to Ks100,000 for the two-bedroomed penthouse, all inclusive of breakfast) This is a fine choice, popular

in particular with tour groups and as the main stop for the Impala shuttle bus. Facilities include a pool, gym and hot-stone massages – perfect post-Kili therapy.

● *Sarova Stanley* (☎ 020-275 7000; ☐ www.sarovahotels.com) corner of Kenyatta Avenue and Kimathi St; room rates vary depending on demand: US$240-420/290-470 for s/c sgl/dbl room only) A luxury hotel with a bit of character, the Stanley first opened its doors to the very well-heeled in 1902 – making it just a few years younger than the city itself. Edward, then Prince of Wales, Ernest Hemingway, and Hollywood's finest from Ava Gardner to Clark Gable have all rested their eminent heads on the Stanley's sumptuously stuffed pillows. Victorian elegance still abounds, though the demands of the modern client have led to the introduction of a shopping arcade, swimming pool and gymnasium. Also plays host to Thorn Tree Café (see p161).

● *Fairmont The Norfolk* (☎ 020-226 5000; ☐ www.fairmont.com; Harry Thuku Rd; room-only prices start at sgl/dbl US$269/ 302 plus 28% tax) Nairobi's *other* historic hotel, and younger by two years, the Norfolk has been oozing class from its premises since it first opened its doors on Christmas Day 1904. Boasts the same facilities as the Stanley plus a fine collection of carriages and classic cars in the central courtyard and a more peaceful, out-of-town feel.

WHERE TO EAT AND DRINK
Kenya's cuisine is virtually indistinguishable from Tanzania's, being hearty, meaty and with an emphasis firmly on quantity rather than quality.

Embodying this description is the legendary tourist-attraction-cum-restaurant, *Carnivore* (Langata Rd, near Nairobi National Park; take a taxi from the town centre), designed specifically for those people whose thought upon seeing the playful gambolling of a young impala for the first time is to wonder what it would taste like coated in a spicy barbecue sauce. Actually, the menu has had to be severely reduced in recent years though you can still find ostrich and antelope migrating across the pages most nights; there are a few vegetarian options too. Vying with the celebrity of Carnivore is ***Thorn Tree Café***, something of a Mecca for travellers. Now on its third acacia, the original idea behind planting a tree in the middle of the courtyard was so that travellers could leave messages for other travellers on its thorns. Unfortunately, trees being trees, the roots of the previous two eventually started to undermine the building itself and had to be destroyed. Furthermore, Health & Safety has intervened and the tree is now encircled by noticeboards where you pin your messages – which reduces the romance (and indeed the raison d'être) of the tree somewhat. And when we looked, none of the messages were by travellers, for travellers, but were mainly announcements of people's birthdays etc. All most disappointing. Anyway, enough moaning: the food here is great, particularly for a post-climb breakfast feed-up (Ks2350) and they have live music (Wed to Sat from 6pm).

For cheaper and more mundane fare, there are any number of **fast-food places** around River Rd and Tom Mboya St, where lunch shouldn't cost more than Ks200 or so (though be warned, 'kebab' is usually a battered sausage containing meat of unknown origin, and not the kind of kebab you'd enjoy on a Friday night after the pubs have closed back in your home country). More upmarket fast-food restaurants include *Pizza Inn*, *Chicken Inn* and *Creamy Inn*, branches of which can be found throughout the city, including near the Hilton Hotel. If you're down near the station, do call in at the restaurant there – with liveried staff and a genteel, restrained atmosphere, it's ideal for those who enjoy a touch of colonial nostalgia, and the prices are good too.

MOVING ON – TO KILIMANJARO
By air
Precision Air (☎ 020-327 4282, Barclays Plaza, Loita St, 🖥 www.precisionairtz .com) fly two to four times daily between Nairobi and Kilimanjaro International (first one leaves around 8.30am, last 10pm).

To get to Nairobi International Airport, bus No 34 (Ks40) leaves from

virtually opposite the Hilton Hotel. Leave plenty of time as this service frequently gets snarled in heavy traffic. Alternatively, a taxi will be about Ks1300.

By coach or shuttle bus
Though there are plenty of **coach** operators willing to take you to Arusha, few can be recommended without hesitation. Far more convenient and comfortable than the coaches are the **shuttle buses**. There are two main companies operating shuttles to Arusha (and several smaller, newer ones). **Riverside** (☎ 0725-999121), on the first floor of Lagos House, Monrovia St, right on Jevanjee Gardens, is the most established. They have two buses, at 8am (which continues on to Moshi) and 2pm (though note that this will probably not arrive in Arusha until after dark). The fare for non-residents is US$25 to Arusha, or US$30 to Moshi.

Impala Shuttle (☎ 020-271 7373) also operates buses to Arusha at 8am and 2pm for US$30. Their offices are in Silver Springs Hotel, a little way from the centre, but their service is the best; if you are staying at the Wildebeest/Upper Hill (see p158) this is the company to use as their office is closer (though still a long drive away).

● **Crossing the border between Kenya and Tanzania** The drive between Nairobi and Arusha is fascinating, not least because you may find yourself sharing the road with camels, zebras, impalas, giraffes and Masai tribesmen on bikes. Despite the chaos of hawkers, warriors and travellers that surrounds the **Namanga crossing**, the border formalities are straightforward enough. On the Kenyan side you'll doubtless have to queue to have your passport stamped, and on the Tanzanian side there maybe a little wait while customs officials cast a cursory eye over your belongings – though these days even that formality is seldom observed and your bags may go through completely unchecked. You can change money at the border though the crossing is renowned for its charlatans so you're better off waiting until Arusha.

ARUSHA, MOSHI & MARANGU

Kilimanjaro International Airport

Is Kilimanjaro the only mountain to have its own international airport? The airport is situated roughly equidistant between Moshi (43km away) and Arusha (50km away), just under 6km to the south of the main road running between the two.

ARRIVAL AND DEPARTURE

Arriving

Arriving is straightforward: the terminal is small and you'll instantly be ushered into Immigration and Passport Control where you fill out a blue arrival form. If you arrived from a country where yellow fever is prevalent – even if you were only changing planes there – you will probably have your **yellow fever certificate** (see p81) checked too. Fail to have it and you'll have to pay (US$20-50) and could be refused entry into the country altogether.

The immigration formalities are usually easily negotiated, especially as Kilimanjaro is also one of only four places in the country where you can pick up a visa on arrival. Once you've made your way through passport control and having collected your baggage, the only thing now separating you from Tanzania is customs from which, safely negotiated, you emerge into the Arrivals Hall, where you'll find a moneychanger offering fair rates for the dollar – though you're better off waiting until you get to town if you can. The ATM that stood in its own separate booth outside is now literally just a hole-in-the-wall – there is no news as to whether it will be replaced or not.

To get to Moshi or Arusha, about 40 or 50 minutes away respectively, costs US$50 in a taxi or you may be lucky enough to get a shuttle bus depending on which airline you flew in with: KLM passengers have the chance to catch a shuttle to Arusha with Impala (US$15), their minibuses leaving when full. Precision Air operate their own shuttle service (Ts10,000) for internal flights, or US$15 for flights from Nairobi/Entebbe. Fly in with any other airline, however, such as Ethiopian, Qatar or Turkish, and you'll have to take a taxi, there being no public transport to and from the airport.

If you were expecting to be picked up and your lift hasn't arrived, there's a nice drinks stall outside where you can enjoy what, in this author's opinion, is some of the best birdwatching to be had in Tanzania outside of the national parks. The stall also serves up the odd samosa, though for something more substantial there's a reasonable canteen, **Delicious Meals Restaurant**, two minutes away just outside the airport grounds, that does a decent *kuku na chipsi* (chicken and chips).

Departing

Leaving Tanzania, things are just as simple. Before heading to the Departure Lounge, if you have any Tanzanian money you want to change you can go and see if the bureau de change in the Arrivals Hall is open (the dollar and Kenyan shilling rates are reasonable but the other rates are a bit stingy). Back at the Departure Lounge, after the initial X-ray the check-in desks are the first thing you see. Tickets sorted and bags checked in, from there you turn right to Passport Control (don't wander past it, even though you'll see others do so – they'll be on a domestic flight so don't need to go through the immigration formalities). Don't be in too much of a hurry to get through to the Departure lounge, for there's even less to do on that side of passport control than there is on this side. Instead, peruse the small string of souvenir shops, have a coffee from the café and check your email using wi-fi (they sell vouchers in at least one of the souvenir shops for US$3 per hour, and the wi-fi seems to cover most of the airport).

Arusha

Arusha may only be Tanzania's fourth largest city but it is, nevertheless, one of considerable consequence. During the days of British rule, Arusha was the symbolic halfway point between Cairo and Cape Town – the two termini of the old British Empire in Africa. (It should be noted, by the way, that the *actual* midpoint between Cape Town and Cairo lies not here but somewhere in central Congo.)

It was also in Arusha that Britain officially gave Tanzania its independence – and it maintains a central role in African affairs today. It is, for example, the home of the spanking new Headquarters of the East African Community – a union between Tanzania, Kenya, Rwanda, Burundi and Uganda that was originally forged in the '70s and has recently been revived. It is also the venue for sorting out issues from all over Africa – including the Tanzanian-brokered peace talks on Burundi and, most famously, the Rwanda War Crimes Tribunal in the Arusha International Conference Centre (AICC), now winding down after 17 years (though its legal successor, the International Residual Mechanism for Criminal Tribunals, will continue in the city). And there's no sign of Arusha's momentum ending any time soon as an enormous amount of investment, much of it from China, floods the city, leading to the construction of innumerable high rises all over the city. This has led to an atmosphere of great excitement – and a real sense that this is a city that's going places. It has also, alas, led to some real problems, not least of which has been the marked increase in traffic – particularly east from the Clock Tower along Nyerere Rd, a distance of about a kilometre that can take 90 minutes during rush hour.

Despite this and the other disadvantages of Arusha – the general noise and chaos – this author, at least, always looks forward to visiting; it wasn't always the case, however, for there was a time when a visit to Arusha was a pretty excruciating affair. Relentless badgering from safari touts (known locally as 'flycatchers') during the day would render one's time in the city tiring at best, while central Arusha was not a good place to be wandering around after dark. The city, however, has wised up to the fact that tourism is the bedrock on which this town is built. Flycatchers are now banned in the city and, apart from the odd souvenir, newspaper- or dope-seller hawking their wares around the Clock Tower area, tourists are largely free to roam unhindered. And they even have full-time policemen stationed round-the-clock in areas where muggings were frequent after dark (which tended to be near the bridges across the three rivers – the Naura, Goliondoi and Themi – that carve the city centre into four).

Though we still wouldn't recommend wandering around alone after dark, the changes introduced by the authorities have benefited the town, and the money pouring in from the east has led to several grand new projects including shiny new hotels, squeaky clean malls and swanky restaurants. The changes have also made it so much easier to spot and appreciate Arusha's charms. These include some of the best tourist amenities in the country, several pretty quarters filled with jacaranda and bougainvillea blossoms and a chaotic and occasionally fascinating central market. Nevertheless, with the call of the wild from Kilimanjaro, Ngorongoro and the Serengeti beckoning, it's a rare tourist who stays long enough to savour them.

WHAT TO SEE AND DO

Very little is the short answer. There are a couple of museums. By **Arusha Monument** there's **Arusha Declaration Museum** (daily 7.30am-6pm; US$4) that could conceivably be worth visiting – but only if you're absolutely sure you've finished preparing for your trek, have written all your postcards, bought all your souvenirs, sent all your emails, cut all your toenails and done all your laundry. Consisting in the main of a few photos and a number of traditional tools and weapons, perhaps the most interesting part is the building itself which is where Nyerere and chums met to hammer out the details of the Arusha Declaration (26-29 January 1967), a declaration that sets out the central tenets of African socialism that was adopted by the government in the following years; that, and a torch which is supposed to be carried around the country every year to promote unity and patriotism among folk (and which is a copy of the torch that was placed on the summit of Kili following independence). We suppose some might find this place provides a useful précis of Tanzanian history from pre-colonial times to the death of Nyerere, and the authorities are to be commended for trying. Overall it's worthy, if not exactly worthwhile.

The **Natural History Museum** (Mon-Fri 9am–6pm, Sat & Sun 9.30am–6pm) is better and, thanks in large part to an influx of photos of local wildlife by Swedish ex-pat Dick Persson, has improved markedly since we last visited. The photos are, in general, very good and tend to concentrate on the more 'unsung' creatures of Tanzania – the frogs, otters, lizards and hyraxes – and the less-visited parts of the country. Add to this a detailed rundown of the history of the Boma and overall this museum provides a fairly diverting way to spend an hour or so, though the entrance fee of Ts6600 is still a bit too high.

Arusha Monument

The **African Cultural Heritage Complex** (Mon-Sat 9.30am-5pm, Sun 9.30am-2pm; free) lies to the west of town on the way to Arusha Airport. It's taken years to come to fruition – we started writing about it back in 2006 and it's only just opened. But we have to say it was almost worth the wait. The most interesting thing about the first, smaller building is the roof, which has been designed to resemble the Kibo summit. Inside, however, you'll find little more than a market for woodcarvings and while there's no denying the artistry that's gone into the sculptures on sale, the designs themselves may be a bit too elaborate to appeal to Western tastes. This place, however, has been rather overshadowed by the huge construction next-door, the design of which has been based on those potent African symbols the spear, the shield and the drum. The reason for these architectural inspirations can be found inside, where a spiral ramp leads you through gallery after gallery of African art, including some fantastic antique bronze sculptures from Benin and wooden totems from all over West Africa on the lower ground floor. Most of the other galleries contain more modern exhibits, largely paintings and photos of various African scenes. As all of the exhibits (including the antiques) are for sale, this giant art gallery could be seen as little more than an upmarket version of the souvenir shop next door. But we think a gentle meander around is a great way of spending an hour or so – and you don't, of course, get any hassle from vendors!

With such a dearth of formal attractions in town, perhaps the most educational and entertaining thing you can do in Arusha is visit a **football game** (Ts1000); it will teach you more about Tanzanians (or at least the male half of the population) and what makes them tick than any papier maché diorama or reconstructed Masai dwelling. The next game is usually chalked up on the noticeboard outside the stadium's main entrance on Col Middleton Rd. Some of the games are rather low-key but attend a big league match and you're in for a treat.

If football's not your game you can always **play pool** (see p183), or go **swimming** (Ts10,000) in the pool at Impala Hotel (see p179).

ARUSHA, MOSHI & MARANGU

Organized tours and courses around Arusha

Via Via (see p182) organizes tours around the city and neighbouring hills. None of these sights will take your breath away, nor is that their intention: they are simply very pleasant escapes from the city and a refreshing way of discovering the country that exists outside the national parks. All prices are per person.

Destinations include Sapuk Waterfall, on the slopes of Meru, which involves at least a couple of hours' walking each way (US$35); Lake Duluti (US$35) which includes a walk in the nearby forest and the chance – for an extra fee – to paddle in a canoe on the water; and a visit to the hot spring at Chemka village (US$50), north of Boma N'gombe.

They also operate a number of courses including a **cookery course** (US$30 plus ingredients), where you spend the morning shopping for ingredients at the local market and the afternoon making something tasty out of them. Or you can take a trip to a **batik workshop** to learn how to print batiks (US$15 plus a further US$10 for materials), or take part in an **African drum-making and dancing workshop** (US$50).

For local tours that take you further afield, the Tanzanian Tourist Board, with help from Dutch development organization SNV, have created **Cultural Tourism Programmes** where you can visit the rural areas of Tanzania and experience 'real' African life, with all profits going towards various development projects. Prices are around U$15-35 per day depending on the group size, though the choice is larger. Amongst the many tours they organize country-wide are trips to **Machame** (🖳 machameculturaltourism.com) to see the waterfalls, caves, old churches, a market, and local coffee farms.

ARRIVAL
By air
Arusha Airport (or 'the little airport' as it's commonly called locally to distinguish it from Kilimanjaro International) lies to the west of the city and serves internal flights only. There's not much to the place other than a tiny 'departure lounge', a great little bookshop crammed with English titles, a souvenir shop or two and a couple of cafés (both Africafé and Msumbi Coffees have concessions here). A taxi into town will set you back about Ts20,000 (though they'll ask for Ts30,000), or you can walk or catch a *boda boda* (motorbike taxi; Ts1000) to the main junction (about one hot, dusty kilometre) and wait for a dalla-dalla to pass by (Ts500). Those who've arrived with Precision Air can catch their shuttle bus (Ts5000).

Not to be confused with Arusha Airport, **Kilimanjaro International Airport** (see p162) lies to the other (eastern) side of town, 44km along and 6km to the south of the road to Moshi.

For details on **going to the airports** see box p184.

By bus
Arriving in Arusha by **public bus**, expect to be dumped (sometimes literally) at the bus station at the southern end of Colonel Middleton Rd in the western half of town, reasonably close to the budget hostels.

If you reach Arusha by **shuttle bus**, on the other hand, tell the driver where you wish to jump out in the town centre and he should drop you there; if not, the chances are you'll be dropped off at the terminal on Simeon Rd just north of Impala Hotel, or at the Impala itself if you took their shuttle. From here you'll have to catch a cab, motorbike or walk to your destination.

ORIENTATION & GETTING AROUND
Arusha is bisected by the **Goliondoi River Valley**, a narrow and shallow dip in the town's topography. The division is more than just geographical: to the west is downtown, the busier, noisier and more fun

part of Arusha, where most of the cheap lodgings can be found. To the east of the valley lies the tourist centre, where most hotels, safari companies and better restaurants are located. This eastern section is further divided by a second river, the **Themi**, that runs along the back of such major landmarks as Arusha Hotel and the AICC.

Arusha is not a big place, most things are within walking distance of each other and **getting around** is not a major hassle, though to get from one half of town to the other it's a good idea to take a **dalla-dalla**; they charge Ts300 for short trips around town or Ts500 for destinations further afield. **Taxis** are distinguishable by their white number plates (other vehicles have yellow ones); they charge around Ts3000 for a trip within the town centre.

Thanks to a flood of cheap motorbikes from Asia, a two-wheeled alternative to the taxi has arrived in the last couple of years. **Boda boda**, or **Toyo**, is the local term for these motorbike taxis; there's no arguing that they are both cheap (Ts5000 will get you from the far east of the city to the far west, even late at night) and the best form of transport for slicing through the traffic. Before hopping eagerly onto one, however, bear in mind that there's already a special wing at Meru Hospital devoted to victims of toyo accidents – drivers, passengers and bystanders – with passengers by far and away the largest contingent, probably because few if any boda boda drivers supply their customers with a crash helmet. As with taxis, the drivers will come and find you, though they can usually be found outside the main hotels and restaurants.

SERVICES
Tourist information
The tourist information office (Mon-Fri 8am-4pm, Sat 8.30am-1pm) is on Boma Rd. Full of brochures, the office has really improved over the last few years and is the best source of information on the city and the safari circuit.

They keep a list of licensed tour agencies in both Moshi and Arusha and a blacklist of those companies to avoid; have a map of the city that they provide to tourists for free; and even have a rundown of bus services from Arusha to East African destinations. They also have a noticeboard where some people advertise for trekking companions. In our opinion, it's the best tourist office in East Africa.

Banks and changing money
The emergence of numerous **cashpoints** (ATMs) means that you should be able to find at least one that takes your card. The most central cashpoint to take foreign bank cards, usually without complaint, is outside the NBC on Sokoine. The Standard Chartered cashpoint at the southern end of Goliondoi Rd is temperamental, the one at Bank Exim over the road is often broken (though if it isn't it *usually* works OK with foreign cards) and the NMB Bank by the Clock Tower seldom accepts foreign cards (though is worth a try if you've exhausted other options). If you've got a vehicle or are staying in the area you may prefer to use Barclays' ATM on the way down to The Outpost on Serengeti Rd or their branch at the TFA Complex.

As for changing money, the **bureaux de change** are far more efficient than the banks. The three Sanya outlets (all on Sokoine; daily 7am-6 or 8pm) are reliable and usually offer close to the best rates in town. They are also just about the only bureau to open on Sunday. You can find one about 50m down from Café Barrista, and one just down from Green Hut House of Burgers with a third near Meru House Inn to the west.

The **AMEX** agent in Arusha is Rickshaw Travels (☎ 027-254 5955) at 184 Engira Rd, behind Kibo Palace Hotel.

Communications
The **post office** (Mon-Fri 8am-4.30pm, Sat 9am-noon) is by the Clock Tower, with a second branch, Meru Post Office (Mon-Fri 8am-1pm, 2-4.30pm, Sat 9am-noon), at the western end of Sokoine near the backpacker hotels.

For **phoning** abroad, TTCL (Mon-Fri 8am-4.30pm, Sat 9am-noon) is on Boma Rd. *(continued on p170)*

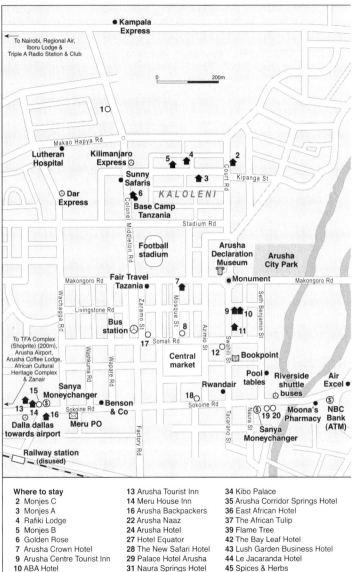

Where to stay

2 Monjes C	13 Arusha Tourist Inn	34 Kibo Palace
3 Monjes A	14 Meru House Inn	35 Arusha Corridor Springs Hotel
4 Rafiki Lodge	16 Arusha Backpackers	36 East African Hotel
5 Monjes B	22 Arusha Naaz	37 The African Tulip
6 Golden Rose	24 Arusha Hotel	39 Flame Tree
7 Arusha Crown Hotel	27 Hotel Equator	42 The Bay Leaf Hotel
9 Arusha Centre Tourist Inn	28 The New Safari Hotel	43 Lush Garden Business Hotel
10 ABA Hotel	29 Palace Hotel Arusha	44 Le Jacaranda Hotel
11 Sinka Court Hotel	31 Naura Springs Hotel	45 Spices & Herbs
	32 Pepe	47 Impala Hotel

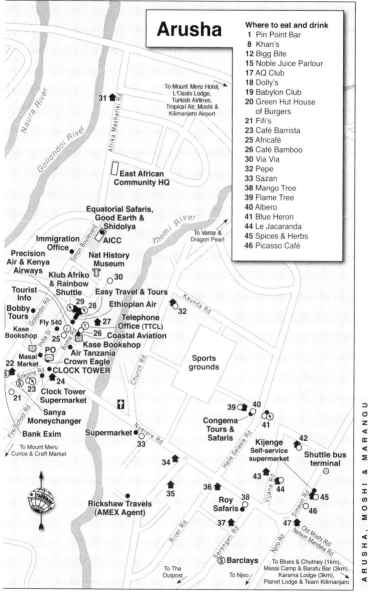

Arusha

Where to eat and drink
1 Pin Point Bar
8 Khan's
12 Bigg Bite
15 Noble Juice Parlour
17 AQ Club
18 Dolly's
19 Babylon Club
20 Green Hut House of Burgers
21 Fifi's
23 Café Barrista
25 Africafé
26 Café Bamboo
30 Via Via
32 Pepe
33 Sazan
38 Mango Tree
39 Flame Tree
40 Albero
41 Blue Heron
44 Le Jacaranda
45 Spices & Herbs
46 Picasso Café

Naura River
Goliondoi River
Afrika Mashariki Rd

31

To Mount Meru Hotel, L'Oasis Lodge, Turkish Airlines, Tropical Air, Moshi & Kilimanjaro Airport

East African Community HQ

Equatorial Safaris, Good Earth & Shidolya

Immigration Office

Precision Air & Kenya Airways

Klub Afriko & Rainbow Shuttle

Tourist Info

Bobby Tours

Kase Bookshop

Masai Market

22

21

AICC

Simeon Boulevard

Nat History Museum

30

Themi River

To Vama & Dragon Pearl

Easy Travel & Tours

Ethiopian Air

29 28

Fly 540

27

Telephone Office (TTCL)

Kaunda Rd

32

25

PO

26

Coastal Aviation

Kase Bookshop

Air Tanzania

Crown Eagle

CLOCK TOWER

24

Goliondoi Rd

India St

Boma Rd

Clock Tower Supermarket

Sanya Moneychanger

Bank Exim

Fire School Rd

Sokoine Rd

23

To Mount Meru Curios & Craft Market

Supermarket

Nyerere Rd

33

34

35

Rickshaw Travels (AMEX Agent)

River Rd

Sports grounds

Church Rd

Congema Tours & Safaris

39 40

41

Halle Selasie Rd

Kijenge Self-service supermarket

42

Shuttle bus terminal

43

44

36

38

Roy Safaris

37

Serengeti Rd

Barclays

To The Outpost

To Njiro

45

Vijani Rd

Simeon Rd

46

47

Niiro Rd

Old Moshi Rd / Nelson Mandela Rd

To Blues & Chutney (1km), Masai Camp & Barafu Bar (3km), Karama Lodge (3km), Planet Lodge & Team Kilimanjaro

ARUSHA, MOSHI & MARANGU

(cont'd from p167) They sell phonecards (Ts1000) which you can then charge with credit for use in the phones outside. There's every possibility that this particular process will be defunct by the time you read this, though hopefully the office will be able to instruct you on any new procedures. A call to Europe is about Ts550 per minute.

Most hotels now offer free **wi-fi** to their guests but if you don't have your own computer finding an **internet** café in Arusha still isn't difficult, especially as most of the big hotels have one. All charge much the same with Ts1000 for half an hour being the norm. The current favourite with most travellers is Café Barrista on Sokoine, especially as they also offer wi-fi facilities which are free if you eat there. Klub Afriko, round the back of New Safari Hotel (see p178), charges Ts1000 for 30 minutes, while the New Safari itself charges double but offers a little more peace and privacy.

Finally, over in the TFA (Shoprite) complex there's Nama Zone (Mon-Sat 8am-6.30pm, Sun 9am-5.30pm), offering lots of technical services and internet at Ts800 for 15 minutes, Ts2500 for an hour.

Airline offices (see also p349)

● **Air Excel** First floor, Subzali Building above Bank Exim on Goliondoi Rd (☎ 027-254 8429; ☐ www.airexcelonline.com; Mon-Fri 8.30am-1pm & 2-5pm, Sat 8.30am-1pm).

● **Air Tanzania** Boma Rd (☎ 027-250 3201; ☐ www.airtanzania.co.tz; Mon-Fri 8am-5pm; Sat & Sun 9am-1pm) Currently Air Tanzania operate only one flight, from Dar to Mwanza. However, rumours are circulating that they'll be opening a second route, a loop from Dar to Arusha and on to Zanzibar, so it's worth checking the latest news at their office.

● **Coastal Aviation** Boma Road (☎ 0752-059650; ☐ www.coastal.co.tz; Mon-Fri 8am-5pm, Sat 9am-1pm).

● **Ethiopian Air** Boma Rd (☎ 027-250 4231/250 6167; ☐ www.flyethiopian.com; Mon-Fri 8.30am-12.30pm & 2-5pm, Sat 8.30am-1pm).

● **Fastjet** (☎ 0685-680533, ☐ www.fast jet.com) There's no office in Arusha yet for

this airline but they are hoping to emulate the business model of such successful budget airlines as Easyjet and Ryanair – who are advertising flights from Arusha to Dar and Kilimanjaro International to Zanzibar (or vice versa) for just Ts32,000 plus taxes and charges. So we thought we had to mention them – and point out that you can book online!

● **Kenya Airways** See Precision Air, below.

● **Precision Air** Boma Rd (☎ 0784-402026; ☐ www.precisionairtz.com; Mon-Fri 8am-5pm, Sat 9am-1pm).

● **Regional Air** Just off Great North Rd/Nairobi Rd (☎ 027-250 4477/4164; ☐ www.regionaltanzania.com; Mon-Fri 8am-5pm, Sat 8am-1pm, Sun 8.30am-12.30pm).

● **Rwandair** Swahili St (☎ 0732-978558; ☐ www.rwandair.com; Mon-Fri 9am-5pm, Sat 9am-1pm).

● **Tropical Air** (☎ 0786-922811, ☐ www .tropicalair.co.tz).

● **Turkish Airlines** Plot 40, opposite Mount Meru Hotel (☎ 0785-111849, ☐ www.turkishairlines.com; Mon-Fri 8.30am-5pm).

● **Zanair** Summit Centre, Sokoine Rd (☐ www.zanair.com; Mon-Fri 8.30am-1pm, 2-5pm, Sat 8.30am-1pm).

Immigration office
The immigration office (Mon-Fri 7.30am-3.30pm) is across the road from the AICC on Afrika Mashariki Rd.

Shopping
You can get most things in Arusha – it's just a question of knowing where to look. Some of the shops seem to have been deliberately set up with tourists and expats in mind, particularly those at the **TFA complex** (**'Shoprite'**) at the western end of Sokoine, where you'll find: a couple of safari operators; Safari Care, a well-stocked camping/trekking shop; several bars, cafés and restaurants; the best English-language bookshop in the city (see p171); and even a massage parlour (☎ 0754-925092; US$30 for a one-hour full-body massage for tourists). This arcade may lack charm, being centred around a dusty parking lot next to a

ARUSHA, MOSHI & MARANGU

supermarket; nevertheless, if you're missing home, this place is unrivalled in Arusha.

● **Books** The chaotic **Kase Bookshop** (Mon-Fri 8am-5pm, Sat 8am-2pm) on Boma Rd by the Air Tanzania office and to the west of the Clock Tower is long established and convenient; **Bookpoint**, near Bigg Bite curry house, is fair too and has recently expanded its English-language section. Best of all, however, is **A Novel Idea** (🖥 www.anovelideatanzania.com; Mon-Sat 9am-5.30pm) in the TFA complex.

● **Electrical goods/cameras Benson & Co**, on Sokoine, should be your first port of call for electrical goods, camera batteries, repairs and so forth. This is also the first place to come if you need to have your phone unlocked (see p85). Note, however, that they're not cheap!

● **Pharmacy Moona's** Pharmacy (Mon-Fri 8.45am-5.30pm, Sat 8.45am-2pm) lies near the eastern end of Sokoine. The staff speak good English.

● **Souvenirs** You won't have any trouble finding souvenirs in Arusha – indeed, often they come and find you. Some of the stuff is poor quality, however. The best place for an overview of what's on offer can be had at **Mount Meru Curios & Crafts Market** (🖥 www.mountmerucurios.co.tz), a vast collection of souvenir stalls collected into one handy site on School Rd (aka Fire Rd, as the fire station is at the bottom of the street) about 300m south of the Clock Tower.

Manage to make it out of here alive and with some money still in your pocket and you can perhaps try **Afreaka Ts**, in the TFA complex, which offers smart, largely African-themed T-shirts (including some decent Kilimanjaro Beer numbers). Just a couple of doors down, **Camphill Handloom Weavers** has some attractive shawls, bags and other cotton items that make for good presents.

Finally, there's a very good variety of goods at **Blue Heron Café** (see p181), which has a couple of rooms of souvenirs stuffed with fabrics, wooden toys, rattan mats and wooden furniture etc; note, however, that this place has fixed prices.

● **Supermarket Shoprite**, in the TFA Complex at the western end of Sokoine,

was Arusha's first full-blown supermarket. Vast and with plenty of choice, most of the customers at this latest branch of the pan-African chain unsurprisingly appear to be expats. If you can't be bothered to schlep all that way, **Kijenge Self-Service Supermarket** by Spices and Herbs hotel/restaurant and the **supermarket** next to the Japanese restaurant Sazan are both OK, while most central of all is **Clock Tower Supermarket** (Mon-Fri 6.30am-9.30pm, Sat 8.30am-9pm, Sun 8.30am-8.30pm) on the main roundabout – which enjoyed a degree of fame in the 1960s as the location for a scene in John Wayne's *Hatari* (see p360) where an elephant runs amok through the aisles!

WHERE TO STAY [see map pp168-9]

As with much of the rest of Tanzania, the hotels in Arusha officially charge different rates for locals and foreigners, particularly for mid-range and high-end hotels. For the prices listed below, we have opted to list the **non-residents' rate** only; the residents' rate is usually lower by 5% or more though not always; sometimes it's just the shilling equivalent of the non-resident price.

We have divided the hotels in approximate price order and, within each category, have **ordered them approximately from west to east** (see map pp168-9).

Camping

Masai Camp (☎ 0754-507131, 🖥 www.masai-camp.com) lies 3km south-east from the centre on Nelson Mandela Rd (aka Old Moshi Rd) and charges US$8pp including hot showers. It's a great place (see also Where to Eat on p182 and Nightlife on p183) but it's not the quietest campsite (indeed, they actively discourage campers looking for peace and quiet from staying on Friday and Saturday nights). They also have a few private rooms (US$18/25 sgl/dbl, though the smarter upgraded rooms are US$40/50; note this is for bed only!).

Budget: under US$20 for a double

The focus for budget travellers these days is the western end of Sokoine Rd, just a few

❏ **Abbreviations**
Throughout this book we have used the following abbreviations when writing about accommodation: **pp** means per person; **s/c** is short for self-contained, a local term meaning that the room comes with a bathroom (ie the room is en suite or a bathroom is attached); while **sgl/dbl/tpl** means single/double/triple rooms. So, for example, where we have written 's/c sgl/dbl/tpl US$35/40/45', we mean that a self-contained single room costs US$35 per night, a self-contained double costs US$40 and a self-contained triple costs US$45.

hundred metres east of Shoprite. *Arusha Backpackers* (☎ 027-250 4474, 🖳 www .arushabackpackers.co.tz) is the sister of the Kindoroko and Backpacker hotels in Moshi and stands in an unpromising position adjacent to the forecourt of a petrol station on Sokoine. Nevertheless, this place is so popular that, in high season at least, you have to book in advance in order to stand a chance of staying here. The rooms are basic but clean and have wi-fi. The highlight, however, is the rooftop restaurant with perhaps the best view of Meru. It's also a great place to stay if you have to catch an early flight for the noise of the traffic outside won't let you sleep beyond 6.30am. Rates, including breakfast, begin at just US$8pp for a place in a four-bed dorm, rising to US$12/20 sgl/dbl, though there are no en suites.

Surviving largely on the overspill from Arusha Backpackers, *Meru House Inn* (☎ 027-250 7803; 🖳 meruhouseinn@hot mail.com; Ts25,000/35,000 sgl/dbl B&B, less Ts5000 if breakfast not required) has been around for a while and is another hotel often patronized by foreign tourists, which is surprising given that it makes little effort to attract them. Still, it's pleasant, relaxed, the manager and his staff have wi-fi, the rooms have wi-fi, there are bathrooms with hot water and there's a cheap café on the first floor and a good Indian restaurant (Noble Juice Parlour – see p181) by the entrance. But do avoid the rooms overlooking either the central courtyard or the road if you want a good night's sleep.

In the first edition of the book the main backpackers area was Kaloleni, a small cluster of streets to the north of the stadium and a few metres east of Colonel Middleton Rd, though with the migration of the tourists to the above establishments this area has fallen on hard times and the hotels that remain now have either closed or found alternative clients, some of whom only want to hire the room by the hour. Nevertheless, for those backpackers who don't like other backpackers, and who would rather stay somewhere authentically African – with all that entails – this area is perfect. (Be warned, however, that the by-law banning flycatchers in Arusha doesn't seem to apply here.) There are still a couple of decent accommodation options. The best is a new place, *Rafiki Lodge* (☎ 0712-782997; 🖳 rafikilodge1@yahoo.com), which is spotless and friendly and the rooms are actually rather lovely – satellite TV, self-contained, mosquito nets etc – and well worth the Ts30,000 (Ts40,000 with air-con).

With each built on or just off Levolosi Rd, the three *Monjes Guest Houses* (☎ 0782-999011, 🖳 www.monjestz.com), labelled A, B and C, are also still fairly reliable. Each charges sgl/dbl Ts18,000/ 25,000, with *Monjes C* and its brighter rooms probably the best, especially if the legendary eatery Pizzarusha returns there as is proposed.

Finally, *L'Oasis Lodge* also have a 'backpackers' section – see p175 for details.

Mid-range: US$20-60 for a double
On the western side of town, the major landmark on Colonel Middleton Rd is the *Golden Rose* (☎ 027-250 7959, 🖳 www .goldenrosehoteltz.com; s/c sgl/dbl/tpl US$30/40/60 B&B), a popular place that's

now dwarfed by its neighbouring conference centre. The hotel's name is apt too, for this is a hotel with something of a gilt complex with many of its rooms decorated in shiny golden hues. Nearby, off Swahili St, **ABA Hotel** (☎ 0755-989175) is a 23-room affair and very comfy, with each room boasting fan, TV, telephone, wi-fi, mosquito nets and its own bathroom with hot water. Rates are a very reasonable at US$15pp including breakfast. It is probably a place that appeals more to the locals, at least when compared to the neighbouring *Arusha Centre Tourist Inn* (☎ 0764-294384; ✉ atihotel@habari.co.tz) which has similar facilities, again with a TV, wi-fi and mosquito net (though no fan) in every room, all of which are en suite. B&B rates are again reasonable at US$30/35 s/c sgl/dbl. Round the corner on Swahili St is a third option in this block: *Sinka Court Hotel* (☎ 0688-891262; ✉ sinka-court-hotel@hotmail.com) has much the same facilities (en suite, TV) though perhaps is slightly smarter, brighter and airier, a difference that's reflected in the price (US$40/50 s/c sgl/dbl, US$55-60 for suites).

Heading across town, *Le Jacaranda* (☎ 027-254 4624; ✉ jacaranda.chez.com; US$50/55 sgl/dbl) is to the east of the centre in a quiet street to the north of Nyerere Rd. I am pleased to see that since the last edition this place has upped its game somewhat. This is a characterful place, its restaurant large and airy, its communal seating areas comfy and laidback and there's even a mini-golf course in the garden. The rooms, however, are the downside: some of the doubles are tired and stark and the singles, most of which lie away from the main hotel proper at the bottom of the garden, feel like monastic cells, with some so small they fit your body like a condom. Still, the food is once more to be recommended, a family bungalow is being built – and I've always had a soft spot for Tinga Tinga art which decorates the exterior walls here and gives the whole place a welcoming smile.

There are several restaurants in the Themi district of town, near Jacaranda, that also offer accommodation. Amongst them are *Pepe* (☎ 0784-399 928; ✉ www.hotel

pepeone.co.tz) with small but lovely self-contained rooms into which are squeezed a TV, a bed with box mozzy net and a fan, while wi-fi pervades every room. Rates are sgl/dbl US$40/45 – add US$5 for breakfast.

Two blocks east, *Flame Tree* (☎ 0783-940802; ✉ flametree.reservation@gmail.com) has similarly simple rooms though still with TV, wi-fi and hot water; rates are sgl/dbl US$35/40. Finally, further east again is the Ethiopian *Spices & Herbs* restaurant (☎ 0754-313162, ☎ 0754-818533; ✉ axum_spices @hotmail.com); this has about 20 en suite rooms built around a central courtyard at the back of their premises. The rooms are simple but clean and airy, with box nets, and *some* have TV, and cost sgl/dbl US$40/50 including breakfast.

Upper-range: US$60-100 for a double
Arusha Tourist Inn (☎ 0754-583455, ✉ www.atihoteltz.com; dbl US$70 B&B, US$60 single occupancy), on Sokoine Rd, is hidden away behind the much tattier Meru House Inn, with which it shares an owner. The 29 en suite rooms come with all the facilities including satellite TV and wi-fi but do lack views; indeed its location verges on the claustrophobic. Still, it's a safe, decent choice, though with no singles.

A relative newcomer to the city's hotel scene (though one that's already starting to look a little ancient, such is the giddy pace of construction around these parts) is *Arusha Crown Hotel* (☎ 027-250 8523; ✉ www.arushacrownhotel.com) on Makongoro Rd by the south-eastern corner of the stadium. Very much a hotel for local businessmen, it's smart and comfy enough though a little bland and the walls cannot entirely block out the noise from the streets below. That said, you do at least get a grandstand view of the football across the road from some rooms. Rates start at US$60/75 s/c sgl/dbl, which in our opinion is fair.

Right in the centre of town, *Arusha Naaz* (☎ 027-250 2087; ✉ www.arushanaaz.net; s/c sgl/dbl/tpl US$45/60/75) comes as a bit of a surprise. The façade looks unpromising and the staff's attitude to their guests can sometimes border on the disdainful. Nevertheless, the rooms are squeaky clean, en suite and all come with TV; there's also a (dazzlingly bright) roof terrace. Try to get a room away from the road if possible.

The Outpost (☎ 027-254 8405; 🖥 www.outposttanzania.com; off map to the south-east) lies down Serengeti Rd to the south of Nyerere Rd, a lane so exclusive that Arusha's usual noise of traffic and touts is replaced by the soothing sound of bird-song and the gentle rhythm of people brushing the dust from the street. Popular with tour groups, The Outpost has its own wi-fi and laundry service and a lovely lounge area kitted out, as with the rooms, in a spartan but relaxed, comfy style. The rooms have TV, are all en suite and there's a small pool and attractive bar/restaurant area. B&B here costs US$60/US$78/90 s/c sgl/db/tpl: pretty good value and a reliably nice hotel.

Virtually opposite Jacaranda, ***Lush Garden Business Hotel*** (☎ 0715-801140, 🖥 www.lushgardenhotels.co.tz) is very smart, swish and hi-tech, with 24 self-

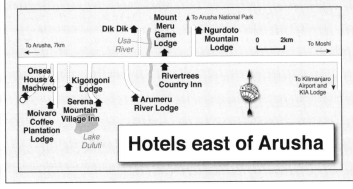

Accommodation around Arusha

Whilst we have spent pages describing the accommodation in Arusha, the fact of the matter is that most of you will have booked your trek before you arrive, and your agency in turn will have arranged your hotel; and it's more than likely that this accommodation won't even be in Arusha but outside of it, where several swish, smart and salubrious lodges are situated, surviving on the patronage of foreign travel companies and their local agents. It's hard to criticize these places except that they do tend to be in the middle of nowhere. The following reviews are **ordered from west to east**.

Arusha Coffee Lodge (☎ 027-250 9279; 🖥 www.elewani.com) consists of 30 luxury chalets that are just gorgeous. Unlike the other hotels in this section, it lies to the west of Arusha on the way to the local airport but is still being used by a couple of trekking companies, particularly those who combine their treks with a safari after-wards. The private chalets on the plantation are served by a pool and they also offer massage service. Another thing in its favour is its renowned restaurant. Now owned by the Elewana chain, prices start at: s/c sgl/dbl US$263/350 in the low season, high season sgl/dbl US$375/500.

Firmly in the luxury bracket, ***Onsea House*** (☎ 0787-112498; 🖥 www.onsea house.com) is a delight. Everything, from the locally made furniture to the outdoor pool and Jacuzzi with views across to Meru, the friendly and conscientious staff and

Hotels east of Arusha

contained rooms and an impressive array of facilities including a computer in each room (yes, really), satellite TV, air-con and even slippers (yes, really again!). Amazingly, it's also very reasonably priced at sgl/dbl US$50/75-80, suites US$115-135. True, you probably weren't dreaming of staying somewhere quite so 'untraditional' when you booked your accommodation in Arusha – but if you can get over that, this is a lovely, comfortable place.

L'Oasis Lodge (☎ 0755-866421, ☎ 027-250 7089; ⌨ www.loasistanzania .com; off map to the north-east) is in an obscure location, a 15-minute walk north of the town, with accommodation in 27 huts, rondavels and 'boma-style' rooms all hidden behind a high wall. The rooms themselves are fine, the food is said to be great and they've got wi-fi, a small pool and, of course, Henry the resident crane. The only quibbles we have, in fact, are that more than one reader has written to say that they've failed to get any sleep due to the barking of the neighbourhood dogs – particularly true for those who've opted for the

the tranquil setting on Namasi Hill, 7km east of Arusha, with views across to Meru, is spot on. One can only imagine they've increased the marriage rates in many Western countries, as people rush for an excuse to stay here. And I haven't yet mentioned the food, prepared by one of the Belgian owners who's been working in Michelin-starred restaurants since he was 16. The rates – s/c sgl/dbl US$210-280/250-340; are not cheap even by Arusha's standards but they are very fair value.

Once upon a time the only problem with Onsea was one of availability, its four double rooms (plus two in the separate cottage by the pool) frequently booked up well in advance. They have alleviated that problem, however, by building a new place next door: Linked by a bridge and with the same sense of understated style, *Machweo Wellness Retreat & Fine Dining* (☎ 0784-833207; ⌨ www.machweo.com) is nevertheless also quite a different entity to its elder sister. For where Onsea House is more homely, cosy and intimate, Machweo, while still exquisitely tasteful, is slightly more 'showy', with rooms boasting 80-channel satellite TVs, some lovely African sculptures loaned by Cultural Heritage (see p165) and even bathtubs in the Honeymoon suites; there's also a spa here too. Rates are the same as at Onsea House.

Not too far away at the end of a bumpy dirt track about 7km east of Arusha, 2km south of the road to Moshi is *Moivaro Coffee Plantation Lodge* (☎ 027-2506315/86, ☎ 0754324193, ⌨ www.moivaro.com), consisting of 40 cottages, each hidden away amongst the lush vegetation of the verdant grounds. Each room is en suite and has a veranda; the lodge also boasts a swimming pool and bar. A massage service is available, too, which will enable you to while away the hours when you're not on the mountain. It can't be easy for a hotel chain to maintain that personal touch and individuality that makes a stay memorable; and I have to say, I did find the service a touch cold and officious the last time I visited. As a result, for the money I think there are more charming options these days. Rates: s/c sgl/dbl/tpl US$132-185/171-250/223-335 for B&B.

Kigongoni Lodge (☎ 0732-978 876, ⌨ www.kigongoni.net) is located in a beautiful hilltop location on an old coffee estate about 11km from Arusha. The 19 rustic cottages are simple but wonderful, with fireplaces, four-poster beds and lovely wooden verandas overlooking the monkey-filled forest below, while Meru and even Kibo loom in the background. The Dutch family who run it are jolly and helpful, the food is good and, to top it all, part of the profit goes to the nearby Sibusiso Foundation, a centre for mentally and physically handicapped children. Throw in the usual facilities, including wi-fi internet and a swimming pool, and you have a very, very pleasant lodge. Rates: s/c B&B US$85-125 per person.   (continued on p176)

cheaper Backpackers Lodge, across the dirt track, which has shared amenities and lacks some of the charm of the main lodge. It must be said there has also been a complaint or two from clients recently about an unreliable hot water supply and I just get the impression they seem to be struggling to keep up with the competition following a couple of changes in senior personnel. Rates: sgl/dbl US$75/100; Backpackers Lodge US$25pp in one of 12 twin-bedded rooms.

One of the places that has probably benefitted from Oasis's (hopefully temporary) decline is *Ilboru Lodge* (☎ 0754-270357; 🖳 www.ilborusafarilodge.com; off

map to the north-west) which ostensibly has many similarities: a location in the dusty suburbs and a layout consisting of brick and thatch rondavels built round a pool for which they charge similar rates (sgl/dbl/tpl US$61-93/78-117/109-152 depending on season). But there the similarity ends, for this place feels more spacious, its rooms bigger, brighter and smarter, and its grounds well maintained by the Dutch owner and his smiling staff. The pool is very large, there is wifi in the grounds and reception, the upstairs restaurant has a large menu (and there's a pancake house too!) and they also offer massage sessions and even Swahili cookery and

Accommodation around Arusha *(cont'd from p175)*

Serena Mountain Village Inn (☎ 027-255 3313, 0787-444015, 🖳 www.serenahotels.com) is one of many Serena properties in Tanzania and yet another lodge that is situated on a coffee plantation, though this time at Tengeru and with the added attraction of Lake Duluti behind. This gorgeous location and the grand, almost baronial reception/restaurant area aren't quite matched by the 42 rooms in concrete bungalows but nevertheless some have full sunken baths and lake views and all have wi-fi. Rates are s/c sgl/dbl US$140/205 low season, US$290/430 high season.

Arumeru River Lodge (☎ 0785-555131, 🖳 www.arumerulodge.com) consists of 10 large, comfortable chalets and a huge, high-roofed makuti reception-cum-restaurant, all standing amongst neatly trimmed gardens amidst the bushes of a coffee estate that lies 20km along and 1km south of the road to Moshi. All the usual facilities are here, including wi-fi (US$5 in the chalets, free in the suites), a small solar-heated pool, satellite TV and a highly regarded restaurant. Rates are s/c sgl/dbl/tpl US$140-160/190-270/240-360 for the garden chalets depending on the season, rising to US$230-260/240-320/315-435 for the suites. Overall, safe and satisfactory without being spectacular.

Dik Dik (☎ 027-255 3499; 🖳 www.dikdik.ch) is homely and in a good location north of the highway. The hotel is named after one of Africa's smallest antelopes and is appropriately petite, particularly when compared to the nearby Ngurdoto (see opposite), save for the high-roofed reception. It boasts just 20 rooms divided between 10 bungalows, each with a fireplace, veranda, wi-fi, hammock and mini-bar; there's a small pool here too and even a viewing tower – from the top of which you can see Kilimanjaro. It's a pleasant, cosy place. Rates: s/c sgl/dbl US$150/200 for B&B. Dik Dik is also a trekking agency, see p189.

The delightful *Rivertrees Country Inn* (☎ 073-297 1667; 🖳 www.rivertrees .com) sits on the banks of the Usa River, 22km east of Arusha. It's a stylishly rustic place, the cosy, slightly 'shabby chic' reception and lounge making good use of old reclaimed wood, while the 18 self-contained guestrooms, two cottages and large thatched River House – which contains two double rooms – are similarly understated and tasteful. But it's the grounds that, for this author at least, are the biggest draw, the riverbanks providing a home to monitor lizards while the Inn's many great old trees offer both welcome shade for residents and a perfect habitat for birds. Indeed, the whole place comes alive with magnificent birdsong throughout the morning. Add

ARUSHA, MOSHI & MARANGU

Tinga-Tinga painting lessons. All in all, very impressive.

Karama Lodge (☎ 027-250 0359, ☎ 0754-475188, 🖳 www.karama-lodge.com) lies 3km south-east of town along Old Moshi Rd/Nelson Mandela Rd; it is beyond Masai Camp and the owners of that actually own this place. An unusual lodge, the Karama is tucked quietly on a hillside facing away from Arusha; it boasts 22 stylish en suite rooms housed in log cabins on stilts, with views of Meru from many. A sauna, pool, massage and yoga room complete the facilities. Rates start as low as

sgl/dbl/tpl US$66/86/126 in low season, rising to US$95/135/170 in the high season.

A couple of kilometres further along Old Moshi Rd/Nelson Mandela Rd is ***Planet Lodge*** (☎ 0736-209966, 🖳 www .planet-lodge.com). We had a couple of clients a year back who insisted that they stay here mainly, we assumed, because of online reviews, as we'd never heard of it. Having now visited it, we found it, in all honesty, to be rather ugly – the 24 concrete 'bandas' with tin roofs looking rather charmless compared to most of the others in this guide. The garden, too, is currently

to this such facilities as wi-fi, a kitchen that bakes its own bread and an attentive, conscientious staff and you have the ideal option for those looking for a little luxury but who aren't bothered about being close to the town. After all, if it's good enough for both a London-based, football-club-owning Russian oligarch and the heir to the British throne – both of whom have stayed in the past couple of years – it'll probably be good enough for you too. Rates: s/c sgl/dbl/tpl US$198/243/320 B&B, or it's US$706 for the River House.

Opposite is another place that's full of character. ***Mount Meru Game Lodge & Sanctuary*** (☎ 027-255 3885, ☎ 0732-297 1771, 🖳 www.intimate-places.com) was established back in 1959 (the founder's son now in charge) although its colonial style harks back to an earlier era. The 17 large, en suite rooms with wi-fi (for which they charge) in wooden bungalows are comfortable and the restaurant is renowned among expats who flee Arusha to dine here at weekends; but it's the **animal sanctuary**, with its rescued elands, ostriches and even buffalo that really sets this place apart. Rates are s/c sgl/dbl US$125-222/US$96-151.

Continuing east, ***The Ngurdoto Mountain Lodge*** (☎ 027-255 5217; 🖳 www.the ngurdotomountainlodge.com) is a massive place just off Moshi Rd on the way to Arusha National Park. The rooms and chalets are en suite and come with TV and mini-bar; some even have their own Jacuzzi. With two restaurants, coffee shop, tennis and badminton courts, swimming pool, health club and even its own golf course, this is just about as good as it gets facility-wise – though it must be said that it's not so much a lodge as a full-on hotel. Probably geared more towards the business client than the tourist, to be fair they've kept their rates the same for a few years now at s/c sgl/dbl US$135/175 up to US$2000 for the presidential villa.

KIA Lodge (☎ 0754 324193; 🖳 www.kialodge.com) is another link in the Moivaro chain and is recommended by more than one reader as a great place to spend your last night in Africa before flying out from neighbouring Kilimanjaro International Airport (to and from which it offers free shuttles). It's decorated in a smorgasbord of Tanzanian styles, too, from the Zanzibar-style reception, the Tinga-Tinga paintings in the restaurant and the Makonde woodcarvings in the rooms. Their hilltop location also allows you unequalled views of both Kili and Meru, as well as distant glimpses of the Pare Mountains and Maasai plains. Lovely. Rates: are the same as for Moivaro Coffee Plantation at s/c sgl/dbl/tpl US$132-185/171-250/223-335 for B&B.

rather immature and shadeless (though labelling the plants is a nice touch). In time it will improve and there's no doubt the service is very attentive and the rooms comfortable with fans and mosquito nets; there's a pool too. Nevertheless, we do remain surprised that it has such an online following. Rates: sgl/dbl/tpl US$70-95/90-118/126-165 depending on season.

Expensive: US$100 and above for a double

Naura Springs Hotel (☎ 027-254 3082/3/4/5; 🖳 www.nauraspringshotel .com; rates sgl/dbl US$120/160) is a soaring, shiny blue-glass landmark north of the AICC. It's not a bad place – a bit dazzling, but the open-air reception is a nice touch and the rooms have all the features you'd expect of a hotel this size (internet access, satellite TV, safes, bathrooms with Jacuzzis); but there are others that have sprung up since its opening about five years ago that are bigger and shinier. One of these stands just a few hundred metres to the south. There are few more potent symbols of the upturns in Arusha's fortunes – and the massive investments pouring in from the Chinese – than *Palace Hotel Arusha* (☎ 027-554 5800, 🖳 www.palacehotelarusha .com), a giant glass-and-steel monolith that reaches skywards, dazzling in the African sunlight. I hardly need tell you that the rooms within are all self-contained and have every sort of modern convenience, from wi-fi to air-con, satellite TV and safe deposit box. Price-wise it's reasonable at sgl/dbl US$125-160/145-185 for rooms, rising to US$280 for the suites.

The arrival – and, more to the point – the location of Palace Hotel Arusha has not been a blessing to everyone. In particular, *The New Safari Hotel* (☎ 027-250 3261/2, 🖳 www.thenewsafarihotel.com; s/c sgl/ dbl/tpl/suites US$90/115/150/200-220) was once the pre-eminent place in this part of town, though now it squats sulking and skulking in the shadows of its new neighbour. There are stories that Hemingway stayed here – though even if he did, it's doubtful he'd recognize the place, especially as it is now owned by the Lutheran Church and thus no alcohol is served. To be fair, the comparisons with its neighbour are a tad unfair, for it remains a decent place, with the gleaming, polished nature of the lobby mirrored by the spotless en suite rooms with TV, wi-fi and mini-bar; they also have a pizzeria and cafeteria on the ground floor that's popular with locals.

Across the road and hidden away behind the phone office is The New Safari's sister, the smart *Hotel Equator* (☎ 027-250 8409; 🖳 www.equator-hotel.com). With every room fitted out with a shower, private balcony, satellite TV, wi-fi, phone and fan, this was once one of the plushest places in the town centre though, like The New Safari, it too has been rather overshadowed, literally and metaphorically, by the arrival of Palace Hotel Arusha. Nevertheless, though it was entirely devoid of any guests when we visited it shows no other signs of decline and the price is fair at s/c sgl/dbl Ts96,000/ 128,000 including continental breakfast.

Perhaps the largest hotel in this category is *Mount Meru Hotel* (☎ 027-2545111, 🖳 www.mountmeruhotel.com; off map to the north-west), once upon a time the Holiday Inn though now fully renovated, restored and reopened by the president of Tanzania after years of being mothballed. It's a bit impersonal, as you may expect from a place this size (it has 178 rooms), but the rooms are comfy and feature all the usual facilities including air-con, wi-fi, satellite TV, mini-bar and so on. Rates start at sgl/dbl US$180/215 and go up to US$410/450 for the Presidential Suite.

No review of Arusha's hotels would be complete without mention of the oldest of the lot, *The Arusha Hotel* (☎ 027-250 7777; 🖳 www.thearushahotel.com), which is actually fairly anonymous despite its location in the very heart of the action by the Clock Tower. Formerly known as the New Arusha, the name change was only sensible considering it opened in 1894 (though the current building dates 'only' from 1927). It remains amongst the swishest and plushest of all the town-centre hotels, with wood-panelled walls and, to use that well-worn brochure phrase, a real 'atmosphere of yesteryear'. The restaurant is, of course, very good, the swimming pool heated and the rooms sumptuous and kitted out with television, wi-fi and, of course, a bathroom. All this luxury doesn't come cheap, however, with rack rates starting at sgl/dbl US$260/300. It should be noted, too, that some are complaining about the drop in the quality of service here recently. For this reason, many people are now migrating a few hundred metres east to *Kibo Palace Hotel* (☎ 027-254 4472; 🖳 www.kibo palacehotel.com), with rooms from sgl/dbl US$170/190 rising to US$400/450 for the suites. With every room en suite and boasting wi-fi, a TV, telephone and safe, this is a great addition to the hotel scene in Arusha, particularly as the service is consistently praised by guests. There's even a small gym and pool for that last-minute Kili workout.

A few metres further along Nyerere Rd, *East African* (☎ 027-205 0075; 🖳 www.eastafricanhotel.com; rooms from sgl/dbl US$90/120) is of a similar age but where Kibo Palace has established a niche in the *mzungu* (tourist) market, the latter continues to survive largely on the patronage of East African businessmen, despite similar facilities. The great lump of gleaming blue glass and concrete along from Kibo Palace is *Arusha Corridor Springs Hotel* (☎ 027-254 5074; 🖳 www.corridor springshotel.com) housing 96 beds in self-contained rooms, air-con, TV, wi-fi and all those other essentials of a luxury hotel. It's actually fairly well priced at just US$70/100 for sgl/dbl, with twins for US$120, all for B&B.

Still further east, *The African Tulip* (☎ 027-254 3004; 🖳 www.theafricantulip .com) is yet another fine hotel in this neck of the forest. Named after the bright orange flowers that grow on the trees along this lane, the Tulip is owned by Roy Safaris (see p191). The rooms are huge and kitted out with every possible modern convenience including flat-screen TVs, remote-controlled air-con, phone and wi-fi. Aside from all this high-tech gadgetry, it's worth mentioning that it's also a very comfortable place in a shiny, glamorous sort of way. Rates are sgl/dbl US$190/230, rising to US$500 for the two-bedroom suites.

Heading to the roundabout one can only guess at the number of forest creatures that were made homeless in order to furnish *Impala Hotel* (☎ 027-2543082, 🖳 www.impalahotel.com) with its wood-heavy reception. It's one of the main business centres in Arusha, with all the trimmings one would expect – a plethora of bars and restaurants (Indian, Chinese, Italian), a pool and conference facilities, and the rooms, all en suite, come equipped with colour television and hot water. Strangely they are all actually quite reasonably priced at s/c sgl/dbl/tpl US$90/110/155 with breakfast.

The Arusha Hotel's long-standing reputation as the best hotel in town is now also being challenged by the arrival of *The Bay Leaf Hotel* (☎ 027-254 3055, 🖳 www.the bayleafhotel.com), a 'boutique hotel' just round the corner from Le Jacaranda. Boasting only six rooms, this is currently one of central Arusha's classiest accommodation options with features including extra king-size beds, flat-screen TVs, wi-fi, and little touches such as bath gowns and slippers, complimentary daily newspapers and even a laundry service (though no pool). Such luxury comes at a price, however, and at The Bay Leaf that price is sgl/dbl US$140/155 for B&B.

Finally, the unusually named *Blues & Chutney* (☎ 0732-971668; 🖳 www.blues andchutney.com; rates s/c sgl/dbl US$120 /160) is a new place south of Old Moshi Rd/Nelson Mandela Rd established by the same people running the excellent Rivertrees (see box p176). The six rooms, all self-contained and with wi-fi, are bright and freshly painted and four have great verandas overlooking the grounds. There's also a shop and massage parlour. Overall, it's a pleasant and tastefully decorated place – though we can't help but feel it's a little overpriced.

WHERE TO EAT AND DRINK
[see map pp168-9]

Arusha is a good place for foodies, with African, Oriental and Indian eateries abounding. Some also advertise 'Continental food', which basically means any dish that doesn't fit into one of the categories above.

Cafés and breakfast spots

On Sokoine in the heart of the tourist land surrounding the Clock Tower, the first place to catch the eye is *Café Barrista* (daily 7.30am-6pm), formerly the venerable Patisserie and recently renovated, with plans to open in the evening. A good menu of burgers, snacks and pizzas is supplemented by some great Mexican dishes. Note: alcohol is not available here.

The renovation at Barrista has happened just in time, for a couple of fierce new rivals have opened nearby. Our favourite of the newbies is *Fifi's* (daily 7.30am-9pm) on Themi Rd, just off Sokoine. More than one resident says they serve the best food in the city centre and the drinks list includes a huge coffee, milkshake and smoothie selection while for food the menu offers Western favourites (sarnis, burgers and salads etc), all well prepared and served with a smile. Another rival is on Boma Rd by the tourist office: *Africafé* (Mon-Sat 7.30am-9pm, Sun 8am-9pm) is a comfy coffee house catering to crowds of caffeine-crazy consumers. The coffee menu is indeed lengthy but what makes this place well worth a visit is once again the food, with great platefuls of some very tasty (if expensive) grub; best value, we think, is the steak and (two) eggs with chips and salad for Ts10,800.

Finally, in the TFA Complex, *Msumbi Coffees* is well-known for its 'boozy coffees' such as Simba's Delight (coffee laced with cognac, Ts6500) and something called a 'granita' (a coffee-flavoured slushy, Ts4000).

Lunches and snacks

As with the category above, the definition here is rather loose: most of the places below also serve dinner as you can tell by the opening hours; furthermore, most of the eateries in the categories above and below also serve snacks and lunches, of course. Nevertheless, in our experience the following tend to be more popular during the day and for this reason we've put them here.

As we're ordering this section approximately from west to east we should start with the establishments in the **TFA complex**. The first is *Ciao Gelati* (Mon-Sat 8.30am-5pm), ostensibly an ice-cream parlour (Ts2500 per scoop) but one that also serves some of the biggest and tastiest salads in Arusha. For the ultimate treat in Arusha *Chocolate Temptation* (Mon-Sat 9am-5pm) is a proper cake shop that specializes in extracting every last milligram of pleasure from the humble cocoa bean. My advice? Come here before climbing to admire the mouthwatering beauty of the confectionery on offer, then promise yourself that, should you reach the summit, you can gorge on anything in the shop, be it a 100g hunk of rocky road (Ts6000) or an entire cake (Ts36,000-60,000). You never know, such an incentive might just be the difference between success and failure...

Moving east, on Sokoine Rd *Dolly's* is a curious place, ostensibly a patisserie though with a vast array of Indian dishes on offer too, all served in spotlessly clean surroundings, making this a favourite for travellers with children.

A little way along the street, *Green Hut House of Burgers* is a bit of a misnomer, for burgers feature but seldom on the menu. This is a great little place for lunchtimes, however, with cheap, simple but filling local fare the order of the day including: *maandazi* (a sort of fried bread; Ts500), *mishkaki* (meat – usually lamb/goat – skewers; Ts1500), *kitumbua* (a sort of rice cake or pattie; Ts600) and several dishes featuring that tasteless Tanzanian staple, *ugali* (a stodgy cornmeal or cassava mush). Note that both locals and tourists have found out about this place so you may find yourself sharing a table with strangers – come before 12.30pm if you'd rather not.

Opposite the tourist office, *Café Bamboo* (daily 7am-9pm) has both been around for years and managed to maintain its high standards. The African music and ethnic design on the walls can't quite eradicate the impression that this is actually a very English-style tearoom – though curiously it's actually more popular with locals than other restaurants around here. The food's good too, with mains Ts8000-10,000 (including a tasty beef stir fry that, refreshingly, contains plenty of meat) or around Ts6000 for vegetarian options.

Blue Heron (🖳 www.blue-heron-tanzania.com; Mon-Thurs 9am-4pm, Fri 9am-10pm, Sat 10am-10pm) occupies, in our opinion, the best grounds in Arusha, a sweet 1950s house set in the middle of some lovely manicured gardens, complete with fountains and some gorgeous mature trees between which pretty yellow birds flit. This place is also notable for its fine souvenir emporium (see p171) as well as some of the comfiest sofas in East Africa. As such, it's a great place to come and write postcards, send emails (they have wi-fi) or, given how long the food takes, write your first novella, To be fair, the food is great and on occasion delightfully hearty, with pizzas for Ts10,000-14,000 and more interesting items including *spaghetti di mare* (Ts17,000), grilled linefish (Ts22,000) and *ceci fritos* and *koroko* (fried salted chickpeas and toasted cashew nuts; Ts7500).

Also in this corner of Arusha there's *Picasso Café* (Mon-Sat 9am-11pm, Sun 9am-5pm), yet another smart café that, with its largely *mzungu* clientele, wouldn't look out of place back home.

Dinner

This isn't a comprehensive guide to dining in Arusha but it does include most of the most popular eateries – at least amongst tourists – in the city.

Asian food... and an Ethiopian There

are a couple of hangouts specializing in Tanzania's hearty, cheap and simple brand of spicy local and Indian cuisine, of which *Khan's* stands out. Long a favourite with locals, it's a garage by day but at around 5pm transforms itself into a barbecue to serve up their take on the chicken-in-a-basket theme, namely 'chicken-on-a-bonnet' (Ts13,000). They also do mixed grills (Ts12,000, or Ts10,000 if there's more than two of you), including chips, naan bread and a serve-yourself table full of salads and spicy sauces. It's just to the north of the Central Market on Mosque St; be

careful around here after dark – take a cab.

There is no shortage of good Indian restaurants in the city. Our first and favourite is *Bigg Bite* (Wed-Sun noon-2.30pm & 6-10pm), one block east of the market, which started off as the first fast-food shack in town and has long been a favourite with expats. Now run by the previous owner's son, Raul, who studied in the UK and is always good for a chat, the place does takeaway (☎ 0754-311474) and even delivers; the food is also both huge and lovely, with Kadai chicken (Ts10,500) a particular treat. The other budget Indian we recommend is *Noble Juice Parlour* (Mon-Sat 8.30am-8.15pm, Sun 9.15am-8pm), beneath Meru House Inn at the western end of Sokoine – pleasant, friendly, and convenient for the budget accommodation in that area. Be warned: some of the dishes are truly fiery at both of these places. Expect to pay Ts8800-9000 for a curry at the latter, Ts9500-12,500 at Bigg Bites.

East of Themi River on or near Nyerere Rd and its continuation, Old Moshi Rd (now renamed Nelson Mandela Rd after the college that's been built further along it out of town), there are several large-scale restaurants that are perfect as venues for that post-Kili celebration (or commiseration) meal. To the north of Nyerere Rd, in particular, are several fine places hidden amongst the jacaranda trees. *The Flame Tree* (☎ 0754-377359; daily 10.30am-10.30pm) on Kenyatta Rd, one block west of the Jacaranda, is now under Chinese management. So what was once the smartest and most tasteful restaurant in town is now an enormous Chinese restaurant with an equally large menu. Nevertheless, some of the dishes are still very tempting with a Kenyan T-bone steak (served in a range of sauces) for Ts27,000, fish dishes for Ts18,000-19,000 (including a delicious prawn pili-pili) and some truly indulgent puddings including a Moshi brownie served with chocolate sauce for Ts7000 and chocolate pithivers (warm puff pastry stuffed with chocolates and nuts ands served with a scoop of vanilla ice cream) for the same price. Some may shudder at the loss of refinement, though to be fair it still pays close attention to detail (intricately folded napkins being just one example) and with the loss of two big Chinese restaurants in recent years, this could be a timely introduction. Situated a few hundred metres to the north of Nyerere Rd on Church Rd, the spacious *Pepe* (☎ 0784-365515; daily 11am-11pm) is an Indian-Italian restaurant with the same high standards of preparation and authenticity afforded to both halves of the menu. The prices are usually fair (Italian mains Ts11,000-13,000, pizzas Ts9000-13,000, while Indian dishes go for Ts8000-14,000); the service can, on occasion, be lackadaisical (though you can avoid this by opting for their takeaway service), but otherwise it's a good choice for a large group looking for a post-trek celebration.

About 500m further north are two top-notch places by the entrance to the Gymkhana Club. *Dragon Pearl* (☎ 027-254 4107; Mon-Fri 11.30am-2.30pm & 6-10.30pm, Sat & Sun 11.30am-10.30pm) is, as you've probably guessed, a Chinese and the best one in town, with a large menu of authentic and generous Asian food and a healthy list of alcoholic drinks too. Our bill for two people each having a starter, main and a beer came to just over Ts60,000. It's a similar budget next door at the Indian restaurant *Vama* (☎ 0784-326325; Wed-Mon 10.30am-2.30pm & 6.30-10pm), where the spicy heat from their lamb vindaloo will have you crying all evening – and probably the next morning too...

As far as I am aware *Sazan* (daily from 6pm), back on Nyerere Rd, is Arusha's only Japanese restaurant. It is presumably looking to capitalize on the increasing numbers of Japanese tourists flocking to Tanzania but who are reluctant to try the local fare.

Prices start at Ts1600 for a simple miso soup, rising to Ts15,000 for 200KCal of sashimi marlin. Whether there are enough Japanese coming to warrant a whole restaurant is a moot point but it is nice to see a place that's willing to serve up something other than pizzas. The restaurant is west of Kibo Palace Hotel.

Finally, for something out of the ordinary a trip to *Spices & Herbs*, the blossom-laden Ethiopian restaurant in the hotel of the same name, could be in order. With vegetarian dishes for around Ts9500 as well as meat dishes (around the Ts15,000 mark), this place has been garnering praise from hungry travellers for years. Try the lamb cooked in Ethiopian butter with onions, green peppers and rosemary (Ts14,500) or their pork chops (Ts15,000) – and you'll see why.

Western food With branches in Honduras, Java and Zanzibar, *Via Via* is a chain of 14 travellers' cafés which is renowned for the good work it does introducing travellers to the local culture. Situated by the old German Boma, it offers live local music every Thursday (see p183) and an array of daytime activities, from drum-making and batik workshops to cookery and Swahili courses (see box p166). And if you don't give a cuss about the culture there's always the food, which includes burgers (Ts12,000-16,000), sandwiches (Ts12,000), pasta (Ts12,000) and a few steak and fish dishes (Ts15,000-18,000) – they are also the only place I've seen that offers fish fingers (Ts10,000).

On Nelson Mandela Rd (formerly Old Moshi Rd), *Barafu Bar*, part of Masai Camp (see p171) is still *the* campsite for the

---

❏ **The top six places to celebrate a climb in Arusha**

In no particular order:
- **Albero** For large groups, with friendly staff and some smashing pizzas.
- **Spices and Herbs** Classy Ethiopian food, good for sharing.
- **Onsea** Posh nosh for the smarter summiteer.
- **Via Via** For those wanting a party afterwards without changing venue.
- **Dragon Pearl** Large venue, large menu, large bar and large portions of food.
- **Vama** Boasting similar qualities to its neighbour above – but with added spice.

overland trucks that trickle into Arusha, though in nothing like the numbers they used to. Indeed, the place has changed somewhat recently. Following complaints from local residents, the noisy old bar that used to stand here has been fitted with a soundproofed roof and they have low-key 'mood' lighting and even place settings for dinner now. It still has a pool table, however, and a comprehensive bar. Food-wise at least half the menu is taken up with pizzas (Ts9000-15,000), which is a bit awkward when pizzas are off the menu that day for some reason, as happened when we visited. We plumped instead for the tuna steak with rice and veg (Ts17,500) – and to be fair, it was very tasty.

Virtually opposite Blue Heron, *Albero* (☎ 0653-575507; daily 11am-when last person leaves) advertises itself as a pizza and pasta place – and indeed their pizzas (Ts10,000-13,000 for 30cm, Ts14,000-18,000 for 36cm) are lovely, and can be delivered too. But what makes this place great is the fact that it still recognizes it's in Africa, with Masai tablecloths and a range of local dishes including *mishikaki* (Ts3000), *mbuzi* (goat cooked in oil; Ts7000), *chips mayai* (egg and chips; Ts5000) and even *ugali* (Ts3000). Given the lively bar built round the fig tree, this is actually a great place to come and celebrate a trek – particularly if you are treating some of your crew too! Other hotels round here that serve good food too are *Le Jacaranda*, with an extensive menu, and *The Outpost*, which does some lovely sizzle plates.

Finally, the best food in town (or, rather, just outside it) is at *Onsea*, where the chef used to work in Michelin-starred restaurants in London. It's food with finesse – they describe it as Belgian and French brasserie-style with an African touch – and usually exquisite, with the menu changing daily. Count on spending about US$50 per head for three courses.

NIGHTLIFE

Arusha is the **nightclub** and **live music** capital of northern Tanzania, attracting rastas and ravers from far and wide.

Unfortunately, as with any large city, the scene changes rapidly and what's recommended here may well be out of date by the time you arrive.

One place that's almost certain to remain, however, is *Triple A* (just north-west off the map on p168), the city's favourite radio station and also one of its most popular nightspots. Open Wednesdays (Ts5000), Fridays (Ts10,000), Saturdays (Ts10,000) and Sundays (Ts5000), the action begins at about 8pm and carries on 'til dawn.

Many of the other venues take it in turns through the week to host their big nights. *Empire Sports Bar* at the TFA Complex, by Shoprite, usually host a live band on Tuesdays and their karaoke night is on Wednesdays, while *Via Via* take over on a Thursday with their live-music evening (Ts7000); visit them during the day to find out what they've got lined up. On Friday the action moves over to *AQ Club* (Ts5000) at Aquiline Hotel by the south-east corner of the bus station, while on Saturday it's either back to the *Empire* for another live band or to *Barafu Bar* at Masai Camp (Ts5000, though the barman said they will shortly make it free). Note that these venues are open throughout the week regardless of whether they are hosting a special night or not.

If you'd rather just drink with the locals, two places seem particularly popular at the moment: *Pin Point Bar* in Plaza Le Manyatta, north of the bus station, is lively (sometimes intimidatingly so); and there's *Babylon Club* by Green Hut House of Burgers on Sokoine which is equally vibrant.

For a game of **pool**, the *Empire* has a table, and *Masai Camp* has a new one.

The mall out at **Njiro** is also a good place to come for an evening's entertainment, be it for the Booglaloo club (Ts5000), the **cinema** (Ts8000 on the upper deck; Ts6000 in the cheap seats) or simply to wolf down pizza and beer at Stiggy's.

Finally, for those who can't live without their weekly dose of English Premier League football, *Mango Tree* (daily 3pm-midnight), *Picasso Café*; (see p181) and *Empire Sports Bar* show most games.

ARUSHA, MOSHI & MARANGU

Moving on
By bus or shuttle

To Moshi Those heading towards Kili will find the **local 'Coaster' buses** are the most convenient way to travel the 81km to Moshi. They run throughout the day from the main bus station, with the last one around 5pm (Ts2500). Always an intimidating place to go, negotiating the bus station is actually fairly straightforward and there'll usually be a tout on hand to point you to the right bus as soon as they see you. Once you're aboard sellers will come to your window with sunglasses and sunhats, papers and perfumes, cake and Coke; everything, in fact, to keep you cool, comfortable, fed and fragrant for the journey.

True, using a Coaster bus is not a particularly pleasant way to travel but other options are thin on the ground, with Moshi ill-served by the **shuttle bus** companies. **Riverside** (☎ 027-250 2639 or ☎ 027-250 3916; 🖳 www.riverside-shuttle.com), with its office in a chemist on Sokoine Rd, have one bus per day at 2pm (US$10), as do **Rainbow Shuttle** (☎ 0787-267324), in the back of New Safari Hotel. The services for both these companies depart from the parking lot up from Impala Hotel on Simeon Rd, though if you book in advance you might get picked up from your hotel – depending on the state of the traffic. The car park at Impala Hotel is home to **Impala Shuttle** (☎ 0784-550012). They, too, operate a daily bus to Moshi (US$10) that starts in Nairobi and calls in at Arusha at around 2pm.

To Nairobi and Kampala Of the **bus** companies, **Dar Express** (3pm; Ts25,000), in offices on Wachagga Rd, offer a good and safe service to Nairobi. **Kampala Express**, who have their offices on the Nairobi-Moshi Road, east of Colonel Middleton Rd, also head to Nairobi and continue onto Kampala (daily, 3.30pm, Ts60,000 to Kampala).

As for the **shuttles**, **Riverside** run two daily to Nairobi, at 8am (arrive 2pm) and 2pm (it's the one from Moshi and is supposed to arrive in Nairobi at 6.30pm). They charge US$25 for foreign tourists.

GETTING TO KILIMANJARO AND ARUSHA AIRPORTS
To Kilimanjaro International
Impala (☎ 027-250 7197) run a **shuttle bus** from their base in the Impala Hotel car park, the shuttle leaving around three hours before the KLM flight – thus allowing passengers who are joining the KLM flight enough time to check-in – and returning when the bus is filled with KLM passengers who've just landed (US$15 each way).

Precision Air/Kenyan Airways also offer a shuttle service to and from KIA for their flights (US$15 if catching a flight to Nairobi or Entebbe, Ts10,000 otherwise). Remember with all shuttles to phone or call in at the airline office beforehand to see if you need to book your place.

A **taxi** to the airport officially costs US$50, though with bargaining this can be reduced slightly.

To Arusha Airport
Precision Air operate a service (Ts5000) for their flights from Arusha Airport. If you're not flying with them, however, you'll have to rely on taxis or public transport. To the west of the post office on Sokoine Rd is the stop for dalla-dallas heading west towards Arusha Airport (listen out for the touts shouting 'Kisongo'), dropping off passengers by the junction a kilometre from the terminal for Ts300; from there you can walk the dusty kilometre or catch a boda boda (about Ts1000). If you're carrying all your luggage, you've got to be seriously tightfisted to opt for this rather than take a taxi from town (Ts15,000 minimum, though Ts20,000-30,000 is more normal).

ARUSHA, MOSHI & MARANGU

Rainbow Shuttle and Impala (see p184) operate identical times and prices. As with all shuttles, they *should* pick you up from your hotel. However, thanks to the massive rise in traffic in the city and the consequent jams and delays to any journey, these days many of the shuttles pick up passengers only if they are staying at hotels near the shuttle bus car park.

To Dar es Salaam Dar Express (see p152; 6/day between 5.50am and 8.30am; Ts28,000, though the 6.30am and 7.30am 'luxury' buses are Ts30,000) and Kilimanjaro Express (7/day; all Ts28,000) are both reliable though it pays to ask

around for the latest information. Buy tickets from their offices in and to the west of Kaloleni; see map p168-9.

By air

Arusha effectively has two airports: Arusha Airport and Kilimanjaro International Airport (see p162) which is less than an hour away. See p170 for details of the airline offices in Arusha and p349 for details of flights.

In our experience the departure tax (US$7 for domestic flights, US$40 for international destinations) is now generally included in the fare. However, it pays to check when reconfirming your flight.

TREKKING AGENCIES

There are around 125 local companies that offer climbs up Kilimanjaro. In terms of value for money and choice, many will say you're better off organizing your trek in Moshi than Arusha. Agencies in Arusha tend to be more expensive for three reasons: firstly, some Arusha agencies are just acting as middlemen for those in Moshi and add their commission on top; secondly, most of the larger and more expensive companies prefer to base themselves in Arusha and enjoy the greater facilities there; and thirdly, the transport costs to Kilimanjaro are that much higher than they are from Moshi.

That said, there are plenty of good-quality, reliable Kilimanjaro trekking companies, so it is well worth investigating what Arusha agents have to offer – which is exactly what we've done here. To find out how we researched this section, please see the box on p186. For details of what to look for in an agency, and what questions to ask, see p36. Three other points need to be mentioned: firstly, note just about all companies offer to drop their prices if there are more than two of you in your group; secondly, don't take everything they advertise at face value – in particular, we found a lot of the success rates hard to believe; and finally, don't be afraid to tell the tour operator you're shopping around; it's the quickest way to get them to give you a good deal.

● African Environments (☎ 027-254 8625; 🖳 www.africanenvironments.com) Established in mid-1987, American-owned African Environments are at the very top end of the market, claiming a 98% success rate on the Lemosho Route – a route they actually pioneered. They were also the first and remain one of the very few companies to equip *all* their expeditions with WFR-trained guides, Gamow hyperbaric bags and oxygen as safety precautions. No surprises, then, that they are widely regarded as just about the most luxurious operator on the mountain and are a favourite with many foreign film crews. They rarely take bookings direct but in their reply to our email they encourage you to contact one of their agents (including Mountain Madness p32, Wilderness Travel p34 and Mountain Travel Sobek p33 to name but three); fail to find

ARUSHA, MOSHI & MARANGU

anything with any of those and then maybe they'll arrange a private trek for you instead. As you'd expect they're expensive (the exact price depending on which of their agents you actually book with), but it's good to see that some of that money filters down to their staff, for they also pay some of the best wages on Kili. In addition to their eight-day Lemosho (which they confusingly call 'Shira') and their nine-day 'Ultimate Kilimanjaro' trek (the Lemosho Route with a climb to the summit via the Western Breach and a night in Crater Camp), they also run a six- or seven-day Machame trail trek.

● **Africa VIP Travel** (☎ 0732-971 775, 🖳 www.africaviptravel.com; Azimio Rd) A fairly small company that doesn't seem to arrange that many treks, though we found their response to our email to be both considerate and comprehensive and the answers they gave showed a decent degree of knowledge. They don't offer the Marangu Route but instead send the majority of their clients on the even-busier Machame, for which they charge US$3540 per person with two nights accommodation at Dik Dik Hotel, airport transfers and both oxygen and a hyperbaric chamber included on the trek. A touch expensive but professional and pleasant.

● **African Walking Company** (🖳 awc-richard@habari.co.tz) Founded by Brit Jim Foster, despite the lack of a website this is the second biggest operator on the mountain thanks to a reputation for reliability and a high standard of treks. As such, they're a favourite with overseas agencies (Africa Travel Resource being one, Peak Planet

---

❏ How we researched this section

As with the previous editions we once again did as much of our research as possible anonymously. In other words, the companies we contacted thought we were just regular punters and had no idea we were researching the next edition of the book. Since the first edition we have noticed some significant changes in the way people book their treks. Where once people would often just buy a ticket to Tanzania and sort out a trek when they arrived, these days almost everybody books their climb via the internet before they set foot on East African soil. So for this edition we, too, mimicked this process, and like most other would-be Kili climbers we began our research online.

Having first checked out each company's website, the next step was to email them in order to find out a bit more about the service they could provide and what they would charge for it. To do this we invented a fictional couple, set up an email address for them, and then sent a standard email to each trekking agency. In it we asked for their prices for two people for a) six days on Marangu, and b) seven days on Machame. We also asked whether they ran treks up the Western Breach (see p300), and if so how much extra this would cost. Finally, we asked why we should book with them above all the other agencies.

Our research didn't stop there, however. We also asked trekkers we met on Kilimanjaro or in Arusha/Moshi of their experiences; consulted all the letters and emails from climbers that we'd received in which recommendations and complaints about agencies often featured; and finally, we talked with KPAP (see box pp47-49) to find out how well or badly each company treated and paid their staff on the mountain.

Please bear in mind that **the reviews are our opinions only**. Remember, too, that things change very quickly in this part of the world, so some of the following will inevitably have altered by the time you begin your research. If you have any advice, comments, praise or criticisms about any of the agencies please contact us using the email/postal address at the front of this book.

and Exodus are others). With so much custom from abroad they don't actually book treks for people who contact them direct – hence the lack of publicity. But if you've signed up with an overseas agency you may well end up with them; and congratulations if you do, for they're one of the best on the mountain. My only gripe (and it's a small one) is that they do have a bizarre approach to the Lemosho Route, urging their climbers instead to take the Shira Plateau Route. Their argument is that the beginning of Lemosho is at 'low altitude' and thus of little use acclimatization wise. There is some merit to that argument, I suppose – though it does rather imply that the sole purpose of climbing Kili is to reach the top, rather than enjoy, in this instance, some of the best forest on the mountain. Most odd. Still, overall very good.

● **African Zoom** (☎ 0732-972218; 🖳 www.africanzoom.com) A small but experienced outfit, pleasant and polite though not with a great volume of Kili treks. Still, their prices are reasonable and their service/treks uncomplicated. Prices: Marangu Route, six days, US$1549 per person; Machame Route, seven days, US$1820pp excluding any accommodation and airport transfers but including oxygen.

● **Arunga Expedition & Safari** (☎ 0732-971780, 🖳 www.aruexpedition.com) Smallish local company, a bit of a one-man-band operation that tries hard to make their clients content and with prices that are certainly reasonable at US$1250 per person for six days on Marangu or US$1450 for seven days on Machame (US$50 less each time if joining a group; US$200 extra if using the Western Breach), including two nights at Arusha Tourist Inn but excluding airport transfers and oxygen (US$60 extra). So you can't really argue with the fees but if you do sign up, please check everything carefully, including the equipment and the guide that will take you – everything, in fact, to make sure your trek is a safe and happy one.

● **Base Camp Tanzania** (🖳 www.basecamptanzania.com; Golden Rose Arcade Building, Conference Centre, First Floor, Colonel Middleton Rd) Half-British husband-and-wife team that's been operating a trekking/safari business for more than a dozen years now and offers a reliable service as befits their background: he's a former overland guide, she is from a family who've worked in tourism for decades. Prices seem reasonable at US$1870 for seven days on Machame, US$1640 for six days on Marangu, including accommodation at Arusha's L'Oasis Lodge or The Outpost and airport transfers – so very reasonably priced. These days organizing the treks themselves, their response when we asked them why we should choose them over other operators, was a blunt "Hate this question so trite :-) our reputation speack (sic) for itself" – which was a bit of a surprise and didn't really answer the query. They don't use the Western Breach, nor do they supply their treks with oxygen (saying that the deterioration in their trekkers' health should never reach the stage where oxygen would be necessary). Overall, not the politest of responses we've had but we understand they're fine when it comes to arranging treks – which is, after all, the important bit.

● **Big Expeditions** (☎ 0754-203 301, 027-254 8449; 🖳 www.bigexpeditions.net; Shule Rd, nr Exim Bank) Around since 2002 but only now really grabbing a decent share of the Kili market thanks in large part to their adoption by US outfit Alpine Ascents. Their itineraries seem fairly standard but they do try to make themselves slightly different by, for example, setting up a table and buffet at Mweka Gate for at least some of those finishing their trek and putting plastic flowers on the picnic tables. Prices: US$1680pp for six days on Marangu or seven days on Machame for US$1800pp for private climbs with oxygen, a hyperbaric chamber and even helicopter rescue included (though see p72) – good value, even though only one night before the trek at Planet Lodge is included.

● **Bobby Tours** (☎ 0786-110786; 🖳 www.bobbytours.com; Goliondoi Rd)
Established way back in 1976, Bobby are a very slick and professional company with
a whole fleet of 4WDs and the swishest offices on Goliondoi. One glance at their oh-
so-thorough website before you arrive in Arusha will give you some idea of how seriously they take their work. They are also surprisingly cheap; indeed, it may be worth
asking them how they can be so cheap, where they make their savings and how much
they pay their crew. Prices: US$1265 for six days on Marangu; US$1450 for seven
days on Machame. Note, however, that there is no accommodation included and when
we asked about oxygen they said that they 'cannot arrange this' – which is a bit of a
concern.

● **Climb Kili** (☎ 0754-282042, 🖳 www.climbkili.com; PPF Building, Kaloleni)
Experienced outfitter with a long list of happy clients and their own agents in both the
UK and America. If there are two of you you can join one of their group climbs or,
for the same price, have a private climb, though it's worth noting that they don't offer
treks on the Marangu Route. Overall, good value and well worth checking out. Prices:
US$2230, with two nights at Arusha's Impala Hotel, airport transfers, oxygen and toi-
let tents included; a climb via Western Breach (with a night at Crater Camp) is
US$350 extra per person.

● **Congema Tours and Safaris** (☎ 0774-444 417, 🖳 www.congemasafaris.com; 51
Haile Sellasie Rd, Albero Italian Restaurant) Fairly small outfit and one praised by
KPAP for being amongst the top half-dozen when it comes to treating their staff well.
Sadly, we failed to get any sort of response from them despite sending several messages (using our pseudonym) via different avenues. Indeed, when KPAP told them I
was trying to contact them they got in touch with me instantly; we wish they'd treat
their potential clients with as much consideration. Still, I promised KPAP I'd review
all the companies they recommended, so even though we have no idea what their service is like or prices are, they've made it into the book. Let's hope they get in touch
soon...

● **Corto Safaris** (☎ 0732-978914, 🖳 www.cortosafaris.com; nr Moivaro Coffee
Plantation Lodge) Based outside Arusha, this French-Tanzanian company was founded in 1994 and is still run by its original owner. Concentrating mainly on the whole
of Tanzania rather than just Kilimanjaro, note that they organize private treks only,
mainly on the Lemosho and Machame routes, with each accompanied by a decom-
pression chamber. Prices: Machame Route, seven days, US$1980 per person; six days
Marangu US$1715pp, though this doesn't cover accommodation in Arusha or airport
transfers.

● **Crown Eagle** (☎ 0754-263085, 🖳 www.crown-eagle.com; Joel Maeda St) A small
outfit occupying second floor offices by the Clock Tower, Crown Eagle has been
going for about a decade now. As for prices: US$1540 per person for six days on
Marangu for a private trek, US$1690pp for a private seven-day Machame trek – with
a discount of about US$200-300 if you're willing to share your trek with others; the
prices include airport transfers and accommodation in Arusha. Reasonably cheap, and
their email was comprehensive, but do check *thoroughly* before booking with them as
to what exactly is included.

● **Destination Tanzania Safaris** (☎ 0754-669 086; 🖳 www.detasa.com) Another
medium-sized operator, this one founded by two mountain guides who still lead
around 60% of the treks themselves. Refuses to touch the Marangu Route because of
its popularity and the supposed lack of opportunities it presents to acclimatize properly. For Machame, the prices include all safety equipment (including oxygen,

hyperbaric chamber and satellite phone), airport transfers and *three* nights' accommodation at Ilboru Lodge; for US$2450 per person all in for seven nights for two people that's pretty reasonable. Also have an office in the US (see p32).

● **Dik Dik** (see also p176; ☎ 027-255 3499; 💻 www.dikdik.ch; Arusha-Moshi Rd) You can tell a Dik Dik expedition on the mountain with their smart luggage crates and mountain gear emblazoned with their logo. No longer operating on the Western Breach but still offering other routes, they never mix groups together – so if you book a trek with them, you won't be lumped with another party (which may be a blessing, or may not). Efficient, reliable and well-run, as you'd expect from a company with significant Swiss input, they describe themselves as a luxury operator and, like their hotel, their treks are smart and fair value. They are also amongst the top half-dozen companies, according to KPAP, when it comes to treating their porters well. Prices: Marangu, six days, US$2830 each for two people; Machame, seven days, US$3360 per person.

● **Duma Explorer** (☎ 0787-079127, 💻 www.dumaexplorer.com; PPF Oloirien Estate, Off #22, Njiro) No relation to the Duma agency in Moshi, this outfit, established in 2004 with considerable American involvement, offer fair prices given the level of their service charging: US$2249 per person for seven days on Machame, US$1749 for six days on Marangu. They're another company that refuse to go up Western Breach; note, too, that hotels in Arusha and airport transfers *aren't* included.

● **Easy Travel & Tours** (☎ 027-250 3929; 💻 www.easytravel.co.tz; Boma Rd) In a prestigious location by New Safari Hotel, Easy Travel & Tours are an efficient and very busy safari company and the representatives for various airlines. Their service is thoroughly reliable, though with so much else going on one gets the feeling that Kilimanjaro treks aren't really their priority. Still, their prices are reasonable: six days on Marangu for US$1365; seven days on Machame US$1625 – with both airport transfers and accommodation at The Outpost included; oxygen is US$100 extra.

● **Equatorial Safaris** (☎ 027-250 2617; 💻 www.equatorialsafaris.com; Room 428, 4th floor, AICC Bldg) Fairly well-established Kili operator with Austrian links who have diversified into offering trips to Rwanda to see the gorillas, treks up Mount Kenya – and even a 68-day program to Everest! Regarding Kili, on their website they offer just Machame, Marangu and Lemosho. As for the treks, alas I didn't meet anybody who had trekked with them when researching this edition, though their reputation for safaris at least is one of competence. Prices: US$1870 for seven days on the Machame Route, US$1620 for six days on Marangu.

● **Fair Travel Tanzania** (☎ 0786 025 886; 💻 www.fairtraveltanzania.com; Top floor, Namvua Plaza Building, Zaramo St) Is this the future of trekking on Kilimanjaro? KPAP would certainly like it to be, for Fair Travel, though relatively new, seem to be setting the standard for porter treatment on the mountain. Approaching the whole issue from a different angle, instead of working out how much they can afford to pay their porters from the money they receive from clients, Fair Travel have begun by working out what a living monthly wage would be for a porter assuming he works on two trips per month – and then pay their staff (and charge their clients) accordingly. As a result, the porters receive US$18 per day – the best wage on the mountain according to KPAP. Another good policy – and wouldn't this make everybody's life easier if it was adopted by everybody? – is that trekkers are not obliged to pay tips; if they do, it is shared *equally* among the entire crew with everyone getting the same amount regardless of their position in the team! Their replies to our emails were polite, eloquent, knowledgeable and thorough (I particularly liked the full breakdown of the price of the trek and where the money goes; see p42) and the charges reasonable at US$2120 per person for two people for six days on Marangu, and US$2250 for seven days on Machame (though airport transfers, accommodation in Moshi/Arusha and oxygen are all extra). Of course, there is a part of me that worries about writing such a lengthy and effusive review – we've been stung before by companies that talk a good talk but then fall short and we have seen similar ventures fail or fall below the lofty standards they preach. So our advice is to check them out – then check with KPAP who'll have the low-down on whether they really are as good as they say.

● **Good Earth** (☎ 0682-530187; 💻 www.goodearthtours.com; Arusha Municipality Rd, Plot 1896) Established tour operator with offices in the AICC Building, and branches in Maryland, USA (see p32) and Vancouver, BC (see p35). Their website rightly boasts that they practise responsible tourism, providing scholarships, books, and supplies to local children and financial support to various environmental groups. They charge US$1590 per person on the Marangu Route (six days), US$1870 on Machame (seven days), both including two nights' accommodation at Planet Lodge and airport transfers. They also offer the Western Breach including a night at Crater Camp for US$350pp on top of the Machame price. Oxygen is US$210 extra for all treks. Cited by KPAP for their admirable treatment of porters.

● **Kindoroko Tours** (☎ 0785-482251; 💻 www.kindorokotour.com; Old Moshi Rd, Christ Church, King Solomon's Building, St Peters) No-nonsense, up-front and offering a pretty good deal, Kindoroko Tours aims squarely at the budget end of the market and are related to the hotel of the same name in Moshi (the boss is the wife of the hotel's owner). They're good value, too, at US$1400 per person for two people for six days on Marangu, or US$1550 for seven days on Machame, this latter price including two nights at Moshi's Bristol Cottages and airport transfers. Note that they don't offer the Western Breach Route because of the risks involved.

● **Maasai Wanderings** (☎ 0755-984925; 💻 www.maasaiwanderings.com; Njiro) Established by an Australian woman and her Tanzanian husband, this company have garnered good reviews down the years, thanks in large part to their considerate treatment of porters. Laudably, they also use some of their profits to support a number of schools and community schemes around Arusha. Seeming to concentrate solely on the Machame Route, currently they organize set departures every other Sunday (seven days, US$1995 per person) with a maximum group size of 12, as well as private treks on other days (US$2295 on the same route). For those looking for a budget trek that also has high ethical values, this company is a decent option – with the fact they concentrate on just one (over-popular) route my only quibble.

● **Nature Discovery** (☎ 027-254 4063; 💻 www.naturediscovery.com) Upmarket company in operation since 1992 that specializes in tailor-made tours; perhaps best known as the trekking partner of large safari operator Thomson. They pretty much ignored the content of the email we sent and concentrated instead on promoting their eight-day Grand Traverse Shira Route (US$3490 per person) – which looks a lovely route, but didn't really answer our questions. When we did get a price from them (after three emails), six days on Marangu is US$3248pp, while seven days on Machame is US$3794pp – with no airport transfers (US$125 extra – the most expensive we've come across) or accommodation included (though their Shira climb *does* include one night at the delightful Rivertrees; see p176). Refreshingly, they also promote Umbwe – the only major company we know that recommends this delightful, tough route. Their upmarket treks always include at least two Wilderness First Responder staff as well as private *flush* toilets; with hot showers, solar-charging kits and a mess tent heater available for a price. Despite the minor grumbles, they're still one of the best.

● **Roy Safaris** (☎ 027-250 2115; 💻 www.roysafaris.com; 44 Serengeti Rd) One of the bigger safari operators and now boasting their very own sumptuous hotel (The African Tulip; see p179) in town. Their reputation rests on their safaris but they seem to know what they're doing on Kili, too, with a good service provided including use of pulse oximeters (see p367) on each trek, all of which are private (ie if you book with them you won't suddenly find yourself lumped with a larger group). Overall they seem pretty competent and reasonable – surprising given the luxury quality of their hotel. Prices: US$1880 per person for six days on Marangu, US$2210pp for seven days on Machame. Given that these treks include two nights at their hotel, where a double is US$230 per night, that represents pretty good value. Airport transfers, however, are an extra US$80.

● **Safari Makers** (☎ 027-254 4446, ☎ 0732-979195; 💻 www.safarimakers.com; Plot #16, Moshono Rd) Reasonably efficient and helpful company, run jointly by a Tanzanian and an American, that offers treks up Kilimanjaro on all the major routes. For Marangu, six days is US$1717 per person; Machame, seven days, US$1988pp with a discount if paying in cash, though neither accommodation in Arusha nor an airport transfer is included and oxygen is US$80 extra.

● **Serengeti Pride Safaris** (☎ 0785-353534, 💻 www.serengetipridesafaris.com) Took the longest while for this lot to answer though to be fair when they did respond they were eloquent, thorough and polite. Claim to have a 98% success rate with their favourite route, the eight-day Lemosho trail, but willing to offer all routes and wisely told us that six-day routes had significantly lower success rates. Prices are fair at US$2530 per person for seven days on Machame – no quote given for the Marangu Route. Overall, not bad – if you can make contact with them!

● **Shidolya** (☎ 027-254 8506, 💻 www.shidolya-safaris.com; Room 218, at the end of the corridor on the 2nd floor, Ngorongoro wing, AICC Bldg) Shidolya are undoubtedly one of the more professional outfits and are also, somewhat surprisingly, cheap by Arusha standards, with seven-day Machame treks for US$1330 per person (US$1580 if taking the Western Breach), or it's US$1280 for six days on Marangu. Note, however, that they charge a whopping US$300 for oxygen and *no* hotel nights or airport transfers are included in this price. They also run Colobus Mountain Lodge in Arusha National Park (see p238) – a good base for exploring the park and climbing Meru.

● **Summits Africa** (☎ 0732-972692 or ☎ 0787-130666; 💻 www.summits-africa.com) This company was formed by the son of one of the founders of Hoopoe Adventure – one of the biggest names in climbing and safaris in recent years. They are also very safety-conscious with oximetry tests for their clients as standard. Such service doesn't come cheap, however, and they are also reluctant to take direct bookings, preferring instead that you use one of their agents such as Aardvark (see p23 & p30). When we did get prices out of them, they offered a 'luxury-spec' trek on Machame for seven days for US$3210 with two nights at Blues & Chutney (see p179), airport transfers and oxygen included.

● **Sunny Safaris** (☎ 027-250 8184; 💻 www.sunnysafaris.com) Previously one of the busier budget agencies but a little quieter now – possibly because their office on Colonel Middleton Road sees far fewer budget travellers than in years gone by when this part of town was Backpacker-Central. The prices they quoted us of US$1900 for seven days on Machame and US$1525 for six days on Marangu seem reasonable,

ARUSHA, MOSHI & MARANGU

though this excludes hotel accommodation (US$35 per person per night extra) and airport transfers (US$70 extra one-way). An oxygen tank is a hefty US$150 on top too. Overall, probably more a safari specialist than a Kili one but they're OK without being outstanding.

● **Tanzania Travel Company** (☎ 0754-294 365; 🖳 www.tanzaniatravelcompany.com) Small company run by Tanzanian naturalist Sam Diah that offers, despite the name, safaris all over East Africa and not just Tanzania. Weirdly, while their website was full of information, finding the relevant stuff – including phone numbers and email address – proved nigh on impossible (we found them eventually on their Facebook page) and the only contact form they had was unwieldy and not fit for purpose; it makes you wonder how they get any bookings at all! Still, it is said that Gane & Marshall (see p26) use them for some treks so maybe they don't require bookings from anywhere else.

● **Team Kilimanjaro** (☎ 0787-77 5895, 🖳 www.teamkilimanjaro.com) Well-established company offering treks on all the routes (although Marangu only reluctantly) including their own takes on Rongai and Lemosho. Sample prices: from US$2057 for six days on their Marangu Route, US$2338 for seven on Machame, the exact price depending on the number of people you're booking for. Two nights at The Outpost or similar are included, as are airport transfers and oxygen on the mountain. Still one of the best – and possibly the best value – of all of them, they're a well organized and efficient company and worth checking out.

● **Team Maasai** (☎ 0787-77 5895, 🖳 climbkilimanjaro.co) If the name doesn't give it away, one look at the wordy website of this new outfit will provide conclusive evidence that this is an offspring of Team Kilimanjaro, though this one staffed almost exclusively by Maasai from the Ngorongoro and Lake Natron regions. Claim to have the cheapest prices anywhere on the internet for fully supported climbs, with seven days for two people on Machame US$1550 per person and six days on Marangu US$1375pp. Accommodation in Arusha, airport transfers and oxygen are all extra.

● **Victoria Expeditions** (☎ 027-250 0444; 🖳 www.victoriatz.com; Silk Club, Seth Benjamin St) Formerly a busy operation that's been going for well over a decade, a success that can be attributed in part at least to a very cheap service, Victoria have been hit by two major blows recently: the loss of their Norwegian boss who did so much to make the agency a success; and the move to new premises in the Silk Club – and away from the backpackers' favourite Mount Meru Hotel, from where a lot of their custom came. The prices remain cheap, however – Marangu six days US$1250, Machame seven days US$1450 for example; as always with budget operators, do check where the savings are being made and if they are paying a fair wage.

❏ Abbreviations

Throughout this book we have used the following abbreviations when writing about accommodation: **pp** means per person; **s/c** is short for self-contained, a local term meaning that the room comes with a bathroom (ie the room is en suite or a bathroom is attached); while **sgl/dbl/tpl** means single/double/triple rooms. So, for example, where we have written 's/c sgl/dbl/tpl US$35/40/45', we mean that a self-contained single room costs US$35 per night, a self-contained double costs US$40 and a self-contained triple costs US$45.

Moshi

Cheaper, quieter, nearer and prettier, Moshi sits in the shadow of Kilimanjaro and, for climbing the mountain, is perhaps a superior base to neighbouring Arusha, 81km away to the west. As the unofficial capital of the Chagga world, most visitors find Moshi a little more interesting too. The missionaries who followed in the wake of Rebmann gave the Chaggas the advantage of a Western education and this, combined with the agricultural fecundity of Kilimanjaro's southern slopes, has enabled the Chaggas to become one of the wealthiest, most influential and most securely self-aware groups in the country. Moshi has reaped the benefits too, prospering to the point where it is now one of the smartest towns in Tanzania (though grim poverty is still not difficult to find, as anybody who has walked around Moshi at night, stepping over the sleeping bodies of the dispossessed lying on the pavements as they do so, can testify).

While the Chaggas are the dominant force in town, Moshi is still a cosmopolitan place, with a large expat community (as well as a huge number of short-term teenage volunteers) and a highly visible Indian minority; this colourful ethnic mixture is reflected in the architecture, with a huge Hindu temple abutting an equally striking mosque and with dozens of small churches and chapels scattered in the streets thereabouts. There also seems to be more civic pride in Moshi than in other parts of the country. Indeed, the only dark cloud for tourists here is the inordinate amount of hassle they suffer from trekking agency touts, 'artists' and the like; the ban that was enforced in Arusha on these 'fly-catchers' can't happen quickly enough here. Look beyond this, however, and you're sure to find Moshi charming, friendly and a lovely place for a stroll. Take an amble any afternoon and you'll pass sewing machinists stitching shirts on sun-baked sidewalks, blade sharpeners spraying sparks from their cycle-powered grinders and smiling schoolkids shouting salutations to the sweaty *mzungu*. It can also boast enough facilities to enable you to organize a trek – and enjoy some long nights of celebration at the end.

PRACTICAL INFORMATION
ARRIVAL
The (sometimes unreliable) Precision Air shuttle is *usually* there to pick up passengers on their flights to **Kili Airport** and take them to Moshi for Ts10,000. Arriving on KLM, Ethiopian, or other internal airlines, however, you'll have to catch a cab to Moshi (US$50). Air Tanzania used to operate a shuttle too but in the absence of any flights – or even a working office – it's safe to assume this has been suspended for the time being.

Flights to **Moshi Airport** are so seldom that hopefully you'll already have transport from there sorted; you'll be lucky to find a taxi waiting at the airport.

Arrive **by bus** and you'll be dropped off at the bus terminal on Mawenzi Rd, 200m south of the Clock Tower, within walking distance of most hotels.

ORIENTATION & GETTING AROUND
According to Harry Johnston (see p113), Moshi could simply mean 'town' or 'settlement', though as with everything Johnston

wrote, this could well be wrong. Indeed, Moshi also translates as 'smoke' – a reference, perhaps, to its situation at the foot of a volcano? What is certain is that Moshi is compact, with almost everything of interest to the holidaying visitor lying on or near the main thoroughfare, **Mawenzi Rd** (aka Nyerere Rd, which is also more commonly known as Double Rd), and its northern extension, **Kibo Rd** (the two names borrowed from the peaks of Kilimanjaro). Together they run all the way from the market at the southern end of town to the roundabout at the northern end with the statue of a soldier facing north towards Kilimanjaro. Separating Mawenzi Rd from Kibo Rd is a second roundabout adorned with a **clock tower** (or should that be 'Coke tower', given the soft-drink sponsorship of the roundabout), the spiritual centre of town. There is a second road running parallel to Double Rd, officially christened **Market St** though known by most people as Single Rd which terminates at the clock tower.

Dalla-dallas drive up and down the main Mawenzi and Market streets for Ts300, though it doesn't take long to walk anywhere. The one exception to this rule is the suburb of **Shanty Town** (see map p203), north-west of the centre, home to a couple of great restaurants, a Chinese and a few fine hotels. A cab to Shanty Town will cost Ts3000 from the town centre; motorbikes (boda boda) around Ts1500.

SERVICES
Banks
The banks don't change money now. In their place, **moneychangers** such as Executive and the wonderfully named God Hates Corruption – Join Him Executive Bureau de Change, stay open later, their rates are fine and they don't charge commission; both of these are in Voda House. The moneychanger with the best rates is currently Trust (spelt 'Trast' on the sign), which also happens to be the most convenient for most of the tourist-friendly hotels.

Just as convenient, there's an **ATM** at Barclays that's on the main drag near most of the budget hotels; another one block west next to Moshi Leopard Hotel, another at the NBC on Kibo Rd (though once upon a time tourists who used this machine found their accounts reduced upon returning home by a sum much greater than that which they withdrew; we believe this problem has been sorted out now); one at Bank Exim on Boma Rd, opposite Abbas Ali's; and there's also one in Nakumatt Supermarket.

Communications
The **post office** (Mon-Fri 8am-4.30pm, Sat 9am-noon) is by the Clock Tower, at the junction with Boma Rd. The **TTCL office** (Mon-Fri 8am-4.30pm, Sat 9am-noon), next to the post office, in theory can sell you phonecards (Ts1000) which you can

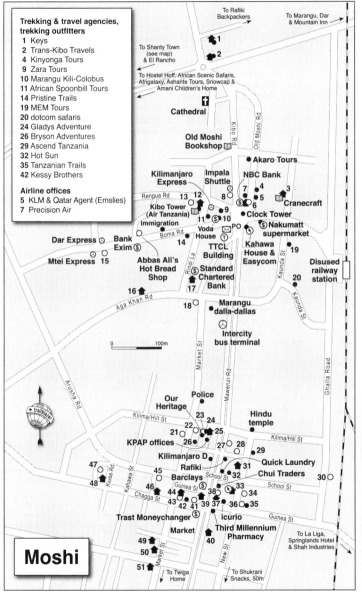

Trekking & travel agencies, trekking outfitters
1 Keys
2 Trans-Kibo Travels
4 Kinyonga Tours
9 Zara Tours
10 Marangu Kili-Colobus
11 African Spoonbill Tours
14 Pristine Trails
19 MEM Tours
20 dotcom safaris
24 Gladys Adventure
26 Bryson Adventures
29 Ascend Tanzania
32 Hot Sun
35 Tanzanian Trails
42 Kessy Brothers

Airline offices
5 KLM & Qatar Agent (Emslies)
7 Precision Air

To Rafiki Backpackers
To Marangu, Dar & Mountain Inn
To Shanty Town (see map) & El Rancho
To Hostel Hoff, African Scenic Safaris, Afrigalaxy, Ashante Tours, Snowcap & Amani Children's Home

1
2

Cathedral
Old Moshi Bookshop
Akaro Tours
NBC Bank
Kilimanjaro Express
Impala Shuttle
Kibo Tower (Air Tanzania)
Immigration
Rengua Rd
13 12
8
7 4
6 5
3
Cranecraft
9
11 10
Clock Tower
Voda House
Nakumatt supermarket
Boma Rd
PO
Bank Exim
Dar Express
14
TTCL Building
Kahawa House & Easycom
19
Mtei Express 15
Abbas Ali's Hot Bread Shop
Standard Chartered Bank
Disused railway station
16
17
Aga Khan Rd
18
Marangu dalla-dallas
Intercity bus terminal
100m
trailblazer
Market St
Mawenzi Rd
Ghalla Road
Police
Our Heritage
Kilima/Hill St
23 24
22
21 25
26
KPAP offices
27 28
29
Hindu temple
Kilima/Hill St
Kilimanjaro D
Rafiki
31
Quick Laundry
Chui Traders
47
45
School St
32
30
48
Barclays
44
Guinea St
38
33
46
43 42 41 39 37 36 35
34
School St
Chagga St
Trast Moneychanger
icurio
Guinea St
49
Market
Third Millennium Pharmacy
50
40
51
New St
To La Liga, Springlands Hotel & Shah Industries
To Shukrani Snacks, 50m
To Twiga Home
Kahawa Rd
Kiusa Rd
Arusha Rd
Kibo Rd
Old Moshi Rd
Rindi La
Kaunda St

Moshi

then load up with credit and use in the phone boxes outside. However, the whole place seemed pretty moribund when we went to check and though they reluctantly sold us Ts1000 credit, they then explained the phones outside weren't working so we had to use one of the office's. (I could be wrong but overall it felt as if TTCL had lost the battle with the mobile phone and was suffering a long, slow demise.)

As with Arusha, **wi-fi** has become common in Moshi with even some of the cheapest hotels offering it as well as many cafés, restaurants and bars. If you need a terminal, **internet** places aren't hard to find. The internet service at Easycom, in the basement of Kahawa House by the Clock Tower, has long been highly regarded (Ts1000 per hour), though Tanzanian Coffee Lounge and Buffalo Hotel are probably

Amani Children's Home

Like many children in Tanzania, Peter was driven to the streets because of extreme poverty and neglect. Born to alcoholic parents who struggled to keep a roof over the family's head and food on the table, Peter was malnourished and sick from an early age. Although Peter was nine when he came to Amani, his physical size alone made him look years younger. With the help of Amani's dedicated team, Peter is healthy and growing fast. He is doing well in school and is looking forward to a positive and happy future.

Despite the Chaggas' reputation among Tanzanians for prosperity and power, the region is not immune to the problems afflicting the rest of the country and that includes the malaise of street children. And while the stories of the children are unique, the general themes of neglect, poverty and desperation are a common theme with all of them.

Whatever each child's reason is for ending up on the streets, the door is always open to them at Amani Children's Home. Founded in 2001 by dedicated Tanzanians, the centre has grown to become the largest in the region, caring for around 80 children at any given time. Most are boys, though around a dozen are girls. Their ages range from 7 to 16, though the majority are between 10 and 14.

Most children come to the centre with the social workers who are employed full time by Amani to meet and rescue children living on the streets. Some are orphans who've lost both their parents, in many cases to AIDS, while others have run away from home because of the physical, mental or sexual abuse they face there. Once on the streets it's a precarious existence. Boys can try to graft a living by collecting scrap metal, begging or stealing; for girls, a life on the streets is even more dangerous, with many ending up as prostitutes.

Once in the Amani Centre, they are washed, fed and given new clothes. Social workers interview the children to learn about their backgrounds, circumstances for being on the street and their suitability for potential reunification with immediate family or relatives. Children quickly adapt to the daily routine, making beds and cleaning the dormitory. They have responsibilities such as washing their clothes and own dishes after each meal. After breakfast most attend school either externally or in Amani's on-site primary education program, which ranges from the Starters class for those who have never been to school or are deemed too old to join the first grade, to Classes A, B and C which are accelerated programs to get children to the educational level they should be attaining at their age. School ends mid-afternoon and then it is free-time for art, games, practising acrobatics, jumping rope; for many kids, the highlight of the day is the afternoon football match.

Despite the security and comparative normality provided by the home – at least compared to their life on the streets – the aim is to eventually reunify the children

more convenient for most people and the latter has longer opening hours – 8am-9pm – and a pretty fast connection too.

Airline offices

Precision Air (☎ 027-275 3498, 🖥 www.precisionairtz.com; Mon-Fri 8am-5pm, Sat, Sun & hols 9am-1pm) are in KNCU Building. **Air Tanzania** (🖥 www.airtanzania.co.tz) are now in Kibo Tower by Nyumbani Hotel but, although somebody must be around to put their advertising boards out in the morning, the lights are always off and the door locked; presumably this will change if and when they start operating flights from Kilimanjaro Airport again. Currently the only number we have for them is the (possibly obsolete) airport one: ☎ 027-255 4319. For other airlines, including KLM

---

with their parents or extended family, having first evaluated that such a move would be appropriate. Indeed, at Amani they create a place for healing with the *upendo* program (upendo is Swahili for 'love'), each staff member serves as 'parent' to several children, supervising them and listening to their problems. Few children have been at the centre since its foundation, with most staying for between 6 and 18 months.

It is both possible and worthwhile to visit the orphanage. One of the most heart-warming aspects of visiting the children is seeing how the older ones look after the newcomers and the more vulnerable. For example, Daudi, an autistic child, is looked after without complaint and treated with both kindness and respect by the other children.

In 2007 Amani made the move from the family house in which it began to a purpose-built centre. At one time in the old house, 65 children shared a bedroom but in the new facility each child has his or her own bunk bed. The growth of Amani is due to the dedication of the staff and careful management of funds. As an essentially secular organization (respecting the children's beliefs and values of Christian and Muslim faiths) the centre is not supported by any one institution or organization but instead relies on donations. Companies such as the Australian travel agents Intrepid Travel and UK-based Private Expeditions, Peace House Africa in the US and the Montreal Canadians hockey team's Childrens Foundation have all helped to support and build upon the volunteers' hard work. The majority of Amani's support, though, comes from individuals and families who visit the centre or hear about its good work and want to help.

Amani welcomes new volunteers and needs those who have a good working knowledge of Swahili, or are willing to learn. Long-term volunteers must be willing to commit to stay for six months or more (by which time Amani reckons your Swahili will be of an acceptable level). But if you can't commit that kind of time, don't despair. The home welcomes foreigners to come and look around the centre and spend some time with the kids. (America's Tusker Safaris, Moshi-based Tanzania Journeys, as well as our own trekking company, Climb Mount Kilimanjaro, are three companies who recommend their clients take time to visit.) Many tourists find that turning up to join in the afternoon football (soccer) game (daily around 3pm) is a good idea, being an easy way to mix and bond with the kids without the need for a common language.

Whether you want to arrange a visit, make a donation or merely find out about their work, have a look at their website (🖥 www.amanikids.org) or call them (☎ 0752-220637, or during office hours ☎ 0732-973579).

Trust us, if you've got a day to spare in Moshi, there's no more rewarding a way to spend it.

ARUSHA, MOSHI & MARANGU

and Qatar, visit **Emslies** (☎ 027-275 2701 or 275 1742) on Old Moshi Rd.

Laundry

Your hotel will probably have some sort of laundry service or you can visit Quick Laundry (Mon-Sat 8am-6pm, Sun 8am-2pm) on School St.

Swimming pools

The YMCA, Impala, Sal Salinero and Keys Hotel all charge Ts5000 to use their pools; in all of these places hotel guests can use the facilities for free.

Shopping

● **Trekking equipment** Finally, Moshi can boast a decent trekking equipment supplier. Indeed, they've now got two! **Gladys Adventure** (Mon-Fri 7am-6pm, Sat & Sun 7am-1pm) is run by the enterprising, eponymous Gladys, who started out trading souvenirs from her curio shop in return for hard-to-come-by bits of trekking equipment with tourists coming off the mountain. Having built up an extensive collection over the decade, Gladys has now moved her operation from her former base 5km out of town to Hill St in the heart of Moshi, just down from the Coffee Shop and round the corner from her trekking agency (see p212). Her collection is extensive, her stuff is good quality and her rental prices are cheap: US$10 for a head torch, pillow US$5, thermarests US$20, bottles US$10 and sleeping bags US$25 – all per trip! Perhaps most usefully of all, she also does a nice line in fleeces and base layers – items that can be really difficult to source in Tanzania. She has also now opened a souvenir shop within her premises.

Gladys' success has inspired a second outfitters, **Ascend Tanzania** (daily 7am-6pm; sample prices: trekking poles US$10, sleeping bags US$25, waterproof trousers US$10, all for a 5- to 7-day trip), to open up on New St, nearly opposite Zebra Hotel. Just one word of caution: while these places are indubitably a godsend, do remember that your agency should be able to supply you with most major bits of equipment that you might have forgotten to bring and it may be included in the price too.

Other items you may well have overlooked but will find extremely useful include: chapsticks (along with mosquito repellent and most other pharmaceutical needs), which can be bought from the Third Millennium **pharmacy** on Mawenzi Rd; and bin liners (or large shopping bags), useful for keeping clothing within your rucksack dry and available from the market or one of the supermarkets mentioned below.

● **Maps and books** about Kili can be bought from **Old Moshi Bookshop** on Rindi Lane at the junction with Kibo Rd, the anonymous **bookshop** on the ground floor of Kibo Tower, **Cranecraft** at Kilimanjaro Crane Hotel which has a decent selection of books about the country, its wildlife and, of course, the mountain, or the **souvenir shop** by Marangu Gate.

● **Supermarkets and other possibly useful stores** Moshi finally has a supermarket worthy of the name. **Nakumatt** (Mon-Sat 8.30am-10pm, Sun 10am-9.30pm) is just down from the Clock Tower, putting others in this area in the shade if not (yet) out of business. Up the hill to the west of the Clock Tower on Boma Rd is **Abbas Ali's Hot Bread Shop** (Mon-Sat 8.30am-6pm), a very pleasant place with great fresh bread and pastries. A convenience store that truly deserves the description is **Kilimanjaro D**, just up from Barclays, and there are branches of **Rafiki Supermarket** opposite, as well as by Moshi Leopard Hotel.

The **central market** does, of course, also sell food – and you'll probably be eating some of it on your trek.

Out in Shanty Town (see map p203), **Woodland Shoppers** is just above 10210 Pizzeria.

● **Souvenir shops** There are plenty of souvenirs to buy in Moshi and as many places willing to flog them to you. One in particular deserves special mention: **Shah Industries** is a leather workshop housed in what used to be a flour mill. It's a strange combination but a beautiful place and a worthy one too: over a third of the workers at Shah Industries have some sort of disability. Definitely worth looking around, it lies to the south-east of town across the train tracks on the way to Springlands Hotel.

Of the 'regular' souvenir shops, the best in terms of choice and quality is **iCurio**, just round the corner from Kindoroko Hotel, with the widest array of stock including a fine line in Kilimanjaro Beer T-shirts. **Our Heritage**, sharing the same building as the Coffee Shop, has a fair array of knick-knacks, while **Cranecraft**, in Kilimanjaro Crane Hotel, has similar stock plus as well as books (see p200). Worth a nose around. **Chui Traders**, near New Castle Hotel on Nyerere Rd, is the place to go for Masai clothes and implements.

WHERE TO STAY   [see map p195]

The following is not an exhaustive list but whilst there are some cheaper places at the southern end of town, many refuse to accept Westerners. Manage to persuade one to let you stay and you can expect to pay around Ts3000 per night, though the chances are it'll be assumed you want bed and broad rather than bed and board. Those looking to **camp** are advised to head to Honey Badger (see box p205). Or you can go to Marangu, where virtually every hotel allows camping in their grounds.

As for hotels that definitely do welcome tourists, in approximate price order they are as follows:

Below US$20 per double

Kilimanjaro Backpackers (☎ 027-275 5159; ☐ www.kilimanjarobackpackers .com; Mawenzi/Double Rd) is a relative of its namesake in Arusha, but while it's around the same price at US$6/10/18 dorm/ sgl/dbl for B&B (all with common bathroom; add US$7-8pp for half-board, another US$6 for full board), it's nowhere near as smart. Nevertheless, it is still hugely popular though do check out a couple of rooms as they vary in size and quality – it's fair to say, for example, that cats could happily enter into the single rooms without fear of being swung around. It boasts wi-fi, fan and mosquito nets and the guests I interviewed were positively enthusiastic about the place; the staff too, in particular the new lad, Bruno, are lovely. Indeed, everything looks smashing ... until you realise there are just two toilets and two showers for up to 28 guests.

The communal areas in *Haria Hotel* (☎ 0763-019395; dorm bed Ts10,000, dbl Ts18,000, s/c dbl Ts25,000), which is on the other side of Double Rd, look slightly scruffy and rundown; this matches the slightly-too-laidback attitude of the staff, though the rooms are actually OK and certainly worth the money, particularly as they boast wi-fi and fans. Note that breakfast is not included, however. The roof terrace is very popular here in the late afternoon.

Still in the same area, *Buffalo Hotel* (☎ 027-275 3736; ☐ www.buffalocom panyltd@yahoo.com), on New St, has clean bright rooms with mosquito nets as well as a fairly popular bar and restaurant downstairs. The hotel has installed cable TV into the en suite rooms (sgl/dbl Ts20,000-25,000/25,000-45,000) and there are also some fairly priced doubles with common facilities (Ts17,000), all rates including breakfast. Note, however, that surprisingly for a hotel in this price bracket, there is no wi-fi.

Just south of the market is *Umoja Lutheran Hostel* (☎ 0769-239860); look for the sign 'KKKT Umoja Hostel'. There's nothing wrong with this place. It's clean, well-run and the al-fresco eating area is certainly pleasant and popular with locals. The rates, too, are decent, at Ts12,000/20,000/ 30,000 sgl/dbl/tpl for rooms with shared bathrooms, or s/c sgl/dbl Ts25,000/30,000, all with breakfast. Nevertheless, it's a rare tourist who stays here. Similarly failing to appeal to the *mzungu* market are *Golden View Hotel* (☎ 0757-365858), on Chagga St, where all the rooms (which are a bit small) have their own balcony, bathroom and mosquito net and rates (s/c sgl/dbl Ts20,000) include breakfast; and *Big Mountain Inn* (☎ 027-275 1862; ☐ p.mti tos@hotmail.com), on Kiusa St, where some very smart rooms are squashed together around a small garden. The baffling price structure could be one of the reasons why tourists seldom venture here: basically, they have some small en suite doubles with air-con which they call 'singles' and for which they charge Ts40,000 (or Ts30,000 without a/c); two people can stay in these rooms (for the same Ts40,000 price) but note you'll only get one free breakfast (an extra breakfast is Ts3500). Alternatively, there are some twin rooms but these cost a less reasonable Ts60,000 (or Ts40,000 without air-con).

Occupying a great central location, **Aa Hotel** (☎ 027-275 3919) is a surprisingly somnolent sort of place – indeed, even the receptionist was asleep when we visited, which at least allowed us to look around unhindered. What we found was a spotless place with murals on the walls of each room, each of which also contained a fan and mosquito net. The prices seem fair too at s/c sgl/dbl/tpl Ts20,000/30,000/40,000, and there are a couple of cheaper doubles with shared facilities for Ts25,000. There could be one obstacle to your staying here, however: as is made clear with a sign on the way in, unmarried couples aren't allowed to share a room.

At the northern end of town by the roundabout, **New Coffee Tree Hotel** (see box p206; ☎ 0752-388311) is a place for those for whom every *shilingi* matters. I've always had a soft spot for this place but, in all honesty, I think I'm pretty much the only *mzungu* who does. Nevertheless, I like the staff, I like the location right next to the Clock Tower and I like the restaurant (see p207) on the top floor. Admittedly, the rooms are basic but they do come with sink and mozzy net and are functional, fine and very fairly priced at only Ts12,000 for a single with shared facilities (and no fan) or Ts15,000/20,000 for en suite twins and doubles/triples (the more expensive ones with TV), all including breakfast.

Continuing northwards, the **YMCA** (☎ 027-275 1754) on the main roundabout has always felt a little rundown. To be fair, the prices of US$15/18 sgl/dbl B&B in rooms with a mosquito net but no fan and with shared bathroom are just about reasonable and guests say it's functional, fine and the pool is lovely.

US$20-50 per double

Kindoroko Hotel (☎ 027-275 4054; 🖥 www.kindorokohotels.com) has long been one of the mainstays of the hotel scene in Moshi, bridging that gap between backpacker places and mid-range hotels.

However, it does feel like it's starting to feel the pinch as other similarly priced hotels establish themselves in town, though it could just be that we visited in the low season. But ignore the sometimes deathly hush along the corridors and it's OK and fairly priced at sgl/dbl/family US$20/30/45 including breakfast.

Zebra Hotel (☎ 0766-998648) is a large but fairly commonplace hotel in the middle of Moshi. Features of their facility-heavy en suite rooms include air-con, satellite TV, direct-dial telephone and room service. The prices are very fair, however, at US$35/40/50 s/c sgl/dbl/tpl or US$55 for 'executive' rooms. If your trekking company has booked a room for you, it's neither a reason to rejoice nor rebel because, unlike a zebra, there's nothing particularly black and white about this hotel; more a fairly unspectacular grey.

Moving to the Clock Tower area but staying in the same price bracket, **Kilimanjaro Crane Hotel** (☎ 027-275 1114; 🖥 www.kilimanjarocranehotelsandsafaris .com) seems to be more of a local businessmen's hotel. It's a decent-enough place, however, with 30 smart rooms, sauna, gym and even a very small pool. Singles, which have showers, TV and telephone, are US$40 each (US$50 with air-con); doubles and triples have both bathtubs and showers and go for US$50 (US$60 with air-con), or it's US$65 for a triple. These rates have stayed the same for quite a few years (since 2006) and as a consequence the hotel is now looking rather good value.

Finally in this bracket, **Lutheran Uhuru Hotel** (☎ 027-275 4512; 🖥 www .uhuruhotel.org) sits in fairly vast grounds in leafy **Shanty Town** (see map p203); don't get this hotel in Shanty Town confused with Lutheran Umoja Hostel in central Moshi. It's a quiet, relaxed place, the only activity coming from the team of gardeners and cleaners maintaining the neat-and-tidiness of it all. The rooms are very pleasant – particularly those in the new Kibo or Kilimanjaro wings – and all are self-contained with mosquito nets and wi-fi. The tariff, in our opinion, is a little high at US$45/55 s/c sgl/dbl in the Mawenzi

Wing (where there's air-con but no TV), US$40/50 in the Kilimanjaro and Kibo wings (TV but no air-con), though there are cheaper rooms in the annex (sgl/dbl US$30/40). Despite this moan, it maintains a healthy trickle of customers and if you don't mind catching some form of transport or walking a fair distance to get to Moshi everyday – or are happy doing nothing all day except watch a battalion of gardeners watering the grass – it's fine.

US$50 and above per double
Beginning in the south of the town, **Osy Grand Hotel** (☎ 0754-421220; 🖳 www .osygrandhotel.com) and **Panama Hotel** (☎ 0756-206615; 🖳 www.panamaho teltz.com) stand close to each other to the west of the market. Both are proud of their facility-stuffed rooms (wi-fi, TV, hot water etc etc) and both are fine – though they seldom cater to the foreign tourist. Prices are s/c sgl/dbl €35/45 in the Osy Grand (add €5 for air-con – no, I don't know why it's priced in euros either), and sgl/dbl US$50/60 in the Panama.

A few hundred metres north **Moshi Leopard Hotel** (☎ 027-275 0884; 🖳 www.leopardhotel.com), on Market St, is an old favourite with tour groups and independent travellers alike. Boasting an excellent terrace bar (from where, if you peer through the branches of the nearby tree, you can see Kibo), the rooms are en suite, very comfy, include a fridge, TV, wardrobe, fan and balcony. As for the rates, the foreigner prices are US$50/60 s/c sgl/dbl, which is fair value but not exceptional. Shame about the staff, who often can't seem to muster a smile between them.

Bristol Cottages (☎ 027-275 5083; 🖳 www.bristolcottages.com), on Rindi Lane, describe themselves as 'The countryside hotel in the middle of town', and though the noise from the buses revving up the hill outside rather shatters that boast, it's true that this is a little blossom-filled idyll and the most convenient upper-bracket hotel in Moshi. The smart cottages, all with large TV and mosquito net, go for US$65/80 s/c sgl/dbl; the new wing, a little noisier due to its proximity to the road, is consequently

slightly cheaper at US$60/70 s/c sgl/dbl, while there are some suites with a mountain view that will set you back US$80/100/120 s/c sgl/dbl/tpl.

Just a few metres up the hill on Aga Khan Rd is another smart place. **Parkview Inn** (☎ 027-275 0711; 🖳 www.pvim.com) was once a bijou B&B boasting just 12 rooms or so but these days thanks to a huge extension it's now a fairly enormous monolith with 44 rooms of elegant (if monotonous) uniformity and the facilities – TV, telephone, wi-fi, air-con and bath or shower – of a large chain hotel. Thankfully, however, it still retains its friendly informality. Rates are US$65/75/120 for s/c sgl/dbl /suite.

Not too far away on Rengua Rd, the old Philip's Hotel has been bought up, spruced up and converted to another link in the **Nyumbani Hotel** (☎ 027-2754432; 🖳 www.nyumbanihotels.com) chain. Mercifully, the rooms are more elegant than the rather overcrowded reception (complete with a hotchpotch of giant Chinese vases, a head of an eland and a stuffed zebra) would have you fear. Rates for these air-conditioned, self-contained rooms with satellite TV and wi-fi start at US$85/100 sgl/dbl B&B. (By the way, the old Moshi Hotel opposite is closed for renovations. Scaffolding has gone up and when we walked past there were definitely hammering sounds coming from the interior. However, after such a long time everything has tumbled into a state of dilapidation, disrepair and decay. It wasn't ready in time for the previous two editions and it won't be for this one; in fact we don't expect it to reopen anytime soon.)

North again, this time on Uru Rd, **Keys Hotel** (☎ 027-275 2250 or 275 1875; 🖳 www.keys-hotel-tours.com) is a traditional-looking family-run hotel and one of the smartest addresses in Moshi. In the main building it's doubles only, all coming with TV, telephone, mini-bar, toilet, shower with hot/cold running water and air-con. There are also 15 small thatch-and-cement cottages in the grounds which are quite fun. All rates (sgl/dbl US$78/91) include continental breakfast.

ARUSHA, MOSHI & MARANGU

Accommodation for volunteers and long-term residents

It seems a little ironic, perhaps, that what is traditionally one of the wealthiest and most developed parts of Tanzania is also the one area that receives more interest from NGOs, charities and the like. As a consequence, Moshi in particular is flooded with volunteers working on any number of projects in the town and surrounding area. This has led in turn to the establishment of several hostels designed specifically to cater for these longer-term residents. And as many of these volunteers will, understandably, want to climb Kili at some point while they're here, it is our duty to cater for them in this book too and look briefly at these hostels.

To begin, we must mention *Hostel Hoff* (☎ 0787-225908; 🖥 www.hostelhoff .com) This place, situated between and just to the north of the two main roundabouts on the way out of Moshi, usually accepts only long-term guests (ie those staying a minimum of one month) and as such is popular with volunteers. Run by an Australian lady who married a local, the gender-divided **dorms** (with mosquito nets and lockable drawers) in the main house are shiny and clean (though the possessions of long-term residents inevitably tend to sprawl out over time onto every available surface). There are a couple of double/twin **rooms** by the toilet block and even a couple of **safari tents** in the back garden (though these are very popular and tend to be taken by those residents who are staying the longest). The price is very reasonable at US$17-19pp per day including buffet breakfast, dinner and laundry; the exact price depends on how long you're staying, which is one reason why it regularly receives rave reviews from its residents. They also now run a successful trekking agency, African Scenic Safaris (see p211).

Karibu Hostel (🖥 www.borntolearntz.org) was built to support the charity Born To Learn which aims to educate the local children. Situated in the pretty village of Mbokome, just before Kiborotoni, towards Honey Badger Campsite (but not as far), it's a 10-minute drive east of Moshi. The hostel has 4-bed and 2-bed **dorms**; rates are US$12pp, US$15 with breakfast.

Twiga Home (☎ 0762-035030; 🖥 www.moshi-hostel.com) is located to the south of town, beyond the airport, though they offer a free shuttle to town three times a day (which is pretty much essential, as it's a half-hour walk to the centre otherwise). And they keep to their promises as far as I can tell. What's more the bar is good, there's wi-fi and satellite TV, the restaurant's decent, the garden pleasant, the staff amiable and the rooms clean and come complete with mosquito nets. It's all very reasonable too at sgl/dbl US$12/18 for rooms with fan, US$14/22 for those with air-con (though they vary according to how long you stay). Indeed, my only gripe *is* the location, which means it can feel a bit lonely if you're staying here by yourself – and scheduling your day around their shuttle is a bit inconvenient. Still, if you can overcome these problems you've got yourself a bargain.

Rafiki Backpackers (☎ 0763730595; 🖥 rafikibackpackers.com) is located out in peaceful Rao, 20 minutes' walk north of town and east of Shanty Town. This hard-to-find hostel (ask for Uhuru Museum – which most locals know, and which is actually a bar – as it's opposite there) is for those who want to stay in a village while still being close enough to the town centre. The owner, Freya, is Belgian and a mine of information; the place itself is clean and cheap at US$12 for a bed (US$15 with breakfast) and use of the kitchen and a fridge. Overall, it's a nice, safe and friendly option – the only problem, as usual, being the distance from town.

However, for the top places in Moshi you have to go to a part of town perhaps misleadingly called **Shanty Town** – a smart area of jacaranda-lined boulevards that's quite unlike any shanty town you've seen or heard about.

The first place you come to is *Kibo Executive Lodge* (☎ 027-2750110; 🖥 www.kiboexecutivelodge-moshi.com), which is typical of Shanty Town, being smart, squeaky clean and pretty luxurious. Established for four years now, it's never quite found its customer base but you can't fault the accommodation, with each of the 10 rooms boasting TV, air-con, shower, bath and wi-fi. Rates are fair at sgl/dbl US$70/80, rising to US$120 for the suites.

If you head north-west on Lema Rd then east off that onto Ameg Rd you come to something of a curiosity. Maybe it's the high concrete walls surrounding the place, maybe it's the uniform whitewashed, green-roofed chalets, or maybe the popular pool where everybody seems to congregate – whatever it is, there's something about *Ameg Lodge* (☎ 027-275 0175, ☎ 0754-058268; 🖥 www.ameglodge.com) that's reminiscent of a 1950s' British seaside holiday camp. Thankfully, the rather bland, shadeless exterior belies some quite stylish rooms, each with shower, satellite TV, fan, veranda and phone. Prices (all rooms are doubles) start at sgl/dbl US$50/94, rising to US$149 for the junior suite with air-con. In addition to the pool, guests are also entitled to use the hotel gym.

Further north and on Lema Rd, *Impala Hotel Kilimanjaro* (☎ 027-275 3443/4 or ☎ 0757-725944; 🖥 www.kilimanjaro.impala hotel.com) is from the same herd as the one in Arusha though where that Impala is more of a business centre, this one is more homely and all the better for it. A lovely pool and friendly staff are just two of its selling points, along with 11 stylish yet inviting en suite rooms with TV and all mod-cons. For those of us who don't live in Tanzania it's US$80/100/140 for s/c sgl/dbl/tpl B&B.

Nearby, *Sal Salinero* (☎ 027-275 2240; 🖥 www.salsalinerohotel.com) is a conglomeration of cottages and standard rooms hidden behind high hedges to the

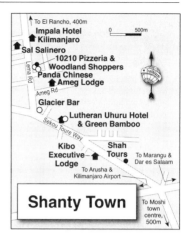

↑ To El Rancho, 400m
Impala Hotel
Kilimanjaro
Sal Salinero
10210 Pizzeria &
Woodland Shoppers
Panda Chinese
Ameg Lodge
Glacier Bar
Lutheran Uhuru Hotel
& Green Bamboo
Kibo
Executive
Lodge
Shah
Tours
To Marangu &
Dar es Salaam
To Arusha &
Kilimanjaro Airport

Shanty Town

To Moshi town centre, 500m

Lema Rd
Ameg Rd
Sekou Toure Way

0   500m

west of Lema Rd. All accommodation comes with air-con, TV and fridge, with many boasting bathtubs too; the executive rooms also have hairdryers. Guests seem to have enjoyed the place, with the cottages getting the best reviews. The sparkling sunkissed pool is very inviting – though currently could do with a bit of a clean. With the prices at sgl/dbl/tpl US$90/120/155 and suites US$180, this may be one of the more expensive places in town but it's also one of the smartest.

Finally, there are two places, both just a little out of town, that are owned and run by trekking agencies. Unless you have booked with one of these agencies it is highly unlikely you will stay here; if you *have* booked with these agencies, the chances are you will get a night or two free at the hotel before and after your trek. The first is the very comfortable *Mountain Inn*, 4km from town on the way to Marangu, which is owned and run by Shah Tours (see p214 for contact details). A pool, sauna and a pretty garden are just some of the attractions here. The second place is the Zara-run (see p216) *Springlands Hotel* (☎ 027-2750011; 🖥 www.springlandshotel.com), 2km to the south of town. Most people who stay here are happy with what they find, the pool being the main attraction.

ARUSHA, MOSHI & MARANGU

Accommodation near Moshi and around Kilimanjaro

The foothills, lower slopes and surrounding plains of Kilimanjaro are dotted here and there with some very pleasant accommodation; it is unlikely you will stay at any of them *unless* you book your trek before you come to Tanzania and the trekking agency happens to put you up in one. And if you do then congratulations – I think that on the whole they offer some of the most pleasant and interesting accommodation in the region. Note that we haven't included all hotels or lodges, of course; almost every village has some sort of accommodation so we have narrowed our survey down to just those that market themselves to tourists. Note, too, that we have not included the hotels in Marangu; you can find these on p219.

The following hotels are ordered from west of Moshi round to the east.

House of West Kili (☎ 0753-426 788, 🖳 www.houseofwestkili.com) Located in **Lawate, Sanya Juu**, this new place (opened 2012) is probably the most suitable candidate if you're looking to cut the travelling time to Londorossi Gate and the start of the Shira or Lemosho routes. Eight huge rooms, with two more planned, sit about 20 minutes' drive from Boma N'Gombe. It's early days yet – the hotel had only been opened a few months when we called in – but the owner also has plans to build an internet café upstairs. There are no TVs; instead the owner hopes you'll participate in a couple of local activities, including bird-watching at the nearby swamp or visiting a local sacred Maasai hill. Rates are US$70pp per night, with meals US$20 each.

Ndarakwai Ranch (☎ 027-250 2713, 🖳 www.ndarakwai.com) Set in 11,000 acres in the **Siha District**, on the lower western slopes of Kilimanjaro; unlike the others in this section this ranch is less a stopover on the way to the mountain than a destination in itself: 15 en suite wi-fi-connected tents on raised wooden platforms, and located on land that teems with 70 species of mammal and 350 species of birds. Beautiful, if above the budget of most trekkers at US$470/770/873 for sgl/dbl/tpl, with game drives extra.

Protea Hotel Aishi Machame (☎ 027-569 41/8; 🖳 www.proteahotels.com) lies in the village **near Kili's Machame gate**. Boasting 30 en suite rooms with wi-fi and telly in each, it's a nice if slightly odd-looking place with a pool and some very precisely manicured grounds; but like many in this section it survives mainly – indeed, almost exclusively – from the business of tour groups; as a result, if you aren't part of a group you may feel a little isolated and lonely.

Stella Maris Lodge (☎ 0686-66 3244, 🖳 stellamarislodge.com) Located on the outskirts of Moshi just south of the road to the airport, in a village that goes by the name of **Mailisita**, blancmange-coloured Stella Maris is a not-for-profit hotel stuffed with facilities (wi-fi, air-con, satellite TV, conference facilities, balconies on all the rooms) where all profit goes to paying the teachers at the attached primary school and buying food for the children under the auspices of Mailisita Foundation (🖳 mailisita .org), a US initiative. Prices are US$70/75/100 for sgl/dbl/two-room suite.

Weru Weru River Lodge (☎ 0753-038608, 🖳 www.weruweruriverlodge.com) Also in **Mailisita** and owned by successful Moshi trekking agent Ahsante (see p211), this is their latest venture, a huge, semi-luxury, facility-filled place with 32 air conditioned veranda-fronted rooms, bar, coffee lounge, swimming pool, wi-fi and two conference halls. The charming wooden fittings and stone floors can't quite compensate for the slightly plain nature of the buildings but all in all it's very impressive and rates are fair at US$85/142 for sgl/dbl; add about US$50 per room for high season.

Kili-konka Holiday Home (☎ 0758-842917, 🖳 www.kilikonka.com) The ultimate in luxury in the region, Kili-konka is a new, private four-bedroom bungalow that you can rent out on a sole occupancy basis for US$800 B&B *a night*! Sounds

WHERE TO EAT AND DRINK
[see map p195]
Four great cafés

As befits a town that grew wealthy on the back of the bean with the caffeine, Moshi has some rather decent little coffee houses. Indeed, there has been a fierce rivalry between them for several years now, though all of them have been rather swept away by a café that manages the difficult feat of being both the newest on the scene – and yet the one with the longest heritage. **KNCU Cafi** (Kilimanjaro Native Coffee Union, better known as **Union Café**; daily 7am-8.30pm) is named after and run by Africa's oldest surviving cooperative, an organization that represents some 60,000 farmers who grow coffee on the lower slopes of Kilimanjaro. It's a history (see box p206) that it is clearly proud of, with the walls adorned with portraits of previous chairmen of the co-op and the building itself, once the HQ of KNCU, retaining many original features (not to mention an industrial coffee roaster that they've just installed – so presumably the smell of coffee is wafting over Moshi as you read this, luring yet more customers to their premises). It's great to see Africa's history being celebrated in this way; this is coffee with a conscience, too, for much of the profit generated is ploughed back into the farming community. As for what you can actually consume here, the coffee (Ts2000-3500) is, of course, both organic and fantastic (the best in Moshi, by common consent), there's a lengthy list of teas too (all Tanzanian) and the menu is Western (including quiche, sandwiches and the inevitable pizzas). The décor is simple and tasteful and the veranda is a lovely place to watch the world go by and enjoy that caffeine buzz. Don't miss this place.

It must be rather galling for the *grande dame* of Moshi's cafés, the **Coffee Shop** (Mon-Fri 8am-8pm, Sat 8am-6pm), on Kilima/Hill St, to be upstaged by a place that has, after all, only just celebrated its second birthday. But it shouldn't be too concerned for it still has plenty of which it should be proud. The food here, including salads, juices, cakes, pies and a wealth of Tanzanian coffees, is very good, the drinks are cold and there's heaps of local information on the noticeboards. Perhaps the best thing about this café, however, is the wonderfully tranquil little garden out back.

A few blocks south, **Tanzanian Coffee Lounge** (Mon-Sat 8am-8pm, Sun 8am-5pm) continues to hold its own, probably because it seems to be going out of its way to supply everything a *mzungu* could want, from internet to ice cream. The service is usually a lot more 'smiley' than at other establishments and the clients tend to be incredibly expensive, which it is, of course, though you do get your own chef, house- and grounds-keeper, security team and on-site manager all included. A fully equipped kitchen, lounge, en suite master bedroom (with two further bathrooms) and wi-fi, iPod docks and microwave are just some of the features. The location is a good one too, just **east of KCMC Hospital** north of Moshi.

Honey Badger Lodge (☎ 0767-551 190, 🖳 www.honeybadgerlodge.com) Having undergone a renovation over the past couple of years following a change of ownership (the son having taken over from his mum who originally ran the place), Honey Badger, 6km east of Moshi on the way to Dar, is now a very attractive place for those who want to get away from it all. Facilities include a pool and 15 smart **en suite rooms** and the best **campsite** in the Moshi area – all set in some lush gardens where tortoises roam. The hotel also supports several charitable initiatives. Well worth a look. Prices: sgl/dbl/tpl US$50/80/90 B&B; add on US$10 per meal; camping US$10. Low-season discounts are available. Internet available at US$5 per day.

Snow Cap Cottages (book through Snow Cap, see p214, in Moshi: ☎ 027-275 4826, 🖳 www.snowcap.co.tz) Swiss-style chalets in a pleasant spot by Rongai Gate, with an open fire, TV room and a well-stocked bar. Prices are US$45pp half-board.

younger too. Despite the name the place feels distinctly 'un-African' – but then that's probably the idea. Food-wise, they serve some decent Mexican food including 'boritos' (Ts10,000) as well as more stan-

dard Western fare including 'sadwiches' (which aren't as bad as they sound) and a large selection of salads.

A fourth coffee lounge, *Aroma* (Mon-Sat 6am-8pm, Sun 6am-1pm) is in a similar

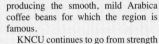

Coffee-growing on Kilimanjaro and the KNCU

Coffee was first planted on the slopes of Kilimanjaro by Catholic missionaries in 1898. Indeed, the first coffee bush they planted, in Kilema district, is still growing. German settlers took over production of the coffee when they arrived and as a consequence local natives were not allowed to grow their own but instead had to work on the settlers' own plantations. Only when the Germans were defeated at the end of World War I and the British took over were the locals able to enjoy some freedom and begin to cultivate their own plantations again as a cash crop, with the churches providing seeds for them to get started. Already in the 1920s the locals were organizing themselves into co-ops to increase their bargaining power and Kilimanjaro Native Planters Association (KNPA), with Joseph Melingo as their first head, was founded in 1925.

Kilimanjaro Native Cooperative Union (KNCU) can trace its roots back to this early organization; though it was officially founded in 1933 it has changed a lot since then. Originally set up to market the coffee of the local farmers who grew their crop on Kili's slopes, the first president was one Charles Cecil Farquharson Dundas, then district commissioner of the Moshi region, who recognized, along with his friend ALB (Ben) Bennett, the need to have primary co-operatives to represent the interests of the farmers. Dundas, incidentally, is mentioned several times in this book thanks to the studies he made of the local Chagga tribes – work he then published in his book *Kilimanjaro and its People*. His work earnt him both an OBE from his government back home (the UK) and the title 'Wasaoye-o-Wachagga' – Elder of the Chagga – from the locals; Bennett, on the other hand, became 'Mbuya-o-Wachagga' – Friend of the Chagga.

But I'm digressing. As befits a union that represents farmers growing crops on Africa's largest mountain, the KNCU went on to become Africa's largest coffee co-op until politics interfered and it was actually banned, along with all the other co-operatives in Tanzania, in 1976. Reinstated in the eighties as KNCU (1984) Ltd, the union currently represents over 70,000 coffee farmers formed into 94 different co-ops – each producing the smooth, mild Arabica coffee beans for which the region is famous.

Union Café, Moshi

KNCU continues to go from strength to strength. They were awarded 'Fair Trade' certification as early as 1993 and has more recently expanded into tourism, not only running the huge New Coffee Tree Hotel on Moshi's main Clock Tower Roundabout but also the ever-popular Union Café. They have also started providing tours of their members' plantations and set up a campsite, idyllically located at Uru-North Msuni, north of Moshi, about a half-hour drive away. You can find out more about each of these on their website at 🖳 www.kncutanzania.com.

vein to the Coffee Lounge but more peaceful and laidback (if that's possible). It also has wi-fi and is quite stylish, with chairs that have been upholstered with coffee sacks and tables made from the cross section of giant trees. Overall, it's quite sophisticated – and is a great choice for those who find themselves at this end of town.

Local food

Beginning at the southern end of town, one steadfastly African joint lies hidden behind a mosque on New St. **Shukrani Snacks** (noon-8pm) is a Somali-run establishment that's popular and cheap. Come here at lunch to try their curry and boiled bananas for just Ts2500 – a great way to fill up.

For more real homegrown East African cooking there are several choices. Currently the most popular amongst *mzungu*, and not just for its location, **Taj Mahal** (daily 7am-10pm) sits right by Kindoroko Hotel and despite the Indian name is actually a great place for local fare such as meat skewers (Ts500 each, though they'll try to rip you for double that) and Zanzibar pizza (a sort of omelette filled with mince and onions and a great way to fill up for just Ts1000). A couple of blocks away, **Chagga Bar and Grill** (daily 8am-10pm) near Moshi Leopard Hotel has a small menu but it includes a huge mountain of *mchemisho kuku* (boiled chicken, vegetables and bananas) for just Ts4000. The place is actually much more tame than it used to be and the food less Chagga and more generally Tanzanian; indeed, they even give you cutlery now. Still, it remains an OK place and the pool table is currently the best in town.

Further up Market St is **Moeen's** (Mon-Sat 8am-10pm), a quieter and perhaps more likeable venue with tasty and huge portions of African food; nothing on the menu costs more than the Ts3500 you'd pay for chicken and chips. Still further along the same road and on the corner with Aga Khan Rd, **Oxygen** (Mon-Sat 7am-9pm, Sun to 1pm) is perhaps the best place to sit and wait for the next dalla-dalla out, with good local food (*nyama chipsi* – meat and chips – Ts3500), wi-fi and a pleasant veranda from which to watch the chaos outside.

Boasting terrific scenery but tardy service, **New Coffee Tree Café** (daily 6am-10pm), on the top floor of the eponymous hotel (see p200), is a light and airy place with sumptuous views towards Moshi in one direction and Kili in the other – both of which you'll have plenty of time to enjoy while you wait the interminably long time for your food. When it does finally put in an appearance, it's tasty, hearty and very good value, with nothing more than Ts6000. Overall, a good place to get away from the heat, hassle, touts and tourists.

Asian food, a burger joint – and somewhere for schnitzel

When the Tanzanian Coffee Lounge closes, the student volunteers migrate en masse to **Indoitaliano** (daily 11am-9.30pm), whose popularity can be ascribed to two factors: a) a good location amongst the hotels near the market, and b) some great food. The name may conjure up all sorts of unappealing fusions but there's no need to be worried: this is really just a straightforward Indian restaurant that happens to make some delightful pizzas too (from Ts9000). Unfortunately, if you are neither in your late teens nor visiting Moshi as a volunteer you may feel out of place here. If this is the case, **Sikh Club** (Mon-Fri 11am-3pm & 6-10pm, Sat & Sun 10am-3pm & 6-10pm) provides welcome sanctuary. It's a lovely peaceful spot with a vast menu and views across a hockey pitch to the hills beyond. They change the chef regularly so it's difficult to judge the food, though the standard is generally pretty high. The food is Indian and the vegetarian selection (mains Ts4500-6500) in particular is without equal in Moshi; their bar is very well stocked too. Just one word of warning: though only a block back from Indoitaliano, the streets around here are particularly dark – it's best not to wander around alone at night.

Nearby is perhaps our favourite place in Moshi. Half of **Milan's** (daily 8am-10pm) is taken up with a typically scruffy snack café of the kind you find all over the country. The other half, however, is rather different: a cute little pink-painted eatery with hand-stitched place mats that boasts an

---

❏ **The top six places in Moshi and Shanty Town to celebrate a climb**
● **Indoitaliano** The old favourite and convenient for many hotels. Book in advance if planning to arrive after 8pm or you're a large group.
● **Panda Chinese** As good as Chinese food gets in the region.
● **Chrisburger** Well it's cheap and cheerful and you can always hang around for the nightclub to open.
● **Salzburger** A quirky evening with great food guaranteed in this Moshi institution, tucked away on the dusty roads west of the main drag.
● **Green Bamboo** Don't be put off by the fact it's part of a religious hostel (even Christians like to let their hair down sometimes) – this is a decent place with great food.
● **El Rancho** Let's just hope that all the things that made this place so great – the extensive bar, oh-so-exquisite food, mini-golf course and air of eccentricity – are left intact when the renovation work is completed.

---

extensive menu of cheap and delicious Indian vegetarian food, including dosas, samosas, bhajis and thalis. No dish is over Ts3800. There are just a couple of minor drawbacks: the service can be fairly desultory, for one thing, and secondly another guidebook has finally discovered it too, so it's not as quiet as it once was. Nevertheless, to my mind this is the best value-for-money place in East Africa.

Some people may be put off by the appearance of *Deli Chez* (Wed-Mon 10am-10pm), which from the outside looks like a fast-food café, though the ground floor décor owes more to the aesthetics of a wedding reception. But upstairs you'll find a very pleasant shaded terrace where the food is fine and fair value; and with both a Japanese and Chinese menu (Ts7000-8000 for mains) this place could provide a welcome break from the same old fare offered by other eateries (though they're not adverse to serving the odd pizza or poppadum too, with a particularly extensive subcontinental menu).

Just north of the Clock Tower roundabout, *Chrisburger* (see also p209) claims to stay open 24 hours and offers very good-value dishes; if you can get a seat on its leafy veranda it's a good place to hide away and watch the world go by. Once again it's great value, with nothing over Ts5000.

On Kenyatta St, *Salzburger* (daily 8am-10pm) is perhaps Africa's most eccentric restaurant, a place that is clearly infatuated with the twee Austrian city after which it is named (and where the boss studied).

Despite the obscure location – it calls itself Africa's best-kept secret – it's a great little eatery and a pleasant escape; and where else can you can munch on *chicken mambo yote* (platter of crispy-skinned chicken blended with vegetables and garnished with onion, green pepper and salad; Ts9500) to the strains of Mozart, or devour *weinerschnitzel* (Ts9000) while the Von Trapps smile down at you from the walls and waitresses swan around in fake leopard-fur waistcoats with matching hats? Good value, and good fun.

In Shanty Town (see map p203)

Moving uptown and upmarket, for a bit of a treat there are several fine places in chic Shanty Town. The first, *El Rancho* (Tue-Sun 12.30-11pm), off Lema Rd, clearly has an identity crisis, being an Indian restaurant with a Mexican name and, weirdly, its own small crazy-golf course too. Despite the confusion this is a lovely, jacaranda-shaded spot, currently undergoing extensive renovation, though presumably it will return to serving the same high standards of food they were renowned for, with mains for Ts6500-12,000. They also have an extensive alcohol selection, which always made this the best place for a post-trek knees-up.

Panda Chinese (Mon-Fri 11am-3pm & 6-10pm, Sat & Sun 11am-10pm) is, as you've probably already guessed from the name, a Chinese restaurant and another standout Shanty Town spot. Some of their dishes, the sizzling beef in Chinese black bean sauce and chicken à la Sichuan (both

Ts10,000) being but two, are a delight and this is a wonderful place to sit with a jasmine tea – or something stronger – and reflect on your trek. Just round the corner, *10210* (pronounced 'ten-to-ten'; Wed-Mon 10am-10pm) is a pizza joint and the sister of Indoitaliano (see p207), which doesn't let its sibling down in any way, serving great pizzas for Ts8000-10,000 and an extensive Indian menu too.

Finally, *Green Bamboo* is a massive place, open all day (8am-late) and specializing in barbecued meat, with 250g of lamb, beef or pork for Ts4500, or it's Ts17,000 for the whole kilogram. There are also pizzas for those who don't fancy meat-munching, and salads to balance all that protein. The main attraction, however, is the lovely (and huge) garden where you can feast on flesh while listening to the strains of 'Bringing in the Sheep' on the Hammond organ being piped through the speakers – the restaurant is, after all, located in the Lutheran Hotel.

NIGHTLIFE
Currently the most popular place for a big night is *Glacier Bar* in Shanty Town on Sekou Toure Way. Open every night (daily, 5.30pm-when last customer leaves), it's hectic at the weekends, particularly on Fridays when they host live bands. Also in Shanty Town, *El Rancho* (see p208) comprises a fine restaurant and the best collection of booze in Moshi.

Back in the town centre, *Pub Alberto*, part of Chrisburger, has a couple of pool tables and a lively atmosphere and continues to gather a reasonable crowd at the weekends, though it's now under serious pressure from *Malindi Club*, a few metres west of Nyumbani Hotel. Entrance is through a set of concrete elephant legs; inside you'll find a cavernous, friendly place serving food and beer and showing football on the telly. A similar experience, though this time nearer most of the hotels, is provided by *East African Pub*, a real rowdy locals' hangout that lovers of English football will adore, with live premiership matches the main entertainment. They also serve a decent plate of *nyama*

choma (grilled meat). Offering a similar experience, though with more Westerners, *Pamoja Café* (8am to when last customer leaves) is a small place along from Indoitaliano. The food is fine, particularly their build-your-own breakfasts, but with a happy hour (5-7pm), premiership football on the big screen and occasionally thumping music, we think it's better for drinking than dining ... and in that respect it's great.

Rapidly losing business as Glacier Bar grows ever more popular, *La Liga* (Tue-Sun 8pm-1am; entrance Ts3000, Fri Ts5000, Sat Ts7000) is a two-floor club on the eastern outskirts of town, one block east of Shah Industries. It's OK though it can feel a little quiet these days.

For those who prefer a less frenetic end to their trip, there are few activities more pleasant than sitting at a **rooftop bar**, sipping a cold beer, staring at Kibo, and thanking God you're not up there! Kilimanjaro Crane Hotel, Nyumbani, Haria and Kindoroko can all help here (and you don't need to be staying at any of them to enjoy the privilege).

MOVING ON
By bus – Arusha and Marangu
Heading to **Arusha**, 'Coaster' buses (the small 30-seat minibuses) leave regularly throughout the day from the bus terminal on Mawenzi (Ts2500). For **Marangu** catch one of the dalla-dallas from the adjacent terminal (Ts1500).

The **shuttles** – Impala, Riverside – charge US$10 for the two-hour journey to Arusha. Services tend to leave at 6.30am and 11am. Riverside (☎ 0755-996453) are in Room 122 on the first floor of Voda House; Impala (☎ 0754-360658), in Impala Hotel and also in town next to Pub Alberto. If you book in advance, you should get picked up from your hotel, though emphasize this when buying your ticket.

By bus – Nairobi and Mombasa
Shuttle buses to Nairobi leave from outside their respective offices (see above). Riverside's leave at 6am and 11am (US$30). Impala also charge US$30 and operate two shuttles but theirs leave at 6.30am and

11.30am. Cheaper are the big **buses**, though for travel to Nairobi they're not recommended due to lack of comfort and the fact that they arrive at the bus terminal there after dark. There is also a bus to **Mombasa**, operated by Simba and travelling via Taveta, which leaves from the bus terminal at 9am daily and cost Ts20,000. They say it takes only six hours – we find this unlikely (eight hours seems more reasonable). Tickets can be bought from the bus terminal.

By bus – Dar es Salaam There are plenty of **bus** companies plying the route to Dar. Be careful, however: as we've already stated, this route is notorious for speeding and, as a result, horrific crashes; the traffic-calming measures installed along the road's length have reduced – but not eliminated – these, and have also helped to increase the total journey time from Moshi to something like 10 hours. The cheaper companies are best avoided; even though they could save you Ts5000 or more it's simply not worth it.

Three have managed to garner a reputation for safety, however: **Dar Express**, on Boma Rd, are still the best in our opinion with buses every half an hour from 7am to 10.30am (Ts28,000, or Ts30,000 on the

'luxury' bus that departs at 9am). Opposite are **Mtei Express**, with three buses daily at 8.30am, 9.30am and 10am (Ts28,000). They are adequate but the main rivals to Dar Express are **Kilimanjaro Express**, with six buses between 7am and 10am (Ts28,000); their offices can be found near Zara Tours' office on Rengua St.

By air
For details of flights out of **Kilimanjaro International**, see p349.

Getting to Kilimanjaro airport takes about 45 minutes from Moshi. There is no public transport and while you can take an Arusha-bound bus from Moshi and jump off at the junction, that still means you have to hitch the final 6km to the airport itself. Precision Air run a shuttle service (Ts10,000) to coincide with their domestic flights; the bus leaves from outside their office 2hrs prior to departure (though do check first). A **taxi** costs US$50 and while bargaining can reduce this, you'll struggle to get much of a discount at night.

Moshi does actually have its own airport and Coastal (🖥 www.coastal.co.tz) do occasionally call in to connect with most of their extensive East African network – but only if there's demand.

TREKKING AGENCIES IN MOSHI

Often cheaper than both Arusha and Marangu, Moshi captures the lion's share of the Kilimanjaro-trekking business, and some of the trekking companies in this town do a roaring trade. But beware: there is still a fair bit of monkey business going on here too, and you do need to be on your guard against cheetahs. For this reason we have compiled the following summary of some of the bigger agencies in town. Before booking with any, read the general advice given on pp36-40 about dealing with the trekking companies. Note, too, that often agencies lower their costs by hitting the wages of the crew; please, if you are going to book with one of these agencies, at the very least increase the amount in tips you pay your crew to compensate for their lower pay.

For details on how we arrived at the following reviews, please see box p186. And if you have any information or reviews on any agency, please send it to us – we'd love to hear from you.

Most companies listed include the following in their prices: airport transfers; a couple of nights in a hotel; transfers to and from Kilimanjaro at the start/end of the trek; park fees; food; basic camping equipment (tents, cooking equipment etc); wages of your staff. Where they don't we have tried to note it in the review.

● **African Scenic Safaris** (ASS; ☎ 0783-080 239, 🖥 www.africanscenicsafaris.com; contact Hostel Hoff, see p202) Recently featured heavily on Lonely Planet's Thorn Tree forum, and as a consequence picked up a lot of business. ASS are one of the cheapest operators on the mountain (Marangu, six days, US$1350, Machame, seven days, US$1600), though they were paying their porters fairly well according to KPAP. Oxygen does not come as standard on the treks though is only US$50 extra. Only operating a few treks at the moment but if they manage to keep their prices low and their ethical standards high they should be receiving a lot more business in the future.

● **Afrigalaxy** (☎ 027-275 0268; 🖥 www.afrigalaxytours.co.tz; CCM Regional Building, Ground Floor, Taifa Rd) A medium-sized company that's been around for about a dozen years but doesn't do too much to promote itself. Regarding treks, they offer a fairly decent service and I received one effusive email about them from a couple of their clients. However, they are one of the companies that perpetuate the myth that Machame is one of the quieter routes, which shows either ignorance or a laziness in not changing the emails they send out. Typical prices are: six days on the Marangu Route US$1250 per person; seven days on Machame for US$1450pp (US$1800 on the Western Breach); prices tumble quickly if there's more than one of you. Clients stay at Buffalo Hotel, airport transfers are US$45 extra but they were evasive when we asked how much they pay their porters (though to be fair, in the document they attached with their email there was, at the end, some sort of 'charter' for the welfare of their crews).

● **African Spoonbill Tours** (☎ 0713-408291, 🖥 www.africanspoonbilltours. com) is located on the first floor of the NHC Building on Rindi Lane near Stanbic Bank and, to their credit, were the first of all the Tanzanian agencies to respond to our initial enquiry though, as with several Tanzanian companies, their email seemed to be a fairly standard 'template' that didn't address many of the questions we set – including, for example, the one that asked how much they pay their porters. Using Buffalo Hotel (see p199) to house their clients, Spoonbill charge US$1630 per person for the seven-day Machame trek, or US$1410pp for six days on Marangu.

● **Ahsante Tours** (☎ 027-2750248; 🖥 www.ahsantetours.com; Plot 29-A Karanga Drive) Though no longer the rock-bottom cheapest, Ahsante are a reliable operator and have been adopted by a number of overseas travel companies (including Explore, Gap Challenge and Discover Adventure) as their agents on Kili. Overall: pretty good. Example prices: US$1770 per person Machame for seven days, Marangu six days US$1520pp; they also operate on the Western Breach, with a seven-day Machame climb via Western Breach US$2070pp. Accommodation is at their new place, Weru Weru River Lodge (see p204); airport transfers are US$80 each way, and oxygen is an extra US$100.

● **Akaro Tours** (☎ 027-275 2986 or ☎ 0754-272124; 🖥 www.akarotours.com; National Social Security Fund Building, Old Moshi Rd) This company has been through a lot of upheaval over the past few years, from the tragic death of its owner to the loss of his former right-hand lady, Teddy, who went to set up her own company. These blows have been hard to bear, the feedback has been mixed recently and the number of clients seem to be dwindling. Still they are cheap at US$1400 per person (add another US$150 to take the Western Breach) for seven days on Machame, US$1200pp for six days on Marangu; oxygen (US$50) and airport transfers (US$50 each) are extra, though two nights at Kilimanjaro Crane Hotel (see p200) are included. Again, you need to ask yourself how they can keep the price so low and pay their porters a living wage – though in their email they *claim* to pay US$10 per day.

● **Bryson Adventures** (☎ 0754-318033; 🖥 www.brysonadventures.com; Mankinga Rd, behind the Coffee Shop) A newish outfit but one that seems to be doing a pretty brisk trade and which has already come to the attention of KPAP for their fair treatment of porters (which perhaps isn't surprising, given the proximity of their offices). Their email was polite, informative and well organized and the prices good too, at US$1320 per person for six days on Marangu and US$1600 for seven days on Machame. Given that this includes two nights at Moshi's Bristol Cottages (see p201), airport transfers and oxygen, we're surprised it's that low so do check all their claims carefully (though, to be fair, the only review I've read about them was an effusive one). Certainly worth checking out.

● **Chagga Tours** (☎ 0754-597 109; 🖳 www.chagga-tours.com; PO Box 7746, office in Kiboriloni, about 3km east of town on the road to Dar) Another outfit that's been undergoing a lot of upheaval recently with the departure of the German part of the partnership, though it is still involved in organizing the Kili[Man] Challenge (see p30). Regarding their climbs, they're slightly pricey at US$1970 for seven days on Machame, US$1575 for six days on Marangu, not including oxygen (US$60 extra) though they do include two nights at Moshi's Keys Hotel (see p201). Also quite renowned for doing cycling tours that go right round Kili.

● **dotcom safaris** (☎ 027-275 4104; 🖳 www.dotcomsafaris.com; Kaunda St) One of Moshi's oldest budget outfits, still clinging to survival by offering fairly basic treks at a pretty cheap price: Machame Route, seven days, US$1430 per person; Marangu Route for six days US$1300pp. Two nights in their own rooms above their office and oxygen on the mountain are included – transfers US$50 extra. The review is necessarily brief because we've yet to meet anyone who's climbed with them, so can't really comment on their service.

● **Evans** (☎ 027-275 2612; 🖳 www.evansadventuresafaris.com; Memorial Stadium, 2km from Moshi) Evans are a typical Moshi outfit, being a longstanding company that aims squarely at the cheaper end of the market. If you're in the market for a budget trek and aren't too concerned about the wages of your mountain crew, they're worth investigating. Prices: US$1375 per person for six days on the Marangu Route; US$1538 for seven days on Machame, or US$1635 if going via the Western Breach. These prices also include two nights at Lutheran Uhuru Hotel and airport transfers.

● **Gladys Adventure** (☎ 0787-111881, 🖳 gladysadventure.com; Hill St) What started out as the best place to go for trekking-gear rental has now become one of the better and busiest trekking agencies in Moshi. Gladys herself is still running the show and her prices seem reasonable and the service great. The differences between the three budget levels of trek are mainly due to the hotels in which you stay before and after the trek. In brief, pre- and post-trek accommodation on the budget climbs (Marangu six days US$1366, Machame seven days US$1710) is at Aa Hotel (see p200), next to their office; Bristol Cottages (see p201) is the hotel they use for their mid-range treks (Marangu six days US$1425, Machame seven days US$1769), while Sal Salinero is the option for the luxury treks (Marangu six days US$1496, Machame seven days US$1886). Western Breach is US$180 extra, oxygen is always included – and overall they're pretty good and well worth checking out.

● **Hot Sun** (☎ 027-275 4037; 🖳 www.hotsunsafaris.com) Another company that will probably come and find you: their office is close to many of the tourist hotels. To be fair, their prices are very cheap, they seemed affable when we visited and their response to our email was succinct and honest. They also seem quite ambitious, with 'reps' in several European countries. Prices: US$1380 for seven days on Machame (US$1450 on Western Breach), with two nights at Buffalo Hotel (see p199) thrown in but oxygen US$150 extra. Note they also advertise open treks on their website that you can join. Worth investigating if you're in town and looking for a basement-budget trek.

● **Kessy Brothers** (☎ 0754-803953; 🖳 www.kessybrotherstours.com) There's little point in telling you where to find this company, for the truth is they'll come and find you if you stay in Moshi for more than a day or so and their adverts are fairly ubiquitous. They're a friendly bunch but with a few negative reviews online and from readers. In response to our email they gave us just one price, a fairly cheap US$1485 per person for seven days on Machame including two nights' accommodation. We couldn't quite credit all their claims – paying their porters US$10 per day for example, seemed particularly far-fetched! – and they also say that oxygen is included in the price, as are airport transfers and even kit hire! If it's true, it's very good value – so if you do decide to go with them, check everything very carefully and make sure it's all written down in a contract.

● **Keys** Keys Hotel (see p201 for contact details) Used by several overseas operators including International Mountain Guides, Tribes Travel and Wild Frontiers. Example prices: US$1570 per person for two people for six days on Marangu or it's US$1766 for seven days on Machame. Prices do not include airport transfers (US$70) but do include two nights at Keys. Experienced and thoroughly competent.

● **Kinyonga Tours and Safaris** (☎ 027-275 2218, 🖳 www.kinyongasafaris-tz.com) Kinyonga's office is now on Old Moshi Rd but they used to operate from the Kilimanjaro Guides' Cooperative hut at Marangu Gate, from where they still hire out equipment to trekkers. Their treks are fairly standard and cover all routes; price-wise, seven days on Machame was US$1500 if joining a group, or US$1700 if it's just the two of you; while for six days on Marangu it's US$1100 or US$1200 for a private trek. Accommodation is at Honey Badger (see p205) and oxygen is included in the price.

● **Marangu Kili-Colobus Travels** (☎ 0754-394 874, 🖳 www.kili-colobus.com; beside Stanbic Bank, Boma Rd) Founded by a group of ex-guides, Marangu Kili-Colobus has been around since 1997 without ever doing anything spectacular enough to merit a bigger write-up in the book than I've already given them. The email they sent included itineraries for every route on the mountain, which suggests that they send the same email to everyone who writes to them regardless of what the correspondent actually asked them – which is just lazy. Sample price: Machame for seven days with Western Breach, US$1550.

● **Moshi Expedition and Mountaineering** (aka **MEM Tours and Safaris**; ☎ 027-275 4234; 🖳 www.memafrica.com; Kaunda St) To be fair to MEM they're a fairly slick and professional agency that belies their location on dusty, dishevelled Kaunda St. The information they provided in response to our email enquiry was comprehensive and useful. Not exactly KPAP's favourite – their treatment of porters is reputed to be less than exemplary – they do at least organize some reasonable treks (private only), offering three standards. At the top is Stellar class, with smarter hotels and a service on the mountain that includes chemical toilets, oxygen, a greater ratio of guides and porters per trekker and two nights in Sal Salinero (see p203). While at the other extreme there's Budget class, with a luggage limit of just 10kg per person (you have to carry anything above this amount yourself!) and there's no accommodation or airport transfers included. For seven days on Machame the prices are US$1700-2100 depending on the class though, uniquely in my experience, the prices of their treks are seasonal and there are some considerable low-season discounts. Note that they do not currently organize treks via the Western Breach, though you can camp in the crater for an extra US$450 per person.

● **Mountain Kingdom Safaris** (MK; ☎ 0773-503 502, 🖳 www.mksafaris.com) With their head office in Dar and a small operations office in Moshi, MK offer only private treks on all the routes. The prices seem fair (Machame US$1816pp for two people for seven days, Marangu US$1511 for six days) though these exclude transfers and hotels and the oxygen is a whopping US$300 extra. Still, their safety record is good and overall they seem knowledgeable and fair; for example, they are one of the few that charges the same price if you go via the Western Breach or not, and only raise the price if you're staying at Crater Camp.

● **Pristine Trails** (☎ 0717-100788, 🖳 www.pristinetrails.com; Boma Rd in the YWCA, opposite Stanbic Bank) Outfit that has been around for over five years now and whose response to our email was one of the clearest and most comprehensible of all we received. Like many companies they offer three standards of trek – in this case Standard (two nights in Moshi Leopard Hotel, see p201, included but no emergency oxygen on the mountain), Luxury (two nights at Bristol Cottages, see p201; trek includes oxygen, toilet and pillows) and Exclusive (two nights at Sal Salinero, see p203; same as Luxury but with shower, sleeping cot, walk-in tents and day-pack porters) – and they also offered a complimentary 'coffee tour' to all their clients, which is a nice touch. Add to this the fact that KPAP are impressed with them and their prices are reasonable (US$1474-2119 per person for six days on Marangu depending on the standard, US$1762-2762 for seven days on Machame; add US$100 for Western Breach); overall this is a company that's well worth checking out.

● **Real Life Adventure Travel** (☎ 0732-972159; 🖳 www.reallifeadventure travel.com) Fairly unknown quantity, though one glance at their website shows they seem to have some sort of American connection, are knowledgeable when it comes to Kilimanjaro and support a number of charitable projects. Prices: US$2565 per person double occupancy for six days on Marangu including two nights at the pleasant Bristol Cottages in Moshi (or similar) and even a day tour of Marangu; US$3120 including *three* nights' accommodation for seven days on Machame; and it's US$3235 for the same deal on the Western Breach.

● **Shah Tours** (☎ 027-275 2370; 🖳 www.kilimanjaro-shah.com; Sekou Toure Way, Shanty Town) Long-established and family run, Shah are the owners of the Mountain Inn. Based in Shanty Town, when it comes to treks they're reliable and also reasonable, in part because their rates include two nights at their Mountain Inn base (see p203). Do watch out for hidden charges: they are the only agency I know, for example, who said they charged extra for the rental of a tent (US$10 per day) and an oxygen tank on the trek is priced at US$180. Costs: six days on Marangu US$1460 per person; seven days on Machame US$1640pp, or US$1790 if ascending via the Western Breach. KPAP alleges that their payment and treatment of porters is still a concern though they themselves claim they pay a generous US$10 to porters per day (each), with guides earning US$20 and cooks US$15 per day.

● **Snow Cap Mountain Climbing Camp** (☎ 027-275 4826; 🖳 www.snowcap.co.tz; CCM Regional Building, Taifa Rd) There's one reason to contact Snow Cap and one reason only: to do the Rongai Route, which they concentrate on more than any other company and which they did more than any other company to help popularize; indeed, they renovated the School Hut, the final hut on the standard Rongai ascent, and built the rather smart Snowcap Cottages on the Kenyan border by the start of the trek (see p205). Their price for seven days on the Rongai Route is US$2103 per person, including a night at the cottages and two nights at Sal Salinero in Moshi (see p203). They do operate on other routes, however, charging US$2162pp for a seven-day Machame trip and US$1890pp for six days on Marangu.

● **Summit Expeditions and Nomadic Experience** (SENE; ☎ 027-275 3233, US toll free 1-866-417-7661; 🖳 www.nomadicexperience.com) Run by the irrepressible force of personality that is Simon Mtuy – an ultra-racer and the holder of the record for the fastest unaided ascent and descent of Kili (see p122) – Summit Expeditions deserve mention for the respect and kindness they show to their porters, with the whole crew, porters included, invited to the post-trek celebratory meal with the trekkers at the end of every climb. Different from other companies in Moshi, SENE concentrate mainly on the Lemosho/ Western Breach Route for which they charge a steep US$3800, though this is for a total of eleven days (with eight on the mountain) and includes a stay at Simon's cottages and farm at Mbahe village, 15 minutes' west of Marangu Gate. They can arrange a Machame climb too (US$3245 for a ten-day package including seven days on Kili and nights at Mbahe), or US$2400 for Marangu Route for a nine-day package with six days on the mountain. Those who trek with this company are often effusive in their praise – I have received some truly glowing reports from delighted trekkers about this bunch – and they're also beloved by KPAP too, mainly for the fact that they are one of the few wholly Tanzanian companies to follow KPAP's guidelines. Not cheap, but by all accounts worth it.

● **Tanzania Experience** (☎ 0786-413334; 🖳 www.tanzania-experience.com) One of the better companies when it comes to treating their porters well according to KPAP, Tanzania Experience have been operating since 2007 on three routes, Marangu, Machame and Lemosho, with scheduled departures as well as private climbs. Prices are average at US$2000pp for two people for six days on Marangu (private climb), US$1960 for six days on Machame (two nights accommodation and airport transfers included, oxygen on the mountain extra). Note they do not offer treks up the Western Breach due to safety concerns.

● **Tanzania Journeys** (☎ 027-275 4296; 🖳 www.tanzaniajourneys.com) Formed in 2006, Tanzania Journeys boast a UK connection, are friendly and profess an ecological and humanitarian outlook. In response to our email we found them honest, well-informed and reasonably priced (Marangu six days US$1805pp, Machame seven days US$2025pp; add US$200 for the Western Breach – though they don't recommend that you take this route), including *three* nights B&B in Moshi's Bristol Cottages (see p201) and transfers from either Kilimanjaro Airport or, unusually, Nairobi.

● **Tanzanian Trails** (☎ 0766-830039, 🖳 www.tanzaniantrails.com; next to Pamoja Café) A relatively new company set up by a former guide and his British wife, Tanzanian Trails operate out of their café of the same name and offer reliable, straightforward treks at a keen price (Marangu, six days, US$1550pp, Machame, seven days, US$1850pp, with Western Breach US$2250pp, including oxygen, airport transfers and two nights at Osy Grand Hotel, see p201). Their response to our email was prompt and clear and they have a keen ethical edge too, working with the Australian NGO Team Vista and offering clients the chance to do some voluntary work prior to their trek. Overall, pretty new but seem to be doing a good job.

● **Trans-Kibo Travels Ltd** (☎ 0754-287618; 🖳 www.transkibo.com; YMCA Building, Kilimanjaro Rd) Some companies surprise you with their tenacity, and Trans-Kibo Travels is definitely one of these. Still operating out of shabby offices in the YMCA, they manage to survive while other, bigger companies stumble and fall. That said, though their email boasts they've been going for over 25 years, I've never met anyone who's actually climbed with them so cannot comment on their service. Still, prices are fair (KPAP would say that it's because they don't pay their mountain staff much) with a six-day trek on the Marangu route just US$1300, while seven days on Machame is US$1500, including accommodation and airport transfers. Prices fall by US$50pp on Marangu and US$100 on Machame if there are six or more of you. For Western Breach add US$200pp.

ARUSHA, MOSHI & MARANGU

● **Trek2Kili** (☎ 0788-360715; 🖳 www.trek2kili.com) North-American and Tanzanian initiative founded by a Canadian woman and her local friend which has been operating for about five years now. They seem to have everything going for them: a good success rate, an association with KPAP and a desire, if their emails are anything to go by, to genuinely treat porters well. They have fair prices too, with US$1550 for six days on Marangu and US$1800 for seven days on Machame, with a portable toilet, airport transfers and two nights at pleasant Bristol Cottages (see p201) thrown in (though oxygen is US$100 extra). Their claim to use only two porters per trekker seems low, perhaps suggesting that the level of service is a little less than some companies; but I'm probably nitpicking, because overall they seem fine and for those after a trek at the budget end of the market, Trek2Kili should be seriously considered.

● **Zara Tours** (☎ 0784-451 000, toll-free 1-866-550-4447; 🖳 www.zaratours.com; Rindi Lane) They may come last in the *Yellow Pages* but they're still the biggest agency on the mountain, even though their presence in the town centre is limited to a small office near the Clock Tower. Even grumbles from some clients about the equipment or service do little to dent their popularity, particularly with overseas agents, with Ultimate Kilimanjaro just one of many companies that uses them. Still, they are competent, no doubt, and it's encouraging to hear rumours that they are becoming more interested in ecotourism and porter welfare. Published costs: Marangu US$1763 for six days; Machame US$1885 for seven days, though there's a premium of US$200 per person if you want a private trek. Airport transfers are US$40 extra; accommodation is, of course, in their own Springlands Hotel (see p203).

Village Education Project Kilimanjaro (VEPK)

This charity was founded in 1994 by Katy Allen, who gave up her (presumably lucrative) career as a lawyer in London to live and teach in Mshiri, a small village on the slopes of Kilimanjaro. The aim of the charity she founded is simple: to provide local children with the education they need to become self-supporting and responsible citizens. While understanding that, in an ideal world, the Tanzanian education system should be doing this, Ms Allen also recognized the shortfall in the standards of teaching in some parts of the country, and in particular rural Tanzania.

Almost 20 years later VEPK now has an extensive primary education program in Tanzania's government primary schools of Moshi Rural District, helping teachers to improve their subject knowledge and teaching methods through regular seminars. They also help to raise the standards of school management through training and supporting headteachers as well as running projects to supply schoolbooks and other teaching materials. VEPK uses both locals and experts from the UK and Australia to train school staff.

In addition to this work with primary schools, VEPK has also branched out into vocational training for older kids, with a school opening in 1999 in Mshiri. Students are taught skills in carpentry, motor mechanics and masonry and they regularly achieve 100% in the end-of-year national exams. The charity has also benefited from the students' training, with many of the classrooms, and much of the furniture, kitchen and lavatory block built by them.

The charity is funded by donations as well as the small amounts they earn from their café (see p218), campsite (see p219) and, of course, from the occasional charity climb. For details on these climbs as well as how to donate directly, please visit their website at 🖳 www.kiliproject.org.

Marangu

According to legend, Marangu got its name when the first settlers in this part of Kilimanjaro, astonished by the lush vegetation, well-watered soils and the countless waterfalls they found here, cried out in delight 'Mora ngu! Mora ngu!' ('Much water! Much water!'). It remains a verdant and extremely attractive place, at least once you move away from the small huddle of shops and hustlers by the bus stop (situated in a part of the town called Marangu Mtoni, which literally translates as 'Marangu in the River') and start to climb up the hill towards Marangu Gate. The town, 14km along the Himo–Taveta highway, is extremely elongated but is in reality little more than two roads running up the mountain, with a filigree of dusty paths running off both.

WHAT TO SEE AND DO

Always one of the prettiest villages on Kili's slopes, for some reason over the past couple of years Marangu has become the unofficial centre of Chagga culture – and it's really fascinating. You can try to find many of the attractions yourself – they're all pretty well signed – but it's much nicer and easier to hire one of the local kids who'll doubtless come up to you to offer themselves as guides (give them around Ts5000 per day); they can also show you some short-cuts which will save time. And while none of these 'Chagga' sights is going to have you rushing to the telephone exchange in order to tell your nearest and dearest back home of the wonders you have seen, nevertheless it's good to see some sort of revival of a fascinating culture that would otherwise be confined largely to the history books. What's more, though your interest in Chagga culture may be slight, the chance to walk around one of the prettiest, homeliest parts of Tanzania should not be passed up; it's a lovely way to spend a day.

The first port of call is usually **Kinukamori Falls** (daily 8.30am-6pm; US$5), just 10 minutes' walk up from the bridge. As lovely as these are, we feel that this is one sight that maybe should have been left as it was, for the addition of a **Hall of Chagga Culture** – an open-air series of statues or dioramas lining the eastern path down to the falls, each depicting some aspect of Chagga culture or history – it seems unnecessary and adds nothing to the beauty of the place. Indeed, with that God-awful statue of a woman about to plunge to her death that's now been installed at the top of the falls, this is one 'enhancement' that is anything but.

Still, some of the other sights are really absorbing. Falling into this category is **Chagga Living Museum** (US$2). The museum is right next to Kilimanjaro Mountain Resort, 10 minutes beyond the market place. The first exhibit is a reconstruction of a thatched Chagga house complete with livestock inside. (We have been told by several people that the Chagga kept their livestock indoors not out of fear they would be rustled by their neighbours but merely to save space outside.) The museum also has a reproduction of a chief's chair (modelled on a real chair owned by one of the local chiefs), as well as displays of traditional Chagga tools, farm implements, rope made from the bark of the *mringaringa* tree, a genealogical look at the history of the Chagga, some drums and a bugle made of kudu horn.

Just before the museum is a turn-off to many people's favourite attraction in Marangu, the delightful **Kilasiya Falls**. The waterfalls are just part of the attraction, for it's the local flora that really catches the eye and many of the plants have been labelled. Reached via a steep muddy path, the falls are exquisite; there are even a couple of natural swimming pools in the gorge for those who fancy a cold dip. It's a great place to have lunch. Like most waterfalls, there's a (negotiable) Ts5000 entrance fee.

Those who've really got a taste for all this Chagga culture may also like to venture east to the village of Mamba Kua Makunde. Walking up the hill from the main road you'll soon hear the sound of the **Chagga blacksmiths**, making anything from weapons to farm implements, often with little children working the bellows to keep the fires hot. It's free, though they'll sting you if you want to take a photo. Nearby, there are some underground **caves** once inhabited by the Chagga. Claustrophobic, dark and difficult for anyone bigger than a smurf to negotiate, they're not the most pleasant of attractions though they are, in their own way, fascinating.

Finally, for modern-day Chagga culture look no further than the twice-weekly **markets** (Monday and Thursday) in the main village square by the junction, which are lively and, by the end of the day, often quite drunken too.

And once you've done all of that? Well don't miss the chance to rest your weary limbs at the **Village Craft Shop** (Mon-Sat 9am-6pm), just behind the market above the river. Part of the Village Education Project Kilimanjaro (see box p216), you can buy souvenirs made by some of the pupils who have benefitted from the charity and there's a decent *café* here too.

PRACTICAL INFORMATION

ARRIVAL
Marangu is reached by **dalla-dalla** from Moshi (Ts1500) in about 60-90 minutes. Passengers are normally dropped by the junction next to the bridge in Marangu Mtoni, though occasionally they will drive up the hill to drop you off on your doorstep. If not, a ride in a **shared taxi** (six people on seats made for four) from the bridge to Marangu Gate costs Ts1000 – make sure you specify you don't want a private hire.

SERVICES
There's a **post office** (Mon-Fri 8am-1pm & 2-4.30pm, Sat 9am-noon) close to the bridge, a **telephone office** and round the

back an **internet facility** (Mon-Sat 8.30am-5.30pm) – though at Ts1500 for 15 minutes, it's better to wait until you get back to Moshi if you can.

WHERE TO STAY
Accommodation in Marangu is fairly luxurious and survives by catering to the tour-group trade. I don't know if there is something in the water here but the people who run many of these establishments are great company – from generous, laugh-a-minute Mark at Mountain Resort to the charming, professional Fred at Kibo Hotel; the kind, thoughtful and intelligent grandparents Lucy and Thomas Kimaro at Coffee Tree Campsite; and not forgetting the louche,

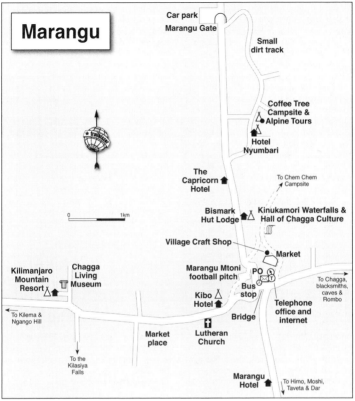

Marangu

Car park
Marangu Gate

Small
dirt track

Coffee Tree
Campsite &
Alpine Tours

Hotel
Nyumbari

The
Capricorn
Hotel

To Chem Chem
Campsite

Bismark
Hut Lodge

Kinukamori Waterfalls &
Hall of Chagga Culture

Village Craft Shop

Market

Kilimanjaro
Mountain
Resort

Chagga
Living
Museum

Marangu Mtoni
football pitch

PO

To Chagga,
blacksmiths,
caves &
Rombo

Kibo
Hotel

Bus
stop

To Kilema &
Ngango Hill

Telephone
office and
internet

Bridge

Market
place

Lutheran
Church

To the
Kilasiya
Falls

Marangu
Hotel

To Himo, Moshi,
Taveta & Dar

0   1km

dapper Mr Moshi at Bismark Hut – all sharp suit, cufflinks, feather in hat and twinkle in eye as he plucks peaches from his tree for you. The accommodation at these places is charming enough as it is but the personalities of these characters – and they *are* characters – provide an extra incentive to spend a night or two in the village.

One way to avoid the high price of staying in a hotel is to camp – an option that all the main hotels provide in addition to a couple of purpose-built places. The latter includes the wonderful *Coffee Tree Campsite* (☎ 0754-691433; 🖳 www.coffee treecampsite.com), which is an immaculate, manicured place to the east of the main

road leading up to Marangu Gate. Camping is US$10 per person (including use of the new glass-sided gas kitchen and the lovely little 'banana office', a lounge that's great to hang out in when it's pouring down), or it's US$12pp for a bed in the cosy chalet and US$20 in their new Mother Nature Home, the exterior of which is decorated with attractive murals of local sites. Tents can also be hired (US$10). **Alpine Tours** are based here, arranging trips to waterfalls and other beauty spots around Marangu.

A second option is *Chem Chem* (contact Dilly Mtuy, ☎ 0754-312086), which is run by the Village Education Project Kilimanjaro charity (see p216). The site lies

1.5km up from the market past Kinukamori Waterfalls; a taxi there will cost Ts6000-7000, or a motorcycle taxi Ts3000.

Another option is **Kilimanjaro Mountain Resort** (see p221); the grounds are gorgeous, the facilities spotless and huge and they charge US$17, or US$30 including tent hire – plus you get to enjoy the bar/restaurant facilities of one of Marangu's most charming and luxurious hotels. Truly a lovely spot.

Camping is also available at **Nyumbani Hotel** (see below; US$10pp), **Kibo Hotel** (see right; US$10pp including use of kitchen and pool) and at **Bismark Hut Lodge** (US$7pp). This last place, run by the raffish and generous Mr Moshi, is also the nearest thing to budget **hotel accommodation** (☎ 0754-318338; sgl/dbl US$15/25) in Marangu. Its name, incidentally, comes from the name of the original first climbers' hut on Kilimanjaro (and which in turn was named after the famous 19th-century German chancellor, of course).

And that, alas, is it for 'cheap' accommodation here. Some of the other places in the village, however, while not 'budget', do at least offer some sort of value for money. Near Coffee Tree Campsite is the friendly **Nyumbani Hotel** (☎ 0754-277300; 🖳 www .nyumbanihotels.com) a sister of the new place in Moshi. Formerly Hotel Nakara – you can still see the signs up outside – presumably the Nyumbani will, like its predecessor, aim to grab its share of the tour-group trade, though independent trekkers are welcome if there's space (rack rates US$90pp for B&B, US$95 half-board, or US$100 full board; single supplement US$20).

On the main road, **The Capricorn Hotel** (☎ 027-275 1309, ☎ 0754-841981;

🖳 www.thecapricornhotels.com) is made up of a number of buildings, some older (and therefore cheaper) than others, and charges US$45-60pp. If you don't mind spending at least US$120pp to stay in the gorgeous Kisera House, up the hill behind the main reception building. More like a home than a hotel, and a particularly smart home at that, there's something decidedly colonial about the décor and furniture at Kisera House, from the plush carpets to the chandeliers and a four-poster bed that's so high it comes with its own set of steps. Then there's the splendid garden, too, a real labyrinth of flowers, birds and streams.

No hotel review of Marangu would be complete without mentioning **Kibo Hotel** (☎ 0754-038747; 🖳 www.kibohotel.com) which, whilst it cannot compete with most of the others here in terms of luxury or comfort, cannot be beaten when it comes to character and history. Recently reopened after a two-year hiatus, the hotel still displays a sign welcoming former US president Jimmy Carter above the entrance – it's a perfect symbol of the faded yet fascinating grandeur of the place, and of the time-warp it appears to be living in now. Indeed, rather comfortingly, the place hasn't changed one iota since we first visited in 2001, save for the ever-growing array of flags, T-shirts and banners from trekking groups that decorate the dining-room walls. Antique German maps and other paraphernalia from the last two centuries adorn reception. The rooms are a tad overpriced (sgl/dbl US$42/66) but I think it's worth it just to wallow in this much nostalgia; it remains an absorbing place to wander around even if you don't intend staying. Lunch (currently US$10) and dinner (US$15) are also available. The

---

❏ **Abbreviations**

Throughout this book we have used the following abbreviations when writing about accommodation: **pp** means per person; **s/c** is short for self-contained, a local term meaning that the room comes with a bathroom (ie the room is en suite or a bathroom is attached); while **sgl/dbl/tpl** means single/double/triple rooms. So, for example, where we have written 's/c sgl/dbl/tpl US$35/40/45', we mean that a self-contained single room costs US$35 per night, a self-contained double costs US$40 and a self-contained triple costs US$45.

urbane, honest manager, Fred Moshi, is gloomy about the prospects of the place and the agencies are largely sending their clients to other establishments now; one can only hope it gets the investment it needs to spruce it up and get the hordes returning again.

Further up the road, 10 minutes past the market and right by Chagga Living Museum, is a relatively new place (by comparison) that makes all the others in Marangu look a little tired. Run by the warm and amiable Mark William Njiu – who was born and raised on site and who, in his capacity as an architect, built the hotel – and his jovial wife Elizabeth, *Kilimanjaro Mountain Resort* (☎ 0754-693461, 💻 www.kilimountresort.com; sgl/dbl/tpl US$133/200/293, full board US$169/272/401) is luxurious and lovely, with sumptuous rooms that boast huge bathrooms with powerful, multi-jet massage showers, digital TVs and their own balconies facing towards Kili's summits. The grounds are gorgeous (with geese and tortoises roaming around), the bar is beautiful, there's internet access (US$5 for 15 mins), a gym, Jacuzzi and massage service (US$40) and the roof terrace is terrific, with views of Kili and Lake Jipe to boot. A new block with state-of-the-art rooms has recently been added, bringing the total number to 42. Several foreign tour agencies have discovered this place – African Walking Company (see p186) amongst them, who use it for their clients heading for the Rongai trek; if you have the time,

energy and money to join them, you won't be disappointed.

Finally, there's another old favourite (and we mean '*old*'!) – the building used to be a farmhouse and it was built in the early 1900s – *Marangu Hotel* (☎ 027-275 6594; 💻 www.maranguhotel.com). The hotel is a couple of kilometres south of town (about a 10-minute walk) on the way to Himo and it stands in 12 acres of gardens (with pool). The food is great too, and rates are sgl/dbl US$65/100 in the low season, US$100/150 in the high. Their main claim to fame, however, is not the hotel, as venerable and comfortable though it may be, but their treks – about which, see below.

MOVING ON

Dalla-dallas back to Moshi leave when full from the main junction at Marangu Mtoni; don't worry about finding one – they'll find you.

There's also a **bus** straight from here to Dar es Salaam: every day at about 7am a Meridian bus drives through on its way from Rombo, further north; the total travel time to Dar is about seven hours. The only other option is to catch a dalla-dalla to Moshi and reserve a seat there; it is in theory possible to stop a Dar-bound bus on the Moshi–Dar highway at Himo, though travellers who try this usually end up waiting for hours for one with a spare seat, and eventually most give up. However, with the improvement in the road north to Taveta, one can easily see more buses passing through between Dar and Kenya.

TREKKING AGENCIES

● **Marangu Hotel** (see above) Few companies can boast the pedigree and experience of Marangu Hotel, which has been sending climbers up Kilimanjaro since – wait for it – 1932! What's more, their reputation is one of the best too – superb guides who work *only* for them, and an endorsement from KPAP who reckon they are the best amongst the 'budget' agencies for their fair treatment of porters. Indeed, all the crew are introduced to the clients at the beginning of the trek and at the end it's customary for everyone to share a celebratory drink together. As for their service, it's efficient without being exceptional, save for the wooden trekking poles they give to each of their clients to keep – a nice touch. Current charges: US$1480 per person for six days on Marangu (two people); US$2035 for seven days on Machame. Note that these prices are exclusive of: accommodation (for which they charge the low-season rates to their climbers of US$70/100 sgl/dbl), oxygen (US$200 per trip) and airport transfers (US$70 from Kili Airport).

ARUSHA, MOSHI & MARANGU

6

SAFE & MINIMUM IMPACT TREKKING

Safe trekking

Came to cave. Men cold. Passed two corpses of young men who died of exposure, a short time ago. The vultures had pecked out their eyes, the leopards had taken a leg from each.

From the diary of **Peter MacQueen** as recorded in his book
In Wildest Africa (1910)

Because of the number of trekkers who scale Kilimanjaro each year, and the odd ways in which some choose to do so, many people are under the mistaken impression that Africa's highest mountain is also a safe mountain. Unfortunately, as any mountaineer will tell you, there's no such thing as a safe mountain, particularly one nearly 6000m tall with extremes of climate near the summit and ferociously carnivorous animals roaming the lower slopes.

Your biggest enemy on Kilimanjaro, however, is likely to be neither the weather nor the wildlife. KINAPA are shy about revealing how many trekkers die on Kili each year, though the most common estimate I've heard is ten. The main culprit behind these fatalities is nearly always the same: the altitude.

The authorities do try to minimize the number of deaths: guides are given some training in what to do if one of their group is showing signs of acute mountain sickness, or AMS, and trekkers are required to register each night upon arrival at the campsite and have to pay a US$20 'rescue fee' as part of their park fees (though what this actually gets you is unclear). But you, too, can do your bit by avoiding AMS in the first place. The following pages discuss in detail what AMS actually is, how it is caused, the symptoms and, finally, how to avoid it. Read this section carefully: it may well save your life. Following this, on p230 you'll find details of other ailments commonly suffered by trekkers on Kilimanjaro.

(Incidentally, for those climbing Meru the above introduction and the following advice are all relevant. Of course, given Meru's lower altitude, the risks of AMS are consequently lower – though this is offset by the slightly higher – though still minimal – risk of attack by wildlife!)

WHAT IS AMS?

AMS, or **acute mountain sickness** (also known as **altitude sickness**), is what happens when the body fails to adapt in time to the lack of air pressure at altitude. In the first edition we stated that 'at Uhuru Peak, the summit of Kilimanjaro, the oxygen present in the atmosphere is only half that found at sea level'. This is not quite the case as reader Janet Bonnema pointed out for the second edition – and her teachings are worth repeating in this fourth edition too. As Janet explains, throughout the troposphere (ie from sea level to an altitude of approximately 10km), the air composition is, in fact, always the same, namely 20% oxygen and nearly 80% nitrogen. So it's not the lack of oxygen that's the problem but the lack of *air pressure*. As Ms Bonnema writes: 'The atmospheric pressure drops by about 1/10th for every 1000m of altitude. Thus the air pressure at the top of Kilimanjaro is approximately 40% of that found at sea level.' In other words, though each breath inhaled is still 20% oxygen, just as it is at sea level, it becomes much harder to fill your lungs since the atmosphere is not 'pushing' so much air into them. As a result, every time you breathe on Kibo you take in only about half as much air, and thus oxygen, as you would if you took the same breath in Dar es Salaam. This can, of course, be seriously detrimental to your health; oxygen is, after all, pretty essential to your physical well-being. All your vital organs need it, as do your muscles. Your lungs load your red blood cells with oxygen and then your heart pumps them round your body delivering oxygen to your muscles and organs as they go.

Problems arise at altitude when that most vital of organs, the brain, isn't getting enough oxygen and malfunctions as a result; because as the body's central control room, if the brain malfunctions, so does the rest of you, often with fatal consequences. Fortunately, your body is an adaptable piece of machinery and can adjust to the lower levels of oxygen that you breathe in at altitude. Unconsciously you will start to breathe deeper and faster, your blood will thicken as your body produces more red blood cells and your heart will beat faster. As a result, your essential organs will receive the same amount of oxygen as they always did. But your body needs time before it can effect all these changes. Though the deeper, faster breathing and heart-quickening happen almost as soon as your body realizes there is less oxygen, it takes a few days for your blood to thicken. With Kilimanjaro, of course, a few days is usually all you have on the mountain, and the changes may simply not happen in time. The result is AMS.

There are **three levels of AMS**: mild, moderate and severe. On Kilimanjaro, it's fair to say that most people will get some symptoms and will fall into the mild-to-moderate categories. Having symptoms of mild AMS is not *necessarily* a sign that the sufferer should give up climbing Kili and descend immediately. Indeed, most or all of the symptoms suffered by those with **mild AMS** will disappear if the person rests and ascends no further that day; assuming they make a full recovery while resting, the assault on the summit can continue. The same goes for **moderate AMS**, though here the poor individual and his or her symptoms should be monitored far more closely to ensure they are not getting any worse and developing into **severe AMS**. This is a lot more serious and sufferers with severe AMS should always descend immediately, even if it means going down by torchlight in the middle of the night.

The following describes the symptoms of the various levels of AMS, while **there's a more comprehensive and more scientific summary of acute mountain sickness on p366**.

What are the symptoms?

The symptoms of **mild AMS** are not dissimilar to the symptoms of a particularly vicious hangover, namely a thumping headache, nausea and a general feeling of lousiness. An AMS headache is generally agreed to be one of the most dreadful you can get, a blinding pain that thuds continuously at ever-decreasing intervals; only those who have bungee-jumped from a 99ft building with a 100ft elasticated rope will know the intense, repetitive pain of AMS. Thankfully, the usual headache remedies should prove effective against a mild AMS headache though do be careful as they can also mask any worsening of symptoms; and do tell your guide as he needs to know your symptoms and what you have taken to ease them in order to judge how well you're faring. As with a hangover, mild AMS sufferers often have trouble sleeping and, when they do, that sleep can be light and intermittent. They can also suffer from a lack of appetite. Given the energy you've expended getting to altitude in the first place, both symptoms can seem surprising if you're not aware of AMS.

Moderate AMS is more serious and requires careful monitoring of the sufferer to ensure that it does not progress to severe AMS. With moderate AMS, the sufferer's nausea will lead to vomiting and the headache will not go away even after pain-relief remedies; in addition the sufferer will appear to be permanently out of breath, even when doing nothing.

With moderate AMS, it is possible to continue to the summit, **but only after a prolonged period of relaxation** that will enable the sufferer to make a complete recovery. Unfortunately, treks run to tight schedules and cannot change their itineraries mid-trek. Whether you, as a victim of moderate AMS, will be given time to recover will depend largely upon how fortunate you are, and whether the onset of your illness happens to coincide with a scheduled rest day or not.

With **severe AMS**, on the other hand, there should be no debate about whether or not to continue: if anybody is showing symptoms of severe AMS it is imperative they **descend immediately**. These symptoms include a lack of coordination and balance, a symptom known as **ataxia**. A quick and easy way to check for ataxia is to draw a 10m line in the ground and ask the person to walk along it. If they clearly struggle to complete this simple test, suspect ataxia and descend. (Note, however, that this lack of coordination can also be caused by hypothermia or extreme fatigue, so ensure the sufferer is suitably dressed in warm clothing and has eaten well before ascertaining whether or not he or she is suffering from ataxia.) Other symptoms of severe AMS include mental confusion, slurred or incoherent speech, and an inability to stay awake. There may also be a gurgling, liquid sound in the lungs combined with a persistent watery cough which may produce a clear liquid, a pinky phlegm or possibly even blood. There may also be a marked blueness around the face and lips, and a heartbeat that, even at rest, may be over 130 beats per minute. These are the symptoms of either HACO and HAPO, as outlined below, while ways to treat somebody suffering from AMS are given on p228.

HACO AND HAPO

Poor Mapandi, a carrier whom I had noticed shivering with fever for the last day or two, stiffened, grew cold and died beside me in the mud.

Peter MacQueen *In Wildest Africa* (1910)

HACO (High Altitude Cerebral Oedema) is a build-up of fluid around the brain. It's as serious as it sounds. It is HACO that is causing the persistent headache, vomiting, ataxia and the lack of consciousness. If not treated, death could follow in as little as 24 hours, less if the victim continues ascending.

Just as serious, **HAPO (High Altitude Pulmonary Oedema)** is the accumulation of fluid around the lungs. It's this condition that is causing the persistent cough and pinkish phlegm. Again, the only option is to descend as fast as possible. In addition, one of the treatments outlined on p228 should also be considered.

GO *POLE POLE** IF YOU DON'T WANT TO FEEL POORLY POORLY – HOW TO AVOID AMS

Haraka haraka haina baraka 'Great haste has no blessing' – a common Swahili saying.

AMS can be avoided. The only surefire way to do so is to **take your time**. Opting to save money by climbing the mountain as quickly as possible is a false economy: the chances are you will have to turn back because of AMS and all your efforts (and money) will be wasted. According to one respected agency, their average success rates based on the number of days their clients' took in getting to the top are as follows:

6 days: 75% of clients made it to the top
7 days: just over 80%
8 days: 90%
9 days or more: over 98%.

As you can see, the longer you take the greater your chance of getting to the top.

According to the Expedition Advisory Committee at the Royal Geographical Society, the recommended acclimatization period for any altitude greater than 2500m is to sleep no more than 300m higher than your previous night's camp, and to spend an extra night at every third camp. But if you were to follow this on Kilimanjaro's Marangu Route, for example, from Mandara

* '*Pole pole*' is a phrase you'll probably hear more than any other on Kili. It's Swahili for 'slowly slowly' and is usually uttered by guides to dissuade their charges from ascending too fast.

Huts you would have to take a further *eight* nights in order to adjust safely to the Kibo Huts' altitude of 4713m – whereas most trekkers take just two days to walk between the two. The EAC realize that the short distances and high per diem cost of climbing Kilimanjaro make this lengthy itinerary impractical, so instead they recommend a pre-trek acclimatization walk on Mount Meru, or Mount Kenya (4895m to Point Lenana, the third highest peak on the mountain and the highest point that non-climbing 'trekkers' can reach). This is an excellent idea if you have the time and are feeling fit; providing you do one of these walks *immediately* before you climb Kili, these treks can be beneficial – and the views towards Kilimanjaro from Meru are delightful too (see pp235-247 for a description of this route).

But what if you don't have the time or money to do other climbs? The answer is to plan your walk on Kilimanjaro as carefully as possible. If you've enough money for a 'rest day' or two, take them. These 'rest days' are not actually days of rest at all – on the Marangu trail, for example, guides usually lead

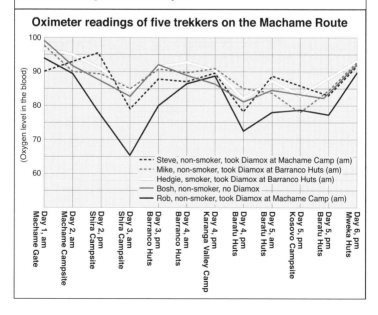

The table below shows the oximeter readings of five trekkers on the Machame Route. You can see how the amount of oxygen in the blood decreases as they ascend the mountain. Perhaps the most interesting feature of the graph, however, is the way that everybody's oxygen saturation declines and climbs at the same places. Despite the differences in each individual's readings, it may interest you to know that all of the climbers made it to the top. For information on pulse oximeters see p367.

Oximeter readings of five trekkers on the Machame Route

(Oxygen level in the blood)

- - - Steve, non-smoker, took Diamox at Machame Camp (am)
- - - Mike, non-smoker, took Diamox at Barranco Huts (am)
Hedgie, smoker, took Diamox at Barranco Huts (am)
——— Bosh, non-smoker, no Diamox
——— Rob, non-smoker, took Diamox at Machame Camp (am)

Day 1, am Machame Gate
Day 2, am Machame Campsite
Day 2, pm Shira Campsite
Day 3, am Shira Campsite
Day 3, pm Barranco Huts
Day 4, am Barranco Huts
Day 4, pm Karanga Valley Camp
Day 4, pm Barafu Huts
Day 5, am Barafu Huts
Day 5, pm Kosovo Campsite
Day 5, pm Barafu Huts
Day 6, pm Mweka Huts

their trekkers up from Horombo to the Mawenzi Hut at over 4500m before returning that same afternoon. But they do provide trekkers with the chance to experience a higher altitude before returning down the slopes, thereby obeying the mountaineers' old maxim about the need to '**climb high**, **sleep low**' to avoid mountain sickness.

The route you take is also important. Some of the routes – the Machame, Lemosho and Shira trails via the Barafu Huts, for example – obey the mountaineers' maxim on the third or fourth days, when the trail climbs above 4500m (around Lava Tower) before plunging down to an altitude of 3986m at Barranco Huts where you spend the night. Some of the shorter trails, however, do not: for example, it is possible for a trekker walking at an average pace on the Marangu, Umbwe or Rongai trails to reach Kibo in three days and attempt an assault on the summit for that third night. This sort of schedule is far too rapid, allowing insufficient time for trekkers to adapt to the new conditions prevalent at the higher altitude. This is why a higher proportion of people fail on these trails and it is also the reason why, particularly on these shorter trails, **it is imperative that you take a 'rest' day on the way up**, to give your body more time to acclimatize.

How you approach the walk is important too. Statistically, men are more likely to suffer from AMS than women, with young men the most vulnerable. The reason is obvious. The competitive streak in most young men causes them to walk faster than the group; that, and the erroneous belief that greater fitness and strength (which most men, mistakenly or otherwise, believe they have) will protect them against AMS. But AMS is no respecter of fitness or health. Indeed, many experienced mountaineers believe the reverse is true: the less fit you are, the slower you will want to walk and thus the greater chance you have of acclimatizing properly. The best advice, then, is to **go as slowly as possible**. Let your guide be the pacemaker: do not be tempted to hare off ahead of him but stick with him. That way you can keep a sensible pace and, what's more, get to know him better and ask him any questions about the mountain and Tanzania that occur to you along the way.

There are other things you can do that may or may not reduce the chance of getting AMS. One is to **eat well**: fatigue is said to be a major contributor to AMS, so try to keep energy levels up by eating as much as you can. Dehydration can exacerbate AMS too, so it is vital that you **drink every few minutes** when walking; for this reason, one of the new platypus-style water bags (Camelbaks), which allow you to drink hands-free without breaking stride, is invaluable (see p61).

Wearing warm clothes is important too, allowing you to conserve energy that would otherwise be spent on maintaining a reasonable body temperature. Although there hasn't been a serious study on this subject, many people swear that carrying your own rucksack increases your chance of succumbing to AMS. Certainly, in our experience, this is true, so, finally, **hire a porter to carry your baggage** (the agencies will assume you want this unless you specify otherwise anyway).

HOW TO TREAT AMS

Sat down beside P.D. in the mud. Gave him one bottle of champagne. Revived him greatly.
Peter MacQueen *In Wildest Africa* (1910)

It is possible that on your trek you will see at least one poor sod being wheeled down Kili, surrounded by porters and strapped to the strange unicycle-cum-stretcher device that KINAPA uses for evacuating the sick and suffering from the mountain. Descent is the most effective cure for AMS but in some severe cases it is not enough. **Diamox** (see box below) is also usually given, though again, if the victim has been suffering for a while, or Diamox is not available, some other treatment may be used such as:

Nifedipine is useful in treating HAPO though is hard to source in Africa and thus is seldom seen on the mountain. To administer the drug, prick a 10mg capsule many times with a pin before giving to the sufferer who should then chew it thoroughly before swallowing. If the victim then shows signs of breathing more easily, this should be repeated 15 minutes later. The drug has the side-effect of lowering blood pressure but can be most effective in helping treat victims of HAPO; some people even continue to ascend if they respond well to the drug – though we don't recommend this. **Dexamethasone** is useful

---

Diamox

Acetazolamide (traded under the brand name Diamox) is the wonder drug that fights AMS and the first treatment doctors give to somebody suffering from mountain sickness. It works because it is a **carbonic anhydrase inhibitor**. This means that the kidneys are forced to expel bicarbonate, thus re-acidifying the blood, which stimulates breathing, thereby allowing a greater amount of oxygen to enter into the bloodstream.

A lot of climbers were initially a bit sceptical about Diamox, worrying whether it actually helped to fight AMS or merely masked the symptoms. It was, after all, developed as a treatment for the eye disease 'glaucoma' and its beneficial effects on AMS sufferers were only noticed much later. Now, however, it seems widely accepted that it really is a most effective drug against altitude sickness. That's not to say that it works for everyone, however; for some reason, some people just don't seem to derive any benefit from the drug at all.

It's worth noting that while Diamox is widely regarded as a boon, there are still many questions to be answered about it. It's not unusual for climbers to be given different prescriptions by their doctors: some will have 125mg tablets, for example, and will be expected to take them twice a day; others (the majority) will have 250mg tablets and will be told to take them either once or, more often, twice per day; while still others will be issued with a single 500 or even 750mg tablet and told to take it only if they are feeling ill.

That last prescription leads us neatly onto the second major question about Diamox. Should the drug be used as a cure for when someone starts developing symptoms of mountain sickness? Or should it be used prophylactically, taking it daily from the start of the walk to prevent AMS occurring in the first place? The disadvantage with doing this, according to one doctor serving on the Annapurna Circuit in Nepal, is that by using Diamox prophylactically, you are using up one possible cure. That is to say, should you begin to suffer from AMS even though you've been taking

for treating severe AMS and, in conjunction with other treatments, in treating HACO. Two 4mg tablets should be given to the HACO sufferer, followed by one tablet every 6 hours until the victim has recovered.

Gamow hyperbaric bag This is a man-sized plastic bag into which the victim is enclosed. The bag is then zipped up and inflated. As it is inflated, the pressure felt by the sufferer inside the bag is increased, thus mimicking the atmospheric conditions present at a lower altitude. The disadvantage with this method is one of inconvenience. The cumbersome bag has to be taken up the mountain and, worst of all, in order to work effectively once the patient is inside, the bag must be kept at a constant pressure. This means that somebody must pump up the bag every two or three minutes. This is tricky when at least two other people are trying to manoeuvre the bag (with the patient inside it) down the slopes. Some of the upmarket trek operators carry one with them and KINAPA are trying to make this compulsory for all groups on the Western Breach. Certainly, while Gamow bags are essential in places where rapid descent is difficult, on Kilimanjaro (save for those staying at Crater Campsite, perhaps) several agencies now consider them to be gimmicky.

Diamox, doctors are going to have to look for another form of treatment to ensure your survival.

At the moment the jury is still out as to what is the best dose and prescription for Diamox, though for what it's worth I find that most people take them prophylactically, either at the very start of the trek or on day three when they are at an altitude of around 3500m or so; 250mg twice a day is the usual regime prescribed from here.

However you decide to take it, there are a couple of **rules you should always follow**: consult your doctor before taking Diamox to discuss the risks and benefits; and secondly, if you do take it, remember to try it out first at home to check for any allergic reaction, as Diamox is a sulfa derivative and some people do suffer from side effects, particularly a strange tingling sensation in their hands and feet.

Are there any other drugs that are as effective as Diamox?
I am grateful to reader Erasmus Schneider for pointing me in the direction of two studies that both suggested that the humble Ibuprofen could also be an effective weapon against altitude illness – and with fewer side effects. The first study, published in 2012 in *National Center for Biotechnology Information* (💻 www .ncbi.nlm.nih.gov) concluded that 'Compared with placebo, Ibuprofen was effective in reducing the incidence of acute mountain sickness.' A second study published in the same journal, concluded that 'Ibuprofen and acetazolamide were similarly effective in preventing high altitude headache. Ibuprofen was similar to acetazolamide in preventing <u>symptoms of</u> AMS [my underlining], an interesting finding that implies a potentially new approach to prevention of cerebral forms of acute altitude illness.' For the moment I would still recommend Diamox over Ibuprofen all the time – as the second study says, it is effective against the symptoms but not necessarily against the cause of altitude sickness – but it will be interesting to hear what other studies have to say in the future.

If you're farting well, you're faring well — other effects of altitude and acclimatization on the human body
In addition to AMS, there are other symptoms suffered by people at high altitude that are not in themselves usually cause for any concern.

The first is the phenomenon of **periodic breathing** (aka sleep apnoea). What happens is that, during sleep, the breathing of a person becomes less and less deep until it appears that he or she has stopped breathing altogether for a few seconds — to the obvious consternation of those sharing the person's tent. The person will then breathe or snore deeply a couple of times to recover, causing relief all round.

Another phenomenon is that of **swollen hands and feet**, more common amongst women than men. Once again, this is no cause for concern unless the swelling is particularly severe. Another one that is far more common among women than men, is **irregular periods**.

The need to **urinate** and **break wind** frequently are also typical of high-altitude living and, far from being something to be concerned about, are actually positive indications that your body is adapting well to the conditions. As is written on an ancient tombstone in Dorset:

> *Let your wind go free, where e'er you be,*
> *For holding it in, was the death of me.*

Oxygen Giving the victim extra oxygen from a bottle or canister does not immediately reverse all the symptoms, though in conjunction with rapid descent it can be most effective. One company, African Travel Resource (ATR), are now supplying their clients (for a fee) with an **ALTOX** system, where oxygen is fed to the client through cannulas inserted in their nose. It sounds uncomfortable but for those who are very worried about altitude, or who *know* they are susceptible, this could be the difference between success and failure.

OTHER POTENTIAL HEALTH PROBLEMS

Coughs and colds
These are common on Kilimanjaro. Aspirin can be taken for a **cold**; lozenges containing anaesthetic are useful for a sore throat, as is gargling with warm salty water. Drinking plenty helps too. A **cough** that produces mucus has one of a number of causes; most likely are the common cold or irritation of the bronchi by cold air which produces symptoms that are similar to flu. It could, however, point to AMS. A cough that produces thick green and yellow mucus could indicate bronchitis. If there is also **chest pain** (most severe when the patient breathes out), a high fever and blood-stained mucus, any of these could indicate **pneumonia**, requiring a course of antibiotics. Consult a doctor.

Exposure
Also known as hypothermia, this is caused by a combination of exhaustion, high altitude, dehydration, lack of food and not wearing enough warm clothes against the cold. Note that it does not need to be very cold for exposure to occur. Make sure everyone is properly equipped, particularly your porters.

Symptoms of exposure include a low body temperature (below 34.5°C or 94°F), poor coordination, exhaustion and shivering. As their condition deteriorates the shivering ceases, coordination gets worse making walking difficult and the patient may start hallucinating. The pulse then slows and unconsciousness and death follow shortly. Treatment involves thoroughly warming the patient quickly. Find shelter as soon as possible. Put the patient, without their clothes, into a sleeping-bag with hot water bottles (use your water bottles filled with hot water and wrapped in something to prevent burning the victim); someone else should take their clothes off, too, and get into the sleeping bag with the patient: there's nothing like bodily warmth to hasten recovery.

Frostbite

The severe form of frostbite that leads to the loss of fingers and toes rarely happens to trekkers on Kilimanjaro. You could, however, be affected if you get stuck or lost in particularly inclement weather. Ensure that all members of your party are properly kitted out with thick socks, boots, gloves and woolly hats.

The first stage of frostbite is known as 'frostnip'. The fingers or toes first become cold and painful, then numb and white. Heat them up on a warm part of the body (eg an armpit) until the colour comes back. In cases of severe frostbite the affected part of the body becomes frozen. Don't try to warm it up until you reach a lodge/camp. Immersion in warm water (40°C or 100°F) is the treatment. Medical help should then be sought.

Gynaecological problems

If you have had a vaginal infection in the past it would be a good idea to bring a course of treatment in case it recurs.

Haemorrhoids

If you've suffered from these in the past bring the required medication with you since haemorrhoids can flare up on a trek, particularly if you get constipated.

Snowblindness

Though the snows of Kilimanjaro are fast disappearing, you are still strongly advised to wear **sunglasses** when walking on the summit – particularly if you plan on spending more than just a few minutes up there – to prevent this uncomfortable, though temporary, condition. Ensure everyone in your group, including porters, has **eye protection**. If you lose your sunglasses a piece of cardboard with two narrow slits (just wide enough to see through) will protect your eyes. The cure for snow-blindness is to keep your eyes closed and lie down in a dark room. Eye-drops and aspirin can be helpful.

Sunburn

Protect against sunburn by wearing a hat, sunglasses and a shirt with a collar that can be turned up. At altitude you'll also need high-factor sunscreen for your face.

Care of feet, ankles and knees

A twisted ankle, swollen knee or a septic blister on your foot could ruin your trek so it's very important you take care to avoid these. Choose comfortable boots with good ankle support. Don't carry too heavy a load. Wash your feet and change your socks regularly. During lunch stops take off your boots and socks and let them dry in the sun. Attend to any blister as soon as you feel it developing.

Blisters   There are a number of ways to treat blisters but prevention is far better than cure. Stop immediately you feel a 'hot spot' forming and cover it with a piece of moleskin or Second Skin/Compeed. One trekker suggests using the membrane inside an egg-shell as an alternative form of Second Skin. If a blister does form you can either burst it with a needle (sterilized in a flame) then apply a dressing or build a moleskin dressing around the unburst blister to protect it.

Sprains   You can reduce the risk of a sprained ankle by wearing boots which offer good support. Watch where you walk, too. If you do sprain an ankle, cool it in a stream and keep it bandaged. If it's very painful you'll probably have to abandon your trek. Aspirin is helpful for reducing pain and swelling.

Knee problems   These are most common after long stretches of walking downhill. It's important not to take long strides as you descend; small steps will lessen the jarring on your knee. It may be helpful to wear knee supports and use walking poles for long descents, especially if you've had problems with your knees before.

Minimum impact trekking

'Manya ulanyc upangenyi cha ipfuve' – 'Do not foul the cave where you have slept' (A Chagga proverb that refers to the habits of the baboon who are said to 'foul their caves' until there comes a point where the stench compels them to find alternative accommodation.)

KINAPA (see p125) does try to keep Kilimanjaro clean. At all huts and campsites, trekking groups have their rubbish weighed by the ranger; if there's any evidence that some rubbish has been dumped (ie if the rubbish carried weighs less at one campsite than at the previous camp) the guide could have his licence temporarily revoked and/or have to pay a heavy fine. It's a system that would appear to have loopholes but until recently Kili *was* a very clean mountain, and though it can be frustrating to have to wait for your guide every morning while the rubbish is weighed, it's a small price to pay for a pristine peak. Sadly, standards appear to have slipped recently and there is now serious concern amongst trekking agents and environmentalists about the state of some of the trails. While it's easy to blame the authorities for the sorry state of Lemosho and other routes, trekkers are just as culpable. After all, much of it is our rubbish.

You can help Kilimanjaro become beautiful once more by following these simple rules (opposite) that apply to almost every mountain anywhere in the world.

SOME GUIDELINES FOR KEEPING THE MOUNTAIN PRISTINE

● **Dispose of litter properly** In theory, all you should have to do is give your litter to your crew: given the stiff punishments they receive for leaving rubbish behind (see opposite), this should ensure all waste is taken off the mountain. Unfortunately, despite all the cleaning crews and the weighing stations at each campsite, some think the litter situation is getting worse. Whatever you decide to do, don't give **used batteries** to porters; keep them with you and take them back to the West where they have the facilities to dispose of them properly (the batteries that is, not the porters).

● **Don't start fires** There's absolutely no need for fires on Kilimanjaro: for cooking, your crew should use kerosene, while for heat, put another layer of clothes on or cuddle up to somebody who doesn't mind being cuddled up to.

● **Use the purpose-built latrines** True, some of them could do with emptying (especially the toilet at the Barranco campsite, which is now so full that the pile of human waste is in danger of developing a snowy summit all of its own), but this is still better than having piles of poo behind all the bushes on the trail and toilet paper hanging from every bough.

● **Leave the flora and fauna alone** Kili is home to some beautiful flowers and fascinating wildlife but the giant groundsels rarely thrive in the soils of Europe and the wild buffalo, though they may look docile when splashing about in the streams of Kili, have an awful temper that makes them quite unsuitable as pets. It's illegal to take flora and fauna out of the park, so leave it all alone. That way, other trekkers can enjoy them too.

● **Boil, filter or purify your drinking water** This will help to reduce the number of non-returnable, non-reusable, non-biodegradable and very non-environmentally friendly plastic mineral water bottles that are used on Kili.

● **Stay on the main trail** The continued use of shortcuts, particularly steep ones, erodes the slopes. This is particularly true on Kibo: having reached the summit, it's very tempting on your return to slide down on the shale like a skier and you'll see many people, especially guides, doing just that. There's no doubt that it's a fast, fun and furious way to get to the bottom, but with thousands of trekkers doing likewise every year, the slopes of Kibo are gradually being eroded as all the scree gets pushed further down the mountain. Laborious as it sounds, stick to the same snaking path that you used to ascend.

● **Wash away from streams and rivers** You wouldn't like to bathe in somebody else's bathwater; nor, probably, would you like to cook with it, do your laundry in it, nor indeed drink it. And neither would the villagers on Kili's lower slopes, so don't pollute their water by washing your hair, body or clothes in the mountain streams, no matter how romantic an idea this sounds. If your guide is halfway decent he will bring some hot water in a bowl at the end of the day's walk with which you can wash. Dispose of it at least 20m away from any streams or rivers.

TOILET ETIQUETTE

The toilets at the various camps come in for a lot of stick from trekkers. And rightly so, too, because for the most part they're bloody awful. KINAPA recognizes as much and is attempting to improve the facilities, with many of the major campsites now boasting gleaming new toilets. But for the moment in a lot of the campsites you'll have to make do with the standard rough wooden sheds with a hole in the floor, the more sophisticated examples of which come with a door.

There's no doubt about it, some of the old 'long-drop' toilets are disgusting. But whatever their state and no matter how unpleasant they may be, you still have a duty to use them (unless you've paid for having a private toilet dragged up the mountain for your use, a privilege which usually costs around US$10 per day). There are few sights on Kilimanjaro more depressing than the clods and streamers of used toilet roll hiding behind rocks and hanging from bushes surrounding each campsite. It's hard to understand why some people think it's OK to sleep in a campsite surrounded by their own shit, rather than spending two minutes inside one of the public loos; but if you happen to be one of them, the following tips may help you overcome your terror of the toilet:

● If you're worried about being disturbed by a fellow trekker, on hearing someone approach try coughing, whistling, screaming or otherwise alerting them to your presence *before* they have a chance to invade your space.
● Conversely, when approaching the toilet, give any occupants inside fair warning of your presence by approaching noisily, treading heavily and knocking before entering. It's only polite.
● If it's the smell that worries you, a bandanna round your nose and mouth can help.
● Visiting the toilet in the early morning – when the stuff inside is frozen solid and the stench is reduced – is also a good plan.
● While you're inside the toilets you have a responsibility to keep things tidy. It can be difficult to maintain balance and aim but if you do miss, do the decent thing and tidy up.

Going outside

If you really, really, really can't wait to reach one of the toilets, the least you can do is deliberate before you defecate. Firstly, make sure you're at least 20m away from both the path and any streams – the mountain is still the main source of water for many villages and they would prefer it if you didn't crap in their H_2O. Secondly, take a trowel with you so you can dig a hole to squat over, and cover this hole with plenty of earth when you've finished. And finally, dispose of your toilet paper properly. One way is to try burning it. One reader has written in to say that it's very difficult to burn soggy toilet paper. The editor of a previous edition, however, conducted a controlled experiment and gave this advice: 'If you light the dry corner of partially wet loo paper and twirl it round so the flame dries the wet bit it *does* all burn up'. Give it a go next time you need to, er, go. Even better, why not adopt the 'pack it in, pack it out' method, ie put the used paper in a bag for disposal in the next toilet – the best approach for keeping the mountain clean.

If we all follow these rules maybe, just maybe, Kilimanjaro will remain Earth's most beautiful mountain – rather than resembling one massive, 5895m-high pile of poo.

MOUNT MERU

7

INTRODUCTION

Mount Meru, which overlooks Arusha from the north, is used by many trekkers as a **warm-up trek** – an *hors d'oeuvre* to the main course of Kili if you like. And a perfect starter it is too: though smaller, it's also quite similar in that to reach its volcanic summit you have first to climb through a number of vegetation zones before embarking on the final night-time march to the highest point on the crater rim and thus the summit itself. What's more, at 4566m it provides the trekker with the perfect opportunity to acclimatize to Kilimanjaro's rarified atmosphere. In other words, the mountain offers a taste of the challenges that lie ahead on Kilimanjaro, whilst also whetting the appetite for the thrills and beauty of that mountain.

However, Meru is worth doing as much for the differences as for the similarities it shares with its neighbour. In particular, there's the greater abundance of **wildlife**. Lying at the heart of Arusha National Park, a reserve that's teeming with animals, it's an odd trekker who doesn't finish the trek with his or her camera filled with pictures of buffalo, giraffe, elephant, bushbuck, dik dik, suni, colobus, blue monkey and warthog. Luckier ones may also see leopard and hyaena, while twitchers will be more than content with the number of birds on offer, from the noisy Hartlaub's turaco to the silver-cheeked hornbill and black-and-white bulbul.

If all this sounds like your idea of a perfect holiday – a safari-and-trek all rolled into one – you're probably right, though there is one point that needs to be emphasized: **do not underestimate Meru**. Though it may be more than a thousand metres lower than Kili, it's still well above the height necessary to bring about **altitude sickness** and with almost everybody taking just over two days before reaching the summit, the risks are great. There is also **more night-time scrambling** to be undertaken on the smaller sibling. Indeed, without a shadow of a doubt our most nerve-racking ascent was a few years ago on Meru and not Kili. True, this had much to do with the fact that there had been heavy rain the evening before the night-time walk to the summit, a downpour which quickly froze and caused the entire trail, from Saddle to summit, to become covered with a layer of ice. Inconvenient on the first part of that night-time walk, on the second half it became positively dangerous, causing us to scribble hurriedly a last will and testament in our notebooks. Indeed, it was thanks only to the hard work of the guides, who dug out footsteps in the ice with a piece of rock or the back of their heels – footsteps in which, taking our lead from King Wenceslas, we then trod – that we gained the summit at all. And it was only by inching our way back down, bottom pressed into the ice, limbs looking for any piece of rock or other non-slippery material to put our weight upon, that we made it back down to write this guide.

So though Meru may not carry the cachet, prestige or the sheer scale of Kili, it's no pushover – and maybe it's no coincidence that the first successful recorded ascent, though still in dispute (being credited to either Carl Uhlig in 1901 or Fritz Jaeger in 1904), occurred at least a dozen years after the conquest of Kilimanjaro. Meru remains an awfully big mountain – the 10th highest peak in Africa in fact – and as such it should be treated with the utmost respect.

PRACTICALITIES

The route
There is only one main route up Meru. It begins at Momela Gate, around 15km from the main Ngongongare entrance to the park where you pay your park fees. Having paid up and driven those 15km, past the plain known as Little Serengeti (Serengeti Ndogo) because of its similarity to Tanzania's most famous park, you arrive at **Momela Gate** (altitude 1597m) where you pick up your ranger and possibly hire your porters.

The route from Momela Gate to the summit is punctuated by **two sets of accommodation huts**: the first are the **Miriakamba Huts (2503m)**, a day's walk from Momela Gate; and the second are the **Saddle Huts (3560m)**, lying a short day's walk from there. From the Saddle Huts it's a further day's walk – or rather, a night's walk – to the summit.

Which path to take Though we just stated above that there's only one path to the summit of Meru, that's not entirely true for, in fact, on this first day there are **two possible paths**, the split between the two occurring just five minutes along the trail. Most trekkers, of course, will want to take both paths, one on the way up and the other on the way down. The question is, therefore, which path to take first?

Regarding these two trails, **the first** is a longer and more circuitous route that follows a 4WD dirt track as it swerves drunkenly and only very approximately along the course of the Ngare Nanyuki (the river you cross on a bridge right at the beginning of the trek) and Jekukumia rivers through the forest before turning north to cross the Crater Plain to the huts. As for the **second option**, this is a much more direct path and, on first sight at least, would appear to be the more tempting. It includes a crossing of the Meru Plain that's alive with Africa's tallest mammal (the giraffe) and its most bad-tempered (the buffalo), and could also take in a diversion to the beautiful Tululusia Falls (if you haven't already visited them on the way up, of course, which is where we describe them on p239). Weirdly, there's very little forest on this route, the path sticking to the top of a grassy, largely tree-less ridge.

Unless you specify otherwise the chances are your ranger/guide will take you on this shorter, steeper path; and it is indeed a wonderful walk. However, we advise you to leave this option until the end and instead **choose the longer trail for your ascent**. Why? Simply because, in our experience, most trekkers are too tired on the last day of their trek to attempt the longer trail on the way down, whatever their intentions when they began their trek. (Indeed, if you're on a three-day trek you may well not even have time to do the longer trail on the last day.) In other words, if you don't take the longer path now, for the ascent, the chances are you'll miss out on it altogether. There's also the matter of acclimatization to consider, for taking over four hours to climb the 906m to Miriakamba Huts is more sensible than taking just two or so, as you would on the shorter trail. So don't be too eager to get amongst the animals on the plain at the foot of Meru but instead choose the longer trail for your ascent and save the shorter trail for the way down; and this is how we've described the trek in the route description beginning on p239.

The cost

Trips up Meru are usually offered by the agencies in Arusha (the best place to organize such a trek) for either three or four days. Note that, unlike Kili, you don't actually need to book this trek through an agency but it is quite tricky to attempt it independently and probably not worth the hassle (see p238 for details). **Don't be misled into thinking that if you book a four-day trek you are more likely to reach the summit because of the extra day's acclimatization**; that extra day is actually spent on the *way down*, not up. So, while we like to have the extra day to descend – it's a bit too much of a rush otherwise to go from the summit to Momela Gate in one day and we were grateful to spend a second night at Miriakamba – if you're on a tight budget you'll save yourself a small fortune in **park fees** by taking a day less. These park fees tend to be a little cheaper than the equivalent charges on Kili and are as follows (all prices from July 2013):

- Conservation fee (formerly known as Park Entrance fee): US$45 per day (US$15 per day for under 16s)
- Hut fee: US$30 per night
- Rescue fee: US$20 per trip
- Guide/ranger fee: US$15 per day

Thus for a four-day/three-night trip you're looking at a total figure of US$350. On top of this you'll probably need to pay the equivalent **porters/guide fees** to enable them to enter and stay in the park. Their conservation fees are charged at Ts2000 per day, while their hut fees are just Ts1500. So, for example, if your agency has supplied you with a guide, cook and four porters, the total amount you'll be paying will be:

- Entrance fee: Ts2000 x 6 people x 4 days = Ts48,000
- Hut fee: Ts1500 x 6 people x 3 nights = Ts27,000
- Making a grand total of: **Ts75,000**

MOUNT MERU

All these fees will be factored into the total amount the trekking agency charges for your trek so needn't concern you too much here. However, you may have noticed in the above examples that there are in fact two guides in the party: one supplied by the agency and one by the park (whom we have called a ranger/guide to avoid confusion). The **ranger/guide** supplied by the park **is compulsory**, for it is he who carries the gun that, should any of the local fauna take an unhealthy interest in your party, could come in very handy. However, these rangers in our experience are often better guides, with good English and a greater knowledge of the park, mainly because they spend most of their time in it. Indeed, on one of our treks we didn't even see the guide who had been supplied by the trekking agency until we got to the Miriakamba Huts at the end of the first day!

Doing it independently

It is this over-supply of guides that leads some tourists to consider doing the whole thing independently without signing up to any trekking agency. True, it *is* tempting but there are a few things to consider first.

For one thing, you will need to **arrange transport to and from the park**; there is public transport, in the form of a dalla-dalla that calls in at the park gate between Arusha and a couple of tiny villages to the north of the park, but it's irregular and it would be difficult to rely on it to get you to and from the park. (It might be an idea to bring a tent in case you miss the last/only dalla dalla and have to sleep at one of the campsites.) Secondly, you'll have to **bring all the food and supplies** you'll need. Thirdly, all this luggage means you'll probably **need to hire porters**, which can be done at Momela Gate at the start of the trail, though you'll need to pay the full Ts15,000 per day wage and to organize them yourself as there'll be no-one to do it for you. What's more, you will still need to take a park ranger – they're compulsory. And while you can pay your park fees by credit card, you'll need to bring a variety as many don't seem to work. So, while the idea of doing the whole trek independently may sound attractive, you do need to have a certain amount of confidence to bring it all off, especially when it comes to organizing your porters, a job that's outside the ranger's remit but is perhaps the most useful purpose of the trekking agency guide.

So, yes, it is possible to go up Meru independently but the saving, money-wise, will be negligible. Indeed, only if you've a real aversion to agencies or fancy the challenge should you attempt it.

Trekking with an agency

Perhaps not surprisingly, therefore, most people choose to sign up with an agency in Arusha. Rates start at around US$700pp for four days. You may want to factor into this fee a night or two at one of the lodges near the park. This will enable you to make an early start in the morning (though treks are officially not allowed to start until 10am anyway, so as not to disrupt the animals' dawn hunt). One such is *Colobus Mountain Lodge* (☎ 027-250 2813), near the western Ngongongare Gate to the park. A good-value 18-banda lodge built around a large *makuti*-thatched reception-cum-bar, the rooms are all clean, airy and bright, while the gardens are flower-filled and attract a range of birds (as does, occasionally, the thatched roof of your banda). It gets mixed reviews but it's good value – if often eerily empty – at around US$100 per room full board.

Another choice is the rather more eccentric **Hatari Lodge** (☎ 0752-553456; 🖥 www.hatarilodge.com), which has real history and character. The lodge is named after the John Wayne film (see p360) that was shot on the farm. Indeed, one of Wayne's co-stars, a German actor called Hardy Krüger, actually ended up giving up Hollywood for Arusha, and bought the farm on which the lodge is set soon after the film was completed. Lying just outside the park's northern boundary, the only realistic way of getting to it is via the park itself so you have to pay the park fees. With a small library, long bar, breakfast terrace and great views of both Kili and Meru, this is a refreshingly different safari lodge with décor and location that are best described as quirky. Prices start at US$240 per person full board in the very low season, rising to US$320 in the high season. If you have the time, come here for a drink even if you're not staying.

STAGE 1: MOMELA GATE TO MIRIAKAMBA HUTS (VIA THE LONGER ROUTE) [MAP A, p241]

Distance: 13.8km; altitude gained: 906m

Though this longer route avoids the fauna-filled Meru Plain, there's still an abundance of wildlife to be seen on this trail. In addition to the beasts of the plain that

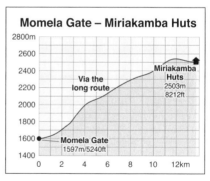

could still be espied behind the screen of acacias, within the first five minutes – no, make that three – of starting one trek up Meru we also encountered dik dik and suni standing motionless in the scrub lining the path, while a little further on a troop of baboons greeted our approach by turning their backs and displaying their red-raw backsides.

It's a hot and dusty start to the trek but a distinctly memorable one; even on this longer route we guarantee you'll see more animals within the first half-hour of your expedition than you would in a month on Kili. If your guide is amenable, you can also take the path off right to visit the impressive **Tululusia Falls**.

The scenery changes slightly as you reach the junction with the path to Campsite 3 and the path bends right (west), with both the gradient and the size of the trees increasing. (These campsites, incidentally, are not for the use of trekkers and can be ignored.) The first junipers, bearded with lichen, appear and the whole trail now takes on a lusher, greener aspect. Continuing up the hill, your guide, bored with the repetitive twists and turns of the official trail, may

The famous arched fig tree

take you on a well-known short-cut, emerging back onto the trail just before a stream with a marshy patch of grassland to the left – nicknamed **Meru's Garden** by the guides and often populated by bushbuck and blue monkey – and the summit beyond. A good opportunity for a photo, methinks. A second photo opportunity occurs just a minute later with the first of several sign-posted **Kilimanjaro viewpoints**.

Regardless of whether you take photos of these places or not, one sight which we can almost guarantee will have you reaching for your Rolleiflex is the **arched fig tree**, a magnificent strangler fig (*Ficus thonningii*) which has now completely enveloped its host and arches across the track. It is reminiscent of those pictures you see of giant redwoods in California which have cars driving through them – though in this instance it is said to have been elephants who have passed through the tunnel formed by the tree, widening the gap as they do so.

The path, illuminated by popcorn cassia (*Cassia didymobotrya*; incorrectly called candle bushes by many guides) in season, heads north soon after to cross an open area with a good view of the summit and possible sightings of buffaloes on the **Itikoni Plain** to the south of the trail. The northerly direction is but temporary, however, the path soon reverting south to acquaint itself with the sweet-water **Jekukumia River** at **Maio Falls**, at 2157m altitude a picturesque spot and a delightful place to break for lunch.

Rested and replete, you now return to the main track as it continues its weaving, wriggling way westwards up the slope. It's a pleasant stroll, the gradient seldom steep and the stands of juniper and podocarpus providing essential shade. The forest is still alive with animals, too, even though they may be more difficult to see. Your ranger/guide, however, should be able to point out the tracks of hyaena, snake, leopard, giraffe or buffalo and your walk will, more than likely, be accompanied by the bark of the bushbuck, call of the colobus monkey (which sounds curiously like a frog) and the broken-klaxon honk of

Leopard track (Mt Meru)

Hartlaub's turaco (which, just to confuse matters, sounds curiously like a monkey). If you're lucky, a crash in the undergrowth or in the branches will give away the precise location of these shy creatures, or indeed of giraffe or buffalo.

The scenery is just as pleasant as before lunch, but by now tiredness and a desire for change will probably have set in, along with a wish that the track, for a few metres at

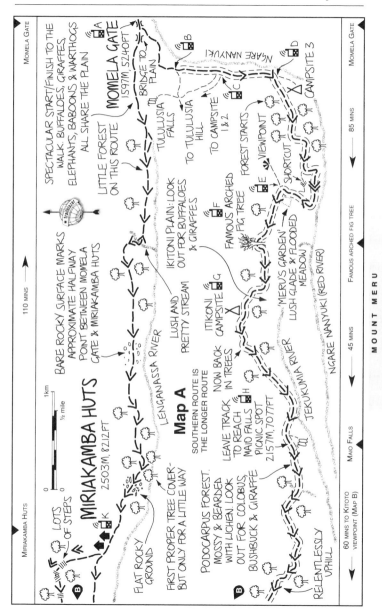

MIRIAKAMBA HUTS | 110 MINS → | ← MOMELA GATE

MOMELA GATE | 85 MINS | FAMOUS ARCHED FIG TREE | 45 MINS | MAIO FALLS | 60 MINS TO KITOTO VIEWPOINT (MAP B)

MOUNT MERU

Map A

SPECTACULAR START/FINISH TO THE WALK. BUFFALOES, GIRAFFES, ELEPHANTS, BABOONS & WARTHOGS ALL SHARE THE PLAIN

MOMELA GATE 1597M, 5240FT

☐A

☐B

NGARE NANYUKI

BRIDGE TO PLAIN

☐C

☐D

CAMPSITE 3

LITTLE FOREST ON THIS ROUTE

TULULUSIA FALLS

TO TULULUSIA HILL

TO CAMPSITE 1 & 2

E VIEWPOINT

SHORTCUT

FOREST STARTS

BARE ROCKY SURFACE MARKS APPROXIMATE HALFWAY POINT BETWEEN MOMELA GATE & MIRIAKAMBA HUTS

★Trailblazer

1km
½ mile

LENGANASSA RIVER

LUSH AND PRETTY STREAM

IKITONI PLAIN: LOOK OUT FOR BUFFALOES & GIRAFFES

☐F FAMOUS ARCHED FIG TREE

MIRIAKAMBA HUTS 2503M, 8212FT

☐K

LOTS OF STEPS

B

FLAT ROCKY GROUND

FIRST PROPER TREE COVER - BUT ONLY FOR A LITTLE WAY

PODOCARPUS FOREST. MOSSY & BEARDED WITH LICHEN. LOOK OUT FOR COLOBUS BUSHBUCK & GIRAFFE

B

RELENTLESSLY UPHILL

SOUTHERN ROUTE IS THE LONGER ROUTE

NOW BACK IN TREES

LEAVE TRACK TO REACH MAIO FALLS 2157M, 7077FT

PICNIC SPOT

☐H

TEKUKUMIA RIVER

ITIKONI CAMPSITE ☐G

'MERU'S GARDEN' LUSH GLADE & FLOODED MEADOW

NGARE NANYUKI (RED RIVER)

least, would follow a straight line. Thankfully, about an hour after leaving the falls the first red hot pokers (Map B) appear (*Kniphofia thomsonii*), a flower that heralds the imminent arrival of **Kitoto Viewpoint**, with views east-north-east over the Momela Lakes and east-south-east over the fauna-filled Ngurdoto Crater, the original centre and raison d'être of Arusha National Park before it merged with Meru to create the current park you find today.

From now until the end of this first stage the path feels more alpine. It's still upwards, at least until you reach a clearing with unrestricted views of the petri-fied lava flow that runs down from the ash cone to the plateau on which you stand – the so-called **Crater Plain**. This plain, though more than 2600m above sea level, still attracts an abundance of game including giraffe, hyaena, leopard and buffalo. On the northern edge of this mini plain is the dry, rocky river-bed of the upper reaches of the **Lenganassa River**, which you follow downhill to your first night's destination.

Miriakamba Huts (Map A) are a smart pair of accommodation huts and accompanying buildings sitting at an altitude of 2503m above sea level. The huts are divided into rooms for four people in two bunk beds and are popular not only with tourists but also, if the amount of dung is anything to go by, buf-falo and elephant too; for this reason, we advise you to take care when nipping out to the loo at night. There are also good views across to Kilimanjaro from the toilets and the viewing platforms at the back of the dining hut.

STAGE 2: MIRIAKAMBA HUTS TO SADDLE HUTS
[MAP A, p241; MAP B, p243]

Distance: 6.1km; altitude gained: 1057m

Everybody has their favourite section of the Meru trek and the walk from the

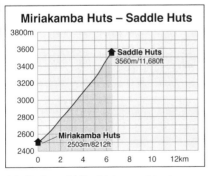

Miriakamba Huts to the lunch stop at Mgongo Wa Tembo is ours. There's something gentle and gorgeously pastoral about the grassy slopes that put one in mind of the rolling hills of England for some reason – the exotic flora and piles of buffa-lo and elephant crap notwith-standing. Indeed, it's the unusual flora – the *Hagenia abyssinica* with its heavy pink/brown blossom, for example, or a species of lobelia (see p244) which resembles in no way the lobelias you'll find in your garden at home – and the continuing presence of the park's larger fauna that add so much to the day. Even the path is impressive, a wooden staircase lead-ing west up the slopes of the ridge towards the Saddle. Then, of course, there are the views over your shoulder of Kilimanjaro glowering at its little brother,

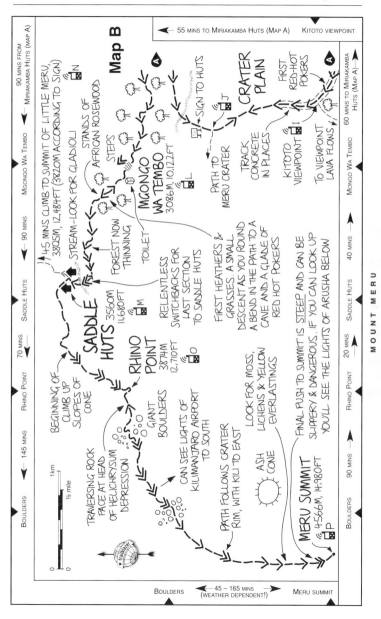

Map B

← 55 MINS TO MIRIAKAMBA HUTS (MAP A)   KITOTO VIEWPOINT

90 MINS FROM MIRIAKAMBA HUTS (MAP A)

45 MINS CLIMB TO SUMMIT OF LITTLE MERU, 3805M, 12,484FT (3820M ACCORDING TO SIGN)

STANDS OF AFRICAN ROSEWOOD

STREAM - LOOK FOR GLADIOLI

STEPS

MGONGO WA TEMBO 3086M, 10,122FT

FOREST NOW THINNING

TOILET

RELENTLESS SWITCHBACKS FOR LAST SECTION TO SADDLE HUTS

SADDLE HUTS 3560M, 11,680FT

SIGN TO HUTS

PATH TO MERU CRATER

CRATER PLAIN

TRACK CONCRETE IN PLACES

KITOTO VIEWPOINT

To VIEWPOINT LAVA FLOWS

FIRST RED-HOT POKERS

60 MINS TO MIRIAKAMBA HUTS (MAP A) →

FIRST HEATHERS & GRASSES. A SMALL DESCENT AS YOU ROUND A BEND IN THE PATH TO A CAVE AND A GLADE OF RED HOT POKERS

BEGINNING OF CLIMB UP SLOPES OF CONE

RHINO POINT 3874M, 12,710FT

GIANT BOULDERS

CAN SEE LIGHTS OF KILIMANJARO AIRPORT TO SOUTH

TRAVERSING ROCK FACE AT HEAD OF HELICHRYSUM DEPRESSION

LOOK FOR MOSS, LICHENS & YELLOW EVERLASTINGS

FINAL PUSH TO SUMMIT IS STEEP AND CAN BE SLIPPERY & DANGEROUS. IF YOU CAN LOOK UP YOU'LL SEE THE LIGHTS OF ARUSHA BELOW

PATH FOLLOWS CRATER RIM, WITH KILI TO EAST

ASH CONE

MERU SUMMIT 4566M, 14,980FT

TRAILBLAZER

1km
½ mile

BOULDERS 145 MINS RHINO POINT 70 MINS SADDLE HUTS 90 MINS MGONGO WA TEMBO 90 MINS FROM MIRIAKAMBA HUTS (MAP A)

MOUNT MERU

BOULDERS 90 MINS RHINO POINT 20 MINS SADDLE HUTS 40 MINS MONGO WA TEMBO

BOULDERS 45 – 165 MINS (WEATHER DEPENDENT!) MERU SUMMIT

its white summit glistening in the sun. It's a great morning's walk. Nor does the interest for trekkers wane much after lunch as the path enters the alpine zone. The trees diminish in size before disappearing altogether, to be replaced by the heathers and ericas that flourish at this altitude. The only problem with the latter half of this second day is that it can become slightly monotonous after a while and impatience and ennui can set in. But don't be in too much of a hurry: from the moment you set off it's vital you take it *pole pole* because of the altitude.

So, from Miriakamba adopt a funereal speed from the word *Twende* ('Go!'). After a few minutes traversing the ridge, the trail heads off up the steps of the mountain's eastern flanks. The path zig-zags for much of the morning, with juniper and hagenia lining the way together with the occasional stand of *Lobelia gibberoa*, whose younger plants display an impressive phallic brush growing out of their tops. Elephants can occasionally be seen along this stretch, so do make sure you stick close to the man with the gun. The path soon bends in a more northerly direction, with great views of Kili to your right framed by the local vegetation. There are some venerable old fallen trees here with some vivid red mountain gladioli growing from the trunks. Following the zig-zags, **Mgongo Wa Tembo** ('Elephant's Back'; about 3086m) is reached, the usual lunch-stop on this second stage with views south over the Crater Plain.

The path continues to climb after the break, soon leaving the forest for something altogether more alpine with *Philippia excelsa* and *Erica arborea* now proliferating. If you're lucky, you may also come across chameleons that, despite being cold-blooded creatures, somehow thrive in this region. It's a bit of a relentless, monotonous trek but it's not long before the **Saddle Huts** (3560m) are reached. As with Miriakamba, these are smart huts that almost put those on Kilimanjaro to shame. Yet despite the altitude the huts still get the occasional visitor from Africa's animal kingdom, including elephants and buffaloes migrating to the grasslands further west. There's little to do up here, allowing you to spend the rest of the afternoon climbing the nearby 3805m **Little Meru**, a simple 45-minute trudge that the guides will often allow you to do by yourself; it's a climb that takes you to an altitude not far short of Rhino Point which you'll be visiting tonight – so remember to climb *pole pole* even though there maybe no-one to regulate your speed. That done, you can relax and prepare yourself for the exertions of the night to come...

STAGE 3: SADDLE HUTS TO THE SUMMIT
(AND BACK TO MIRIAKAMBA HUTS) [MAP B, p243]

Distance: 5.5km; altitude gained: 1006m

The ascent – Saddle Huts to the Summit

And so to the final ascent, and if the height of Meru is invaluable for acclimatizing, so this night-time march is wonderful preparation for that final push to Kili's Uhuru Peak. True, this walk is shorter and, unlike the relentless zig-zags taking you up Kibo's slopes, more varied and direct. But the experience of waking up at some godforsaken hour to undertake a chilly high-altitude trek up a very big African volcano, before contouring around the crater rim to reach the highest point as the sun rises to the east, is useful training indeed.

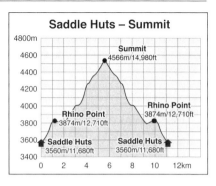

Saddle Huts – Summit

The stage begins with a crossing of the Saddle before bending south to the start of the climb. It's a walk that sees you leave behind the larger vegetation – the ericas and philippias – on a winding path that eventually joins the crest of a ridge that brings you out at **Rhino Point** (3874m), the climb's first landmark. Thereafter the route bends west and, having descended to cross a **rockface** at the head of a lush (by the standards of this altitude) depression, then climbs to follow the lip of the Meru Crater. For the next couple of hours the path follows the course of the crater rim. Being night, of course, you'll have to wait for views of the crater itself until the morning, though beyond it you should be able to see, in the distance, the lights of various settlements as well as Kilimanjaro International Airport and even, in the far distance, Mererani tanzanite mine, working away through the night. Eventually, about 3½ hours after setting off, the crater rim begins to bend noticeably south. As it does, hopefully at the same time the eastern horizon will start to turn pink and orange

MOUNT MERU

Mount Meru – Route to the Summit

with the onset of the new day, and the silhouette of Kili can clearly be discerned, with both Kibo and Mawenzi summits visible.

The summit (4566m) also seems tangibly closer, too, so it's disheartening to discover that it's still a minimum of an hour away – or nearer three if it's

been snowing and your guides have to create a path in the ice using nothing but the heels of their boots as spades and bits of rocks as shovels! It can be a little terrifying, too, with one false step sending you plummeting down the icy slopes. Take care!

At the summit (which used to be called, rather quaintly, Socialist Peak, though they've since taken away the sign) there's little save a flag, a sign and a box containing a book where you can sign your name.

On the summit of Mount Meru

There are also, of course, great views over Arusha to the west and Kili to the east, with Meru's perfect ash cone below you.

The descent – The Summit to Miriakamba Huts

Photos taken and hands shaken, it's time for the descent – and isn't it wonderful to be able to walk at a speed of your choosing again! It's also interesting to see how different in daylight the path looks. Look back from **Rhino Point**, for example, to the climb up to the crater rim – was it really that steep? Notice, too, while renegotiating the descent from the summit, all the mini bumps and craters to the north and west of Meru which were hidden on the way up.

Pressure from guides for a big tip

One of the uglier aspects of many Meru climbs is the pressure exerted by guide and ranger in tandem on the poor trekker to pay a sizeable tip. Sit in the Miriakamba or Saddle Huts and you'll see them sidle up to their clients, innocently ask them how their dinner was, make a light bit of chit chat – and then launch into a speech about how much they are expecting to receive in gratuities.

It's a revolting practice. I have heard tales of people paying fortunes after being subjected to such pressure and of other trekkers being left in tears after being forced to hand over far more than they were initially expecting. Suffice to say, I think it's well within your rights to tell these gentlemen in no uncertain terms to get lost. Furthermore, you could also tell them that if they are to get a tip (which, of course, they are entitled to if they have carried out their job professionally) **it is entirely up to you how much you'll pay**, and that if they don't leave you alone the tip will be reduced in size accordingly. If they continue, report them to both the park authorities and the agency with which you climbed. (By way of a guideline, I would pay somewhere around US$40-50 per day per climber for the whole crew).

I am a great supporter and admirer of the guides and rangers and the work they do – but this is a disgusting practice and should be stamped out.

The descent back to the Saddle, though wearying, shouldn't take more than 2½-3 hours. Those who've opted to spend four days on the mountain will take an hour or so back at the **Saddle Huts**, packing their bags, eating some well-earned food and maybe getting a little shut-eye, before the two-hour return stroll down to Miriakamba where they'll be spending the night. Those on the three-day trip will also have an hour to recover at the Saddle Huts, though for them the walk down is, of course, that much longer. If you're reading this at the Saddle Huts after your ascent to the summit, you'll probably appreciate now why we suggested taking the long route on the first stage and saving the shorter route for now.

STAGE 4: MIRIAKAMBA HUTS TO MOMELA GATE
(VIA THE SHORTER ROUTE)   [MAP A, p241]

Distance: 6.5km; altitude lost: 906m

One of the advantages Meru has over Kilimanjaro is that this last stage, though short, is in no way an anti-climax, whereas the last day on Kili often feels like something to endure rather than enjoy. The descent from Miriakamba is hard on your knees, of course, but by way of compensation there's some unusual flora (check out the pink *Impatiens* growing right on the path and the hardy Sodom's apple trees, *Solanum sodomaeum*, growing by the side of it), a charming little river to cross and, of course, a crossing of the buffalo- and warthog-filled Meru Plain at

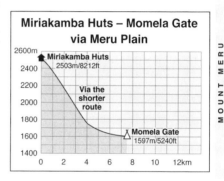

the very end, with Kili as an awe-inspiring backdrop.

If you haven't already seen them this walk could also include a brief diversion to the impressive **Tululusia Falls**, just a few minutes off the path to the south before the plain. Isn't it curious, by the way, how there's so little forest on this route compared to the dense, dark cloud forest on the first day – even though they both cover the same altitude?

Even with the diversion you should find yourself back at Momela Gate just two hours or so after setting off. There'll just be time to distribute tips, collect your certificates (one for Mount Meru, possibly one for Little Meru too) and say your farewells to your companions. It's been a wonderful walk, hasn't it? You've seen some beautiful birds, flowers and animals, taken in some breath-taking views and through sheer bloodymindedness climbed to the very summit of Tanzania's second highest mountain.

Now it's time for the highest...

MOUNT MERU

TRAIL GUIDE & MAPS

Using this guide

ABOUT THE MAPS IN THIS GUIDE

Scale
Most of the **trekking maps** in this guide are drawn to the same scale, namely 26mm to 1km (1²/₃ inches to the mile). The exceptions are the maps which depict the final ascent to the top, ie the trails up to the Kibo summit (Map Nos 6, 13, 18 & 33), which is usually made at night. On these maps the scale has been doubled (ie 52mm to 1km or 3¹/₃ inches to the mile) to allow for more detail to be drawn on them.

Walking times
The times indicated on the maps should be used only as an approximate guide. **They refer to walking times only and do not include any time for breaks and or food.** Overall you may find you need to **add around 30-50%** to our times depending on your walking speed and the time taken for rest breaks to get an idea of the total time you'll spend on the trail.

Gradient arrows
You will also notice that we have drawn '**gradient arrows**' on the trekking maps in this book. The arrows point uphill: two arrows mean that the hill is steep, one that the gradient is reasonably gradual. If, for example, you are walking from A (at 80m) to B (at 200m) and the trail between the two is short and steep, it would be shown thus: A – – – – >>– – – – B.

The Marangu Route

Because this trail is popularly called the '**Tourist Trail**' or '**Coca Cola trail**', some trekkers are misled into thinking this 5- or 6-day climb to the summit is simply a walk in the (national) park. But remember that a greater proportion of people fail on this route than on any other. True, this may have something to do with the fact that Marangu's reputation for being 'easy' attracts the more inexperienced, out-of-condition trekkers who don't realize that they are embarking on a **36.55km uphill walk**, followed immediately by a

In the following descriptions, the treks have been divided into stages, with each stage roughly corresponding to a day's trekking. For this reason, throughout the text the words 'stage' and 'day' have been used interchangeably.

36.55km knee-jarring descent. But it shouldn't take much to realize that Marangu is not much easier than any other trail: with the Machame Route, for example, you start at 1811m and aim for the summit at 5895m. On Marangu, you start just a little higher at 1905m and have the same goal, so simple logic should tell you that it can't be that much easier. Indeed, the fact that this route is often completed in 5-6 days as opposed to the 6-7 days it takes to complete Machame would suggest that this route is actually more arduous – and gives you some idea of why **more people fail on this trail** than on the so-called 'Whiskey Route'.

The main reason why people say that Marangu is easier is because it is the only route where you **sleep in huts** rather than under canvas. The accommodation in these huts should be booked in advance by your tour company, who have to pay a deposit per person per night to KINAPA in order to secure it. To cover this, the tour agencies will probably ask you to pay them some money in advance too. This deposit is refundable or can be moved to secure huts on other dates, providing you give KINAPA (and your agency) at least seven days' notice.

(Bear in mind if you're booking with a Tanzanian agency for a trek the next day, you should ask your agency to show you a receipt confirming they have paid a deposit for your accommodation on the trek. Otherwise, you may find yourself being turned away at Marangu Gate at the start of the trek because your company didn't book your accommodation and there's no room.) Incidentally, there are currently 84 spaces at Mandara Huts, 160 at Horombo – the extra beds are necessary because this hut is also used by those *descending* from Kibo – and 60 at Kibo.

(cont'd on p252)

Kilimanjaro seen from Lake Jipé
(from *The Kilima-njaro Expedition – A Record of Scientific Exploration in Eastern Equatorial Africa* **HH Johnston**, 1886)

WHAT'S IT LIKE ON THE MOUNTAIN?

Fun. It really is. Sure, the last push to the summit is hard, as some of the quotes used later in this book clearly indicate, but don't let that put you off. Kilimanjaro is a delightful mountain to climb:

But we had much to compensate us for all we had to give up. The charm of the mountain scenery, the clear, crisp atmosphere, the tonic of 'a labour we delight in' and the consciousness now and again of success achieved, all went far to make our fortnight's arduous toil a happy sequence of red-letter days.
Hans Meyer *Across East African Glaciers*

The days are spent walking through spectacular landscapes which change every day as you pass through different vegetation zones. The pace is never exhausting, as you have to walk slowly in order to give yourself a chance to acclimatize. What's more, at the end of the day, while the guides are cooking your dinner, you are free to wander around the campsite and, as you bump into the same people time and again over the course of the trek, a sense of community soon develops. Then as night falls, and you tuck into the huge plates of food cooked by your crew, the stars come out, stunning everyone into silence. This is the favourite time of day for most people: rested, replete with food and with a day of satisfactory walking behind and a good night's sleep ahead, it's natural to feel a sense of comfort and contentment, with the thought of wild animals possibly lying nearby serving to add a pleasing frisson of excitement.

Bed? It's too early. I feel too good. Aaah, I wonder if there'll ever be another time as good as this. **Gregory Peck**, in the film version of *The Snows of Kilimanjaro*

Of course, walking up from less than 2000m or thereabouts to 5895m does, as you can probably imagine, take a lot of effort and the night walk to the summit is unarguably tough. But short of actually carrying you up, your crew will do everything in their power to make your entire experience as comfortable as possible. In fact, they'll spoil you: not only do they carry your bag, but at the end of the day's walk you'll turn up at camp to find your tent has already been erected, with a bowl of hot water lying nearby for you to wash away the grime of the day. A few minutes later and a large plate of popcorn and biscuits will be served with a mug of steaming hot tea or coffee.

Accommodation on the trail

I got back in time to see P.D. lying on sloping ground, slipping off the stretcher, and in great pain. Small fire had been made under the root of a great tree. Rain soon came on and wiped out the fire ... tent was not put up and we were all in great misery. Men with tent lost in the darkness. Thought if the rain stopped we could go on in the moonlight. Rain did not stop. **Peter MacQueen** *In Wildest Africa* (1910)

Unless you are on the Marangu Route, accommodation on the mountain will be in tents brought up by your porters. (Do not be tempted to sleep in any of the caves as that is against park regulations.) On the Marangu Route, camping is forbidden; instead people have to sleep in huts along the route. (You will see people camping on this route but they are trekkers who took the Rongai Route to ascend and are now descending on Marangu.) The sleeping arrangements in these huts are usually dormitory-style, with anything from four to twenty beds per room.

Confusingly, away from the Marangu Route **many of the campsites are actually called 'huts' but don't be fooled**: they are called huts because of the green shacks you'll find at these campsites which are usually inhabited by the park rangers. Trekkers used to be allowed to sleep in these huts too, but no longer.

The only other buildings you will possibly see along the trail are the **toilets**. Most are of the same design, namely a little wooden hut with a hole in the floor. Some are in better condition than others; all we will say is that some people are terrible shots, while other latrines are in desperate need of emptying before the contents become Kilimanjaro's fourth peak. Smart new ones are now being built at many of the bigger camps.

Food on the trail
Remember to tell your agency if you have any special dietary requirements – because meat, nuts, gluten and dairy form a substantial part of the menu on Kilimanjaro.

A typical **breakfast** will involve eggs (boiled or fried), porridge, a saveloy (possibly with some tomatoes too), a piece of fruit such as a banana or orange, some bread with jam, honey or peanut butter and a mug of tea, hot chocolate or coffee.

Lunch is sometimes prepared at breakfast and carried by the trekker in his or her daypack, though the more expensive companies have tables set up and cook food on site. (This practice is reportedly being phased out by the authorities who are concerned at the environmental damage this causes.) This packed lunch often consists of a boiled egg, some sandwiches, a banana or orange, and some tea kept warm in a flask and carried by your guide.

At the end of the day's walking, **afternoon tea** is served with biscuits, peanuts and, best of all, salted popcorn. The final and biggest meal of the day, **dinner** usually begins with soup, followed by a main course including chicken or meat, a vegetable sauce, some cabbage or other vegetable, and rice or pasta; if your porters have brought up some potatoes, these will usually be eaten over the first few days as they are so heavy.

Drink on the trail
Porters will collect **water** from the rivers and streams along the trail. Some of this they will boil and maybe purify for you at the start of the day to carry in your water bottles. On the lower slopes you can collect water yourself from the many streams and purify it using a filter or tablets. Note, however, that as you climb ever higher water becomes more scarce. On the Machame trail, for example, the last water point is at Karanga Valley, the lunch-stop before Barafu; on Marangu, it's just before the Saddle. For this reason it is essential you carry enough bottles or containers for *at least* three litres.

In camp, **coffee** and **tea** are served and maybe **hot chocolate** too – all usually made with powdered milk. Remember that caffeine, present in coffee and tea, is dehydrating, which can be bad for acclimatization. Caffeine is a diuretic too (ie you will want to urinate frequently – something you should already be doing a lot as you adapt to the higher conditions).

What to put in your daypack
Normally you will not see your main backpack from the moment you hand it to the porter in the morning to at least lunchtime, and maybe not until the end of the day. It's therefore necessary to pack everything you may need during the day in the bag you carry with you. Some suggestions, in no particular order:

- sweets
- water and water purifiers
- camera and batteries plus spare
  film or memory card
- this book/maps
- sunhat/sunglasses and suncream

- toilet paper and trowel
- plastic bag for rubbish
- rainwear
- walking sticks/knee supports
- medical kit, including chapstick
- lunch (supplied by your crew)

(cont'd from p249) If any one of those is already booked to capacity on the night you wish to stay there, you won't be allowed to start your trek and will have to change your dates.

The fact that you do sleep in huts makes little difference to what you need to pack for the trek, for sleeping bags are still required (the huts have pillows and mattresses but that's all) though you can dispense with a ground mat for this route. Regarding the sleeping situation, it does help if you can get to the huts early each day to grab the better beds. This doesn't mean you should deliberately hurry to the huts, which will reduce your enjoyment of the trek and increase the possibility of AMS. But do try to **start early each morning**: that way you can avoid the crowds, beat them to the better beds, and possibly improve your chances of seeing some of Kili's wildlife too.

In terms of **duration**, the Marangu Route is one of the shorter trails, taking just five days for both the ascent and descent. Many people, however, opt to take an extra day to acclimatize at Horombo Huts, using that day to visit the Mawenzi Huts at 4535m. From a safety point of view this is entirely sensible and aesthetically such a plan cannot be argued with either, for the views from the path to the huts across the Saddle to Kibo truly take your breath away – assuming you have some left to be taken away after all that climbing.

One aspect of the Marangu Route that could be seen by some as a drawback is that it is the only one where you **ascend and descend via the same path**. However, there are a couple of arguments to counter this perception: firstly, between Horombo and Kibo Huts there are two paths and it shouldn't take too much to persuade your guide to use one trail on the ascent and a different one on the way down; and there's a Nature Trail alternative on the descent from Mandara Huts to the gate as well. Both of these are described in the book on p335 and p336 respectively. Secondly, we think that the walk back down the Marangu Route is one of the most pleasurable parts of the entire trek, with the gradients more gentle than on other descents and splendid views over the shoulder. Furthermore, it offers you the chance to greet the crowds of sweating, red-faced unfortunates heading the other way with the smug expression of one for whom physical pain is now a thing of the past and whose immediate future is filled with warm showers and cold beers.

❏ **Mobile (cell) phone reception on the Marangu Route**

Those with a mobile (cell) phone will find that the Marangu Route has poor reception in general. It depends which network you're with, but I found that there is little to no reception at the Mandara Huts (though I did get reception at the nearby **Maundi Crater**), and the first real chance of getting reception was at **Horombo Huts**; reception there was patchy but walk around and you should be able to find some places where you can connect with the outside world. After that, reception at Kibo Huts was pretty much non-existent so you have to wait until **Stella Point** and **Uhuru Peak** before regaining contact with the outside world again.

Trekkers' experiences

Of course, everybody's experience of climbing Kili is different. The majority of letters we get are of the 'had the time of my life' variety, which are particularly lovely to receive, especially as it's great to know other people enjoyed the experience as much as we always do:

What a fab trip! And yes, We all made it to the top (one of us with a humungous, vice-like headache, but our good guide carried her pack on the last leg)!! And best of all, we all came back friends!   Anneliese Dibetta (Canada)

A few letters also contain some useful advice:

If I can make any strong recommendations it is the truth and value of 'pole pole'... I redefined the phrase pole pole and from the first step to the last I went the pace I needed to do to keep my heart rate even and not get out of breath. More often than not I was way behind the group, always had one of the guides or assistant guides with me and not once did I feel pressured to go faster. It was the key to my success.
                                                                      Clare Wickens (US)

I found the trail up the Western Breach to be tough but not necessarily dangerous. I think the 'toughness' came from being at the altitude we were at – which raised both the level of exertion needed to climb and the fatigue I was experiencing from the trip so far – more than the trail itself. As I watched the porters trot by with large loads (five dozen eggs on one guy or our dining table and chairs) I realized how easy the trail really was even though at the time I was feeling taxed by it. Patti Wickham (US)

One general observation would be that although everyone said how much it was to do with altitude, I didn't realise the extent of it. I thought I'd tire easily and be breath-less, but didn't understand how half the people would have headaches, and people would be running out of the dining hall to vomit. I was mentally prepared for some-thing physically demanding, but not for feeling ill and having a headache for days on end...

As you come up to Kibo, a few people said they start to get excited and want to get it over with quickly. I'd say it's worth advising them to make sure they keep going slowly, and warn them that a lot of people suddenly feel really tired during the last 5-10 minutes of the walk.   Richard Evans (UK)

One or two of them were quite encouraging too:
Two of us were not really in good enough shape to complete Kili by any route, no scrambling experience, and no strong expectation of summiting, but by taking seven days and by doing the scramble in the daylight, all made it to the summit, and back down to Mweka Gate, happy, safe and sound.   John Wickham (US)

That's not to suggest, of course, that everyone has a pleasant time...

I've had a lovely few days but now I have a headache and feel like shit. Please leave me alone. Thank you. Overheard at Barafu Camp and shouted by an anonymous German hiding inside his tent while his group readied themselves for the final climb.

For a couple of days I thought you must have a great job: travel around the world and write about it. I now know better. I feel sorry for you. I thought climbing Kilimanjaro was hell. I would ask for a big raise in your salary if I were you...
                                                                      Mark Burgmans (Holland)

STAGE 1: MARANGU GATE TO MANDARA HUTS
[MAP 1, p255; MAP 2, p257]

Distance: 8.3km (8.75km if taking the Nature Trail); altitude gained: 818m

The woods are lovely, dark & deep,
But I have promises to keep,
And miles to go before I sleep.
Robert Frost as seen on a sign-
writer's wall in Moshi

As the headquarters of KINA-
PA (Kilimanjaro National
Park), you might expect
Marangu Gate (altitude 1905m/
6256ft) to have the best facilities of all the gates and it does-
n't disappoint. Not only does
the gate have the usual **registration office** but there's also a

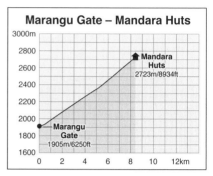

Marangu Gate – Mandara Huts

Mandara Huts 2723m/8934ft

Marangu Gate 1905m/6250ft

picnic area, a smart new toilet block and a **shop** that has a good collection of
books and souvenirs. There's also a small booth run by Kilimanjaro Guides
Cooperative by the entrance to the car park where you can **hire any equipment**
you may have forgotten to bring along, from essentials such as hats and fleeces,
sleeping bags and water bottles to camping stuff that you almost certainly won't
need on the trail such as stoves and so forth, which should be provided by your
agency. (Incidentally, the authorities have even bigger plans for this gate, with
blueprints for a whole new visitor centre already drawn up, including a conference hall, internet café and a museum dedicated to the mountain.)

Having gone through the laborious business of **registering** (a process that
usually takes at least an hour, though it can be quicker if you manage to get here
before the large tour groups arrive), you begin your trek by following the
trekkers' path which heads left off the road (which is now used solely by
porters). You may still find the odd eucalyptus tree around the gate, one of the
few non-native plants on the mountain. They were introduced, according to the
version I've heard, by the first chief park warden of Kilimanjaro, a man who
married a relative of Idi Amin – the former despot of Uganda later shooting him
in an argument, so the story goes. As an 'alien' species and one that consumes
a lot of water, the eucalyptus trees are slowly being eradicated by the authorities from the national park itself. (It has to be a gradual process, however: look
through the trees to your right just after you start out and you'll see a big open
area – the ugly result of eradicating the trees too quickly.)

This first day's walk is a very pleasant one of just over 8km and though the
route is uphill for virtually the entire time, there are enough distractions in the
forest to take your mind off the exertion, from the occasional troop of **blue
monkeys** to the vivid red *Impatiens kilimanjari*, a small flower that has almost
become the emblem of Kilimanjaro. The path soon veers towards and then follows the course of a **mountain stream**; sometimes through the increasingly

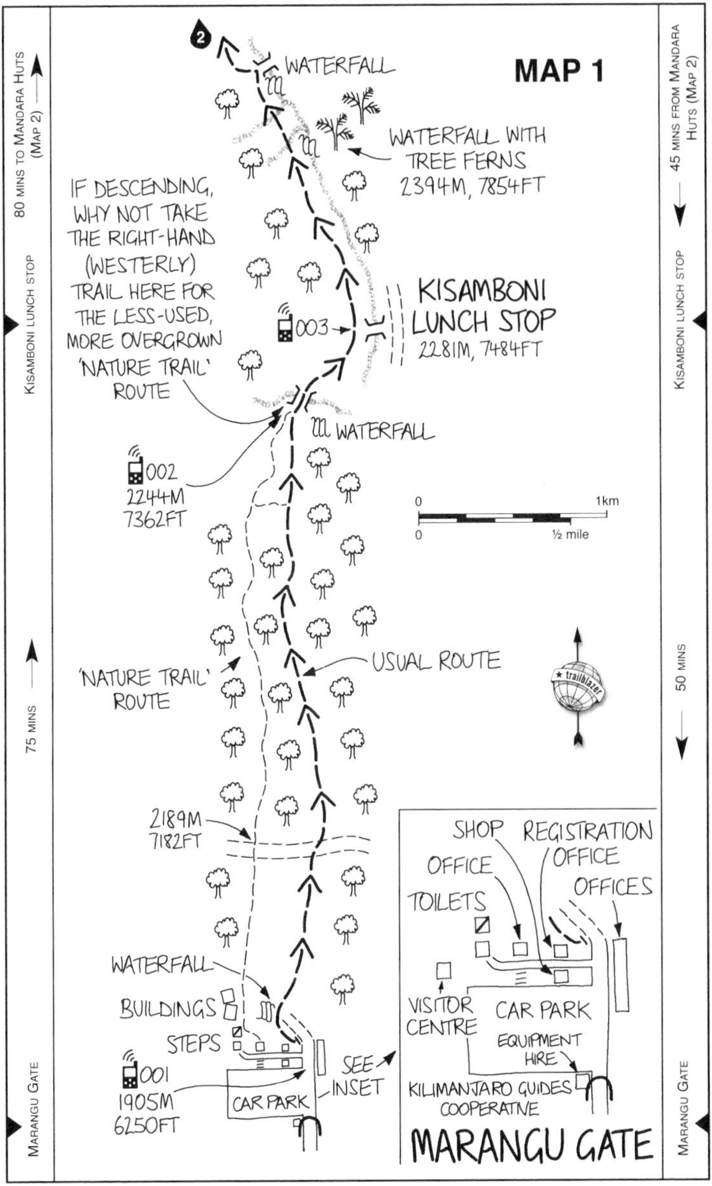
MAP 1
80 MINS TO MANDARA HUTS (MAP 2)
45 MINS FROM MANDARA HUTS (MAP 2)
KISAMBONI LUNCH STOP
75 MINS
50 MINS
MARANGU GATE
2
WATERFALL
WATERFALL WITH TREE FERNS 2394M, 7854FT
IF DESCENDING, WHY NOT TAKE THE RIGHT-HAND (WESTERLY) TRAIL HERE FOR THE LESS-USED, MORE OVERGROWN 'NATURE TRAIL' ROUTE
003
KISAMBONI LUNCH STOP 2281M, 7484FT
WATERFALL
002 2244M 7362FT
0 1km
0 ½ mile
USUAL ROUTE
'NATURE TRAIL' ROUTE
trailblazer
2189M 7182FT
WATERFALL
BUILDINGS
STEPS
001 1905M 6250FT
CAR PARK
SEE INSET
SHOP
REGISTRATION OFFICE
OFFICE
OFFICES
TOILETS
VISITOR CENTRE
CAR PARK
EQUIPMENT HIRE
KILIMANJARO GUIDES COOPERATIVE
MARANGU GATE

impenetrable vegetation to your right you can glimpse the occasional small **waterfall**.

After about 1¼ hours a wooden bridge leads off the trail over this stream to the picnic tables at **Kisamboni** and a reunion with the 4WD porters' trail. This is the halfway point of the first stage and in all probability it is here that you will be served lunch.

> *... ferns and heaths were plentiful, the last-named preponderating as we got higher up. At a height of 6,300 feet, however, all these were merged in the primaeval forest, in which old patriarchs with knotted stunted forms stood closely together, many of them worsted in the perpetual struggle with the encroachments of the parasitical growths of almost fabulous strength and size, which enfolded trunks and branches alike in their fatal embrace, crippling the giants themselves and squeezing to death the mosses, lichens, and ferns which had clothed their nakedness. Everything living seemed doomed to fall prey to them, but they in their turn bore their own heavy burden of parasites; creepers, from a yard to two yards long, hanging down in garlands and festoons, or forming one thick veil shrouding whole clumps of trees. Wherever a little space had been left amongst the many fallen and decaying trunks, the ground was covered with a luxurious vegetation, including many varieties of herbaceous plants with bright coloured flowers, orchids, and the modest violet peeping out amongst them, whilst more numerous than all were different lycopods and sword-shaped ferns.*
> **Lieutenant Ludwig von Höhnel**
> *Discovery by Count Teleki of Lakes Rudolf and Stefanie* (1894)

Returning to the trail and turning right, you continue climbing north for 30 minutes to another bridge, again leading off to the right of the trail; your path, however, heads off to the left, directly away from the bridge. The trail is a little steeper now as you wind your way through the forest. It is a very pretty part of the walk, with varieties of *Impatiens* and, draped amongst the trees, the white-flowered *Begonia meyeri-johannis* edging the path; though by now you may be feeling a little too tired to enjoy it to its fullest.

Press on, and 15 minutes later yet another bridge appears which you *do* take. Like some sort of botanical border post, the bridge heralds the first appearance of the **giant heathers** (*Erica excelsa*) on the trail, with masses of **bearded lichen** liberally draped over them; though the forest reappears intermittently up to and beyond Maundi Crater it's the spindly heathers and stumpy shrubs of the second vegetation zone, the alpine heath and moorland, that now dominate.

From this bridge, the first night's accommodation, **Mandara Huts** (2723m), lies just 35 minutes away. If you have the energy, a quick 15-minute saunter to the parasitic cone known as **Maundi Crater** is worthwhile both for its views east over Kenya and north-west to Mawenzi and for the wild flowers and grasses growing on its slopes. On the way to the crater, look in the trees for the bands of semi-tame monkeys, both blue and colobus, that live here and are particularly active at dusk.

In all the route descriptions, do remember that the times we quote are approximations and, more importantly, refer to walking times only with no time spent resting, taking photos etc. Add on 30-50% to get an estimate of the total time spent on the trail.

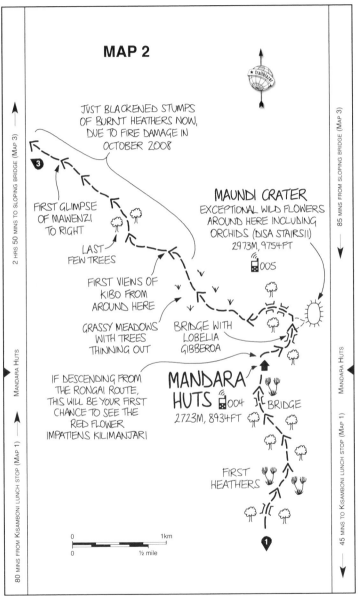

MAP 2

JUST BLACKENED STUMPS
OF BURNT HEATHERS NOW,
DUE TO FIRE DAMAGE IN
OCTOBER 2008

FIRST GLIMPSE
OF MAWENZI
TO RIGHT

LAST
FEW TREES

FIRST VIEWS OF
KIBO FROM
AROUND HERE

GRASSY MEADOWS
WITH TREES
THINNING OUT

BRIDGE WITH
LOBELIA
GIBBEROA

MAUNDI CRATER
EXCEPTIONAL WILD FLOWERS
AROUND HERE INCLUDING
ORCHIDS (DISA STAIRSII)
2973M, 9754FT
005

IF DESCENDING FROM
THE RONGAI ROUTE,
THIS WILL BE YOUR FIRST
CHANCE TO SEE THE
RED FLOWER
IMPATIENS KILIMANJARI

MANDARA
HUTS 004
2723M, 8934FT

BRIDGE

FIRST
HEATHERS

0   1km
0   ½ mile

2 HRS 50 MINS TO SLOPING BRIDGE (MAP 3)

85 MINS FROM SLOPING BRIDGE (MAP 3)

MANDARA HUTS

MANDARA HUTS

80 MINS FROM KISAMBONI LUNCH STOP (MAP 1)

45 MINS TO KISAMBONI LUNCH STOP (MAP 1)

TRAIL GUIDE AND MAPS

Incidentally, Mandara Huts are the only huts on the mountain to be named after a person rather than a place. Mandara was the fearsome chief of Moshi, a warrior whose skill and bravery on the battlefield was matched only by his stunning cupidity off it. Mandara once boasted that he had met every white man to visit Kilimanjaro, from Johannes Rebmann to Hans Meyer, and it's a fair bet that all of them would have been required to present the chief with a huge array of presents brought from their own country. Failure to do so was not an option, for those who, in Mandara's eye (he had only one, having lost the other in battle), were insufficiently generous in their gift-giving, put their lives in peril. The attack that led to the death of Charles New (see p113), for example, was said to have been orchestrated by Mandara after New had 'insulted' him by refusing to give the chief the watch from his waistcoat. Read any of the 19th-century accounts of Kilimanjaro and you'll usually find plenty of pages devoted to this fascinating character – with few casting him in a favourable light.

STAGE 2: MANDARA HUTS TO HOROMBO HUTS
[MAP 2 p257; MAP 3, p259]

Distance: 12.5km; altitude gained: 998m

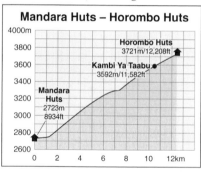

Mandara Huts – Horombo Huts

Horombo Huts
3721m/12,208ft

Kambi Ya Taabu
3592m/11,582ft

Mandara
Huts
2723m
8934ft

On this stage, in which you gain almost a kilometre in altitude, you say a final goodbye to the forest and spend the greater part of the day walking through the bleaker landscape of Kilimanjaro's moorland. If the weather's clear you will get your first really good look at the twin peaks of Kili, namely spiky Mawenzi and snow-capped Kibo; they will continue to loom large, and will doubtless appear in just about every photo you take, from now to the summit. The proteas, giant groundsels (*Dendrosenecio kilimanjari*) and phallic lobelias (*Lobelia deckenii*) also make their first appearance, with the former growing in some abundance towards the latter part of the walk and especially around Horombo Huts.

The whole landscape as far as the eye could reach was a medley of dull grey lava slabs, dotted with the red-leafed protea shrub (Protea Kilimandscharica) and stunted heaths, which became smaller and smaller as we rose higher. Not a sound disturbed the silence of this uninhabited mountain mystery; not a sign of life broke the stillness save a little ashy-brown bird that hopped about the boulders, flipping its tail up and down. And to add to the impression created by the eerie scene, huge senecios lifted to a height of 20ft their black stems and greyish-yellow crowns and stood spreading out their arms in the deep moist gullies, like ghostly sentinels of the untrodden wilds.

Eva Stuart Watt *Africa's Dome of Mystery* (1930)

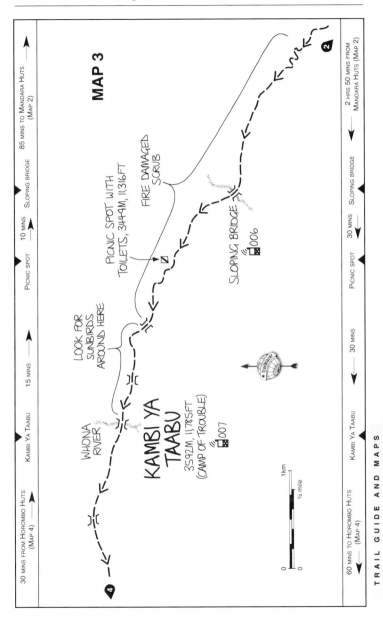

MAP 3

85 MINS TO MANDARA HUTS (MAP 2)

SLOPING BRIDGE

10 MINS

PICNIC SPOT

PICNIC SPOT WITH TOILETS, 3449M, 11,316FT

FIRE DAMAGED SCRUB

2 HRS 50 MINS FROM MANDARA HUTS (MAP 2)

15 MINS

KAMBI YA TAABU

LOOK FOR SUNBIRDS AROUND HERE

WHONA RIVER

KAMBI YA TAABU 3592M, 11,785FT (CAMP OF TROUBLE)

007

SLOPING BRIDGE

006

30 MINS FROM HOROMBO HUTS (MAP 4)

60 MINS TO HOROMBO HUTS (MAP 4)

KAMBI YA TAABU

30 MINS

PICNIC SPOT

30 MINS

SLOPING BRIDGE

1km

½ mile

0

0

TRAIL GUIDE AND MAPS

The day begins with a stroll through the monkey forest towards Maundi Crater. After 15 minutes you cross a small bridge and, leaving the last significant expanse of forest behind, enter a land of tall grasses and giant heathers. **Wild flowers** rarely seen elsewhere, such as the pinkish *Dierama pendulum*, abound in this little bumpy corner of the mountain. Crossing bridges over (often dry) water courses, past the slowly disappearing evidence of a large fire that raged in October 2008, if it's a clear day you may be able to make out, atop one of the many undulations, some **picnic tables** and toilets amongst the heather; this will be your lunch stop, reached after a fairly trying 30-minute climb from the **sloping bridge**. The guides typically call this the halfway point in the day but they're being unnecessarily pessimistic: Horombo Huts lie just 90 minutes away, the path tracing a generally westward course across a number of (dry) stream beds including the head of the Whona River that runs through a valley known as **Kambi Ya Taabu**, which translates, rather melodramatically, as the 'Camp of Trouble'!

Horombo Huts (3721m) are generally regarded as the most pleasant of those on the route: small A-frame shelters partitioned down the middle, with each side holding beds for four people. They cater for a transient population of around 160 trekkers plus porters and guides as well as a more permanent

---

Mawenzi

Though less than 8km of nothingness (namely the Saddle) separates the foot of one from the foot of the other, the twin peaks of Kibo and Mawenzi could scarcely be more different. Where Kibo is all gentle slopes and a perfectly circular crater, Mawenzi is spiky, steep, and rises to a series of peaks like the back of a stegosaurus. Furthermore, where the former is at least partially covered in glaciers, the other stands naked, or at least wears no permanent raiment of ice, its sides too steep to allow the glaciers a secure-enough footing. And while Kibo is easily accessible to walkers, any assault on Mawenzi involves some serious preparation, specialist equipment and no small amount of technical skill.

Indeed, the only similarity between the two peaks is their enormity: Mawenzi's **Hans Meyer Peak**, at 5149m, is the third highest in Africa (after Kibo and Mount Kenya, 50m taller). Its smaller size when compared to Kibo can be ascribed to the fact that the Mawenzi volcano died out first, while the forces that formed Kibo continued to rage for a few thousand years after Mawenzi had become extinct, pushing Kibo above the height of its older brother. Erosion then caused the collapse of Mawenzi's entire north-east wall, releasing the waters of a lake that had formed in its crater down into the valley below.

The jagged appearance of its summit is due to the formation of **dykes**. This is where lava, pushed into gaps in the crater rim, solidified over time and, being harder than the original rock, remained while the softer rock eroded. Today, this hardened lava is also rather shattered, which, combined with its steep gradients, makes Mawenzi extremely dangerous to climb. John Reader, in his book *Kilimanjaro*, tells of two Austrian climbers who perished on their descent from the summit of Mawenzi, with the body of one of them found dangling by a rope snagged to the rocks. Such is the difficulty associated with any climb of Mawenzi that, rather than risk clambering up the peak to recover the corpse, the park authorities decided instead to hire a marksman to shoot at the rope with a rifle.

population of four-striped grass mice whose numbers are now almost at plague proportions; indeed, some of them have now forsaken their grassy homeland to scavenge in the main dining hall. The huts are also the busiest, catering not just for those ascending the mountain but those coming back down too, as well as those who spend the day here acclimatizing. As such the whole place tends to get rather busy.

Speaking of which, if you have opted for an **acclimatization day** the chances are you'll be led by your guide on the northern route (aka Mawenzi Route, see box p260) past the **Zebra Rocks** and up to the **Mawenzi Huts** at 4535m (see Map 4, p262). Not only will this afford you magnificent views of your ultimate destination across the Saddle, but it is also, of course, wonderful exercise to help you to cope with the thin air of Kibo later on. The benefits of taking this extra day may not be immediately apparent but will hopefully manifest themselves later on as you saunter up Kibo with at most a minor headache, while littering the trail around you are the weeping, retching bodies of the AMS-sufferers who opted not to take the extra day. Oh, and the huts are also near enough to allow you to return to Horombo for a late lunch!

STAGE 3: HOROMBO HUTS TO KIBO HUTS
[MAP 4 p262; MAP 5, p263]

Distance: 9.5km (10.3km on the Mawenzi alternative); altitude gained: 993m

The path to Kibo from Horombo now divides; almost invariably you will be led along the southern (left-hand) route, which we describe now. If your guide is amenable, however, you may like to ask him on the return from Kibo to use the more northerly route, particularly if you did not take a day to acclimatize at Horombo (those who did will be familiar with much of this northerly path, which we have called the Mawenzi Route and describe, starting at Kibo Huts, on p335).

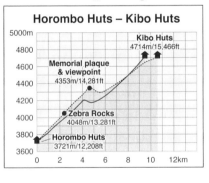

Horombo Huts – Kibo Huts

Kibo Huts
4714m/15,466ft

Memorial plaque & viewpoint
4353m/14,283ft

Zebra Rocks
4048m/13,281ft

Horombo Huts
3721m/12,208ft

The 9.5km **southern path** seems rather steep at first as it bends left (north-west) and up through the thinning vegetation of the moorland. Looping north, just under 30 minutes after leaving Horombo you come to the tiny mountain stream known as **Maua River** (3914m). You should fill up your water bottles here, for the water from this point on is rather brackish. The terrain climbs steadily after Maua, passing the **junction** with the porters' path (ie the Southern Circuit) – this section being largely used by porters as a short-cut to Barafu.

Soon after, some of Kili's many parasitic cones move into view for the first time. The **last water point**, well signposted and rather incongruously furnished

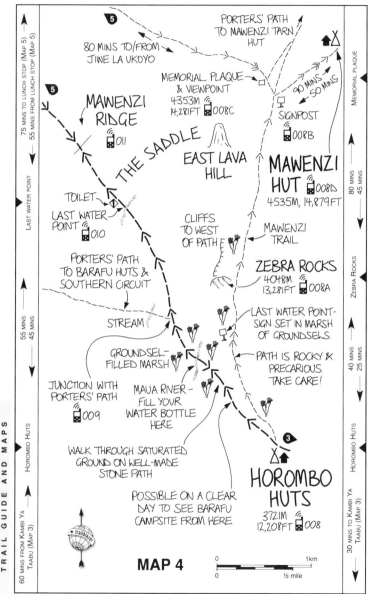

PORTERS' PATH TO MAWENZI TARN HUT

80 MINS TO/FROM JIWE LA UKOYO

MEMORIAL PLAQUE & VIEWPOINT
4353M
14,281FT 008C

SIGNPOST
008B

MAWENZI RIDGE
011

THE SADDLE

EAST LAVA HILL

MAWENZI HUT 008D
4535M, 14,879FT

TOILET

LAST WATER POINT
010

CLIFFS TO WEST OF PATH

MAWENZI TRAIL

PORTERS' PATH TO BARAFU HUTS & SOUTHERN CIRCUIT

ZEBRA ROCKS
4048M
13,281FT 008A

STREAM

LAST WATER POINT- SIGN SET IN MARSH OF GROUNDSELS

GROUNDSEL- FILLED MARSH

PATH IS ROCKY & PRECARIOUS. TAKE CARE!

JUNCTION WITH PORTERS' PATH
009

MAUA RIVER - FILL YOUR WATER BOTTLE HERE

WALK THROUGH SATURATED GROUND ON WELL-MADE STONE PATH

HOROMBO HUTS
3721M
12,208FT 008

POSSIBLE ON A CLEAR DAY TO SEE BARAFU CAMPSITE FROM HERE

trailblazer

MAP 4

0   1km
0   ½ mile

75 MINS TO LUNCH STOP (MAP 5)
55 MINS FROM LUNCH STOP (MAP 5)

LAST WATER POINT

55 MINS
45 MINS

HOROMBO HUTS

60 MINS FROM KAMBI YA TAABU (MAP 3)

MEMORIAL PLAQUE

80 MINS
45 MINS

ZEBRA ROCKS

40 MINS
25 MINS

HOROMBO HUTS

30 MINS TO KAMBI YA TAABU (MAP 3)

90 MINS
50 MINS

with picnic tables, marks the beginning of the uphill approach to **Mawenzi Ridge**, beyond which lies the approach to the **Saddle**, the dry, barren terrain separating Kilimanjaro's two major peaks. With the **Middle Red Hill**, a large parasitic cone, ahead of you to the right, you find yourself descending into a rather flat, extremely windswept and dramatic landscape, the only decoration provided by a few tufts of grass, some hardier floral species such as the aptly named everlastings, and a number of boulders and smaller stones, some of which have been arranged into messages by previous trekkers. It is for these kinds of views that you brought your camera, for the light at this altitude is frequently superb, and while many of your photos may end up in the fire it's a fair bet that a few will be destined for the mantlepiece. The path loops almost due north between the Kibo summit on your left and the Middle Red on your right, whose western slopes shelter trekkers from the often howling wind and more often than not provide the venue for **lunch**.

Your path for the afternoon continues northwards across the Saddle; it's a bit of a weary trudge on a steadily inclining path to **Jiwe La Ukoyo**, a former

KIBO HUTS   45 MINS →   JIWE LA UKOYO   50 MINS →   LUNCH STOP   55 MINS TO LAST WATER POINT (MAP 4) →

TO SCHOOL HUT

📱015

25

6

JIWE LA UKOYO 📱014

SIGN FOR
KIBO CIRCUIT 📱013

KIBO HUTS
4714M 📱016
15,466FT

TOILETS &
PICNIC TABLE

THE SADDLE
OFTEN EXTREMELY
WINDY

BIG BOULDER

80 MINS
BETWEEN
JIWE LA UKOYO
& MEMORIAL
PLAQUE

4

TRIPLETS

MAP 5

LUNCHSTOP 📱012
& TOILETS

MIDDLE
RED HILL

0   1km
0   ½ mile

FEELS LIKE A ROAD –
A WIDE TREK CROSSING
THE ALPINE DESERT

4

KIBO HUTS ← 75 MINS   JIWE LA UKOYO   50 MINS   LUNCH STOP ←   75 MINS FROM LAST WATER STOP (MAP 4)

TRAIL GUIDE AND MAPS

campsite with some toilet huts and a huge boulder (*jiwe* means 'rock' in Swahili). It is also the meeting point between the two main paths from Horombo. Thereafter the path turns sharply westwards towards the **Kibo Huts**, which nestle snugly on the lowest slopes of the summit after which they were named. Though the huts look close, you still have around 1¼ hours' walking from Jiwe La Ukoyo; it's a tough walk too, a gradual but relentless uphill slog to round off what has already been a fairly wearying day.

The huts themselves are basic, built of stone and rather chilly. A sign on the door of the main hut tells you that you are now at 4750m (though we think it's a little bit lower than this at 4714m); a second sign warns you that Gillman's Point is still five hours away...

STAGE 4: KIBO HUTS TO GILLMAN'S POINT AND UHURU PEAK
[MAP 6, p265; MAP 33, p347]

Distance: 6.25km; altitude gained: 1181m

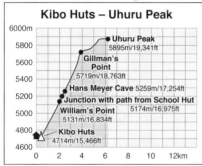

Kibo Huts – Uhuru Peak

- Uhuru Peak 5895m/19,341ft
- Gillman's Point 5719m/18,763ft
- Hans Meyer Cave 5259m/17,254ft
- Junction with path from School Hut 5174m/16,975ft
- William's Point 5131m/16,834ft
- Kibo Huts 4714m/15,466ft

And so you come to the testing part of the walk. No matter how tough you have found the trekking so far, it was but a leisurely stroll compared to what lies ahead of you tonight. The path to Gillman's Point on the crater rim has been in your sights since the previous after-noon when you crossed the Saddle and saw it rearing up at an angle of 16° (John Reader's estimate) behind the Kibo Huts. We think that one of the reasons why this route has a higher failure rate than any of the others is down to the difficulty of this last stretch, which seems steeper and the ground less solid than on other routes. The stretch between Gillman's and Uhuru Peak also sees a high percentage of people giving up, pre-sumably because of the greater distance, even though the gradient is less steep and the hard stuff is, in theory at least, largely behind them.

All of which means that the chances of failure on this route are high – and of making it, but throwing up or passing out along the way, are even higher. Just remember the golden rule: when it comes to climbing Kibo, there is no such thing as too slow. The mountain was formed around 500,000 years ago and has remained much the same ever since, so I think it's reasonable to assume it will still be there in the morning, no matter what time you arrive at the top.

I find a rhythm and try to lose my thoughts to it but feel the first pain of a stomach cramp and then another, and I feel the nausea starting and the headache that I recognise all too well ... The pain is sharp in my head and my cramping is still with me; if I feel this way how is Danny doing with no sleep and nothing in his stomach from the vomiting after dinner?
Rick Ridgeway, *The Shadow of Kilimanjaro – On Foot Across East Africa*

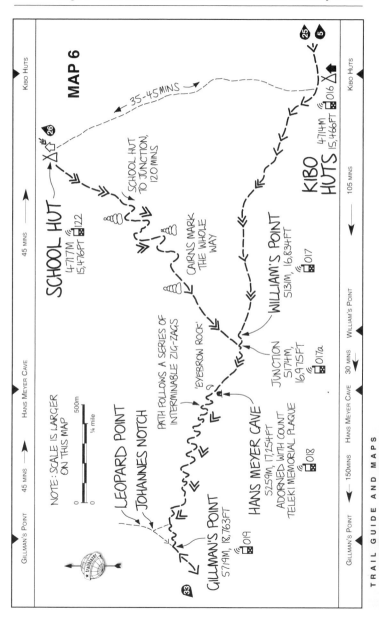

MAP 6

KIBO HUTS

35-45 MINS

SCHOOL HUT →
4717M
15,476FT 📷122

SCHOOL HUT TO JUNCTION
120 MINS

CAIRNS MARK
THE WHOLE
WAY

KIBO
HUTS
4714M
15,466FT 📷016

WILLIAM'S POINT
5131M, 16,834FT
📷017

JUNCTION
5174M,
16,975FT 📷017a

'EYEBROW ROCK'

LEOPARD POINT
JOHANNES NOTCH

NOTE: SCALE IS LARGER
ON THIS MAP

PATH FOLLOWS A SERIES OF
INTERMINABLE ZIG-ZAGS

HANS MEYER CAVE
5259M, 17,254FT
ADORNED WITH COUNT
TELEKI MEMORIAL PLAQUE
📷018

GILLMAN'S POINT
5719M, 18,763FT 📷019

500m
0
¼ mile
0

trailblazer

What you can't see from Kibo Huts, and yet what is rather good about this path, is that there are a number of landmarks on the way – the main ones being William's Point at 5131m and Hans Meyer Cave at 5259m – that act as milestones, helping both to break up the journey and to provide you with some measure of your progress. **William's Point** – or rather, the large east-facing rock immediately beneath it – lies 1¾ hours from Kibo Huts and is usually the first major resting point. **Hans Meyer Cave**, a small and undistinguished hollow adorned with a plaque commemorating the Hungarian hunter, Count and *bon viveur* Samuel Teleki, who rested here in 1887, is 30 minutes further on.

From Hans Meyer Cave, it's a case of following the scree **switchbacks**; if you've mastered the art of walking in a zombie-like trance, now is the time to put that particular technique into action.

> *By some transcendental process I seemed to take on the characteristics of a Shire* [horse], *my head lowered, resolute, I just plunked one foot in front of t'other, mentally munching nothingness.* **Sebastian Snow** *The Rucksack Man,* writing about his attempt to walk from Tierra del Fuego to Alaska across the Americas. It's a good example to follow for your walk to Gillman's Point

This part, as you pinball back and forth on a stretch of fine scree bounded by two boulder-strewn slopes, is extremely exposed and if there's any wind about, you will almost certainly feel it here. If you bought one in Moshi, now is the time to put on your balaclava: your friends will be too concerned with their own situation to laugh at you. By the way, look behind you and you'll see a line of torches snaking up the slope in a scene that feels almost Biblical.

Gradually the zig-zags begin to reduce in size like the audiograph of an echo. You are now entering the final phase of the climb to Gillman's, though it

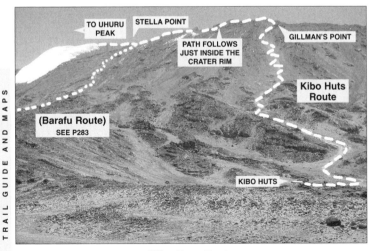

Kibo Huts Route

takes an hour to complete and you'll probably be breathless the whole way. It's easy to get lost in the dark on this final stretch, so don't be too surprised if you see other trekkers to the left and right of you on a different path. If your guide is at least halfway competent, however, you should find yourself at the crater's edge at **Gillman's Point** (5719m; if, upon arrival at the crater rim, you find no signpost welcoming you to Gillman's, the chances are the guide has got his bearings slightly wrong and has led you to the slightly lower point of **Johannes Notch**. No matter: Gillman's is just a three-minute scramble up to your left.)

Gillman's Point is 960m above Kibo Hut [we actually make it 1005m], *that is almost the equivalent of three Empire State Buildings standing one on top of another. The horizontal distance between Kibo Hut and Gillman's Point is roughly 3000 metres, so the gradient averages about 1:3.3 and the distance covered on the way up is about 3300m – the equivalent of nine Empire State Buildings laid end to end up the incline.*   **John Reader** *Kilimanjaro*

If the wind is not too high, Gillman's is a good spot to sit for a few minutes, get your head together, contemplate the star-spangled night with the silhouette of Mawenzi to the east, and congratulate yourself on having earned a nice certificate for making it to the crater rim, having completed the hardest part of the trek. At least, it's the hardest part physically; the hardest part from a psychological point of view now awaits as you try to muster up the energy and enthusiasm to tackle the walk to **Uhuru**. Because if Kilimanjaro is the Roof of Africa, all you've done so far is get to the attic.

Though the time varies throughout the year, as a rough guide you need to be at Gillman's at around 4.45am in order to have a chance of seeing the sunrise at Uhuru at around 6am. If you've no chance of making it by then, consider seeing the sunrise from somewhere along the way: from Stella Point, for example, or overlooking Rebmann Glacier, or from one of the lesser peaks before Uhuru.

See Map 33 on p347 for details of the summit and the walk around the crater rim. The first part of this walk is undulating as you ride the rim's peaks and troughs; you may well need your head torch as you walk in the moon-shadow. From **Stella Point**, 30-45 minutes to the south of Gillman's, the path begins to climb more steadily. Though nothing like as steep as that which has gone before, at this stage any incline is a major challenge. Don't be too disheartened by the many false summits you will encounter along the last part; instead, distract your mind from the pain you are feeling by looking at the huge and beautiful icefields to your left and the sheer, desolate enormity of the crater on your right. A gorgeous dawn at the summit, and a certificate back at Marangu Gate, are the prizes that await...

> *Is it so small a thing*
> *To have enjoy'd the sun,*
> *To have lived light in the spring,*
> *To have loved, to have thought,*
>   *to have done;*
> *To have advanc'd true friends,*
>   *and beat down baffling foes?*
>   **Matthew Arnold**
>   *Empedocles on Etna* (1852)

For details of what you can actually see at the summit, turn to p344, while for a description of the designated descent path, turn to the **Marangu Route descent** on p334.

TRAIL GUIDE AND MAPS

The Machame Route

Then they began to climb and they were going to the East it seemed, and then it darkened and they were in a storm, the rain so thick it seemed like flying through a waterfall, and they were out and Compie turned his head and grinned and pointed and there, ahead, all he could see, as wide as all the world, great, high, and unbelievably white in the sun, was the top of Kilimanjaro. And then he knew that there was where he was going.
Ernest Hemingway, *The Snows of Kilimanjaro*

Ask any guide or tour agent which is their favourite walk on Kilimanjaro and often they will choose this, the Machame-Mweka Route (usually just shortened to the Machame Route, a convention we have adopted here). Though some of them doubtless say this because it's easier to organize – requiring no hut-booking or long-haul driving – it is not difficult to see why the route is so popular: beginning on the south-western side of the mountain, the path passes through some of the mountain's finest features, including the **cloud forest** of Kili's southern slopes, the dry and dusty **Shira Plateau** and the delightful groundsel-clad **Barranco Campsite**.

Furthermore, you have a choice of ascent routes to the summit with thrill-seekers opting for the daunting **Western Breach Route**, while the majority head for the lengthy, long-winded climb up the **Barafu Trail**, with Rebmann Glacier edging into your field of vision on your left as dawn breaks behind Mawenzi on your right. Furthermore, unlike the Marangu Route, on Machame you don't use the same path to descend but instead you come down via the Mweka Route, a steep but very pretty trail encompassing inhospitably dry mountain desert and lush lowland forest in a matter of a few hours.

For all these reasons, Machame is now the busiest on the mountain. Indeed, it must be said that it is now, on certain days at certain times of the year, simply *too* popular – which will doubtless put many people off. Another reason could be that while the Machame Route is widely reckoned to be that much harder than the Marangu Route (and is thus nicknamed the Whiskey Route, in

---

❏ **Mobile (cell) phone reception on the Machame Route**
It depends which network you're with, of course, but mobile (cell phone) reception on the Machame Route seems to be OK by the standards of Kilimanjaro. I couldn't get any reception up to **Machame Huts**, however, and it was only on the second morning as we left the forest that reception was resumed. At **Shira Caves** the porters climb up the rocks surrounding the camp to use their phones. At **Lava Tower** there is fair reception, and while you have to wander around the camp to get anything at both **Barranco** and **Karanga**, it is good at **Barafu**, intermittent at **Stella Point** and fine, so we are told, at **Uhuru Peak**. The **Millennium Camp**, on the descent, also has good mobile reception. If you are taking the Western Breach Route, please see the box on p290 for a summary of your mobile reception from Lava Tower.

opposition to Marangu's softer soubriquet of the 'Coca Cola trail'), the proportion of trekkers who reach the top using this route is marginally but significantly higher. This could be down to a number of factors: the Machame Route allows people to acclimatize better because it's longer (**40.16km to the summit via Barafu, or 36.7km via the Western Breach**, as opposed to 35.5km on Marangu); when it comes to climbing the slopes of Kibo, the Barafu Route is more straightforward than the route from Kibo Huts to Gillman's, as it is largely conducted on the firm terrain of a ridge rather than sliding, shifting shale; or maybe the Machame's higher success rate is merely an indication that more experienced, hardened trekkers – ie the very people who are presumably most likely to reach the summit – are more inclined to choose this route.

The following description assumes you will be taking the Barafu Route to the summit. This walk via Barafu traditionally lasts for six days and five nights, though it is now more common for trekkers to opt for an extra night during the ascent, usually at Karanga Camp, halfway between Barranco and Barafu camps. Not only does the extra day aid acclimatization but it also reduces from almost six to three the number of hours walked on the day that precedes the exhausting midnight ascent to the summit, thereby allowing trekkers more time to recover their faculties, relax and prepare themselves for the final push to the top.

Incidentally, those daredevils wishing to try their hand at the Arrow Glacier/Western Breach Route, will leave the regular Machame Route on the third day; the map on p276 and the box on p277 indicate where. You can then find a description of that path to the summit on p300.

STAGE 1: MACHAME GATE TO MACHAME HUTS
[MAP 7, p271; MAP 8, p273]

Distance: 10.75km; altitude gained: 1210m
Coming from Moshi, the drive to Machame Gate, at an altitude of 1811m, takes just under an hour. On the way to the gate ask the driver to point out the house of the local chief, a simple yet large bungalow on the left-hand side of the road. Passing through **Machame village** you'll soon arrive at the gate itself, a small collection of buildings huddled around a 4WD car park. **Register** in the office and make sure you use the toilet facilities on site – you may not think much of them now but, believe me, compared to some of the latrines on the trail these are heavenly.

Back at the car park, porters are busy haggling over who is going to take what, guides are reporting to KINA-PA reception to wrestle with the red tape, while the trekkers are packing away their lunchboxes

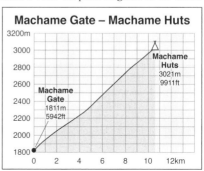

Machame Gate – Machame Huts

Machame Huts 3021m 9911ft

Machame Gate 1811m 5942ft

TRAIL GUIDE AND MAPS

and quietly steeling themselves for the rigours ahead. To one side of this chaos is the beginning of the trail...

This 10km+ first day is a long and sweaty one. It starts with a 3km amble up a 4WD track, a wide snaking trail that cuts through the kind of deep, dark enchanted forest that Hansel and Gretel would be familiar with. Green moss hangs thickly from the branches that creak and groan in the wind; it's a magical start to a wonderful adventure. After 45 minutes the 4WD road comes to an end, the gentle curves and steady incline giving way to a narrower, steeper but now beautifully renovated pedestrians-only path that continues all the way to Machame Huts. Looking to the side of the path you'll notice that the vegetation is already changing as you progress deeper into the **cloud forest**, the scarlet and yellow *Impatiens kilimanjari* and pink *Impatiens pseudoviola* now flourishing between the roots of the 30-metre tall trees; tree ferns also proliferate here.

Ninety-five minutes or so from the end of the 4WD track, the path widens momentarily to form several small **clearings** (one of which has en suite toilet facilities) that make for popular lunch stops. Those who've already drunk their water bottles dry can replenish their supplies from the stream down in the valley to the west. Listen out for the primate-like call of the black (actually dark green) and red turaco which nests around here, and watch your lunch too: it's not uncommon for the forest rodents to sneak into lunchboxes and drag off a samosa or two.

The post-prandial path varies little from that which has gone before, though the gradient increases slightly the higher you climb. As the forest gradually begins to thin out you'll notice that you are actually walking on a narrow forested spine between two shallow valleys. A stream – more audible than visible – runs briefly to the right of the trail.

Around two hours after lunch the second signpost of the day appears, this time warning against the careless discarding of cigarette butts; as well as dispensing some sound advice, this sign also marks the border between the cloud forest and the heath, where long grasses dominate and the robust trees of the forest give way to the spindly, tree-like giant heathers. *Kniphofia thomsonii* (known to you and me as red hot pokers) make their first appearance at this altitude, as do several other wild flowers and shrubs such as the bushy *Philippia excelsa*. With the forest thinning, Kibo peak hoves into view for the first time to the east.

It is only 20 minutes from the signpost to **Machame Huts** (3021m), a series of level pitches cut into the grass, each with its own toilet. Make sure you sign your name in the **registration book** and aim to pitch your tent as high as possible for the best views: by the green hut is a good spot, affording views to the east up to Kibo and south-west towards Mount Meru. Look out for the birdlife too, which is abundant round here, with olive thrush, common stonechats and flocks of montane white-eye all resident, in addition to the usual seedeaters and alpine chats that are ubiquitous on the mountain.

By the way, having climbed to 3021m you are now higher than the top of Mawson Peak, at 2745m the highest point in Australia.

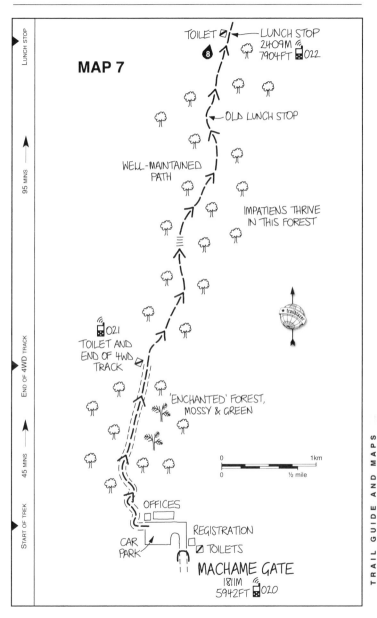

TOILET ← LUNCH STOP
2409M
7904FT 022
8

MAP 7

← OLD LUNCH STOP

WELL-MAINTAINED
PATH

IMPATIENS THRIVE
IN THIS FOREST

trailblazer

021
TOILET AND
END OF 4WD
TRACK

'ENCHANTED' FOREST,
MOSSY & GREEN

0   1km
0   ½ mile

OFFICES

REGISTRATION

CAR
PARK   TOILETS

MACHAME GATE
1811M
5942FT 020

LUNCH STOP

95 MINS

END OF 4WD TRACK

45 MINS

START OF TREK

TRAIL GUIDE AND MAPS

STAGE 2: MACHAME HUTS TO SHIRA CAVES
[MAP 8, p273; MAP 9, p274]

Distance: 5.3km; altitude gained: 818m

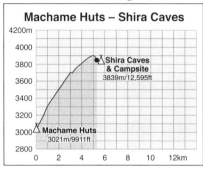

This leg of the trek is short but a little strenuous as you ascend from 3021m up to the Shira Plateau, finally coming to a halt at the Shira Caves at just over 3839m. Parts of this walk are a bit steep and the skinny, naked heathers at this altitude provide little shade from the heat; what's more, the path is extremely dusty, at least after lunch, so if you have gaiters you'll probably be thankful for the protection they provide (and remember to keep your camera bag tightly closed too to prevent dust inveigling into any valuable equipment). In spite of all this, by taking it slowly, resting frequently and enjoying the en-route views that encompass Kibo, Meru and all points in between, this day needn't be too taxing.

The walk starts as it goes on for much of the morning, with a steepish climb north up through forests of stunted, twisted heather bushes; while ahead of you in the distance is the lip of Shira Plateau. The path winds its way up to the top of a ridge formed by a petrified lava flow, occasionally allowing trekkers some splendid **views** over Machame Huts and the village below as well as the flat Tanzanian plains beyond. Giant groundsels (*Dendrosenecio kilimanjari ssp cottonii*), the squat, chunky trees with the green-leaf crown, begin to dot the path and Kilimanjaro's desiccated **helichrysums**, ubiquitous above 3000m, appear here for the first time, like living pot pourri. Note, too, how most of the vegetation not only diminishes in size as you climb higher but the taller plants seem to bend as one towards the plateau, as if pointing the way.

After passing a number of **viewpoints** and clambering from one side of the ridge to the other, the gradient of the trail increases exponentially towards the **lunch stop**, hidden from view behind a rocky outcrop. The effort expended in reaching there is worth it, for while munching your sandwiches you can savour yet more views of Kibo as well as all points south. Note, however, that the renovated path ends here.

By observing the line of porters and trekkers on the path ahead you can pick out the afternoon's trail, which initially continues north and up, before bending fairly sharply to the north-west, cutting a near horizontal line beneath the rim of the plateau. But though the worst of the day's climbing is behind you, don't be fooled into thinking this is an easy section, for the path on this north-westerly trail undulates considerably as it climbs over rocks and boulders and it can be tiring in the searing afternoon heat. As a distraction, the first of Kilimanjaro's

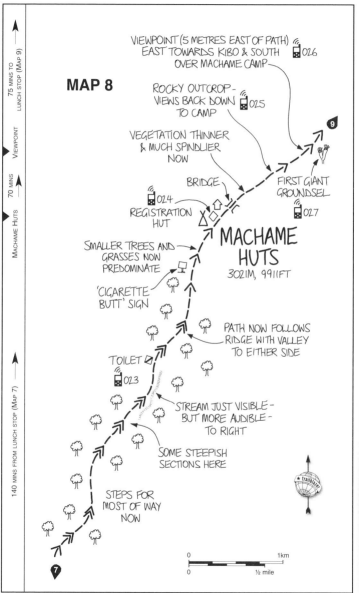

MAP 8

VIEWPOINT (5 METRES EAST OF PATH)
EAST TOWARDS KIBO & SOUTH
OVER MACHAME CAMP

026

ROCKY OUTCROP –
VIEWS BACK DOWN
TO CAMP

025

VEGETATION THINNER
& MUCH SPINDLIER
NOW

BRIDGE

FIRST GIANT
GROUNDSEL

027

024
REGISTRATION
HUT

MACHAME
HUTS
3021M, 9911FT

SMALLER TREES AND
GRASSES NOW
PREDOMINATE

'CIGARETTE
BUTT' SIGN

PATH NOW FOLLOWS
RIDGE WITH VALLEY
TO EITHER SIDE

TOILET

023

STREAM JUST VISIBLE –
BUT MORE AUDIBLE –
TO RIGHT

SOME STEEPISH
SECTIONS HERE

STEPS FOR
MOST OF WAY
NOW

7

9

0   1km
0   ½ mile

trailblazer

75 MINS TO LUNCH STOP (MAP 9)   VIEWPOINT   70 MINS   MACHAME HUTS   140 MINS FROM LUNCH STOP (MAP 7)

TRAIL GUIDE AND MAPS

celebrated moorland **lobelias** (*Lobelia deckenii*), both phallic and cabbage-shaped and growing to a height of around two metres, appear by the trail.

Just under an hour after lunch the plateau is gained and the path continues northwards. Look out for Shira Plateau's distinctive, shiny black **obsidian** rock (see p91). Your camp for the night is **Shira Caves Campsite**. (Note that this campsite is not on older maps, though the caves are.)

Looking west from Shira Caves Campsite, ask your guide to point out **Shira Cathedral** and **East Shira Hill** which line the southern boundary of Shira Plateau, and, behind them to the far west, **Johnsell Point** and **Klute Peak**,

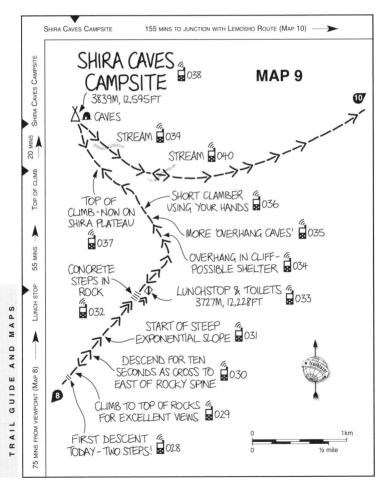

SHIRA CAVES CAMPSITE   155 MINS TO JUNCTION WITH LEMOSHO ROUTE (MAP 10) →

SHIRA CAVES CAMPSITE
3839M, 12,595FT 038

MAP 9

CAVES

STREAM 039

STREAM 040

TOP OF CLIMB - NOW ON SHIRA PLATEAU 037

SHORT CLAMBER USING YOUR HANDS 036

MORE 'OVERHANG CAVES' 035

OVERHANG IN CLIFF - POSSIBLE SHELTER 034

CONCRETE STEPS IN ROCK 032

LUNCHSTOP & TOILETS 3727M, 12,228FT 033

START OF STEEP EXPONENTIAL SLOPE 031

DESCEND FOR TEN SECONDS AS CROSS TO EAST OF ROCKY SPINE 030

CLIMB TO TOP OF ROCKS FOR EXCELLENT VIEWS 029

FIRST DESCENT TODAY - TWO STEPS! 028

trailblazer

0   1km
0   ½ mile

SHIRA CAVES CAMPSITE | 20 MINS | TOP OF CLIMB | 55 MINS | LUNCH STOP | 75 MINS FROM VIEWPOINT (MAP 8)

TRAIL GUIDE AND MAPS

the highest points of the Shira Ridge, the western rim of the oldest of Kili's three craters. Mount Meru, too, is still visible to the west on the horizon.

Incidentally, by reaching this camp you are now at a higher altitude than Mafadi (3450m), the highest peak in South Africa.

STAGE 3: SHIRA CAVES CAMPSITE TO BARRANCO HUTS
[MAP 9, p274; MAP 10, p276; MAP 11, p279]

Distance: 10.75km via Lava Tower; altitude gained: 147m (788m up to Lava Tower Camp, then 641m descent to Barranco)

Camp-life on Kilimanjaro is a capital school for the practice of self-denial.
Hans Meyer *Across East African Glaciers*

During this section of the trek you cover over 10km as you move from the western to the southern slopes of Kilimanjaro; by the end of it you may feel slightly disappointed to learn that, for all your efforts, you will have gained just 147m in height, from Shira Caves at 3839m to Barranco, situated at an altitude of 3986m. Nevertheless, this leg of the trek is vital for acclimatization purposes, for during the day you will climb to a respectable

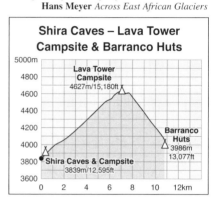

Shira Caves – Lava Tower Campsite & Barranco Huts

Lava Tower Campsite 4627m/15,180ft

Barranco Huts 3986m 13,077ft

Shira Caves & Campsite 3839m/12,595ft

4627m if taking the path via Lava Tower. (There's another path via the new and unofficial **Sheffield Campsite**, 4547m, which is great for those who can't quite manage the climb up to Lava Tower; and a third and older trail which is lower still.) Don't be surprised, therefore, if by the end of it you have a crashing headache: this is normal and is only cause for concern if it is accompanied by other symptoms of mountain sickness, or if the pain hasn't disappeared by the morning.

The day begins with a steady, gentle ascent through the dry, boulder-strewn terrain of Shira Plateau towards the western slopes of Kibo (the summit of which, from this angle, is said by some trekkers to resemble the profile of a Native American Indian chief at rest. No, I can't really see it either.) At first the path meanders somewhat, rising and falling regularly as it negotiates the gentle folds of the plateau before finally settling on a roughly easterly direction, with a steady, shallow incline for most of the next 6km. Notice how the vegetation has declined until only a few everlastings and lichen manage to cling to life. Ahead, facing you down, is the brilliant white smear of Penck Glacier.

Soon after the **junction with the Lemosho Route** the path loops to the south-east and divides. Not too long ago it was only those people who opted to tackle the summit on the more difficult Western Breach Route who headed east

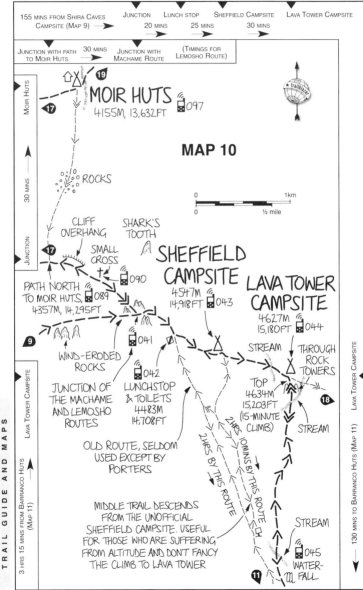

155 MINS FROM SHIRA CAVES CAMPSITE (MAP 9) →   JUNCTION   LUNCH STOP   SHEFFIELD CAMPSITE   LAVA TOWER CAMPSITE
20 MINS   25 MINS   30 MINS

JUNCTION WITH PATH TO MOIR HUTS   30 MINS →   JUNCTION WITH MACHAME ROUTE   (TIMINGS FOR LEMOSHO ROUTE)

MOIR HUTS   097
MOIR HUTS   19
17
4155M, 13,632FT

MAP 10

ROCKS

0   1km
0   ½ mile

30 MINS

CLIFF OVERHANG   SHARK'S TOOTH
SMALL CROSS   090
JUNCTION   17
PATH NORTH TO MOIR HUTS, 089
4357M, 14,295FT

SHEFFIELD CAMPSITE
4547M 14,918FT   043

LAVA TOWER CAMPSITE
4627M 15,180FT   044

STREAM   THROUGH ROCK TOWERS

9   041

WIND-ERODED ROCKS   042
JUNCTION OF THE MACHAME AND LEMOSHO ROUTES   LUNCHSTOP & TOILETS 4483M 14,708FT

TOP 4634M 15,203FT (15-MINUTE CLIMB)   18
STREAM

OLD ROUTE, SELDOM USED EXCEPT BY PORTERS

2 HRS JOINING BY THIS ROUTE
2 HRS BY THIS ROUTE

MIDDLE TRAIL DESCENDS FROM THE UNOFFICIAL SHEFFIELD CAMPSITE. USEFUL FOR THOSE WHO ARE SUFFERING FROM ALTITUDE AND DON'T FANCY THE CLIMB TO LAVA TOWER

STREAM
045
WATER-FALL

11

LAVA TOWER CAMPSITE

3 HRS 15 MINS FROM BARRANCO HUTS (MAP 11)   TRAIL GUIDE AND MAPS

LAVA TOWER CAMPSITE   130 MINS TO BARRANCO HUTS (MAP 11)

> ❏ **Ascent of Kibo via the Western Breach/Arrow Glacier Route**
> The Western Breach Route is a harder, shorter, more dangerous and less popular alternative trail than the standard route via Barafu Huts. But it's also a great walk that allows you to explore the crater floor and all its features – the Furtwangler Glacier, Reusch Crater and Ash Pit, to name but three – as well as affording supreme views of the Shira Plateau, Barranco Valley and the summit of Mount Meru. The route starts at the Lava Tower Campsite. You can find a full description of the Arrow Glacier/Western Breach Route starting on p300.

towards **Lava Tower**; these days, however, most guides recognize the acclimatization benefits of taking this climb and also opt for this route, even if they then divert off down to Barranco Huts. As for the more southerly route, this is now largely the preserve of porters and those trekkers who aren't doing so well and need to descend quickly to Barranco. (This more gentle, southerly trail bends round to the right past the **lunchstop** and onto the highest point of *this* walk, 4530m, before descending quickly via a series of zigzags into a gully. It then bends south-east once more, following the contours of Kibo's lower reaches as it crosses two more streams. Less than an hour later the trail meets with the old **Umbwe Route** – see p326 – a junction that is marked by a proliferation of signposts, from where it's downhill all the way to Barranco.)

Back at Lava Tower the higher route splits again. The route up to Arrow Glacier soars above, while the path to Barranco drops steeply south to a stream, and rises and falls a couple of times before plummeting, finally and fabulously, into the delightful **Barranco Valley**, rich in groundsel and lobelia. A huge gouge in the southern face of Kibo to the south-west of Uhuru Peak, the valley is in places 300m deep and was formed when a huge landslide swept southwards down from the summit about 100,000 years ago.

From **Barranco Huts campsite** (3986m) and its environs you'll have spectacular views of Kibo's southern face, the Western Breach and the mighty Heim Glacier, with glacial moraine tumbling southwards towards the camp. Few are the trekkers who do not rank this campsite as their favourite on this trail. Indeed, so beautiful is it that it's tempting to linger outside one's tent after dark and savour the sights and scenery of this most

'...an extraordinary arborescent plant, since named *Senecio Johnstonii*... Its trunk was so superficially rooted and so rotten that, in spite of its height and girth, I could pull it down with one hand.
(from *The Kilima-njaro Expedition*, **HH Johnston**, 1886; note that the tree he is talking about and depicting is no longer called *Senecio johnstonii* but *Dendrosenecio kilimanjarii ssp cottonii*).

TRAIL GUIDE AND MAPS

spectacular site – though in reality, the cold soon chases most people into their sleeping bags.

By the way, though you have gained only 147m since this morning, by climbing to Lava Tower Campsite (4627m) you have reached an altitude that's just 7m shy of the highest mountain in Switzerland, the Dufourspitze; bother to climb up Lava Tower itself, which takes about 15 minutes or so, and you'll be 57m higher.

STAGE 4: BARRANCO HUTS TO BARAFU HUTS
[MAP 11, p279; MAP 12, p280]

Distance: 8.5km; altitude gained: 676m

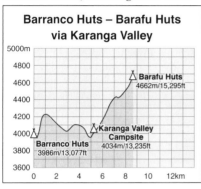

**Barranco Huts – Barafu Huts
via Karanga Valley**

Barafu Huts
4662m/15,295ft

Karanga Valley
Campsite
4034m/13,235ft

Barranco Huts
3986m/13,077ft

At this altitude this is a long stage; so long that many trekkers prefer to tackle it over two days, camping for the night above Karanga Valley. Make sure you fill your containers in the valley below the campsite as this is the last place to get water on the Machame Route and, if the cold wind's rushing through, it's possibly the last place you'd want to be stopping at too, though its beauty cannot be denied. As you walk along the path today the great glaciers of Kili's Southern Icefields – the Heim, Kersten and Decken glaciers – will appear on your left one after the other. Curiously, although this stage sets you up nicely for the final push to the summit, by the end of the day you will actually be further away from Uhuru Peak (as the lammergeyer flies) than you were at the start of the day at Barranco.

The hardest part of the day occurs right at the beginning, with a near-vertical scramble to the east of the campsite up **The Barranco Wall** or **Breach Wall** (now more commonly called the **Breakfast Wall**, as it is usually tackled after breakfast). In my experience most trekkers actually get a real kick out of this climb, probably because it provides such a welcome change from the relentless *pole pole* trudge of the previous stages. You'll have to stash your walking poles away for this first section, because at times you'll need to use both hands to haul yourself up the groundsel-dressed slopes. False summits along the way shouldn't discourage you, for after about 80 minutes you'll reach the true summit of the wall; here you can sit on the bare rock and enjoy the views south and east, with the great Heim Glacier over your shoulder to the north, and relish the prospect of the relatively gentle descent into the next gully below.

At the bottom of this pretty little gully, and having crossed the small stream that flows through it, you come to a **flat gravel area**, possibly once a camping spot and, by the amount of loo roll hanging from the bushes, a popular pit stop too. To the north-east a path snakes towards a high pass, once open only to porters and now closed to everybody. Your guide will lead you away from this short-cut to Barafu and bring you instead along an easier trail cutting south-east into a series of mini-valleys. Climbing out of these valleys, the path then cuts across a barren, **'desert' slope** where the silence and stillness are positively deafening, before finally descending down the western, lusher slopes of the **Karanga Valley**.

Ferns, heather and other greenery reappear for a while as you descend along the rock-and-mud path, a path that you share in places with a mountain stream. Karanga Valley is, in the words of John Reader, 'narrow, steep and exquisite'. It is also your last place to collect water before the summit, so it is vital you fill all your water bottles here. Try to collect your water from as high a point in the stream as possible and purify it: giardia could be present. The valley itself is like

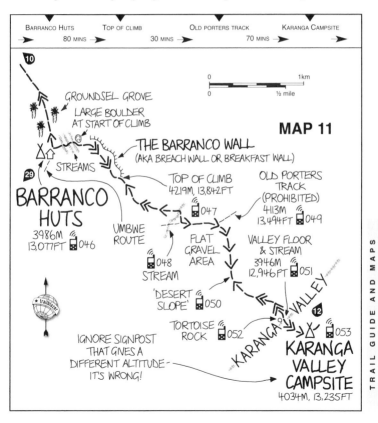

BARRANCO HUTS	TOP OF CLIMB	OLD PORTERS TRACK	KARANGA CAMPSITE
80 MINS →	30 MINS →	70 MINS →	

10

GROUNDSEL GROVE
LARGE BOULDER
AT START OF CLIMB

0 _____ 1km
0 _____ ½ mile

MAP 11

THE BARRANCO WALL
(AKA BREACH WALL OR BREAKFAST WALL)

29

STREAMS

BARRANCO HUTS
3986M
13,077FT 📱046

UMBWE ROUTE

TOP OF CLIMB
4219M, 13,842FT
📱047

OLD PORTERS TRACK
(PROHIBITED)
4113M
13,494FT 📱049

FLAT GRAVEL AREA

📱048
STREAM

VALLEY FLOOR & STREAM
3946M
12,946FT 📱051

'DESERT SLOPE' 📱050

KARANGA VALLEY

TORTOISE ROCK 📱052

12

📱053

IGNORE SIGNPOST THAT GIVES A DIFFERENT ALTITUDE - IT'S WRONG!

KARANGA VALLEY CAMPSITE
4034M, 13,235FT

trailblazer

a small oasis of green, albeit a cold and windswept one; beautiful shimmering green **malachite sunbirds** nest around here – you may spot them feeding on the lobelias.

Those who plan to cover this leg in two days rather than one will camp at the top of the next climb, a very steep 20-minute ascent on a switchback path. This is the somewhat misnamed **Karanga Valley Campsite** (4034m; I say misnamed because, of course, it's above the valley and not in it; also, *karanga* is Swahili for 'peanut' – yet I doubt nuts have ever grown up here!), an unlovely place, windswept and ramshackle, with something of the atmosphere of a refugee camp about it. At this altitude it's often hemmed in by clouds which unfortunately obscure its best feature, namely the lovely views it affords of Kibo's southern face. By the way, for those who are staying here the distance from Barranco to Karanga is **5.1km** and despite all your efforts you will now be just **48m** higher than when you set off from Barranco.

At the campsite the trail takes a leftward turn, heading in a north-easterly direction on a steady incline, with the Kersten and Decken glaciers a permanent presence to your left. The scenery now becomes even more barren as you make your way between the boulders and over the shattered rocks and stones of this misty mountain slope. Even the trail is faint. Only the occasional cairn marking out the way gives an indication that man has passed this way before (unless, of course, some bastard has dropped litter). If George Lucas is looking for somewhere wild, inhospitable and unearthly as a location for his next Star Wars instalment, he could do a lot worse...

At the top the path bends more to the east and descends into a shallow valley that, if anything, is even drier and more blighted than the previous section. Once again, the Southern Icefields loom ominously to your left, with Rebmann Glacier appearing for the first time.

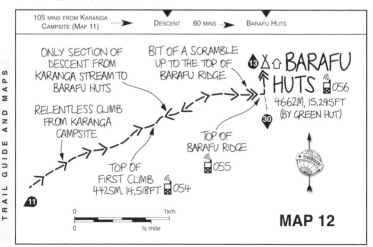

105 MINS FROM KARANGA CAMPSITE (MAP 11)   DESCENT   60 MINS →   BARAFU HUTS

ONLY SECTION OF DESCENT FROM KARANGA STREAM TO BARAFU HUTS

BIT OF A SCRAMBLE UP TO THE TOP OF BARAFU RIDGE

13 △ ⌂ BARAFU HUTS 056
4662M, 15,295FT (BY GREEN HUT)
30

RELENTLESS CLIMB FROM KARANGA CAMPSITE

TOP OF BARAFU RIDGE 055

TOP OF FIRST CLIMB 4425M, 14,518FT 054

11

★ trailblazer

0   1km
0   ½ mile

MAP 12

Barafu Huts (4662m), your destination for this leg, lies at the end of this valley, reached after a short scramble up the cliff-face and a 15- to 25-minute walk almost due north. Barafu means 'Ice' in Swahili and the camp is probably called this because of its proximity to Rebmann Glacier, away to the north-west. It's an appropriately chilly spot but it has its advantages: the views of the climb that you face are good, and they've installed some new toilets too (and not before time; according to one popular rumour, a woman died at Barafu when the toilet she was sitting in collapsed and slid down the hillside – which is not the most dignified way of meeting your Maker). By the way, at 4662m you are now higher than Mount Elbert, at 4401m the highest mountain in the Rocky Mountains.

Try to get some food and rest as soon as possible and sort out your preparations for the next stage before it gets dark: you've got a long night ahead.

STAGE 5: BARAFU HUTS TO STELLA POINT AND UHURU PEAK
[MAP 13, p282; MAP 33, p347]

Distance: 4.86km; altitude gained: 1233m

But now, apparently, the mountain was inhabited by fiery beings who baffled man's adventurous foot: the mountain receded as the traveller advanced, the summit rose as he ascended; blood burst from the nostrils, fingers bent backwards... even the most adventurous were forced back. **Richard Burton** in *Progress of Expedition to East Africa*, reporting the rumours he had heard about Kilimanjaro while residing in Tanga (circa 1857).

And so you come to the final ascent. For the past five days or so you've enjoyed some wonderful walking and miles of smiles; now it's time to do the hard yards.

The climb itself is a rigorous, vigorous push to Stella Point and the crater rim, followed by a 45-minute trudge up to Uhuru Peak, the highest point in Africa. It's tough, no doubt about it, but if you man-

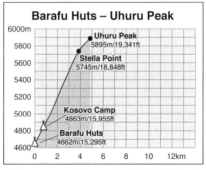

Barafu Huts – Uhuru Peak

- Uhuru Peak 5895m/19,341ft
- Stella Point 5745m/18,848ft
- Kosovo Camp 4863m/15,955ft
- Barafu Huts 4662m/15,295ft

age to avoid sickness or injury there's no reason why you shouldn't be clutching a certificate come tomorrow evening.

This final stage usually begins at around midnight; this not only allows trekkers the chance to see sunrise from the summit but also leaves enough daylight to allow for the long descent to the next night's campsite, with an hour's recuperation back at Barafu on the way. As such, you can leave most of your **luggage** at Barafu while you tackle the ascent, though you should take any valuables with you (there have been a few robberies from tents left unguarded), as well as your **camera**, spare film and batteries and all your **water**, which should be kept in **insulated bottles** or it'll freeze up and be useless on the ascent.

TRAIL GUIDE AND MAPS

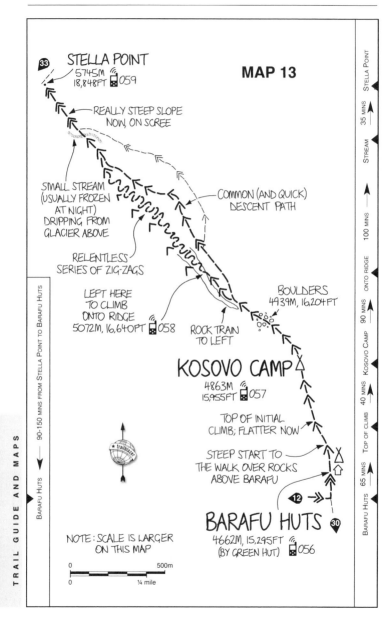

MAP 13

STELLA POINT
5745M
18,848FT 📻 059

REALLY STEEP SLOPE
NOW, ON SCREE

SMALL STREAM
(USUALLY FROZEN
AT NIGHT)
DRIPPING FROM
GLACIER ABOVE

COMMON (AND QUICK)
DESCENT PATH

RELENTLESS
SERIES OF ZIG-ZAGS

LEFT HERE
TO CLIMB
ONTO RIDGE
5072M, 16,640FT 📻 058

BOULDERS
4939M, 16,204FT

ROCK TRAIN
TO LEFT

KOSOVO CAMP
4863M
15,955FT 📻 057

TOP OF INITIAL
CLIMB; FLATTER NOW

STEEP START TO
THE WALK OVER ROCKS
ABOVE BARAFU

BARAFU HUTS
4662M, 15,295FT 📻 056
(BY GREEN HUT)

NOTE: SCALE IS LARGER
ON THIS MAP

0   500m
0   ¼ mile

TRAIL GUIDE AND MAPS

90-150 MINS FROM STELLA POINT TO BARAFU HUTS

BARAFU HUTS ← ← ← ← ← ← ←

STELLA POINT
35 MINS
STREAM
100 MINS
ONTO RIDGE
90 MINS
KOSOVO CAMP
40 MINS
TOP OF CLIMB
65 MINS
BARAFU HUTS

Cameras, particularly digitals and feature-heavy SLRs, have been known to freeze in these conditions as well so keep them (or at the very least their batteries) insulated, preferably by putting them in an inside pocket or wrapped in clothing in your daypack. Wear most of your **clothes** too – you can always take a layer or two off in the unlikely situation you find yourself getting too hot – and have your **head-torch** readily to hand when you wake up so you don't have to spend time and energy looking around for it before you go.

Good luck!

At 4am by the light of a hurricane lamp, and wrapped in everything that could give warmth, I started with Mawala, the headman, and Jonathan, our guide, on the long uphill pull of 4000ft over loose scree and fissured rocks. The cold was intense, and Mawala got two of his toes frost-bitten ... our breathing had become so difficult that we could barely drag ourselves along and had to sit down every few yards to recover breath, now and again sucking icicles and nibbling Cadbury's Milk Chocolate. Yet the steep ascent was mostly over projecting ridges of lava slabs and presented no real obstacle beyond the extreme altitude. Here and there, however, we struck a bed of loose shingle, which mockingly carried us backwards at every footstep almost the whole distance of our tread.

Eva Stuart Watt *Africa's Dome of Mystery* (1930)

The way to the summit starts, as you've probably already observed from Barafu, by scrambling over the **small cliffs** at the northern end of the camp in what is the steepest part of the trek save for the final push to Stella Point. Passing through the unofficial **Kosovo Camp (4863m)** about 1¾ hours into the trek, you may be pleased to know that you are higher than Mont Blanc, the highest mountain in Western Europe (4807m).

Barafu Route

Climbing still further, the path now ascends to a rocky ridge, in the shadow of which you initially walk before taking a sharp left to surmount it and walk along its spine. You are now heading directly for the summit and Stella Point, a direction you will maintain for nearly the entire night. The **switchback path** begins in earnest once you leave the ridge and continues for most of the next two hours or more. It is pointless describing the scenery on this section, for the chances are you won't be able to see much beyond the radius of your torch-beam and you probably won't be keen on surveying the landscape now anyway. If it's a clear night, however, you may be able to see Rebmann Glacier ahead of you to your left, with the ice-free Stella Point a little to its right in the distance. Picking your way through the trail of knackered trekkers and exhausted assistants, ignore the sound of people retching and sobbing and remember to keep your pace constant and very slow, even if you feel fine: you've come this far, and now is not a good time to get altitude sickness.

Though you probably won't notice it, the path actually drifts slightly to the north over these three hours, before crossing a **stream** that is usually frozen at night. You are now just 35 minutes from Stella Point (5745m), but it's a painful, tear-inducing half-hour on sheer scree. The gradient up to now has been steep, but this last scree slope takes the biscuit; in fact, it takes the entire tin. In just about everybody's opinion this is the hardest part of the climb, when the cold insinuates itself between the layers of your clothes, penetrating your skin, chilling your bones and numbing the marrow until finally, inevitably, it seems to freeze your very soul. The situation seems desperate at this hour and you can do nothing; nothing except keep going. It's one thing to fail to reach the summit because of altitude sickness; quite another to fail from *attitude* sickness.

The situation was appalling, there was a grandeur and a magnificence about the surroundings which were almost too much for me; instead of exhilarating, they were oppressive.
Charles New, the first person to reach the snowline on Kilimanjaro, in his book *Life, Wanderings, and Labours in Eastern Africa* (1873)

The ground underfoot is just one more obstacle at this stage, the distinctive **shale and gravel slopes** of Kibo causing you to slip back with every step. Everybody has their own way of tackling this, with some trekkers stabbing their poles hard into the ground to aid their balance, while others walk with a Chaplinesque gait, their feet splayed outwards to stem the slide back. Whatever way you choose, you'll find it hard work.

Lift one foot and then the other, just enough to place it higher; don't use any more energy than you need to and breathe deeply between each move. Rhythm is everything, rhythm and pacing, and when you are in it your thoughts go and it is dreamlike, but you are still here in the moment, the cone beam of light coming from your forehead tying you through the blackness to the lava slope of this mountain that in your mind you see rising to a rare glacial height above the acacia-studded plain of Africa.
Rick Ridgeway *The Shadow of Kilimanjaro – on Foot across East Africa* (1999)

Make it to Stella and you can afford to relax a little. To give you an idea of your achievement, you are now higher than the summit of Russia's Mount Elbrus, at 5642m the highest peak in Europe.

If you really, absolutely, positively, definitely can't do any more, take comfort from the fact that you have already matched the feat of respected climber HW Tilman, for whom Stella Point was the highest point reached on his first attempt on the summit; and you can always use his excuse – he thought that this *was* the highest point – too. (Mind you, as if to prove that it was ignorance and not a lack of fortitude that prevented him from reaching Uhuru, he then went on to conquer the much-harder Mawenzi Peak a few days later.) Take comfort, too, from the fact that you have also earned yourself a certificate; a certificate, moreover, that's identical – save for a couple of words – to the one they give you if you reach the summit. But for most trekkers, those two words – 'UHURU PEAK' – are everything. Words that are worth all the money, time and energy one has spent in getting to this point; and which are certainly worth the extra 45 minutes it takes to stagger around the crater rim (see Map 33, p347), passing minor pinnacles such as **Elveda** and **Hans Meyer** points before finally arriving, just as Hans Meyer himself did over a century ago, at **Uhuru Peak**: the true summit of the mountain and the highest point in the whole continent. You are now enjoying an unrivalled view of Africa – nobody on this great chaotic, crazy, charismatic continent is currently gazing down from as lofty a vantage-point as you.

From the summit, it's usual for trekkers who took the Machame Route up to take the **Mweka Route** back down; and this you'll find described on p337.

Machame village in the late nineteenth century. Engraving by **Alexandre Le Roy** from *Au Kilima-Ndjaro* published in 1893.

The Lemosho & Shira Plateau
routes – an introduction

Without doubt Kibo is most imposing as seen from the west. Here it rises in solemn majesty, and the eye is not distracted by the sister peak of Mawenzi, of which nothing is to be seen but a single jutting pinnacle. The effect is enhanced by the magnificent flowing sweep of the outline, the dazzling extent of the ice-cap, the vast stretch of the forest, the massive breadth of the base, and the jagged crest of the Shira spur as it branches away towards the west.

Hans Meyer *Across East African Glaciers* (1891)

These two treks have been put together simply because they have a lot of features in common, the main one being that both involve a crossing of the expansive Shira Plateau which stretches out for around 13km to the west of Kibo. This plateau is actually a **caldera**, a collapsed volcanic crater: when you are walking on the plateau, you are actually walking on the remains of the first of Kilimanjaro's three volcanoes to expire, over 500,000 years ago; it was then filled by the lava and debris from the later Kibo eruption.

The plateau also has a reputation for its **fauna**, largely thanks to its proximity to both Amboseli National Park in Kenya and the West Kilimanjaro Wildlife Corridor, from where herds of elephant, eland, buffalo, and big cats such as lion and leopard have been known to wander. Indeed, not so many years ago trekkers on these routes had to be accompanied by an armed ranger to protect them against encounters with predators. That said, to be honest you will be very, *very* lucky to see any evidence of visiting wildlife on the plateau, save for the odd hoofprint or two and the occasional sun-dried lumps of scat and spoor. So, while the proximity of Africa's finest wild beasts adds a certain frisson of excitement to the walk, don't choose either of these trails purely on the strength of their reputation for spotting game: it's an awful long way to come just to see some desiccated elephant shit.

The first thing to know about these two routes is that **it is common for the Lemosho Route to be referred to as the Shira Plateau Route** (or just Shira Route), particularly by foreign agencies keen to promote the fact that you'll be walking across the Shira Plateau. This, of course, is confusing so you should ask your agency to indicate *exactly* which of the two routes you will be taking. Another way to check is to see where your first night's accommodation will be; if it's Big Tree Campsite (Mti Mkubwa in Swahili), it's the Lemosho Route that you'll be following, regardless of what your trekking agency calls it.

The journey to Londorossi

Getting to the start of the Lemosho/Shira Routes is a bit of a bind. Your immediate destination is Londorossi Gate, the starting point for both treks, but before you get there you first have to suffer a two-hour African massage (the local

❑ **How we have ordered this section**

The difficulty with writing a description of the trails that cross the Shira Plateau is that there is no one official Lemosho Route and no one official Shira Plateau Route either.

So, for simplicity's sake, we have assumed in the following descriptions that from Shira 1 Campsite the **Lemosho Route** will head towards Shira 2/Shira Huts (either straight there or via the Cathedral) and from there to Lava Tower. We have ordered it this way as this is the route most people follow when they book a Lemosho trek. From Lava Tower it's more common to go round the southern side of Kibo and head to Barranco Campsite, a route you can read about on p275. That said, the **Lemosho Route is also the most common trail taken by those who are looking to climb via the Western Breach**, and this is the route we take in the following description.

For the **Shira Route**, on the other hand, we have assumed that from Shira 1 people will head to Moir Huts and from there round the northern side of Kibo on the Northern Circuit, simply because the very few companies that use this route will often take that path.

But do bear in mind that the various stages of these routes are interchangeable; it is just as feasible for you to start off on the Shira Plateau Route, for example, and head round to Barranco Campsite, or begin on the Lemosho Route and head to Moir Huts and the Northern Circuit – or indeed to ignore both options and head up the Western Breach!

The simple fact is, there are **several paths** on the plateau and a number of possible campsites too, and each year the guides slightly alter the routes taken by their trekkers. For these reasons, the descriptions of these routes may not tally exactly with your own experience on the plateau; so look at the itinerary your company has provided and that way you can see which parts are relevant to you.

---

euphemism for any sort of vehicular ride on a typically rutted African track). As a result of the extra effort and petrol required to get here, these two trails often cost a little more than the more accessible Marangu, Umbwe and Machame trails.

Thus, for much of the first day you won't be walking anywhere but will be strapped into the back of a jeep as it glides along the Arusha–Moshi highway before turning off at **Boma Ya Ng'ombe** ('Cattle Corral'; 26km from Moshi). From there it bounces along for another hour past **Sanya Juu** (22km from the turn-off and virtually the last place to get supplies), **Ngarenairobi** and **Simba Farm** (a huge estate to the left of the road). Your guide will have to alight briefly at a small hut to pay a fee to the Forest Authority before you finally pull up near the village and gate of Londorossi.

It's a weird place, a Spaghetti Western outpost stuck in the middle of Africa, made entirely of wood, divided up and shut off from the outside world by high wooden fences designed to keep the local fauna at bay. The gate, where you can register and pick up a **permit**, is slightly separate and stands in its own compound.

From here, the two trails divide and are described separately overleaf.

The Lemosho Route

The Lemosho Route is a relatively new variation on the traditional Shira Plateau Route (described on p305), which is seldom used nowadays. Indeed, though many people book what they think is a trek on the Shira Route – as that is what the trekking agencies often call it – it is usually the Lemosho Route on which they will actually be walking.

Although these things change quite often, currently the Lemosho route is one of the quietest on the mountain (only the Umbwe Route, which has a reputation for being the most difficult trail, and the Shira Route, which largely follows a road for its first couple of days, are less popular). At the risk of this situation changing (we can't help but feel somewhat responsible for the explosion in popularity of the Rongai Route due to our warm review of it in a previous edition), it is currently our favourite of the official trails, a 7- to 8-day yomp (though some companies take as many as 10 days) through the remote and pristine cloud forest of West Kilimanjaro and across the Shira Plateau to the highest point in Africa and back down again. The assault on the summit is conducted via either the tricky **Western Breach Route** (see p300) or via Barranco, Karanga Valley and Barafu to Stella Point on the **Barafu Route** (a description of which begins on p277). One or two companies also offer a route that utilises the Northern Circuit (see p324), and an ascent to the summit via School Huts and Gillman's Point (see p266). Either way, the usual **descent route is the Mweka trail** (see p337).

Colobus monkey
(from *The Kilima-njaro Expedition*, **HH Johnston**, 1886)

It is the first day or so, when you are walking through the forests on Kilimanjaro's western slopes, that is the real reason why this trail has overtaken the old Shira Plateau Route as the main path attacking Kilimanjaro from the west. With the latter you are often driven all the way up to the plateau, thereby missing out on some fine forest, which you experience only through a car window. Indeed, take the Cathedral diversion and use the Barafu Route to get to the summit and it's the **longest ascent route on Kilimanjaro at 46.26km** (though it can be just 32.8km if taking the direct route to Shira Huts and then the Western Breach).

Other advantages with this route? Well from personal experience I think the birdlife is the most diverse and interesting of any on the mountain; though I admit I can't actually back this up with any statistical proof, the fecundity of the forest means many species are able to thrive under its canopy. What's more, the Lemosho Route allows for more variations and diversions from the main route than any other trail. As well as side trips to the minor peaks of Kilimanjaro's third summit, the Shira Ridge – usually done as an acclimatization walk on the second day – you can also branch off the main path to visit the **Shira Cathedral**, on the southern side of the plateau, on day three. Again, such a side trip is useful for acclimatization purposes and no extra days need to be taken to do this. Other side trips that *do* require an extra day include a trek to Moir Huts, on the north-western side of the mountain; and, if taking the Western Breach Route to the summit, a diversion to see Reusch Crater and Ash Pit. Indeed, one of the joys of the Lemosho Route is the variety of different trails one can take and itineraries one can build – there is no one standard 'Lemosho Route'.

Though it's a great route, Lemosho is not without its **drawbacks**. For one thing, we reckon it to be the **wettest route**; though meteorology doesn't back us up, in our experience it always seems to rain on this side of the mountain more than anywhere else. Though it varies from month to month, the amount of **rubbish** on the trail and especially at the campsites can be distressing too. How anyone could be stupid enough to drop sweet wrappers in somewhere as lovely as the western forest is beyond me, while those who leave used batteries on the ground at campsites deserve shooting. Don't hesitate to leave messages in the suggestion boxes at Shira Huts or write to KINAPA if the trail and campsites are in a bad state when you arrive. I, too, would welcome your reports on the latest situation – for better or worse; send us an email to the usual address (📧 postmaster@climbmountkilimanjaro.com) and I promise to reply – get enough of them and I'll let KINAPA know too.

STAGE 1: LONDOROSSI GATE TO MTI MKUBWA/BIG TREE CAMP
[MAP 14, p291]

Distance: 4.8km; altitude gained: 396m

Park fees paid and luggage weighed at Londorossi, you jump back on the coach/car as it takes you up the slopes past largely denuded hills and little wooden shacks incongruously furnished with satellite dishes. (As these dishes indicate, the inhabitants aren't particularly poor even though the conditions of their houses would indicate otherwise; in fact, the reason why they live in crudely erected wooden shacks is because they aren't actually allowed to build any permanent construction this high up on Kili.) Some of these settlements have actually been

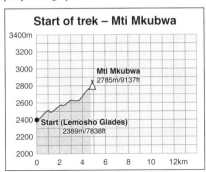

Start of trek – Mti Mkubwa

Mti Mkubwa 2785m/9137ft

Start (Lemosho Glades) 2389m/7838ft

dignified with names, including **Gezaulale** and the last 'village' before the forest, **Chaulale**. Considering the cold climate, it won't surprise you to learn that as well as the tree plantations that abound, potatoes and carrots are the main crops in these parts.

Eventually, 10 minutes after Chaulale and having entered the forest, your vehicle will give up trying to negotiate the muddy path – either at the official start of the track, marked by a couple of toilets, or some distance before it if the road or your vehicle is in a particularly poor state – and it will be time to alight, grab your daypack and make your own way up the slopes. Even if you aren't having lunch now and have no need for the toilets, do delay setting off just for a few moments to see if the colobus monkeys that hang around here put in an appearance. (This place, by the way, is sometimes called **Lemosho Glades**.)

It may already be late in the day by the time you start walking, although the first night's camp lies only around two hours from the end of the road. There are enough steep gradients in these two hours to check all your equipment is comfortable and your limbs are in full working order. The conditions are often misty and quite cool on this first stage through the forest; ideal weather for walking, if not for taking photos.

As you can tell from the map opposite, landmarks in the forest are few; nevertheless, it's still a splendid start to your trek. At times there is an almost Jurassic quality to the trail, a feeling that you've stumbled into some Lost World – a sense that I can ascribe only to the untamed nature of the forest on this side of the mountain and the complete lack of any evidence that humanity has passed this way. It's just wonderful. It helps too, of course, that throughout today you'll be sharing the forest with colobus and blue monkey and the rarely encountered buffalo, elephant, lion and leopard. Indeed, it wasn't uncommon a few years back for trekkers to be accompanied by armed rangers to ward off any over-curious animals. In addition to the fauna, you'll be sharing the path with many of the celebrities of Kilimanjaro's floral kingdom, including the two most prominent *Impatiens* species, *kilimanjaro* and *pseudoviola*, as well as millions of soldier ants; while watching over the whole shebang are those giants without which there would be no forest, in particular the camphor, podocarpus and hagenia trees. Look out, too, for the *Lobelia gibberoa* and ask your guide to

TRAIL GUIDE AND MAPS

❏ **Mobile (cell) phone reception on the Lemosho Route**
Trekkers with mobile (cell) phones will find little opportunity to use them on the first half of the Lemosho Route. The first place we have ever managed to get reception was after leaving the forest on the second morning, though this happened only once; the first place where it's just about certain you'll get reception is by the **Cathedral** on the third morning. **Shira Huts** has reception if you're prepared to search for it on the boulders around the campsite, and reception is OK at **Lava Tower**. Thereafter it depends on which route you're taking. For the Western Breach, reception is fair at **Arrow Glacier**, you can sometimes get it at **Crater Camp** too and, so it is said, at the **summit**.

If you're taking the Barafu Route to the top, see the box on p268 for a summary of mobile reception on this section of the route.

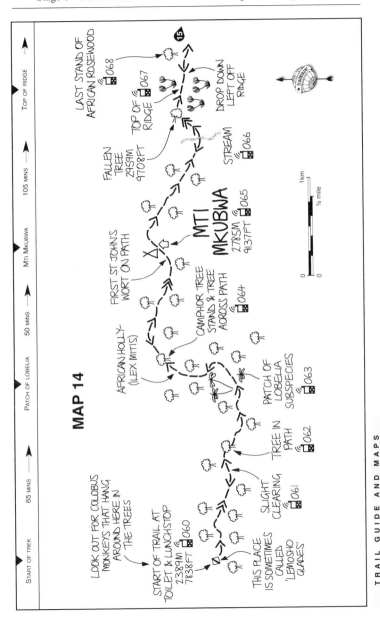

point out the *Dracaena afromontana*, locally known as the *masale*, which though seemingly unimpressive is held in high esteem by the Chagga (see box below).

Your destination for this first stage is the campsite known officially (ie by nobody) as the **Forest Camp**, and unofficially (ie by everybody) as **Mti Mkubwa**, or **Big Tree Camp** (2785m), for obvious reasons. Lying at the top of a ridge in the shade of a wonderful spreading podocarpus, as with all the campsites on Kili there's little to it other than a piece of flat ground, a couple of long-drop toilets and a ranger's hut. But it's still many people's favourite stopping point on the trail, with the noise of the turaco and colobus in the trees at both dusk and dawn making for a quintessential African night.

STAGE 2: MTI MKUBWA/BIG TREE CAMP TO SHIRA 1 CAMPSITE
[MAP 14, p291; MAP 15, p295]

Distance: 7.9km; altitude gained: 719m

You've spent a whole day travelling, registering, walking and sweating and you are still some way short of the plateau, which you will finally reach towards the end of this second stage, leaving the forest for the moorland as you do so. Many trekkers' favourite stage on the trail, this 4hr+ walk (though with all the breaks you'll need it will take a full day) is something of a red-letter day too. For not only do you forsake forest for moorland and get your first proper views of the Shira

---

Dracaena afromontana – the Chagga's constant companion

Known as *masale* by the locals, the inedible and – at least compared to some of the beautiful plants on Kilimanjaro – rather unedifying *Dracaena afromontana* has nevertheless been cultivated and used by the Chagga since time immemorial, to the extent where it's now almost their tribal emblem. Nobody knows why this should be but it's clear that where the outside world sees an unspectacular green plant of little practical use, the Chagga see a shrub whose spiritual qualities and symbolism are far more important than the practical and nutritional value inherent in other plants.

You'll probably first come across the *dracaena* in one of the mountainside villages where it's still commonly used as a boundary marker, with a row of them planted to form a fence to demarcate the extent of a person's property. According to some Chagga guides, this is because *dracaena* is able to ward off evil spirits which, so it is said, are unable to pass through a line of them. The plant was also traditionally a symbol of contrition and an appeal for clemency. If you were in dispute with a neighbour, for example, or had somehow wronged somebody, the best way to ask for forgiveness would be to give them a *dracaena* plant. Do so, and they'd have to have a very strong reason for not pardoning you.

Indeed, in some Chagga villages it is said that the *dracaena* is a Chagga's constant companion, accompanying a person throughout their life from their first breath to their last. There's some truth to this, too, because in some Chagga villages it was customary to give the sap of the plant to newborns before they took their mother's milk for the first time; while when it came to burying a village chief, the corpse would traditionally have been wrapped in dracaena leaves before being interred.

Plateau and its accompanying ridges and peaks but it is on this stage that, finally and famously, you get your first views of Kibo.

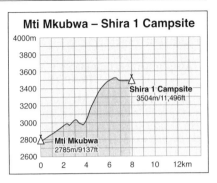

Mti Mkubwa – Shira 1 Campsite

Shira 1 Campsite
3504m/11,496ft

Mti Mkubwa
2785m/9137ft

These rewards are not gained without effort, however; during today you'll be climbing over 700m, taking you above 3500m and into the realm of dastardly HACO and its evil twin, HAPO (see p225). So do make sure you go *pole pole* if you don't want to feel poorly poorly.

The day begins just as the last one left off, as you head in a general easterly direction and generally upwards too, though with plenty of minor variations as you negotiate the folds and creases of Kili's forested slopes. Eventually you find yourself heading north-east to climb to the top of a ridge, the point where you actually gain the top being marked by a large **fallen tree**. As with many of the larger trees in this neck of the woods, this giant used to show signs of having been scorched around the trunk – the unmistakable handiwork of honey-seekers who burn the hollow inside the tree in order to smoke out the bees, making it easier to gain access to their produce.

Heading east and up along the ridge, it's not long before the trees start to diminish in size and number, to be replaced by their hardier cousins in the heather and stoebe families. These soon begin to crowd you in on both sides but not enough to obscure your view north over the valley. It's a valley you eventually join, too, as you continue your eastward and upward progress, contouring gently to the valley floor to reacquaint yourselves with the decorative **African rosewood**, *Hagenia abyssinica*, here making one last stand.

The relentless uphill is finally interrupted by a short descent to what was once a popular lunchstop – popular, that is, until the litter left there drove guides and their trekkers to find another dining-room to frequent and, no doubt, despoil too. This better **lunchspot** lies at the top of the next ridge; while there's no water up here (whereas there is in the original picnic site down below) the views are better, particularly to the north over the Ngare Nairobi River and the 4x4 road of the Shira Plateau Route beyond. From this new lunchspot the path once again points east then bends south, following the ridge, before heading east once more to contour around the slope of what is – though you may not realize it just yet – the northern extremity of the **Shira Ridge**.

The path's gradient, steep since lunch, flattens out as you contour along this northern slope and drops at the **first sight of Shira Plateau**. This is the moment you've been waiting for all day: standing at 3536m above sea level, the Shira Ridge to your right, snow-capped Kibo ahead, the plateau unfurled at your feet with your next two days' trekking mapped out for you upon its face. More immediately, beneath you lies the green uniport of **Shira 1 Campsite** (3504m), a spot that's popular with four-striped grass mice, streaky seed-eaters and white-necked ravens as well as the usual foreign itinerants in lurid Gore-Tex.

STAGE 3: SHIRA 1 CAMPSITE TO SHIRA HUTS
[MAP 15, p295; MAP 16, p297; MAP 17, p299]

Distance: 6.9km (10.1km via the Cathedral); altitude gained: 391m

As mentioned in the introduction, one of the advantages of the Lemosho Route is the number of variations one can take. And this third stage is perhaps the one with the greatest number of options, for not only are there are several destinations, there are also different ways of reaching them.

In order to introduce some sort of clarity and simplicity, we've chosen as our destination for this third stage the Shira Huts (also known as Shira 2), simply because it's to there that most people head. But it is not unheard of for some companies, such as Tusker Safaris, to head on to Moir Huts, on the north-western side of Kibo, before dropping back south to Barranco, or even to carry on round the Northern Circuit (as used on Team Kilimanjaro's TK Lemosho Route, AWC's North Route and Nature Discovery/Thomson's Grand Traverse) as we've mentioned elsewhere.

There are **two main ways of getting to Shira Huts** from Shira 1: the regular direct trail slicing north-west to south-east across the plateau, or the new and increasingly popular alternative detour via Shira Cathedral on the plateau's southern rim. Though it's not too strenuous, this latter option does provide some useful if marginal acclimatization as you climb to 3862m before briefly dropping again. Furthermore, as if the lack of a blinding AMS headache later on wasn't reward enough, there are also the views from the top of the Cathedral across the plateau and towards Kibo; as it takes only a day and thus no more time than the regular route, we recommend you select this option if given the choice. (Though if you do choose this variation try to set off early as the clouds often roll in by mid morning, obscuring any decent views.) However, as it is the alternative route to the main trail, we have described it second (beginning on p296).

Shira 1 Campsite to Shira Huts: the regular route

This 'traditional' trail may lack the pzazz of the younger alternative but that's not to dismiss it altogether. After all, no stroll across the Shira Plateau could ever be described as dull. Shira Huts is the main campsite on the plateau, equipped with a rangers' office, some smart toilets and a particularly prominent

TRAIL GUIDE AND MAPS

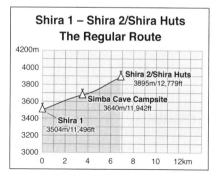

**Shira 1 – Shira 2/Shira Huts
The Regular Route**

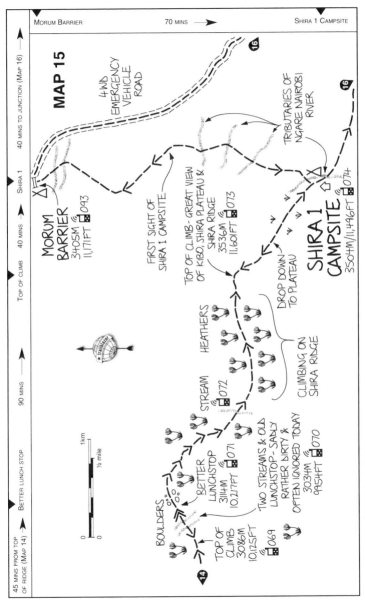

MAP 15

MORUM BARRIER   70 MINS →   SHIRA 1 CAMPSITE

40 MINS TO JUNCTION (MAP 16) →

4WD EMERGENCY VEHICLE ROAD

TRIBUTARIES OF NGARE NAIROBI RIVER

MORUM BARRIER
3405M
11,171FT   📷 093

FIRST SIGHT OF SHIRA 1 CAMPSITE

TOP OF CLIMB - GREAT VIEW OF KIBO, SHIRA PLATEAU & SHIRA RIDGE
3536M
11,601FT   📷 073

SHIRA 1 CAMPSITE
3504M/11,496FT   📷 074+

DROP DOWN TO PLATEAU

CLIMBING ON SHIRA RIDGE

HEATHERS

STREAM   📷 072

BETTER LUNCHSTOP
3114M
10,217FT   📷 071

TWO STREAMS & OLD LUNCHSTOP - SADLY RATHER DIRTY & OFTEN IGNORED TODAY
303M
995FT   📷 070

BOULDERS

TOP OF CLIMB
3086M
10,125FT   📷 069

1km
½ mile
0
0

SHIRA 1 →

TOP OF CLIMB →

90 MINS →

BETTER LUNCH STOP →

45 MINS FROM TOP OF RIDGE (MAP 14) →

40 MINS →

16

16

14

TRAIL GUIDE AND MAPS

suggestion box, as if to invite criticism from trekkers; given the filthy state of the campsite when we last visited, it's probably going to get it too.

To get to Shira Huts involves just under three hours of steady uphill walking. From Shira 1 you head south-east through the heath and moorland of the plateau; watch out for buffalo tracks and those of other animals – klipspringer, dik dik – that cross the plateau in search of salt and fresh grazing. Come to think of it, watch out for buffaloes themselves – encountering one can ruin your holiday. Cross the unimpressive trickle of the waterway that will, further down the slopes, become the torrent of the Ngare Nairobi, and about 85 minutes from breaking camp you reach the plateau's crossroads. It is here that the Lemosho Route meets the 4x4 track of the Shira Plateau Route; here too that you meet the deep-ish creek of the Simba River. Shame, then, that such an important landmark should be marked only by a couple of toilets belonging to **Simba Cave Campsite** (3640m), used largely by those on the (old) Shira Route (see p305). The **cave** itself is a rather forlorn effort lying north-east of the junction.

From here it's another 40-45 minutes of marching past the junction with the path to Moir Huts and to the top of a ridge, from where you can see the green roof of your destination, **Shira Huts** (3895m). It's a fairly direct 35-minute path that takes you there, crossing a couple of shallow ridges and a stream along the way.

By the way, on arriving at Shira Huts you will be higher than the top of Großglockner, at 3798m the biggest mountain in Austria.

Shira 1 Campsite to Shira Huts via Shira Cathedral

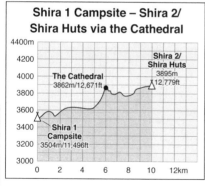

Shira 1 Campsite – Shira 2/ Shira Huts via the Cathedral

The Cathedral
3862m/12,671ft

Shira 2/ Shira Huts
3895m
12,779ft

Shira 1 Campsite
3504m/11,496ft

This route begins by following the regular trail as it heads south-east across the southern half of the plateau, turning off south by a big and distinctive boulder just after crossing the Ngare Nairobi. (Note that from this boulder you can already see your final destination on this stage, the Shira Huts, in the far distance.) It's a long trek across to the foot of the Cathedral, with **Shira Cone** (aka Cone Place) the only major landmark nearby, but it's not a trek that's lacking in interest. In all probability you should see the first *lobelia deckenii* of your trek, standing sentinel-straight as they peer above the grass to check on your progress. You may also see many animal tracks on the trail, including klipspringer, eland and dik dik, hoofprints that betray this path's origins as a trail used by animals in search of salt and fresh grazing. Crossing many (probably dry) **stream-beds**, all of which, when filled with water, feed into the Ngare Nairobi, you start to climb through heather trees to the foot of the rounded hump known as the **Cathedral** (3862m). The summit is gained

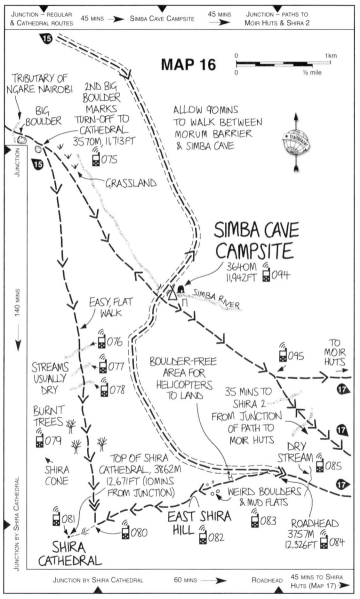

JUNCTION – REGULAR & CATHEDRAL ROUTES · 45 MINS → · SIMBA CAVE CAMPSITE · 45 MINS → · JUNCTION – PATHS TO MOIR HUTS & SHIRA 2

15

MAP 16

0   1km
0   ½ mile

TRIBUTARY OF NGARE NAIROBI

ALLOW 90MINS TO WALK BETWEEN MORUM BARRIER & SIMBA CAVE

BIG BOULDER

2ND BIG BOULDER MARKS TURN-OFF TO CATHEDRAL 3570M, 11,713FT

15

JUNCTION

075

GRASSLAND

SIMBA CAVE CAMPSITE 3640M 11,942FT 094

SIMBA RIVER

140 MINS

EASY, FLAT WALK

076

077

078

STREAMS USUALLY DRY

BOULDER-FREE AREA FOR HELICOPTERS TO LAND

095

TO MOIR HUTS

17

35 MINS TO SHIRA 2 FROM JUNCTION OF PATH TO MOIR HUTS

17

BURNT TREES

079

DRY STREAM 085

17

TOP OF SHIRA CATHEDRAL, 3862M 12,671FT (10MINS FROM JUNCTION)

SHIRA CONE

WEIRD BOULDERS & MUD FLATS

083

ROADHEAD 3757M 12,326FT 084

JUNCTION BY SHIRA CATHEDRAL

081

080

EAST SHIRA HILL 082

SHIRA CATHEDRAL

JUNCTION BY SHIRA CATHEDRAL · 60 MINS → · ROADHEAD · 45 MINS TO SHIRA HUTS (Map 17) →

TRAIL GUIDE AND MAPS

soon after, the whole expedition from Shira 1 taking just under 3¼ hours. Panorama-wise, not only are there the delights of the plateau ahead, including Moir Huts to the north-east and Kibo to your right, but behind and to the east of the Cathedral your guide should be able to point out the faint traces of the Machame Route etched into the slopes.

From the summit you make your way north-east across **East Shira Hill** and the other undulations of the crater rim, eventually arriving at a strange muddy area sprinkled with boulders, the lack of vegetation being due to poor drainage according to one guide. The eastern end of this area has been converted into a makeshift **helipad**, until now used largely by film crews to fly in supplies, including the IMAX crew during the 40 days they spent on the mountain to film their *Kilimanjaro: To the Roof of Africa* documentary. Just a couple of minutes later you come to the **roadhead** – the final termination of the 'rescue road' that emergency vehicles use when ferrying people from the mountain (and the continuation of the road that those on the old Shira Route take to gain access to the plateau, though they alight at Morum Barrier – see p306). It may be the end of the road, but you still have a further 45 minutes up to the **Shira Huts** (3895m) and the day's end.

STAGE 4: SHIRA HUTS TO LAVA TOWER CAMP/BARRANCO HUTS
[MAP 17, p299; MAP 10, p276]

Distance: 10.1km to Barranco Huts (6.7km to Lava Tower); altitude gained: 91m (732m to Lava Tower Campsite, then 641m descend to Barranco Huts)

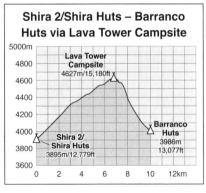

If you've spent the last three days marvelling at the silence and solitude of the Lemosho Route and wondering what all those reports about overcrowding on Kilimanjaro were about, today should answer that. For it is on this stage that the tranquil Lemosho Route (where, if you're lucky, it is still possible to feel as if you're the only group on the mountain) merges with the over-popular Machame Route. Nor is it just solitude you'll be bidding farewell to on this stage. The Shira Plateau also takes a final bow and as a result you'll be leaving the World of Heather for the Land of Lichen. True, those opting for the trek round the southern side of Kibo will reacquaint themselves with heathers, stoebes, lobelias and senecios at the magical Barranco Valley. But from now until the summit, the Barranco and other valleys excepted, it is the alpine desert that prevails.

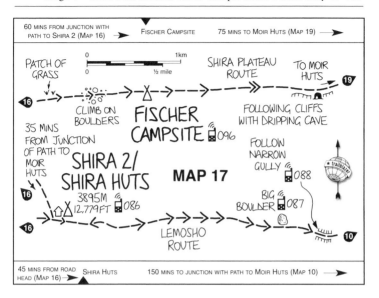

60 MINS FROM JUNCTION WITH PATH TO SHIRA 2 (MAP 16) → ▼ FISCHER CAMPSITE   75 MINS TO MOIR HUTS (MAP 19) →

PATCH OF GRASS

0 _____ 1km
0 _____ ½ mile

SHIRA PLATEAU ROUTE   TO MOIR HUTS

19

16

CLIMB ON BOULDERS

FISCHER CAMPSITE 📱096

FOLLOWING CLIFFS WITH DRIPPING CAVE

35 MINS FROM JUNCTION OF PATH TO MOIR HUTS

16

SHIRA 2/ SHIRA HUTS

3895M 12,779FT 📱086

MAP 17

FOLLOW NARROW GULLY 📱088

BIG BOULDER 📱087

★trailblazer

16

→ → → → → → → LEMOSHO ROUTE

10

45 MINS FROM ROAD HEAD (MAP 16) → SHIRA HUTS   150 MINS TO JUNCTION WITH PATH TO MOIR HUTS (MAP 10) →

As mentioned on p288, there are two alternative routes to the summit – and it's on this stage that the two paths diverge. You can read about both of them on p277 onwards (regular route via Barranco Valley and the Barafu Route) and p300 onwards (Western Breach Route).

But you have to get to the Machame Route first and that involves about three hours of uphill walking. As you probably expect, it's an easterly climb up the fairly gentle slope of the Shira Plateau, gradually forsaking the heather and moorland for something altogether more barren, where lichen-covered boulders predominate. Look out for the shiny black obsidian rock (see p91) on the trail, not forgetting to look up occasionally to see Meru in the distance over your right shoulder. There are few steep passages to this stage, save for a brief clamber up a **narrow gully**; 10 minutes more of clambering on a fairly steep gradient and suddenly you find the path flattening out, just before the junction with the little-used path to Moir Huts (Map 10, p276); the hut itself lies about 30 minutes away (see p308). This junction is a popular place to rest and, if the mist that swirls around Kibo is in a particularly benign mood, a great place for photos too. There's also a path from here to the foot of **Shark's Tooth** (25 mins), the pointy little peak sitting to Kibo's west. The regular trail, however, bends right (south) to chop through a gully, from where it curves again to follow, approximately, a line of overhanging rocks. Arching south again, you now climb up to the top of the neighbouring ridge... and there, marked by some weird mushroom-rock formations, you meet the main Machame Route that has been contouring that ridge from the Shira Caves.

TRAIL GUIDE AND MAPS

Soon after, the path loops to the south-east and divides. It is here that those who have opted to tackle the summit on the more difficult Western Breach Route branch off east towards the Lava Tower. The majority of trekkers heading to Barranco will also follow this deceptively lengthy and fairly steep uphill trek, passing through the unofficial **Sheffield Campsite** (from where there is a further trail heading south to Barranco) and on to **Lava Tower Campsite** (4627m), squeezed between Kibo and the tower itself. Though not the most direct path to Barranco, this route is useful in order to gain some much-needed altitude that could be vital in the battle against mountain sickness.

If you are taking the longer route via Barafu, turn to p277 for a description of your trek; while if you're continuing on the Western Breach, read on.

THE WESTERN BREACH ROUTE TO UHURU PEAK

Over the years the Western Breach Route has acquired a certain aura and a reputation as the hardest of the summit routes. Nor is this reputation entirely undeserved. Though it's the shortest time-wise, it's also the steepest (with the mean gradient of the route said to be 26°) and there's a bit of non-technical and very basic scrambling involved. What's more, and most worryingly, this trail is subject to occasional rockfalls and there are a couple of places where your guide should stop and listen out for any heading in your direction. In January 2006 three American climbers perished in a rockslide near Arrow Glacier (see box below). Following on from this, KINAPA brought in some legislation to regulate trekking on this route. All trekkers must now wear protective helmets during their climb on this route; many agencies ask their clients to sign disclaimers too.

It's interesting to see the reactions of the trekking agencies to the route. Some, such as Zara, the biggest operator on the mountain, shy away from it;

The Western Breach disaster

On Wednesday 4 January, 2006, three climbers were killed in a rockfall on the Western Breach Route. Another member of their party, together with four porters, were injured in the incident. The rockslide was caused by the collapse of a glacial deposit, estimated to weigh up to 39 tonnes. The rocks are believed to have tumbled some 150m and were travelling at 39m per second when they hit the climbers.

Though the accident occurred almost a decade ago the repercussions are still with us. The route was closed for over a year following the tragedy while studies were made into the accident and its causes, finally reopening in late 2007. Even then, many in the trekking community were unhappy that it had been reopened at all, particularly as the course of the path was unchanged so the trail still went through a 'death zone' – between 5210m and 5310m (17,093ft and 17,421ft) – where rockfalls were more likely. KINAPA's only concession to safety was to insist that trekkers wear safety helmets on the route – a stipulation that some agencies consider to be futile in the face of a full-scale rockfall. This is why many companies now insist that trekkers sign waiver forms clearing the agency of liability should any accident occur. Despite the concerns, there have been no major incidents on this route since the 2006 tragedy.

others, such as SENE, positively recommend it. Such reactions are an indication of just how diverse the opinions are about this path.

That said, to hear some people talk about the Western Breach you'd think you'd have to have the climbing capabilities of your average housefly in order to make it to the top. Suffice to say: you don't. Yes, this route is a little trickier in parts. And yes, after snowfall the route up can be icy and an ice axe may be required in extreme conditions. But as with all the routes in this book no technical climbing know-how is necessary – just the ability to haul yourself up with your hands on occasion when required.

So what are the benefits of doing this route? Well, firstly, the Western Breach is the only one that enters directly into the crater as opposed to peaking at the top of the rim that rises above the crater floor. As such, this is the most convenient route to take if you want to explore Ash Pit, Reusch Crater, Furtwangler Glacier and the other features of the summit. (Though it's possible to visit these features even though you climbed to the summit on other routes, few trekkers actually do so; whatever their intentions before they reach the top of Kibo, by the time trekkers get there via Gillman's or Stella Point they're usually too knackered or in too much pain to spend the two hours-plus necessary to explore the crater.) And the other main benefit of climbing via the Western Breach is, of course, the kudos that comes with having conquered the hardest non-technical route Kilimanjaro has to offer.

Note that once upon a time the Western Breach was the one trail to the summit that was often tackled during the day rather than at night, traditionally by those intending to camp on the summit. Despite this, the general consensus

Western Breach Route

amongst Kili connoisseurs is that it is still much easier to tackle 'The Breach' at night, when the scree, shale and rocks are frozen and thus less likely to move when you step on them. Furthermore, after dark the occasionally vertiginous drops are invisible, which makes climbing for vertigo sufferers much easier. Indeed for safety reasons KINAPA now insist that everybody is away from Arrow Glacier Campsite by 5am, in order that they are clear of the area with the greatest risk of rockfall by 7am (ie the first hour after sunrise). There are still a few groups who tackle it by day but, like both the other routes up Kibo, the Western Breach is now mostly attempted at night.

Do note, finally, that this route, though the shortest way to the top, is often the most expensive if you intend to camp at the summit because it is usual for porters to receive a premium to climb up Kibo. This is understandable; on all other routes they don't go above around 4700m (ie the altitude of the last campsite/huts), whereas here they have to go to the crater (above 5700m) and carry all their load up the trickiest route too.

Stage 5: Lava Tower Campsite to Arrow Glacier Campsite
[Map 18, p303]

Distance: 2.5km; altitude gained: 244m

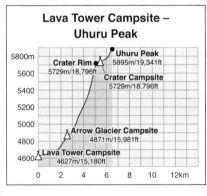

By our reckoning this particular leg, even if taken *pole pole*, lasts little longer than 75 minutes, yet it's not unusual for trekking agencies to set aside an entire day for it. In one respect this seems a little over-cautious and does lead to a situation where, that hour aside, you'll be spending the rest of your day freezing your butt off inside your tent. On the other hand, it's a good idea to take your time at this altitude. After all, save for the Crater Camp this is the highest place where you can pitch your tent on the mountain (the altitude of Arrow Glacier Campsite being 4871m); and that kind of altitude should always be taken seriously.

Furthermore, the walk, though only 75 minutes or so in duration, is still quite exhausting, it being uphill all the way. You begin by crossing a stream or two (one of which, **Bastions Stream**, runs below Lava Tower) before climbing steeply in a south-easterly direction to the top of a ridge. Near the top of the climb you pass an old trail running directly from Lava Tower to the Western Breach Route that bypasses Arrow Glacier Campsite altogether; it's a path that's seldom used these days and unless your guide points it out to you, it's easily missed. Descending for a few seconds to a stream and then climbing to a second ridge, by following the direction of *that* ridge eastwards you soon come to

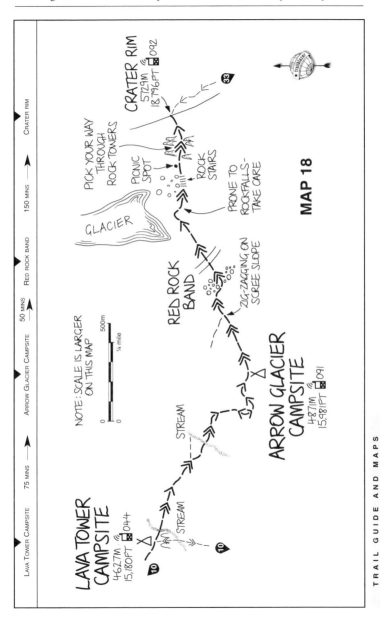

MAP 18

LAVA TOWER CAMPSITE | 75 MINS | ARROW GLACIER CAMPSITE | 50 MINS | RED ROCK BAND | 150 MINS | CRATER RIM

CRATER RIM
5729M
18,796FT 092

PICK YOUR WAY THROUGH ROCK TOWERS

PICNIC SPOT

ROCK STAIRS

PRONE TO ROCKFALLS – TAKE CARE

GLACIER

RED ROCK BAND

ZIG-ZAGGING ON SCREE SLOPE

NOTE: SCALE IS LARGER ON THIS MAP

500m

¼ mile

ARROW GLACIER CAMPSITE
4871M
15,981FT 091

STREAM

LAVA TOWER CAMPSITE
4627M
15,180FT 044

STREAM

STREAM

TRAIL GUIDE AND MAPS

Arrow Glacier Campsite. Engulfed by avalanches and often subject to the vagaries of the extreme conditions up here, this place has always been a bit of a mess and little has changed. Whilst the rubbish is depressing, it's the toilets that are the most revolting spectacle, with the ones that haven't been destroyed now home to an entirely new geological form: neither stalactite nor stalagmite, but stalacshite. Console yourself with the thought that if you're not spending a night on the summit, you probably won't be spending a full night here but should be away by 2am. Happy Camping!

Incidentally, you are now just 6m lower than the summit of the Vinson Massif – at 4877m, the highest point in Antarctica.

Stage 6: Arrow Glacier Campsite to Uhuru Peak
[Map 18, p303; Map 33, p347]
Distance 4km; altitude gained: 1024m (see profile p302)

Though we've talked as if there is one set path from campsite to crater rim, this isn't actually the case; the path changes as snow and rockfalls dictate. Every guide has his own way of tackling the ascent, too. As such, the map on p303 and the description that follows may differ from the exact route you end up taking. But whatever route you take, rest assured it will be steep, and it will be exhausting.

Having said that each path up the Western Breach is unique, your guide will doubtless aim for the rocky ridge that you can see from Arrow Glacier Campsite which runs from the rock towers near the crater down towards the camp (and is often called the 'Stone Train'). It will take around 1¾ hours before you properly join this ridge (soon after crossing a second stream), a walk that includes the most dangerous part of the ascent, where **rockfalls** are frequent. Furthermore, this area is often also covered in snow and many a guide has lost the path here. Successfully gain the ridge and about 15 minutes later you'll find yourself at the foot of the so-called **Rock Stairs** – natural steps that, after the shifting scree and rocks of the previous 1¾ hours, come as something of a relief. These stairs are also viewed as a 'Point of No Return' by the porters who, once they see that you've reached here, consider there's no turning back and thus break camp and march off to Mweka (unless you're planning to sleep at Crater Camp, of course, in which case they'll be right behind you).

The stairs take about 40 minutes to tackle altogether, at the end of which you find yourself on a small, flat space that's often used as a **picnic spot** by those tackling the Western Breach during the day. Dirty and chilly, a more inhospitable picnic spot it would be hard to find, though you do get great views down to Barranco Campsite. Beyond the picnic site the stairs are replaced by a path that's just as steep, though you have to tackle this section without the benefit of any steps. The trail picks its way between the **rocky towers** guarding the crater; but persevere for another 40 minutes and you'll find yourself finally gaining the **crater rim (5729m)**, with **Furtwangler Glacier** on your left the first of many spectacular sights up here. Walking on level ground for a change, it takes around 10 minutes to reach **Crater Campsite** (also 5729m), set amongst boulders at the foot of the climb up to Uhuru.

The path up to **Reusch Crater** and **Ash Pit Viewpoint**, 40 minutes away, bends north round and behind Furtwangler Glacier. For more details on what's up here, see p344.

The **stiff switchback climb** up to **Uhuru Peak**, 50 minutes away, lies to the south of the campsite, clearly etched into the crater wall. It's a hard climb and you'll be cursing every zigzag and switchback on the way. But keep going: the sense of achievement at the top is beyond compare. And it's a feeling that will stay with you all the way down, and all the way back to your home country. Because if you get to the summit, you'll believe you can do anything.

Oh, to be able to bottle that feeling...

The Shira Plateau Route

This is the older of the two trails that cross the Shira Plateau and, in our opinion, is definitely the inferior. That said, a couple of the biggest companies operating on the mountain – African Walking Company in particular – insist this is the better route, for reasons we shall come to in a moment.

Our problems with this route are twofold. Firstly, and in our opinion most importantly, you miss out on the forest zone on the way up (it's a very rare trekker who, these days, begins their walk before Morum Barrier which lies at the start of the Shira Plateau); and it's not just any old forest either, for the jungle on this western side of Kili is the best on the mountain. That, we think, is little short of unforgivable.

The second problem we have is that the Official Shira Route is actually a 4WD track used by emergency vehicles. In other words, you'll be walking on a track that's been designed with vehicles in mind – which can never be as fun as walking on a trail made for pedestrians. Though to be fair to the companies that do offer this route, most of them these days seem to turn off the 'road' as soon as they can in favour of one of the many other paths that criss-cross the plateau – in effect ending up on one of the Lemosho Route variants – and some don't actually walk on the road at all.

All of which begs the question: why do the companies who patronize this route think it's better than Lemosho? Well from what we can gather, it's simply

---

❏ **Mobile (cell) phone reception on the Shira Plateau Route**
I am afraid that the Shira Route – or at least the version of it described here – has perhaps the worst reception of all the trails. On my last trek on this trail I failed to get reception pretty much the whole way round. You can sometimes have success at one of the **Pofu Camps** on the Northern Circuit and, before that, you may be lucky enough to get something on the **ridge above Moir Huts** which the guides say is reliable – though I failed. There is little reception at Third Cave so, after that, the next time you'll be able to use your mobile phone will be at **Gillman's** (possibly), **Stella** or **Uhuru Peak**.

because they reckon that if you are going to have a 7- or 8-day trek, if you can spend those days at a higher altitude (Morum Barrier is at 3405m), you should be able to acclimatize better and thus have a better chance of reaching the top than if you spent one or two of those days at a lower altitude trudging up Kilimanjaro's western slopes. All of which may be true – though to our mind this still doesn't compensate for missing out on the forest of the western slopes, which you now see only through a car window.

So I guess it comes down to a matter of opinion and taste: if your sole reason for setting foot on the mountain is to get to the summit, the Shira Plateau Route *may* be a better route for you. But if you have any interest in the more complete experience, one that includes both ascending and descending via *all* the various vegetation zones, Lemosho wins hands down.

STAGE 1: LONDOROSSI GATE TO MORUM BARRIER, SHIRA 1 OR SIMBA CAVE CAMPSITE   [MAP 15, p295; MAP 16, p297]

Morum Barrier to Shira 1: Distance: 3.75km; altitude gained: 99m
Morum Barrier to Simba Cave Campsite: 6.5km; altitude gained: 215m

A journey of a thousand miles begins with a single step, said the inscrutable 6th-century BC philosopher Lao-tzu. Thankfully, for those of you who have chosen

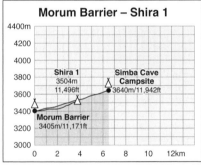

this route, your own journey will be a lot shorter than 100 miles and your first step will be onto a bus that will convey you to **Londorossi Gate** (p289). It is a rare trekker who begins his or her walk here, however, so – ramblers registered and permits purchased – you'll rejoin the bus as it conveys you up the slopes, through pine plantations, forest and moorland, with the occasional monkey or baboon crossing your path and the Ngare Nairobi River a capricious companion to your right.

Eventually the twisting track bifurcates in the shadow of Morum Hill. A few metres on from this divide are the remnants of what was clearly some sort of concrete gatepost – the remnants of the old **Morum Barrier** (3405m). Several information boards also stand nearby and there's a toilet here too.

It's a lonely place: the landscape windswept, the flora dry and scrubby, the fauna virtually non-existent. Indeed, it almost feels as if humanity has abandoned this corner of the mountain and coming across the remains of the barrier always puts me in mind of that moment when Charlton Heston comes across the Statue of Liberty at the end of *Planet of the Apes*. Rather than sink to your knees and bewail the demise of *Homo sapiens*, however, as Charlton did, we advise you to keep your spirits up and get walking. Incidentally, by driving to 3405m you are only 2m short of the *combined* altitudes of the highest points of Scotland, Wales and England – namely Ben Nevis (1344m), Snowdon (1085m) and Scafell Pike (978m) respectively – and you haven't even started walking yet!

Morum Barrier marks the start of the Shira Plateau, where you'll be spending the next couple of days. Occasionally, groups turning up late are forced to **camp** here though if everything has gone smoothly thus far it's more usual to walk to one of the campsites on the plateau, with Shira 1 or Simba Cave Campsite being the only realistic choices.

Shira 1 (3504m) is reached via a narrow trail that heads south from the information boards. The trail crosses several streams but the whole walk takes only 70 minutes or so; from Shira 1 you then continue along the Lemosho Route to Shira 2 (possibly via the Cathedral, as described on p296) and Lava Tower (see p298); or your trekking company may have opted to head towards Moir Huts and possibly continue from there round the Northern Circuit, which we describe on p308.

Those who instead opted to stay at **Simba Cave Campsite (3640m)** – reached by walking along the road for about 90 minutes – have essentially the same options. The campsite, adorned with several weatherbeaten old wooden toilets as well as the cave, marks the main junction between the road and the Lemosho Route. (Incidentally, we don't know of any company that still uses the 'road' after Simba Cave, with more easterly footpaths, described on p296, superior alternatives.)

STAGE 2: SIMBA CAVE CAMPSITE TO MOIR HUTS
[MAP 16, p297; MAP 17, p299; MAP 19, p309]

Distance: 6km; altitude gained: 515m

Around 45 minutes from Simba Cave lies a **junction** marked with little more than a simple sign, with direction arrows usually scraped into the dirt too. Nevertheless, it's quite an important place, where the regular Lemosho Route and the route to Moir Huts divide. Those heading to Shira 2/Shira Huts should see p296; while those heading towards Moir Huts and the Northern Circuit should read on.

From the junction with the main trail a 135-minute path picks its way between boulders, around or over petrified lava flows, and through grassy swards. The main 'landmark' is the **disused Fischer Campsite**, named after Scott Fischer who did much to pioneer this route with his company Mountain Madness and who perished on the slopes of Everest. Hunt around for (or get your guide to

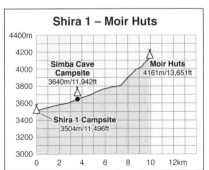

Shira 1 – Moir Huts

show you) the small plaque that commemorates him and admire the resplendent giant groundsels that thrive in this chilly location. Just over an hour's schelp afterwards the path curves in the shadow of some **low cliffs** past an impressive **dripping cave** just before the **Moir Huts** (4155m). Set in a lovely sheer-sided valley that sees few visitors, the campsite is more peaceful than almost any other on the mountain; alas, it also means the cleaning crews seldom drop by, so there's often plenty of rubbish around and lots of shattered animal bones. Furthermore, apart from the three toilets, the only other building is a ruined pyramid-shaped hut, built as a sleeping shelter but now sadly vandalized. As a result, the whole camp does feel a bit cold and bleak. Even the white-necked ravens don't bother scavenging around here, the pickings presumably being too slim, and the silence as a result can be positively deafening. A rare touch of warmth and pleasure, however, is provided by the seedeaters which, lacking the social graces of their brethren at lower altitudes, happily hop into your tent in search of crumbs. There's also a great deal of pleasure to be had in views that take in both the Shira Ridge – where you have just come from – and snow-laden Kibo where, all being well, you hope to be going...

STAGES 3 & 4: THE NORTHERN CIRCUIT (MOIR HUTS TO THIRD CAVE CAMPSITE)   [MAP 19, p309; MAP 20, p311]

At first sight, the Northern Circuit, which drapes around the northern face of Kibo, appears to offer little to the Kili climber, especially when compared to its counterpart the Southern Circuit. For one thing, the northern trail lacks such attractions as the lovely Barranco Valley and its photogenic campsite, the charm of the sunbird-flitted Karanga Valley, the busy excitement of Barafu Campsite and the scrambling challenge of the Breakfast Wall. Furthermore, the Southern Circuit is nearer to civilization, with Moshi and the neighbouring villages both visible, on occasion, and just a day's walk away, which may prove vital if you run into difficulty and need to descend quickly. In contrast, there is no such descent available on the Northern Circuit; if you need to evacuate from this side of Kibo you'll have to walk to the Shira Plateau or the Saddle and work out how to get back down from there.

So far, so unattractive. But there is one quality the Northern Circuit has that its southern neighbour lacks: **solitude**. For while the Southern Circuit resounds to the footfall of just about every trekker who opted for the Machame, Umbwe, Lemosho and Shira routes – not to mention their crews – the Northern Circuit sees very few people. True, visit in the high season and you may bump into trekkers who have signed up to one of the 'alternative' routes offered by the big companies such as Team Kilimanjaro, African Walking Company or Nature Discovery/Thomson; but even at that time there's every possibility you will have the whole path to yourself. For the Northern Circuit is not part of any of the 'official' routes but instead exists to offer those who want to avoid the crowds the chance to do so. Indeed, so seldom is this path used at certain times of the year that often there is no actual 'path' to follow – just a series of cairns that mark out the route.

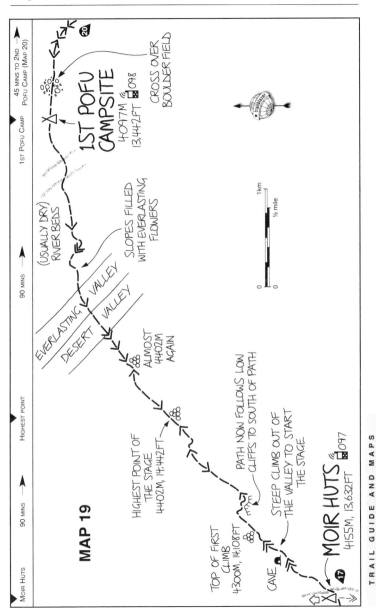

MAP 19

MOIR HUTS — 90 MINS — HIGHEST POINT — 90 MINS — 1ST POFU CAMP — 45 MINS TO 2ND POFU CAMP (MAP 20)

❷⓿

1ST POFU CAMPSITE
4,097M
13,442FT

CROSS OVER BOULDER FIELD

(USUALLY DRY) RIVER BEDS

SLOPES FILLED WITH EVERLASTING FLOWERS

EVERLASTING VALLEY

DESERT VALLEY

ALMOST 4,402M AGAIN

HIGHEST POINT OF THE STAGE 4,402M, 14,442FT

PATH NOW FOLLOWS LOW CLIFFS TO SOUTH OF PATH

TOP OF FIRST CLIMB 4,300M, 14,108FT

STEEP CLIMB OUT OF THE VALLEY TO START THE STAGE

CAVE

MOIR HUTS 4,155M, 13,632FT

❶❼

1km
½ mile

The path can be completed in one day – though it is more normally divided into two stages, with a night spent at one of three **Pofu Camps**. Altitude-wise, and assuming you are going from west to east ie from Moir Huts to Third Cave Campsite, you actually lose a little in altitude – from 4155m to 3936m. This, however, fails to convey the sometimes quite large and sweaty climbs and descents you have to make on your way round and you will in fact climb to 4402m at one point; as such, this route is pretty good for acclimatization.

Though we have written this from west to east, this is one of those paths which sees walkers heading in both directions. I do apologise but those of you walking from east to west (having come, usually, from the Rongai Route) will have to read this description backwards, as it were...

Moir Huts to Second Pofu Campsite   [Map 19, p309; Map 20, p311]
Distance: 9.2km; altitude _lost_: 122m (247m up to the high point then 369m descent to Pofu)

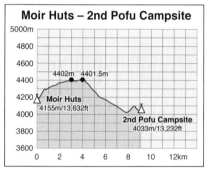

As mentioned before, peace and solitude are the main characteristics of this path. In terms of acclimatization, you actually achieve the lofty altitude of 4402m today before falling to the Second Pofu Camp at 4033m. It won't be unusual, therefore, for people to feel some symptoms of altitude sickness (often a headache) by the time they arrive at one of the Pofu Campsites. So do try to go *pole pole* and to drink lots to avoid this; and furthermore, don't set off from Moir Huts if you're feeling any effects of the altitude as you are going to even more remote places.

The walk begins with perhaps the steepest climb of the day, a relentless slog up a barren slope to exactly 4300m. Cairns both mark the top of the ascent and the way forward, as you spend your day making your way around Kibo's northern face, dropping down into the many north–south valleys before clambering back out of them. Though this can get a little monotonous, note how the character of each valley is different to its neighbours, with some decorated with everlastings, others blanketed in heathers, and still others virtually pure, lifeless desert. Eventually, after three hours, you'll come to the **first of the Pofu Camps** – this one said to be preferred by Nature Discovery/Thomson – followed in short order by some **boulders** that you need to scramble over to reach the **second** (45 mins) and most popular of the three possible Pofu campsites.

It has to be said that the three Pofu Camps are all fairly uncharismatic places, perched on chilly ridges between the valleys and with not a toilet between them (hopefully your agency will have packed one for you to use). It

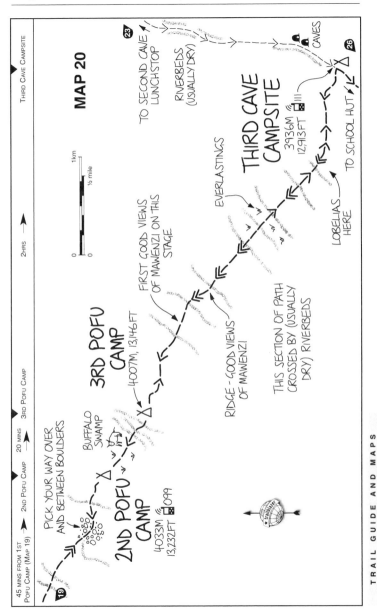

MAP 20

THIRD CAVE CAMPSITE

2HRS →

45 MINS FROM 1ST POFU CAMP (MAP 19) → 2ND POFU CAMP → 20 MINS → 3RD POFU CAMP

23
TO SECOND CAVE LUNCHSTOP

RIVERBEDS (USUALLY DRY)

CAVES

26

THIRD CAVE CAMPSITE

3936M 12,913FT

TO SCHOOL HUT

LOBELIAS HERE

EVERLASTINGS

THIS SECTION OF PATH CROSSED BY (USUALLY DRY) RIVERBEDS

FIRST GOOD VIEWS OF MAWENZI ON THIS STAGE

RIDGE - GOOD VIEWS OF MAWENZI

3RD POFU CAMP

4007M, 13,146FT

BUFFALO SWAMP

PICK YOUR WAY OVER AND BETWEEN BOULDERS

2ND POFU CAMP

4033M 13,232FT

19

0   1km
0   ½ mile

will probably come as no surprise to you that we think a cleaning crew is definitely required around here; though the number of trekkers passing this way is small, over time the mess they and their crews have left has built up considerably. Unfortunately, there's not much to distract you from the mess except to sit and watch the mist roll in and, on occasion, clear again, giving you the chance to spot the eland that are said to hang about in these parts and after which the campsites are named. If the skies are clear enough you should get a full frontal view of Kibo, while Mawenzi peers coyly over your shoulder and the lights of Kenya twinkle in the far distance below.

Second Pofu Campsite to Third Cave Campsite   [Map 20, p311]
Distance: 6.8km; altitude _lost_: 97m

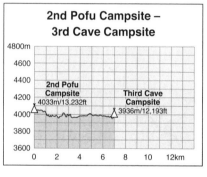

Unsurprisingly this stage continues in pretty much the same vein as the previous one as the path continues on its merry traverse around the northern slopes. Once again the trekker is asked to negotiate numerous valleys, mostly dry, one or two slightly more fecund, and one at the very start of the day that is, so it is said, favoured by buffalos in search of water during the dry season. The gradients aren't quite as dramatic on this stage and the day slightly shorter though you'll still find yourself pretty puffed out by the time you reach **Third Cave Campsite**. The reason for this is clear when you look at the gradient profile and see how much ascending and descending you have to do on this stage. The views, however, provide ample compensation, with Kibo to your right and Mawenzi gradually looming larger and larger ahead of you, though you won't see much of the glorious Saddle that separates them until the next stage.

For details of Third Cave Campsite, please see p321, while for details of your trail from here you'll need to consult this book in conjunction with the itinerary your agency has provided – with School Hut, Kibo Huts and even Mawenzi Tarn just three of the possible destinations.

The Rongai Route

Please convey to the seven blind climbers who reached the summit of Kilimanjaro my warm congratulations on their splendid achievement.
Queen Elizabeth II in a telegram to Geoffrey Salisbury who, with his team of young,
blind African trekkers, used the Rongai Route for their attempt on the mountain.

Probably due to the improvement in the road heading from Marangu to the Kenyan border that leads to the start of this trek, the Rongai Route has become inordinately popular over the past couple of years. Where once you had a 50:50 chance of having the trail to yourself, these days you'll be lucky indeed to avoid the hordes.

While many will see the Rongai's new-found popularity as a drawback, it can't be denied that it is deserved – even though, at first glance, this trail seems decidedly unattractive. The lower slopes at the very start of the trail have been denuded by farmers and now present a cultivated and unexciting landscape, the 'forest' for the first hour here being nothing more than a pine plantation. Nor is the 'proper' native forest that you do eventually walk through that spectacular either, being little more than a narrow band of (albeit pretty) woodland which soon gives way to some rather hot and shadeless heathland. Indeed, the parched character of Kili's northern slopes often means trekking parties have to carry water along the way (often all the way from the Second Cave lunchstop to the School Hut if taking the regular Rongai Route without the diversion to Mawenzi Tarn); your agency should have supplied you with enough porters for this. And then there's the expense: if you are booking your trek in Moshi, Arusha or Marangu, the cost of a Rongai trek can be higher than all other trails except Lemosho/Shira Plateau due to the expense of travelling to the start of the trek.

So why, if this route is more expensive, far-flung and barren than all the others, has it become so popular? Well for one thing, there's the **wildlife**. Because of its proximity to Amboseli, your chances of seeing the local fauna

---

❏ **Mobile (cell) phone reception on the Rongai Route**
Mobile reception on the Rongai Route is not great, though it's better if you are taking the Mawenzi Tarn variation. As always, reception depends a lot on which network you are with. Guides say you can get reception by the **Hut at Simba Camp** – though I have to say I've never managed it. One place where I do always get reception, however, is at the popular resting place on the large flat rock during the second morning. **Second Caves** also has reasonable reception. Thereafter, however, on the regular Rongai Route the chances to use your phone are limited.

Those taking the trail via Mawenzi Tarn will find reception at **Kikelelwa** comes and goes; while at **Mawenzi Tarn** it is also intermittent, though more reliable by the toilets. Crossing the Saddle there is usually no reception, so the next time you'll be able to use your mobile phone will be at **Gillman's** (possibly), **Stella** or **Uhuru Peak**.

❏ **What's this route called again?**
The name **Rongai Route** is actually something of a misnomer. It may be the name that everybody uses but, strictly speaking, it's not the correct one. The real, original Rongai Route used to start at the border village of the same name but was closed several years ago by the authorities who decided that two trails on a side of the mountain that few trekkers visit was unnecessary. You will still see this route marked on older maps but nowadays all trekkers who wish to climb Kilimanjaro from the north follow a different trail, also known as the **Loitokitok Route** after the village that lies near the start. Just to confuse the issue still further, this isn't officially the correct name either, for along the trail you'll see various signs calling this trail the **Nalemuru Route** – or, occasionally, Nalemoru – though this name is rarely used by anyone.

---

here are greater than on any other route bar those starting in the far west below Shira Plateau. During the research for the first edition of this book we encountered a troop of colobus monkeys, while later that same day we came across an elephant skull, with elephant droppings and footprints nearby; and at night our little party was kept awake by something snuffling around the tents (a civet cat, according to our guide, though presumably one wearing heavy hobnail boots to judge by the amount of noise it was making). Buffaloes and eland also frequent the few mountain streams on these northern slopes (though, as previously mentioned, these streams, never very deep, are almost always dry except in the rainy season and consequently the buffaloes choose to bathe elsewhere for most of the year – though occasionally they head up the slopes in search of salt. There's a dead buffalo wedged in the rocks between Third Cave and School Hut that, given the conditions, will probably be there for many years.) The **flora** is different here too, with its juniper and olive trees. And if at the end of the **26.8km** (37.65km if taking the Mawenzi Tarn Diversion) ascent to Uhuru Peak you do feel you've somehow missed out on some of the classic features of Kili – lobelias, for example, or the giant groundsels, which don't appear regularly on the northern side except near Kikelelwa Camp on the diversion up to Mawenzi Tarn – fear not, as both can be found in abundance on the 36.55km-long Marangu Route, **the designated descent** for those coming from Rongai.

Furthermore, opt for the extra day – which we strongly advise, for reasons not only of acclimatization – and you will spend that extra night at **Mawenzi Tarn Hut**, which not only allows you to savour some gobsmacking views across to Kibo from the top of the ridge above the tarn but also gives you the chance the following day to walk across the Saddle, many people's favourite part of the mountain. And finally, when it comes to the ascent, we found the walk from School Hut to Gillman's Point to be *marginally* easier than that from Kibo Huts (though admittedly the two do share, for the last three or four hours or so to the summit, the same path). Other advantages include the drive to the start: from Moshi the road passes through a rural Chagga heartland, so giving you the chance to see village life Chagga-style (see p139), which we heartily recommend. Furthermore, if you manage to find other trekkers to join you and split the cost, the transport should not be too expensive.

PREPARATION

The journey to Loitokitok and Rongai Gate

What was once one of the more arduous aspects of trekking on the Rongai Route – getting to the start – has since become much easier thanks to the improvement of the road from a muddy, dusty track to a fully fledged tarmac highway. A journey that used to take half a day or more can now be completed in just a couple of hours. But though the journey may be a lot easier it still retains some interest, mainly because it takes you through several Chagga villages.

From **Marangu Gate**, where you'll stop to pick up your permit, your vehicle will return down the hill to **Marangu Mtoni** before continuing round the dry, eastern side of the mountain, through the villages of **Mwika** and **Mrere**, host to a big market on Saturday, in the heart of the Rombo District. After them, in order, the villages of **Shauritanga** (site of a horrific tragedy in June 1994, when 42 schoolgirls were burnt to death in a dormitory fire started by a candle), **Olele**, **Usseru**, **Mashima** and **Kibaoni** emerge in fairly rapid succession before, eventually, you arrive at **Tarakea**, the largest settlement. There is also a border post with Kenya in Tarakea; presumably your driver will know *not* to take the road leading to it but instead to keep on hugging the road which now heads northwest. (Incidentally, though not an official crossing point for *mzungu*, we know of several foreigners who have, with some negotiation, managed to get through.)

The wooden settlement of **Loitokitok** lies a few minutes on from Tarakea, where a track on the left branches up to the park gate, situated at around 2000m. From the gate you can see the smart *Snow Cap Cottages* (see p205 for contact details), which resemble (from this distance at least) Swiss-style chalets.

STAGE 1: RONGAI GATE TO SIMBA CAMPSITE
[MAP 21, p316; MAP 22, p317]

Distance: 7km; altitude gained: 638m

It is an inauspicious start to the trek. Having registered with the park official in his wooden booth-cum-office, and possibly having taken your lunch in the smart little tourist **shelter** behind it, your guide will take you up the slopes through what, for many trekkers, is one of the least exciting parts of Kilimanjaro, a hot and dusty blemish of **pine plantations** followed by fields of potato and maize, pockmarked here and there with the wooden shacks of those who eke out a living from the soil. (The pine in question, incidentally, is *Pinas caribas*, or Caribbean pine; native, according to one trekker, to a small

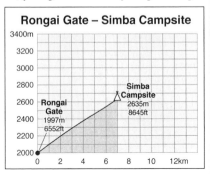

Rongai Gate – Simba Campsite

Rongai Gate 1997m 6552ft

Simba Campsite 2635m 8645ft

TRAIL GUIDE AND MAPS

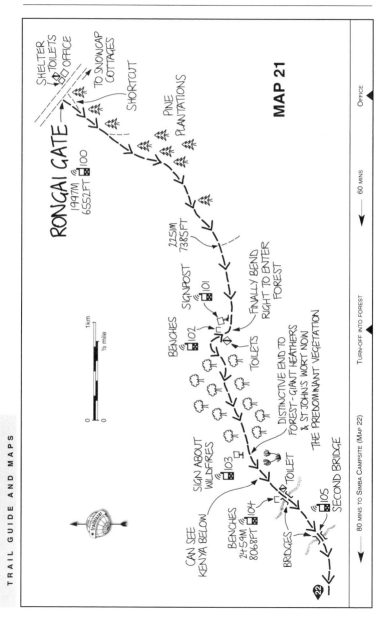

SHELTER
TOILETS
OFFICE
TO SNOWCAP COTTAGES
SHORTCUT

RONGAI GATE
1997M
6552FT 100

MAP 21

PINE PLANTATIONS

2151M
7385FT

SIGNPOST
101

FINALLY BEND RIGHT TO ENTER FOREST

BENCHES
102

TOILETS

DISTINCTIVE END TO FOREST - GIANT HEATHERS & ST JOHNS WORT NOW THE PREDOMINANT VEGETATION

SIGN ABOUT WILDFIRES
103

CAN SEE KENYA BELOW

BENCHES
2459M
8068FT 104

BRIDGES

TOILET

105
SECOND BRIDGE

22

1km
½ mile
0

OFFICE

60 MINS

TURN-OFF INTO FOREST

80 MINS TO SIMBA CAMPSITE (MAP 22)

valley in Belize where it struggles to grow but which thrives in the climatic conditions present on this side of the mountain.) True, there is more native forest just off the path to the right – but for some reason the path for this first hour steadfastly refuses to enter it, preferring instead to stick to the perimeter of the plantations; while you may have some interest in studying the living conditions of rural Tanzanians, I'm guessing that the opportunity to walk past fields of vegetables was not one of the main reasons why you signed up to climb this mountain.

It is just about an hour before you turn right and escape into the lush green haven of the forest. When you do so, you'll be disappointed to find just how quickly the tall trees of the montane forest give way to the more stunted vegetation of the **heathland**, such as giant heathers and St John's wort. It's tempting to blame the untrammelled agriculture for the paltry amount of decent rainforest here. No doubt the farmers have played their part but the truth of the matter is that this side of Kili has never had much in the way of rainforest – simply because it never gets much in the way of rain. Besides, this narrow band of forest is still teeming with wildlife, in particular **colobus monkeys**, with a troop often grazing by the entrance to the forest.

Leaving the forest on a trail that slowly steepens, about 50 minutes afterwards you cross a stream and a few minutes later reach the first campsite on this route, known as the **Simba (or Sekimba) Campsite**, at an altitude of 2635m.

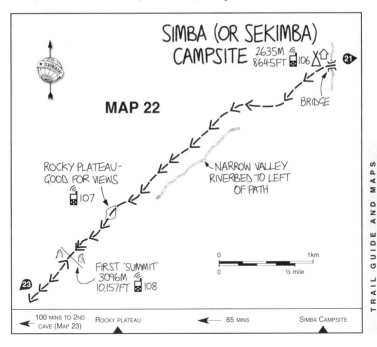

It's always good to get to a campsite, and this one in particular is pleasant: surrounded by heathers, with creatures snuffling about the tent at night and birdsong to wake you in the morning, this spot has a pleasingly wild, isolated ambience.

STAGE 2: SIMBA CAMPSITE TO THIRD CAVE CAMPSITE
[MAP 22, p317; MAP 23, p319]

Distance: 5.8km to Second Cave Campsite; 3.3km to Third Cave Campsite (9.1km in total); altitude gained: 852m to Second Cave; Second Cave to Third Cave 449m; 1301m in total

This stage perhaps lacks the variety of other stages. For most of the day you will be walking up slopes flanked with heather with the twin peaks of Kilimanjaro

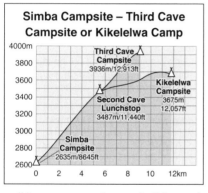

Simba Campsite – Third Cave Campsite or Kikelelwa Camp

Third Cave Campsite 3936m/12,913ft

Kikelelwa Campsite 3675m 12,057ft

Second Cave Lunchstop 3487m/11,440ft

Simba Campsite 2635m/8645ft

keeping a watchful eye as you progress. If you're on a five-day trek, during this stage you will bid farewell to those lucky trekkers who opted to take the extra day and visit the Mawenzi Tarn Hut; they will go their own way after lunch. (That route is described on p320.) For the 'five-dayers', by the end of today you will have ascended more than 1300m. But there's no gain without pain and today is long, involving almost 4½ hours of steady walking on a steep, dusty path. Take comfort from the fact that tomorrow is much easier, and that you have already ascended almost 2000m from the gate, and are now well over halfway to the summit.

If you haven't already been doing so, this is also the time to take things deliberately *pole pole* ('slowly slowly' in Swahili) – you're reaching some serious altitudes now, and mountain sickness stalks the unwary.

The path at the start of this 9.1km stage is, perhaps surprisingly, a westward one, its goal seeming to be the northern slopes of Kibo rather than the eastern slopes you will eventually climb. The heathers are gradually shrinking in size now too and while some trees still cling on at this altitude, they are few in number and scattered. For these reasons, the first part of this stage is rather shadeless and very hot. After 45 minutes a **river bed** (dry for the best part of the year) joins you from the left and the path follows its course for most of the next hour. Look back occasionally and, weather permitting, you should be able to see a number of villages on the Kenyan side of the border, the sunlight glinting off the metal roofs. Continuing upwards, the path steepens slightly and begins to turn more to the south. The terrain up here is rather rocky and bumpy. The path continues south-south-west, rounding a few minor cliffs and hills and crossing

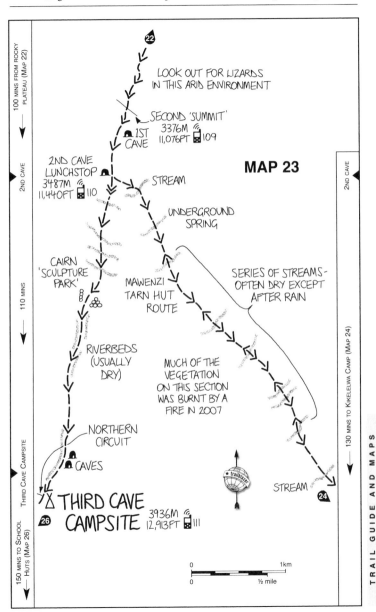

22

LOOK OUT FOR LIZARDS
IN THIS ARID ENVIRONMENT

SECOND 'SUMMIT'
3376M
11,076FT 📱 109

🏠 1ST
CAVE

2ND CAVE
LUNCHSTOP 🏠
3487M
11,440FT 📱 110

STREAM

MAP 23

UNDERGROUND
SPRING

CAIRN
'SCULPTURE
PARK'

MAWENZI
TARN HUT
ROUTE

SERIES OF STREAMS-
OFTEN DRY EXCEPT
AFTER RAIN

RIVERBEDS
(USUALLY
DRY)

MUCH OF THE
VEGETATION
ON THIS SECTION
WAS BURNT BY A
FIRE IN 2007

NORTHERN
CIRCUIT

🏠 CAVES

△ THIRD CAVE
26 CAMPSITE 3936M
12,913FT 📱 111

STREAM

24

0   1km

0   ½ mile

trailblazer

100 MINS FROM ROCKY PLATEAU (MAP 22)

2ND CAVE

110 MINS

THIRD CAVE CAMPSITE

150 MINS TO SCHOOL HUTS (MAP 26)

2ND CAVE

130 MINS TO KIKELELWA CAMP (MAP 24)

TRAIL GUIDE AND MAPS

a number of false summits, before eventually flattening out and arriving at a small, waterless cave. As inviting as the cave and the shade it offers now appear, this is not your lunch stop. That lies 20 minutes further on through lizard country of bare rocks and long grasses and is known as the **Second Cave** (3487m).

Before setting off in the afternoon, make sure you are on the correct trail, for the path to the Mawenzi Tarn Hut branches off at this point (see below): if your destination is the Third Cave Campsite but you find yourself heading south-east, reconsider.

The path to the Third Cave begins behind and above the caves. Crossing a wide and usually dry riverbed, which in the rainy season is sometimes used as a playground by buffaloes, the path continues drifting southwards across

---

❑ THE MAWENZI TARN HUT ROUTE
[MAP 23, p319; MAP 24, p322; MAP 25, p323]

This alternative path is wonderful. Great views, lovely scenery and a useful way to acclimatize. If you can afford the extra day on the mountain, don't hesitate.

From Second Cave to Kikelelwa Campsite
Distance: 5.95km; altitude gained: 188m

From Second Cave, the usual lunchstop on the second day, the path takes an abrupt south-easterly turn directly towards the jagged peak of Mawenzi. Traversing open moorland the path meanders and undulates; assuming you've already walked from Simba Camp this morning, you will feel rather drained by the time you stumble into **Kikelelwa Camp** (3675m), situated by a couple of caves by the Kikelelwa River, with giant groundsels and lobelias flourishing nearby. (Incidentally, I don't know why this should be so but whenever I have walked this stretch of the path – which must be a good half-dozen times now – it has always been either raining or very misty. That said, it has always brightened up in the evening to reveal Kibo's snowy summit peaking over the ridge that separates the campsite from the Saddle.) Compared to the morning where you gained over 850m, this afternoon's walk increases your altitude by less than 200m, though the distances of the two parts are about the same and, given the amount of climbs and falls, this latter walk is just as exhausting.

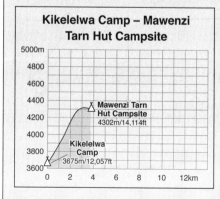

Kikelelwa Camp – Mawenzi Tarn Hut Campsite

Mawenzi Tarn Hut Campsite 4302m/14,114ft

Kikelelwa Camp 3675m/12,057ft

Kikelelwa Camp to Mawenzi Tarn Hut Campsite
Distance: 3.75km; altitude gained: 627m

Though this stage to Mawenzi Tarn is relatively short at less than 4km and is usually completed in a morning (allowing time for a brief acclimatization trek in the afternoon for those who feel up to it), it's also steep as you gain over 600m, the path shedding the moorland vegetation as it climbs steadily.

increasingly arid terrain, the 'dry flower' helichrysum now interspersed amongst the heathers. The halfway point between Second and Third Caves is marked, surreally, by a '**cairn sculpture park**' where (presumably) the more creative trekkers and porters have left dozens of elegantly arranged rocks and stones artfully balanced into pillars, peaks and other forms; a good place to take a break, methinks. As huge rocks begin to appear to left and right, temporarily obscuring Mawenzi and Kibo, the unmistakable outline of toilet huts appear ahead on the trail, a sure sign that the campsite is nearing, this time to your left across another **broad riverbed**. This is the **Third Cave Campsite** (3936m) and the **last water point** before the summit.

For the continuation of this route, please go to p324.

Mawenzi Tarn Hut Campsite (4302m) is situated in one of the most spectacular settings, in a cirque beneath the jagged teeth of Mawenzi. There's a small ranger's hut here and a toilet block.

Assuming the walk here was trouble-free you will have most of the afternoon to go on an acclimatization climb up the ridge to the west; if you're lucky, the sky will be clear, affording you fantastic views of Kibo, though in all probability you'll merely catch the odd glimpse through the clouds that usually roll in across the Saddle in the afternoon. But no matter, for you'll get the same views tomorrow morning when the skies should be clearer and the sun will be behind you too. The views back down to the Tarn – which, to be honest, is little more than a puddle with delusions of grandeur – are great too.

Mawenzi Tarn Hut Campsite to Kibo Huts
Distance: 8.9km; altitude gained: 412m
This lovely day begins with a slight retracing of your steps before you strike out westwards, crossing the ridge and dropping down the slope to tiptoe along the beautifully barren Saddle's northern edge.

With views like screensavers to east and west, it's a rare trekker indeed who doesn't rate this day as their favourite on the mountain. The flora is sparse but do look out for eland which are said to stroll up here.

You have two destinations at the end of this third day: School Hut (Map 6) or, more usually these days, Kibo Huts. Both lie on the lower slopes of Kibo and both are just a few hours' walk away. Depending on which hut you end up at, see p325 for the continuation of your walk up to Gillman's from School Hut, or p264 for the walk up to Uhuru from Kibo Huts.

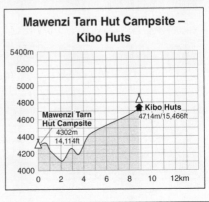

Mawenzi Tarn Hut Campsite – Kibo Huts

Mawenzi Tarn Hut Campsite 4302m 14,114ft

Kibo Huts 4714m/15,466ft

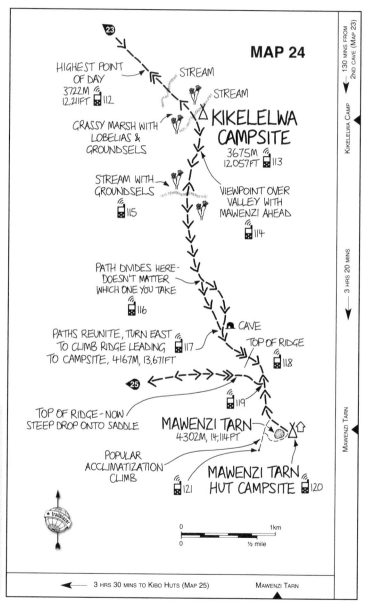

MAP 24

HIGHEST POINT
OF DAY
3722M
12,211FT 📱112

STREAM

STREAM

GRASSY MARSH WITH
LOBELIAS &
GROUNDSELS

△ KIKELELWA
CAMPSITE
3675M
12,057FT 📱113

STREAM WITH
GROUNDSELS
📱115

VIEWPOINT OVER
VALLEY WITH
MAWENZI AHEAD
📱114

PATH DIVIDES HERE-
DOESN'T MATTER
WHICH ONE YOU TAKE
📱116

PATHS REUNITE, TURN EAST
TO CLIMB RIDGE LEADING
TO CAMPSITE, 4167M, 13,671FT
📱117

CAVE
TOP OF RIDGE
📱118

25

📱119

TOP OF RIDGE - NOW
STEEP DROP ONTO SADDLE

MAWENZI TARN
4302M, 14,114FT

POPULAR
ACCLIMATIZATION
CLIMB
📱121

MAWENZI TARN
HUT CAMPSITE 📱120

0   1km
0   ½ mile

130 MINS FROM
2ND CAVE (MAP 23)

KIKELELWA CAMP

3 HRS 20 MINS

MAWENZI TARN

◀ 3 HRS 30 MINS TO KIBO HUTS (MAP 25)   MAWENZI TARN

TRAIL GUIDE AND MAPS

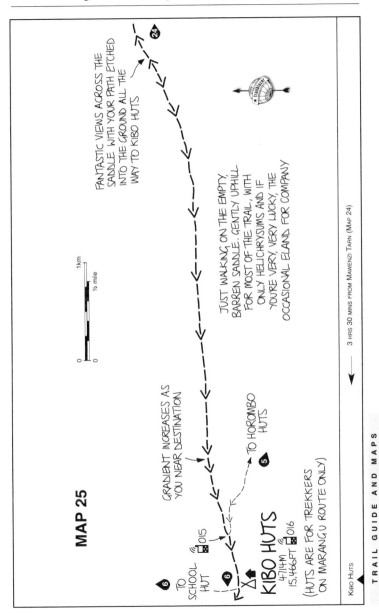

MAP 25

FANTASTIC VIEWS ACROSS THE SADDLE WITH YOUR PATH ETCHED INTO THE GROUND ALL THE WAY TO KIBO HUTS

JUST WALKING ON THE EMPTY, BARREN SADDLE. GENTLY UPHILL FOR MOST OF THE TRAIL, WITH ONLY HELICHRYSUMS AND IF YOU'RE VERY, VERY LUCKY, THE OCCASIONAL ELAND FOR COMPANY

GRADIENT INCREASES AS YOU NEAR DESTINATION

TO HOROMBO HUTS

TO SCHOOL HUT

015

016

KIBO HUTS
4711M 15,466FT

(HUTS ARE FOR TREKKERS ON MARANGU ROUTE ONLY)

3 HRS 30 MINS FROM MAWENZI TARN (MAP 24)

1km
½ mile
0
0

STAGE 3: THIRD CAVE CAMPSITE TO SCHOOL HUT
[MAP 23, p319; MAP 26, p325]

Distance: 4.8km; altitude gained: 781m

This stage is little more than an *hors d'oeuvre* for the main course, which will be served at around midnight tonight. Yet it may surprise you to find out that over the course of this stage you climb 781m. By the end of it you'll be on the

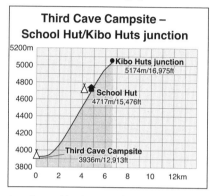

Third Cave Campsite – School Hut/Kibo Huts junction

- Kibo Huts junction 5174m/16,975ft
- △ ▲ School Hut 4717m/15,476ft
- △ Third Cave Campsite 3936m/12,913ft

eastern slopes of Kibo, with splendid views across the Saddle to Mawenzi just a few minutes' walk away.

Looking south-west from the Third Cave Campsite, you should be able to see much of today's path snaking over the undulations of Kibo. The path begins by retracing the last few steps of yesterday back to the **river bed**, which forks just a few minutes after the campsite into two distinct tributaries. The path, too, divides at this junction and is signposted, with your trail heading off to the right (west), crossing the western tributary and continuing on towards the foot of Kibo. It's a slow slog southwards up the hill. Even the heathers struggle to survive up here, disappearing for the last time less than an hour outside camp; only the everlastings and the occasional yellow senecio continue to thrive, providing a welcome relief from the relentless greys and browns of the rocky soil.

After about 75 minutes a summit of sorts is reached, whereafter the path now heads more to the west, directly towards Kibo. A porters' path bisects the trail around here, a path so seldom used that the junction is easily missed. No matter, for your path is clear as it bends more to the south, traversing **Kibo's eastern slopes** with the western face of Mawenzi now in full view to your left. Soon after, your guide may take you off the trail and down the hill a little on a porter's path to see the main sight of the day: a buffalo carcass, well preserved by the dry conditions, wedged between rocks. One can only imagine that the buffalo – presumably up here looking for salt which they like to lick off the cliffs – became

caught between the rocks and couldn't get out again.

The last bit of the walk is steep and the difficulty in getting oxygen into your lungs will leave you feeling quite exhausted. But after just over an hour from the western bend in the path, you finally reach the

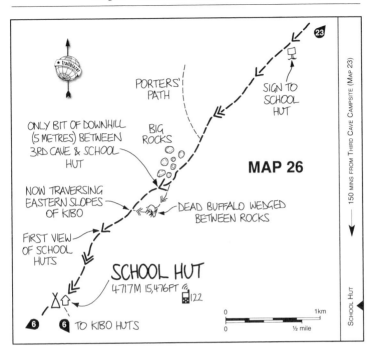

PORTERS' PATH

SIGN TO SCHOOL HUT

ONLY BIT OF DOWNHILL (5 METRES) BETWEEN 3RD CAVE & SCHOOL HUT

BIG ROCKS

MAP 26

NOW TRAVERSING EASTERN SLOPES OF KIBO

DEAD BUFFALO WEDGED BETWEEN ROCKS

FIRST VIEW OF SCHOOL HUTS

SCHOOL HUT
4717M 15,476FT 122

TO KIBO HUTS

150 MINS FROM THIRD CAVE CAMPSITE (MAP 23)

SCHOOL HUT

0   1km
0   ½ mile

School Hut (marked as the Outward Bound Hut on some maps, its former name and one that KINAPA would prefer you didn't use), sitting in the shadow of some rather daunting cliffs. The hut sits at an altitude of about 4717m – virtually the same as Kibo Huts. Incidentally, the Kibo Huts, larger and permanently manned by park staff, are the first place to head if you need help. They lie just 35-45 minutes to the south, the path beginning by the southernmost toilet hut.

STAGE 4: SCHOOL HUT TO UHURU PEAK VIA JUNCTION WITH KIBO HUTS ROUTE [MAP 6, p265]

Distance: 1.9km to Kibo Huts route, plus 4km to Uhuru Peak (5.9km in total); altitude gained: 457m to Kibo Huts route, plus 721m to Uhuru Peak, 1178m total (see p264 for the Kibo Huts to Uhuru Peak profile)

The higher we climbed the rarer grew the atmosphere and the more brilliant the light of the stars. Never in my life have I seen anything to equal the steady lustre of this tropical starlight. The planets seemed to grow with a still splendour which was more than earthly, ... Assuredly, the nights of lower earth know nothing of this silver radiance.

Hans Meyer *Across East African Glaciers* (1891)

There is no direct trekking route from the School Hut to the crater rim. Instead, the path heads south from the huts to join up with the 'Tourist trail' running

TRAIL GUIDE AND MAPS

from Kibo Huts towards Gillman's Point – the trail we have dubbed the Kibo Huts Route. Your trail joins it between William's Point (5131m) and Hans Meyer Cave (5259m). In our experience, it takes slightly – though only slightly – less time from School Hut to this junction than it does from Kibo Huts, so you may wish to start this stage a little later than you would if walking from Kibo Huts – say at 12.15-12.30am rather than midnight.

Finding the start of the path from the School Hut can be a little tricky in the dark so we recommend you or your guide conduct a little reconnaissance while it's still light to ensure he knows where you're supposed to go. Once you're on the path, which starts with a scramble up the rocks behind the School Hut, the trail becomes fairly clear, being marked with cairns the whole way. A repetitive pattern emerges during the walk: generally you are walking in a south-westerly direction over scree, but every so often the path turns more westerly and climbs more steeply over solid rock – these being petrified lava flows. At the end, a short descent brings you into the Kibo Huts 'valley' and a union with the path up to Gillman's. After the isolation of the previous two hours, the number of trekkers on this path comes as something of a shock. Hans Meyer Cave lies just 20 minutes above you along a series of switchbacks.

For details of the path up to Gillman's Point from Hans Meyer Cave, turn to p266. For the descent you'll be using the Marangu Route, details of which can be found on p334.

The Umbwe Route

If Marangu is the 'Coca Cola Route' and Machame has the nickname 'The Whiskey Route', what does that make Umbwe, (in)famous as the shortest (**24.35km***from gate to summit if taking the Western Breach Route, though it's **27.71km** if trekking via Barafu, making it longer than the standard Rongai Route), the steepest and hardest of the trails on Kili? Sure, Machame is *fairly* steep here and there. But on Umbwe, the gradient is such that in a couple of places on the first day you can stand upright on the trail and kiss it at the same time. What's more, since the Machame path has been renovated, it's now only on the Umbwe route that you'll be trekking on tree roots for much of the first day. So while Machame is still popularly called 'The Whiskey Route', since its recent renovation that 'whiskey' has been rather watered down; and when compared to the unadulterated Umbwe Route, Machame starts to seem like pretty small beer.

That said, the Umbwe Route is still **a non-technical climb**. Taxing, but not technical. All you need are an iron will and calves of steel; this is truly a trek to

---

* It should be mentioned that if you don't visit Barranco Camp but head straight from the Umbwe Route to Arrow Glacier – as speed ascent record holder Kilian Jornet did (see p7) – the distance is even shorter at about 21.2km.

test your mettle. The difficulty is that it's so damn relentlessly uphill. Indeed, looking back on the first couple of days we can think of very few places where you actually descend, the longest being the five minutes or so at the end of the second stage when you walk down to Barranco Campsite.

As far as rewards go, while your calves and thighs will curse the day God paired them with somebody who would want to undertake such a climb, your heart and lungs will be thankful for the workout. Your eyes, too, will be grateful you chose Umbwe as they feast upon the scenery, particularly on the second morning as you leave the forest and find yourself walking on a narrow ridge between spindly heathers. The gobsmacking views on either side of the trail here are amongst the most dramatic the mountain has to offer, save for those on the summit itself. Your ears, too, will be glad they're stuck to the side of your head rather than anyone else's for they'll enjoy the break, this being the quietest trail of them all (with only Nature Discovery/Thomson of the big agencies positively promoting Umbwe) – at least until the end of the second day when you find yourself joining the hordes at Barranco Camp, the busiest on the mountain. Once at Barranco, you can either follow the majority round to Barafu and access the summit via Stella Point; or, if you hanker after the quieter, more dramatic option once again, you can join the path up to Lava Tower and continue to the summit via the Western Breach (see p300). This latter option is the connoisseur's choice, no doubt, though be warned that it's an extremely risky strategy unless you take at least one – and preferably two – acclimatization days en route to Arrow Glacier Campsite. Otherwise, the trip from Moshi up to Arrow Glacier Campsite, an increase in altitude of almost 4000m, will have taken you just three days which is far too rapid. Do this and you can kiss your summit certificate – and possibly a lot more – goodbye.

So that's Umbwe: dramatic views, blessed solitude and some terrific, invigorating walking – and all without the clutter and chatter of other trekkers. Those who know the mountain consider it Kili's best-kept secret. And it's hard to argue with that.

STAGE 1: UMBWE GATE TO UMBWE CAVE CAMPSITE
[MAP 27, p329; MAP 28, p331]

Distance: 9.6km; altitude gained: 1293m

The first stage of this trek transforms itself from a tiring tramp on a 4WD trail to a terrific trek on tree roots. It's normal to start this stage fairly late in the day for permits for this route are issued not at Umbwe Gate but at Marangu; if you specifically want to start early it might be worth asking your agency if they can fetch the permit the day before. (This may not be such a bad idea, for one guide told us of one occasion when, owing to torrential rain that washed away the road leading to Umbwe, the group he was leading didn't actually arrive at Umbwe Cave Campsite until 10pm!)

As the closest gate to Moshi, getting to the start of the trail should be uncomplicated as long as the road is intact. Turning off the Moshi–Arusha road just 10 minutes after leaving the former, you bid farewell to the joys of tarmac

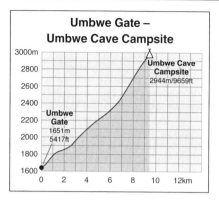

**Umbwe Gate –
Umbwe Cave Campsite**

Umbwe Cave
Campsite
2944m/9659ft

Umbwe
Gate
1651m
5417ft

by heading north on a mud track to Umbwe. Passing banana plantations (with much of the produce in this region going to make banana wine, bottled in Arusha) you soon reach the gate, where there's little save for some toilets and a couple of friendly and under-worked rangers. This is also the place where you should pay your forest fee – the only route other than Lemosho where you must fork out for the forest before you can begin (as usual, your trekking agency will sort this out).

After the usual faffing around at the gate, you eventually begin your walk by setting off on a 4WD road. With monkeys (blue and colobus) crashing in the trees, turacos gliding above them, chameleons stalking amongst the shrubbery and some of Kilimanjaro's more celebrated flora putting in an appearance, including a profusion of *Impatiens pseudoviola* and, further on, its more glamorous, beautiful, and rarer cousin, *Impatiens kilimanjari*, it's a fine start. Look out, too, for *Lobelia gibberoa*, with its strange phallic brush growing out of the top of the plant. This route is one of the few places where you can find them on the mountain, though they appear in greater abundance on Mount Meru. If it's the weekend, you'll also be sharing the path with dozens of kids collecting fodder, probably illegally, from the forest.

No matter how interesting this initial walk is, after almost two hours it comes as something of a relief when the road finally ends and the Umbwe route 'proper' begins. It's a path that continues the north/north-north-east trend of the road, though in our opinion it's considerably more charming. For much of it you'll be walking not on the soil but actually on tree roots. These can be your

---

❏ Mobile (cell) phone reception on the Umbwe Route

Mobile reception on the Umbwe Route is not great, though as always it depends a lot on which network you are with. I've never managed to get a signal in the forest on this route, though on the second morning after struggling through the giant heathers I do often get reception – intermittently. At Barranco reception is not good, though on the ridge before entering camp it's OK. Then up to **Lava Tower** and **Arrow Glacier** it is fine, even up to **Crater Camp** and, so I've been told, the summit.

As for those heading to the summit via Barafu, while it's not great at Karanga I've always got pretty good reception at **Barafu**; while at **Stella**, if you walk around enough, you can get it there too.

On the descent, it's usually OK at **Millennium Camp** but declines after that until you leave the forest.

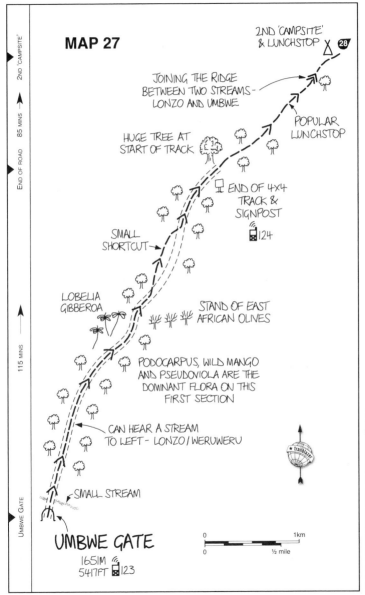

MAP 27

2ND 'CAMPSITE' & LUNCHSTOP 28

JOINING THE RIDGE BETWEEN TWO STREAMS - LONZO AND UMBWE

HUGE TREE AT START OF TRACK

POPULAR LUNCHSTOP

END OF 4X4 TRACK & SIGNPOST
124

SMALL SHORTCUT

LOBELIA GIBBEROA

STAND OF EAST AFRICAN OLIVES

PODOCARPUS, WILD MANGO AND PSEUDOVIOLA ARE THE DOMINANT FLORA ON THIS FIRST SECTION

CAN HEAR A STREAM TO LEFT - LONZO / WERUWERU

SMALL STREAM

UMBWE GATE

1651M
5417FT 123

0   1km
0   ½ mile

2ND 'CAMPSITE'

85 MINS

END OF ROAD

115 MINS

UMBWE GATE

TRAIL GUIDE AND MAPS

best friend, providing steps up a trail which would otherwise be too steep; or, if it's been raining, they can be your worst enemy, causing you to slip and swear.

Almost an hour after leaving the road you reach a **popular lunch-stop**; halfway between here and a second possible lunch-stop/campsite you realize you've actually **joined a ridge** – and a spectacular one at that, with the great forested ravine of the Umbwe River on one side and the more modest dip of the Lonzo Stream on the other. No doubt you've also noticed that the trail is getting increasingly steeper. Indeed, this ridge is one of the steepest parts of the entire trek; in places you'll be using the tree roots to haul yourself up with your hands. Luckily, there are plenty of tree roots around. The forest around here is rich and dark, the forest canopy minimizing the amount of light that filters through to the path. Distract yourself from the muffled screaming coming from your calf muscles by admiring the beauty of the forest here, the trees all knobbled, gnarled and heavy with moss. In between breaths, check out the beautiful red *Impatiens kilimanjari*, too, growing between those same tree roots that are helping you progress along the route.

An hour after joining the ridge you reach the first heathers on the trail. As those who've trekked on other routes will know, this often heralds the end of the first day and so it is here with the destination on this first stage, **Umbwe Cave Campsite** (2944m), lying just 10 minutes away. More a glorified overhang than a proper cave, the adjacent campsite dribbles up the ridge and is a charming spot, a quiet place hidden in the upper reaches of the forest with *Impatiens kilimanjari* dotted here and there amongst the tents.

Let's just hope you started your trek in time to reach it.

STAGE 2: UMBWE CAVE CAMPSITE TO BARRANCO HUTS
[MAP 28, p331; MAP 29, p332]

Distance: 4.75km; altitude gained: 1042m
This second stage of the Umbwe Route is a showcase for the weird and wonderful. It's the stage where you move from the forest, past a magical stretch of

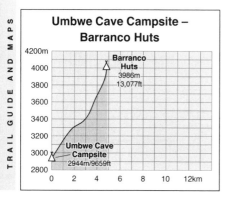

giant heathers and on to the moorland zone where giant groundsels – surely the strangest plants on Kilimanjaro – grow in abundance. The walking, as with yesterday's stage, is pretty much uphill all the way, though again is tiring rather than technical and thus nothing to fear. By the end you will have reached Barranco Huts, a wonderful spot serving a number of routes and on the border of the alpine desert. Note that Machame Route trekkers will have taken three days to get to this camp, and those on the Lemosho Route four. It gives you some idea just how steep the Umbwe Route is; it should also remind you, if you didn't know before, of the importance of building in rest days and of taking it *pole pole* from now on.

The stage starts with a tramp through one of the prettiest sections – no, make that *the* prettiest section – of heathland on the entire mountain, the sunlight penetrating through the giant heathers to dapple the carpet of soft mossy grass. We've never seen heather forest so thick, so uniform, so laden with bearded lichen nor so gorgeous. Though normally lumped together with the moorland above it, here, as with the Mweka Route that you'll be tackling on the way down, the heather zone is so very distinct from it. As the path veers to the left you notice you're overlooking the vertiginous valley of the Lonzo Stream (a tributary of the Weru Weru) while veer right and you find yourself staring down the giddying ravine of the Umbwe – and you suddenly realize you're balanced on a knife-edge ridge. Vertigo sufferers should perhaps concentrate instead on Kibo which, if the weather's on your side, glistens magnificently ahead.

Around 40 minutes after breaking camp you reach **Jiwe Kamba**, or 'Rope Rock', the name providing a clue as to how trekkers used to tackle this section. The rope's gone now and though larger groups still bring their own, it's no

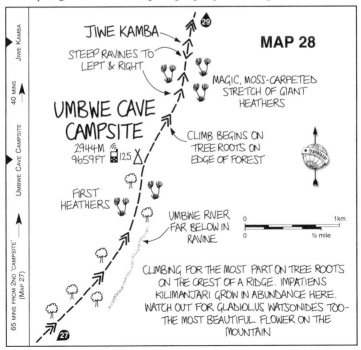

BARRANCO HUTS

DRIFT EAST OFF RIDGE TO...

BARRANCO HUTS

3986M
13,077FT 📱046

CLIMB UP SOUTHERN SLOPE OF
'BARRANCO RIDGE' WHERE
LOBELIAS AND HELICHRYSUMS
DOMINATE

NOW ON NEW
ROCKY RIDGE

ROCKY OUTCROP
SURROUNDED BY
EVIDENCE OF FIRE

★ trailblazer

📱126
POPULAR LUNCH STOP
ON RIDGE - VIEWS OF
MOSHI

PATH DRIFTS
NE TO JOIN
RIDGE

PATH GOES THROUGH
ROCKY OUTCROPS-
FIRST GROUNDSELS
APPEAR

MAP 29

ROCKY & STEEP-
USE HEATHERS TO PULL
YOURSELF UP

28

0　　　　　　　　1km

0　　　　½ mile

BARRANCO HUTS
65 MINS
ROCKY OUTCROP
55 MINS
ROCKY OUTCROPS
65 MINS FROM JIWE KAMBA (MAP 28)

TRAIL GUIDE AND MAPS

problem if you didn't – it's just a few careful steps to the top, rope or no rope.
The going is a little rockier from now on and you'll soon find yourself using the
vegetation flanking the path to haul yourself up. As you progress further north
the first helichrysums appear, their paper texture and white colour contrasting
with the scarlet mountain gladioli, *Gladiolus watsonides*, which survives in both
the forest and heathland zones and surely rivals the impatiens and orchids as the
most beautiful flower on the mountain. Continue still further and amongst the
tussock grass and rocky outcrops the first **groundsels** also put in an appearance.

The ridge which you've been following eventually merges with a new one
which you also climb and then follow, still heading north and with Mount Meru
now a spectator in the distance to the west. Climbing to yet another rocky ridge,
this one with clear signs of having suffered fire damage, you continue your
progress north towards what we will call Barranco Ridge, which you start to
climb before turning off right and down to **Barranco Huts** campsite (3986m).
For a description, please turn to p277.

It is at Barranco that you have a choice to make: left, north-west and up for Lava Tower Campsite, Arrow Glacier Campsite and the path via the Western Breach to the summit. Or right, east and up to Karanga, Barafu and the path up to the summit via Stella Point. Presumably you will have already decided one way or the other. If you've opted for the more popular route via Barafu Huts, turn to p278 for the continuation of this trail. Whereas if you're gunning for the Western Breach, read on...

STAGE 3: BARRANCO HUTS TO LAVA TOWER CAMPSITE
[MAP 11, p279; MAP 10, p276]

Distance: 3.5km; altitude gained: 641m
Many of the trails on Kili started as porters' routes, ie the porters established them before the guides and their clients adopted them and, eventually, the authorities too. Furthermore, it is of course the nature of porters to find the quickest route from A to B, with little thought given as to whether it's a pretty or attractive route.

So it is with today's trail from Barranco up to Lava Tower, the start of the climb up to the Western Breach. It's a short-cut that was established by porters hurrying down from Arrow Glacier or Lava Tower round to the Mweka Route, in order to meet their clients arriving down from the summit. This trail has become

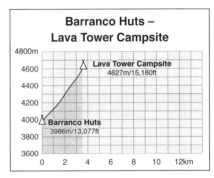

so established as to render the previous route just about obsolete. (That previous route, by the way, continued along the crest of the ridge to the west of Barranco Campsite to the signposted junction at the head of the Barranco Valley and is still marked on most maps, though it's a rare guide – indeed, anyone – who'll follow it these days.)

The only problem with this new route is that, as previously mentioned, it *is* a short-cut, and one moreover used by porters to *descend* from the mountain. As such, as an ascent route many people find it entirely too short and will have succumbed to the pain of altitude sickness by the stage's end. We therefore recommend you take this into consideration and maybe factor two nights at Barranco into your itinerary, with the rest day spent sauntering up to the head of the valley to help you get used to the rarified atmosphere.

The stage begins with a walk up the Barranco Valley. Come here later in the day and you'll find yourself hiking against a tide of trekkers on the Machame, Lemosho and Shira routes all coming the other way down the same path. But assuming you've started walking in the morning it will probably be just you and your crew, allowing you to enjoy undisturbed views of Kibo through the stands of **groundsels**. About 25 minutes after setting off you leave the main path by a **waterfall** as you continue north, eventually crossing the **stream** you've been following since the day's beginning (and, indeed, as further down it turns into the Umbwe River, since the start of the whole trek). Recrossing it further upstream, you'll find yourself on a slightly gentler trail which continues straight ahead over two streams and on, steeply, up to **Lava Tower**. The entire walking, without breaks, would have taken you just 3¼ hours and you'll probably be at Lava Tower by lunch, allowing you plenty of time to savour this grim camp-site's uniquely chilly, godforsaken 'charm'.

For details of the rest of the walk from Lava Tower to the summit, please turn to p302.

The descent routes

MARANGU ROUTE

Stage 1: Uhuru Peak to Gillman's Point to the Horombo Huts
[Map 33, p347; Map 6, p265; Map 5, p263; Map 4, p262]

Distance: 15.75km; (16.55km for Mawenzi alternative); altitude lost: 2174m
Few people remain at the summit for long: weariness, the risk of hypothermia and the thought of a steaming mug of Milo at the Kibo Huts are enough to send most people scurrying back down. There are **two main ways** of doing this: the **first** is to follow exactly the course from Gillman's to Kibo that you took get-

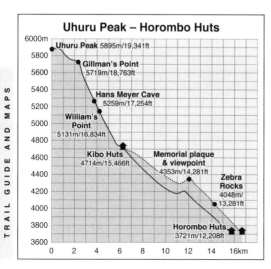

ting up here, carefully retracing every zig and zag like somebody who has dropped a contact lens on the way up but can't quite remember when or where. It is precisely those people who are in greatest need of getting down fast who usually use this slower method to descend.

The **second way** is to cut straight through the switchbacks and simply head vertically downwards in a sort of ski-style, using the now defrosted scree to act as a brake on your momentum as you push against it with the sides of your boots. After the tedium of the previous night's *pole pole*, heel-to-toe exercise, the sheer abandon of this method and the rapid progress made – it takes just over 90 minutes to travel from Gillman's to the huts this way – comes as something of a relief. Take care, however: far more people are injured going down than going up. Furthermore, do remember that every year at least 20,000 pairs of feet tread on this part of the mountain and, at the risk of sounding like a killjoy, pushing down all that scree cannot be doing the mountain any good. Indeed, may we politely request that you use this faster method only if you need to descend rapidly? Otherwise, stick to the switchbacks which will be far less damaging to the mountain – and safer too!

Upon returning to Kibo Huts, your guide should allow you to rest for an hour at least before moving on again to the **Horombo Huts**. If you ascended on the Marangu Route, heed the advice given at the beginning of Stage 3 (see p261) and ask your guide to take you back via a different route to the one on which you ascended. This usually means returning via the Saddle on the Mawenzi Route, a route we describe in the box below. If you return via the southerly, 'usual' route, expect it to take 3¼ hours from Kibo Huts.

If you took the Marangu Route up the mountain, you'll be sleeping in the huts again; while those who took the Rongai Route, which also uses this path to descend, will be camping outside them.

❏ **Returning via the Mawenzi Route**   **[Map 5, p263; Map 4, p262]**
This is the more interesting path between Kibo Huts and Horombo Huts, encompassing entire groves of giant groundsels (*Senecio kilimanjari*), Zebra Rocks and perhaps the best panorama of them all on Kili. It is also seldom used.

From Kibo Huts the path descends once more to **Jiwe La Ukoyo** (see p263). Though there appears to be but one path from Jiwe, there is in fact another, much fainter path heading more directly towards Mawenzi across The Saddle. If you cannot make it out at first don't worry, just aim for Mawenzi and you will soon notice a faint but distinct path etched into the earth bisecting the Saddle. Ten minutes after Jiwe a junction with the even-fainter **Northern Circuit** is reached (a signpost is the only evidence that there is a junction here at all), and 35 minutes after that the path begins to rise and fall as it follows the contours of Mawenzi's lower reaches.

After another 35 minutes following this undulating terrain you come to a summit of sorts, from where you can rest by a **memorial plaque** and gaze back over what is, in my humble opinion, the finest **panorama** this mountain has to offer: the alpine desert of The Saddle, with a string of parasitic cones leading from the foreground to the foot of Kibo and with Mawenzi just over your shoulder. Spectacular. From here, the path runs due south through heather, past the path leading to Mawenzi Hut and on to **Zebra Rocks** (a collection of rockfaces stained by water that resemble the flanks of a zebra), then down between the groundsel gullies until, 70 minutes from the unforgettable panorama and 2½ hours since leaving Jiwe La Ukoyo, the roofs of **Horombo Huts** appear beneath you.

TRAIL GUIDE AND MAPS

Stage 2: Horombo Huts to Marangu Gate
[Map 4, p262; Map 3, p259; Map 2, p257; Map 1, p255]
Distance: 20km (20.75km on Nature Trail – see below); altitude lost: 1816m
Don't be in too much of a hurry to finish your trekking, for today holds lots of treats for those who take the time to enjoy them. If you have come from the Rongai Route this is the first time you will have seen forest so thick and vast on

Kilimanjaro, and it's worth taking the time to appreciate the different flora on this side of the mountain. But even if you ascended by the Marangu Route, it still warrants a second look on the way down. Much of the scenery may be old hat to

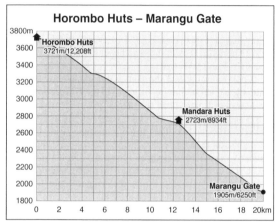

you by now but remember you've still paid US$70 in park fees alone for the privilege of walking in the forest today, so you may as well make the most of it. And just as Lee Marvin in *Paint Your Wagon* sang that he'd never seen a town 'that didn't look better looking back', so most people will agree that the forest

❑ **Marangu Nature Trail**   **[Map 1, p255]**
A nice alternative for those who have already climbed via the Marangu Route and don't fancy taking exactly the same route back down is to divert off after one of the trail's many bridges onto the signposted nature trail.

Only fractionally longer than the regular route, this trail's main attraction is that it is so rarely used; indeed, when we last walked along this path it was quite overgrown and it was clear it hadn't been trekked in a while. This attraction could also be its main disadvantage – the path does have to divert around the occasional fallen tree and there are places where a number of alternative trails present themselves, so you need a guide whom you trust to know where he is going. Assuming you have one this really is a pleasant alternative to the main trail and possibly for the first time on your entire trek you may get an inkling of just how Meyer, New, Teleki, von der Decken and all the other explorers of the 19th century must have felt as they carved their path through the forest. As a reward for taking the route less travelled the path culminates in a lovely waterfall – though it's only really 'active' during the rainy season. From there it's a simple climb up some steps back to the main trail, with the gate just yards away.

seems so much more welcoming when you're walking *downhill* through it – and the views of Kibo are that much more appealing from over the shoulder, knowing you'll never have to climb it again.

It takes about 2 hours 20 minutes to return from Horombo Huts to the **Mandara Huts** which are, typically, the final lunchstop of the trail. From there, it's back into the forest and down to the **gate**, a journey of some 95 minutes. Name registered, tips dispersed and with certificate clutched close to your bosom, it's time to return to the land of hot showers and flush toilets. Your adventure is at an end – and civilization will rarely have felt so good.

THE MWEKA ROUTE

The Mweka Route (20.6km from summit to civilization) is the designated descent route for the Machame, Lemosho/Shira and Umbwe routes. As such, it is a very busy route though repair work a few years ago ensured that it is once more in good condition.

Stage 1: Uhuru Peak to Barafu Huts and Mweka Huts
[Map 33, p347; Map 13, p282; Map 30, p339; Map 31, p341]
Distance: 11.5km; altitude lost: 2789m

What goes up must come down and that includes you. The path back to Barafu is little more than a retracing of your steps of the previous night (assuming you climbed this way and not the Western Breach Route), though there is a slightly

quicker, if more hair-raising approach: descending from Stella Point, after 10 minutes or so you reach a **boulder** which earlier that morning you would have walked around: it's the same boulder that marks the very steep last 30 minutes or so to the crater rim.

This boulder also marks the start of a **straight ski-run down** through the gravel that bypasses the zigzags of the regular route. Some people prefer to make it down as quickly as possible so choose this trail; others find it too taxing on both nerves and knees and opt for the **gentler descent**. Before deciding which is for you, read the advice about erosion at the top of p335 and if possible take the slower option. Note, too, that with the 'faster'

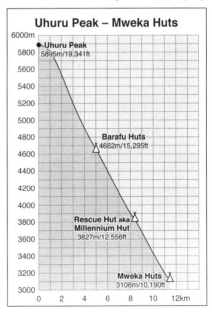

Uhuru Peak – Mweka Huts

- Uhuru Peak 5895m/19,341ft
- Barafu Huts 4662m/15,295ft
- Rescue Hut aka Millennium Hut 3827m/12,556ft
- Mweka Huts 3106m/10,190ft

TRAIL GUIDE AND MAPS

Waterfall at the foot of Kilimanjaro. Engraving by Alexandre Le Roy from *Au Kilima-Ndjaro (Afrique Orientale)* published in 1893.

descent it's not so easy to find your way back to Barafu: at one point you must turn right to rejoin the main path to camp or you risk ending up lost in the valley below. A Korean trekker was believed to have done this in 2008 – and has never been seen again. The entire descent takes about two hours from Stella Point, less if you take the 'fast' route.

You probably feel, on returning to camp, that you have earned the luxury of a brief rest at **Barafu**, and indeed you have. But make sure it *is* brief, for you still have another 140 minutes of knee-knackering downhill before you reach Mweka Huts, your probable home for the night. A pretty monotonous 140 minutes it is, too, as you head off due south and down for the entire 6.64km. In its defence, the descent is both large (dropping from 4662m to 3106m) and fairly gradual, which can only be good news for AMS sufferers. There is also some interest to be had in seeing how the vegetation changes along the way: at first, only the incredibly hardy yellow senecios are able to survive at the high altitude, but they are soon joined by their dry-looking cousins in the *helichrysum* family; soon after that the first heathers appear, to be joined a little later by the proteas. However, it must be said that the **actual path is the worst on the**

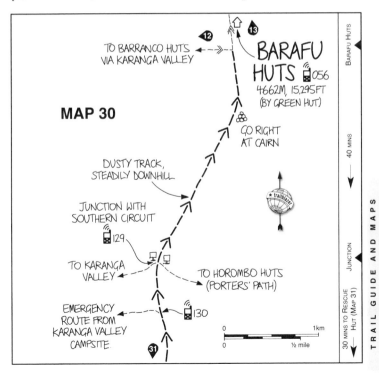

MAP 30

TO BARRANCO HUTS
VIA KARANGA VALLEY

12

13

BARAFU
HUTS 🔋056
4662M, 15,295FT
(BY GREEN HUT)

GO RIGHT
AT CAIRN

DUSTY TRACK,
STEADILY DOWNHILL

JUNCTION WITH
SOUTHERN CIRCUIT
🔋129

TO KARANGA
VALLEY

TO HOROMBO HUTS
(PORTERS' PATH)

EMERGENCY
ROUTE FROM
KARANGA VALLEY
CAMPSITE

130

31

0   1km
0   ½ mile

BARAFU HUTS ◀

40 MINS ▼

JUNCTION

30 MINS TO RESCUE ◀ HUT (MAP 31)

TRAIL GUIDE AND MAPS

mountain, full of loose rocks that shift when trodden upon, causing already weary trekkers to stumble, fumble, fall and swear their way down, particularly the stretch before Millennium Huts.

Around 40 minutes or so from Barafu you come to a **junction**, often marked with a signpost or two, with the little-used Southern Circuit: to your left on the slopes you can see paths from Horombo Huts on the Marangu Route, while to your right are those coming from the Karanga Valley. Another path, an emergency trail from Karanga Campsite for those suffering from altitude, joins the Mweka Route just above the green-roofed rescue hut. This hut was originally established to help out the suffering during the millennium when the mountain was swamped by thousands hoping to see the new era in from the summit. It's remained ever since and, now called the **Rescue Hut** or **Millennium Huts** (or even **High Camp**; 3827m), is a campsite for those who prefer something a little quieter than the Mweka Huts; it's also a useful site to use when the Mweka campsite has been flooded by heavy rain. There is also a water source nearby – another advantage over the Mweka Huts and one of the reasons, perhaps, why more and more groups are choosing to stay here.

Immediately afterwards, giant heathers grow for the first time by the dusty path and, further down, the vanilla-coloured **protea** makes its first appearance, and thereafter dominates the pathside vegetation. The protea's presence ensures a healthy population of **malachite sunbirds** live around here too, as well as the little green **montane white-eyes** – so-called because of the distinctive white ring around their eyes. **Chameleons**, surprisingly, also make the heather their home.

You first glimpse **Mweka Huts** (3106m) about 40 minutes before you actually get there as you descend on a ridge between two valleys towards a small heather-clad hill. Rounding this, the path widens and flattens before turning south-west and climbing for a few seconds on the final section to the camp – the only ascent of the entire walk from Barafu. Mweka Huts is unremarkable; the eco-toilets they installed that we raved about in the last edition are now sadly a bit of a blemish on the campsite: malodorous, fly-filled and shit-stained, they're in need of some TLC – or at least a clean.

By the way, you may wish to share out your tips at Mweka Huts before you depart on this last leg: as porters all walk at different speeds, this may be the last time the whole group is together.

Stage 2: Mweka Huts to Mweka Gate   [Map 31, p341; Map 32, p343]
Distance: 9.1km; altitude lost: 1473m

By now you'll probably just want to get off the mountain as quickly as possible – which would actually be rather a shame, for this last section follows a very pretty forest trail alive with birdsong and flowers. Indeed, the variety, quantity and sheer beauty of the flora is incredible. This path has now thankfully been fully restored following years of over-use. Towards the end of 2001 it was so eroded that in parts trekkers found themselves walking in a 2ft deep trench. The worst bits of that path have now been abandoned altogether (in one place a bridge has actually been built to convey the new path across the old), and the new trail is in much better shape. The only complaint we have is that the

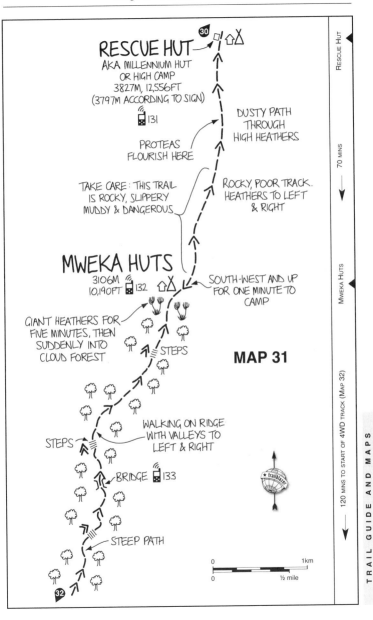

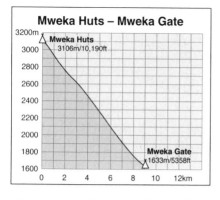

Mweka Huts – Mweka Gate

Mweka Huts
3106m/10,190ft

Mweka Gate
1633m/5358ft

authorities have decided to build steps on the steep parts, which we are sure is good for combatting erosion – but after five days or so of climbing, your knees will be screaming for mercy by the end. It's a lovely section of forest but whether your mind can concentrate on anything other than the pain in your joints is another matter.

This stage begins in similar fashion to much of the previous one, by heading south and down. Less than five minutes after you start walking, you find yourself in **cloud forest**, the border between this and the giant heather forest so definite and distinct that you could almost draw a line in the ground between the two. Once again walking on a narrow ridge between two valleys, look around and notice how the trees now grow in height and girth, how the moss that grows upon them is thick, green and hearty where before it was stringy and limp, and how flowers such as the *Impatiens kilimanjari* once again make an appearance, and in abundance too. Its cousin *Impatiens pseudoviola* also lines the path, while the occasional, beautiful vivid red mountain gladiolus flourishes here and there, the delicate white flowers of the wild blackberry grow in clusters and the alabaster-white petals of the *Begonia meyeri johannis* litter the trail towards the end.

Around two hours after breaking camp, you'll find yourself walking on the **start of the 4WD track** down to the gate which lies a further 45 minutes away. At **Mweka Gate** (1633m) you can usually buy a souvenir T-shirt to advertise the fact you reached the summit (curiously, there are no suitable T-shirts for those that did not). You must also sign the last **registration book** at the nearby park office, from where those who were successful can collect the appropriate certificate. If you're with a company that has 4WD vehicles you might be met at the gate; the rest have to walk 10 minutes further down the hill to the lower station, where there are a couple of shops and a bar. Those who succeeded in reaching Uhuru Peak can usually be seen standing around, their certificates dangling casually yet deliberately from their hands so they are clearly visible to passers-by, in much the same way that Ferrari owners are wont to display their car keys. Your mountain odyssey is almost at an end: from here, it's a 30-minute drive back to the land of power showers, flush toilets and cold, cold beer. You've earned it – though if you do plan to celebrate in Moshi, please take more care than Hans Meyer did upon his return to town in 1889:

In the evening, to show there was no ill-feeling, I treated the natives to a display of fireworks, in the course of which a spark from a rocket set fire to one of the men's huts.

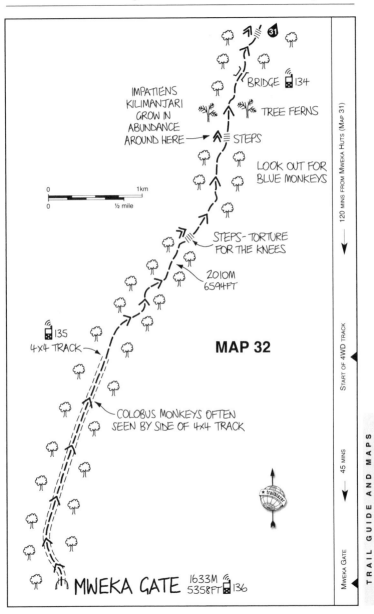

IMPATIENS
KILIMANJARI
GROW IN
ABUNDANCE
AROUND HERE →

BRIDGE 📱134

TREE FERNS

👣 STEPS

LOOK OUT FOR
BLUE MONKEYS

STEPS – TORTURE
FOR THE KNEES

2010M
6594FT

📱135
4X4 TRACK

MAP 32

COLOBUS MONKEYS OFTEN
SEEN BY SIDE OF 4X4 TRACK

0 _____ 1km
0 _____ ½ mile

★ trailblazer

MWEKA GATE 1633M
5358FT 📱136

120 MINS FROM MWEKA HUTS (MAP 31)

START OF 4WD TRACK

45 MINS

MWEKA GATE

TRAIL GUIDE AND MAPS

THE SUMMIT

What's at the top?

The crater of Kilimanjaro is a primeval place and decidedly uncomfortable, yet I was drawn to it. The idea of spending some days and nights awoke a compelling mixture of reverential fear and wonder; similar, I suspect, to the compulsion which draws some people unquestioningly to church. And like churches, the crater also invites contemplation of the eternal mysteries.
John Reader *Kilimanjaro* (1982)

It's only when you reach the top of Kibo that you realize the mountain really is a volcano and all you have done is climb to the crater rim.

The rim itself is largely featureless, though as the highest point on the mountain it has assumed a pre-eminent role and is the focus of all trekkers. Many of the bumps and tumescences on it have been dignified with the word 'Spitze' or 'Point' as if they were major summits in their own right. Heading clockwise around the rim from **Gillman's**, these features in order are: **Bismark Towers**, **Stella Point** (the aim of those climbing from Barafu), **Elveda** and **Hans Meyer points** and **Uhuru Peak**; while just to the north of Gillman's is **Johannes Notch**, **Leopard Point** and **Hans Meyer Notch**. The distance between Gillman's and Uhuru is a little over 2km, with the crater rim rising 176m between the two. The floor of the crater, covered in brown shale and rocks and boulders of all shapes and sizes, lies between 25m (at Gillman's) and 200m (at Uhuru Peak) beneath this rim.

Trudging around the rim to Uhuru is achievement enough. There are, however, plenty of other diversions to keep you on the summit for longer ...

WALKING ON THE SUMMIT   [Map 33, p347]

For most people the conquest of Uhuru Peak and a nice certificate that says as much is reason enough to climb Kilimanjaro. Some trekkers, however, always want to do just that little bit more and if you still have some energy to burn once you've reached the summit you may care to take a quick tour around the crater itself. **Warn your**

(Opposite) Struggling past the Rebmann Glacier on the Crater Rim.

guide in advance of your intentions – preferably before you've even started your trek – as some react badly to the idea of spending any longer on the summit than is absolutely necessary; a little gentle cajoling along with a few hints about the size of the tip that awaits them at the end of the trip should do the trick. Make sure, too, that your guide knows his way around up there: you'll probably be a little short of humour as well as breath on the crater rim and following an ignorant guide while he tries in vain to locate the correct path to the Reusch Crater will do little to lighten your mood.

The standard way to reach **Reusch Crater**, Kibo summit's very own parasitic cone, is to ascend via the Western Breach, where a trail of sorts heads off to the north round Furtwangler Glacier away from Uhuru Peak to the crater. For this reason, it is far more common for those who have climbed via the difficult Arrow Glacier/Western Breach Route to visit Reusch than those who ascended by one of the other paths. But those who arrived at the crater rim at either Gillman's or Stella Point needn't despair, for there is also a porters' trail from near Stella Point that crosses the crater floor to join up with the path to Reusch.

The actual climb up to the rim of Reusch Crater is relatively short but surprisingly tiring; if you didn't know you were at altitude before, you will now! This walk can take as little as 30 minutes from the campsite, though that's assuming that you are in fairly good shape; and on the summit this is a very big assumption. Having reached Reusch, check out the bright yellow sulphurous deposits, largely on its western side, and the fumaroles that occasionally puff smoke – proof not only that Kili is a volcano, but that it is also an active one. The smell of sulphur is all-pervasive in this crater and the earth is hot to touch.

Within Reusch Crater is the 120m-deep **Ash Pit** which, though it does not conspicuously contain ash, is said to be one of the most perfect examples of this sort of formation in the world. At 360m across it's also one of the largest. If you reach the Ash Pit, you can truly say you have conquered this mountain.

The faces behind the features

Most Kilimanjaro climbers are aware that Uhuru is Swahili for 'Freedom' and the highest point in Africa was christened this after Tanzania achieved independence in 1961. But do you know after what or whom other features of Kibo are named? Some of them are relatively easy: **Rebmann Glacier** is obviously named after the first European to see Kilimanjaro (see p105), while neighbouring **Decken Glacier** is named after another eminent Victorian, Baron von der Decken, the first man to seriously attempt to climb the mountain. His travel partner, Otto **Kersten**, also has a glacier named after him next to the Baron's; while next is **Heim Glacier**, named after Albrecht Heim, world-renowned glacier expert. Hermann **Credner** and Albrecht **Penck** are two other German geologers/geographers who are celebrated in the names of glaciers on Kili; in

(Opposite) Top: Descending back to Barafu Camp after reaching the summit.
Middle: The joy of reaching the summit!
Bottom: The Ash Pit at the heart of the Reusch Crater.

Penck's case twice, with both a Great Penck and Little Penck Glacier. The Great Penck and Credner Glacier together form the Northern Icefield.

There's also **Furtwangler Glacier**, sadly much reduced recently, which sits on the crater floor and is named after the first man to ski down the side of Kilimanjaro. Herr Furtwangler also has a point on the crater rim named after him, as does the leopard (Leopard Point), which was found frozen in the ice back in the early years of the 20th century.

Meanwhile, **Hans Meyer**– the first man to the summit, of course – has both a Point and a Notch named after him. Another man who *may* have a Notch named after him is the first European to see Kili, Johannes Rebmann (in addition to the glacier we just mentioned). I say 'may' as there is also a theory that Johannes Notch is in fact named after Hans Meyer's guide Yohani Kinyala Lauwo (see p50) – Johannes being the German 'version' of Yohani. If it is named after Mr Lauwo, it's the only feature on the summit of Kili that's named after a Tanzanian. To the south of Johannes Notch, Bismark Towers are named in tribute to Otto von Bismark (or Bismarck), German chancellor who united the German states and who was in office when Hans Meyer first conquered Kili.

Two of the most well-known points on the crater rim, **Gillman's** and **Stella Point**, are named after quite obscure figures. The former, for example, was *probably* named after the first man to reach the crater rim after the mountain had come under British protection, one Clement Gillman, who reached this point (but no higher) in 1921. While Stella Point is named after the wife of Dr Kingsley Latham, a member of the Mountain Club of South Africa, and marks the point that they both reached in 1925. Latham then went on to discover the frozen leopard mentioned previously, from which Pastor Richard Reusch took an ear as a souvenir (see p121) – and after whom the inner crater was named following his 25th ascent of the mountain. His wife is also celebrated on the mountain: **Elveda Point**, which is one of the false summits on the way to Uhuru Peak. Reusch, incidentally, went on to climb the mountain 65 times – a record, we believe, for a non-native.

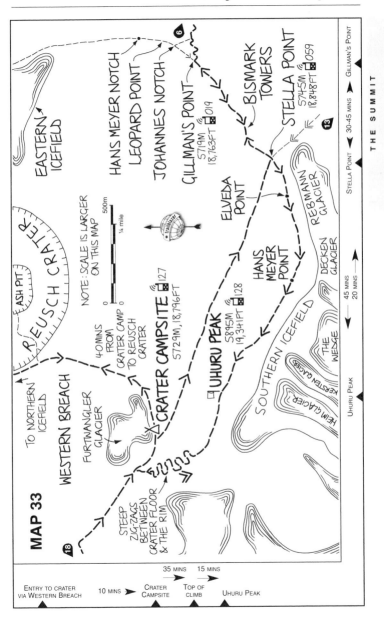

MAP 33

THE SUMMIT

Gillman's Point ◀ 30-45 MINS ▶ Stella Point ◀ 45 MINS / 20 MINS ▶ Uhuru Peak

GILLMAN'S POINT
5719M, 18,763FT 🏠 019

STELLA POINT
5745M, 18,848FT 🏠 059

HANS MEYER NOTCH
LEOPARD POINT
JOHANNES NOTCH

BISMARK TOWERS

ELVEDA POINT

HANS MEYER POINT
5895M, 19,341FT 🏠 128

REBMANN GLACIER

DECKEN GLACIER

SOUTHERN ICEFIELD

THE WEDGE

KERSTEN GLACIER

HEIM GLACIER

EASTERN ICEFIELD

ASH PIT

REUSCH CRATER

To Northern Icefield

WESTERN BREACH

FURTWANGLER GLACIER

40 MINS FROM CRATER CAMP TO REUSCH CRATER

CRATER CAMPSITE 🏠 127
5729M, 18,796FT

UHURU PEAK

STEEP ZIG-ZAGS BETWEEN CRATER FLOOR & THE RIM

NOTE : SCALE IS LARGER ON THIS MAP

0 — 500m
0 — ¼ mile

trailblazer

ENTRY TO CRATER VIA WESTERN BREACH → 10 MINS → CRATER CAMPSITE → 35 MINS → TOP OF CLIMB → 15 MINS → UHURU PEAK

APPENDIX A – SWAHILI

Of the two main languages you will encounter, **Swahili**, the national tongue, is undoubtedly the more useful and the one you will see written on signs and notices. There are plenty of Swahili dictionaries around: street vendors sell little green versions in Arusha or you can pick one up in souvenir stores for about a sixth of the price they charge.

The other language, **Chagga** and its various dialects, is common around Kili but it is unlikely you'll hear it outside the region. You will, however, curry favour with porters and guides on Kilimanjaro by learning a few words; see the box on p138 for a brief introduction. Chagga dictionaries are rare though you'll find one mentioned on p358.

Basics

Yes	*Ndiyo*
No	*Hapana*
Good Morning	*Jambo*
My name is...	*Jina langu ni...*
How are you?	*Habari gani?*
Please...	*Tafadhali...*
Thanks (very much)	*Ahsante (sana)*
Do you speak English?	*Unasema Kiingereza?*
Help!	*Saidia!*
How much is it?	*Kiasi gani?*
Slowly, slower	*Pole, pole-pole*
Let's go!	*Twendai!*

Places

Bank	*Banki*
Launderette	*Kufulia*
Post office	*Posta*

Days of the week

Monday	*Jumatatu*
Tuesday	*Jumanne*
Wednesday	*Jumatano*
Thursday	*Alhamisi*
Friday	*Ijumaa*
Saturday	*Jumamosi*
Sunday	*Jumapili*

Travel

Bus station	*kituo cha mabasi*
Airport	*kiwanja cha ndege*
Port	*bandari*
Train station	*stesheni*
Ticket office	*wanapouza tikiti*
When will we arrive at...?	*tutafika...jini?*
Is this the direct way to...?	*hii ni njia fupi kwenda...?*

Food and drink

Beans	*Maharagwe*
Bread	*Mkate*
Chicken	*Kuku*
Coffee	*Kahawa*
Cold	*Baridi*
Eggs	*Mayai*
Fish	*Samaki*
Meat	*Nyama*
Orange	*Chungwa*
Pork	*Nyama ya nguruwe*
Vegetables	*Mboga*
Venison	*Nyama ya porini*
Water	*Maji*

Numbers

1	*moja*	10	*kumi*	70	*sabini*
2	*mbili*	11	*kumi na moja*	80	*themanini*
3	*tatu*	12	*kumi na mbili*	90	*tisini*
4	*nne*	20	*ishirini*	100	*mia*
5	*tano*	21	*ishirini na moja*	200	*mia mbili*
6	*sita*	30	*thelathini*	1000	*elfu*
7	*saba*	40	*arobaini*	2000	*elfu mbili*
8	*nane*	50	*hamsini*		
9	*tisa*	60	*sitini*		

APPENDIX B – FLIGHT SCHEDULES: KILIMANJARO & ARUSHA AIRPORTS

FLIGHTS TO AND FROM KILIMANJARO AIRPORT

International flights

The situation regarding flights into Kilimanjaro (JRO) has improved of late with a couple more major international airlines flying into JRO thereby supplementing the services operated by KLM, Ethiopian Airlines and Kenya Airways.

Qatar Airways (⌨ www.qatarairways.com) offer a daily service, particularly useful for those flying from Asia (who've always been a little hard done by before now when it comes to getting to Kili), arriving daily and departing 2-3 hours later (currently at either 10.50 or 16.20) back to Doha.

Turkish Airlines (⌨ www.turkishairlines.com) fly six times weekly from Istanbul. At the moment they seem to offer the cheapest deals and the service is good too – the only problem being that they arrive in the middle of the night, and depart again an hour later (currently at 02.10); make sure your agency is willing to offer airport transfers at this time!

KLM (⌨ www.klm.com) fly every day in the high season to Tanzania, touching down in Kilimanjaro on their way to Dar. In 2012 it looked suspiciously as if they were winding down their service to East Africa when their office in Arusha closed. But they are still flying every day in the high season so hopefully we were just being unnecessarily pessimistic. Flights leave Schiphol (Amsterdam) at around 10.10am, arriving the same day at Kili at 8.35pm (total travel time 8hrs 25 mins). If you're coming from the UK, where KLM have a great network, that links various airports around the country to Amsterdam's Schiphol Airport, they could well be the most convenient airline. Those flying from the US will also find KLM a good option: flights from New York to Amsterdam are around twice daily (or five times if you include their partner Delta Airlines), three of them arriving no later than 7.35am which will enable you to transfer for the flight to Kilimanjaro; they also fly from Los Angeles but any onward connection to Kilimanjaro would currently involve an overnight stop in Amsterdam. KLM's flight leaves Kilimanjaro Airport for Dar at about 8.50pm daily in the high season before returning to Europe.

Ethiopian Airlines (⌨ www.ethiopianairlines.com) operate a pretty comprehensive pan-African network and are renowned for being cheap and also one of the most reliable of African airlines. They fly at least daily from Addis Ababa to Kilimanjaro via Nairobi, though half the time their flights arrive in the middle of the night (currently 3.20am). From London they have flights to Addis Ababa six times weekly; from the States, they have a flight from Washington Dulles Airport daily which is usually perfect for the morning connecting flight to Kilimanjaro as long as everything runs smoothly. Ethiopian Airlines' planes tend to hang around for an hour at Kilimanjaro Airport from the moment they arrive before returning to Addis.

Kenya Airways (⌨ www.kenya-airways.com) also advertise flights to Kilimanjaro, though they will actually carry you only as far as Nairobi and one of their partners, Precision Air, will fly you from there. Nevertheless, it's a good service, flying daily at 8pm from London to Nairobi, arriving at around 6.30am.

A couple of minor airlines also advertise flights to JRO from Europe including **Edelweiss Air** (⌨ www.edelweissair.ch), a small Swiss airline that fly into Kilimanjaro and the Kenyan coastal city of Mombasa in the summer (July-October), once a week on a Sunday night from Zurich, arriving (and flying out) the next morning.

Condor Air (⌨ www.condor.com) are a German outfit flying every Thursday from Frankfurt, arriving early Friday morning at Kilimanjaro International and beginning the return leg about an hour later.

Regional and domestic airlines to Kilimanjaro Airport

For a good overview of regional airlines – and the chance to book tickets – visit the website ⌨ **www.alternativeairlines.com**.

Precision Air (⌨ www.precisionairtz.com), partner of Kenya Airways, fly around four times per day between Nairobi and Kilimanjaro. They also have around 3-4 flights from Dar every day. They have at least two flights a day from Kili to Dar, and also fly to Nairobi three times a day (currently 6am, 10.55am and 2pm).

Regional Air (⌨ www.regionaltanzania.com) now include Kilimanjaro in their journey round Manyara and Serengeti national parks, as does **Coastal Aviation** (⌨ www.coastal.co.tz).

There's a new budget airline in town: **Fastjet** (⌨ www.fastjet.com) fly from Kili to Zanzibar for as little as US$20 each way (plus taxes) three times a week, and twice daily between Kili and Dar.

Rwandair fly to Kili from Kigali directly on a Friday, and via Dar on a Wednesday and Sunday. They currently fly to Kigali directly on Wednesday and Sunday, and via Dar on Friday.

Rumours of **Air Tanzania** (⌨ www.airtanzania.co.tz) flying to Kili or Arusha abound but I've yet to see any concrete evidence of this (such as, for example, a plane) so I remain sceptical – though the offices are open in Moshi and Arusha again. **Fly540** (⌨ www.fly540.com) have, for the moment at least, suspended their flights to Kilimanjaro from Nairobi, though they maintain an office in Arusha and it is hoped they will resume in the future.

FLIGHTS TO AND FROM ARUSHA AIRPORT

Air Excel (☎ 027-254 8429; ⌨ www.airexcelonline.com) have daily flights from various destinations in the Serengeti (Grumeti, Kleins, Seronera) as well as Lake Manyara, before finally arriving at Arusha at 12.10pm. They also have a daily flight from Dar at 4.20pm, and one from Zanzibar at 4.55pm. They have daily flights to the Serengeti (Grumeti, Kleins, Seronera) as well as Lake Manyara and a daily flight to Dar and Zanzibar.

Coastal Aviation (⌨ www.coastal.co.tz) have daily flights from Grumeti, Lobo, Mwanza, as well as the south and Selous. Their 12.15pm flight arrives at Dar at 2.20pm, then continues on to Selous, Mafia and Kilwa. They also serve the Serengeti, Ngorongoro, Tanga and other Tanzanian destinations.

Regional Air (⌨ www.regionaltanzania.com) operate flights from Serengeti and Manyara. They also run daily flights to Manyara and on to the Serengeti, with another route taking in Zanzibar and Dar.

Zanair (⌨ www.zanair.com) operate a daily flight (except Thursday) from Zanzibar to Arusha, arriving at 12.50pm. They have a daily flight to Zanzibar at 2pm.

ZantasAir (⌨ www.zantasair.com) run private charters all over Tanzania and are useful if none of the above offers a flight that fits your schedule.

APPENDIX C – TANZANIAN & KENYAN DIPLOMATIC MISSIONS

TANZANIAN EMBASSIES AND CONSULATES ABROAD

- **Australia** 3rd Fl, MPH Bldg 23 Barrack St, Perth WA 6000; ☎ 08-9221 0033; 🖳 www.tanzaniaconsul.com; also Level 2, 222 La Trobe St, Melbourne 3000; ☎ 03-9667 0243
- **Belgium** Avenue Franklin Roosevelt 72 – 1050 Brussels; ☎ 02-640-6500;
- **Canada** 50 Range Rd, Ottawa, Ontario K1N 8J4; ☎ 613-232-1500; 🖳 www.tzrep ottawa.ca
- **China** 8 Liang Ma He Nan Lu, Sanlitun, Beijing 100600; ☎ 010-6532 1719; 🖳 www.tanzaniaembassy.org.cn
- **Congo (DRC)** 142 Boulevard 30 Jin BP 1612, Kinshasa
- **Denmark** Gothersgade 21 DK – 1123 Copenhagen; ☎ 33 16 49 00; 🖳 robert@tan zania-consulate.dk
- **Egypt** 9 Abdel Hamid Loutfy St, Dokki-Cairo; ☎ 02 337 4286; 🖳 tanrepcairo@in finity.com.eg
- **Ethiopia** Addis Ababa; ☎ 01 511063
- **France** 13 ave Raymond, Pointcare, 75116 Paris; ☎ 01 53 70 63 66; 🖳 ambtan zanie@wanadoo.fr
- **Germany** 11 14050 Berlin, Charlotten-burg, Westend; ☎ 030-303 0800; 🖳 www.tanzania-gov.de
- **India** EP-15C, Chanakyapuri, New Delhi-110 021, ☎ 11-2412 2864; 🖳 tanzrep@del2 .vsnl.net.in
- **Italy** Via Cesare, Beccaria 88, Rome; ☎ 06-3600 5234; 🖳 tanzarep@pcg.it; also Via Santa Sofia 12, Milan; ☎ 02-5830 7534
- **Japan** 21-9, Kamiyoga 4 Chome, Setagaya-Ku, Tokyo 158-0098; ☎ 03-425 4531/3, 🖳 www.tanzaniaembassy.or.jp
- **Kenya** Taifa Road Re-insurance Plaza, 9th Floor, Nairobi; ☎ 20-311 948; 🖳 high com@tanzaniahc.or.ke
- **Mozambique** Ujamaa House, Maputo; ☎ (263-4) 721870; 🖳 safina@zebra.uem.mz
- **Netherlands** Parallelweg Zuid 215, 2914 LE Nieuwerkerk aan den IJssel, Amsterdam; ☎ 0180-320939; 🖳 www.tan zania.nl/
- **Nigeria** 11 Ganges St, Ministers Hill, Maintana, Abuja; ☎ 234 9 413 2313; 🖳 tan abuja@lytos.com
- **Russia** Pyatnitskaya, Ulitsa 33, Moscow; ☎ 231 8126; 🖳 tanmos@wm.west-call.com
- **Rwanda** 15 avenue Paul VI, BP 3973, Kigali; 🖳 tanmos@wm.west-call.com
- **South Africa** 845 Goont Ave, Pretoria; ☎ 012-342 4371; 🖳 tanzania@cis.co.za
- **South Korea** Hyundai Corporation, Hyundai Bldg 2F 140-2, Kye-dong Chrongro-ku, Seoul; ☎ 02-7446-1172
- **Sweden** Wallingatan 11, Box 7255, 111 60, Stockholm; ☎ 08 5032 0600/1; 🖳 www .tanemb.se
- **Switzerland** 47 Avenue Blanc, CH 1202 Geneva; ☎ 022 731 8920; 🖳 mission.tanza nia@itu.ch
- **Uganda** 6 Kagera Rd, Kampala; ☎ (41) 257357; 🖳 tzrepkla@imul.com
- **UK** 3 Stratford Place, London W1C 1AS; ☎ 020-7569 1470; 🖳 tanzaniahigh commission.co.uk
- **USA** 1232 22nd Street NW, Washington DC 20037; ☎ 202-939-6125/7; 🖳 www.tan zaniaembassy-us.org
- **Zambia** Ujamaa House, No 5200, United Nations Ave, 10101 Lusaka; ☎ 227698/227702; 🖳 tzreplsk@zamnet.zm
- **Zimbabwe** Ujamaa House, 23 Baines Ave, Harare; ☎ 04-721870, 722627

KENYAN EMBASSIES AND CONSULATES ABROAD

- **Australia** Qe Insurance Building, 33-35 Ainslie Ave, Civic Sq, Canberra, ACT 2601; ☎ 02-6247 4788; 💻 www.kenya.asn.au/
- **Belgium** Ave Winston Churchill 208, 1180 Brussels; ☎ 02 3401040; 💻 www.kenyabrussels.com
- **Botswana** Plot 786 Independence Ave, Gaborone; ☎ 395 1408; 💻 Kenya@info.bw
- **Burundi** PTA Bldg, 2nd Fl, West Wing, Chaussée du Prince Louis Rwagasore, Mutanga, Bujumbura; ☎ 22-258160; 💻 www.kenyaembassyburundi.com
- **Canada** 415 Laurier Avenue East, Ottawa, Ontario, K1N 6R4; ☎ 613-563-1773/4/6; 💻 www.kenyahighcommission.ca
- **Congo (DRC)** 4002 Ave de Louganda, Commune de Gombe, Kinshasa; ☎ 8 1700 8203/00/07; 💻 kenem-drc@jobantech.cd
- **Egypt** 29 El Kods EL Sharif St, Mohandesseen, Giza, Cairo; ☎ 02-345 3628; 💻 kenemb-cairo.com
- **Ethiopia** Fikre Mariam Rd, High 16 Kebelle 01, Addis Ababa; ☎ 11 6610033; 💻 kengad@telecom.net.et
- **France** 3 rue Freycinet, 75116 Paris; ☎ 01 56 62 25 25; 💻 paris@amb-kenya.fr
- **Germany** Markgrafenstr 63, 10969 Berlin; ☎ 030 2592 6650; 💻 www.kenyaembassyberlin.de
- **India** 34 Paschimi Marg, Vasant Vihar, New Delhi, 110057; ☎ 11 2614 6537/38/40; 💻 www.kenyamission-delhi.com
- **Ireland** 11 Elgin Rd, Ballsbridge, Dublin; ☎ 01-6136380; 💻 www.kenyaembassyireland.net
- **Israel** 15 Abba Hillel Silver, 3rd Floor, Ramatgan 52136, Tel Aviv; ☎ 03 575 4633; 💻 www.kenyaembassyisrael.org
- **Italy** Via Archimede 164, 00197, Rome; ☎ 06 8082717; 💻 www.embassyofkenya.it
- **Japan** 3-24-3 Yakumo, Meguro-ku, Tokyo 152-0023; ☎ 03-3723 4006/7; 💻 www.kenya rep-jp.com
- **Netherlands** 21 Nieuwe Parklaan, 2597 LA The Hague; ☎ 070-350 4215
- **Rwanda** Chancery Plot No 1716, Kacyiru Avenue Del Lumuganda, Kacyiru, Kigali; ☎ 583332-6
- **South Africa** 302 Brooks St, Menlo Park, 0081 Pretoria; ☎ 12 362 2249; 💻 kenrep@mweb.co.za
- **Spain** Paseo De La Castellana 143 2 APL, 28046 Madrid; ☎ 91 571 09 25; 💻 www.kenya embassyspain.es
- **Sudan** Premises No 516, Block 1 West Giraif, Khartoum; ☎ 15577 2808; 💻 kenemb@yahoo.com; also Juba ☎ 811 823664
- **Sweden** Birger Jarlsgatan 37, 2nd Floor, 103 95 Stockholm; ☎ 08 218300/4/9; 💻 Kenya.embassy@telia.com
- **Tanzania** PO Box 5231, Dar es Salaam; ☎ 22 266 8285/6
- **Uganda** Corner Acacia Ave & Lower Kololo Terrace, Kampala; ☎ 006-41-258232/5/6; 💻 kenyaahicom@africaonline.co.ug
- **UK** 45 Portland Place, London W1B IAS; ☎ 020-7636 2371; 💻 www.kenyahighcommission.net
- **USA** 2249, R St NW, Washington DC 20008; ☎ 202-387-6101; 💻 www.kenyaembassy.com
- **Zambia** 5207 United Nations Ave, PO Box 50298, Lusaka; ☎ 01 250722; 💻 kenhigh@zmnet.zm
- **Zimbabwe** 95 Park Lane, PO Box 4069, Harare; ☎ 04 704820; 💻 kenhicom@africaonline.co.zw

APPENDIX D – RECOMMENDED READING LISTENING AND WATCHING

MAPS

Maps of Kilimanjaro are available in Arusha, Moshi and probably your own country. The best one we've found, however, is reliably available only online: **Kilimanjaro Kibo** (1:80,000) is written in both English and German and is by some distance the most accurate map available for the mountain. With profiles of a couple of the routes, GPS points, town plans on Arusha and Moshi, descriptions of the vegetation zones and a review of the retreat of permanent ice, this is also the most informative and useful map. You can order a copy by visiting the publisher's website at 💻 www.climbing-map.com.

The most common map we see is the cartoonish **New Map of the Kilimanjaro National Park**, by Giovanni Tombazzi, which is bright and colourful though in all honesty it's a little inaccurate and the cartoon style means it's of little practical use. Still, it's packed full of information and the flora guide on the reverse is useful. The scale, by the way, is about 1.1cm to 1km (or 1:90,909), with a close-up of the summit on the reverse drawn at a scale of 5.4cm to 1km (about 1:18,518.5). They also publish a similar-style map to Meru. NB Make sure you get the **New Map** as the old one really is out of date. Giovanni also does a map of **Arusha National Park** in a similar style though we think it's inferior to the official map produced by TANAPA **Arusha National Park – The Tourist Map**.

Back on Africa's highest mountain, **Tourist Map of Kilimanjaro** (1:100,000) by the Ordnance Survey (1989) is the biggest and most beautiful, though once again of little practical use: the routes themselves have been drawn, seemingly without thought of precision, over the top of what looks an accurate topographical map. Well over a decade old, it's a little out of date too. As such, it's better in a frame on your wall at home than in your backpack.

Another one that would perhaps be better in a frame – because it is beautiful – is the **Satellite View of Kilimanjaro** (1:90,000), a blue-coloured bird's-eye view of the mountain with contours, roads and routes drawn on top and, unusually but refreshingly, a study of the Chagga people on the reverse as well as gradient profiles.

A third map, **Kilimanjaro** (1:50,000), by Mark Savage, is harder to track down – though the shop at Marangu Gate stocks some. The descriptions of the trails are not brilliant and the map itself is a little ugly, though it is more up to date than the above and the black-and-white drawings of wild flowers are good – though would be far more useful in colour.

The Canada-based ITM (International Travel Maps) series has recently produced **Kilimanjaro**, a colourful 1:62,500 map of the mountain, as well as a separate 1:6,250,000 road map of the area.

Finally, **Original City Map – Arusha and Moshi**, distributed by Toke Tanzania (💻 www.toku-tanzania.com; last published 2012) offers very good maps of the two cities. There's also **Explore the Slopes of Mount Kilimanjaro**, another cartoon-style affair which also has a (very simple) plan of Moshi centre and some few basic facts about the region. Definitely another that is more decorative than useful – but charming in its own way.

Online maps

A couple of companies have produced GPS maps of the Kilimanjaro region that you can upload to your computer and then plot the waypoints on. I'm afraid I am not entirely enamoured of either. The best is by **GPS travelmaps** (💻 www.gpstravelmaps.com). The basic map itself seems very detailed and it's a useful base for putting on your own GPS readings. The other map is **Tracks 4 Africa**'s (💻 tracks4africa.co.za).

RECOMMENDED READING

Please note that many of the following are rare and a number are extremely difficult to find. Among those that are readily available are Hemingway's *The Snows of Kilimanjaro* (and the recently published *Under Kilimanjaro*, the rather long-winded novel-cum-memoir-cum-tribute-to-Africa that recounts Papa Hemingway's time in Kenya); the comprehensive and wonderful book-of-the-IMAX-film *Kilimanjaro, Mountain at the Crossroads*, by Audrey Salkeld – possibly the most beautiful and absorbing souvenir of your climb that money can buy (the book that is, not Audrey); and John Reader's excellent (though rather bulky) *Kilimanjaro*, which you may have more luck tracking down in Tanzania than in your home country. If you're visiting Zanzibar after Kilimanjaro, you may want to wait and buy your reading material for the mountain there: some of the bookshops in Stonetown have fine selections.

Biography and personal accounts

Many of the following books, particularly those written during the great days of exploration in the 1800s, are now out of print and, short of a miraculous discovery in a secondhand bookstore, the only place you're going to find them is at the British Library or a similar institution abroad. The internet is, of course, another source. For example, I've successfully tracked down online the English translation of Hans Meyer's account of his conquest of Kili (see first entry below); now all I've got to do is find the £5750 the dealers are asking for it. The online auction house eBay is a good place to begin your search. The Canadian-based Voyager Press also have some good stuff on Kili, particularly old reports from the Royal Geographic Society.

For those books that *are* still in print, your best bet is in Tanzania itself, either in the small souvenir shop by Marangu Gate or, somewhat surprisingly, in the large bookshops in Stonetown, Zanzibar. Failing that, you could always try online bookshops such as Abebooks and Amazon, on which you will usually be able to track down a copy.

The explorers...

● *Across East African Glaciers – An Account of the First Ascent of Kilimanjaro* Dr Hans Meyer, translated from the German by EHS Calder (George Philip and Son, 1891) Perhaps the most fascinating book ever written about the mountain, Meyer's beautiful work describes his unprecedented ascent of Kilimanjaro, all illustrated with some lovely sketches by ET Compton. Splendid stuff. Now available in a much less-charming – but much more affordable – reprint by Kessinger Press.

● *An Essay on the Sources of the Nile in the Mountains of the Moon* Charles T Beke (Neill and Company, 1848) This short work is of interest not only because it was published at the same time as Rebmann's ground-breaking visit to Kilimanjaro but also, though written around 160 years ago, the author still takes as his starting point the work of Ptolemy written 1800 years before, thus giving an indication of just how little was known about Africa at that time.

● *Discovery by Count Teleki of Lakes Rudolf and Stefanie* Lieutenant Ludwig von Höhnel, translated by Nancy Bell (Longmans, Green and Co, 1894) Lengthy, two-volume account of the Hungarian count as he shoots and slaughters his way through East Africa's fauna, written by his companion von Höhnel. Only about a sixth of the book deals specifically with Kili, though that sixth is interesting both for the account of their attempt to climb Kili and their dealings with Chagga chiefs Mandara (whom they try to avoid) and Mareale.

● *Life, Wanderings, and Labours in Eastern Africa* Charles New (Cass Library of African Studies, 1971, originally 1873) Charles New set off in 1871 to spread the gospel to Africa's heathen population but it was as an explorer that he is remembered, becoming the first white man to cross the African snow-line during a visit to the Chagga region. This book was written in the months spent in England between his first and second trips, on the latter of which he fell ill and died. Once again, though the account of his time on the slopes of Kili occupies only about a third of the book, it is for the most part fascinating, as much for his description of Mandara and the Chaggas as it is for his climb up the mountain.

● **The Church Missionary Intelligencer** (Seeleys, 1850) Definitely one you'll have to look for in the British Library, this august organ was the first to publish Rebmann's accounts of his three trips to Kilimanjaro, as well as Krapf's subsequent visit to the Usambara region. Volume 1, May 1849, contains most of the relevant texts.

● **The Kilima-njaro Expedition – A Record of Scientific Exploration in Eastern Equatorial Africa** HH Johnston (Kegan Paul, Trench and Co, 1886; republished by Gregg International Publishers, 1968) Widely dismissed as exaggeration going on fabrication, this is nevertheless a very entertaining read thanks to Johnston's sense of humour and the scrapes into which he gets. Just possible to find second-hand or pick up the reprint by Kessinger Publishing.

● **Tracts Relating to Missions** (Printed by A Lankester, 1878) Yet another work whose habitat is restricted almost entirely to the British Library these days, this collection of missionary accounts includes one by the Rev A Downes Shaw entitled **To Chagga and Back — An Account of a Journey to Moshi, the Capital of Chagga, Eastern Equatorial Africa**.

● **James Hannington, First Bishop of Eastern Equatorial Africa – A History of his Life and Work** EC Dawson (Seeley and Co, 1887) I have to confess I had never heard of this book – nor indeed the bishop – until I came across a copy on eBay (for a tenner!). And fascinating it is too, for though the bishop's own efforts on Kili are fairly paltry, not getting much above the treeline, his diary entries about the Chagga chief Mandara and the region in general are fascinating, and this book is filled with mentions of the great explorers (Johnston, Thomson etc) he encountered during his time in East Africa before he was speared to death in Uganda on the orders of a local king.

...and those who followed in their wake

With the rise of self-publishing you can now find a slew of memoirs printed by those who've conquered Kili, both in traditional paper format and, even more so as ebooks. I have to say I found most a little dull but that could be because I've climbed the mountain a few times now, whereas those who haven't, or who haven't yet, may find them both useful and fascinating. But there are several other books here that I really enjoyed:

● **Africa's Dome of Mystery** Eva Stuart Watt FRGS (Marshall, Morgan and Scott Ltd, 1930) Brought up in East Africa, Ms Stuart-Watt describes her life among the Chagga people, including an account of her climb to Kibo's crater rim. Interesting, if only for the fact that there are few accounts of Kibo from this period under British rule.

● **Bicycles up Kilimanjaro** Richard and Nicholas Crane (Oxford Illustrated Press 1985) These two cycled up Kili with Mars Bars taped to their handlebars to finance the construction of windmills for pumping water in East Africa. The only other person I met who had read this book said he enjoyed it, but I didn't.

● **Duel for Kilimanjaro** Leonard Mosley (Weidenfeld & Nicolson, 1963) Account of the East African campaign during World War I. The fact that I stuck with it to the end, even though my interest in military history is slight, is testament to how well this book is written and what an absorbing story it is. The British, by the way, come across as comically incompetent.

● **Snow on the Equator** HW Tilman (Bell and Son Books, 1937, republished as part of **The Eight Sailing/Mountain Exploration Books** by Baton Wicks, 1989) Inaccurate account (Kilimanjaro is not an extinct volcano, for example, but a dormant one) by coffee planter, explorer, mountaineer and all-round show-off Harold William Tilman. Nevertheless a very entertaining read and, for all his bluster, Tilman comes across as an entirely likeable fellow.

● **The Road to Kilimanjaro** Geoffrey Salisbury (Minerva Press, 1997) Though mainly autobiographical, recounting Salisbury's busy life, this book includes a heart-warming, humbling account of an expedition in 1969 by the author to the summit of Kilimanjaro on the Loitokitok (Rongai) Route with a group of eight totally blind African youths, all but one of whom made it to the top.

● *Making the Climb: What a Novice Climber Learned About Life on Mount Kilimanjaro* John C Bowling (Beacon Hill Press, 2007) Tedious account of a climb by the president of Olivet Nazarene University (Chicago, USA) that's reminiscent of the dullest of sermons you used to have to sit through as a child – including a liberal sprinkling of prayers throughout the chapters. Read it if you must, but only as a way to build up stamina; for if you manage to finish it before your own trek then climbing the mountain will feel like a breeze. Very, very dreary indeed.

● *Kilimanjaro: Hakuna Matata* Chris Baker (🖳 www.lulu.com, 2007) There's nothing unusual about this person's climb, nor is there anything special about Mr Baker or his writing style. Nevertheless, as a straightforward account of what it's like to climb Kilimanjaro I really think this book is very good and the fact that profits go to KPAP can only be a good thing. Also has an accompanying website: 🖳 www.kilimanjaro-hakuna-matata.com.

● *The Shadow of Kilimanjaro – On Foot Across East Africa* Rick Ridgeway (Bloomsbury 1999) Well-written account of a walk that begins on the summit of Kilimanjaro and ends at Malindi on the Kenyan coast. Though Kilimanjaro is dealt with in a matter of pages at the front of the book, the narrative style is absorbing and this book is well worth reading.

● *On Top of Africa – the Climbing of Kilimanjaro and Mount Kenya* Neville Shulman (Element Books, 1995) Tale of the conquering of these two African giants by the author, along with the help of Zen philosophies and his own personal *shin* spirit.

● *In Wildest Africa* Peter MacQueen, FRGS (George Bell and Sons, 1910) Account of one of the first tourists to visit Kilimanjaro, coming here during the German occupation. Includes a description of their ascent up Kili, during which some of their porters died, more were frightened by snow and fled (taking the food with them); MacQueen only managed to find his way down by following the trail of porters' corpses left behind from an expedition five months previously. He went on to reach a highly credible 19,200ft, the highest, at that time, by an English speaker.

● *Kilimanjaro via the Marangu Route: "Tourist Route" my ass* Phil Gray (iUniverse Inc, 2006) This book has had some pretty negative reviews on the internet and it is indeed pretty cynical, but it's not as bad as some people will have you believe. Mr Gray seems an amiable fellow, never one to tell it straight when there's the possibility of a gag, and I found the book a readable account of his climb.

● *Kissing Kilimanjaro – Leaving it all on top of Africa* Daniel Dorr (The Mountaineers Books, 2010) Pretty standard account of a pretty standard trek – or rather, treks, for the author returned to climb Rongai having first failed on Machame. Overly thorough and a little too comprehensive, there are too many longeurs to make this an absorbing read. Still, for those seeking a step-by-step account (sometimes literally) of what it's like up there, it's OK – though my goodness the ending is rather melodramatic!

● *Kissing Kibo – Trekking to the Summit of Mount Kilimanjaro via the Lemosho Route* Sheree Marshall (iUniverse, 2010) Though I found it to be the most error-strewn of the titles here, I have to admit that this book wasn't written for a pedant like me and the author, a middle-aged African-American divorcée, is a lot more engaging than the other author who enjoys making out with mountains, Mr Dorr (see above). The book is also, mercifully, a lot more succinct (Ms Marshall is in Tanzania by page seven, for example, while it takes Mr Dorr 49 pages to reach the same point). Also one of the few accounts of a trek on the Lemosho Route, which makes a change, and includes at the end of the book plenty of practical advice – though given the wealth of mistakes that litter this book, I wouldn't necessarily follow them religiously.

● *A Girl's Guide to Climbing Kilimanjaro – What you need to know and bring to have a wonderful and comfortable climb* Rachel Durchslag & Jackie Payne (CreateSpace, 2012) I don't usually review other guidebooks (or indeed read them) but I thought that the standpoint taken by this book was sufficiently different to mine – I am a man, after all – that it would be worth seeing what they had to say without fear of being accused of unfairly slating the competition. That said, I couldn't find much that they say in their book that I don't say in this one. So I asked a female friend who's climbed Kili for her unbiased opinion, though she was even more scathing and summed up the book in one simple word: pointless.

● *Zombies on Kilimanjaro – A Father/Son Journey above the Clouds* Tim Ward (Changemakers Books, 2012) I was looking forward to reading this book: the praise on the back cover suggested it was going to be a fun read, the book is one of the more recent publications on the mountain and, unlike many of the other titles reviewed here, the author has some sort of previous experience when it comes to writing. However, the description of the climb gradually takes a back-seat to the author's turgid analysis of his relationship with his son and his obsession with the theory of memes until, by the time I finally reached the last page, I felt more drained than I have ever done climbing the mountain. A real test of stamina.

● *Kilimanjaro – One Woman's Journey to the Roof of Africa and Beyond* Deb Denis (Marion Grace Publishing, 2012) Another comprehensive account of one person's climb, covering not only why and when she did it but, most important of all, how she did it. Clearly venturing out of her comfort zone, Deb spent one year preparing for her African adventure, which begins in one of the smallest countries on the continent and ends on its largest mountain. The story of her journey – in both the physical and the personal sense – is an entertaining and thought-provoking one.

● *Kilimanjaro – One Man's Quest to go over the Hill* MG Edwards (Brilliance Press 2012) Man on the verge of a mid-life crisis attempts to climb Kili via the Marangu Route. Maybe I'm biased – he got in touch with me to ask if it was OK to use our maps – but I thought this one of the better accounts written recently.

● *Climbing Kilimanjaro at 70* Richard A Wolfe PhD (Ingalls Publishing 2010) The title pretty much sums up the contents as septuagenarian nuclear engineer Dr Wolfe manages to fulfil an ambition that he first dreamed of when a young projectionist at his local cinema and watched *The Snows of Kilimanjaro* about forty times.

Fiction

● *Home on Kilimanjaro* Margaret Chrislock Gilseth (Askeladd Press, 1998) Novel written by a lady who spent four years teaching in Marangu for the Lutheran Church, written largely from the point of view of her 11-year-old son.

● *The Snows of Kilimanjaro* Ernest Hemingway (Arrow Books, 1994) Short story about a writer plagued by both a gangrenous leg and a rich wife, written by an honorary game warden based in Loitokitok in the early 1950s. Was always regarded as his most autobiographical work until the publication of...

● *Under Kilimanjaro* Ernest Hemingway (Kent State University Press, 2005) Hemingway called it fiction but with himself and his wife as the lead characters and the events that are described presumably pretty close to the truth, this book could just as easily have been pigeonholed in the Biography category above. Long and funereally paced, it has its moments but is probably for fans and aficionados only.

● *Kilimanjaro Burning* John H Robinson (Birch Book Press, 1998) Entertaining enough, but other than in being set in Tanzania it's not really relevant to the mountain. Nevertheless, good at evoking the country, its sights and smells, for those who know the area.

● *Bingo Bear was here – A Toy Bear's Climb to the Top of Africa's Highest Mountain* Gwill York Newman (Sunstone Press 2003) It goes against one's nature to criticize a children's book but when the author implies that Kilimanjaro is in Kenya in the preface, thereby insulting an entire nation, I think the gloves are off. Anyway, this is about the adventures of a stuffed koala from Cleveland, Ohio, as he accompanies the author and her husband to the top of Africa's highest mountain. Which is in Tanzania. The author lives in New Mexico, by the way, and has since climbed with Bingo in other mountainous places including Kashmir and the American Rockies. Which she probably thinks are in France.

Chagga language, history and lifestyle

● *Chagga – A Course in the Vunjo Dialect of the Kichagga Language of Kilimanjaro, Tanzania* Bernard Leeman and Trilas Lauwo (published in Europe by Languages Information Centre) The best Chagga language book we could find; this tome, written by an Australian who worked as a teacher in the region, deals with the basic structure and grammar and is an ideal introduction to the tongue.

● *History of the Chagga People of Kilimanjaro* Kathleen M Stahl (Mouton & Co, 1964) Highly detailed account of the Chaggas, probably more for those with an academic interest in the subject, but proof that contrary to popular opinion the Chagga do have an absorbing – and surprisingly lengthy – history.

● *Hunger and Shame – Child Malnutrition and Poverty on Mount Kilimanjaro* Mary Howard and Ann Millard (Routledge) Comparatively rich by African standards it may be but, as this book proves, the Kilimanjaro region still suffers from more than its fair share of grinding poverty. With views from family members, health workers and government officials, this book discusses the moral and practical dilemmas of malnourishment.

● *Kilimanjaro and its People* The Honourable Charles Dundas OBE (H, F and G Witherby, 1924; reprinted by Frank Cass & Co, 1968) Probably still the most authoritative account of the Chagga people, this tome is a little dry in places (particularly the rather involved history section) and outdated too (very few of the more extreme Chagga practices, described on pp137-43 of this book, are still conducted today); nevertheless the sections on religion, witchcraft and ritual ceremonies are completely fascinating and offer the most comprehensive insight into how the Chaggas *used to be*, at least, if not how they are today.

Field guides to the fauna

● *Pocket Guide to Mammals of East Africa* Chris Stuart and Mathilde Stuart (Struik, 2009) Around 160 pages of nice photos of animals both fierce and fascinating.

● *Kilimanjaro – Animals in a Landscape* Jonathan Kingdon (BBC Publications 1983) Born in Tanganyika, Kingdon is an artist specializing in the flora and fauna of his homeland. This book, based on a BBC series, contains examples of his work as well as an extended commentary on the creatures that live on the mountain.

● *Birds of East Africa: Kenya, Tanzania, Uganda, Rwanda, Burundi* Terry Stevenson and John Fanshawe (Helm Field Guides, 2004) Bird guides tend to be amongst the most beautiful books around and this one is no different, with gorgeous drawings by Brian Small, John Gale and Norman Arlott. Reckoned to be *the* authoritative guide.

● *Birds of Kenya and Northern Tanzania* Dale A Zimmerman (Helm Field Guides, 2005) Another in the series, just as beautiful – and only slightly less weighty than the one above.

Field guides to the flora

Strangely, there is no comprehensive book on the flora of the region or country. There is *Field Guide to Common Trees and Shrubs of East Africa* Najma Dharani (Struik, 2002) but this, alas, has little relevance to the mountain itself.

Coffee-table books

● *Kilimanjaro* John Reader (Elm Tree Books, 1982) Excellent, beautifully written coffee-table book with detailed accounts both of the history and geology of Kili as well as the author's experience of photographing it.

● *Kilimanjaro: The Great White Mountain* David Pluth (Camerapix, 2001) Another tome that will have your coffee-table groaning.

● *Kilimanjaro: To the Roof of Africa* Audrey Salkeld (National Geographic Books, 2002) The best-looking book on Kilimanjaro, this mighty tome includes detailed sections on history and geology as well as some excellent photographs of the mountain. If you only buy one book about the mountain – other than the one you're holding now, of course! – make it this one.

FOR YOUR LISTENING PLEASURE

The following is some appropriate music to take up the mountain with you; appropriate, but not necessarily any good. And we have to wonder: have any of the following artists actually been anywhere near the mountain?

● **Babyshambles** *Killamangiro* Celebrity junkie and Kate Moss's ex is also, apparently, a rock star. This 2005 offering was Pete Doherty's first single with new band Babyshambles following his acrimonious departure from The Libertines.

● **Miles Davis** *Filles de Kilimanjaro* Before he went all funky and weird on us with his *Bitches Brew* album – great album cover, unlistenable tunes – Miles Davis recorded this album in 1968 with his 'second great quintet', featuring Wayne Shorter on trumpet and keyboard god Herbie Hancock.

● **Medwyn Goodall** *Snows of Kilimanjaro* 'As uplifting as catching the first sight of the mountain rising up out of the African plains – as inspirational as gazing down from the summit – *Snows of Kilimanjaro* is a perfect musical tribute to the inner strength of those who rise above adversity.' At least, that's what the blurb says and as it was made in support of a charity climb, I'm not going to disagree. Whatever I may really think.

● **Iration Steppas Meet Dennis Rootical** *Kilimanjaro* A 1995 10-inch single from British dubmasters. Rare; check out the Summit Mix on side two.

● **Lange presents Firewall** *Kilimanjaro* Trance-dance CD from 2004, including 8-minute-long original mix, 9-minute 23-second Lange remix and 7-minute 51-second 'B-side', *Touched*. Not special.

● **Letta Mbulu** *Kilimanjaro* Soulful disco with Afrobeats. Quite groovy but difficult to find except on compilation.

● **The Rippingtons** *Kilimanjaro* Guitarist Russ Freeman's instrumental follow-up to *Moonlighting*, their successful debut. Jazzy, smoothish and with world-music influences.

● **Teardrop Explodes** *Kilimanjaro* One of Britain's loveable oddballs, Julian Cope – last seen in public travelling around Britain to write about stone circles – first came to public attention with the release of this 1980 debut album. Includes their greatest hit, 'Reward', which is bound to stir up memories amongst those who grew up in the '80s. Like me. Described as post-punk by aficionados – shorthand for passionate, angry yet melodic.

● **Toto** *Africa* Bearded '80s crooner's worldwide smash includes the line 'Sure as Kilimanjaro rises like Olympus above the Serengeti'. Which, of course, it doesn't.

● **The Twinkle Brothers** *Kilamanjaro* I so wanted to like this record. Liked the cover; liked the band's name, and even liked the deliberate misspelling (it was deliberate, wasn't it?) Besides, apart from a couple of Bob Marley LPs I don't have much reggae in my collection. Thankfully, though a little too reggae-lite for my liking in places, overall it's pretty good and with a bass deep enough to upset the neighbours.

● **Mountain Mocha** *Kilimanjaro* (various titles) This is more like it, an oddball bunch of Japanese funksters from the outskirts of Tokyo named after a mountain in Africa and playing smashing grooves to which, if I could dance, I would. Remind me most of James Brown's various backing bands – JBs, Maceo & the Macks etc; must be great fun to see live. Their self-titled first album, by the way, is my favourite (and has a lovely painting of Kili on the cover).

● **Quartette Tres Bien** *Kilimanjaro* Another record that, like Mountain Mocha Kilimanjaro, reminds me that collecting isn't entirely a futile waste of money, the Quartet Tres Bien were a St Louis-based jazz combo who recorded in the mid-60s. This slice of swinging fights a constant battle with cheese throughout both sides, but when they're winning – such as on the brooding title track – they're smashing.

...AND SEVEN RELEVANT FILMS

● *Hatari!* Long on time but short on quality, this 151-minute 1963 epic starring John Wayne in typical derring-do mode as well as Hardy Krüger (see p239) and the preposterously named Red Buttons is not great, though if you can ignore the paper-thin plot, stilted acting, constipated dialogue and questionable attitude towards the wildlife, women and locals, there's some enjoyment to be had in glimpsing the region as it was in the early '60s. The scenes where they hunt and capture the animals (made, of course, without the benefit of CGI) are also very impressive and the score by Henry Mancini is reliably hummable (particularly the signature tune 'Elephant Walk').

● *Kilimanjaro – to the Roof of Africa* The 2002 film of the book – or was it the book of the film? Whatever, this IMAX film recounting the experiences of a group of trekkers on the mountain is beautifully shot by film-maker David Breashears. It's the best documentary if you want to know what it's like to climb the mountain, as well as a gorgeous and evocative souvenir for those who have already done so.

● *Killers of Kilimanjaro* With scarcely a swash left unbuckled, this 1959 tale follows the adventures of trouble-shooter Robert Adamson (Robert Taylor) who, arriving in deepest Africa with Jane Carlton (played by the luscious Anne Aubrey) to oversee the completion of a cross-continental railroad, finds he has all manner of continental clichés to contend with, from slave traders (ruthless) to tribes (savage) and, of course, the local fauna (Grrrr!). Will he make it out alive? And complete the railroad too? And get together with Jane? Probably, yes. It's not great but I quite enjoyed it and it has a certain charm. Usually available on eBay, if you're interested.

● *The Mines of Kilimanjaro* Italian offering from 1986 that's been dubbed into English. Tobias Hoesl stars as Dr Ed Barkely who travels to East Africa in search of his professor's killers. But as Robert Taylor (see *Killers of Kilimanjaro*, above) could have told him, this part of the world is chock-a-block with danger, from savage tribes (in this case, the Gundors), Chinese gangsters (?) and even Nazis (???). And after that, things get *really* weird! But as Robert Taylor could *also* have told him, there are compensations in the form of some lovely scenery and equally comely female company, with Elena Pompei as Eva Kilbrook. All in all, an appalling film but unfortunately not bad enough to be funny – making it possibly the worst couple of hours of cinematic 'entertainment' you will ever experience.

● *In the Shadow of Kilimanjaro* It's 1500 men versus 90,000 flesh-eating baboons that have been driven mad by a drought: the odds look bad but if anybody can find a way out of this 1986 dilemma, John Rhys Davis and Timothy Bottoms can.... Grab a beer and some chocolate, settle into your favourite armchair, disengage your brain and enjoy this truly rubbish but succulent slice of '80s ham and corn. Available on eBay.

● *Snows of Kilimanjaro* Henry King's 1952 film version of Ernest Hemingway's semi-autobiographical work, with Gregory Peck in the leading role, Susan Hayward as his devoted belle and Ava Gardner as the lost love he pines for – and when you see Ava in this film, you can't blame him. Of course it's the most highbrow film of the seven here and I should like it – but, personally speaking, give me killer baboons any day.

● *Volcano above the Clouds* From the Nova PBS stable comes this hour-long documentary from 2003 about a team climbing the Lemosho/Western Breach Route. Ostensibly it's about the team's attempts to discover how much the glaciers' disappearance will affect the water supply and to see whether the volcano is still active, but really it's just a documentary of a climb – and for that it's OK. Contact Nova direct, or I found it via Amazon marketplace.

APPENDIX E – GPS WAYPOINTS

Each GPS waypoint was taken on the route at the reference number marked on the map as below. Note the position format we are using is known as UTM UPS; the map datum is WGS 84 (37 M); you can change both of these on a Garmin GPS by going to Units Setup on the Settings menu, then changing the Position Format and Map datum where necessary.

Note that by some of the waypoints there is a small 'c', which denotes that the waypoint was not found by us and thus we cannot vouch for its accuracy.

Any comments on any of the waypoints and their accuracy will be gratefully received. Thanks.

MOUNT MERU

Map	Ref	GPS waypoint	Description
Map A	A	37M 261065 9642331	Momela Gate
Map A	B	37M 260557 9642021	Turn-off to Tululusia Hill
Map A	C	37M 260452 9641613	Turn-off to Campsite 1 & 2
Map A	D	37M 260430 9640906	Campsite 3
Map A	E	37M 259270 9640892	Turn-off to viewpoint
Map A	F	37M 258686 9641090	Famous arched fig Tree
Map A	G	37M 258127 9641264	Itikoni Campsite
Map A	H	37M 256701 9640742	Maio Falls diversion
Map B	I	37M 254592 9641371	Kitoto Viewpoint
Map B	J	37M 254338 9642470	Turn-off to Meru Crater
Map A	K	37M 255495 9642787	Miriakamba Huts
Map B	L	37M 253925 9643310	Mgongo wa Tembo
Map B	M	37M 252564 9644015	Saddle Huts
Map B	N	37M 252628 9644638	Little Meru
Map B	O	37M 251603 9643468	Rhino Point
Map B	P	37M 249943 9641219	Meru summit

KILIMANJARO – ASCENT ROUTES

The Marangu Route

Map	Ref	GPS waypoint	Description
Map 1	001	37M 335295 9641479	Marangu Gate
Map 1	002	37M 335341 9644784	Bridge
Map 1	003	37M 335676 9645120	Bridge to Kisamboni
Map 2	004	37M 334809 9648242	Mandara Huts
Map 2	005	37M 335400 9648732	Maundi Crater
Map 3	006	37M 330631 9651540	Sloping bridge
Map 3	007	37M 328280 9652715	Kambi ya Taabu
Map 4	008	37M 326490 9652894	Horombo Huts
Map 4	009	37M 325328 9654221	Junction with porters' path
Map 4	010	37M 324892 9655246	Last water point
Map 4	011	37M 324379 9655970	Mawenzi Ridge
Map 5	012	37M 323192 9657409	Lunchstop with toilets
Map 5	013	37M 322614 9658810	Sign for Kibo Circuit
Map 5	014	37M 322447 9658958	Jiwe la Ukoyo
Map 5	015	37M 321300 9659306	Junction with path to Mawenzi Tarn
Map 5 & 6	016	37M 320991 9659232	Kibo Huts

Map 6	017	37M 319713 9659625	William's Point
Map 6	017A	37M 319599 9659653	Junction of paths from School and Kibo Huts
Map 6	018	37M 319400 9659750	Hans Meyer Cave
Map 6 & 33	019	37M 318632 9660028	Gillman's Point
Map 33	128	37M 317075 9659821	Uhuru Peak

The Machame Route (via Barafu Huts and Stella Point)

Map 7	020	37M 304266 9649064	Machame Gate
Map 7	021	37M 304409 9650814	Toilet and end of 4WD track
Map 7	022	37M 305373 9654229	Lunch-stop and toilet
Map 8	023	37M 306531 9656282	Toilet
Map 8	024	37M 307321 9657714	Machame Registration Hut
Map 8	025	37M 307748 9658051	Rocky outcrop
Map 8	026	37M 308080 9658257	Viewpoint
Map 8	027	37M 308137 9658337	First giant groundsel
Map 9	028	37M 308233 9658449	First descent of day
Map 9	029	37M 308315 9658560	Climb to top of rocks for views
Map 9	030	37M 308515 9658753	Ten-second descent
Map 9	031	37M 308807 9659087	Start of steep slope
Map 9	032	37M 309122 9659438	Concrete steps in rock
Map 9	033	37M 309123 9659466	Lunchstop and toilets
Map 9	034	37M 309299 9659975	Overhang in cliff
Map 9	035	37M 309192 9660158	Further overhang caves
Map 9	036	37M 309175 9660179	Short clamber using your hands
Map 9	037	37M 308977 9660464	Top of climb – now on Shira Plateau
Map 9	038	37M 308443 9661064	Shira Caves Campsite
Map 9	039	37M 308730 9660835	Stream
Map 9	040	37M 309299 9660600	Stream
Map 10	041	37M 312517 9661462	Junction of the Machame & Lemosho routes
Map 10	042	37M 312859 9661292	Lunchstop and toilets
Map 10	043	37M 313415 9661041	Sheffield Campsite
Map 10	044	37M 314131 9660747	Lava Tower Campsite
Map 10	045	37M 313959 9658662	Waterfall
Map 11	046	37M 314325 9657792	Barranco Huts
Map 11	047	37M 315177 9657333	Top of climb ie Barranco Wall (aka Breakfast Wall)
Map 11	048	37M 315779 9657062	Stream
Map 11	049	37M 316167 9656961	Old porters track
Map 11	050	37M 316315 9656386	Desert slope
Map 11	051	37M 316983 9656046	Valley floor and stream
Map 11	052	37M 316851 9656077	Tortoise Rock
Map 11	053	37M 317089 9655848	Karanga Campsite
Map 12	054	37M 318707 9656657	Top of climb
Map 12	055	37M 319724 9656918	Top of Barafu Ridge
Map 12 & 13	056	37M 319762 9657263	Barafu Huts
Map 13	057	37M 319592 9658015	Kosovo Campsite
Map 13	058	37M 319249 9658326	Turn left to climb on to the ridge
Map 13 & 33	059	37M 318040 9659630	Stella Point
Map 33	128	37M 317075 9659821	Uhuru Peak

The Lemosho Route (via Western Breach Route)

Map 14	060	37M 294046 9667904	Start of Lemosho Route at toilet
Map 14	061	37M 295058 9667784	Slight clearing
Map 14	062	37M 295082 9667762	Tree in path
Map 14	063	37M 295789 9667751	Patch of lobelia
Map 14	064	37M 296078 9668489	Camphor tree stand and tree across path
Map 14	065	37M 297174 9668591	Mti Mkubwa
Map 14	066	37M 298279 9668000	Stream
Map 14	067	37M 299074 9668169	Top of ridge
Map 14	068	37M 299193 9668178	Last stand of African rosewood (left of path)
Map 15	069	37M 299516 9668155	Top of climb
Map 15	070	37M 299765 9668304	Two streams and old lunchstop
Map 15	071	37M 300087 9668487	Better lunchstop
Map 15	072	37M 300897 9667634	Stream
Map 15	073	37M 302211 9667729	Top of climb – first view of Kibo
Map 15	074	37M 303210 9666760	Shira 1 (campsite)
Map 16	075	37M 304514 9665765	Boulder where path to Shira Cathedral route turns off
Map 16	076	37M 304809 9663689	First stream
Map 16	077	37M 304843 9663552	Second stream
Map 16	078	37M 304873 9663387	Third stream
Map 16	079	37M 304884 9662988	Burnt trees
Map 16	080	37M 305059 9661945	Junction with path to Shira Cathedral
Map 16	081	37M 304823 9661850	Top of cathedral
Map 16	082	37M 306091 9662268	East Shira Hill
Map 16	083	37M 306328 9662360	Weird boulders and mud flats
Map 16	084	37M 306876 9662437	Roadhead
Map 16	085	37M 307312 9662331	Dry stream
Map 17	086	37M 308314 9662240	Shira Huts (campsite)
Map 17	087	37M 310497 9662179	Big boulder
Map 17	088	37M 311028 9662077	Narrow gully
Map 10	089	37M 311568 9661987	Path north to Moir Huts
Map 10	090	37M 312105 9661769	Small cross
Map 10	043	37M 313415 9661041	Sheffield Campsite
Map 18	044	37M 314131 9660747	Lava Tower Campsite

Western Breach Route to Uhuru Peak

Map 18	091	c 37M 315109 9660256	Arrow Glacier Campsite
Map 18	092	c 37M 316482 9660666	Crater Rim
Map 33	127	37M 316829 9660194	Crater Campsite
Map 33	128	37M 317075 9659821	Uhuru Peak

The Shira Plateau Route

Map 15	093	37M 303371 9669714	Morum Barrier
Map 16	094	37M 306221 9664795	Simba Cave Campsite
Map 16	095	37M 307186 9663697	Junction with path to Moir Huts
Map 17	096	37M 308711 9663477	Fischer Camp

The Northern Circuit

Map 19	097	37M 311025 9663594	Moir Huts
Map 19	098	37M 316614 9666951	1st Pofu Campsite
Map 20	099	37M 317958 9666354	2nd Pofu Campsite
Map 20	111	37M 323357 9663335	Third Cave Campsite

The Rongai Route

Map 21	100	37M 332794 9672735	Rongai Gate
Map 21	101	37M 330548 9671175	Signpost
Map 21	102	37M 330486 9671195	Benches
Map 21	103	37M 329351 9670985	Sign about wildfires
Map 21	104	37M 328834 9670717	Benches
Map 21	105	37M 328371 9670227	Second bridge
Map 22	106	37M 327535 9670053	Simba (or Sekimba) Campsite
Map 22	107	37M 325494 9668733	Rocky plateau
Map 22	108	37M 324934 9668209	First 'summit'
Map 23	109	37M 324279 9667203	Second 'summit'
Map 23	110	37M 324041 9666423	Second Cave (lunch-stop)
Map 23	111	37M 323357 9663335	Third Cave Campsite

The Mawenzi Tarn Hut Route

Map 23	110	37M 324041 9666423	Second Cave (lunch-stop)
Map 24	112	37M 326938 9662833	Highest point of day
Map 24	113	37M 327477 9662418	Kikelelwa Camp
Map 24	114	37M 327418 9661909	Viewpoint over valley and photo stop
Map 24	115	37M 327332 9661625	Stream with groundsels
Map 24	116	37M 327506 9660758	Path divides; both options OK
Map 24	117	37M 327787 9660261	Paths reunite
Map 24	118	37M 328098 9659970	Top of ridge
Map 24	119	37M 328116 9659841	Junction with path to Kibo Huts
Map 24	120	37M 328485 9659458	Mawenzi Tarn Campsite
Map 24	121	37M 328083 9659117	Top of acclimatization climb
Map 24	119	37M 328116 9659841	Junction with path to Kibo Huts
Map 25	015	37M 321300 9659306	Junction with path to Horombo Huts
Map 25	016	37M 320991 9659232	Kibo Huts
Map 26 & 6	122	37M 320675 9660736	School Hut
Map 6	017 A	37M 319599 9659653	Junction of paths from School and Kibo Huts
Map 6	018	37M 319400 9659750	Hans Meyer Cave
Map 6 & 33	019	37M 318632 9660028	Gillman's Point
Map 33	059	37M 318040 9659630	Stella Point
Map 33	128	37M 317075 9659821	Uhuru Peak

The Umbwe Route via Western Breach

(For the route to the summit via Barafu Huts and Stella Point, please see waypoints 046-049 & 128)

Map 27	123	c 37M 308823 9647262	Umbwe Gate
Map 27	124	c 37M 308500 9649200	End of 4x4 road & signpost
Map 28	125	c 37M 312323 9654092	Umbwe Cave Campsite
Map 29	126	c 37M 312900 9556000	Lunchstop on ridge
Map 29 & 11	046	37M 314325 9657792	Barranco Huts
Map 10	045	37M 313959 9658662	Waterfall
Map 10 & 18	044	37M 314131 9660747	Lava Tower Campsite
Map 18	091	c 37M 315109 9660256	Arrow Glacier Campsite
Map 18	092	c 37M 316482 9660666	Crater Rim
Map 33	127	37M 316829 9660194	Crater Campsite
Map 33	128	37M 317075 9659821	Uhuru Peak

KILIMANJARO – DESCENT ROUTES

The Marangu Route
See p361 for the Marangu Trail waypoints and use them in reverse until Map 4 where you have the option of doing the Mawenzi Route.

The Mawenzi Route

Map 4	008A	37M 325945 9654684	Zebra Rocks
Map 4	008B	37M 326374 9656687	Signpost and junction
Map 4	008C	37M 326240 9656836	Memorial plaque and viewpoint
Map 4	008D	37M 327617 9657468	Mawenzi Hut

The Mweka Route

Map 33	128	37M 317075 9659821	Uhuru Peak
Map 33 & 13	059	37M 318040 9659630	Stella Point
Map 13 & 30	056	37M 319762 9657263	Barafu Huts
Map 30	129	37M 319091 9654859	Junction with path to Karanga Valley on one side and a porters' path on the other
Map 30	130	37M 319086 9654264	Emergency route from Karanga Valley
Map 31	131	37M 319144 9653675	Rescue (aka Millennium Hut)
Map 31	132	37M 318558 9650985	Mweka Huts
Map 31	133	37M 317765 9649028	Bridge
Map 32	134	37M 317256 9647528	Second bridge
Map 32	135	37M 316526 9645691	Start of 4x4 road
Map 32	136	37M 315674 9643991	Mweka Gate

Map key

Symbol	Meaning	Symbol	Meaning	Symbol	Meaning
♠	Where to stay	⊠	Post Office	Ⓒ	Mosque
○	Where to eat	Ⓢ	Bank/exchange office	✚	Church/cathedral
Λ	Campsite	ⓘ	Tourist Information	◔◕	Bus station/stop
⇧	Hut	▦	Library/bookstore	Ⓣ	Telephone office
◻	Building	Ⓝ	Internet	┉▢┉	Rail line & station
☑	Public toilet	⊤	Museum/gallery	●	Other

Symbol	Meaning	Symbol	Meaning	Symbol	Meaning
╱	Main trail	⇗	Steep slope		Tree fern
╱	Other trail	⌇	Cliff		Heather
╱╱	4WD track		Bridge and river		Boulders
╱╱	Road		Trees	008	GPS waypoint
⬈	Slope		Groundsel	32	Map continuation

APPENDIX F – AMS ARTICLES

See p223-30 for AMS information. The first article here was sent in by Gerald (Joe) Power, Director of Cardiac Anaesthesia at Princess Alexandra Hospital, Brisbane, Australia. It is a more scientific – and accurate – summary of altitude sickness, its causes and treatments, and we are very grateful to him for taking the time to write and send this in to us; nice one Joe!

Altitude sickness occurs as a result of there being less oxygen in the air you breathe as you ascend through the atmosphere. Although the percentage of oxygen stays the same, the amount of oxygen, best represented by the pressure it exerts, decreases. At sea level, the atmosphere exerts a pressure of 760 millimetres of Mercury (mmHg) or 101 kilopascals (kPa). Oxygen represents 21% of this total and correspondingly exerts a 'partial pressure' of 152mmHg or 21kPa.

The importance of this pressure can be illustrated by the example of a river – water flowing from a high to a low point under the influence of gravity. The greater the difference in height between these two points will influence how rapidly the water flows. Likewise oxygen has to diffuse (flow) from the lungs, into the blood and then into the tissues. This process is influenced by many factors, the most important being the pressure of the oxygen in the air you breathe into your lungs. Human life has evolved to survive comfortably when that pressure is close to 21kPa.

As one ascends higher in the atmosphere, this pressure decreases and consequently the rate at which the oxygen is able to diffuse from the lungs into the tissues decreases. This, however, is not met with a decreased requirement of oxygen in the tissues.

At the summit of Kilimanjaro, the atmospheric pressure is approximately 349mmHg or 48kPa. This is roughly half the pressure at sea level. The partial pressure of oxygen is 9.2kPa, which represents a significant reduction from that at sea level. If a person were to be exposed to this pressure with no acclimatization (for example if you flew to the summit of Kilimanjaro in a helicopter), loss of consciousness would most likely be the result.

Altitude sickness comes as a result of the abnormal response of the human body to the oxygen starvation that occurs with altitude. The response of the brain to low oxygen supply is to dilate the arteries supplying blood to it. This results in an increase in the pressure in the brain and if the normal regulation breaks down, swelling (oedema) of the brain occurs and if severe, this can cause death.

The lungs have a normal physiological response to decreased levels of oxygen in the air, whereby the small arteries constrict and decrease the blood supply to an area of the lung. Under normal circumstances, this reflex is essential to allow the correct matching of blood supply and ventilation in the lungs. At altitude, this response can become unregulated and will result in fluid filling the air sacs (alveoli) in the lungs.

Not everyone responds in the same manner to altitude. Research done in the 1980s on Mt Everest, and in low pressure simulators, revealed that certain individuals do not respond appropriately to falling levels of oxygen. Under normal circumstances, the rate at which someone breathes is predominantly controlled by the level of carbon dioxide in the blood. A reserve reflex is to be able to respond to decreasing oxygen pressure by increasing your breathing. Individuals who lack this response appear to be susceptible to developing mountain sickness.

The key element to minimizing altitude sickness is through acclimatization. A gradual ascent of the mountain allows the heart, lungs, brain and blood to adjust to the decreased oxygen pressure. The physiological response includes an increased respiratory rate (made easier by the air being thinner) and increased heart rate to supply more blood to the tissues. Over time, the amount of haemoglobin in the blood will increase as this allows more oxygen to be carried to the tissues.

Factors that will increase the likelihood of developing altitude sickness are those that worsen the supply of oxygen to the tissues – dehydration, hypothermia, fatigue and drugs that depress or interfere with respiration.

Diamox (acetolzalamide) was first proposed as an aid to acclimatization in the 1960s. In brief, as a person breathes harder with altitude, the levels of carbon dioxide in the blood fall. This has the effect of removing some of the stimulus that a person requires to breathe. This effect is particularly important when one falls asleep. Diamox reduces the impact of the falling carbon dioxide levels and helps to maintain normal breathing.

The treatment of altitude sickness is to restore the oxygen pressures to normal. This is most effectively achieved by descending from altitude. Temporary measures include using bottled oxygen or a Gamow bag (portable pressure chamber). In the event of the development of cerebral oedema, intravenous steroids help to limit the swelling of the brain.

References JF Nunn, *Applied Respiratory Physiology;* JB Wes, *Tolerance to severe hypoxia: lessons from Mt. Everest; Acta Anaesthesiol Scand 1990:34; S94 18-23*

Is pulse oximetry a reliable predictor of who will get AMS?

Over the past few years most of the better trekking agencies have been equipping their mountain teams with a nifty little gadget called a **pulse oximeter**. This matchbox-sized bit of kit, when clipped to a subject's finger, provides, in a matter of seconds, readings for both the pulse (which is normally equivalent to the subject's heart rate) and their blood oxygenation (SaO_2), ie the percentage of haemoglobin that is saturated with oxygen (Haemoglobin is the 'vehicle' that carries oxygen from the lungs to the body tissues; the greater the oxygenation reading, the more efficiently oxygen is being delivered around the body). All very interesting, of course – but what do these figures actually tell us, if anything, about one's chances of suffering from altitude sickness if one continues to climb?

For the answer, I am grateful to Jo Middleton, my teacher on a Wilderness First Responder course, for sending me a highly readable and simple-to-follow article that he found in a 2012 edition of *Wilderness and Environmental Medicine*. The article, entitled *Pulse Oximetry and Predicting Acute Mountain Sickness: Are We Asking the Right Questions?*, summarised the studies that had been done on the link between oximetry readings and altitude sickness.

The first serious study was done in 1998 on Denali in Nepal. Surveying 102 climbers at 4200m, they concluded that 84% SaO_2 was their 'cut-off': in other words, the 21 trekkers who went on to develop altitude sickness all recorded an SaO_2 reading below 84%. Unfortunately, there were 56 other people who also registered SaO_2 scores of below 84% and yet did *not* end up with altitude sickness.

Subsequent studies seemed to confirm that oximeters are, at best, unreliable predictors of who will suffer from AMS. In particular, a study on the Mexican volcano Pico De Orizaba (5640m) and published in 2012 found that the average SaO_2 readings (taken at 4260m) of those who subsequently suffered from altitude sickness, when compared to those who didn't, differed by only 0.3%!

All of which would suggest that oximeters are pretty useless when it comes to predicting how well a climber is going to acclimatize. The researchers, however, insist that their science is sound and the link between pulse oximetry and AMS *should* – in theory – be strong. So certain are they of this that instead they think the data collection in the above studies must have been flawed. But until a study is done that satisfies their standards, we have to assume the readings given by pulse oximeters are only of limited use when it comes to guessing who is going to acclimatize well – and who isn't. And for those who record a high oxygenation reading of above approximately 89% when at around 4000m, congratulations – it appears you *should*, according to these studies, acclimatize well; while for those who register a reading below this figure, don't panic – there's a good chance you'll be OK too!

ACKNOWLEDGEMENTS

For this fourth edition I would like to thank those trekkers, locals and expats who kindly offered advice and suggestions.

In no particular order (and Tanzanian unless otherwise stated), thanks are due to: Karen Valenti (US) at KPAP, as ever, for all her information and company; Jo Middleton (UK) for providing me with the article on pulse oximetry; Eric Knox (US) of Indiana State University for his help in identifying the various groundsel species; Velly, the receptionist at Buffalo Hotel, for always making me feel so welcome; and Bruno Mathias for performing a similar role at the Kindoroko and Backpacker hotels. Janet Bonnema (US) for her lesson on air pressure and burning damp toilet roll (!); John Rees-Evans of Team Kilimanjaro and his wife Rebecca for their hospitality; Alastair Gillies (Ross County) for his company on Meru and Kili and info on the nightlife of Arusha; guides Simon Kaaya, Freddie Achedo, Joshua Ruhimbi, Deo Shayo, Nick Basso and Alex Minja; thanks to Frank Mtei for his help with the Chagga language guide and Amina Malya and Vincent Munuo for checking it; Kristy Kim and Kathleen Mahoney at Amani Children's Orphanage; Dr Doug Hardy for his help with the climate section of the book; Tom Hennigan (US) for his help with American insurance companies; Darlene Roquemore (US), Felicia and Melanie Wilson for their advice on where to eat at the cheaper end in Moshi; Shane Little, who was cycling across Africa, and Nathan Shitundi for the company in Moshi; Richard and Alisea at Pamoja Café in Moshi. Jessica Cochems (US); Dr Jusphat Peter (Ken); Shaphiy H Msiru – sorry for spelling your name wrong last time! – and all the crew at TK; David Yesayah Joseph for his help with information about the nightlife in Tanzania and the tours of Via Via; Mark William Njiu at Mountain Resort, Marangu; Lucy and Thomas Kimaro at Coffee Tree Campsite in Marangu; Fred Moshi at Kibo Hotel, Marangu; Mr Tumainili Moshi at Bismark Hotel, Marangu; Johnny P Tarimo for guiding me around Marangu; Victoria Dance and Gabriela Sanchez de la Cuesta in Nairobi for their advice; Göran Orsander (Sweden); and last, but most definitely not least, Mr ME Lufungulo, Chief Park Warden at KINAPA, for giving up some of his time to talk to me about plans for the future of the park.

I hope you all find that, thanks to your input, this fourth edition is even better than the previous three.

At Trailblazer I would like to thank Nick Hill for transforming my childlike scribbles into maps of beauty; Anna Jacomb-Hood for editing this edition and for the index; Nicky Slade for proof-reading; and Bryn, as ever, for making the whole thing possible.

INDEX

Abbreviation for Mount Meru: (MM)
Page references in **bold** type refer to maps

TRAILBLAZER'S LONG-DISTANCE PATH (LDP) WALKING GUIDES

We've applied to destinations which are closer to home Trailblazer's proven formula for publishing definitive practical route guides for adventurous travellers. Britain's network of long-distance trails enables the walker to explore some of the finest landscapes in the country's best walking areas. These are guides that are user-friendly, practical, informative and environmentally sensitive.

● **Unique mapping features** In many walking guidebooks the reader has to read a route description then try to relate it to the map. Our guides are much easier to use because walking directions, tricky junctions, places to stay and eat, points of interest and walking times are all written onto the maps themselves in the places to which they apply. With their uncluttered clarity, these are not general-purpose maps but fully edited maps drawn by walkers for walkers.

● **Largest-scale walking maps** At a scale of just under 1:20,000 (8cm or 3¹/₈ inches to one mile) the maps in these guides are bigger than even the most detailed British walking maps currently available in the shops.

● **Not just a trail guide – includes where to stay, where to eat and public transport** Our guidebooks cover the complete walking experience, not just the route. Accommodation options for all budgets are provided (pubs, hotels, B&Bs, campsites, bunkhouses, hostels) as well as places to eat. Detailed public transport information for all access points to each trail means that there are itineraries for all walkers, for hiking the entire route as well as for day or weekend walks.

Coast to Coast *Henry Stedman*, 6th edition, £11.99
ISBN 978-1-905864-57-7, 256pp, 110 maps, 40 colour photos

Cornwall Coast Path (SW Coast Path Pt 2) 4th edition, £11.99
ISBN 978-1-905864-44-7, 352pp, 130 maps, 40 colour photos

Cotswold Way *Tricia & Bob Hayne* 2nd edition, £11.99
ISBN 978-1-905864-48-5, 192pp, 60 maps, 40 colour photos

Dorset & South Devon (SW Coast Path Pt 3) *Stedman & Newton*, £11.99
ISBN 978-1-905864-45-4, 336pp, 88 maps, 40 colour photos

Exmoor & North Devon (SW Coast Path Pt I) *Stedman & Newton*, £11.99
ISBN 978-1-905864-43-0, 192pp, 60 maps, 40 colour photos

Hadrian's Wall Path *Henry Stedman*, 3rd edition, £11.99
ISBN 978-1-905864-37-9, 224pp, 60 maps, 40 colour photos

North Downs Way *John Curtin*, 1st edition, £9.99
ISBN 978-1-873756-96-6, 192pp, 80 maps, 40 colour photos

Offa's Dyke Path *Keith Carter*, 3rd edition, £11.99
ISBN 978-1-905864-35-5, 240pp, 98 maps, 40 colour photos

Peddars Way & Norfolk Coast Path *Alexander Stewart*, £11.99
ISBN 978-1-905864-28-7, 192pp, 54 maps, 40 colour photos

Pembrokeshire Coast Path *Jim Manthorpe*, 4th edition, £11.99
ISBN 978-1-905864-51-5, 224pp, 96 maps, 40 colour photos

Pennine Way *Keith Carter & Chris Scott*, 3rd edition, £11.99
ISBN 978-1-905864-34-8, 272pp, 138 maps, 40 colour photos

The Ridgeway *Nick Hill*, 3rd edition, £11.99
ISBN 978-1-905864-40-9, 192pp, 53 maps, 40 colour photos

South Downs Way *Jim Manthorpe*, 4th edition, £11.99
ISBN 978-1-905864-42-3, 192pp, 60 maps, 40 colour photos

West Highland Way *Charlie Loram*, 5th edition, £11.99
ISBN 978-1-905864-50-8, 208pp, 60 maps, 40 colour photos

'The same attention to detail that distinguishes its other guides has been brought to bear here'.
THE
SUNDAY TIMES

TRAILBLAZER TREKKING GUIDES
Europe
Corsica Trekking – GR20
Dolomites Trekking – AV1 & AV2
Scottish Highlands – The Hillwalking Guide
Tour du Mont Blanc
Walker's Haute Route: Mt Blanc to the
Matterhorn
South America
Inca Trail, Cusco & Machu Picchu

Africa
Kilimanjaro
Moroccan Atlas – The Trekking Guide
Australasia
New Zealand – The Great Walks
Asia
Nepal Trekking & The Great Himalaya Trail
Sinai – the trekking guide
Trekking in the Everest Region
Trekking in Ladakh

Sinai – the trekking guide *Ben Hoffler*, 1st edn, £14.99
ISBN 978-1-905864-41-6, 288pp, 74 maps, 30 colour photos
Trek with the Bedouin and their camels and discover one of the
most exciting new trekking destinations. The best routes in the High
Mountain Region (St. Katherine), Wadi Feiran and the Muzeina
deserts. Once you finish on trail there are the nearby coastal resorts
of Sharm el Sheikh, Dahab and Nuweiba to enjoy.

Inca Trail, Cusco & Machu Picchu
Alexander Stewart, 5th edn, £13.99
ISBN 978-1-905864-55-3, 320pp, 65 maps, 35 photos
The Inca Trail from Cusco to Machu Picchu is South America's
most popular trek. Practical guide with detailed trail maps, plans
of Inca sites, guides to Lima, Cusco and Machu Picchu. Now
includes the Santa Teresa Trek, the Choquequirao Trail and the
Vilcabamba Trail. Two challenging new treks included linking the
above treks. With a history of the Incas by Hugh Thomson.

Tour du Mont Blanc
Jim Manthorpe 1st edn, £11.99
ISBN 978-1-905864-12-6, 208pp, 60 maps, 30 colour photos
At 4810m (15,781ft), Mont Blanc is the highest mountain in west-
ern Europe, and one of the most famous mountains in the world.
The trail (105 miles, 168km) that circumnavigates it, passing
through France, Italy and Switzerland, is the most popular long dis-
tance walk in Europe. Includes Chamonix and Courmayeur guides.

Dolomites Trekking Alta Via 1 & Alta Via 2
Henry Stedman, 2nd edn, £11.99
ISBN 978-1-873756-83-6, 192pp, 59 maps, 38 colour photos
AV1 (9-13 days) & AV2 (10-16 days) are the most popular long-
distance hikes in the Dolomites. Numerous shorter walks also
included. Places to stay, walking times plus detailed guides to
Cortina and six other towns.

Moroccan Atlas – the trekking guide
Alan Palmer, 1st edn, £12.99
ISBN 978-1-873756-77-5, 268pp, 54 maps, 40 colour photos
The High Atlas in central Morocco is the most dramatic and beautiful section of the entire Atlas range. Towering peaks, deep gorges
and huddled Berber villages enchant all who visit. With 44 detailed
trekking maps, 10 town and village guides including Marrakech.

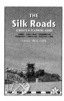

TRAILBLAZER TITLE LIST

Adventure Cycle-Touring Handbook
Adventure Motorcycling Handbook
Australia by Rail
Australia's Great Ocean Road
Azerbaijan
Coast to Coast (British Walking Guide)
Cornwall Coast Path (British Walking Guide)
Corsica Trekking – GR20
Cotswold Way (British Walking Guide)
Dolomites Trekking – AV1 & AV2
Dorset & Sth Devon Coast Path (British Walking Gde)
Exmoor & Nth Devon Coast Path (British Walking Gde)
Hadrian's Wall Path (British Walking Guide)
Himalaya by Bike – a route and planning guide
Inca Trail, Cusco & Machu Picchu
Japan by Rail
Kilimanjaro – the trekking guide (includes Mt Meru)
Mediterranean Handbook
Morocco Overland (4WD/motorcycle/mountainbike)
Moroccan Atlas – The Trekking Guide
Nepal Trekking & The Great Himalaya Trail
New Zealand – The Great Walks
North Downs Way (British Walking Guide)
Norway's Arctic Highway
Offa's Dyke Path (British Walking Guide)
Overlanders' Handbook – worldwide driving guide
Peddars Way & Norfolk Coast Path (British Walking Gde)
Pembrokeshire Coast Path (British Walking Guide)
Pennine Way (British Walking Guide)
The Ridgeway (British Walking Guide)
Siberian BAM Guide – rail, rivers & road
The Silk Roads – a route and planning guide
Sahara Overland – a route and planning guide
Scottish Highlands – The Hillwalking Guide
Sinai – the trekking guide
South Downs Way (British Walking Guide)
Tour du Mont Blanc
Trans-Canada Rail Guide
Trans-Siberian Handbook
Trekking in the Everest Region
Trekking in Ladakh
The Walker's Anthology
The Walker's Haute Route – Mont Blanc to Matterhorn
West Highland Way (British Walking Guide)

For more information about Trailblazer and our
expanding range of guides, for guidebook updates or
for credit card mail order sales visit our website:

www.trailblazer-guides.com

Kenya / Tanzania

BORDER REGION

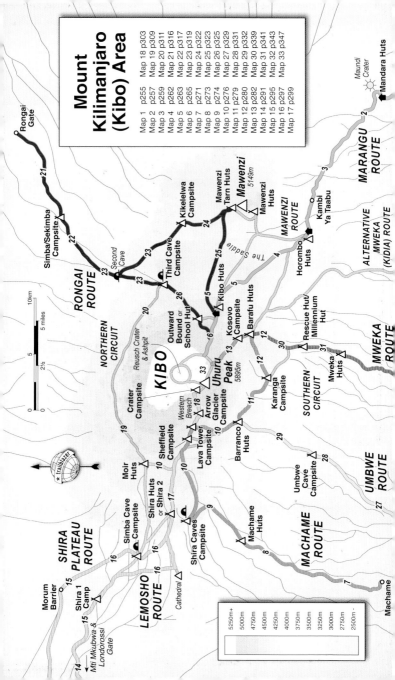

Mount Kilimanjaro (Kibo) Area